History of the Jews

(Volume IV)

H. Graetz

Alpha Editions

This edition published in 2020

ISBN : 9789354003691

Design and Setting By
Alpha Editions
email - alphaedis@gmail.com

CONTENTS.

CHAPTER I.

CULTIVATION OF THE KABBALA, AND PROSCRIPTION OF SCIENCE.

1270—1328 C.E.

CHAPTER II.

THE FIRST EXPULSION OF THE JEWS FROM FRANCE, AND ITS CONSEQUENCES.

1306—1328 C.E.

CHAPTER III.

THE AGE OF THE ASHERIDES AND OF GERSONIDES.

CHAPTER IV.

THE BLACK DEATH.

CHAPTER V.

THE AGE OF CHASDAÏ CRESCAS AND ISAAC BEN SHESHET.

CHAPTER VIII.

CAPISTRANO AND HIS PERSECUTION OF THE JEWS.

1442—1474 C.E.

CHAPTER IX.

THE JEWS IN ITALY AND GERMANY BEFORE THE EXPULSION FROM SPAIN.

1474—1492 C.E.

CHAPTER X.

THE INQUISITION IN SPAIN.

CHAPTER XV.

THE KABBALA AND MESSIANIC FANATICISM. THE MARRANOS AND THE INQUISITION.

CHAPTER XVI.

STRIVINGS OF EASTERN JEWS FOR UNITY. SUFFERING IN THE WEST.

CHAPTER XVII.

THE JEWS IN TURKEY. DON JOSEPH NASSI.

1566—1600 C.E.

CHAPTER XVIII.

THE JEWS IN POLAND.

1566—1600 C.E.

CHAPTER XIX.

SETTLEMENT OF JEWS IN HOLLAND. FEEBLE ATTEMPTS AT ENFRANCHISEMENT.

HISTORY OF THE JEWS.

CHAPTER I.

CULTIVATION OF THE KABBALA, AND PROSCRIPTION OF SCIENCE.

Progress of the Kabbala—Todros Halevi and his Sons—Isaac Allatif and his Kabbalistic Doctrines—Adventurous Career of Abraham Abulafia—He assumes the Character of Messiah—Opposition of Ben Adret—The Prophet of Avila—Joseph Jikatilla and his Kabbalistic Mazes—The Impostor Moses de Leon—Forgeries of the Kabbalists—Origin of the Zohar—Its Doctrines and Influence—Shem-Tob Falaquera—Isaac Albalag—Levi of Villefranche—Samuel Sulami and Meïri—Abba-Mari's Exaggerated Zeal—Jacob ben Machir Profatius and the Controversy regarding the Study of Science—Asheri—The Poet Yedaya Bedaresi.

1270—1328 C.E.

THE secret science of the Kabbala, which hitherto had assumed a modest deportment and been of a harmless character, began to foment discord in Ben Adret's time, ensnare the intelligence and lead astray the weak. What it lacked in intrinsic truth and power of conviction, it endeavored to supply by presumptuousness. It had already spread from Gerona, its original seat, and from northern Spain by way of Segovia to southern Spain, as far as the Castilian capital, Toledo, the Jewish community of which had before strenuously opposed obscurantism. In the city of Toledo the Kabbala won the adherence, among others, of one man who, by his noble birth, his princely state, his high position, his wealth and learning, gave it great weight. This man, whose influence is even now not fully recognized, was Todros ben Joseph Halevi, of the noble Toledan family of Abulafia (born 1234, died after 1304). He was a nephew of that Meïr Abulafia who had been so obstinate an adversary of Maimuni and rationalistic thought. Todros Abulafia took as a model his uncle, who in his old age had laid his hands on his head, and blessed him. When he grew up, he applied himself to the Talmud and to secret lore; but he must have been a man of affairs, too, for he obtained an honorable position at the court of Sancho IV, and was in special favor with the wise queen, Maria de Molina, as a physician and financier. By the Jews he was esteemed and venerated as their prince (Nasi). When the king and queen of Spain held a meeting in Bayonne with the king of France, Philip le Bel, to settle their mutual hostilities (1290), Todros Abulafia was in the train of the former, and received the most flattering homage from the Jews of southern France. Todros, like his uncle, was a determined opponent of philosophy and its devotees. He had no words bitter enough against the would-be wise people who hold everything which appears incompatible with logic as incredible and impossible. Even Maimuni, whom he highly respected, he censured for undervaluing the importance of the sacrifices so greatly as to explain them merely as a concession to the heathen propensities of the people, and for calling the offering of incense an expedient for purifying the air. He waged vehement warfare against the philosophy which denies the existence of evil spirits, which to him was identical with doubting the existence of angels. Having been initiated into the secret science by one of the earliest Kabbalists, perhaps by Jacob of Segovia, who formed a school of his own, Todros valued it as divine wisdom, to uncover whose veil to laymen was fraught with danger. The recognition of the secret doctrine by a person of so high a position could not but produce some effect. His sons, Levi and Joseph, likewise plunged headlong into its study. Two of the four Kabbalists of his time, who developed the Kabbala, and extended its influence, ranged themselves under the banner of Todros Abulafia, and dedicated their compositions to him. These four Kabbalists of the first rank, who established new theories with more or less success, were Isaac Ibn-Latif, Abraham Abulafia, Joseph Jikatilla, and Moses de Leon, all Spaniards. They obscured the mental light, with which men of intellect, from Saadiah to Maimuni, had illumined Judaism, and substituted for a refined religious belief, fantastic and even blasphemous chimeras. The intellectual degradation of the Jews in the following centuries is to a large extent their work. They led astray both their own times and posterity through designed or unintentional imposition, and the injuries which they inflicted on Judaism are felt even at the present day.

The least harmful of these four was Isaac ben Abraham Ibn-Latif or Allatif (born about 1220, died about 1290). He no doubt owed his origin to the south of Spain, for he was acquainted with Arabic. Nothing is known of his history beyond the fact that he was on friendly terms with Todros Abulafia, to whom he dedicated one of his works. His writings, as has been said by one who came after him, seem to "stand with one foot on philosophy and with the other on the Kabbala." But Allatif only toyed with philosophical formulæ, their meaning does not seem to have become known to him. He was not of a thoughtful nature, and did not enrich the Kabbala, although he attempted to give himself the appearance of following original methods, and avoided the usual Kabbalistic expressions. Allatif started with the thought that a philosophical view of Judaism was not the "right road to the sanctuary," and that it was, therefore, needful to seek a higher conception, but, instead of making the way clear, he concealed it by empty allusions and unmeaning phrases. Allatif laid more weight than his predecessors on the close connection between the spiritual and the material world—between God and His creation. For the Godhead is in all, and all is in it. In soul-inspiring prayers the human spirit is raised to the world-spirit (Sechel ha-Poel), to which it is united "in a kiss," and, so influencing the Divinity, it draws down blessings on the sublunar world. But not every mortal is capable of such spiritual and efficacious prayer; therefore, the prophets, the most perfect men, were obliged to pray for the people, for they alone knew the power of prayer. The unfolding and revelation of the Deity in the world of spirits, spheres and bodies, were explained by Isaac Allatif in mathematical formulæ. Isaac Allatif must, however, be considered a clear thinker, when compared with his enthusiastic contemporary, Abraham Abulafia, who endeavored to establish a new order of things by Kabbalistic sophisms.

Abraham ben Samuel Abulafia (born 1240, in Saragossa, died 1291) was an eccentric personage, full of whims, and fond of adventures. Endowed with a lively mind and with more than a moderate amount of knowledge, he renounced the ways of common sense to throw himself into the arms of enthusiasm. His whole life from his entry into manhood was a succession of adventures. His father, who had instructed him in the Bible and the Talmud, died when his son was a youth of eighteen, and two years later Abraham undertook a journey of adventure, as he relates, in order to discover the mythical river Sabbation or Sambation, and to become acquainted with the supposed Israelite tribes dwelling on its banks, no doubt with a Messianic purpose. His mind was in a constant tumult. He wrestled for clearness, but fell ever deeper into mazes and illusions. One thing, however, became evident to him, that the philosophy with which he had much occupied himself offered no certainty, and, therefore, no satisfaction to the religious mind thirsting after truth. Even the trite Kabbala as commonly accepted, with its doctrine about the Sefiroth, did not satisfy his soul, since both only nursed the pride of knowledge. He, a Kabbalist, criticised the unsoundness of this mystic theory so severely and correctly that it is surprising that he should have conceived still more insane notions. Abraham Abulafia sought after something higher, for prophetic inspiration, which alone opens the fountain of truth, without traversing the laborious path of systematic application.

At length Abulafia believed that he had found what his soul was yearning for, and that through divine inspiration he had come upon a higher Kabbala, in relation to which the lower mystical doctrine and philosophy were only handmaids. This Kabbala alone, he maintained, offers the means of coming into spiritual communion with the Godhead, and of obtaining prophetic insight. This means was far from new, but the firm conviction of its effectiveness and his application of it are peculiar to Abulafia. To decompose the words of Holy Writ, especially the all-hallowed name of God, to use the letters as independent notions (Notaricon), or to transpose the component parts of a word in all possible permutations, so as to form words from them (Tsiruf), or finally to employ the letters as numbers (Gematria), these are the means of securing communion with the spirit-world. But this alone is not sufficient. He who desires to render himself worthy of a prophetic revelation, must adopt an ascetic mode of living, must remove himself from the turmoil of the world, shut himself up in a quiet chamber, deliver his soul from earthly cares, clothe himself in white garments, wrap himself up with Talith and Phylacteries, and devoutly prepare his soul, as if for an interview with the Deity. Besides, he must pronounce the letters of God's name at intervals, with modulations of the voice, or write them down in a certain order, at the same time making energetic movements, writhing and bending forward till the mind becomes dazed, and the heart filled with a glow. Then the body will be surprised by sleep, and a sensation will arise, as if the soul were released from the body. In this condition, if it become lasting through practice, the divine grace is poured into the human soul, uniting with it in a kiss, and the prophetic revelation follows quite naturally. This means of working himself up into a state of ecstasy Abulafia certainly practiced, exciting his heated fancy to delirium. He considered his Kabbala to be prophetic inspiration, by means of which he alone could penetrate into the secrets of the Torah. For the plain sense of the words and the simple practice of the religious precepts were merely for the uninitiated, like milk for children. Experts, on the other hand, find the higher wisdom in the numerical value of the letters and in the manifold changes of the words.

In this way he laid down his Kabbala, in antithesis to the superficial or baser Kabbala, which occupies itself with the Sefiroth, and, as he gibingly said, erects a sort of Decem-unity instead of the Christian Trinity. He lectured on his Kabbala in Barcelona, Burgos, and Medina-Celi. So low was the general intelligence, that this half-insane enthusiast found old and young to listen to him. Two of his disciples, Joseph Jikatilla, and Samuel, alleged to be a prophet, both of Medina-Celi, proclaimed themselves to be prophets and workers of miracles. Abulafia appears, nevertheless, to have aroused opposition in Spain, or at least not to have found any real sympathy; he left his native country a second time, betaking himself once more to Italy, where he reckoned upon stronger support. In Urbino for the first time he produced prophetic writings, and alleged that God had spoken with him. At last he conceived the mad idea of converting the pope to Judaism (Sabbath-eve, 1281). The attempt cost him dear. He was arrested two days later in Rome, languished twenty-eight days in prison, and escaped the stake only through the circumstance that God, as he expressed it, had caused a double mouth (or tongue?) to grow in him. Possibly he told the pope that he, too, taught the doctrine of the Trinity. After this he was allowed to walk about Rome in freedom. Thence Abulafia proceeded to the island of Sicily, and in Messina he met with a favorable reception, gaining six adherents. Here he finally proclaimed that he was not only a prophet but the Messiah, and set forth his claims in writing (November, 1284). God, he said, had revealed to him His secrets, and had announced to him the end of the exile and the beginning of the Messianic redemption. The gracious event was to take place in the year 1290. Mysticism has always been the ground on which Messianic fancies have thriven.

Through strictly moral deportment, ascetic life and revelations veiled in obscure formulæ, perhaps also through his winning personality and boldness, Abraham Abulafia found many in Sicily who believed in him, and began to make preparations for returning to the Holy Land. But the intelligent part of the Sicilian congregation hesitated to join him without investigation. They addressed themselves to Solomon ben Adret, to obtain information from him respecting Abraham Abulafia. The rabbi of Barcelona, who was acquainted with Abulafia's earlier career, sent an earnest letter to the community of Palermo, in which he severely condemned the self-constituted Messiah as illiterate and dangerous. Naturally, Abulafia did not allow this attack to remain unanswered, but proceeded to defend himself from the denunciation. In a letter he justified his prophetic Kabbala, and hurled back Ben Adret's invectives in language so undignified that many thought the letter not genuine.

But his abusive retort was of no avail, for other

congregations and rabbis, who may have feared that a persecution might be the consequence of his fantastic doctrines, also expressed themselves against Abulafia. He was harassed so much in Sicily that he had to leave the island, and settle in the tiny isle of Comino, near Malta (about 1288). Here he continued to publish mystical writings, and to assert that he would bring deliverance to Israel. Persecution had embittered him. He leveled charges against his brethren in faith, who in their stubbornness would not listen to him: "Whilst the Christians believe in my words, the Jews eschew them, and absolutely refuse to know anything of the calculation of God's name, but prefer the calculation of their money." Of those who exclusively occupied themselves with the Talmud, Abulafia said that they were seized by an incurable disease, and that they were far inferior to those skilled in the higher Kabbala. Abraham Abulafia, besides twenty-six on other subjects, composed at least twenty-two so-called prophetic works, which, although the product of a diseased brain, were used by the later Kabbalists. What at last became of the prophetic and Messianic enthusiast and adventurer is not known.

His extravagant conduct did not fail to produce evil consequences, even in his own time, and was as infectious as an epidemic. About the same time there arose in Spain two enthusiasts, of whom one was probably Abraham Abulafia's disciple. One of them made his appearance in the small town Ayllon (in the district of Segovia), the other in the large congregation of Avila. Both proclaimed themselves to be prophets, and announced in mystic language the advent of the Messianic kingdom. Both found followers. The adherents of the prophet of Avila related, that in his youth he had been ignorant, and could neither read nor write; that an angel, who appeared to him in his sleeping, and sometimes also in his waking moments, suddenly endowed him through higher inspiration, with the power of writing a comprehensive work, full of mystical ideas, and a diffuse commentary (without which at that time no fairly respectable book could be conceived). When the people of Avila and remote congregations heard of this they wondered greatly. The story excited extraordinary interest, and the representatives of the congregation of Avila consulted Solomon ben Adret, the last commanding authority of that time, as to whether they should accept this new prophecy.

Himself a partial follower of the secret science, subscribing only to the Biblical and the Talmudical miracles, the rabbi of Barcelona replied that he would have considered the affair of the prophet of Avila as arrant fraud, if trustworthy people had not attested its truth. Still he could not possibly recognize him as a prophet, for he lacked the principal conditions which the Talmud lays down as essential to prophecy: outside of Palestine, prophecy is altogether impossible; the age is not suitable for prophetic revelation, and the prophetic spirit can not rest upon a perfectly ignorant person. It was incredible that a man should go to bed an idiot and get up a prophet. The story required the most painstaking and impartial investigation.

In spite of the warning of the most honored rabbi of the time, the prophet of Avila pursued his course, and fixed the last day of the fourth month (1295) as the beginning of the Messianic redemption. The easily influenced and ignorant multitude made preparations for its coming, fasted, and spent money lavishly in alms, that they might be found acceptable in the Messianic kingdom, and be permitted to partake of its bliss. On the appointed day, the deluded people, dressed as on the Day of Atonement, hastened to the synagogues, and waited there to hear the trumpet-blasts announcing the Messianic advent. But the expected Messiah did not show himself, nor was there any sign of him. Instead, they are said to have noticed on their garments small crosses, for which they were totally unprepared, and which partly sobered and partly terrified them. It is possible that some of the incredulous in the congregation had fastened the crosses secretly on their garments, either to practice a joke upon their credulous brethren, or to point out to what end Messianic charlatanry was destined to lead them, and thus cure them of their delusion. Some of the impostor's followers are said to have gone over to Christianity in consequence of this incident; others, to have been plunged into melancholy, because they could not explain the presence of the crosses. What became of the prophets, or beguiled deceivers, of Ayllon and Avila is not related. Like Abraham Abulafia they were lost sight of, and have importance only as the excrescences of a diseased state. It is possible that another disciple of Abulafia, Joseph Jikatilla, who also was looked upon as a performer of miracles, and had his dwelling not far from Ayllon, played a part in the mad or deceitful pranks of the prophets of Ayllon and Avila. Joseph ben Abraham Jikatilla (born in Medina-Celi, died in Penjafiel, after 1305), heard, at the age of twenty years, an exposition of the bewildering secret doctrine of Abulafia, and whilst the latter still was in Spain, he composed a Kabbalistic book of his own, in which he exhibits the same eccentricities as his master. He, too, occupied himself with the mysticism of letters and numbers, and with the transposition of letters. Joseph Jikatilla's writings are in reality only an echo of Abraham Abulafia's fancies; the same delusion is apparent in both. But far more influential and more pernicious than these three Kabbalists, Allatif, Abulafia, and Jikatilla, was Moses de Leon, whose ascendancy was felt both by his contemporaries and posterity. Although a contemporary and fellow-specialist unmasked his performances, Moses de Leon succeeded in introducing into Jewish literature and thought a book which gave the Kabbala a firm foundation and wide extension, in brief, raised it to the zenith of its power. The question about Moses ben Shem Tob de Leon (born in Leon about 1250, died in Arevalo, 1305) is only whether he was a selfish or a pious impostor. His intention was certainly to deceive and lead astray, and in this respect he appears much baser than Abulafia, who at all events was sincere and naïve in his delusion. A sciolist, who had mastered neither the Talmud nor any other subject thoroughly, Moses possessed the skill to use deftly the little that he knew, to write easily and fluently, to discover a connection between the most remote things and verses of Scripture piled up in the chamber of his memory, and to couple them with playful wit. Even the Kabbala was not present to him as a system; he knew merely its forms and technical terms, and employed them in a skillful manner.

Of careless prodigality, Moses de Leon expended everything that he had without reflecting what would remain for the morrow; he made use of the Kabbala which had come into fashion to procure for himself a rich source of revenue. He led a wandering life, lived a long time in Guadalaxara, then in Viverro, in Valladolid, and finally in Avila. At first he published his intellectual productions under his own name (about 1285). His writings, however, were not sufficiently noticed, and brought him but little fame and money. Moses de Leon then hit upon a much more effective means for opening hearts and purses. He commenced the composition of books under feigned but honored names. If he put the doctrines of the Kabbala, worn threadbare, to be sure, into the mouth of an older, highly venerated authority, some imposing name from the dazzling past,—taking care, of course, to make the coloring and the method of presentation archaic—would not such a composition be eagerly swallowed? Would he not be richly rewarded if he hinted that he was in possession of so costly a treasure? Moses de Leon knew well the credulity of those who devoted themselves with more or less earnestness to the study of the Kabbala; how they eagerly sought for every word which they were led to think originated from ancient times. For, since the secret science had been promulgated, and had striven for recognition, doctrines which sounded Kabbalistic had been fathered upon old and illustrious names, and thus had found acceptance. But Moses de Leon did his work much more cleverly than most forgers. He found the most likely author for the secret doctrine, against whom there could be little or no objection, in the person of the Tanaite Simon bar Yochaï, who is said to have spent thirteen years in a cave, solitary and buried in profound reflection, and whom ancient mysticism represented as receiving revelations. Simon bar Yochaï was assuredly the right authority for the Kabbala. But he must not be permitted to write or speak Hebrew, for in this language the Kabbalists would recognize the echo of their own voices. He must express himself in Chaldee, in a half obscure language, peculiarly fit for secrets, and sounding as if from another world. And thus there came into the world a book, the book Zohar (brilliancy), which for many centuries was held by Jews as a heavenly revelation, and was and partly is even now regarded by Christians as an old tradition. But seldom has so notorious a forgery so thoroughly succeeded. Moses de Leon well knew how to produce the proper effect on credulous readers. He made Simon bar Yochaï appear in splendor, surrounded by a halo, in the book Zohar, and impart his revelation to a circle of select pupils (sometimes twelve, sometimes six), "scholars who shine with heaven's light." "When they assembled to compose the Zohar, permission was granted to the prophet Elijah, to all the members of the celestial conclave, all the angels, spirits, and higher souls to act in sympathy with them, and the ten spiritual substances (Sefiroth) were charged with the duty of revealing to them deeply hidden secrets, reserved for the time of the Messiah." Or in another version: Simon bar Yochaï summoned his followers to a great council, and heard the flapping of the wings of the celestial host, who also had assembled to listen to the disclosure of mysteries till then unknown even to the angels. The Zohar glorifies its author excessively. It calls him the holy light, who stands higher than the greatest prophet, Moses, "the faithful shepherd." "I swear by the holy heavens and the holy earth," the Zohar makes Simon bar Yochaï exclaim, "that I behold now what no other mortal since Moses ascended Sinai for the second time has beheld, aye, even more than he. Moses knew not that his countenance shone; I, however, know that my countenance shines." On account of God's love for the writer of the Zohar, his generation merited the revelation of truths till then hidden. As long as he who illumines everything lives, the sources of the world are opened and all secrets are disclosed. "Woe to the generation forsaken by Simon bar Yochaï." He is almot deified in the Zohar. His disciples once broke out into ecstatic praise that he had mounted the degrees to heavenly wisdom, which none of his predecessors had done; and of him it is written in Scripture, "All men are to appear before the lord," *i. e.*, before Simon bar Yochaï. This extravagant glorification and self-deification, sufficient to mark a forgery, are not without design. They were to meet the objection, how the Kabbala, so long unknown, and kept secret by the prudent Kabbalists—for they had hesitated to impart any of it in writing—how this mysterious wisdom could all at once come to light, and be revealed to every one's knowledge. The Zohar frequently uses the following excuse: As the time in which Simon bar Yochaï lived was especially meritorious and rich in grace, and as the Messianic period was near, the veil which had concealed the book so long could now be drawn aside.

There are certainly very few compositions which have exercised so much influence as the Zohar, or which can be compared with it in regard to the remarkable nature of its contents and form. It is a book without beginning or end, of which it is unknown whether it once formed part of a whole, whether the extant portions originally belonged to it, or were added later, or whether at an earlier period more of it was in existence. It consists of three principal parts, with appendices and explanatory comments. The absence of form in this farrago made it possible for certain portions to be imitated. It is so easy and tempting to imitate its wild though sonorous style. Thus the forgery was counter-forged. It is not positively certain whether the Zohar is to be regarded as a running commentary to the Pentateuch, as a theosophic manual, or as a collection of Kabbalistic sermons. And its contents are just as curious, confused and chaotic as its form and external dress. The Zohar with its appendages in no wise develops a Kabbalistic system like Azriel's, neither does it unfold an idea like Abraham Abulafia, but plays with the Kabbalistic forms as with counters — with the En-Sof, with the number of the Sefiroth, with points and strokes, with vowels, accents, with the names of God and the transposition of their letters, as well as with the Biblical verses and Agadic sayings — casts them about in eternal repetition, and in this manner produces sheer absurdities. Occasionally it gives a faint suggestion of an idea, but in a trice it evaporates in feverish fancies, or dissolves in childish silliness.

The underlying principle of the Zohar (if we may speak of principles in reference to this book) is that the historical narratives and religious statutes of the

Bible were never intended to be understood in a plain, simple sense, but that they contain something higher, mysterious, supernatural. "Is it conceivable," the Zohar makes one of Simon bar Yochaï's circle exclaim, "that God had no holier matters to communicate than these common things about Esau and Hagar, Laban and Jacob, Balaam's ass, Balak's jealousy of Israel, and Zimri's lewdness? Does a collection of such tales, taken in their ordinary sense, deserve the name of Torah? And can it be said of such a revelation that it utters the pure truth?" "If that is all the Torah contains," remarks Simon bar Yochaï (or Moses de Leon), "we can produce in our time a book as good as this, aye, perhaps better. No, no! the higher, mystical sense of the Torah is its true sense. The Biblical narratives resemble a beautiful dress, which enraptures fools so that they do not look beneath it. This robe, however, covers a body, *i. e.*, the precepts of the Law, and this again a soul, the higher soul. Woe to the guilty, who assert that the Torah contains only simple stories, and therefore look only upon the dress. Blessed are the righteous, who seek the real sense of the Law. The jar is not the wine, so stories do not make up the Torah." Thus the secret lore of Moses de Leon naturally has free play to pervert everything and anything, and give it the seal of sublimity, and in this manner to promulgate a false doctrine, not only absurd, sometimes even blasphemous and immoral. All laws of the Torah are to be considered as parts and constituents of a higher world; they resolve themselves into the mysteries of the masculine and feminine principle (positive and negative). Only when both parts meet, does the higher unity arise. Consequently, whenever any one transgresses one of the laws, he obscures the brilliant image of the higher world.

It is almost impossible to give an idea of the abuse which the Zohar, or Moses de Leon, practices in the interpretation of Holy Writ, and how he twists the sense of the words. In the verse, "Raise your eyes to heaven, and see who has created this," a profound mystery is supposed to reside, which the prophet Elijah learned in the celestial school, and revealed to Simon bar Yochaï; namely, that God had been unknown and obscure before the creation of the world, in a manner existing, and still not existing. He was the "Who" (the unknown subject). The creation is part of His self-revelation. It was by the creation that He first proclaimed Himself as God.

The Zohar is particularly concerned with that side of man which is an eternal riddle to man,—the soul, its origin and end. Like the older Kabbalists, the Zohar assumed the pre-existence of the souls in the brilliant world of the Sefiroth. They are there wrapped in a spiritual robe, and entranced in the contemplation of God's light. When the souls are about to enter this world they assume an earthly garment, the body; but as soon as they are to leave the earth, the angel of death divests them of this earthly garment. If a soul lives piously and morally here below, it receives its former heavenly robe, and can once more enjoy the blissful ecstasy of God's presence; if not, particularly if it departs from the world impenitent, it wanders about naked and ashamed till purified in hell. The nakedness of the soul, paradise and hell—depicted in fantastic, baroque, and terrible images—are themes for which the Zohar often and gladly makes digressions. What happens to the soul during sleep, and the shadows of life—sin, impurity in small and great things—are likewise favorite subjects for discussion in the Zohar, to which it frequently reverts, presenting them in the greatest variety of guises and repetitions. One of the older Kabbalists arrived at the notion that to the higher world, the world of light, of holiness, and of angels, there was a sharp antithesis—a world of darkness, of unholiness, of Satan, in short the principle of evil, which was likewise developed into ten degrees (Sefiroth) at the creation of the world. In spite of their opposite characters, the two worlds are of one origin, forming opposite poles, and are in the same relation to each other as the right side is to the left. Accordingly, evil is called in the language of the Kabbalists the left or other side. The Kabbalists gave another representation of the Satanic empire. On the border of the world of light, the world of darkness is situated, and encompasses it as the shell surrounds the kernel of the fruit. Hence the Zohar metaphorically designates evil, or sin, with its ten degrees, as shell (Kelifa). This side is the favorite topic of the Zohar; for here it can apply its peculiar exposition of the Scriptures. The ten Sefiroth of the left side, the Satanic kingdom, are enumerated and denominated by names which savor of barbarism. The names sound like those of the princes of the demons in the book of Enoch, and are perhaps borrowed thence: Samael or Samiel, Azael, Angiel, Sariel, Kartiel. The Zohar identifies all blasphemers and wicked people with the evil principle of the "shells" (Kelifoth)—the first serpent, Cain, Esau, Pharaoh, and Esau's empire, Rome, and the civil and spiritual power of Christendom in the Middle Ages, which rested on violence and injustice. Israel and righteous people, on the other hand, belong to the world of light, the right Sefiroth. "He who goes after the left side (sin), and defiles his actions, draws upon himself the impure spirits; they attach themselves to him, nor do they ever leave him." The laws of the Torah have no other object than to effect and cherish the union of the souls with the world of light. Every transgression of them brings the souls to the world of darkness, evil spirits, and impurity. The Zohar coarsely represents the connection of the souls with light or with darkness by the image of wedded union, as, in general, it asserts the masculine and feminine principle in the higher world, even in reference to the Deity. As long as Israel lives in exile, the divine unity is deficient and disrupted; God will become one only in those days when the Mistress (Matronita) will espouse the King.

Moses de Leon would have left a gap, if he had not spoken of the Messianic period—the keynote of the Kabbala—and determined its date. In fact, the sudden revelation of the doctrine so long held secret rests on the assumption that the time of the Messiah is near. But here the forger betrays himself. Instead of indicating a period or a year for the appearance of the Messiah approximating the age of Simon bar Yochaï (in the second century), the Zohar, with its casuistical playing with letters and numbers, demonstrated that it would happen in the beginning of the fourteenth century, therefore in the lifetime of the author. "When the sixtieth or the sixty-sixth year will pass the threshold of the sixth thousand, the Messiah will show himself;" but some time will pass before all nations will be conquered, and Israel be gathered together. The Messiah will first be summoned to appear on earth from his secret abode in Paradise, "the bird's nest," where he has been dwelling in bliss since the beginning of the world. A bloody conflict will then break out in the world. Edom and Ishmael (Christian and Mahometan nations) will vehemently contend with one another, and eventually both will be annihilated by a mightier conquering people. Signs and miracles will presage the time, and the resurrection of the dead and a general diffusion of the Kabbalistic knowledge of God will constitute the end of the world. Moses de Leon intended to arouse in the minds of his contemporaries the hope that they would behold the time of the Messiah with their own eyes. He was perhaps as much a victim to Messianic enthusiasm as Abraham Abulafia. Despite the Zohar's endeavor to exalt rabbinical Judaism and its law, and by a mystical explanation to give every custom, however trivial, a special signification and higher import, it carps at and criticises the Talmud and its method, though in an obscure, equivocal manner, and with the most innocent air in the world. It represents the study of the Kabbala as of much higher importance than the study of the Talmud, and even of the Bible. The Kabbala has the power of soaring, and is able to follow the flight of the Deity in His inscrutable guidance of things; the Talmud, on the other hand, and its adherents, have clipped wings, and cannot elevate themselves to higher knowledge. The Zohar compares the Mishna (Talmud) with a lowly slave; the Kabbala, on the other hand, with a powerful mistress. The former has to do with inferior matters, with "clean and unclean," with "permitted and prohibited," with "what is and is not fit to be used." As long as this woman rules with her "now pure, at another time impure blood," the union of the Father with the Matrona (God with Israel) cannot take place. In the Messianic period, on the other hand, when the higher knowledge will awake, and gain the ascendency, the Kabbala will once more assert its dominion over the slave (Talmud), as in the time of the lawgiver Moses. The Zohar lastly compares the study of the Talmud with a rugged, unproductive rock which, when struck, gives out scanty drops of water, causing only disputes and discussions. The Kabbala, on the other hand, is like a spring flowing abundantly, to which only a word needs to be spoken to cause it to pour out its refreshing and vivifying contents.

When the Zohar or Midrash of Simon bar Yochaï was published, it aroused the greatest wonder among the Kabbalists. They seized upon it with avidity. Moses de Leon received vast multitudes of orders to send copies. The question, whence all at once had come so comprehensive a work of an old teacher of the Mishna, not a trace of which had been known till then, was thus answered: Nachmani had exhumed it in Palestine, had sent it to his son in Catalonia, by a whirlwind it had been carried to Aragon or Alicante (Valencia), where it had fallen into the hands of Moses de Leon, who alone possessed the original document. The repute of the newly discovered Kabbalistic treasure soon spread through the whole of Spain. The school of Abulafia at once gave the Zohar the tribute of its acknowledgment, and considered it indisputably genuine. Moses de Leon's wildest hopes were more than realized. There were, of course, Kabbalists who doubted that the Zohar had originated with Simon bar Jochaï and his school, but none the less did they pay homage to the book as to a pure source for Kabbalistic theories. When the Kabbalist Isaac of Accho, who had escaped the massacre that had ensued upon the capture of that city, arrived in Spain, and saw the Zohar, he was staggered, and became desirous of coming to the root of the question, whether this alleged ancient Palestinian work was really genuine, as he had been born and educated in the Holy Land, had associated with Nachmani's pupils, and yet had never heard a syllable about it. When he met Moses de Leon in Valladolid, the latter took a solemn oath that he had in his house at Avila an old copy of the book from the hand of Simon bar Yochaï, and pledged himself to submit it to Isaac of Accho for examination. But Moses de Leon became ill on his journey home, and died in Arevalo (1305). The veil around the origin of the Zohar was wrapped still closer. Two influential men of Avila, David Rafan and Joseph de Avila, had indeed discovered the simple truth from Moses de Leon's wife and daughter. Moses de Leon had never possessed the original copy, but had evolved it out of his own inner consciousness, and had written it with his own hand. His wife frankly related that she had often asked her husband why he published the productions of his own intellect under a strange name, and that he had answered that the Zohar would not, under his own name, have brought him any money, but assigned to Simon bar Yochaï it had been a lucrative source of income.

Thus wife and daughter, without being aware of the full gravity of their assuredly unassailable testimony, unmasked Moses de Leon as a forger. Nevertheless, the Zohar met with the unqualified applause of the Kabbalists, because it supplied a want which would have had to be provided for in one way or another. The Kabbalistic doctrine, which had already gained so much weight, had hitherto been without firm basis; it had no other authority than the very doubtful one of Isaac the Blind. Now the dignified figure of a teacher of the Mishna in communion with departed spirits and celestial hosts and angels confirmed the truths which were not only doubted by many at the time, but absolutely ridiculed. Should they, then, not cling to it and defend it? What Moses de Leon put into the mouth of Simon bar Yochaï, "Many will range themselves round the book Zohar, when it becomes known, and nourish their minds with it at the end of days," actually happened soon after his death. If the Zohar did not bring the Kabbalists anything essentially new, it exhibited to them what they did know in so peculiar a form and language, that they were wonderstruck. Everything in it is contrived for effect, for illusion, and for fascination. The long discussions which Simon bar Yochaï holds with his circle or with the "faithful shepherd," have dramatic power, especially the scene in which, in premonition of his speedy dissolution, he imparts once more what he so often had proclaimed. Full of effect, and, upon minds easily accessible to faith, of transporting and overwhelming influence, are the oft-recurring exclamations in the Zohar: Woe, woe to those who believe, or do not believe, or fail to respect, this and that. Sometimes short prayers are interspersed, which, being elevated and imaginative, are peculiarly fitted to fill the soul with mysterious awe. Even the characteristic terms introduced instead of the usual Kabbalistic forms are calculated to arouse interest by their double sense. The author designated God and the higher spiritual substances (Sefiroth) collectively or in their single parts and effects, as father, mother, the prototype of man, bride, matron, the white head, the large and the small face, the mirror, the higher heaven, the higher earth, lily, apple-orchard, and so on. The pious were gained over to the side of the Zohar, as it attributes to every religious custom and every practice a higher import, a higher sanctity, and a mysterious effect.

So a new text-book of religion was by stealth introduced into Judaism. It placed the Kabbala, which a century before had been unknown, on the same level as the Bible and the Talmud, and to a certain extent on a still higher level. The Zohar undoubtedly produced good, in so far as it opposed enthusiasm to the legal dry-as-dust manner of the study of the Talmud, stimulated the imagination and the feelings, and cultivated a disposition that restrained the reasoning faculty. But the ills which it has brought on Judaism outweigh the good by far. The Zohar confirmed and propagated a gloomy superstition, and strengthened in people's minds the belief in the kingdom of Satan, in evil spirits and ghosts.

Through its constant use of coarse expressions, often verging on the sensual, in contradistinction to the chaste, pure spirit pervading Jewish literature, the Zohar sowed the seeds of unclean desires, and later on produced a sect that laid aside all regard for decency. Finally, the Zohar blunted the sense for the simple and the true, and created a visionary world, in which the souls of those who zealously occupied themselves with it were lulled into a sort of half-sleep, and lost the faculty of distinguishing between right and wrong. Its quibbling interpretations of Holy Writ, adopted by the Kabbalists and others infected with this mannerism, perverted the verses and words of the Holy Book, and made the Bible the wrestling-ground of the most curious, insane notions. The Zohar even contains utterances which seem favorable to the Christian dogma of the Trinity of the Godhead. The mystics dismembered the fair form of Holy Writ, indulged in mad sport, and stupefied all sense for truth, but they were scarcely more guilty in this respect than the so-called philosophers of the time. Maimuni's attempt to bring Judaism and its religious literature into consonance with reason, to give certain too realistic verses of the Bible a philosophical, or at least a tolerable sense, and place religious precepts on the basis of an intelligible, acceptable purpose, encouraged half-learned men to explain everything and anything in the same way. Hence the allegorizing of the Scriptures, the Agada, and the rites, was carried to an incredible extreme. These pseudo-philosophers divested the stories of the creation and of the patriarchs of their historical character, and interpreted them as philosophical commonplaces, in which they sported with Aristotelian and Maimunist terms, as the Zohar with Kabbalistic terms. Abraham and Sarah, for example, denote to the allegorists matter and form, Pharaoh denotes vicious desires, Egypt the body, the land of Goshen the heart, Moses the divine spirit, and the Urim and Thummim, which the High Priest wore on his breast in the Temple, were the astrolabe of the astronomers, with which they calculated time, longitude and latitude. If there had been at that time any Jewish thinkers of the first rank, they would have made serious efforts to put a stop to this childish proceeding, whether Kabbalistic or pseudo-philosophical. But the age of Ben Adret happened to be poor in great intellects. Even the two chief representatives of the philosophy of that time, Shem-Tob Falaquera and Isaac Albalag, were not above mediocrity, and were themselves tainted with the current errors.

There were, however, certain men of bolder spirit, who from philosophical premises drew conclusions endangering the stability of Judaism. Like their predecessors, the Alexandrine allegorists, many intelligent and consistent thinkers were induced at this time to disregard the ceremonies of Judaism by assigning erroneous purposes to religious precepts. As the ceremonies are intended simply to awaken certain religious, philosophical, or moral feelings, they argued, it is sufficient to call up these thoughts, to be penetrated by them, to occupy one's mind constantly with them, while the observance of religious customs is superfluous. Several members of this school denied Moses' prophetic character, accepting him only as an ordinary lawgiver, such as other nations had, and thus rejected the divinity of the Torah. The pseudo-philosophers cast a doubt upon the very fundamentals of Judaism, and thereby provoked a reaction injurious to free inquiry.

The chief authority of this allegorical school was a man of vast erudition, but full of crotchets, who, without desiring it, occasioned violent conflicts. This was Levi ben Abraham ben Chayim, of Villefranche, not far from Perpignan (born about 1240, died after 1315). Coming from a respectable family of scholars, he was deeply read in the Talmud; but he was more attracted by Maimuni's philosophy and Ibn-Ezra's astrology, being a warm adherent of the belief of the latter in the influence of the stars over human destiny. Of a volatile rather than a solid mind, Levi ben Chayim had no perfect conception of Maimuni's aims. To him Judaism resolved itself into philosophical platitudes, which, preposterous and childish as they sound to us, were, strange to say, regarded by the people of early times as profound wisdom. Ben Chayim was the disseminator of that superficial method satisfied with formulæ instead of thoughts. He composed two chief works, one in verse, the other in prose, a kind of encyclopædia, in which he applied the theory derived from Maimuni to all branches of knowledge. In these books he translated the historical narratives in the Bible into philosophical generalities, explained the standing still of the sun on the occasion of Joshua's victory as a natural occurrence, and in general, adopted any method of expounding which depends on word-twisting. Levi ben Chayim repudiated the allegorical interpretations of laws; in fact, he denounced the allegorists as heretics, and desired to preserve the historical character of the biblical narratives as much as possible. Like his prototype, Ibn-Ezra, he tried to keep secret his deepest convictions, so that not even his friends could fathom his ideas. This Judaism, disfigured by absurd philosophical interpretations, was not only privately taught, but preached in the synagogues.

The home of this pseudo-philosophy was the not insignificant congregation of Perpignan, the capital of the province of Roussillon, which belonged to the kingdom of Aragon. Although the Jews had no enviable lot, and were compelled to live in the most miserable part of the town, that assigned to lepers, they nevertheless preserved a taste for science and free inquiry, and eagerly awaited the new theories taught by the exponents and followers of Maimuni's philosophy. Here poor Levi of Villefranche had found a place of refuge at the house of a rich and influential man, Don Samuel Sulami or Sen Escalita, whose piety, learning and liberality were praised beyond measure by his contemporaries. "From

Perpignan to Marseilles there is not another who can be compared with Samuel Sulami in knowledge of the Law, benevolence, piety and humility. He gives charity in secret, his house is open to every traveler; and he is indefatigable in getting books for his collection." He corresponded on learned topics with Ben Adret, and took interest in the philosophical interpretation of the Bible and the Agada. Even the rabbi of Perpignan was a friend of free thought and a determined enemy of mummified orthodoxy and the unreflecting faith of the literalist. This was Don Vidal Menachem ben Solomon Meïri (born Elul, 1249, died about 1306), little celebrated in his own time, but none the less of great importance. Though not of commanding influence, he possessed an attractive personality. He had what nearly all his contemporaries sorely lacked, moderation and tact. These qualities are revealed particularly in Meïri's style. Nearly all the Jewish authors of Spain and Provence wrote their prose and verse in a redundant, bombastic style, as if the whole literary thesaurus of the Bible were needed to express a meager idea. The much-admired model of this time, the moral poet Yedaya Bedaresi, is so prolix in saying the most ordinary platitude, that one has to peruse whole pages of his apology, reflections, and miscellaneous writings before coming across a tolerable idea. The style in vogue, a mosaic of Biblical phrases, favored verbosity. But Don Vidal Meïri forms a glorious exception to this practice, his style being terse and clear. In his commentaries to the tractates of the Talmud which relate to ceremonial duties, he proceeds throughout in a methodical manner, advances from the general to the particular, arranges his material in lucid order, and seeks to give the reader information, not to confuse him. Of a similar character is Meïri's exposition of Holy Writ. The philosophers and mystics always endeavored to find some higher meaning in it, the simple explanation being too prosaic for them, and accordingly they put upon the Bible their own extravagant nonsense. Not so Meïri. He certainly assumed that there are many commands and narratives in the Bible which point to something higher than the literal meaning, but the majority of them must, he maintained, be taken quite literally. Meïri was naturally dissatisfied with the extravagant mannerisms of the allegorists, but it did not enter his mind to reject the good together with the bad, to interdict learning because of its abuse.

These proceedings were not regarded quite so calmly by certain bigots, dwelling in the city which had produced the obscurantist Solomon of Montpellier, the proscriber of Maimuni and his compositions, and author of so much dissension and evil. Although pseudo-philosophical extravaganzas were not more dangerous than the follies of the Kabbalists, the watchers of Zion nevertheless overlooked the latter, and waged energetic warfare with the former, so that the philosophers obtained more weight than they would otherwise have had. The bigots of Montpellier well-nigh kindled the fire of discord in Jacob. The first instigator of this ill-timed zeal belonged to that class of men who mark off the province of faith according to an exact rule, denounce every movement and opinion which transgress their limit as heresy, and desire to have them rooted out with anathemas and scourges, where possible with fire and sword— a class of men in whom fanatical zeal cannot be separated from a kind of egoism. To this category belonged Abba-Mari ben Moses, of Montpellier, or, as his aristocratic title ran, Don Astruc En-Duran de Lünel. Of a respectable family, and of great influence in the capital of Languedoc, Abba-Mari was certainly not without culture, and he had great veneration for Maimuni and his compositions; but he had irrevocably attached himself to the Jewish creed as laid down by Nachmani, and was indignant if any one ventured to consider it from the point of view of another system. He did not object to miraculous tales; on the contrary, the more the better. The conclusions of philosophy and science, which denied the possibility of these miracles, in no way disturbed him. In the choice between Moses and Aristotle, or between the authorities of the Talmud and the upholders of philosophy, he was not for a moment doubtful to whom to give the preference. To be sure, this narrow-minded point of view is justifiable; but Abba-Mari wanted to thrust his opinion upon every one else, and to persecute all who thought otherwise. Not only did he hold in abomination the allegorical exegesis publicly preached, but he reprobated the study of all profane literature as the cause of this aberration. He regretted that the scourge could no more be brought into requisition to silence those who filled their minds with such learning as endangered religion.

Abba-Mari, however, did not possess sufficient authority to proceed against Levi of Villefranche and his school. He addressed himself to the most influential rabbi of the time, Ben Adret of Barcelona, and charged that their perversities would accomplish the dissolution of Judaism, if a restraint were not put upon them. He importuned Ben Adret to exercise his great influence. The rabbi naturally found the circumstance deplorable that "strangers had forced their way through the gates of Zion." He exhorted Abba-Mari to organize a party to oppose this extravagant movement, but positively refused his support, as he did not like to interfere in the affairs of congregations abroad. Other bigots, however, took up the cause, and hurried it to a crisis, among them Don Bonafoux Vidal, of Barcelona, and his brother, Don Crescas Vidal, who had moved to Perpignan, both highly respected and learned, but as intolerant as Abba-Mari. Don Crescas made a proposition, which met with much applause. The study of science, and the reading of profane literature in general, was to be prohibited to Jewish youths till their thirtieth year. Only men of mature age, "who had filled their minds with the Bible and the Talmud, were to be allowed to warm themselves by the strange fires of philosophy and the natural sciences." Although Ben Adret did not feel disposed to take measures against the study of science, he nevertheless considered it his duty to persecute the provoker of so much animosity. He took umbrage at the pious Samuel Sulami for granting a heretic shelter in his house, thus giving him an opportunity to spread his pernicious views. He harassed Samuel Sulami so unmercifully, and subjected his conscience to such torment, that the man, not very remarkable for strength of character, became shaken in his previous convictions. When a daughter of his died he believed that it was a punishment for his sinfulness, and renounced his hospitality to Levi. Many members of the congregation of Perpignan bitterly resented the suspicion of heresy cast upon Levi, and as they knew Ben Adret to be a man of stainless character, they vented their dissatisfaction on the instigator, Abba-Mari, to whom they imputed sordid ulterior designs and personal motives.

Abba-Mari and his allies, who felt themselves helpless without powerful support, labored without intermission to inflame the zeal of the Barcelona rabbinate, that it might forbid free inquiry and the study of science. At the same time they promised the co-operation of the whole congregation of Montpellier, which, being the chief one in southern France, would draw other communities after it. Ben Adret and his college, imagining from Abba-Mari's exaggerated description that Judaism was in the greatest danger, were at last determined to take up the matter, but desired first to sound the congregation of Montpellier as to its feeling on the subject, and for this purpose sent a letter to be read before the members in case they felt disposed to join them in interdicting the study of the natural sciences. But as soon as the proposed ban against the sciences became known, decided opposition arose among the most important men of the congregation.

There was at that time in Montpellier a man, who by reason of his family, position, wealth and knowledge, was held in high estimation by his people, and who had imbibed a love for the sciences with his mother's milk. Jacob ben Machir Tibbon, known in Christian circles as Don Profiat, or Profatius (born about 1236, died after 1312), was descended on one side from the celebrated Meshullam of Lünel, the first to promote a revival of learning in southern France, and on the other side he was related to the Tibbonides. From his birth he was taught to look upon Judaism and science as twin sisters, dwelling together in the utmost harmony. Like all educated Jews of his time, he was well grounded in Jewish literature, the Bible, and the Talmud, practiced medicine as his profession, but devoted himself with particular zeal to mathematics and astronomy. His accurate observation of the inclination of the earth's axis to the orbit was taken by later master astronomers as the basis of their investigations. As he had acquired a knowledge of Arabic, he was able to translate useful scientific works from that language into Hebrew. His wealth of knowledge was not employed as a means of gratifying his vanity or ambition, but he properly regarded it as the distinction of man, enabling him to arrive at self-knowledge. Jacob Tibbon maintained that in the happy time of the Jewish people science had its home in their midst, but exile and suffering had banished it, and its former exponents now had to become students in order to learn the results arrived at by foreign nations. In his scientific labors Jacob ben Machir had a very noble end in view. He aimed at elevating his co-religionists in the eyes of the Christian world, and silencing the sneers of their enemies, who tauntingly said that they were destitute of all knowledge.

This man was now asked to assist in banishing science from the Jewish world. If Abba-Mari wished to carry out in Montpellier his scheme of holding the Jewish youth aloof from the study of the sciences, he was bound to take Jacob ben Machir into consideration. For he was held in high esteem by his congregation on account of his many excellent traits and his meritorious achievements, and had the greatest influence with the members entitled to a vote. Indeed, he was the first to whom Abba-Mari disclosed the project, supported by the Barcelona rabbinate, against the study of the profane sciences, and he reckoned upon Jacob's co-operation. With impressive decisiveness, Profiat not only refused participation, but pointed out the sad consequences of so serious a step, and importuned him to omit the public reading of Ben Adret's letter. Abba-Mari and his ally, Todros of Beaucaire, nevertheless persisted in their determination, and summoned the members of the congregation to an important conference in the synagogue on a Sabbath (Elul-August, 1304). It was immediately apparent that the zealots had deceived themselves, or had been too confident in their assertion that the Jews of Montpellier would give unanimous consent to the interdict to be laid on science. A portion of the congregation even abstained from taking part in the deliberations, and Jacob ben Machir raised an emphatic protest against the proposed enslaving of the intellect. A violent discussion ensued, and the meeting dispersed without coming to a resolution. Soon a party, consisting of advocates of science, and of friends, adherents and parasites of the highly esteemed leader, rallied round Jacob Machir, the most distinguished representative of science. The obscurantists and the simple-minded attached themselves to Abba-Mari, so that the congregation became a prey to division and conflict. Each party endeavored to gain supporters, both within and without the community.

It became a point of honor with Abba-Mari to bring the affair to a conclusion conformable to his own views, for his defeat had exposed his true position to Ben Adret and the Barcelona congregation. After the unfavorable issue of the first deliberation in the synagogue, he hardly ventured to answer the man whom he had assured of a unanimous adoption of his proposal. He, therefore, worked very energetically in collecting at least twenty-five signatures of members of the congregation, to give Ben Adret proof that he did not stand alone in his extreme views.

It was no less a point of honor with Jacob Tibbon not to allow the interdiction of science to come into force. For he and the Tibbonides believed that the attacks were directed chiefly against their highly-venerated ancestors, Samuel Ibn-Tibbon and Jacob Anatoli, because the latter's book of sermons (Malmed) had been the first to explain away Biblical tales and religious laws, and at that time was used in certain quarters for Sabbath devotions. Ben Adret, at Abba-Mari's instigation, did, indeed, treat Anatoli, the favorite of the Tibbonides, with scorn. Of Samuel Ibn-Tibbon, the translator of Maimuni's works, and propagator of his theories, the austere bigots had not a good word to say. Judah ben Moses, his great-grandson, consequently became the soul of what may be called the Tibbonide party, which agitated against Abba-Mari's plan. To attract outsiders, the Tibbonides gave out that the adversaries of science once more had in view the denunciation of Maimuni and his compositions as heretical, and that Abba-Mari wanted to take up the position of Solomon of Montpellier. This was a very happy party manœuvre; it won over even those who had shown indifference to the burning topic of the day, for they thought themselves in duty bound to take up arms on behalf of Maimuni's honor. The Tibbonide party, thus strengthened, sent a trenchant and pointed letter to Ben Adret and the Barcelonians, to ask them to reconsider their decision. It is true, they were not able to offer any convincing reasons for the admission of science into the Jewish curriculum; but the arguments which they set forth in its favor were considered satisfactory in a superficial age. They appealed to King Solomon's wisdom, "from the cedar of Lebanon to the hyssop on the wall," which, they said, referred to nothing but natural science. From the Talmud, too, reasons were adduced for the study of science. They would not admit the validity of the reply that it was not intended to interdict research generally, only to prohibit immature young men from its pursuit. That, they said, was an evasion of the main point at issue. For a man not familiar with science before his thirtieth year was permanently incapable of engaging in its study, and in advanced age could never retrieve the loss. The Tibbonides, moreover, protested that they were branded as heretics, because along with the Torah they paid homage to the profane sciences. They did not recognize the superiority of any one in piety and orthodoxy. Lastly, the Tibbonides exhorted Ben Adret and his college to bury the hatchet of denunciation and discord. The spirited and defiant tone assumed by Jacob ben Machir and his adherents greatly provoked the Barcelonians. The tension increased. Bitter and caustic letters flew hither and thither. Both sides labored to gain new adherents in other congregations, and to draw over the waverers. The communities of Argentière, Aix, Avignon and Lünel, through their representatives, declared in favor of Abba-Mari and his followers. In Perpignan, the chief seat of the much-assailed enlightenment, a relative of Abba-Mari agitated in his favor. The latter was particularly desirous of securing the assistance of a man who, by reason of his noble birth and highly honorable position, had powerful influence in Perpignan and elsewhere. This was Kalonymos ben Todros of Narbonne, thought to be a descendant of the house of King David. Kalonymos did not at first appear inclined to take part in the proscription of science; but Abba-Mari from the one side and Ben Adret from the other assailed him with such pertinacity that at length he promised his consent and co-operation. As the Tibbonide party had also gained new adherents, Ben Adret himself shrank from pushing the controversy to extremes, and decided not to issue the decree of excommunication till at least twenty congregations had declared themselves unequivocally in favor of it.

Whilst in southern France and Spain the balance was inclining now to one side, now to the other, in the dispute about the admission of scientific studies into Jewish circles, the German communities were passing through a series of the most deplorable events, which drove to Spain a man who spoke the deciding word in favor of the excommunication and proscription of free inquiry. He was of high morality, rare disinterestedness, of pure aspiration and sincere piety, and possessed profound Talmudical learning, but was filled with the fanatical hate of his countrymen against profane knowledge. The emigration of Asheri or Asher from Germany to Spain inaugurates an unhappy period for the Spanish and Provençal Jews in their efforts for the progress of culture.

Asher ben Yechiel (born about 1250, died 1327) of the Rhine district, sprang from ancestors who centered their whole world in the Talmud. A disciple of the celebrated Meïr of Rothenburg, Asher acquired the acute Tossafist method, composed

Tossafist works, but had a finer sense of system and order than this school. After the death of his master, whose corpse the unprincipled emperor, Adolph of Nassau, refused to give up for burial without remuneration, Asheri was reckoned among the most influential rabbinical authorities of Germany. A paroxysm of persecutions of the Jews broke out in his time, far worse than those during the crusades; it robbed thousands of innocent men of their lives, or sentenced them to a lot worse than death. A civil war raged at that time in Germany between Adolph of Nassau and Albrecht of Austria, who were contending for the empty glitter of the German crown. This strife promised impunity for audacious attacks on the Jews, who were proscribed by the church and society, and an opportunity was easily found. A report was spread that the Jews of the little town of Röttingen (in Franconia) had desecrated a sacramental wafer and pounded it in a mortar, and blood was said to have flowed from it. A nobleman of the place, named Rindfleisch, took up the cause of the host alleged to have been desecrated, declared that he had received a mission from heaven to root out the accursed race of Jews, and gathered a credulous, besotted mob around him to assist in his bloody intentions. He and his troops first of all consigned the Jews of Röttingen to the flames (7th Iyar—20th April, 1298). From this place the rabble of slaughterers, under Rindfleisch's leadership, traveled from town to town, always swelling their numbers with others of their description, and destroyed all the Jews who fell into their hands, even those converted to Christianity. Rindfleisch, impelled by audacity and spurious enthusiasm, fairly forced the inhabitants of various towns to ill-treat their Jewish fellow-citizens brutally. The great community of Würzburg was completely blotted out (12th Ab—24th July). In Nuremberg the Jews had at first fled for refuge into the fortress, but being attacked there, too, they took to arms, and though assisted by humane Christians, were overpowered at last, and all butchered (22d Ab—1st August). Asheri's relative and fellow-student, Mordecai ben Hillel, who had compiled a very important rabbinical work, fell at about the same time, together with his wife and five children. Many parents, lest their children from fear of death should renounce their faith, threw them with their own hands into the flames, and plunged in after them. In Bavaria the congregations of Ratisbon and Augsburg were the only ones to escape the slaughter. In the first city, where they had the right of citizenship from time immemorial, the mayor protected them with great zeal. In Augsburg, too, the mayor and council defended them against the destroyers, Rindfleisch and his horde.

This bloody persecution spread from Franconia and Bavaria to Austria, swept away more than a hundred and forty congregations and more than 100,000 Jews, and lasted nearly half a year. The Jews of Germany all trembled, and were prepared to meet destruction. This would certainly have come if the civil war in Germany had not been brought to an end by the death of Emperor Adolph, and the election of Albrecht. The second Habsburger energetically restored the country to a state of peace, brought to book the perpetrators of the outrages on the Jews, and imposed fines on the towns which had participated in them, on the ground that he had suffered losses in his purse through the immolation of his "servi cameræ" and their goods. The majority of the Jews baptized through fear returned to Judaism, apparently with the connivance of the emperor and the representatives of the church. The after-throes of this massacre were likewise bitter enough. The wives of those who had perished could not authenticate the death of their husbands through Jewish witnesses, as no men remained alive competent to give testimony. They could appeal only to the statement of baptized Jews, whose evidence was considered by many rabbis to be invalid according to the Talmudical marriage laws. Asheri, however, was sensible enough to unbend from this strictness, and allowed the widows to marry again on the evidence of baptized Jews returned to Judaism.

Asheri did not feel very secure in Germany after this bloody massacre, or perhaps he was threatened with danger on the part of Emperor Albrecht. It was said that the emperor demanded of him the sum of money which the Jews were to pay as ransom for the imprisoned Meïr of Rothenburg, for which Asheri had become security. He accordingly left Germany (summer of 1303), and traveled from one country to another with his wife, his eight sons and grandsons, and on account of his reputation, he was everywhere treated with the utmost respect, especially in Montpellier, even before the breaking out of the controversy. He finally settled in Toledo, the largest city of Spain (January, 1305). With joy the illustrious German rabbi was installed by the Toledo congregation in the vacant rabbinate. With Asheri the dismal spirit of over-piety, so hostile to knowledge, entered into the Spanish capital.

Asheri did not conceal his antipathy to profane culture. He could not conceive how pious Jews, in southern France and in Spain, could occupy themselves with subjects outside of the Talmud. With the utmost scorn he discountenanced the very aspiration of the Spanish and Provençal Jews on which they prided themselves. He thanked his Creator that He had protected him from the baneful influence of science. He did not give the southern Frenchmen and the Spanish Jews credit for thoroughness even in knowledge of the Talmud, and maintained that the German and northern French

Jews alone had inherited wisdom from the time of the destruction of the Temple. A man like this, incapable of appreciating the sciences, and harboring enmity to everything not in the Talmud, was bound to exercise an influence prejudicial to knowledge. Next to him Solomon ben Adret himself appeared more or less of a freethinker. Abba-Mari forthwith availed himself of the man, from whom he expected effectual support for his party. He requested him to express his views on the pending question. Asheri, of course, gave Abba-Mari his unqualified approval, but was of opinion that he did not go far enough, for the evil would not be eradicated, if the pursuit of the sciences were allowed at a ripe age. The poison of heresy had spread too far, every one was infected by it, and the pious were open to the reproach that they shut their eyes to it. His proposal was that a synod should be convoked, and a resolution be taken that study was to be devoted solely to the Talmud, while the sciences were to be pursued only when it was neither day nor night—that is, not at all. This exclusive fidelity to the Talmud, which rejected all compromise, advocated by an energetic man of pure character, made an overpowering impression on the unsettled minds of Spanish Jews. Ben Adret himself, who had hitherto always hesitated to lead the movement, all at once declared that he was prepared to pronounce the ban, if Abba-Mari and the prince, Kalonymos, would prepare it. An officious zealot, Samson ben Meïr, disciple of Ben Adret, took upon himself to collect assenting signatures from twenty congregations. Toledo was especially reckoned upon, having been swayed by Asheri's mind, and next, Castile generally, which as a rule followed the guidance of the head community.

How artificial and opposed to the sentiment of the majority this zeal was, became apparent especially in the congregation of Montpellier, styled the tower of

Zion by Abba-Mari's party. In this congregation the zealots did not venture to collect signatures for the sentence of excommunication. As if in defiance, one of the Tibbonides announced that he would give a reading from Anatoli's book of sermons on a certain Sabbath, and immediately drew a numerous audience. Abba-Mari, who had repeatedly boasted to Ben Adret of his mighty influence, and had persuaded him that the whole congregation, except a few deluded people, were on his side, now had to admit that Montpellier was not to be reckoned upon in this affair. In the consciousness that their party was in a minority in southern France, the two leaders, Abba-Mari and Kalonymos, of Narbonne, made the ecclesiastical ban unexpectedly mild, both as to wording and contents. First, the reading of works on natural science and of metaphysical books only was to be prohibited, all other branches of learning being expressly allowed. Secondly, the writings of Jewish authors, even those dealing with natural science or metaphysics, were to be excluded from the inhibition. Abba-Mari, with a view to meeting his adversaries half-way, had made the proposal to fix the period when the study of every department of learning was to be allowed, not at the thirtieth, but at the twenty-fifth year of the student's age. Ben Adret, however, who could not tolerate half-measures nor brook retreat, had now become more severe. He who formerly had to be driven and urged on, now became the propeller. Asheri's influence is not to be mistaken. On the Sabbath of Lamentation in commemoration of the destruction of Jerusalem, he and his colleagues ordered the anathema against the study of the sciences to be read amid solemn ceremonies, the scroll of the Law in the arms of the reader (4th Ab—26th July, 1305). Whoever read any scientific book before the twenty-fifth year of his age was liable to the penalty of excommunication. The ban was to remain in force for half a century. The philosophical expounders of Holy Writ were doomed in the hereafter, and in this world subjected to excommunication, and their writings condemned to be burnt. As no exception was made of scientific works composed in Hebrew, according to the formulation of the ban, not only Anatoli's book of sermons was exposed to proscription, but also Maimuni's philosophical writings. Ben Adret and his college allowed only the study of medicine, on the ground that its practice is permitted in the Talmud. This was the first heresy-tribunal in Jewish history, and Ben Adret was at its head. The Dominicans had found docile emulators among the Jews.

According to the communal system in the Middle Ages, every congregation was independent, and the resolutions of one congregation had no force with another. The ban accordingly had validity only in Barcelona, unless some other congregation confirmed it. Ben Adret, however, labored to have it adopted by other congregations. The sentence, signed by Ben Adret, his two sons, and more than thirty of the most influential members of the Barcelona congregation, was dispatched to the congregations of Spain, Languedoc, northern France, and Germany. But the ban was not so readily adopted as the authorities of Barcelona had flattered themselves it would be. Jacob ben Machir and his party had already received notice that a blow was being meditated against them, and accordingly made preparations for a countermove. They resolved from the first to frustrate the effect of the ecclesiastical interdict of the study of science. They drew up a resolution in Montpellier which contained three important points. A sentence of excommunication was to fall upon those who, out of religious scruples, ventured to debar or withdraw their sons, whatever their youth, from the study of any science whatsoever, regardless of the language in which it was treated; secondly, upon those who presumed to utter an irreverent or abusive word against the great Maimuni, and, lastly, also upon those who presumed to denounce a religious author on account of his philosophical system. The last point was introduced for the sake of Anatoli's memory, which his opponents had vilified. Thus there was ban against ban. Jacob Tibbon and his friends caused their resolution in favor of science and its advocates to be announced in the synagogue, and the great majority of the congregation of Montpellier took his side. Party zeal, however, impelled the Tibbonides to take an ill-advised step, which threatened to produce the same evil consequences as had ensued at the time of the first conflict in Montpellier with the obscurantists. As Jacob ben Machir Profatius and others of his party had influence with the governor of the city, they wished to secure his assistance in the event of their opponents' endeavoring violently to carry the Barcelona interdict into effect. The governor, however, explained to them that he was interested only in one point: that the Jewish youth should not be prevented from reading other than Talmudical works. He should strongly deprecate any attempt to discourage the study of extra-Talmudical literature, because, as he frankly expressed himself, he would not consent to their being deprived through fear of excommunication of the means to potential conversion to Christianity. To the other points he was indifferent.

Abba-Mari and his party were now in despair on account of the activity of their opponents. As the resolution in favor of the unrestricted study of science had been adopted by the majority of the community, according to rabbinical law it was binding on the minority as well, and therefore on their leader, and they could not legally stand by the interdict of Barcelona. Thus the zealots, the provokers of the conflict, had their hands tied, and were caught in their own net. They did what they could; they protested against the resolution of the Tibbonides, and advertised their protest far and wide. But they could not conceal that they had suffered a defeat, and were obliged to consult certain authorities as to whether the resolutions of the Tibbonides were binding on them. Ben Adret was thus placed in an embarrassing position. The party of Jacob ben Machir believed, or wished to have it believed, that the prohibition of the rabbis of Barcelona in reference to the study of scientific books, was meant to apply to Maimuni's works, too. They obtained the credit of having taken up the cudgels in behalf of Maimuni's honor, and of contending for the glory of Judaism; whilst their opponents, Ben Adret included, through their narrow-mindedness and obstinacy, were exposing their religion to the scorn of educated Christians. The vindicators of science seemed to be continually gaining in public opinion. There now appeared on their side a young poet, whose eloquent defense, written in a highly imaginative style, made a great impression. It gives a faithful picture of the feeling and excitement which agitated the souls of the champions of science, and, therefore, awakens interest even in the present day. In a modest manner, but with manly spirit, the poet tells Ben Adret truths which he never had the opportunity of hearing in his own circle. This young poet, more famous through his letter than through his verses, was Yedaya En-Bonet ben Abraham, better known under the name of Bedaresi (of Béziers) and under the poetical pseudonym of Penini (born about 1280, died about 1340). Yedaya Penini, son of the bombastic poet, Abraham Bedaresi, had more talent as a poet than his father. He possessed a lively imagination and overflowing wealth of language, and lacked only restraining tact, and a dignified, universally acceptable, uplifting aim for poetry. This deficiency gave his poems the appearance of empty grandiloquence and artificiality. He had inherited the defect of his father, inability to control the superabundance of words by the law of beauty. He was too ornate, and he moralized, instead of elevating and impressing. In his seventeenth year Yedaya Bedaresi wrote a book of morals (Pardes), and in his earliest years, whilst his father was still alive, he composed a prayer of about one hundred verses, in which all the words begin with the same letter (Bekashoth ha-Memin), and which his father, and perhaps his contemporaries, admired, but which is nevertheless very insipid. An admirer of Maimuni and Ibn Ezra, Bedaresi considered science and philosophy of equal importance with Judaism, or, like most thoughtful men of that time, he believed that the one contained the other.

Bedaresi conceived that his deepest convictions had been assailed by Ben Adret's anathema, and that it had in reality been directed against Maimuni's name, and, therefore, he could not restrain himself from addressing a sharp rebuke to the excommunicators. As he lived in Montpellier and was certainly attached to Jacob ben Machir's party, it is quite probable that he wrote the defense of Maimuni and of science, sent to Ben Adret, at their instigation (December, 1305, or January, 1306). This missive, like most of those written in this controversy, was intended not only for the individual addressed, but for the Jewish reading public in general. After Bedaresi had expressed his respect for the upright, learned rabbi of Barcelona, he remarked that he and his friends were not indignant about the ban, for science was invulnerable, and could not be injured by the fulmination of excommunicators. They were only hurt that Ben Adret should brand the Jewish congregations of southern France as heretics and renegades, and expose them to contempt in his message to many congregations and countries. Ben Adret, he continued, had allowed himself to be taken in tow by Abba-Mari, and had made a mountain of a mole-hill. From time immemorial, from Saadiah's age, science was not only tolerated in Judaism, but cherished and fostered, because its importance in religious knowledge was indisputable. Moreover, the denouncers of heresy were not consistent; they excluded the science of medicine from the ban, although this science, like every other, had a side which was in conflict with religion. How could they dare impugn the writings of Maimuni, whose dazzling personality outshone all his great predecessors? At the end, Yedaya Bedaresi observed that violent faction fights had broken out in Montpellier. Did they wish to continue to foment party strife, that the absence of unity among the Jews might occasion the Christians unholy satisfaction? "We cannot give up science; it is as the breath to our nostrils. Even if Joshua would appear and forbid it, we could not obey him, for we have a warranty, who outweighs you all, Maimuni, who has recommended it, and impressed it upon us. We are ready to set our goods, our children, and our very lives at stake for it." In conclusion, he invited Ben Adret to advise his friends in Montpellier to relinquish heresy hunting, and desist from stirring the fire of discord.

At the same time, furious disputes broke out in the church, between King Philip IV of France and Pope Boniface VIII, but here the subject of the dispute was not ideal good, not science and free research, but purely dominion, power and mammon. There was war to the knife between the chiefs of the two parties. The king accused the pope of heresy, simony, covetousness, perjury, and impurity. And the pope released the subjects from their oath to their hereditary king, and gave away his empire. The Jewish hostilities had neither the same wide range, nor yet the same bottomless wickedness.

Ben Adret and several who had signed the decree of excommunication, Moses Iskafat Meles and Solomon Gracian, were so unpleasantly affected by Bedaresi's letter, and feared its effect so much, that they hastened to offer the explanation that they had in no wise animadverted upon Maimuni's writings, whom they revered in the highest degree. They even exhorted Abba-Mari's party to make peace with their opponents, to vindicate their dignity before their common enemy. But the controversy was now at a stage when it could no longer be settled peaceably. The mutual bitterness was too violent, and had become too personal. Each party claimed to be in the right from its own standpoint; neither could consent to a compromise nor make concessions. Each adhered to its own principles; the one sought to enforce the freedom of science, the other protested that Jewish youth, before maturity, must be guarded from the deleterious poison of knowledge. Whilst the adherents of Abba-Mari were seeking legal decisions to prove the ban of their opponents unauthorized, a sad event happened, which, like a whirlwind, tore friends asunder, and dashed enemies against each other.

CHAPTER II.

THE FIRST EXPULSION OF THE JEWS FROM FRANCE, AND ITS CONSEQUENCES.

Philip le Bel—The Jews of France plundered and banished—Estori Parchi; Aaron Cohen; Laments of Bedaresi—Eleazar of Chinon, the Martyr—Return of the Jews to France; their Precarious Position—Progress of the Controversy regarding the Study of Philosophy—Abba-Mari and Asheri—Death of Ben Adret—Rabbinical Revival in Spain—Isaac Israeli II—Samuel and the Queen Maria Molina—Don Juan Emanuel and Judah Ibn-Wakar—The Jews of Rome—Robert of Naples and the Jews—Peril of the Jews in Rome—Kalonymos ben Kalonymos, his Satires—Immanuel and Dante—The Poet Judah Siciliano—Leone Romano and King Robert—Shemarya Ikriti—Position of Karaism—Aaron the Elder and the Prayer-Book of the Karaites.

1306—1328 C.E.

PHILIP IV, le Bel, at that time the king of France, one of those monarchs who made arrogant and unprincipled despotism familiar to Europe, suddenly issued a secret order (21st January, 1306), imposing the strictest silence, to the higher and lower officials throughout his kingdom, to put all the Jews of France under arrest on one and the same day, without warning of any kind. Before the Jews had fully recovered from fasting on the Day of Lamentation in remembrance of the destruction of Jerusalem, and as they were about to begin their daily business, the constables and jailors appeared, laid hands upon them, and dragged young and old, women and children, to prison (10th Ab—22d July). There they were told that they had to quit the country within the space of a month, leaving behind both their goods and the debts owing to them. Whoever was found in France after that time was liable to the penalty of death. What could have induced this prudent rather than clerical prince so suddenly to change his sentiments towards the Jews? It was certainly not clerical intolerance, nor was it yielding to the will of the people. For the French, even in the Middle Ages, were not bigoted, and it was not their wish to remove the Jews to free themselves from usurers. Avarice was the first motive of this cruel order. For Philip's feud with the pope, and his war with the rebellious Flemish, had so exhausted his treasury, and had rendered necessary so unsparing an extortion of money that, as the ballads of the time scoffingly said, "The fowl in the pot was not secure from the king's grasp." The king wanted to replenish his coffers from the property of the Jews. Another circumstance is said to have moved him to this hard-hearted resolution. The German emperor Albrecht, who at that time was not on good terms with Philip, had demanded the surrender of the kingdom of Arles; further, that he should deliver up Jesus' supposed crown of thorns, and lastly, that he should acknowledge the authority of the successor of Vespasian, Titus, and Charlemagne over the French Jews, *i.e.*, yield to him a portion of the hard-earned property of the Jews. Philip is said to have consulted his lawyers, to decide to whom the authority over the Jews appertained, and as they adjudged it to the German emperor, the idea occurred to him to fleece the Jews of their property, and to send his "servi cameræ" naked and bare to Albrecht. Before the world the king covered his act of violence, inhuman as it was unstatesmanlike, with the excuse that incredible outrages of the Jews had rendered their expulsion imperative. That he had aimed at the possessions of the Jews was shown by his relentless plundering. The officials left the unhappy Jews nothing beyond the clothes they wore, and to everyone not more than seemed necessary for a day's living (12 gros Tournois). Wagonfuls of the property of the Jews, gold, silver and precious stones were transported to the king; and less valuable objects were sold at a ridiculously low price. At the appointed time (September, 1306), they were banished, about 100,000 souls, from the country which their ancestors had inhabited, in part at the time of the Roman republic, long before Christianity had spread into France. Some who could not separate themselves from their property and the country which they loved went over to Christianity. The whole congregation of Toulouse is said to have been guilty of this cowardice, which scarcely seems credible. The celebrated seats, at which so much intellect had been displayed, the colleges of Rashi, Tam, and the Tossafists: Troyes, Paris, Sens, Chinon, Orleans; the places in which a higher culture had had its temple: Béziers, Lünel, Montpellier, whence the combatants for and against science were plunged into common misery,—all these schools and synagogues were sold to the highest bidder or given away. A German or an English king might have destroyed the holy places of the Jews—King Philip le Bel made a present of a synagogue to his—coachman. An approximate idea can be formed of the sums which the expulsion and robbery of the Jews brought in to the king, if it is kept in mind that the sale of the Jewish goods in the house of the prefect of Orleans alone brought in 337,000 francs.

How many of the refugees, reduced to beggary, fell victims to the hardships of their journey cannot be known. The bitter plaints of those oppressed by the heavy affliction sound mournful and touching even at this distance of time. Estori Parchi, then a youth of many accomplishments and noble heart, a relative of Jacob ben Machir, whose parents had emigrated from Spain to southern France, thus describes his sorrow: "From the house of study have they torn me; naked was I forced as a young man to leave my ancestral home, and wander from land to land, from people to people, whose tongues were strange to me." Parchi at length found a resting-place in Palestine. Another fugitive, the learned Aaron Cohen of Narbonne, poured forth this elegy: "Unhappy me, I saw the misery of the banishment of the sons of Jacob, like a herd of cattle driven asunder. From a position of honor I was thrown into a land of darkness." The sudden turn of fortune which changed rich men into beggars, and exposed the delicate and those used to the comforts of life to bitter privation, filled the bombastic poet Yedaya Bedaresi with gloomy reflections. In vivid colors he painted the trouble and pain of life, and man's helplessness and nothingness. His "Trial of the World" (Bechinath Olam), suggested by personal observation and bitter experience, consequently makes a depressing and mournful impression, and reflects faithfully the melancholy feelings of the ill-starred race.

The expulsion of the Jews from France by the stony-hearted Philip le Bel did not come off without martyred victims. Those who transgressed the time of grace, yet rejected solicitations to abjure their faith, were punished by death. A martyr of this time, Eleazar ben Joseph of Chinon, is specially famous. He was a learned, noble-minded man, a correspondent of Ben Adret, master of many distinguished disciples, among them the youthful Parchi, one of the last of the Tossafist school. He was condemned to the stake, although no crime could be laid at his door except that he was a Jew. With him died two brothers. The expatriated Jews dispersed in all parts of the world; many traveled to Palestine. But the majority remained as near as possible to the French borders, in Provence proper, at that time partly under German suzerainty, in the province of Roussillon, which belonged to the Aragonian king of Majorca, and in that island. Their intention was to wait for a favorable change of fortune, which would permit them to return to the land of their birth. They had not speculated falsely. King Philip himself was induced by avarice to unbend from his severity.

The vehement struggle in Montpellier about permitting Jewish youth to engage in the study of the sciences, remarkable to relate, continued after the banishment from France (September, 1306), and the mutual hatred of the two parties was in no way abated by suffering. A portion of the Tibbonide party had settled in Perpignan, which belonged to the king of Majorca, who was no favorer of the Jews. At his command copies of the Talmud were once more delivered up to the *auto-da-fé;* but as he hoped to gain some advantage by the settlement of intelligent, industrious Jews, he suffered them. Abba-Mari and another portion of the congregation of Montpellier at first took up their abode in the town of Arles, but as he could not stay there, he, too, emigrated to Perpignan (January, 1307). But the opposing party, which had influence with the king or governor, endeavored to hinder his settlement in that place. Abba-Mari's partisans, by making representations to the king, succeeded in obtaining permission for him to live in Perpignan. Here the controversy raged anew. Solomon ben Adret and Asheri, particularly the latter, whose decision of character had acquired for him the chief authority, again interfered. Asheri declared that he had given his signature in a half-hearted manner to the decree prohibiting young men from occupying themselves with profane studies; for, according to his opinion, it was too great a concession to permit it at the age of twenty-five. Science ought to be prohibited altogether, for it inevitably lures on to unbelief. The defenders of science were to be condemned without mercy, since the afflictions of exile had made no impression on them, suffering had not broken their spirit of defiance, and had not chastened their hardness of heart.

This view, that qualities prejudicial to Judaism were inherent in science, gained supremacy after Ben 'Adret's death (1310), when Asheri was acknowledged in Spain and in the neighboring countries as the only authority in religious matters. Asheri, his sons and companions who had migrated with him from Germany, transplanted from the Rhine to vivacious Toledo that spirit of honest, but tormenting, narrow-minded and intolerant piety; that gloomy disposition which regards even harmless joy as a sin; that feeling of abjectness, which characterized the German Jews of the Middle Ages, and they inoculated the Spanish Jews with it. The free activity of the mind was checked. Asheri concentrated all his mental power on the Talmud and its exposition. His chief work was a compilation of the Talmud for practical use (1307—1314). On all occasions he endeavored to enforce a difficult, painful, and severe discipline. If any one desired to express his thoughts on any department of knowledge whatsoever, he had to array his subject in the garments of contrite orthodoxy. When the erudite Isaac ben Joseph Israeli II, of Toledo, published an astronomical work (1310), he had to adjust it to Talmudical standards, and introduce it by a confession of faith, for only in this manner could he find grace in Asheri's eyes.

At about this time, during Asheri's rabbinate in Toledo, prominent Jews once more obtained influence at court. King Ferdinand IV (1295—1312) had a Jewish treasurer named Samuel, whose counsels he followed in political matters too. The dowager queen, Maria de Molina, who had held the reins of government during her son's minority, with feminine passionateness hated the favorite Samuel, who is said to have nourished the enmity between mother and son. One day, when Samuel was in Badajos, and was preparing to accompany the king to Seville, he was attacked by an assassin, and so severely wounded that he was left for dead. It is not known who instigated the deed. The king had such care and attention devoted to Samuel, that he recovered from his wounds.

Don Ferdinand's death brought in its train a time of unquiet, of civil war, and social anarchy for Spain. As the Infante Alfonso was still a child in the cradle, several persons, the clever Maria de Molina, the young queen-mother Constantia, and the uncles of the young king contended for the guardianship and the regency, and provoked faction feuds in the country (1312—1326). Donna Maria de Molina, who conducted the government, did not extend her hate against her son's Jewish counselor to the community to which he belonged. As in the lifetime of her husband she had had a Jewish favorite, Todros Abulafia, so during her regency she had a Jewish treasurer, Don Moses. When the council of Zamora (1313) renewed canonical laws hostile to the Jews, the cortes of Burgos demanded the exclusion of Jews from all honors and offices, and the pope issued a bull that Christians were to be absolved from their debts to Jews on account of usury, the wise regent submitted only in part. She ordered that Jews should not bear high-sounding Christian names, nor enter into close intercourse with Christians; but she most emphatically declared herself against the unjust abolition of debts, and published a law that no debtor could make himself free of his obligation to professors of the Jewish faith by appealing to a papal bull.

The regency of Don Juan Emanuel inaugurated an improvement in the condition of the Castilian Jews (1319—1325). The regent was a friend of learning, himself an author and poet, and was consequently held in esteem by educated Jews. A Jew of Cordova, Jehuda ben Isaac Ibn-Wakar, found high favor in his eyes, and probably acted as his treasurer. At his solicitation Juan Emanuel once more invested the rabbinate with penal jurisdiction, which the Jews had partly lost during the regency of Maria de Molina, and had practiced only privately.

Jehuda Ibn-Wakar, however, was an admirer of Asheri, and, like the latter, of excessive piety, desiring to have every religious transgression punished with the utmost severity. When a Cordovan uttered a blasphemy in Arabic, Ibn-Wakar asked Asheri what was to be done with him, and the latter replied that his tongue should be cut out. A beautiful Jewess having had intercourse with a Christian, Don Juan Manuel resigned her to the punishment of the Jewish court, and Jehuda Ibn-Wakar condemned her to have her face disfigured by the removal of her nose, and Asheri confirmed the sentence.

The southern Spanish and Castilian congregations still lived in peace, and in the undisturbed possession of their goods; on the other hand, the northern Spanish, and still more the southern French congregations were exposed to bloody attacks by fanatical hordes, which the church had unfettered, and then could not restrain. Jews once more lived in France. Louis X had recalled them nine years after their banishment (1315). This king, himself seized by a desire to abrogate the ordinances of his father and indict his counselors, had been solicited by the people and the nobility, who could not do without the Jews, to re-admit them into France. He accordingly entered into negotiations with them in reference to their return. But the Jews did not accept his proposal without deliberation, for they well knew the inconstancy of the French kings, and the fanatical hatred of the clergy against them. They hesitated at first, and then submitted their conditions. These were, that they be allowed to reside in the same places as before; that they should not be indictable for former transgressions; that their synagogues, churchyards, and books be restored to them, or sites be granted for new places of worship. They were to have the right of collecting the money owing to them, of which two-thirds should belong to the king. Their former privileges, as far as they were still in force, were to be again extended to them, or new ones conceded. King Louis accepted all these conditions, and granted them also the right of emigration under certain restrictions. In order to conciliate the clergy, he, on his side, imposed the conditions that they wear a badge of a certain size and color, and hold neither public nor private disputations on religion. Two high officials (prud'hommes, auditeurs des Juifs) were appointed to superintend the re-settlement of the Jews. Their residence in France was fixed for twelve years; if the king should resolve to expel them again after the expiration of that period, he put himself under the obligation to give them a year's warning that they might have time to make their preparations. The king published this decree, declaring that his father had been ill-advised to banish the Jews. As the voice of the people solicited their return, as the church desired a tolerant policy, and as the sainted Louis had set him the precedent of first banishing and then re-admitting them, he had, after due consultation with the prelates, the barons, and his high council, permitted the return of the Jews. The French Jews streamed back in masses to their former dwelling-places, regarding this event as a miraculous redemption. When Louis X died a year after, and his brother Philip V, the Long, ascended the throne, he extended their privileges, and protected them especially from the enmity of the clergy; so that they and their books could be seized only by royal officers. But they were not free from vexation by the degenerate clergy, who insisted that the Jews of Montpellier, who thought they could venture on certain liberties, should re-affix the Jew-badge on their dress. At one time they accused the Jews of Lünel with having publicly outraged the image of Christ on the Purim festival; at another time they ordered that two wagonfuls of copies of the Talmud be publicly burned in Toulouse. Such occurrences, however, were mere child's play compared with what they had to endure from the bigoted multitude.

Philip V had the idea, repugnant to the spirit of the time, of undertaking a crusade to wrest the Holy Land, after so many vain attempts, from the hands of the infidels. This enterprise appeared so foolish to the discerning, that even Pope John XXII, the second of the popes that resided in Avignon instead of at Rome, dissuaded him from it. Nevertheless, the fancy, as soon as it was known, inflamed the minds of the rude populace. A young man of excited imagination gave out that a dove had settled at one time on his head, at another, on his shoulder, and when he had sought to seize it, it had transformed itself into a beautiful woman, who urged him to gather a troop of crusaders, assuring him of victory. His utterances found credulous hearers, and the lower people, children, and swine-herds attached themselves to him. A wicked priest and an unfrocked Benedictine monk used the opportunity to force their way to the front, and thus arose in northern France (1320) a numerous horde of forty thousand shepherds (Pastoureaux, Pastorelli, Roïm), who moved in procession from town to town carrying banners, and announced their intention of journeying across the sea to deliver the so-called holy sepulcher. Their attention was immediately turned to the Jews, possibly because they wanted to raise money for the purchase of weapons by robbing the Jews of their possessions, or a Jew, as is related, had made sport of their childish heroism. The massacre of the Jews by the shepherds (Gesereth-ha-Roïm) is another bloody page in Jewish history.

Nearly all the crusading enterprises had commenced with the murder of Jews; so this time. The shepherd-gangs which had collected near the town of Agen (on the Garonne) cut down all the Jews they met on their march from this place to Toulouse, if they refused to be baptized. About five hundred Jews had found refuge in the fortress of Verdun (on the Garonne), the commandant having placed a strong tower at their disposal. The shepherds took it by storm, and a desperate battle took place. As the Jews had no hopes of rescue, they had recourse in their despair to self-destruction. The unhappy people selected the oldest and most respected man of their number to slay them one after the other. The old man picked out a muscular young assistant in this ghastly business, and both went to work to rid their fellow-sufferers of their miserable lives. When at last the young man, after slaying his aged partner, was left alone, the desire of life came strong upon him; he declared to the besieging shepherds that he was ready to go over to them, and asked to be baptized. The latter were just or cruel enough to refuse the request, and tore the renegade to pieces. The Jewish children found in the tower were baptized by force. The governor of Toulouse zealously espoused the cause of the Jews, and summoned the knights to take the approaching shepherds prisoners. Thus many of them were brought in chains to the capital, and thrown into prison. But the mob, which sympathized with them, banded together, and set them at liberty, the result being that the greater part of the congregation of Toulouse was destroyed. A few seceded to Christianity. On the capture of the shepherds near Toulouse, the Jews in the neighborhood, who had been granted shelter in Castel-Narbonnais, thought that they were now free of all danger, and left their place of refuge. They were surprised by the rabble, and annihilated. Thus perished almost all the Jews in the neighborhood of Bordeaux, Gascogne, Toulouse, Albi, and other towns of southern France. Altogether, more than 120 Jewish congregations in France and northern Spain were blotted out through the rising of the Shepherds, and the survivors were so impoverished by spoliation that they were dependent upon the succor of their brethren in other parts, which flowed to them in abundance even from Germany.

The following year, too, was very unfortunate for the Jews, the trouble again beginning in France. This persecution was occasioned by lepers, from whom it has its name (Gesereth Mezoraim). The unhappy people afflicted by leprosy in the Middle Ages were banished from society, declared dead as citizens, shut up in unhealthy quarters, and there tended after a fashion. Once, when certain lepers in the province of Guienne had been badly provided with food, they conceived and carried into effect the plan of poisoning the wells and rivers, through which many people perished (1321). When the matter was traced back to the lepers, and they were examined under torture, one of them invented, or somebody suggested to him, the lying accusation that the Jews had inspired them with the plan of poisoning the waters. The charge was generally believed; even King Philip V had no doubt about it. Sometimes it was asserted that the Jews wanted to take revenge for the sufferings experienced at the hands of the Shepherds the year before; again, that they had been persuaded by the Mahometan king of Granada to cause the Christians to be poisoned; or it was suggested that they had done it in league with the Mahometan ruler of Palestine, to frustrate the intended crusade of King Philip. In several places Jews were arrested on this accusation, unmercifully tortured, and some of them burnt (Tammuz—July, 1321). In Chinon a deep pit was dug, fire kindled in it, and eight Jewish men and women thrown in, who sang whilst dying. The mothers had previously cast in their children, to save them from forcible baptism. Altogether five thousand are said to have suffered death by fire in that year. Many were banished from France, and robbed by the heartless populace. Philip was convinced later on of the untruth of the accusation; but as the Jews had been accused, he seemed to think that the opportunity might be used to swell the treasury. Accordingly, the congregations were condemned by Parliament to a penalty of one hundred and fifty thousand pounds (Parisian); they were to apportion the contributions among themselves. Deputies (procureurs) from northern France (de la langue française) and from Languedoc, met and enacted that the southern French Jews, decimated and impoverished by the previous year's massacre, were to contribute forty-seven thousand pounds, and the remainder was to be borne by the northern French Jews. The wealthiest Jews were put under arrest as security for the payment of the fine, and their goods and debts distrained.

In the same year a great danger threatened the oldest of the European communities. Misfortune came upon it the more unexpectedly as till then it had tasted but little of the cup of misery which the Jews of England, France and Spain so often had to drink to the dregs. It was because Rome did not belong to the pope, but to the families of Orsini and Colonna, to the Ghibellines and Guelphs—the great and minor lords, who fought out their party feuds in that city—that the Jews were left untouched by papal tyranny. It was well for them that they were little considered.

At about this time the Roman Jews had made an advance in material welfare and intellectual culture. There were some who possessed houses like palaces, furnished with all the comforts of life. Since the time when, through the concurrence of favorable circumstances, they had tasted of the tree of knowledge, learning and poetry were cherished by the Italian Jews. The seeds which Hillel of Verona, Serachya ben Shaltiel and others had scattered, commenced to bear fruit. When the flower of intellectual glory in southern France began to decay through the severity of Talmudical rigorists and the bloody persecutions, it unfolded itself in Italy, especially in Rome. At that time the first rays of a new cultural development, breaking through the gloom of priestcraft and the rude violence of the Middle Ages, appeared in Italy. A fresh current of air swept the heavens in Italy in the beginning of the fourteenth century, the epoch of Dante, thawing the icy coat of the church and of knightdom, the two pillars of the Middle Ages. A sense of citizenship, the impulse towards liberty, enthusiastic love for science, were the striking symptoms of a new spirit, of a striving for rejuvenescence, which only the emperor, the embodiment of rude, ungainly knighthood, and the pope, the incarnation of the stern, unbending church, failed to perceive. Every greater or lesser Italian lord made it a point of honor to encourage art and science, and patronize poets, artists and learned men at his court. Nor were the Jews overlooked at this juncture. One of the most powerful Italian princes, Robert of Anjou, king of Naples, count of Provence (Arelat), vicar-general of the Papal States and for some time titular lieutenant of the Holy Roman empire, was a friend of science, a warm admirer also of Jewish literature, and consequently a protector of the Jews. Several Jewish littérateurs were his teachers, or at his instance undertook scientific and theological works.

Either in imitation of the current practice or from sincere interest in Jewish literature, rich Jews, who played the part of small princes, invited Jewish authors into their circle, lightened their material cares by liberal support, and stimulated their activity by encouragement. Thus it came to pass that three

Jewish Italian men of letters had the courage to compete with the Spaniards and Provençals. These were Leo Romano, Judah Siciliano, and above all the poet Immanuel Romi, who once more ennobled neo-Hebrew poetry, and raised it to a higher level. The Roman congregation at that time displayed exceptional interest in Jewish writings. Of Maimuni, the embodiment of science for them as for the rest of the Jewish world, they possessed the copious Religious Codex, and the translation of his "Guide;" but of his luminous Mishna commentary, composed originally in Arabic, only those parts which Charisi and Samuel Ibn-Tibbon had done into Hebrew. The representatives of the Roman congregations, to whom probably the poet Immanuel also belonged, wished to have a complete edition of the work, and sent a messenger to Barcelona to Ben Adret expressly for the purpose of procuring the remaining parts. The affair was not so simple as the Roman Jews had imagined. The greater portion of the anxiously desired commentary of Maimuni on the Mishna, on account of peculiar difficulties, was not yet rendered into Hebrew. The greatest obstacle was the circumstance that the Spanish Jews, except those in Toledo and in the neigborhood of the kingdom of Granada, had forgotten Arabic. Ben Adret, who wished to oblige the Roman congregation, endeavored to get the required portions translated into Hebrew. He encouraged scholars, learned both in Arabic and the Talmud, to undertake this difficult task, and Joseph Ibn-Alfual and Jacob Abbassi of Huesca, Solomon ben Jacob and Nathaniel Ibn-Almali, the last two physicians of Saragossa, and others divided the labor among themselves. Jewish literature is indebted for the possession of this most valuable work of Maimuni to the zeal of the Roman congregation, of Ben Adret, and these translators.

The Roman community was roused from its peaceful occupations and undisturbed quiet by a rough hand, and awakened to the consciousness that it existed under the scourge of priestcraft and the caprice of its rulers.

It is related that a sister of the pope (John XXII), named Sangisa, had repeatedly exhorted her brother to expel the Jews from the holy city of Christendom. Her solicitations had always been fruitless; she therefore instigated several priests to give testimony that the Jews had ridiculed by words and actions a crucifix which was carried through the streets in a procession. The pope thereupon issued the command to banish all the Jews from Roman territory. All that is certain is that the Jews of Rome were in great danger during that year, for they instituted an extraordinary fast, and directed fervent prayers to heaven (21 Sivan—18 June, 1321), nor did they fail to employ worldly means. They sent an astute messenger to Avignon to the papal court and to King Robert of Naples, the patron of the Jews, who happened to be in that city on state affairs. The messenger succeeded, through the mediation of King Robert, in proving the innocence of the Roman Jews in regard to the alleged insulting of the cross and the other transgressions laid to their charge. The twenty thousand ducats, which the Roman community is said to have presented to the sister of the pope, silenced the last objections. The Jews of Rome entered their school of trouble later than the Jews of other countries. For that reason it lasted the longer.

Whilst King Robert was residing in southern France, he seems to have made the acquaintance of a learned, genial Jewish satirist, Kalonymos ben Kalonymos, and to have taken him into his service. This talented man (born 1287, died before 1337) possessed solid knowledge, was familiar with the Arabic language and literature (which was very remarkable in a Provençal), and in his youth (1307–1317) translated medical, astronomical, and philosophical writings from that language into Hebrew. Kalonymos ben Kalonymos was not merely a hewer of wood and drawer of water, an interpreter in the realm of science; he had intellect enough to make independent observations. Disregarding the province of metaphysical speculation, he was more interested in pure ethics, which he especially wished to inculcate in his co-religionists, "because neglect and ignorance of it leads men to all kinds of perversities and mutual harm." He did not treat the subject in a dry, uninteresting style, but sought to clothe it in attractive garments. With this end in view, Kalonymos adapted a part of the Arabic encyclopedia of science (which was in circulation under the name of "Treatises of the Righteous Brethren") for a dialogue between man and beasts, giving the theme a Jewish coloring.

In another work, "Touchstone" (composed at the end of 1322), Kalonymos ben Kalonymos held up a mirror for his Jewish contemporaries, in which they could recognize their perversities, follies, and sins. To avoid giving himself the appearance of an irreproachable censor of morals, he enumerated his own sins, more in satire than as a confession. Kalonymos whimsically satirized even Judaism. He wished he had been born a woman, for then he would not have had to bear the burden of six hundred and thirteen religious laws, besides so many Talmudical restrictions and rigorous ordinances, which could not possibly be fulfilled, even when a man tried with the most exacting conscientiousness. As a woman, he would not have to trouble himself with so much reading, to study the Bible, the Talmud, and the subjects belonging to it, nor torment himself with logic, mathematics, physics, astronomy, and philosophy. By and by Kalonymos' satire grew deeply serious. The degradation of his Jewish co-religionists, and the bloody persecutions occasioned by the Shepherds and the lepers, dispelled his mocking humor, and satire was changed into lamentation. In Rome, which King Robert assigned to him as a place of residence, Kalonymos, having been furnished with letters of recommendation, obtained entry into a joyous, vivacious, imaginative circle of men, by whom he was stimulated to write a peculiar parody. He composed a treatise for the Jewish carnival (Purim), in which he imitated the tenor and spirit of the Talmud, its method, controversies, and digressions, with considerable wit. It is a fine parody, exciting laughter at every step, and one can not tell whether it was intended as a harmless carnival joke or as a satire on the Talmud. Kalonymos occupied a position of importance in the Roman congregation. Handsome in form, of abundant accomplishments, solid character, all his excellencies enhanced by the good opinion of King Robert of Naples, he was everyone's favorite. The Italian Jews were proud of him. But Kalonymos was not a true poet, still less an artist.

Much more gifted, profound, and imaginative was his older friend and admirer, Immanuel ben Solomon Romi (born about 1265, died about 1330). He was an anomaly in the Jewish society of the Middle Ages. He belonged to that species of authors whose writings are all the more attractive because not very decent. Of overflowing wit, extravagant humor, and caustic satire, he is always able to enchain his readers, and continually to provoke their merriment. Immanuel may be called the Heine of the Jewish Middle Ages. Immanuel had an inexhaustible, ready supply of brilliant ideas. And all this in the holy language of the Prophets and Psalmists. Granted that the neo-Hebrew poets and thinkers, the grammarians and Talmudists, had lent flexibility to the language, but none of Immanuel's predecessors had his power of striking from it showers of sparkling wit. But if, on the one side, he developed the Hebrew language almost into a vehicle for brilliant repartee, on the other side, he robbed it of its sacred character. Immanuel transformed the chaste, closely-veiled maiden muse of Hebrew poetry into a lightly-clad dancer, who attracts the attention of passers-by. He allows his muse to deal with the most frivolous and indelicate topics without the slightest concealment or shame. His collection of songs and novels tends to exert a very pernicious and poisonous effect upon hot-blooded youth. But Immanuel was not the hardened sinner, as he describes himself, who thought of nothing but to carry on amours, seduce the fair, and deride the ugly. He sinned only with the tongue and the pen, scarcely with the heart and the senses.

Though he often indulges in unmeasured self-laudation, this simple description of his moral conduct must still be credited: "I never bear my enemies malice, I remain steadfast and true to my friends, cherish gratitude towards my benefactors, have a sympathetic heart, am not ostentatious with my knowledge, and absorb myself in science and poetry, whilst my companions riot in sensual enjoyments." Immanuel belonged to those who are dominated by their wit, and cannot refrain from telling some pointed witticism, even if their dearest friends are its victims, and the holiest things are dragged in the mire by it. He allowed himself to be influenced by the vivacity of the Italians and the Europeanized Jews, and put no curb upon his tongue. What is remarkable in this satirist is that his life, his position, and occupation seem to have been in contradiction with his poetical craft. In the Roman community he filled an honorable position, was something like a president, at all events a man of distinction. He appears to have belonged to the medical profession, although he made sport of the quackery of physicians. In short, he led the domestic life of his time, a life permeated by morality and religion, giving no opportunity for excess. But his honorable life did not prevent him from singing riotous songs, and from writing as though he were unconscious of the seriousness of religion, of responsibility and learning. Immanuel was acquainted, if not on intimate terms, with the greatest poet of the Middle Ages, the first to open the gates of a new epoch, and to prognosticate the unity of Italy in poetic phrase. Probably they came to know each other on one of Dante's frequent visits to Rome, either as ambassador or exile. Although their poetic styles are as opposite as the poles—Dante's ethereal, grave, and elevated; Immanuel's forcible, gay, and light—they, nevertheless, have some points of contact. Each had absorbed the culture of the past; Dante the catholic, scholastic, and romantic elements; Immanuel the biblical, Talmudical, Maimunist, philosophical, and neo-Hebraic products. Both elaborated this many-hued material, and molded it into a new kind of poetry. The Italians at that time were full of the impulse of life, and Immanuel's muse is inspired by the witchery of spring. He wrote ably in Italian, too, of which a beautiful poem, still extant, gives evidence. Immanuel was the first to adapt Italian numbers to the neo-Hebraic lyre. He introduced the rhyme in alternate lines (Terza rima in sonnet form), by which he produced a musical cadence. His poems are not equally successful. They are wanting not in imagination, but in tenderness and grace. His power lies in poetical prose (Meliza), where he can indulge in free and witty allusions. In this style he composed a host of short novels, riddles, letters, panegyrics, and epithalamia, which, by clever turns and comic situations, extort laughter from the most serious-minded readers.

In one of his novels he introduces a quarrelsome grammarian of the Hebrew language, a verbal critic who takes the field in grammatical campaigns, and is accompanied by a marvelously beautiful woman. Immanuel enters into a hair-splitting disputation that he may have the opportunity of coquetting with the lovely lady. He suffers defeat in grammar, but makes a conquest in love. Immanuel's description of hell and paradise, in which he imitated his friend Dante, is full of fine satire. Whilst the Christian romantic poet shows gravity and elevation in his poetical creation, represents sinners and criminals, political opponents and enemies of Italy, cardinals and popes, as being tortured in hell, metes out, as it were, the severe sentences of judgment day; his Jewish friend, Immanuel, invents scenes in heaven and hell for the purpose of giving play to his humorous fancy. Dante wrote a divine, Immanuel a human, comedy. He introduces his pilgrimage to heaven and hell by relating that he once felt greatly oppressed by the burden of his sins, and experienced compunction; at this juncture his young friend Daniel, by whose untimely death he had lately been deeply affected, appeared to him, and offered to guide him through the dismal portals of hell and the elysian fields of the blessed. In the chambers of hell Immanuel observes all the wicked and godless of the Bible. Aristotle, too, is there, "because he taught the eternity of the world," and Plato, "because he asserted the reality of species" (Realism). Most of all he scourges his contemporaries in this poem. He inflicts the torment of the damned upon the deriders of science; upon a Talmudist who secretly led a most immoral life; upon men who committed intellectual thefts, and upon those who sought to usurp all the honors of the synagogue, the one to have his seat by the Ark of the Covenant, the other to read the prayers on the Day of Atonement. Quack doctors are also precipitated into hell, because they take advantage of the stupidity and credulity of the multitude, and bring trusting patients to a premature grave. His young, beatified guide goes with him through the gates of Paradise. How the departed spirits rejoice at the poet's approach! They call out, "Now is the time to laugh, for Immanuel has arrived." In the description of paradise and its inhabitants, Immanuel affects to treat his theme very seriously; but he titters softly within the very gates of heaven. Of course, he notices the holy men, the patriarchs, the pious kings and heroes of the Jewish past, the prophets and the great teachers, the poets, Jehuda Halevi and Charisi, the Jewish philosopher Maimuni. But next to King David, who fingers the harp and sings psalms, he observes the harlot Rahab who concealed the spies in Jericho, and Tamar who sat at the cross-roads waiting. Dante excludes the heathen world from paradise, because it did not acknowledge Christ, and had no share in the grace of salvation. Immanuel sees a troop of the blessed, whom he does not recognize, and asks their leader who they are. "These are," answers the latter, "righteous and moral heathens, who attained the height of wisdom, and recognized the only God as the creator of the world and the bestower of grace." The pious authors, David, Solomon, Isaiah, Ezekiel, on seeing Immanuel, darted forward to meet him; each one thanks him for having expounded his writings so well, and here older and contemporary exegetists come in for their share of Immanuel's sly satire.

Neo-Hebraic poetry, which began with José ben José, and reached its zenith in Ibn-Gebirol and Jehuda Halevi, attains its final stage of development in Immanuel. The gamut had now been run. After Immanuel, the Hebrew muse became silent for a long time, and it required a fresh and powerful stimulus to awaken it from slumber to new energy. Verses were, of course, written after his days, and rhymes polished, but they are as far removed from poetry as a street-song from a soul-stirring melody.

The fate of Hebrew poetry is illustrated in Immanuel's career. For a long period he was popular, every one sought his friendship, but in old age he fell into neglect and poverty. His own statement is that his generosity dissipated his means. He was as much derided as he had formerly been praised. He left Rome with his family, traveled about, and found repose at length at the house of a wealthy, influential friend of art (Benjamin?) in Fermo, who interested himself in him, and encouraged him to arrange the verses and poems written at different periods of his life into a symmetrical whole.

The praises which Immanuel bestows on his own productions, and his boast that he casts the old poets into the shade, certainly tend to produce a bad impression. Nevertheless, like every expert in his profession, he was far removed from that repulsive vanity which perceives its own depreciation in the recognition of another. To true merit Immanuel gave the tribute of his warmest praise, and modestly conceded precedence to it. Not only did he extol the highly honored Kalonymos, basking in the sunshine of the king's favor, with the most extravagant figures of speech, but he praised almost more heartily the poet Jehuda Siciliano, who lived in straitened circumstances. He gave him the palm for poetical verse, maintaining his own superiority in poetical prose. But for Immanuel, nothing would have been known of this poet. Poor Siciliano had to waste his power in occasional poems for his subsistence, and was thus unable to produce any lasting work. With glowing enthusiasm Immanuel eulogizes his cousin, the young and learned Leone Romano, Jehuda ben Moses ben Daniel (born about 1292), whom he calls the "Crown of Thought." In paradise he allots to him the highest place of honor. Leone Romano was the teacher of King Robert of Naples, and instructed him in the original language of the Bible. He knew the language of learned

Christendom, and was probably the first Jew to pay attention to scholastic philosophy. He translated for Jewish readers the philosophical compositions of Albertus Magnus, Thomas Aquinas, and others. Leone Romano composed original works of exegesis, set forth in philosophical method. Greatly as his contemporaries admired his learning and intellect, which had achieved so much when he had scarcely arrived at man's estate, he exercised no influence whatever on posterity.

The Roman society which promoted science and poetry may be said to have included also the grandson of a Roman emigrant who took up his abode in Greece, Shemarya Ikriti (Cretan) of Negroponte (flourished 1290—1320). He stood in close relation with the Roman community and King Robert. Familiar with Talmudical literature, as he probably was rabbi in Negroponte, he devoted himself to philosophical speculations, and was, perhaps, well read in the Greek philosophical literature in its original language. In his youth, Ikriti, like many of his contemporaries, occupied himself with translations of philosophical works. Later on he conceived a plan of practical utility, in which he thought he could turn his knowledge to account. He sought to smooth over the difference between the Rabbanites and the Karaites, and lastingly to reconcile the sects at enmity with each other for centuries, "that all Israel may once more be united in one fraternal bond." Shemarya of Negroponte was the first, perhaps the only Rabbanite, who, if he did not extend the hand of reconciliation to Karaism, at least showed a friendly disposition towards it. He recognized that both parties were in error; Karaism was wrong in rejecting Talmudical traditions unconditionally; but the Rabbanites sinned against truth in placing the Talmud in the forefront, and overlooking the Bible. In Greece there may have been Karaites at that time who had come from Constantinople. To these Shemarya Ikriti addressed himself to incline their minds towards union with the mother community.

For the difficult task of bringing discordant faiths into harmony, much intelligence and energy were required, and Shemarya could furnish only good will. He was not deficient in knowledge, but his mental grasp was not sufficiently powerful. At the instance of King Robert, who interested himself in Jewish literature, he wrote a commentary on the Bible, and forwarded to him, with a dedication, the books first completed (1328). It read as follows: "To our noble king Robert, adorned like King Solomon with the crown of wisdom and the diadem of royalty, I send this exposition of the cosmogony and the Song of Songs." His Biblical commentaries were set forth with great diffuseness, covered a great range, and were not calculated to appeal to the Karaites, and draw them over to the side of rabbinical Judaism. His attempt at reconciliation miscarried, perhaps was not made in the proper spirit; for there was a disposition on the part of some Karaites to treat his overtures favorably, and his efforts would not have failed, if they had been conducted with skill. Nevertheless, Ikriti was held in such esteem in his time that the Roman congregation took an interest in his labors, entered into correspondence with him, while the Karaites assiduously read his works, and in later times considered him a member of their own party.

Karaism was still dragging itself along in its decaying, stiffening form. Internal schisms remained unaccommodated. Different Karaite congregations celebrated the festivals at different times: the Palestinians, according to the observation of the new moon, and the extra-Palestinian congregations, in common with the Rabbanites. Their extremely severe marriage laws were not finally settled even at this epoch. Karaism at that time had three centers—Cairo in Egypt, Constantinople in the Byzantine Empire, and Sulchat (Eski-Crim) in the Crimean peninsula. Some importance was possessed by Aaron ben Joseph the Elder, physician in Constantinople (flourished about 1270—1300). He came originally from the Crimea, made extensive voyages, and acquired a knowledge of medicine and philosophy. Aaron I also made himself intimate with Rabbanite literature to a degree that few of his sect attained. He made use of Nachmani's commentary on the Pentateuch, and from this circumstance arose the mistake of later Karaites, that Aaron had sat at Nachmani's feet. His familiarity with Rabbanite literature had a beneficial effect on his style; he wrote much more clearly and intelligibly than most of the Karaite authors. He was even disposed to accept the tradition of the Talmud.

He completely fixed the Karaite prayer book (Siddur Tefila), hitherto in an unsettled condition, incorporating into it hymns written by Gebirol, Jehuda Halevi, Ibn-Ezra, and other Rabbanite liturgical poets. Aaron himself possessed very little poetical genius, and his metrical prayers, with which he enriched the prayer book of the Karaites, have no great poetical merit, but by the admission of hymns written by Rabbanites into his compilation, he showed that he knew how to appreciate the devout sublimity in the prayers of the Spanish Jews, and that he was not altogether devoid of taste. If Shemarya, of Negroponte, had undertaken to effect a reconciliation between the Rabbanites and the Karaites in a more intelligent and energetic manner, there can be no doubt that Aaron would willingly have offered his assistance, provided, of course, that he had known of Shemarya's attempt. There was not wanting among Karaites a strong inclination for union. Owing to the activity of Abraham Maimuni II, a great-grandson of the renowned Maimuni, who had succeeded to the post of Chief (Nagid) of the Rabbanite communities in Egypt after the death of his father David, an important Karaite congregation in Egypt on one day openly acknowleged the teachings of the Rabbanites. In Palestine, too, frequent conversions of Karaites to Talmudical Judaism took place. On this account the rabbis of the time were more favorably disposed towards them. On the one hand, the strict Talmudist Samson of Sens denounced the Karaites as heathens, whose wine was not to be partaken of by orthodox Jews; on the other hand, Estori Parchi, who had been banished from Provence, and who, emigrating to Palestine, had settled in Bethshan, recognized them as co-religionists, led astray by erroneous notions, but not to be rejected.

CHAPTER III.

THE AGE OF THE ASHERIDES AND OF GERSONIDES.

Condition of Palestine—Pilgrims and Immigrants—Shem Tob Ibn-Gaon—Favorable Position of the Jews in Castile under Alfonso XI—Persecution in Navarre—Joseph de Ecija and Samuel Ibn-Wakar—Increase of Anti-Jewish Feelings—Abner-Alfonso of Burgos, Convert to Christianity, and Persecutor of the Jews—Gonzalo Martinez—Fall of Martinez and Deliverance of the Jews—Decline of the Study of Science—The Study of the Talmud prosecuted with Renewed Vigor—Jacob and Judah Asheri—Isaac Pulgar, David Ibn-Albilla—The Provençal Philosophers Ibn-Kaspi, Leon de Bagnols, and Vidal Narboni—Decline of the Study of the Talmud in Germany—Emperor Louis of Bavaria and the Jews—Persecution by the "Leather-Arms."

1328—1350 C.E.

THE Holy Land was once more accessible to its children. The Egyptian sultans, into whose power it passed after the fall of Accho and the expulsion of the Christians, were more tolerant than the Christian Byzantine emperors and the Frankish crusading kings. They did not hinder the coming of Jewish pilgrims who desired to lighten their over-burdened hearts by praying and weeping over the ruins of the past, so rich in recollections, or at the graves of their great men there interred; nor did they oppose the settlement of European exiles, who again cultivated the soil of the land of their fathers. The long, firm, yet mild, reign of the Mameluke sultan, Nassir Mahomet (1299—1341), was a happy time for the Jews who visited Palestine. Whilst under the rule of the Christian governors of the country no Jew was permitted to approach the former capital, at this time Jewish pilgrims from Egypt and Syria regularly came to Jerusalem, to celebrate the festivals, as in the time when the Temple shone in all its splendor. The Karaites established special forms of prayer for those who went on pilgrimages to Jerusalem: at their departure, the whole congregation assembled to give utterance in prayer to the bitter-sweet emotions connected with Zion. The immigrants who settled in Palestine engaged in agriculture. They came to feel so thoroughly at home there that the question was mooted whether the laws of tithes, of the year of release, and others ought not to be again carried into effect. In consequence of the freedom and tolerance which the Jews were enjoying, many enthusiastic spirits were again seized by the ardent desire to kiss the dust of the Holy Land. Emigration to Palestine, especially from the extreme west, became very common at this time.

A pupil of Meïr of Rothenburg, named Abraham, a painstaking copyist of holy writings, considered his dwelling in the Holy Land a mark of divine grace. Two young Kabbalists, Chananel Ibn-Askara and Shem Tob Ibn-Gaon from Spain, also traveled thither, probably to be nearer the source of the mystic doctrines, which fancy assigned to this country, and took up their residence in Safet. But instead of obtaining fresh information upon the doctrines of the Kabbala, one of them—Ibn-Askara died in his youth—introduced new features of the science. Shem Tob ben Abraham Ibn-Gaon, from Segovia (born 1283, died after 1330), whose teacher in the Talmud had been Ben Adret, and in the Kabbala Isaac ben Todros, was a zealous adherent of the secret science, and described even Maimuni as a Kabbalist.

The congregation of Jerusalem was at this time very numerous. A large portion of the Rabbanite community led a contemplative life, studied the Talmud day and night, and became engrossed with the secret lore of the Kabbala. There were also handicraftsmen, merchants, and several acquainted with the science of medicine, with mathematics and astronomy. The artistic work of the famous calligraphers of Jerusalem was in great demand, far and near. Hebron, too, possessed a vigorous community, whose members engaged chiefly in the weaving and dyeing of cotton-stuffs, and in the manufacture of glass wares, exported in large quantities. In the south of Palestine, in company with Mahometans, Jewish shepherds again pastured their flocks after the manner of the patriarchs. Their rabbi was also a shepherd, and delivered discourses upon the Talmud in the pasture fields for such as desired to obtain instruction.

Although the Holy Land was the goal of ardent, longing hearts, yet it was no more a center for the dispersed of the Jewish race than it had been for a long time previous. It could not produce an original leader of any sort, and lived upon the crumbs of culture dropped by the Jews in Europe. The Kabbala, studied in Palestine since the time of Nachmani, was an exotic plant which could never flourish very well there, and degenerated into rankest superstition. The Holy Land did not even produce a Talmudical authority of widespread renown; also for earnest rabbinical studies it had become dependent upon Europe. The leadership of Judaism in the days after the death of Ben Adret and Asheri remained with Spain, not as formerly Aragon, but Castile, where the family of Asheri and their views prevailed. Here lived Talmudical authorities whose decisions were considered final. Here was still to be found, if not a flourishing state of science, at least appreciation of scientific research. In Castile, under the rule of the powerful and intelligent Alfonso XI, the Jews were in so prosperous a condition that, compared with other countries in Europe, this period may be called a Golden Age. Several clever Jews in succession, under the modest title of ministers of finance (Almoxarif), exercised an influence upon the course of politics. Not only the court, but also the great nobles, surrounded themselves with Jewish counselors and officers. In place of the humble, servile bearing, and the degrading badge which the church decreed for the Jews, the Jewish Spaniards still bore their heads erect, and clothed themselves in gold and silk. Dazzled by the glitter of this favorable state of affairs, some recognized the fulfillment of the old prophecy, "the scepter shall not depart from Judah," which Christians had so often employed in their attacks on Judaism.

It is scarcely to be wondered at, if the Spanish Jews were unduly elated because of the promotion of a few from their midst to state offices. Such prominent public men were for the most part a protecting shield for the communities against the avaricious and turbulent lower orders of the nobility, against the stupid credulity and envy of the mob, and the serpent-like cunning of the clergy, lying concealed but ready to attack the Jews. Jewish ministers and counselors in the service and the retinue of the king, clothed in the costume of the court, and wearing at their sides the knightly sword, by these very circumstances, without special intercession, disarmed the enemies of their brethren in faith and race. The impoverished nobles, who possessed nothing more than their swords, were filled with envy of the rich and wise court Jews; but they were compelled to stifle their feelings. The masses, guided by appearances, did not venture, as was done in Germany, to ill-treat or slay any Jew they chanced across, as an outlaw and a pariah, because they knew that the Jews were held in high favor at court. They often overrated their influence, believing that the Jews at court could obtain a hearing with the king at any time. Even the haughty clergy were obliged to restrain themselves so long as Joseph of Ecija, Samuel Ibn-Wakar, and others, were in a position to counteract their influence.

If the Castilian Jews compared the condition of their brethren in neighboring countries with their own, they must certainly have felt exalted, and entitled to be proud of their lot. In Aragon, at this time united into one kingdom with the islands of Majorca and Sicily, the persecuting spirit of the church, which Raymond de Penyaforte had stirred up, and Jayme I had perpetuated by means of oppressive laws, was rampant. In Navarre, which for half a century had belonged to the crown of France, the hatred against the Jews burned with a frenzy hitherto to be met with only in Germany. The last of the Capets, Charles IV, was dead, and with the accession of Philip VI to the French throne the House of Valois began. It is noteworthy that even Christians believed that the extinction of the lineal successors of Philip le Bel was retribution for his merciless expulsion of the Jews from France. The people of Navarre strove to separate themselves from the rule of France, and form an independent state. It is not known in how far the Jews stood in the way of their project. Anyhow it is certain that suddenly, throughout the whole country, a bloodthirsty enmity arose against the Jews, prompted by envy of their riches, and fostered by the monks. A Franciscan, named Pedro Olligoyen, made himself most prominent in goading on the deluded mob against the innocent Jews. In the large congregation of Estella a most horrible massacre began on a Sabbath (23d Adar—5th March, 1328). The infuriated mob raised the cry, "Death to the Jews, or their conversion."

In vain did the Jews attempt to defend themselves in their streets; the inhabitants of the city, strengthened by troops from other places, besieged them, and took by storm the walls which surrounded the Jewish quarter, breaking them down and slaying almost all the Jews of the city. They also set fire to the Jewish houses, and reduced them to ashes. The description by an eye-witness of his own sufferings gives only a feeble idea of the horrors of this savage massacre in Estella. The murderers had slain the parents and the four younger brothers of Menachem ben Zerach, then barely twenty years old, afterwards a scholar of commanding influence. He himself was wounded by the murderers and knocked down, lying on the ground unconscious, from evening till midnight, beneath a number of corpses. A compassionate knight, a friend of Menachem's father, searched for him beneath the pile of corpses, took him to his house, and had him carefully tended till he recovered from his wounds. Similar scenes of barbarity were enacted in other parts of the country, especially in Tudela, the largest community in Navarre, and in the smaller ones of Falcos, Funes, Moncilla, Viana and others, but nowhere to so frightful an extent as in Estella. Over six thousand Jews perished in these massacres. Only the Jews of the capital, Pampeluna, appear to have escaped these savage attacks. The people of Navarre at length succeeded in their desire; their country was separated from France, and obtained a king of its own, Philip III, Count of Evreux and Angoulême. As soon as he was crowned, the relatives of the murdered entreated him to mete out justice. At first, Philip prosecuted the guilty persons in real earnest; he ordered the ringleaders, the Franciscan Pedro Olligoyen and others to be cast into prison, and laid a fine upon the cities in which these crimes had been committed. But, in course of time, he liberated all the imprisoned, and remitted the fine as an act of grace. He took good care, too, not to let the stolen property and the possessions of persons without heirs escape him; they had to be surrendered to him, just as in Germany. There was no objection to the Jews' being slaughtered, but the royal treasury was not to suffer loss on that account. This king and his successors imposed new burdens upon the wretched people. The Jews of Navarre now began to sink into degradation like those of Germany.

The sun that was shining upon them in Castile at this time was, strictly speaking, only a false sun, but its glimmer, compared with the gloom wherein the congregations of other countries were steeped, gives at least momentary pleasure. Alfonso XI, as soon as he came of age, and obtained the sovereignty (1325—1380), had two Jewish favorites, Don Joseph of Ecija and Samuel Ibn-Wakar. The former, whose full name was Joseph ben Ephraim Ibn-Benveniste Halevi, had a pleasing exterior, understood music, and knew how to ingratiate himself with those in power. At the recommendation of his uncle, the king had made him not only minister of finance (Almoxarif), but also his confidential counselor (privado), whose opinion he highly valued. Joseph of Ecija possessed a state carriage, knights accompanied him as an escort on his journeys, and hidalgos dined at his table. On one occasion the king dispatched him on a very important and honorable mission which almost cost him his life. He was besieged by the citizens of Valladolid in the palace of the Infanta, and they demanded his surrender with tumultuous clamor. Some of Joseph's retinue succeeded in escaping from the city, and they hastened at full speed to the king, to whom they related what had taken place. Alfonso rightly considered this a revolt against his sovereignty. He marched rapidly against Valladolid, and summoned the knights of Old Castile to join him. For the sake of his Jewish favorite, he besieged the former capital of his kingdom, burnt many houses, and would have destroyed the place entirely, had not more moderate persons intervened, and explained to the king that the people were not so much embittered against Don Joseph as against Don Alvar Nuñez, whose influence was most hateful to them. Don Alfonso thereupon condescended to remove Alvar from his public offices, whilst Don Joseph continued in favor with the king.

The other favorite of King Alfonso was his physician, Don Samuel Ibn-Wakar (Abenhuacar). This man had a scientific education, was an astronomer, and perhaps the astrologer of his master. Although he occupied no public office, and took no part in state affairs, yet, through the favor of the king, he possessed very great influence. There existed between Don Joseph of Ecija and Ibn-Wakar the jealousy which is common among courtiers who bask in the rays of the same sun. On account of their rivalry, these two favorites sought to injure each other, and thus they and their co-religionists incurred the hatred of the people.

Some wealthy Jews, probably relying upon the favorable position of their friends at court, carried on money transactions in an unscrupulous manner. They extorted a high rate of interest, and mercilessly persecuted their dilatory Christian debtors. The king himself encouraged the usury of the Jews and Moors, because he gained advantage therefrom. The complaints of the people against the Jewish and Mahometan usurers grew very numerous. The cortes of Madrid, Valladolid and other cities made this point the subject of petitions presented to the king, demanding the abolition of these abuses, and the king was compelled to yield to their entreaty.

The minds of the people, however, remained embittered against the Jews. The cortes of Madrid thereupon called for several restrictive laws against the Jews, such as, that they should not be allowed to acquire landed property, and that Jewish ministers of finance and farmers of taxes should not be appointed (1329). Alfonso replied, that, in the main, things should continue as they had been before. Don Samuel Ibn-Wakar rose even higher in the royal favor. Don Alfonso intrusted him with the farming of the revenues derived from the importation of goods from the kingdom of Granada.

He, moreover, obtained the privilege empowering him to issue the coinage of the realm at a lower standard. Joseph of Ecija now became jealous and offered a higher sum for the right of farming the import-taxes from Granada. When he thought he had supplanted his rival, the latter dealt him a severe blow. Ibn-Wakar succeeded in persuading the king that it would be more advantageous to the people of Castile to carry the protective system to its uttermost limits, and prohibit all imports from the neighboring Moorish kingdom (1330—1331).

Whilst the two Jewish courtiers were striving to injure each other, the enemies of the Jews were busily at work to imperil their reputation and the existence of all the Castilian congregations. They inflamed the minds of the people by representing to them that, owing to the depreciation in the value of money, brought about by the farmer of the coinage, Ibn-Wakar, the price of the necessaries of life had risen, these articles being exported to the neighboring countries, where they were bartered for silver, which had a higher value in their own land. The enemies of the Jews also brought the influence of the church to bear to arouse the prejudices of the king against all the Jews. Their champion was a Jew, who no sooner had embraced Christianity, than he became a fanatical persecutor of his brethren. This was the infamous Abner, the forerunner of the baptized and unbaptized Jew-haters, who prepared, and at length accomplished, the humiliation and banishment of the Spanish Jews.

Abner of Burgos, or as he was afterwards called, Alfonso Burgensis de Valladolid (born about 1270, died about 1346), was well acquainted with biblical and Talmudical writings, occupied himself with science, and practiced medicine. His knowledge had destroyed his religious belief, and turned him not only against Judaism, but against all faiths. Troubled by cares for his subsistence, Abner did not obtain the desired support from his kinsmen in race. He was too little of a philosopher to accept his modest lot. His desires were extravagant, and he was unable to find the means to satisfy them. In order to be able to live in ease and splendor, Abner determined, when nearly sixty years of age, to adopt Christianity, although this religion was as little able to give him inward contentment as that which he forsook. As a Christian, he assumed the name of Alfonso. The infidel disciple of Aristotle and Averroes accepted an ecclesiastical office; he became sacristan at a large church in Valladolid, to which a rich benefice was attached, enabling him to gratify his worldly desires. He attempted to excuse his hypocritical behavior and his apostasy by means of sophistical arguments.

Alfonso carried his want of conscientiousness so far that not long after his conversion to Christianity he attacked his former brethren in faith and race with bitter hate, and showed the intention of persecuting them. Owing to his knowledge of Jewish literature, it was easy for him to discover its weak points, employ them as charges against Judaism, and draw the most hateful inferences. Alfonso was indefatigable in his accusations against the Jews and Judaism, and composed a long series of works, in which he introduced arguments partly aggressive, partly defensive of his new faith against the attacks upon it by the Jews. In his abuse of Judaism, the Hebrew language, in which he composed with much greater ease than in Spanish, was made to do service.

Alfonso had the brazen impudence to send one of his hateful writings to his former friend, Isaac Pulgar. The latter replied in a sharply satirical poem, and pressed him close in his polemical writings. The Jews of Spain had not yet become so disheartened as to suffer such insolent attacks in silence. Another less renowned writer also answered Alfonso, and thus a violent literary warfare broke out.

Alfonso of Valladolid, however, did not content himself with polemical writings; he boldly presented himself before King Alfonso XI, and laid his accusations against the Jews before him. He raked up anew the remark of the Church Father Jerome and others, that the Jews had introduced into their book of prayer a formula of imprecation against the God of the Christians and his adherents. The representatives of the Jewish community in Valladolid, probably summoned by the king to justify themselves, emphatically denied that the imprecation originally leveled against the Minim (Nazarenes) referred to Jesus and his present followers. Alfonso, however, would not admit the validity of this exculpation, and pledged himself to prove his charges against the Jews in a disputation. The king of Castile thereupon commanded the representatives of the Valladolid community to enter upon a religious discussion with the sacristan. It took place in the presence of public officials and Dominicans. Here Alfonso Burgensis repeated his accusations, and was victorious, inasmuch as, in consequence of this disputation, King Alfonso issued an edict (25th February, 1336) forbidding the Castilian communities, under penalty of a fine, to use the condemned prayer or formula of imprecation. Thus the enemies of the Jews succeeded in winning over the king, who was really well-disposed towards the Jews. More ominous events were to happen.

King Alfonso was not very constant; he transferred his favor from one person to another. He took into his confidence a man unworthy of the distinction, named Gonzalo Martinez (Nuñez) de Oviedo, originally a poor knight, who had been promoted through the patronage of the Jewish favorite, Don Joseph of Ecija. Far from being grateful to his benefactor, he bore deep hatred against him who had thus raised him, and his hostile feeling extended to all Jews. When he had risen to the post of minister of the royal palace, and later to that of Grand Master of the Order of Alcantara (1337), he revealed his plan of annihilating the Jews. He lodged a formal charge against Don Joseph and Don Samuel Ibn-Wakar, to the effect that they had enriched themselves in the service of the king. He obtained the permission of the king to deal with them as he chose, so as to extort money from them. Thereupon Gonzalo ordered both of them, together with two brothers of Ibn-Wakar, and eight relatives with their families, to be thrown into prison, and confiscated their property. Don Joseph of Ecija died in prison, and Don Samuel died under the torture to which he was subjected. This did not satisfy the enemy of the Jews. He now sought to destroy two other Jews, who held high positions at court—Moses Abudiel and (Sulaiman?) Ibn-Yaish. He implicated them in a charge, pretending all the while to be friendly towards them. Through their downfall Gonzalo Martinez thought to carry into effect his wicked plan against the Castilian Jews without difficulty.

The Moorish king of Morocco, Abulhassan (Alboacin), whose help was implored by his oppressed co-religionists in Granada, had sent a very large army under the command of his son, Abumelik, over the straits to undertake a vigorous campaign against Castile. On the reception of this news, terror spread throughout Christian Spain. King Alfonso forthwith appointed Gonzalo Martinez, Master of the Order of Alcantara, as general in charge of this war, and invested him with plenary power. But funds were wanting; at the deliberation on ways and means of procuring them, Gonzalo propounded his plan for depriving the Jews of their wealth, and then expelling them from Castile. By this means, large supplies of money would flow into the royal treasury; for all the Christians who were dunned by the Jews would willingly pay large sums of money to rid themselves of their enemies. Fortunately this proposal met with opposition in the royal council, and even from the most prominent clergyman in Castile, the archbishop of Toledo. The latter urged that the Jews were an inexhaustible treasure for the king, of which the state should not deprive itself, and that the rulers of Castile had guaranteed them protection and toleration. Don Moses Abudiel, who obtained information concerning the council held to decide on the weal or woe of the Jews, advised the congregations to institute public fasts, and to supplicate the God of their fathers to frustrate the wickedness of Gonzalo. The latter marched to the frontier against the Moorish army, and secured an easy victory. It happened, fortunately for the Spaniard, that the Moorish general, Abumelik, fell pierced by an arrow, and his army, filled with dismay at this event, was defeated and put to rout. The vainglory of the Grand Master of Alcantara now attained a high pitch. He thought to obtain such great importance in Spanish affairs that the king would be compelled to approve of all measures proposed by him. He was, indeed, filled with that pride which precedes a fall.

The feeble hand of a woman was the cause of his downfall. The beautiful and sprightly Leonora de Guzman, who had so enthralled the king with her charms that he was more faithful to her than to his wife, hated the favorite Gonzalo Martinez, and succeeded in making the king believe that he spoke ill of him. Alfonso desiring to learn the real truth of the matter sent a command to Gonzalo to present himself before him in Madrid; he, however, disobeyed the royal command. To be able to defy the anger of the king, he stirred up the knights of the Order of Alcantara and the citizens of the towns assigned to his government, to rebel against his sovereign, entered into traitorous negotiations with the king of Portugal and with the enemy of the

Christians, the king of Granada. Alfonso was forced to lead his nobles against him, and besiege him in Valencia de Alcantara. In mad defiance, Gonzalo directed arrows and missiles to be aimed at the king, which mortally wounded a man in the vicinity of Alfonso. But some of the knights of the Order of Alcantara forsook their Grand Master, and surrendered the stronghold to the king. There remained nothing for Gonzalo except to yield. He was condemned to death as a traitor, and was burnt at the stake (1336), and thus ended the man who had sworn to annihilate the Jews. The Castilian congregations thereupon celebrated a new festival of deliverance, in the same month in which the evil plans of Haman against the Jews had recoiled on his own head. Alfonso again received the Jews into his favor, and raised Moses Abudiel to a high position at his court. From this time till the day of his death, Alfonso XI acted justly towards his Jewish subjects.

It may be thought that, under these on the whole favorable circumstances, the Jews occupied themselves with their intellectual culture, which had already developed its full blossom; but it was not so. Castile in particular, and all Spain, at this epoch, were very deficient in men who cultivated Jewish science. The Talmud constituted the only branch of study which intellectual men attended to, and even here there was no particular fertility. Decrease in strength manifested itself even in the study of the Talmud. The most famous rabbis of this period had so great a mistrust of their own powers that they no longer dared take an independent view of anything, and relied more and more upon the conclusions of older authorities. They made it very convenient for themselves by slavishly following Maimuni's Code in practical decisions, deviating from it only in such particulars as Asheri had objected to. The latter had pretty well succeeded, if not in altogether destroying the inclination of the Spanish Jews to engage in scientific inquiry, at least in bringing science into disrepute, and thus weakening its study. The distinguished supporters of philosophy henceforth no more came from Spain; the few that came into prominence were from southern France. These were Ibn-Kaspi, Gersonides and Narboni. Asheri and his sons, who inherited his hostility to science, in causing the view to become general throughout Spain, that a man should not engage in higher questions concerning Judaism and its connection with philosophy, did not consider that by this means the spirit of the Spanish Jews would become enfeebled and incapacitated for Talmudical investigations, too. The Jewish sons of Spain were not so well suited for the study of narrow Talmudism as the German Jews. Prevented from occupying themselves with science, they lost their buoyancy of spirit, and became unfit for the studies permitted. Even their pleasure in song and their poetical talents died away. Occasionally a poem was still produced, but it consisted merely of rude and unimaginative rhymes. In time they were no better than the German Jews, whom they had before so greatly despised. Even their prose style, on which the Spanish Jews had formerly bestowed so much care, degenerated for the most part into spiritless verbosity. The charming writer, Santob de Carrion, who as early as the time of Alfonso XI had clothed his thoughts in beautiful Spanish verse, was a solitary poet, whose song awoke no echo.

The eight sons of Asheri, his relatives, who had emigrated with him from Germany to Toledo, together with his numerous grandsons, dominated Spanish Judaism from this time onwards. They introduced a one-sided Talmudical method of instruction deeply tinged with a gloomy, ascetic view of religion. The most famous of the sons of Asheri were Jacob (Baal ha-Turim) and Jehuda, both intensely religious, and of unselfish, self-sacrificing dispositions; they were, however, limited to a very narrow range of ideas. Both were as learned in the Talmud as they were ignorant in other subjects, and possessed every quality calculated to bring the decay of religion into accord with the increasing sufferings of the Jews in this third home of their race.

Jacob ben Asheri (born about 1280, died 1340) was visited by bitter misfortunes. His life was one chain of sufferings and privations; but he bore all with patience, without murmur or complaint. Although his father, Asheri, had brought much wealth with him to Spain, and had always been in good circumstances, yet his son, Jacob, had to suffer the bitterest pangs of poverty. Nevertheless, he received no salary as a rabbi: in fact, he does not appear to have filled that post at any time. As with all the family of Asheri, both sons and grandsons, the Talmud constituted his exclusive interest in life; but he displayed more erudition than originality. His sole merit consists in the fact that he brought the chaos of Talmudical learning into definite order, and satisfied the need of the time for a complete code of laws for religious practice.

Owing to his German origin and to his residence in Spain, Jacob Asheri became familiar with the productions of the different schools and authorities in their minutest details. He was thus well suited to control this chaotic mass and reduce it to order. On the basis of the labors of all his predecessors in this field, especially of Maimuni, Jacob compiled a second religious code (in four parts, Turim, shortened to Tur, about 1340). This work treated solely of religious practice, that is, of the ritual, moral, marriage and civil laws. He omitted all such things as had fallen into disuse since the destruction of the Temple and because of altered circumstances. With the composition of this work, a new phase in the inner development of Judaism may be said to begin.

Jacob's code forms part of a graduated scale, by means of which it can be ascertained to how low a level official Judaism had sunk since the time of Maimuni. In Maimuni's compilation thought is paramount; every ritual practice, of whatever kind, whether good or bad, is brought into connection with the essence of religion. In Jacob's code, on the other hand, thought or reasoning is renounced. Religious scrupulousness, which had taken so firm a hold of the German Jewish congregations, inspires the laws, and imposes the utmost stringency and mortifications. Maimuni, in accepting religious precepts as obligatory, was guided entirely by the Talmud, and but seldom included the decisions of the Geonim as invested with authority. Asheri's son, on the contrary, admitted into his digest of religious laws everything that any pious or ultra-pious man had decided upon either out of scrupulosity or as a result of learned exposition. In his code, the precepts declared to be binding by rabbinical authorities far outnumbered those of Talmudic origin. One might almost say that in Jacob Asheri's hands, Talmudical Judaism was transformed into Rabbinism. He even included some of the follies of the Kabbala in his religious digest.

Jacob's code is essentially different from that of Maimuni, not only in contents, but also in form. The style and the language do not manifest the conciseness and lucidity of Maimuni's. Notwithstanding this, his code soon met with universal acceptance, because it corresponded to a want of the times, and presented, in a synoptical form, all the ordinances relating to the ritual, to marriage, and civil laws binding on the adherents of Judaism in exile under the rule of various nations. Rabbis and judges accepted it as the criterion for practical decisions, and even preferred it to Maimuni's work. A few of the rabbis of that age refused to forego their independence, and continued to pronounce decisions arrived at by original inquiry, and therefore paid little heed to the new religious code. The great majority of them, on the other hand, not only in Spain, but also in Germany, were delighted to possess a handy book of laws systematically presenting everything worth knowing, making deep, penetrative research superfluous, and taxing the memory more than the understanding. Thus Jacob's Tur became the indispensable manual for the knowledge of Judaism, as understood by the rabbis, for a period of four centuries, till a new one was accepted which far surpassed the old.

His brother, Jehuda Asheri, was on a par with Jacob in erudition and virtue, but did not possess similar power of reducing chaos to order. He was born about 1284, and died in 1349. After the death of his father, the community of Toledo elected him as Asheri's successor in the rabbinate of the Spanish capital. He performed the functions of his office with extraordinary scrupulousness, without respect of persons, and was able to call the whole community to witness that he had never been guilty of the slightest trespass. When Jehuda Asheri, on account of some small quarrel with his congregation, resolved to take up his abode in Seville, the entire community unanimously begged of him to remain in their midst, and doubled his salary. In spite of this show of affection, he did not feel comfortable in Spain, and in his will he is said to have advised his five sons to emigrate to Germany, the original home of his family. The persecution of the German Jews, during the year of the epidemic pestilence, probably taught them that it was preferable to dwell in Spain. By reason of his position in the most important of the congregations and of his comprehensive rabbinical learning, Jehuda Asheri was regarded as the highest authority of his age, and was preferred even to his brother Jacob.

Seeing that even the study of the Talmud, so

zealously pursued in Spain, had fallen into this state of stagnation and lassitude, the other branches of science could not complain that they made no progress, or were not attentively cultivated. The study of the Bible, Hebrew grammar, and exegesis were entirely neglected; we can recall hardly a single writer who earnestly occupied himself with these subjects. Owing to the energetic zeal of Abba-Mari, the interdict of Ben Adret, and the pronounced aversion of Asheri, reasoning had fallen into disrepute and decay. The truly orthodox shunned contact with philosophy as the direct route to heresy and infidelity, and pseudo-pious people behaved in a yet more prudish fashion towards it. It required courage to engage in a study inviting contempt and accusations of heresy. The Kabbala, too, had done its work, in dimming the eyes of men by its illusions. There were but few representatives of a philosophical conception of Judaism in those days; these were Isaac Pulgar, of Avila, David Ibn-Albilla of Portugal, and Joseph Kaspi of Argentière, in southern France.

Levi ben Gerson, or Leon de Bagnols, was more renowned and more talented than any of these. He was also called Leo the Hebrew, but more usually by his literary name Gersonides (born 1288, died about 1345). He belonged to a family of scholars, and among his ancestors he reckoned that Levi of Villefranche who had indirectly caused the prohibition of scientific study. In spite of the interdict of Ben Adret forbidding the instruction of youths in science, Gersonides was initiated into it at a very early age, and before he had reached his thirtieth year he was at work at a comprehensive and profound work upon philosophy. Gersonides was gifted with a versatile and profound intellect, and averse to all superficiality and incompleteness. In astronomy he corrected his predecessors, and made such accurate observations that specialists based their calculations upon them. He invented an instrument by means of which observations of the heavens could be made more certain. This discovery filled him with such ecstasy that he composed a Hebrew poem, a kind of riddle, upon it, though he was an unpoetical man, and had his head filled with dry calculations and logical conclusions. He also wrote works upon the science of medicine, and discovered new remedies. At the same time he was held in very high repute by his contemporaries as a profound Talmudist, and inspired by his love for systematic arrangement, wrote a methodology of the Mishna.

Maestro Leon de Bagnols, as he was called as a physician, fortunately did not belong to the Jews of France proper: he successively lived in Orange, Perpignan, and in Avignon, at this time the home of popedom. Therefore, he had not been a sufferer in the expulsion of his co-religionists from this land; but his heart bled at the sight of the sufferings which the exiles were made to undergo. He moreover escaped from the effects of the rising of the Shepherds, and the subsequent bitter calamities. At about the same time, his fertile powers of production began to put forth fruit, and he began the series of writings which continued for more than twenty years (1321—1343). None of his writings created such a sensation as his work on the philosophy of religion (Milchamoth Adonaï). In this he set forth the boldest metaphysical thoughts with philosophical calmness and independence, as if paying no heed to the fact that by his departure from the hitherto received notions upon these questions, he was laying himself open to the charges of heresy and heterodoxy. "If my observations are correct," he remarked, "then all blame leveled against me, I regard as praise." Leon de Bagnols belonged to a class of thinkers seldom met with, who, with majestic brow, seek truth for its own intrinsic value, without reference to other ends and results which might cause conflict. Levi ben Gerson thus expressed his opinion upon this subject: Truth must be brought out and placed beneath the glare of open daylight, even if it should contradict the Torah in the strongest possible manner. The Torah is no tyrannical law, which desires to force one to accept untruth as truth, on the contrary, it seeks to lead man to a true understanding of things. If the truth arrived at by investigation is in harmony with the utterances of the Bible, then so much the better. In his independence of thought, the only parallel to Gersonides among Jewish inquirers is Spinoza. Unlike many of his predecessors, he would not look upon science as a body of occult doctrines designed for an inner circle of the initiated. He moreover refused to follow slavishly the authorities in philosophy regarded as infallible. He propounded independent views in opposition not only to Maimuni and Averroes, but also to Aristotle. Leon de Bagnols did not establish a perfect and thoroughly organized system of the philosophy of religion, but treated of the difficulties which interested the thinkers of the age more incisively than any of his predecessors.

In spite of his great ability, Gersonides exercised very little influence upon Judaism. By the pious, he was denounced as a heretic, because of his independent research, and his ambiguous attitude towards the doctrine of the creation. They took the title of his chief work, "The Battles of the Lord," to mean "Battles against the Lord." So much the warmer was his reception by Christian inquirers after truth. Pope Clement VI, during the lifetime of the author, commanded his treatise upon astronomy and the newly-invented instrument to be translated into Latin (1342).

Of a similar nature was another representative of philosophical Judaism of this age, Moses ben Joshua

Narboni, also called Maestro Vidal (born about 1300, died 1362). His father Joshua, who belonged to a family in Narbonne, but resided in Perpignan, was so warmly interested in Jewish, that is to say Maimunistic, philosophy, that in spite of the interdict hurled against all who studied the subject, he instructed his son therein when he was thirteen years old. Vidal Narboni became an enthusiastic student. He divided his admiration between Maimuni and Averroes, his writings consisting chiefly of commentaries upon their works. His travels from the foot of the Pyrenees to Toledo and back again to Soria (1345—1362) enriched and amended his knowledge. He was interested in anything worth knowing, and made observations with great accuracy. No calamities or troubles succeeded in damping his zeal in the inquiry after truth. In consequence of the Black Death, an infuriated mob fell upon the community at Cervera. Vidal Narboni was compelled to take to flight with the rest of the congregation; he lost his possessions, and, what was more painful to him, his precious books. These misfortunes did not disturb him; he took up the thread of his work where it had been interrupted. He accomplished no entirely independent or original work; he was a true Aristotelian of Averroist complexion. Narboni conceived Judaism as a guide to the highest degree of theoretical and moral truth: the Torah has a double meaning—the one simple, direct, for the thoughtless mob, and the other of a deeper, metaphysical nature for the class of thinkers—a common opinion in those times, Gersonides alone demurring. Narboni, too, gave expression to heretical views, that is, such as are contrary to the ordinarily accepted understanding of Judaism, but not with the freedom and openness of Levi ben Gerson. He rejected the belief in miracles, and attempted to explain them away altogether, but defended man's freedom of will by philosophical arguments. Death overtook him in the very midst of his labors when, advanced in years, he was on the point of returning to his native land from Soria, on the other side of the Pyrenees, where he had spent several years.

Though the Karaite, Aaron ben Elia Nicomedi, may be reckoned among the philosophers of this time, he can scarcely be admitted into the company of Levi ben Gerson and the other Provençal thinkers. His small stock of philosophical knowledge was a matter of erudition, not the result of independent thought. Aaron II, of Nicomedia (in Asia Minor, born about 1300, died 1369), who probably lived in Cairo, was indeed superior to his ignorant brother Karaites, but several centuries behind the Rabbanite philosophers. His thoughts sound like a voice from the grave, or as of one who has slumbered for many years, and speaks the language of antiquity, not understood by the men of his own day.

Aaron ben Elia was not even able to indicate the end aimed at by his work, "The Tree of Life." Without being himself fully conscious of his motives, he was guided in its composition by jealous rivalry of Maimuni and the Rabbanites. It vexed him sorely that Maimuni's religious philosophical work, "The Guide," was perused and admired not only by Jews, but also by Christians and Mahometans, whilst the Karaites had nothing like it. Aaron desired to save the honor of the Karaites by his "Tree of Life." He sought to detract from the merits of the work of Maimuni, and remarked that some of the statements to be found in the book had been made by Karaite philosophers of religion. Notwithstanding this, he followed Maimuni most minutely, and treated only of those questions which the latter had raised; but he sought to solve them not by the aid of philosophy, but by the authority of the Bible.

The history of this period, when dealing with

events in Germany, has nothing but calamities to record: bloody assaults, massacres, and the consequent intellectual poverty. Asheri and his sons were either deluded or unjust when they preferred bigoted Germany to Spain, at that time still tolerable, and cast longing looks thitherwards from Toledo. From the time of Asheri's departure till the middle of the century, misfortune followed upon misfortune, till nearly all the congregations were exterminated. On account of this state of affairs, even the study of the Talmud, the only branch of learning pursued in Germany with ardor and thoroughness, fell into decay. How could the Germans gather intellectual strength, when they were not certain about one moment of their lives, or their means of sustenance? Their state in a most literal way realized the prophetical threat of punishment: "Thy life shall hang in doubt before thee; and thou shalt fear day and night. In the morning thou shalt say, Would God it were even! and at even thou shalt say, Would God it were morning! for the fear of thine heart wherewith thou shalt fear." Emperor Louis, the Bavarian, is reported to have been favorably inclined towards the Jews, which is said to have made them proud. But this is idle calumny both against the emperor and the Jews. No German ruler before him had treated his "servi cameræ" so badly, pawned them and sold them, as Louis the Bavarian. He also imposed a new tax upon the Jews, the so-called golden gift-pence. As the emperors had gradually pawned all the revenues derived from their "servi cameræ" to enable them to satisfy their immediate necessity for money, Louis the Bavarian was driven to cogitate upon some new means of obtaining supplies from them. He promulgated a decree (about 1342), which commanded that every Jew and Jewess in the German Empire above the age of twelve, and possessed of at least more than twenty florins, should pay annually to the king or the emperor a poll-tax of a florin. He probably derived his right, if, indeed, the question of right was considered in reference to the treatment of Jews, from the fact that the German emperors were in possession of all the prerogatives once claimed by those of Rome. As the Jews, since the days of Vespasian and Titus, had been compelled to pay a yearly tax to the Roman emperors, the German rulers declared themselves the direct heirs to this golden gift-pence.

Hitherto the massacres of Jews in Germany had taken place only at intervals, and in a few places; but now, under the reign of Louis, owing to riots and civil wars, they became much more frequent. During two consecutive years (1336—1337), a regularly organized band of peasants and rabble, who called themselves "the beaters of the Jews," made fierce attacks upon them with unbridled fury and heartless cruelty. Two dissolute noblemen were at the head of this troop; they gave themselves the name of Kings Leather-arm (Armleder) from a piece of leather which they wore wound round the arm. In this persecution, as in that of Rindfleisch, the fanaticism and blind superstition inculcated by the church played an important part. One of the Leather-arms announced that he had received a divine revelation which directed him to visit upon the Jews the martyrdom and the wounds which Jesus had suffered, and to avenge his crucifixion by their blood. Such a summons to arms seldom remained unanswered in Germany. Five thousand peasants, armed with pitchforks, axes, flails, pikes, and whatever other weapons they could lay hands upon, gathered around the Leather-arms, and inflicted a bloody slaughter upon the Jewish inhabitants of Alsace and the Rhineland as far as Suabia. As frequently happened during such barbarous persecutions, numbers of Jews, on this occasion also, put an end to their own lives, after having slain their children to prevent their falling into the hands of the Church. Emperor Louis the Bavarian did indeed issue commands to protect the heretic Jews (April, 1337), but his help came too late, or was of little effect. At length the emperor succeeded in capturing one of the Leather-arms, whom he ordered to be executed.

At about the same time a bloody persecution, prompted by the frenzy of avarice, was set on foot in Bavaria. The councilors of the city of Deckendorf (or Deggendorf) desired to free themselves and all the citizens from their debts to the Jews, and enrich themselves besides. To carry out this plan, the fable of the desecration of the host by the Jews, with the accompaniment of the usual miracles, was spread abroad. When the populace had been incited to a state of fanatical frenzy, the council proceeded to execute the project which it had secretly matured outside the town, so as not to arouse any suspicion among the Jews. On the appointed day (30th September, 1337), at a signal from the church bell, the knight Hartmann von Deggenburg, who had been initiated in the conspiracy, rode with his band of horsemen through the open gates into Deckendorf, and was received with loud rejoicing. The knight and the citizens thereupon fell upon the defenseless Jews, put them to death by sword and fire, and possessed themselves of their property. In honor of the miracles performed by the host that had been pierced by the knives of the Jews, a church of the Holy Sepulcher was erected, and appointed as a shrine for pilgrims; and the puncheons which the Jews had used, together with the insulted host, were placed beneath a glass case, and guarded as relics. For many centuries they were displayed for the edification of the faithful,—perhaps are still displayed. The lust for slaughter spread abroad into Bavaria, Bohemia, Moravia, and Austria. Thousands of Jews perished by different forms of torture and death. Only the citizens of Vienna and Ratisbon protected their Jewish inhabitants against the infuriated mob. The friendly efforts of Pope Benedictus XII were of little avail against the brutal spirit of the then Christian world.

CHAPTER IV.

THE BLACK DEATH.

Rise of the False Accusation against Jews of Poisoning the Wells—Massacres in Southern France and Catalonia—The Friendly Bull of Pope Clement VI—Terrible Massacres in all Parts of Germany—Confessions wrung from the Jews on the Rack—The Flagellants as a Scourge for the Jews—King Casimir of Poland—Persecution in Brussels—The Black Death in Spain—Don Pedro the Cruel and the Jews—Santob de Carrion and Samuel Abulafia—Fall of Don Pedro and its Consequences for the Jews—Return of the Jews to France and Germany—The "Golden Bull"—Manessier de Vesoul—Matathiah Meïr Halevi—Synod at Mayence.

1348—1380 C.E.

THE assistance of the pope was of very little use to the Jews, and the protection of the German emperor was like the support of a broken reed. Within ten years they learned this comfortless experience; for soon came most mournful days for the Jewish communities in most parts of Europe where the cross held sway, to which the slaughter by the Leather-arms and the brutal atrocities of Deckendorf were but a weak prelude.

The glimpse of good fortune which the Spanish Jews enjoyed under Alfonso XI served only to bring down upon their brethren in the other Christian countries a widespread, intense, indescribably cruel persecution with which none of the massacres that had hitherto taken place can be compared. The destroying angel called the Black Death, which carried on its ravages for over three years, made its way from China across lands and seas into the heart of Europe, heralded by premonitory earthquakes and other terrifying natural phenomena. Sparing neither rank nor age, it left a devastated track behind, sweeping away a fourth part of all mankind (nearly 25,000,000) as with a poison-laden breath and stifling every noble impulse. In Europe the invisible Death with its horrors turned the Christians into veritable destroying angels for the Jews. Those whom the epidemic had spared were handed over to torture, the sword, or the stake. Whilst neither Mahometans nor Mongols who suffered from the plague attacked the Jews, Christian peoples charged the unhappy race with being the originators of the pestilence, and slaughtered them *en masse*. The church had so often and impressively preached that infidels were to be destroyed; that Jews were worse than heretics, even worse than unbelieving heathens; that they were the murderers of Christians and the slayers of children, that at last its true sons believed what was said, and carried its doctrines into effect. Owing to the prevailing misery, discipline and order, obedience and submissiveness were at an end, and each man was thrown upon his own resources. Under these circumstances, the effects of the education of the church appeared in a most hideous form. The Black Death had indeed made itself felt among Jews also; but the plague had visited them in a comparatively milder form than the Christians, probably on account of their greater moderation, and the very careful attention paid their sick. Thus the suspicion arose that the Jews had poisoned the brooks and wells, and even the air, in order to annihilate the Christians of every country at one blow.

It was charged that the Spanish Jews, supposed to be in possession of great power and influence over the congregations of Europe, had hit upon this diabolical scheme; that they had dispatched messengers far and wide with boxes containing poison, and by threats of excommunication had coerced the other Jews to aid in carrying out their plans, and that these directions issued from Toledo, which might be viewed as the Jewish capital. The infatuated populace went so far as to name the man who had delivered these orders and the poison. It was Jacob Pascate, said they, from Toledo, who had settled in Chambery (in Savoy), from which as a center he had sent out a troop of Jewish poisoners into all countries and cities. This Jacob, together with a Rabbi Peyret, of Chambery, and a rich Jew, Aboget, was said to have dealt largely in the manufacture and sale of poisons. The poison, prepared by the Jewish doctors of the black art in Spain, was reported to be concocted from the flesh of a basilisk, or from spiders, frogs and lizards, or from the hearts of Christians and the dough of the consecrated wafers. These and similar silly stories invented by ignorant, or, perhaps, malicious people, and distorted and exaggerated by the heated imagination, were credited not alone by the ignorant mob, but even by the higher classes. The courts of justice earnestly strove to learn the real truth of these rumors, and employed the means for confirming a suspicion used by the Christians of the Middle Ages with especial skill—torture in every possible form.

As far as can be ascertained, these tales concerning the poisoning of the brooks and wells by Jews first found credence in southern France, where the Black Death as early as the beginning of the year 1348 had obtained many victims. In a certain town of southern France, on one day (the middle of the month of May), the whole Jewish congregation, men, women, and children, together with their holy writings, were cast into the flames. From that place the slaughter spread to Catalonia and Aragon. In these provinces, in the same year, anarchy was rife, because the nobles and people had revolted against the king, Don Pedro, in order to secure certain of their privileges against the encroachments of the monarch. When the tales of the poisoning of the wells had taken firm root in the minds of the people of these countries also, the inhabitants of Barcelona gathered together on a Saturday (towards the end of June), slew about twenty persons, and pillaged the Jewish houses. The most distinguished men of the city received the persecuted people under their protection, and aided by a terrible storm, loud thunder and flashes of lightning, they made a successful attack upon the deluded or plunder-seeking assailants of the Jews.

A few days later the community at Cervera was attacked in a similar manner, eighteen of its members killed, and the rest compelled to flee. The Jewish philosopher, Vidal Narboni, happened to be in the town, and in the assault he lost his possessions and his books. All the congregations of northern Spain knew themselves in danger of being attacked; they instituted public fasts, implored mercy from heaven, and barricaded those of their quarters which were surrounded by walls. In Aragon, however, the higher classes came to the help of the Jews. Pope Clement VI, who had taken so much interest in the astronomical works of Gersonides, and who, terrified at the approach of death, had shut himself up in his room, still felt for the sufferings of an innocent, persecuted people. He issued a bull in which, under pain of excommunication, he prohibited anyone from killing the Jews without proper judicial sentence, or from dragging them by force to be baptized, or from despoiling them of their goods (the beginning of July). This bull was probably of some use in southern France, but in the other parts of the Christian world it produced no effect. One country followed the example of another. The ideally beautiful region surrounding Lake Geneva next became the scene of a most frightful persecution. At the command of Amadeus, duke of Savoy at that time, several Jews suspected of poisoning were arrested and imprisoned in two small towns, Chillon and Chatel, on Lake Geneva. A commission of judges was appointed to inquire into the charges brought against the prisoners, and, if convicted, they were to be severely punished. In this country, then, a prince and his tribunal believed the preposterous fable of the poisoning by Jews. On the Day of Atonement (15th September, 1348), three Jews and a Jewess in Chillon were made to undergo torture: the surgeon Valavigny, from Thonon, Bandito and Mamson, from Ville-Neuve, and, three weeks later, Bellieta and her son Aquet. In their pain and despair, they told the names of the persons from whom they had received the poison, and admitted that they had scattered it in different spots near wells and brooks. They denounced themselves, their co-religionists, their parents and their children as guilty. Ten days later the merciless judges again applied the torture to the enfeebled woman and her son, and they vied with each other in their revelations. In Chastelard five Jews were put to the torture, and they made equally incredible confessions of guilt. Aquet made the wild statement that he had placed poison in Venice, in Apulia and Calabria, and in Toulouse, in France. The secretaries took down all these confessions in writing, and they were verified by the signatures of their authors. To remove all doubts concerning their trustworthiness, the crafty judges added that the victims were only very lightly tortured. In consequence of these disclosures, not only the accused who acknowledged their crime, but all the Jews in the region of Lake Geneva and in Savoy were burnt at the stake.

The report of the demonstrated guilt of the Jews rapidly made its way from Geneva into Switzerland, and here scenes of blood of the same horrible description were soon witnessed. The consuls of Berne sent for the account of the proceedings of the courts of justice at Chillon and Chastelard. They then put certain Jews to the torture, extracted confessions from them, and kindled the funeral pyre for all the Jews (September).

The annihilation of the Jews on the charge of poisoning was now systematically carried out, beginning with Berne and Zofingen (canton Aargau). The consuls of Berne addressed letters to Basle, Freiburg, Strasburg, Cologne, and many other places, with the announcement that the Jews had been found guilty of the crime imputed to them; and also sent a Jew, bound in chains, under convoy, to Cologne, that every one might be convinced of the diabolical plans of the Jews. In Zurich the charge of poisoning the wells was raised together with that of the murder of a Christian child. There, also, those who appeared to be guilty were burnt at the stake, the rest of the community expelled from the town, and a law passed forbidding them ever to return thither (21st September). The persecution of the Jews extended northwards with the pestilence. Like the communities around Lake Geneva, Jews in the cities surrounding Lake Constance, in St. Gall, Lindau, Ueberlingen, Schaffhausen, Constance (Costnitz), and others, were burnt at the stake, put to the wheel, or sentenced to expulsion or compulsory baptism. Once again Pope Clement VI took up the cause of the Jews; he published a bull to the whole of Catholic Christendom, in which he declared the innocence of the Jews regarding the charge leveled against them. He produced all possible reasons to show the absurdity of the accusation, stating that in districts where no Jew lived the people were visited by the pestilence, and that Jews also suffered from its terrible effects. It was of no avail that he admonished the clergy to take the Jews under their protection, and that he placed the false accusers and the murderers under the ban (September). The child had become more powerful than its parent, wild fancy stronger than the papacy.

Nowhere was the destruction of the Jews prosecuted with more thoroughness and more intense hatred than in the Holy Roman Empire. In vain the newly-elected emperor, Charles IV, of Luxemburg, issued letter after letter forbidding the persons of the Jews, his "servi cameræ," to be touched. Even had he possessed more power in Germany, he would not have found the German people willing to spare the Jews. The Germans did not commit their fearful outrages upon the Jews merely for the sake of plunder, although a straightforward historian of that epoch, Closener of Strasburg, remarks that "their goods were the poison which caused the death of the Jews." Sheer stupidity made them believe that Jews had poisoned the wells and rivers. The councils of various towns ordered that the springs and wells be walled in, so that the citizens be not poisoned, and they had to drink rain water or melted snow. Was it not just that the Jews, the cause of this evil, should suffer?

There were some too sensible to share the delusion that the Jews were the cause of the great mortality. These few men deserve a place in history, for, despite their danger, they could feel and act humanely. In the municipal council of Strasburg, the burgomaster Conrad (Kunze) of Wintertur, the sheriff, Gosse Sturm, and the master workman, Peter Swaber, took great trouble to prove the Jews innocent of the crimes laid at their door, and defended them against the fanatical attack of the mob and even against the bishop. The councilors of Basle and Freiburg likewise took the part of the unhappy people. The council of Cologne wrote to the representatives of Strasburg that it would follow the example of the latter town with regard to the Jews; for it was convinced that the pestilence was to be considered as a visitation from God. It would, therefore, not permit the Jews to be persecuted on account of groundless reports, but would protect them with all its power, as in former times. In Basle, however, the guilds and a mob rose in rebellion against the council, repaired with their flags to the city hall, insisted that the patricians who had been banished on account of their action against the Jews, should be recalled, and the Jews banished from the city. The council was compelled to comply with the first demand; as to the second, it deferred its decision until a day of public meeting, when this matter was to be considered. In Benfelden (Alsace) a council was actually held to consider the course to be followed with regard to Jews. There were present Bishop Berthold of Strasburg, barons, lords, and representatives of the towns. The representatives of Strasburg bravely maintained the cause of the Jews, even against the bishop, who either from malice or stupidity was in favor of their complete destruction. Although they repeatedly demonstrated that the Jews could not be the cause of the pestilence, they were out-voted, and it was decided to banish the Jews from all the cities on the upper Rhine (towards the close of 1348).

The Jews of Alsace, through the decision of Benfelden, were declared outlaws, and were either expelled from the various places they visited, or burnt. A hard fate overtook the community of Basle. On an island of the Rhine, in a house especially built for the purpose, they were burnt to death (January 9th, 1349), and it was decided that within the next two hundred years no Jew should be permitted to settle in that city. A week later all the Jews of Freiburg were burnt at the stake with the exception of twelve of the richest men, who were permitted to live that they might disclose the names of their creditors, for the property of the victims fell to the community. The community of Speyer was the first sacrifice amongst the communities of the Rhineland. The mob rose up and killed several Jews, others burning themselves in their houses, and some going over to Christianity. The council of Speyer took the property of the Jews, and confiscated their estates in the neighborhood. The council of Strasburg remained firm in its protection of the Jews, sending out numerous letters to obtain proofs of their innocence. But from many sides came unfavorable testimony. The council of Zähringen said that it was in possession of the poison the Jews had scattered. When tried it proved fatal to animals. The council would not let it go out of its hands, but would show it to a messenger.

A castellan of Chillon had the confessions of the Jews tortured in the district of Lake Geneva copied, and sent them to the council of Strasburg. Only the council of Cologne encouraged Wintertur to support the cause of the Jews, and to take no notice of the demands of their enemies. At length the trade-guilds rose against Wintertur and his two colleagues, who were deposed from office. A new council was chosen that favored the persecutions of the Jews. In the end, the entire community of Strasburg—2,000 souls—were imprisoned. The following day, on a Sabbath (14th February, 1349), they were all dragged to the burial ground. Stakes were erected, and they were burnt to death. Only those who in despair accepted the cross were spared. The new council decreed that for a period of a hundred years no Jew should be admitted into Strasburg. The treasures of the Jews were divided amongst the burghers, some of whom were loth to defile themselves with the money, and, by the advice of their confessors, devoted it to the church.

Next came the turn of Worms, the oldest Jewish community in Germany. The Jews of this town had the worst to fear from their Christian fellow-citizens, Emperor Charles IV having given them and their possessions to the town in return for services, so that "the city and the burghers of Worms might do unto the Jews and Judaism as they wished, might act as with their own property." When the council decreed that the Jews should be burnt, the unfortunates determined to anticipate the death which awaited them from the hangman. Twelve Jewish representatives are said to have repaired to the town hall and begged for mercy. When this was refused to them, they are said to have drawn forth the weapons concealed in their clothes, to have fallen on the councilors, and killed them. This story is legendary; but it is a fact that nearly all the Jews of Worms set fire to their houses, and that more than 400 persons were burned to death (10th Adar —1st March, 1349). The Jews of Oppenheim likewise burnt themselves to death to escape being tortured as poisoners (end of July). The community of Frankfort remained secure so long as the rival emperors, Charles IV and Gunther of Schwarzburg, were fighting in that neighborhood; the latter holding his court in Frankfort. When he died, and the contest was ended, the turn of the Jews of Frankfort came to be killed. On being attacked they burned themselves in their houses, causing a great conflagration in the city. In Mayence, where the Jews had hitherto been spared, a thief, during a flagellation scene, stole his neighbor's purse. An altercation arose, and the mob seized the opportunity to attack the Jews. They had, no doubt, been prepared, and 300 of them took up arms, and killed 200 of the mob. This aroused the anger of the entire Christian community, which likewise took to arms. The Jews fought a considerable time; at length, overpowered by the enemy, they set fire to their houses (24th August). Nearly 6,000 Jews are said to have perished in Mayence. In Erfurt, out of a community of 3,000 souls, not one person survived, although the council, after their slaughter in the whole of Thuringia, including Eisenach and Gotha, had long protected them. In Breslau, where a considerable community dwelt, the Jews were completely destroyed. Emperor Charles gave orders to seize the murderers and give them their due punishment.

But he had taken no steps to hinder the horrible slaughter enacted everywhere, although informed of the plots against the Jews. In Austria, also, the outcry was made that the Jews were poisoners, and terrible scenes ensued. In Vienna, on the advice of Rabbi Jonah, all the members of the congregation killed themselves in the synagogue. In Krems, where there was a large congregation, the populace of the town, assisted by that of a neighboring place named Stein and the villages, attacked the Jews, who set fire to their houses and died (September, 1349), only a few being saved.

In Bavaria and Suabia, persecution was also rife, and the communities of Augsburg, Würzburg, Munich, and many others succumbed. The Jews of Nuremberg, through its extensive commerce, possessed great riches and grand houses, and were the especial objects of dislike to the Christians. Their destruction was so imminent that Emperor Charles IV freed the council from responsibility if they should be injured against its wish.

At length their fate was fulfilled. On a spot afterwards called Judenbühl (Jews' hill), the followers of the religion of love erected a pile, and all those who had not emigrated were burnt or killed. The council of Ratisbon did its utmost to save the community, the oldest in the south of Germany. For here also the mob demanded the annihilation or banishment of the Jews. The dukes of Bavaria, the sons of Emperor Louis, who favored the persecution of the Jews, had given the people permission in writing to "treat the Jews as they liked, according to honor or necessity, and banish them with or without justice." Margrave Louis of Brandenburg, son of Emperor Louis, one of the partisans of the rival emperor, Gunther of Schwarzburg, showed his religious feeling by giving orders to burn all the Jews of Königsberg (in Neumark), and to confiscate their goods. So inhuman were people in those days that the executioner boasted of his deed, and gave documentary evidence that Margrave Louis had commanded the Jews to be burnt. In North Germany there lived but few Jews, except in Magdeburg, but there, too, they were burnt or banished. In Hanover (in 1349) the flagellants were rampant. Outside of Germany, amongst the nations still uncivilized, there were comparatively few persecutions. Louis, King of Hungary, an enthusiast for his faith, drove the Jews out of his land, not as poisoners, but as infidels, who opposed his scheme of conversion, although he had given them equal rights with the Christians and privileges besides. The Hungarian Jews who remained true to their faith emigrated to Austria and Bohemia. In Poland, where the pestilence also raged, the Jews suffered but slight persecution, for they were favored by King Casimir the Great. At the request of some Jews who had rendered services to him, the king, after his ascent upon the throne (October 9th, 1334) confirmed the laws enacted nearly a century before by Boleslav Pius, duke of Kalish, or rather by Frederick the Valiant, archduke of Austria, and accepted by the king of Hungary and various Polish princes. Holding good only in the dukedom of Kalish and Great Poland, they were extended by Casimir to the whole of the Polish empire. Thirteen years later, Casimir altered the laws by which the Jews were permitted to lend money at interest, but we must not deduce that he was inimical to the Jews, for he expressly states that he made this limitation only at the request of the nobility. In the years of the pestilence, too, Casimir appears to have protected the Jews against the outbreaks of the misguided multitude, for the accusation of the poisoning of wells by the Jews had traveled from Germany across the Polish frontier, and had roused the populace against them. Massacres occurred in Kalish, Cracow, Glogau, and other cities, especially on the German frontier. If the number of Jews stated to have been killed in Poland (10,000) be correct, it bears no relation to the enormous multitudes who fell as victims in Germany. Later (1356) Casimir is said to have taken a beautiful Jewish mistress named Esther (Esterka), who bore him two sons (Niemerz and Pelka) and two daughters. The latter are said to have remained Jewesses. In consequence of his love to Esther, the king of Poland is supposed to have bestowed special favors and privileges on some Jews, probably Esther's relations. But the records, handed down by untrustworthy witnesses, cannot be implicitly believed.

At all events, the Jews of Poland fared better than those of Germany, seeing that they were placed on an equality, if not with the Roman Catholics, yet with the Ruthenians, Saracens, and Tartars. The Jews were permitted to wear the national costume and gold chains and swords, like the knights, and were eligible for military service.

As on the eastern frontier of Germany, the Jews on the western side, in Belgium, were also persecuted at the period of the Black Death. In Brussels a wealthy Jew stood in great favor with the duke of Brabant, John II. When the flagellants came, and the death of his co-religionists was imminent, this Jew entreated his patron to accord them his protection, which John willingly promised. But the enemies of the Jews had foreseen this, and ensured immunity from punishment through the duke's son. They attacked the Jews of Brussels, dragged them into the streets, and killed all—about 500.

In Spain, the congregations of Catalonia, which, after those of Provence, supplied the first victims, conceived a plan to prevent the outrages of fanaticism. They determined to establish a common fund in support of their people who should become destitute through a mob or persecution. They were to choose deputies to entreat the king (Don Pedro IV) to prevent the recurrence of such scenes of horror. Other concessions were to be sought, but the plan was never carried into effect, owing to delay on the part of the Jews of Aragon, and also probably because too much was expected of the king. The Jews under Aragonian rule were still behind those in the kingdom of Castile.

In Castile also the Black Death had held its gruesome revelries; but here the population, more intelligent than elsewhere, did not dream of holding the Jews responsible for its ravages. In Toledo and Seville the plague snatched away many respected members of the community, particularly from the families of Abulafia, Asheri, and Ibn-Shoshan. The grief of the survivors is vividly depicted in such of the tombstone inscriptions of the Toledo Jewish cemetery as have come down to us. King Alfonso XI was amongst the victims of the insidious plague, but not even a whisper charged the Jews with responsibility for his death. During the reign of Don Pedro (1350—1369), Alfonso's son and successor, the influence of the Castilian Jews reached a height never before attained. It was the last luster of their splendid career in Spain, soon to be shrouded in dark eventide shadows. The young king, only fifteen years of age when called to the throne, was early branded by his numerous enemies with the name of "Pedro the Cruel." His favors to the Jews had a share in procuring him this nickname, although he was not more cruel than many of his predecessors and successors. Don Pedro was a child of nature with all the good and the bad qualities implied; he would not submit to the restrictions of court etiquette, nor allow himself to be controlled by political considerations. Through the duplicity and faithlessness of his bastard brothers, sons of Alfonso's mistress, Leonora de Guzman—the same who had unconsciously saved the Jews from imminent destruction—the king was provoked to sanguinary retaliation. The instinct of self-preservation, the maintenance of his royal dignity, filial affection, and attachment to an early love, had more to do with his reckless, bloody deeds than inherent cruelty and vengeance. The young king, destined to come to so sad an end, involving the Castilian Jews in his fall, was from the beginning of his reign surrounded by tragic circumstances. His mother, the Portuguese Infanta Donna Maria, had been humiliated and deeply mortified by her husband at the instigation of his mistress, Leonora de Guzman. Don Pedro himself had been neglected for his bastard brothers, and particularly for his elder half-brother, Henry de Trastamara. The first important duty of his reign, then, was to obtain justice for his humiliated mother, and degrade the rival who had caused her so much misery. That he tolerated his bastard brothers is a proof that he was not of a cruel disposition. His severity was felt more by the grandees and hidalgos, who trampled on justice and humanity, and ill-treated the people with cavalier arrogance. Only in these circles Don Pedro had bitter enemies, not amongst the lower orders, which, when not misled, remained faithful to him to death. The Jews also were attached to him. They risked property and life for their patriotism, because he protected them against injustice and oppression, and did not treat them as outcasts. The Jews certainly suffered much through him, not in the character of patient victims, as in Germany and France, but as zealous partisans and fellow combatants, who shared the overthrow of their leader with his Christian followers.

Shortly after Don Pedro had ascended the throne, when the grief caused by the death of King Alfonso XI was still fresh, a venerable Jewish poet ventured to address to the new monarch words of advice in well-balanced Spanish verses. This poet, Santob (Shem Tob) de Carrion, from the northern Spanish town of that name (about 1300—1350), a member of a large community, has been entirely neglected in Jewish literature. Christian writers have preserved his memory and his verses. Santob's (or as abbreviated, Santo's) poetical legacy deserves to be treasured. His verses flow soft and clear as the ripples of an unsullied spring, dancing with silvery brightness out of its rocky hollow. He had not only thoroughly mastered the sonorous periods of the Spanish language, at that time in a transition state between tenderness and vigor, but had enriched it. Santob embodied the practical wisdom of his time in beautiful strophes. His "Counsels and Lessons," addressed to Don Pedro, have the character of proverbs and apothegms. He drew upon the unfailing wealth of maxims of the Talmud and later Hebrew poets for his verse, and the sweetness of his poetry was derived from various sources.

Santob's verses are not always of this gentle, uncontroversial character. He did not hesitate to speak sternly to those of his co-religionists who had become wealthy by the king's bounty, and he denounced the prejudice with which Spanish Christians regarded whatever was of Jewish origin. Even to the young king he was in the habit of indulging in a certain amount of plain speaking; and in his stanzas, more than 600 in number, he often drew for his majesty's benefit suggestive pictures of virtue and vice. He reminded the king, too, of promises made to Santob by his father, and bade him fulfill them. From this it would appear that our Jewish troubadour, who wooed the muse so successfully, was not a favorite of fortune. Little, however, is known of him beyond his verses, and we have no knowledge of the reception which his representations met at the hands of Don Pedro.

To other prominent Jews the king's favor was unbounded. Don Juan Alfonso de Albuquerque, his tutor and all-powerful minister, recommended for the post of minister of finance a Jew who had rendered him great services, and the king appointed Don Samuel ben Meïr Allavi, a member of the leading family of Toledo, the Abulafia-Halevis, to a state situation of trust, in defiance of the decision of the cortes that Jews should no longer be eligible. Samuel Abulafia not only became treasurer-in-chief (Tesoreo mayor), but also the king's confidential adviser (privado), who had a voice in all important consultations and decisions. Two inscriptions referring to Don Samuel, one written during his lifetime, the other after his death, describe him as noble and handsome, instinct with religious feeling, a benevolent man, "who never swerved from the path of God, nor could he be reproached with a fault."

Another Jew who figured at Don Pedro's court was Abraham Ibn-Zarzal, the king's physician and astrologer. Don Pedro was, indeed, so surrounded by Jews, that his enemies reproached his court for its Jewish character. Whether the protection he extended to his Jewish subjects was due to the influence of these Jewish favorites or to his own impulses is unknown. On opening for the first time the cortes of Valladolid (May, 1351), he was presented with a petition, praying him to abolish the judicial autonomy enjoyed by the Jewish communities and their right to appoint their own Alcaldes; he replied that the Jews, being numerically a feeble people, required special protection. From Christian judges they would not obtain justice, or their cases would be delayed.

Whilst the relatives of the young king were intriguing to arrange a marriage between him and Blanche, daughter of the French Duc de Bourbon, he fell in love with Maria de Padilla, a clever, beautiful lady of a noble Spanish family. It is said that he was formally married to her in the presence of witnesses. At any rate, he caused the marriage proposals to Blanche to be withdrawn; but the

Bourbon princess, either of her own accord, or at the instance of her ambitious relatives, insisted on coming to Spain to assume the diadem. Her resolve brought only sorrow to herself and misfortune to the country. The nearest relatives of the king strained every nerve to procure the celebration of the marriage, and in this they succeeded; but Don Pedro remained with his bride only two days. The result of this state of things was that to the old parties in the state another was added, some grandees taking part with the deserted queen, others with Maria de Padilla. To the latter belonged Samuel Abulafia and the Jews of Spain. The reason assigned was that Blanche, having observed with displeasure the influence possessed by Samuel and other Jews at her husband's court, and the honors and distinctions enjoyed by them, had made the firm resolve, which she even commenced to put into execution, to compass the fall of the more prominent Jews, and obtain the banishment of the whole of the Jewish population from Spain. She made no secret of her aversion to the Jews, but, on the contrary, expressed it openly. For this reason, it is stated, the Jewish courtiers took up a position of antagonism to the queen, and, on their part, lost no opportunity of increasing Don Pedro's dislike for her. If Blanche de Bourbon really fostered such anti-Jewish feelings, and circumstances certainly seem to bear out this view, then the Jews were compelled in self-defense to prevent the queen from acquiring any ascendency, declare themselves for the Padilla party, and support it with all the means in their power. Dissension and civil war grew out of this unhappy relation of the king to his scarcely recognized consort. Albuquerque, who was first opposed to the queen, and then permitted himself to be won over to her side, fell into disgrace, and Samuel Abulafia succeeded him as the most trusted of the king's counselors. Whenever the court moved, Samuel, with other eminent grandees, was in attendance on the king.

One day Don Pedro's enemies, at their head his bastard brothers, succeeded in decoying him, with a few of his followers, into the fortress of Toro. His companions, among whom was Samuel Abulafia, were thrown into prison, and the king himself was placed under restraint (1354). Whilst a few of the loyal grandees and even the Grand Master of Calatrava were executed by the conspirators, the favorite Samuel was, strange to say, spared. Later on he succeeded in escaping with the king. Having shared his royal master's misfortune, he rose still higher in his favor, and the esteem in which he was held by the king was largely increased by his successful administration of the finances, which he had managed so as to accumulate a large reserve, of which few of Don Pedro's predecessors had been able to boast. The treacherous seizure of the king at Toro formed a turning point in his reign. Out of it grew a fierce civil war in Castile, which Don Pedro carried on with great cruelty. In this, however, the Jewish courtiers had no hand; even the enemies of the Jews do not charge the Jewish minister with any responsibility for Don Pedro's excesses. The bastard brothers and their adherents endeavored to seize the chief town, Toledo. Here Don Pedro had numerous partisans, amongst them the whole of the Jewish community, and they contested the entrance of the brothers. One of the gates was, however, secretly opened to them by their friends, and they immediately attacked the quarters in which the Jews lived in large numbers. In Alcana street they put to the sword nearly 12,000 people, men and women, old and young. But in the inner town they failed to make any impression, the Jews having barricaded the gates and manned the walls, together with several noblemen belonging to the king's party (May, 1355). A few days later Don Pedro entered Toledo. By his adherents in the city he was received with enthusiasm, but he dealt out severe retribution to all who had assisted his brothers.

Samuel Abulafia, by the wisdom of his counsels, his able financial administration, and his zeal for the cause of Maria de Padilla, continued to rise in the favor of the king. His power was greater than that of the grandees of the realm. His wealth was princely, and eighty black slaves served in his palace. He seems to have lacked the generosity which would have suggested employing some portion of his power and prosperity for the permanent benefit of his race and religion. He certainly "sought to promote the welfare of his people," as an inscription tells us; but he failed to understand in what this welfare consisted. Against injustice and animosity he protected his brethren, promoted a few to state employment, and gave them opportunities for enriching themselves, but he was far from being what Chasdaï Ibn-Shaprut and Samuel Ibn-Nagrela had been to their co-religionists. Samuel Abulafia appears to have had little sympathy with intellectual aspirations, or with the promotion of Jewish science and poetic literature. He built synagogues for several of the Castilian communities, and one of especial magnificence at Toledo, but not a single establishment for the promotion of Talmudic study.

The Abulafia synagogue at Toledo which, transformed into a church, is still one of the ornaments of the town, was, like most of the Spanish churches of that period, built partly in the Gothic, partly in the Moorish style. It consisted of several naves separated from each other by columns and arches. The upper part of the walls is decorated with delicately cut arabesques, within which, in white characters on a green ground, the eightieth Psalm may be read in Hebrew. On the north and south sides are inscriptions in bas-relief, reciting the merits of

Prince Samuel Levi ben Meïr. The community offers up its thanks to God, "who has not withdrawn His favor from His people, and raised up men to rescue them from the hands of their enemies. Even though there be no longer a king in Israel, God has permitted one of His people to find favor in the eyes of the king, Don Pedro, who has raised him above the mighty, appointed him a councilor of his realm, and invested him with almost royal dignities." The name of Don Pedro appears in large and prominent letters, suggesting that this prince, in intimate relations with the Jews, belonged, one may say, to the synagogue. In conclusion, the wish is expressed that Samuel may survive the rebuilding of the Temple, and officiate there with his sons as chiefs of the people.

This large and splendid synagogue was completed in the year 1357. For the following year the beginning of the Messianic period had been predicted, a century before, by the astronomer Abraham ben Chiya and the rabbi and Kabbalist Nachmani, and, a few decades before, by the philosopher Leon de Bagnols. As this prophecy was not literally fulfilled, many Jews began to regard the eminence attained by Samuel and other leading Jews as a suggestion of the scepter of Judah. It was a dangerous aberration, whose pitfalls were fully appreciated by Nissim Gerundi ben Reuben (about 1340—1380), rabbi of Barcelona, the most important rabbinical authority of his day. Justly fearing that the belief in the coming of a Messiah would suffer discredit by the non-fulfillment of such prophecies, he preached against the calculation of the end of the world from expressions in the book of Daniel.

Don Samuel exercised too decided an influence over the king to avoid making enemies. Even had he been a Christian, the court party would have devised schemes to bring about his fall. Attempts were made to stir up the Castilian population against the

Jews, particularly against the Jewish minister, not only by Don Pedro's bastard brother, Don Henry, and Queen Blanche, but by all formerly in the king's service. Don Pedro Lopez de Ayala, poet, chronicler, and the king's standard-bearer, has given us, in one of his poems, a picture of the feelings of the courtiers for favored Jews: "They suck the blood of the afflicted people; they lap up their possessions with their tax-farming. Don Abraham and Don Samuel, with lips as sweet as honey, obtain from the king whatever they ask." Samuel's fall was desired by many. It is even said that some Toledo Jews, envious of his good fortune, charged him with having accumulated his enormous wealth at his royal master's expense. Don Pedro confiscated Samuel's entire fortune and that of his relatives, 170,900 doubloons, 4,000 silver marks, 125 chests of cloth of gold and silver and 80 slaves from the minister, and 60,000 doubloons from his relatives. According to some writers, an extraordinary quantity of gold and silver was found buried under Samuel's house. Don Pedro ordered his former favorite to be imprisoned at Toledo and placed upon the rack at Seville, in order to force him to disclose further treasures. He, however, remained firm, revealed nothing, and succumbed under the torture (October or November, 1360). His gravestone recites in simple phrase how high his position had been, and how his soul, purified by torture, had risen to God. Concerning Don Pedro, the inscription has not a single condemnatory expression.

Samuel Abulafia's death did not change the friendly relations between the king and the Jews. They remained faithful to him, and he continued to confer important distinctions on members of their body. They consequently came in for a share of the hatred with which the enemies of the king regarded him. The king resolved to put to death his detested consort (1361). Whatever the character of the queen, whether she was a saint or the reverse, whether or not she had deserved her fate, the method of her death must ever remain a stain on Don Pedro's memory. In spite of the animosity with which De Ayala regarded the Jews, there is no intimation in his chronicle that any of Don Pedro's Jewish favorites were concerned in this crime. It was reserved for a later period to invent fables identifying them with the king's guilt. A story was forged to the effect that a Jew had administered poison to the queen on the king's order, because she had insisted on the expulsion of the Jews from Spain. A French romance, in which an endeavor is made to varnish the deeds and misdeeds of the French adventurers who fought against Don Pedro and the Jews, attributes the queen's death to a Jewish hand.

Don Pedro announced publicly, before the assembled cortes at Seville, that his marriage with Blanche of Bourbon had been illegal, inasmuch as he had been previously married to Maria de Padilla. He called witnesses, among them a few of the clergy, and these confirmed his statement on oath. Through the murder of Blanche, and its consequences, an opportuntity offered itself to Don Henry de Trastamara to obtain allies for the dethronement of the king, and of this he was not slow to avail himself. The Bourbons in France and the king promised him aid, and allowed him to enlist the wild lances of the so-called great or white company, who, at the conclusion of the war with England, were rendering France insecure. The pope, displeased at the favors shown by Don Pedro to the Jews, also supported Don Henry, and placed the king of Spain under the ban.

To invest his rebellion with a tinge of legality and win the feelings of the people, Don Henry blackened his brother's character, picturing him as an outcast who had forfeited the crown because he had allowed his states to be governed by Jews, and had himself become attached to them and their religion. Don Henry carried his calumnies so far as to state that not only his mistress, Maria de Padilla, was a Jewess, but that Don Pedro himself was of Jewish extraction.

With the mercenaries of the "white company," graceless banditti, Henry crossed the Pyrenees to make war on and, if possible, depose his brother. At the head of these French and English outlaws stood the foremost warrior of his time, the hero and knight-errant, Bertrand du Guesclin (Claquin), celebrated for his deeds of daring, his ugliness, and his eccentricity, who, like the Cid, has been glorified by legend. The Jews consistently cast in their fortunes with those of the Don Pedro party, and supported it with their money and their blood. They flocked to its standard in the field, and garrisoned the towns against the onslaughts of Don Henry and Du Guesclin. The wild mercenaries to whom they were opposed avenged themselves not only on the Jewish soldiers, but also on those who had not borne arms.

The approach of the enemy compelled Don Pedro to abandon Burgos, the capital of Old Castile, and at an assembly of the inhabitants it was prudently resolved not to contest Don Henry's entrance. On taking possession of the town, where he was first proclaimed king (March, 1360), Henry levied a fine of 50,000 doubloons on the Jewish community, and canceled all outstanding debts due from Christians to Jews. The Jews of Burgos, unable to pay this large contribution, were compelled to sell their goods and chattels, even the ornaments on the scrolls of the Law. Those who could not make up their share of the contribution were sold into slavery. The whole of Spain fell to the conqueror in consequence of Don Pedro's neglect to concentrate round himself that portion of the population on which he could rely, or to buy over the free lances of the "white company," as he had been advised. The gates of Toledo, the capital, were opened to the victor, although Don Pedro's party, to which the Jews belonged, strongly counseled defense. Upon the Toledo community Don Henry also levied a heavy fine for its fidelity to the legitimate king. Don Pedro's last refuge was Seville, which he also lost.

Once again fortune smiled on Don Pedro, after he was compelled to cross the Pyrenees as a fugitive, and leave the whole of his country in the hands of the enemy. The heroic Prince of Wales, called the Black Prince from the color of his armor, being in the south of France, undertook to come to the aid of the deposed monarch both for the sake of a legitimate cause, and in expectation of rich rewards in money and land. Henry de Trastamara was compelled to leave Spain (1367). The whole of the peninsula hailed the victor Don Pedro and his ally, the Black Prince, with enthusiasm, as it had previously rejoiced at the triumph of his brother and the wild Constable of France, Bertrand du Guesclin. Soon, however, the scene changed. The Black Prince left Don Pedro, and Don Henry returned with new levies from France. The northern towns of Spain again fell before his arms. The citizens of Burgos opened their gates to the conqueror, but the Jews remained true to the unfortunate Don Pedro. Assisted by a few loyal noblemen, they bravely defended the Jewry of Burgos, and were subdued only by the superior strength of the enemy. They obtained a favorable capitulation, providing for their undisputed continuance in the town, but they were forced to pay a war indemnity of one million maravedis.

This time the Christian population was desirous of profiting by the revolt against Don Pedro. The cortes of Burgos represented to Henry that the

Jews, having been favorites and officials under the former king, were largely responsible for the civil war, and that he should sanction a law to exclude them in future from all state employment, including the post of physician to the king or queen, and also from the right of farming taxes. To this Don Henry replied that such a practice had not been countenanced by any former king of Castile. He would, however, not consult with the Jews at his court, nor permit them the exercise of functions which might prove detrimental to the country. From this it is evident that Henry had no particular aversion to the Jews. Possibly, he feared that by oppressing them he might drive them to acts of desperation.

Don Pedro still counted many adherents in the country. Most of the Jewish communities remained true to him, and Jews served in his army, and fought against the usurper for the king, who to the last treated them with special favor. Even when in despair he was obliged to call to his assistance the Mahometan king of Granada, he impressed upon that monarch the duty of protecting the Jews. Notwithstanding this, the Jews endured indescribable sufferings at the hands of both friend and foe. Don Pedro being entirely dependent on the auxiliaries of the Black Prince and on those of the Mahometan king, his wishes with respect to the Jews were not regarded. The community of Villadiego, celebrated for its benevolence and the promotion of learning, was utterly destroyed by the English. The same evil fortune befell Aguilar and other communities. The inhabitants of Valladolid, who paid allegiance to Don Henry, plundered the Jews, demolished their eight synagogues, despoiled them of their treasures, and tore up the sacred writings. A period of shocking degeneracy followed. Wherever Don Henry came, he laid the Jews under heavy contributions, precipitating them into poverty, and leaving them nothing but their lives. The Mahometan king, Don Pedro's ally, carried three hundred Jewish families as prisoners from Jaen to Granada. Still worse was the treatment of the violent Du Guesclin. A prey to French Jew-hatred, he could not look upon Jews as his equals in party strife and war, but only as slaves who had dared draw the sword against their masters. The misery was so great at this time that many Jews became converts to Christianity.

The community of Toledo suffered most severely. In emulation of Don Pedro's Christian adherents, they made the greatest sacrifices for the defense of the town, and endured a long and frightful siege. The famine during the investment was so great that the unfortunates consumed, not only the parchment of the Law, but even the flesh of their own children. Through hunger and war the greater portion of the Toledo community perished—according to some 8,000 persons, according to others more than 10,000. At last, at Montiel, Don Henry defeated his brother, who had been abandoned by all his partisans (14th March, 1369). Don Pedro's end was tragic. When the brothers met, Henry is said to have hurled these insulting words in his face: "Where is the Jew, the son of a harlot, who calls himself king of Castile?" They then closed in a struggle. Don Pedro was overcome, and beheaded by his brother's general, Du Guesclin. Pope Urban V could not contain his delight on hearing the news of Don Pedro's death. "The church must rejoice," he wrote, "at the death of such a tyrant, a rebel against the church, and a favorer of the Jews and Saracens. The righteous exult in retribution." The humiliation and abasement of the Spanish Jews, which the papacy had so long failed to accomplish, was obtained unexpectedly by the civil war in Castile. At Montiel they suffered a defeat pregnant with consequences fatal to their future.

Had a traveler, like Benjamin of Tudela, journeyed through Europe in the latter half of the fourteenth century, with the object of visiting, enumerating, and describing the various Jewish communities, he would have had a dismal picture to give us. From the Pillars of Hercules and the Atlantic Ocean to the banks of the Oder or the Vistula, he would have found in many districts no Jews at all, and elsewhere only very small, poverty-stricken, wretched communities, still bleeding from the wounds inflicted by the plague-maddened populace. According to human calculation, the destruction of the Jews in western and central Europe was imminent. Those who had survived the pitiless massacre, or been spared a desperate suicide, had lost courage. Communal ties were for the most part rent asunder. The recollection of the scenes of horror through which they had passed long agitated the small number of surviving Jews, and left them no hope of better times. Lord Byron's elegiac lines—

> "The wild dove hath her nest, the fox his cave,
> Mankind their country—Israel but the grave,"

are applicable to the whole of the mediæval history of the Jews, but to no period more than to this. Western and central Europe had become for the descendants of the patriarchs and the prophets one vast grave, which insatiably demanded new victims.

It is remarkable that the Jews had become indispensable to the Christian population, in spite of the venomous hatred with which the latter regarded them. Not only princes, but cities, and even the clergy, had a mania for "possessing Jews." A few years after the terrible frenzy which followed the Black Death, German citizens and their magistrates hastened to re-admit the Jews; they soon forgot their vow, that for a hundred or two hundred years no Jew should dwell within their walls. The bishop of Augsburg applied to Emperor Charles IV for the privilege "to receive and harbor Jews." The electors, ecclesiastical as well as secular, were bent upon curtailing the exclusive right of the German emperor to possess serfs of the chamber (servi cameræ), and upon acquiring the same right for themselves. Gerlach, archbishop of Mayence, especially exerted himself to wrest this privilege from Emperor Charles IV, his success being to no small extent due to the desire of the emperor to retain his popularity amongst the electors. At an imperial Diet held at Nuremberg in November, 1355, where a kind of German constitution, known as the "Golden Bull," was promulgated, the emperor conferred on the electors, in addition to the right of discovery of metal and salt mines, the privilege to hold Jews; that is to say, he yielded to them this source of revenue in addition to such sources as deposits of metal and salt. But it was only to the electors that the emperor conceded this right; he retained his rights over the "servi cameræ" living under the rule of the minor princes and in cities. The archiepiscopal elector of Mayence lost no time in utilizing the new privilege, and immediately employed a Jew to obtain others for him. Thus the Jews were at once repelled and attracted, shunned and courted, outlawed and flattered. They were well aware that it was not for their own sake that they were tolerated, but solely on account of the advantages they afforded the authorities and the population. How, then, could they be expected not to devote themselves to money-making, the sole means by which they were enabled to drag out a miserable existence?

In France, as in Germany, financial considerations induced the rulers to consent to the re-admission of the Jews. The embarrassments resulting from frequent wars with England, particularly felt after the captivity of King John (September, 1356), threatened to reduce this chivalrous land to the condition of a province of the English crown. Money especially was wanting. Even to ransom the imprisoned king the assembled States-General did not vote supplies, or they burdened their grant with heavy conditions. The third estate rose in rebellion, and encouraged the peasants to throw off the yoke of the nobles. Anarchy reigned throughout the country. At this juncture the Jews, with their financial skill, appeared to the dauphin Charles, who acted as regent during the captivity of the king, as providential deliverers of the state. A clever Jew, Manessier (Manecier) de Vesoul, actively negotiated the return of the Jews to France, whence they had been so frequently banished. The dauphin-regent had granted permission to a few Jews to return, but if the impoverished state or court was to reap any real benefit from such return, it was necessary that it should take place on a large scale. Hence, the plan which Manessier submitted to the prince was approved in every detail, and the return of the Jews for twenty years was authorized under the most favorable conditions. Neither the Jews nor their representative, Manessier, cared to take advantage of so important an offer without the consent of the imprisoned king. The plan was accordingly submitted to him for confirmation. At the instance of Manessier de Vesoul, the Jews at the same time laid before the king a memorial setting forth that they had been unjustly expelled from France, and that they could not forget the land of their birth. The imprisoned monarch then issued a decree (March, 1360), by which, with the consent of the higher and lower clergy, the higher and lower nobility, and the third estate, permission was granted to all Jews to enter France and reside there for twenty years. They were allowed to take up their abode in any part of the country, in large and small towns, villages and hamlets, and to possess, not only houses, but also lands.

The head of every Jewish family was, however,

compelled, on entering the country, to pay a sum of fourteen florins (florins de Florence) for himself, and one florin for each child or other member of his family; besides this, he became liable to an annual Jew tax of seven florins, and one for each individual of his household. On the other hand, the emigrants were to enjoy extensive privileges. They were not amenable to the jurisdiction of the ordinary courts or officials, but had a special justiciary in the person of Count d'Etampes, a prince of the blood royal, who acted as their protector (gardien, conservateur), and whose duty it was to appoint investigating judges and commissioners, and to safeguard the interests of the community when endangered. Cases of misdemeanor and crime amongst themselves were to be tried by two rabbis and four assessors. From the decisions of this tribunal there was no appeal. The property of the convicted Jewish criminal, however, became forfeited to the king, to whom, in addition, the rabbis had to pay the sum of one hundred florins. For past misdemeanors and crimes the king granted them a complete amnesty. They were protected against the violence of the nobles and the petty annoyances of the clergy. They could not be forced to attend Christian services or discourses. Their furniture, cattle, and stores of grain and wine, as well as their sacred books, not merely the Bible, but copies of the Talmud also, were to be guaranteed against confiscation, so that the public burning of the Talmud at Paris could not be repeated. The amplest protection was given their trade. They were allowed to charge 80 per cent interest (4 deniers on the livre) on loans, and to take pledges, their rights upon which were safeguarded by a fence of laws. Manessier de Vesoul himself, the active and zealous negotiator of these privileges, was appointed to a high position at court. He became receiver general (procureur or receveur-general), and in this capacity was responsible for the punctual payment of the Jew taxes, his commission being nearly 14 per cent. The result of the granting of these privileges was that the Jews entered France in large numbers, even foreigners being permitted to settle there, or take up a more or less protracted residence.

The extensive privileges granted to the Jews excited envy. The Christian physicians, exposed to the competition of Jewish doctors, complained that the latter had not passed a public examination, and denounced them as charlatans. The judges and officials, without power over the Jews and having no opportunity for extorting money from them, complained that they abused their privileges. The clergy, indignant at the favored position of the Jews, but having no real grievance, complained that they no longer wore the prescribed badge. The feeble king allowed an order to be extorted from him, to some extent in contradiction of his own decree, by which only such Jews were to be permitted to practice medicine as had passed an examination, and all Jews, not excepting those even who enjoyed especial privileges (Manessier and his family), were to wear a red and white wheel-shaped badge (rouelle) of the size of the royal seal. Finally the Jews were re-committed to the jurisdiction of the ordinary courts, and the earlier arrangements annulled.

As soon as the politic dauphin ascended the throne, under the title of Charles V, and adopted a strict system of government, to deliver himself from dependence on the States-General (May, 1364), he proceeded to assure himself of the sources of revenue possessed by the Jews. He restored the privileges partly abolished by his father, lengthened the period of residence by six years, and secretly granted permission to Hebrew money dealers to exceed the charge of 80 per cent on loans. At the instance of Manessier de Vesoul, always zealous in the interests of his co-religionists, the Jews were again withdrawn from the jurisdiction of the ordinary tribunals, and committed to the care of their official protector, Count d' Etampes. The clergy, whose hatred of the Jews bordered on inhumanity, were rendered powerless. In the south of France, the heads of the church had threatened with excommunication any Christians who should trade with Jews, or provide them with fire, water, bread, or wine, and by this means, had so stirred up the fanaticism of the people, that the lives and property of the Jews were imperiled. To counteract this, the governor of Languedoc issued, in the name of the king, an ordinance informing the officials, both lay and ecclesiastical, that all who exhibited hostility toward the Jews would be unsparingly punished in person and substance.

During the reign of Charles V (1364—1380), then, the condition of the Jews was at least endurable. Manessier remained receiver general of the Jew taxes for the north of France (Langue d'Oyl), and the same functions were discharged by Denis Quinon in Languedoc. On the complaint of the latter that a few Jewish converts, in conjunction with the Christian clergy, had forced their former brethren to attend the churches to hear sermons, the king issued a rescript (March, 1368) severely prohibiting all such unseemly compulsion. Subsequently, Charles prolonged the period for remaining in the country by ten years, and later on by six more. All this was brought about by the indefatigable Manessier (1374). His zeal in the Jewish cause and the advantages the king derived from his exertions were rewarded by the exemption of himself and his family from every kind of tax, contribution and service to the crown (1375).

Although the German and French Jews appeared to revive after their dreadful sufferings, it was only a material revival; their spirit remained dead. Their intellectual powers had disappeared. In France, where, during more than two centuries, from Rashi to the last of the Tossafists, the study of the Talmud had been carried to its most flourishing point, and where remarkable acuteness and intellectual depth had been developed, the new emigrants exhibited so astonishing an ignorance that they were obliged to commence their studies anew. The indulgences of the kings, John and Charles, certainly spoke of rabbis who should be invested with authority to try Jewish criminals ; but there was not a single profound Talmudist among them ; indeed, according to the avowal of contemporary writers, not more than five of even mediocre attainments. The only devotee of Talmudical study, Matathiah ben Joseph Provenci, has left nothing in writing to testify to his ability. Held in such esteem by Charles V that he and his family were exempted from wearing the distinctive badges prescribed by law, and apparently related to the receiver general, Manessier de Vesoul, Matathiah was in the best position to deal with the prevailing ignorance. He re-established a college at Paris, assembled pupils, expounded the Talmud to them, ordained them to rabbinical offices, and caused copies of the Talmud to be written. In consequence of his energy and his comparatively great learning, he was chosen by the newly established French communities to the office of chief rabbi and chief justice in civil and penal cases, his appointment being confirmed by the king. His school had to supply the communities with rabbis, but his pupils enriched rabbinical literature by their contributions as little as he himself. Even Provence, once so fruitful of Jewish literature, had become intellectually impoverished.

In Germany, where the rabbis had once been so proud of their traditional knowledge, the Black Death, with its attendant persecutions and banishments, had so thinned the ranks of the Jews that extraordinary intellectual decay had set in. The illiterate and the superficial, in the absence of better men, were inducted into rabbinical offices. This mischievous practice was vigorously opposed by Meïr ben Baruch Halevi, a rabbi, who, in his time, passed for a great authority in Germany (1370—1390). Rabbi at Vienna, as his father had been before him, Meïr Halevi (Segal) ordered that no Talmudical student should exercise rabbinical functions unless authorized by a rabbi of standing. Until then it had been the practice for anyone who felt able and willing to assume the rabbinical office without further ceremony, or, if he perchance settled in the neighborhood of his teacher, to obtain permission from him. As from the time of Gershom of Mayence there had always been great Talmudists in Germany, public opinion counteracted the abuse of this liberty; for had an unqualified person arrogated to himself the exercise of rabbinical functions, he would have incurred general derision and contempt. After the Black Death, however, this deterrent lost much of its force through the scarcity of Talmudists. The order of Meïr of Vienna, that every rabbi should be ordained, that he should earn the title (Morenu), and that, without such preparation, he should be precluded from dealing with matrimonial matters, marriages and divorces, was dictated by the exigencies of the times, not the presumptuousness of its author. The insignificance of even the most respected of the German rabbis of this period is apparent from the fact that not one of them has left any important Talmudical work; that, on the contrary, they all pursued a course productive of mental stagnation. Meïr Halevi, his colleague Abraham Klausner, and Shalom, of Austria, rabbi at Neustadt, near Vienna, devoted themselves exclusively to writing down and perpetuating the customs of the communities (Minhagim), to which, formerly, but very little attention had been given. They and their disciples, Isaac Tyrnau of Hungary, and Jacob Mölin (Maharil) have left behind them nothing but such insipid compilations. If the Austrian school, which at this time preponderated, was so wanting in intellectuality, how much more the Rhenish, from which only names have come down to us.

Through the disasters that resulted from the Black Death, the memories of old times had become so obliterated that the Rhenish rabbis found themselves compelled, in consequence of differences of opinion on points of marriage law, to convene a synod, exclusively for the purpose of restoring old regulations. At the meeting at Mayence (15th Ab—5th August, 1381) a few of the rabbis, together with some of the communal leaders, renewed the old decisions of Speyer, Worms and Mayence (Tekanoth Shum); as, for instance, that the childless widow should be released, without extortion or delay, from the obligation of marrying her brother-in-law, and should receive a definite portion of the property left by her husband. Among the rabbis who took part in this synod there is not one name of note.

CHAPTER V.

THE AGE OF CHASDAÏ CRESCAS AND ISAAC BEN SHESHET.

The Jews of Spain after the Civil War—Joseph Pichon and Samuel Abrabanel—The Apostates: John of Valladolid—Menachem ben Zerach, Chasdaï Crescas, and Isaac ben Sheshet—Chayim Gallipapa and his Innovations—Prevôt Aubriot and the Jews of Paris—The French Rabbinate—Revival of Jewish Influence in Spain—The Jews of Portugal—The Jewish Statesmen, David and Judah Negro—Rabbis and Clergy—Persecutions in Germany and Spain—The First Germs of the Inquisition—Second Expulsion of the Jews from France—The Convert, Pessach-Peter—Lipmann of Mühlhausen.

1369—1380 C. E.

The heart of the Jewish race had become not less crippled and sickly than its members. In Spain disintegrating forces were at work on the firm nucleus of Judaism, which had so long defied the corroding influences of ecclesiastical and civil animosity. The prince, whom the Jews at the dictates of their loyalty had so sturdily resisted, against whom they had even taken up arms; the bastard, Don Henry de Trastamara; the rebel who had brought civil war upon his native land, and flooded it with a marauding soldiery; the fratricide, who had burst the bonds alike of nature and law, had, after the victory of Montiel, seized the scepter with his blood-stained hands, and placed the stolen crown of Castile on his guilty head. Of the large Jewish population, a considerable proportion had, during the protracted and embittered civil war, met death on the field of battle, in the beleaguered towns, and, armed and unarmed alike, at the swords of the mercenaries of the "white company."

The Jewish community of Toledo, the Castilian capital—the "Crown of Israel" of the Middle Ages, and, in a measure, the Jerusalem of the Occident—

did not number, after the raising of the siege, as many hundreds of Jews as previously thousands. The remainder of the Jews of Castile had been reduced to beggary by the depredations and confiscations of friend and foe. Not a few, in their despair, had thrown themselves into the arms of Christianity. A striking picture of the unhappy condition of the Castilian communities at this period is furnished by a contemporary writer, Samuel Çarça: "In truth, plunderers followed on plunderers, money vanished from the purse, souls from the bodies; all the precursory sufferings of the Messianic period arrived —but the Redeemer came not!"

After Don Henry's victory, the Jews had good reason to tremble. One pretext for making war on his brother was the favor shown by Don Pedro to Jews. Now he had become the arbiter of their destinies. Would he not, like another Vespasian or Hadrian, place his foot on the necks of the vanquished? The gloomiest of their anticipations, however, were not realized. Don Henry II was as little able to dispense with the Jews as his predecessors, or the French and German princes. Jews were the only financiers able to keep the state exchequer in prosperity and order, and for this purpose Don Henry stood in need of them more than ever. During the war he had incurred debts for the payment of the troops with which Du Guesclin had assisted him, and for help received in other quarters he had made promises which had to be redeemed. The country had become impoverished by the protracted war. Who was to procure the necessary sums, and provide for the systematic collection of the taxes, if not the Jews? Henry was not blind to the merits of the Jews exemplified in their constancy to his brother. Instead of punishing the conquered, he appreciated their fidelity, saying: "Such subjects a king must love and reward, because they maintained proper loyalty to their conquered king unto death, and did not surrender to the victor."

Don Henry, then, was guilty of the conduct which, in the case of his brother, he branded as a crime in the eyes of all Christendom; he employed able Jews in the service of the state, confiding to them the finances in particular. Two Jews from Seville, Don Joseph Pichon and Don Samuel Abrabanel, he appointed to important posts, the former as receiver general of taxes, and Almoxarif to the king, by whom he was held in high esteem. Other Jews, distinguished for their ability or their wealth, had access to Don Henry's court.

If the king bore the Jews no grudge for the part they had taken in the war against him, the general population was not so magnanimous. The nobility and the commonalty could not forgive their having confronted them as foes in the besieged towns and on the open battle-fields. A passion for vengeance, linked with the usual Jew-hatred, blinded them to the benefits which the Jews contributed to the welfare of the state, and their only thought was how to gratify their resentment. The Jews, being the vanquished, ought, as they thought, to be reduced to a kind of serfdom. The hostile feeling of the populace manifested itself on the assembling of the first cortes at Toro (1371). Here the enemies of the Jews opened the attack. The cortes expressed to the king their displeasure that this "evil, audacious race," these enemies of God and Christendom, were employed in "high offices" at court and by the grandees of the realm, and that the farming of the taxes was confided to them, by which means feeble Christians were held in subjection and fear. The cortes accordingly made explicit demands upon the crown with respect to the Jews. From that time forward they were not to be eligible for any kind of state employment; they were to live in Jewish quarters separated from the Christian population, be forced to wear Jew-badges, be prohibited from appearing in public in rich apparel, from riding on mules, and from bearing Christian names. To Don Henry these demands were very unwelcome, but he dared not refuse some concessions. The majority he dismissed with the remark that in his treatment of Jews he only followed the example of his ancestors, especially that of his father, Alfonso XI. The two restrictions conceded were, if not of material significance, yet calculated to have a sinister effect. These were that the Castilian Jews should don the degrading badges, and give up their Spanish names. The pride of the Jews, equal to that of the grandees and the hidalgos, was deeply wounded. A century and a half had elapsed since the canonical law concerning the Jew-badge, the outcome of papal intolerance and arrogance, had been promulgated. During the whole of that period the Jews of Castile had been able to prevent its application to themselves, but now they also were to be compelled to wear the stigma on their garments. They who had been accustomed to hold their heads high, and rejoice in sounding titles, were, like the German Jews, to slink along with downcast eyes, and be called by their Oriental names. They could not accustom themselves to this humiliating situation.

In consequence of an outcry made by some of his subjects, who had been ruined by loans from Jewish creditors, and complained of usurious interest, Don Henry made encroachments upon their private rights. He decided that if the Christian debtors discharged their obligations within a short space of time, they need refund only two-thirds of the principal borrowed.

The misery resulting from the civil war and the new restrictions exercised a depressing effect on the Castilian Jews. Their most prominent men, those who had access to court, and possessed wealth and influence, especially Samuel Abrabanel, exerted themselves to remedy the gloomy state of affairs.

They particularly endeavored to restore the abased, impoverished, and disorganized community of Toledo; but it was beyond their power to revive the scholarly culture and intellectual distinction to which the Toledo community had been as much indebted for its leading position as to the prosperity of its members. The unhappy war, and the evils following in its trail, had stunted the Jewish mind, and diverted it from intellectual to material interests. Disorganization proceeded with great strides. Indifference to scientific work resulted in so general an ignorance, that what formerly every tyro was familiar with now passed for transcendent wisdom. We have an example of the mawkishness to which the new Hebrew poetry had fallen in the verses of the poetaster Zarak (Zerach) Barfat, who, in a poetical paraphrase of the book of Job, completely marred the beauties of that work of art. Just at this period men of learning and ability were urgently required, for representatives of Christianity began to make earnest and energetic attacks on Judaism to obtain converts from amongst its adherents.

Don Henry had much to thank the clergy for; they had sanctified his usurpation, and acquiesced in his arrogated succession. From gratitude and a false conception of religiousness, he conceded much to them. At his command, Jews were again forced to take part in religious debates, in which there was much to lose and nothing to gain.

Two baptized Jews received from the king the privilege of holding religious discussions in every province and town of Castile, which they might compel Jews to attend.

One of these apostates was John of Valladolid. At Burgos the discussion took place before Archbishop Gomez of Toledo. At Avila the whole community was compelled to repair to the great church (1375), where the debate was carried on in the presence of many Christians and Mahometans.

Moses Cohen de Tordesillas, who was as familiar with Christian as with Jewish theological authorities, appeared on behalf of the Jews. He entered upon his dangerous enterprise with trepidation, for he had had an opportunity to form an estimate of Christian charity. During the civil war, Christian marauders had robbed him of all his possessions, and had even personally ill-used him in order to force him to embrace Christianity. All these trials he had suffered with the courage of strong convictions, but he had become so poverty-stricken that he had to accept support from the community of Avila.

Moses de Tordesillas did not find his part in the discussion too difficult. The apostate John of Valladolid laid stress on the proposition that the dogmas of Christianity—the Messianic claim, the Divinity and Incarnation of Jesus, the Trinity, and the Virginity of the "Mother of God"—could be demonstrated from the Old Testament. It was consequently not difficult for his Jewish opponent to confute his arguments. After four debates John was obliged to abandon his task, vanquished. This, however, did not conclude the matter. A pupil of the apostate, Abner-Alfonso, appeared soon after, and challenged Moses de Tordesillas to a debate on the Talmud and Agadic texts. In case of refusal, he threatened publicly to impeach the Talmud as the source of anti-Christian sentiments. Moses was again forced to meet a series of silly assertions and charges, and to drag himself through the thorny length of another controversy. By the advice of the Avila community, he committed to writing the principal arguments used in these discussions under the title, "Ezer ha-Emuna," and sent them to his Toledan brethren for use under similar circumstances. Moses de Tordesillas' disputations, notwithstanding the difficulties of his position, were characterized by calmness and equanimity. Not a word of abuse or invective escaped him, and he counseled his Toledo brethren not to permit themselves to be tempted by their zeal to vexatious expressions, "for it is a fact," he said, "that the Christians possess the power and disposition to silence truth by force." Toledo, formerly recognized as the teacher of Jewry, was now obliged to play the part of pupil, and follow formularies in the disputations to which its members might be invited.

As if the more far-seeing Jews had anticipated the approach of the gloomiest era of Spanish Judaism, they provided their co-religionists for the coming struggle with casque and buckler, so that the inexorable foe might not surprise them unarmed. A Spanish Jew, contemporary with Moses de Tordesillas, compiled a polemical work, more exhaustive than its predecessor, defending Judaism and attacking Christianity. Shem-Tob ben Isaac Shaprut of Tudela had at an early age been forced into the position of a defender of his brethren against proselytizing attempts. Cardinal Don Pedro de Luna, who later on, as Pope Benedict XIII, brought so much confusion into the church and evil on the Jews, was possessed of a perfect mania for conversion and religious controversy. At Pampeluna he summoned Shem-Tob ben Shaprut to a debate on original sin and salvation, and the latter was compelled to sustain his part in the presence of bishops and learned prelates. The war between England and Castile, the scene of which was Navarre, obliged Shem-Tob ben Shaprut, with many other Jews, to quit the country (1378) and settle in the neighboring town of Tarazona, in Aragon. Observing here that Jews of the stamp of John de Valladolid were extremely zealous in the promotion of religious discussions, the conversion of weaklings, and the maligning of Jewish literature, he published (1380) a comprehensive work ("Eben Bochan"), unmasking the speciousness of the arguments deduced by Christian controversialists from the Bible and the Talmud. The work is written in the form of a discussion between a believer in the unity of God and a Trinitarian. To enable the Jews to use weapons out of the Christian armory, Shem-Tob ben Shaprut translated into Hebrew extracts from the four Gospels, with incisive commentaries. Subsequently the anti-Jewish work of the apostate Abner-Alfonso fell into his hands, and he refuted it, argument by argument.

These polemical works did not prove of far-reaching importance; at any rate, their effect was not what their authors had expected. The Jews of Spain did not so much stand in need of writings as of men of force of character, commanding personality and dignity, able to raise, if not the masses, at least the half-educated classes, and imbue them with somewhat of their own spirit. The ban against scientific studies, pronounced by excessive fear and extreme religiousness, notably avenged itself. It dwarfed the intelligence of the people, and deprived them of that capacity for appreciating the signs of the times which only a liberal education can develop. Even faith suffered from this want of culture in the rising generation. Only one Jew of profound philosophic genius stands out prominently in the history of this period, and the influence he exerted over a rather small circle was due less to his superior intelligence than to his position and Talmudic knowledge. The majority of the Spanish rabbis, if not actually hostile, were indifferent to the sciences, especially to religious philosophy. Only laymen devoted themselves to such pursuits, and they were neither exhaustive in their inquiries nor creative in their speculations. It is characteristic of this period that Maimuni's philosophical "Guide of the Perplexed" was entirely neglected, the fashion being to read and discuss Ibn-Ezra. The fragmentary nature of the writings of this commentator, the ingenuity and acuteness, the disjointedness of thought, the variety of matter, which characterize his work, appealed to the shallowness of this retrograde generation. Shem-Tob ben Shaprut, Samuel Çarça, Joseph Tob-Elem, Ezra Gatiño, and others wrote super-commentaries on Ibn-Ezra's commentary on the Pentateuch. The solution of riddles propounded by Ibn-Ezra, and the discovery of his secrets, and explanations of his obscurities, seriously exercised the minds of large circles of students.

The Talmud, with which the more thoughtful minds, prompted by a religious bias, continued to be engaged, fared no better than secular learning. Here, also, a state of stagnation, if nothing worse, had supervened. The rabbis of some large communities were not even able to discharge one of their chief duties, the explanation of the Talmud to their disciples. A French Talmudist, Solomon ben Abraham Zarfati, who had settled at Majorca, could venture to speak slightingly of the Spanish rabbis, not excepting the celebrated Nissim Gerundi, and compare them disparagingly with the French and German rabbis. A measure of the average intelligence of the rabbis of this period is yielded by the works of Menachem ben Zerach, chief rabbi of Toledo, even after its misfortunes a very important Jewish community.

Menachem ben Aaron ben Zerach (born 1310, died 1385) counted several martyrs in his family. His father, Aaron, was one of the unfortunates whom the cupidity and tyranny of a French king had banished. With the limited means spared by legalized robbery he had settled in Estella, a not inconsiderable Navarrese community. His father, mother, and four brothers perished in the massacre of Jews instigated by a Dominican friar. Young Menachem was severely wounded in this outbreak, and might have succumbed but for the assistance of a nobleman of his father's acquaintance. On his recovery he devoted himself daily to Talmudical study, and later on attended the celebrated school of the Asheride Judah of Toledo. After he had passed his fortieth year, Menachem ben Zerach became chief of an academy, the care of which was confided to him by the Alcala (de Henares) community. During the civil war in Castile he was wounded and plundered by the lawless soldiery, and of his entire fortune, only his house, field, and collection of books remained. Don Samuel Abrabanel assisted him in his distress, so that he was enabled to recover somewhat from his misfortunes. Through his interposition Menachem was called from Alcala to assume the rabbinate of Toledo, where he opened an academy. As the disciple and successor of Jehuda Asheri, considerable Talmudical attainments were with justice expected of him. But he did not rise above the mediocrity of his times. To remedy the increasing ignorance of religious forms and duties, he wrote a compendium of theoretic and practical Judaism ("Zeda la-Derech," 1374), as comprehensible as it was short, for the use of prominent Jews, who, employed at court and by the grandees, had not sufficient leisure to search an extensive literature for instruction. His work is interspersed with scientific elements—psychological and religio-philosophical—but it is weak and commonplace, full of platitudes, and its several parts do not cohere. Even the Talmudical elements are neither profound nor original. The only redeeming feature is that it is conceived in a warm, sympathetic spirit, distinguishing it from the usually dry rabbinical disquisitions.

Only two men of this time are raised by their character and learning above the dead level of prevailing mediocrity: Chasdaï Crescas and Isaac ben Sheshet. They both lived in the kingdom of Aragon, where the Jews under Pedro IV and Juan I were neither so poor nor so oppressed as their brethren in Castile. Chasdaï Crescas and Isaac ben Sheshet were not sufficiently great to dominate their contemporaries, or prescribe their own views as rules of conduct; they were, however, the foci of large circles, and were frequently appealed to for final decisions on complicated and difficult questions. Both worked earnestly for the maintenance and furtherance of Judaism, for the preservation of peace in the communities at home and abroad, and for the consolation and re-animation of the broken in spirit, notwithstanding that their means were limited, and the times unpropitious.

Chasdaï ben Abraham Crescas (born 1340, died 1410), originally of Barcelona, and subsequently of Saragossa, where he ended his days, did not belong to the class of ordained rabbis, but he had been educated on Talmudical lines, and was an accomplished Talmudist. His wealth and his occupations seem to have indisposed him for this honorable position. Chasdaï Crescas was in close relation with the court of Juan I, of Aragon, was frequently consulted on important state questions, and also had much intercourse with the grandees of the kingdom. In the views of the various schools of philosophy he was well versed; the independence and depth of thought he evinced in dealing with them stamp him an original thinker. His ideas, of course, were largely based upon religious, or rather Jewish convictions, which, however, he presented in an original form. Chasdaï Crescas was the first to recognize the weak points of the prevailing Aristotelianism, and he attacked it with irresistible force. Of his youth nothing is known, and it is impossible to say under what influences those ripe powers of mind were developed which enabled him to question the authority not only of Maimonides and Gersonides, but of Aristotle himself. His ancestors were learned Talmudists, and his grandfather enjoyed a reputation equal to that of the famous Asheri family. In Talmudical studies he was a disciple of Nissim Gerundi, of Barcelona. Chasdaï Crescas was kind and gentle, a friend in need, and a faithful defender of the weak. During the unhappy days which broke upon the Jews of Spain in his lifetime, he devoted all his powers to the mitigation of the disasters which befell his brethren.

Similar in character, but fundamentally opposed to him in the disposition of his mind, was his friend and senior, Isaac ben Sheshet Barfat (Ribash, born 1310, died about 1409). A native of Barcelona, and having studied under Ben Adret's son and pupils, Isaac ben Sheshet may, in a measure, be considered a disciple of Ben Adret. He acquired his teacher's capacity for seizing the spirit of the Talmud and expounding it lucidly, and far surpassed him in hostility to secular studies. Ben Adret had permitted the circumstances of his times to extort from him the prohibition of such studies, as far as raw youths were concerned; Ben Sheshet, in his rigid orthodoxy, took the view that even mature men should hold aloof from them, although at that period there was but little fear of heresy. The physical sciences and philosophy, he held, should be completely avoided, as they were calculated to undermine the two essential supports of the Torah, the doctrines of the creation, and of a Providence; because they exalted reason over faith, and generated doubts of miracles. In Gersonides, and even Maimuni, Ben Sheshet found illustrations of the pernicious effects of philosophic speculation. He granted that they were men of incomparable genius, but he insisted that they had been seduced by philosophy to adopt heterodox views, and explain certain miracles of the Bible rationalistically. Ben Sheshet was of high moral character; his disposition was kindly, and on several occasions he willingly sacrificed his personal interests to advance the common good and to promote peace. But when he suspected the violation of a Talmudical precept or the non-observance of even an unessential custom, his mildness was immediately transformed into most obdurate severity.

On account of his Talmudical learning, his clear, penetrating intellect, and his irreproachable character, he was much sought after. The important community of Saragossa elected him its rabbi. Immediately on taking office, Isaac ben Sheshet gave an illustration of the tenacity with which he clung to the letter of the Law, even when it conflicted with the spirit. He observed, with regret, that the practice obtained of reading the book of Esther on the feast of Purim in a Spanish translation, for the benefit of the women. This practice had been introduced into other Spanish communities, and was not only applauded by all men of common sense, but had even been authorized by a few rabbis, who considered it unobjectionable from a Talmudical point of view. Ben Sheshet raised a cry of alarm, as if Judaism had been threatened with ruin. He called to his assistance the authority of his teacher, Nissim Gerundi, and together they opposed the excellent custom with sophistical argument. They appear to have been successful in abolishing it.

Still more characteristic of Isaac ben Sheshet is his quarrel with Chayim ben Gallipapa, a rabbi, stricken in years, whose opinions differed from those of the rabbi of Saragossa. This man (born 1310, died 1380), rabbi of Huesca and Pampeluna, was a singular figure in the Middle Ages, whom it is difficult to classify. Whilst the rabbis of the time, particularly since the rise of the Asheride teaching, exceeded all bounds in the imposition of burdensome observances, and always, in cases of doubt, decided in favor of their most rigorous fulfillment, Gallipapa took the opposite view, and maintained that the aim of all Talmudical exegesis should be to disencumber life. The times, he considered, had improved, and neither the ignorance of the people nor the fear of defection was so great as to warrant such severity. This principle was no mere theory with Gallipapa, for he followed it practically. The freedom he suggested concerned matters of comparative insignificance, but at that time every trifle was regarded as important. On certain dogmas, also, Gallipapa held independent views. The Messianic belief which, since the time of Maimonides, had become an article of faith, to deny which was heresy, he boldly set aside. Gallipapa considered that the prophecies, in Isaiah and Daniel, of the great prosperity of Israel in the future, had been fulfilled in the days of the Maccabees, and wrote a work on the subject. Against this hardy innovator, a storm naturally arose. A neighboring rabbi, Chasdaï ben Solomon, of Tudela, a man of not over-fine sensibilities, denounced him to Isaac ben Sheshet, and the latter lectured the venerable Gallipapa, who had sent disciples into the world, as if he had been a mere schoolboy. He adjured Chayim Gallipapa to avoid scandal and give no opportunity for schism amongst his brethren. The modest attempt at reform went no further.

This severe tendency in matters of religion was the natural outcome of the prevailing spiritual needs; and it must be confessed that the more rigorous, the better it was adapted to them. Isaac ben Sheshet and his friend Chasdaï Crescas, who, although no enemy of secular learning, entertained the same view as his colleague, and defended his orthodoxy on philosophic grounds, were considered, after the death of Nissim Gerundi, the most eminent rabbinical authorities of their day, not in Spain only. From far and near, inquiries were addressed to them, principally to Isaac ben Sheshet, but also to Chasdaï Crescas. The proudest rabbis and the largest communities invoked their counsel, and were content to abide by their decisions. The court of Aragon also regarded them as the leaders of the Jewish communities, but this operated to their disadvantage. In consequence of the denunciation of some malevolent pĕrson, the ground of which is unknown, the king, Don Pedro IV, ordered Chasdaï Crescas, Isaac ben Sheshet, his brother, Crescas Barfat, the aged Nissim Gerundi of Barcelona, and two others, to be thrown into prison. After a long time, they were released on bail. We may believe Isaac ben Sheshet, when he assures us that he and his fellow-prisoners were all innocent of the offense or crime laid to their charge. Their innocence must have come to light, for they afterwards remained unmolested.

The authority of Chasdaï Crescas and Isaac ben Sheshet was appealed to by the French communities to settle an important point in a dispute about the chief rabbinate of France. A change, largely the outcome of the political condition of the country, had come over the circumstances of these communities. Manessier de Vesoul, the zealous defender and protector of his co-religionists, was dead (about 1375—1378). Of his four sons—Solomon, Joseph, Abraham, and Haquinet—the eldest succeeded to his father's post of receiver general of the Jew taxes and political representative of the French Jews, and the second became a convert to Christianity. Solomon and his brothers enjoyed the same esteem at the royal court as their father. They were exempted from wearing the humiliating Jew badge, and they diligently cared for the interests of their brethren. Among Jews, however, they do not seem to have obtained the consideration that their father had enjoyed. On the death of the king, Charles V, their importance ceased altogether. The regent Louis, Duke of Anjou, confirmed, for a consideration, the privileges acquired by the French Jews (14th October, 1380), and prolonged their term of sufferance in the land by another five years. His protection, however, did not reach far, or rather it involved the Jews in his own unpopularity. The impoverished population of Paris, driven to despair by burdensome taxation, loudly and stormily demanded redress of the young king and the regent. Egged on by a nobility involved in debt, they included the Jews in their outcry, and demanded that the king should expel from the country "these shameful usurers who have ruined whole families." The people did not stop at words; at the instigation of the nobles, they attacked the houses of the Jews (November 16th, 1380), robbed the exchequer of the receiver general (of the Vesoul family), pillaged their dwelling-houses, destroyed the bonds of the debtors, appropriated the accumulated pledges, murdered a few Jews, and tore children from the arms of fleeing and weeping Jewish mothers to baptize them forthwith. A large number of Jews saved themselves by flight to the fort Châtelet. The regent was much irritated by this violent outbreak, but was unable to punish the offenders at once on account of the excited state of the people. He ordered that the Jews be reinstated in their homes, and the plunder restored to them. Few complied with the order. The prevôt of Paris, Hugues Aubriot—a man of considerable energy, who had beautified and enlarged the French capital—also interested himself in the Jews. In particular, he brought about the restitution of the stolen and baptized children. For this he was violently attacked by men whose learning should have taught them better. Aubriot, by his orderly administration, had made enemies of the university professors and students, who denounced as criminal his interference for the benefit of the Jews. He was accused before the bishop of Paris of having held intercourse with Jewish women, and even of being a secret adherent of Judaism. He was found guilty of heresy and infidelity, and made to pay with imprisonment for his humane conduct towards the Jews. Not only in Paris, but also in other towns where the people rose against heavy taxation, Jews fell victims to the popular excitement. Four months later, similar bloody scenes were enacted in Paris and the provinces when the rising of the Maillotins (so called from the mallets with which the insurgents were armed) took place. For three or four days in succession Jews were again plundered, ill-treated, and murdered (March 1st, 1381). The king, Charles VII, or rather the regent, attempted to protect the Jews and to obtain some indemnification of their losses. They were, however, unable to recover from the blow they had received. In these tumults the sons of Manessier de Vesoul appear either to have lost their lives, or, at any rate, their position of influence.

This change in the fortunes of the French Jews brought in its train a violent communal dispute, the excitement of which extended far and wide. The chief rabbi, Matathiah Provenci, had been gathered to his fathers. The communities had elected his eldest son, Jochanan, in his place, and the king had confirmed their choice. He had been in office five years, and was projecting the establishment of an academy, when a former pupil of his father, one Isaiah ben Abba-Mari, arrived in France from Savoy with the authorization of the German chief rabbi, Meïr ben Baruch Halevi, granting to him alone the right to maintain an academy and ordain pupils as rabbis. Whoever exercised rabbinical functions without his authority and, especially, meddled with marriages and divorces, was threatened with excommunication. All unauthorized documents were declared null and void. By virtue of his authority, and in consequence of Jochanan's refusal to subordinate himself to him, Isaiah relieved him of his office (about 1380—1390). The Vesoul family being extinct or having lost prestige, Jochanan found himself without influential support. Many of the French Jews, however, were extremely wroth at this violent, imperious behavior of the immigrant rabbi. They condemned the presumptuousness of the German rabbi, Meïr Halevi, in treating France as though it were a German province, and protested against his dictating laws to the French communities, as it had always been the custom to regard each community, and certainly the Jews of each country, as independent. The result was a storm of indignation, which increased considerably when Isaiah proceeded to appoint his own relatives to the various rabbinates. It being impossible to settle the dispute by an appeal to the home-authorities, Jochanan turned with his grievance to the two foremost representatives of Spanish Judaism, Chasdaï Crescas and Isaac ben Sheshet. Both these "Catalonian grandees," as they were called, pronounced in favor of Jochanan. This decision, however, was not destined to bring about lasting peace, for the days of the Jews in France were numbered.

The storm on this occasion arose in Spain, and convulsed for a time the entire Jewish race. The golden age of the Spanish Jews had passed away; still they were more firmly established in the Peninsula than in any other country. It required a series of violent shocks, extending over an entire century, to completely uproot them, whilst in France they were swept away by a breath, like twigs planted in quicksand. For the sanguinary drama which commenced towards the end of the fourteenth century, and ended in the latter part of the fifteenth, the Spanish Jews were themselves largely to blame. It is true that the many had to suffer for the few, for when the enemies of the Jews complained of their obsequious attendance at court and on the grandees, of their wealth accumulated by usury, and their flaunting in silks and satins, blame was due only to a few of the most prominent, for whose follies and extravagances the masses were not responsible. Indeed, there were Jews who complained that their moral sense was deeply wounded by the selfishness and covetousness of their wealthy brethren. "For these troubles," says one, "the titled and wealthy Jews are greatly to be held responsible; their only consideration is for their position and money, whilst for their God they have no regard." In fact, the union that had previously been the chief source of strength among the Spanish Jews, was broken up. Jealousy and envy among the Jewish grandees had undermined fraternal feeling, which formerly had induced each to merge his interests in those of the community at large, and all to combine for the defense of each. Generosity and nobility of mind, once the brilliant qualities of the Spanish Jews, had now become almost extinct. A contemporary writer pictures their degeneracy in darkest hues, and if only one half of what he tells us is true, their decline must have been grave indeed.

"The majority of wealthy Jews," says Solomon Alami in his "Mirror of Morals," or "Letter of Warning," "who are admitted to royal courts, and to whom the keys of public exchequers are confided, pride themselves on their dignities and wealth, but give no thought to the poor. They build themselves palaces, drive about in splendid equipages, or ride on richly caparisoned mules, wear magnificent apparel, and deck their wives and daughters like princesses with gold, pearls, and precious stones. They are indifferent to their religion, disdain modesty, hate manual labor, and live in idleness. The wealthy love dancing and gaming, dress in the national costume, and go about with sleek beards. They fill themselves with dainties, whilst scholars starve on bread and water. Hence, the rabbis are despised, for all classes prefer to have their sons taught the lowest of handicrafts to bringing them up to the study of the Law. At sermon time, the great resign themselves to sweet slumber, or talk with one another, and the preacher is frequently disturbed by men and women at the back of the synagogue. On the other hand, how devout are the Christians in their houses of worship! In every town the noble live at variance with one another, and stir up discord on the most trivial questions. Still worse is the jealousy with which they regard each other; they slander one another before the king and the princes."

It is certainly true that at this period secret denunciations, once almost unknown among the Jews, were exceedingly rife, even rabbis being occasionally the victims. As the aged Nissim Gerundi, Isaac ben Sheshet, Chasdaï Crescas, and their friends were victimized by the conspiracy of some miserable calumniator, so an attempt was made to ruin the rabbi of Alkolea de Cinca, En-Zag Vidal de Tolosa, by representations to the queen of Aragon.

The rabbis, who, with one or two assessors, constituted courts of justice for criminal cases, dealt severely with such traitors, and even sentenced them to death. In the communities of Castile, Aragon, Valencia, and Catalonia, the privilege of passing death-sentences was of great antiquity. The Jewish courts required for the execution of such sentences special sanction from the king in a sealed letter (Albala, Chotham); but, if necessary, this could be obtained through the medium of Jewish courtiers, or by bribery. Such proceedings, however, only increased the evil they were designed to cure. The accused were made short work of without exhaustive inquiry, or sufficient testimony, and this naturally infuriated their relatives and friends. It did not unfrequently occur that utterances were construed as treasonable which had no such character. The ill-advised action of the Jewish court of Seville (or Burgos) on an unfounded charge of disloyalty to the community preferred against an eminent and beloved co-religionist was, if not the actual cause, at any rate the occasion of the first widespread and sanguinary persecution of the Jews in Spain, the final result being the total expulsion of the Jews from the Peninsula.

Joseph Pichon, of Seville, high in favor with the king of Castile, Don Henry II, whose receiver general of taxes he had been, was accused of embezzlement by some jealous Jewish courtiers. He was imprisoned by the king, condemned to pay a fine of 40,000 doubloons, and then set free. He afterwards retrieved his reputation, and became extraordinarily popular among the Christian population of Seville. To avenge his wrongs, or possibly with a view to his own vindication, he had entangled his enemies in a serious accusation, when Don Henry died. His son, Don Juan I, was crowned at Burgos, the capital of Old Castile (1379). During the coronation festivities, a Jewish court of justice (at Burgos or Seville) condemned Pichon as an enemy to the community and a traitor (Malshim, Malsin), without affording him an opportunity of being heard in defense. Some Jews, having access to the court, asked permission of the young king to execute a dangerous member of their own body without mentioning his name. Confidants of the king are said to have been bribed to obtain the royal signature to this decree. Provided with the king's warrant and the death sentence of the rabbinical college, Pichon's enemies repaired to the chief of police (Alguacil), Fernan Martin, and obtained his assistance at the execution. Early on the morning of the 21st August, two or three Jews, together with Martin, entered Pichon's house whilst he was yet asleep, and awoke him under the pretext that his mules were to be seized for debt. As soon as he appeared at the door of his dwelling, he was arrested by the Jews intrusted with the carrying out of the sentence, and, without a word, beheaded.

Whether Pichon had deserved death, even according to rabbinical law, or whether he fell a victim to the intrigues of his enemies, is not known. It is not difficult to understand that so cruel an act should have stirred up widespread indignation. The anger of the young king knew no bounds when he learnt that his coronation festivities had been stained with the murder of one who had rendered his father substantial services, and that his own sanction had been surreptitiously obtained. He immediately ordered the execution of the Jews who had carried out the sentence, and of a Jewish judge of Burgos. Even the chief of police, Fernan Martin, was ordered to be put to death for the assistance he had given; but at the intercession of some nobles, his life was spared, and his punishment commuted to the chopping off of one hand. This incident had other grave consequences. The king at once deprived the rabbis and Jewish courts of justice of jurisdiction in criminal cases, on the ground of their abuse of the privilege. At the first meeting of the cortes at Soria (1380), he made this restriction a permanent statute. By its terms the rabbis and communal leaders were thenceforth prohibited from decreeing punishments of death, dismemberment, or exile, and in criminal cases were to choose Christian judges. One of the reasons assigned was that, according to the prophets, the Jews were to be deprived of all power and freedom after the advent of Jesus. The still exasperated king then arraigned the Jews on other charges. He accused them particularly of cursing Christians and the Christian church in their prayers, and with receiving Mahometans, Tartars, and other foreign persons into the pale of Judaism, and having them circumcised. These alleged practices were forbidden under heavy penalties. The feeling against the Jews was not limited to the king and the court circle. The entire population of Castile was roused by the apparently unjust execution of Joseph Pichon, and by the circumstance that his death was not the work of irresponsible individuals, but of the foremost leaders of the Jewish community. In Seville, where Pichon had been very popular, the fury against the Jews rose to such a height that, had the opportunity presented itself, summary vengeance would have been taken.

Accusations against the Jews and petitions for the restriction of their liberties became the order of the day at the meetings of the cortes, as formerly at the councils of the Visigothic kings. The infuriated Don Juan acquiesced in this agitation, in so far as it did not tend to the detriment of the royal finances. At the cortes of Valladolid (1385), he granted the petition for the legalization of the canonical restrictions, presented by the clergy, and accordingly prohibited the living together of Jews and Christians, and the suckling of Jewish infants by Christian nurses, under pain of public whipping. He also consented to the passing of a law excluding Jews (and Mahometans) from the post of treasurer to the king, queen, or any of the royal family.

Curiously, it was the quarrel over the chief rabbinate of Portugal that snatched the crown of that country, at the moment when it was within his grasp, from this monarch, who cannot be said to have been wholly hostile to the Jews. By a treaty with King Ferdinand of Portugal, it had been agreed that, male heirs to the crown failing, he, or rather his second wife, the Portuguese Infanta Beatrice (Brites), should have the first right to the succession. In Portugal the Jews had always been tolerated, and, up to the time of their expulsion from the country, suffered no persecution. During the reign of King Ferdinand (1367—1383), their position was exceptionally happy. Since the thirteenth century (1274), the government of the community had been more completely in its own hands than in any other European country. Some of their peculiar institutions dated even further back. At the head of the Portuguese Jews was a chief rabbi (Ar-Rabbi Mor), possessing almost princely privileges. On account of the importance of the office he was always appointed by the king, who conferred it as a reward for services rendered to the crown, or to add to the dignity of some particular favorite. The chief rabbi used a special signet, administered justice in all its branches, and issued decrees under his own sign-manual with the addendum: "By the grace of my lord, the king, Ar-Rabbi Mor of the communities of Portugal and Algarve." It was his duty to make an annual circuit of all the Portuguese communities, to investigate their affairs, invite individuals to lay before him their grievances, even against the rabbis, and remedy abuses wherever they existed. On these journeys he was accompanied by a Jewish judge (Ouvidor), a chancellor (Chanceller) with his staff, a secretary (Escrivão), and a sheriff (Porteiro jurado), to carry out the sentences of his court. The chief rabbi or Ar-Rabbi Mor, appointed in each of the seven provinces of the kingdom provincial rabbis (Ouvidores) subject to him. These rabbis were established in the seven principal provincial Jewish centers, Santarem, Vizeu, Cavilhão, Porto, Torre de Montcorvo, Evora and Faro. They governed the provincial communities, and were the judges of appeal for their several districts. The local rabbis were elected by the general body of contributing members of the community; but the confirmation of their election and their investiture proceeded from the chief rabbi, under a special deed issued in the name of the king. The judicial authority of the rabbis extended to criminal cases, and they retained this privilege much longer than their Spanish brethren. Public documents had to be written in the vernacular. The Jewish form of oath was very simple, even in litigation with Christians; it required nothing but the presence of a rabbi and the holding up of the Torah.

The king, Don Ferdinand, had two Jewish favorites, who supervised his monetary affairs: Don Judah, his chief treasurer (Tesoreiro Mor), and Don David Negro, of the highly-respected Ibn-Yachya family, his confidant and counselor (Almoxarif). When this frivolous and prodigal monarch died, and the regency was undertaken by the queen, Leonora —a princess whose beauty rendered her irresistible, but who was hated for her faithlessness and feared for her vindictiveness and craft—the municipal authorities of Lisbon approached her with an urgent prayer for the abolition of sundry unpopular measures of the late king. Among other things they asked that Jews and Moors should no longer be allowed to hold public offices. Leonora craftily replied that during the lifetime of the king she had exerted herself to procure the exclusion of Jews from public offices, but her representations had always been unheeded. Immediately after the king's death she had removed Judah and David Negro from the public service, and dismissed all the Jewish receivers of taxes. She nevertheless retained Judah in her immediate circle, anticipating that, on account of his wealth and experience, he might prove of use to her. Leonora's scheme to obtain absolute authority and share the government with her paramour was frustrated by the still craftier bastard Infante Don João, Grand Master of Avis. In the art of winning public favor and turning it to account, Don João was a master, and he soon brought things to such a pass that the queen regent was forced to leave the capital. Burning for revenge, Leonora invoked the aid of her son-in-law, King Don Juan of Castile, with the result that a sanguinary civil war was commenced. In opposition to the aristocratic faction, supporting the queen regent and the Castilians, there arose a popular party, which enthusiastically espoused the cause of Don João of Avis. Leonora was obliged to fly before the hatred of her people and take refuge in Santarem. Among her escort were the two Jewish grandees, Judah and David Negro, who had escaped from Lisbon in disguise. Hither came King Juan of Castile; and Leonora, in order to be enabled to take full vengeance on her enemies, renounced the regency in his favor, and placed at his disposal all her adherents, comprising the entire Portuguese nobility, together with a large number of fortresses. The idea of the Castilian king in undertaking this enterprise was to unite the crowns of Portugal and Castile; but for the realization of this project a thorough understanding between Leonora and her son-in-law and her ungrudging co-operation were indispensable. This important harmony was disturbed by a question as to the appointment of a chief rabbi, and owing to this dispute their agreement was transformed into bitter and disastrous enmity.

The rabbinate of Castile became vacant in 1384. Leonora, desiring to obtain the appointment for her favorite Judah, made application to the king on his behalf. At the instance of his wife Beatrice, he conferred the dignity upon David Negro. Leonora's anger at this rebuff was expressed with vehemence. She is reported to have said to her circle of adherents: "If the king refuses so trivial a favor, the first I have asked of him, to me, a woman, a queen, a mother, one who has done so much for him, what have I and what have you to expect? Even my enemy, the Grand Master of Avis, would not have treated me thus. You will do better to go over to him, your legitimate master." Leonora transferred to her son-in-law, King Juan, all the hatred with which she had formerly regarded the Grand Master of Avis. She organized a conspiracy to murder him, the details of which she confided to the former treasurer Judah. The plot was, however, discovered by the chief rabbi elect, David Negro, who saved the king's life. Don Juan immediately caused the queen dowager to be arrested and thrown into prison. Judah also was imprisoned, and ordered to be executed, but at the energetic intercession of his rival, David Negro, his life was spared. This quarrel with and imprisonment of his mother-in-law cost Don Juan all support in Portugal. Thenceforth he encountered resistance on every side, and was obliged to resort to forcible measures for the subjugation of the country. His plans, however, all failed, and in the end he found himself compelled to renounce his hope of a union of the two lands.

A few rabbis intrigued to obtain rabbinical office, and involved their several communities in much unseemly strife, as, for example, David Negro and Judah, Isaiah ben Abba-Mari and Jochanan in France, Solomon Zarfati and En-Vidal Ephraim Gerundi in the Island of Majorca, and Chasdai ben Solomon and Amram Efrati in Valencia, but it must be acknowledged that such incidents were of rare occurrence. To the majority, the rabbinate was as a holy priesthood, the duties of which they sought to discharge in all purity of heart and deed, with devotion and self-denial. They were generally examples to their communities, not only in learning and piety, but in high-mindedness, conscientiousness, and the purity of their morals. Even the less worthy cannot be charged with anything more serious than a desire for place, and a certain degree of irascibility. It would be a gross libel on their memory to compare them with the servants of the church during the same period. At no time in its history had Christianity more reason to be ashamed of its representatives than during the fourteenth and the succeeding century. Since the papacy had established itself at Avignon, it had become a perfect hot-bed of vice, the contagion of which spread over the clergy down to the lowliest friar. Besides, there arose passionate strife between pope and anti-pope, between one college of cardinals and another, dividing the whole of Christendom into two huge, bitterly hostile camps. It was only natural that the clergy should infect the lay world with their immeasurable dissoluteness and vice. Yet these degenerate, inhuman and degraded Christian communities presumed to treat the modest, virtuous, pious Jews as outcasts and accursed of God. Although superior in everything save wickedness and the virtues of a robber chivalry, they were denied the commonest rights of man. They were baited and slaughtered like beasts of the field. In Nördlingen the entire Jewish community, including women and children, was murdered (1384). All over Suabia they were persecuted, and in Augsburg they were imprisoned until a ransom of 20,000 florins was paid. A characteristic illustration is furnished by the following occurrence: The rabbis and communal leaders of central Germany had determined to hold a synod at Weissenfels, in Saxony, for the purpose of deliberating upon certain religious questions, and adopting resolutions of public utility (1386). They had provided themselves with safe-conduct passes from the Saxon princes, it being unsafe for Christians to travel on the public highroads, and, of course, much more so for Jews. Nevertheless, a party of German robber-nobles, anticipating rich booty, waylaid the travelers on their return journey, and, having plundered and ill-used them, threw them into prison, and liberated them only on the payment of a ransom of 5,000 groschen. The rabbis and their companions complained to the princes of this attack, and the latter, indignant at the disrespect with which their authority had been treated, summoned the noble marauders to answer the charges urged against them. The line of defense adopted by the spokesman of the accused was that they had no idea of disregarding the safe-conduct passes of the princes, but that they held the opinion that the Jews, the enemies of the church, did not deserve the protection of Christian authorities. The speaker continued that, for his own part, wherever he met the enemies of Christ, he would give them no quarter. A defense of this kind could not fail to obtain applause.

Its spirit was that of the majority of the Christians of that day. The accused were absolved from blame, and the Jews dismissed without redress, "for the defense captivated the princes."

The art of poetry, which should beautify life, began to work like poison on the moral atmosphere of the Jews. For some centuries past romantic works had variously portrayed the character of a creditor, who, as equivalent for a debt, claimed a certain portion cut from the body of his creditor, either a liege lord from his vassal, or a nobleman from a burgher.. At first this was harmless fiction, but afterwards it was turned against the Jews, as though only a Jewish Shylock could be capable of such hardness of heart as to insist on the payment of a pound of flesh from a Christian. Thus cannibal hatred of Christians was foisted on the Jews, and received credence. Romances took up the theme, and made it popular.

The depraved, dissolute clergy—a class of men who, in an age of public decency, would have been objects of universal contempt, or might have earned the corrections of a Bridewell—affected to feel insulted by contact with the Jews, and, under the pretext that their cloth was disgraced by them, caused new scenes of horror and cruelty. In Prague, since the time of Charles IV the chief city of Germany, a bloody persecution was set on foot by their agency. A local priest—perhaps one of those whom Emperor Wenceslaus had caused to be pilloried with their concubines—passed through the Jewish quarter on Easter Sunday (April 18th, 1389) with the host, to visit a dying person. Jewish children playing in the street—it was one of the latter days of the Passover feast—were throwing sand at one another, and a few grains happened to fall upon the priest's robe. His attendants immediately turned upon the children, and cruelly beat them. Their cries quickly brought their parents to their rescue, whereupon the priest fled to the market-place, loudly proclaiming that his holy office had been profaned by Jews. To invest the incident with the necessary importance, he exaggerated it, and said that he was pelted with stones until forced to drop the host. The citizens and lower orders of Prague immediately banded themselves together, and, armed with murderous weapons of every description, made a violent attack upon the houses of the Jews. As usual, they offered their victims the choice between death and baptism, but they found them steadfast in their faith. Many thousands perished in the massacre, which lasted a whole day and night. Several of the Jews, among them their venerable rabbi, first took the lives of their wives and children, and then their own, to escape the cruelties of their enemies. The synagogue was laid in ashes, and the holy books and scrolls torn and trodden under foot. Not even the burial ground escaped the fury of these Christian zealots. The corpses in the streets were stripped of their clothing, left naked, and then burnt.

For the same offense—that is, for no offense at all—the communities in the vicinity of the Bohemian capital were "confined, oppressed, ill-treated and persecuted." The reigning pope issued a bull condemning the outrages (July 2d, 1389), and based his action upon the edict of Pope Innocent IV, which enacted that Jews should not be forcibly baptized, nor disturbed in the observance of their festivals; but he failed to produce an impression on the consciences of the faithful. It was in vain, too, that the Jews appealed to their liege lord, the German emperor Wenceslaus, in whose capital the persecution had originated. This prince—who, had he not been an emperor, would certainly have been a freebooter —was a man of sense only on the rare occasions when he was not intoxicated. His reply to the representations of his Jewish subjects was that they had deserved the attacks made upon them, as they had had no right to show themselves outside their houses on Easter Sunday. For the goods and chattels they had left behind them he exhibited more concern, promptly ordering them to be appropriated to his empty exchequer. This was the measure of his general attitude towards the Jews. During several years he attempted to possess himself of their monetary claims on his Christian subjects, and to carry out his design he convened (1385) a conference of representatives of the Suabian cities, which met at Ulm. Despite the impoverishment of the German communities, he exacted from every Jew, even from every Jewish youth and maiden, the so-called "golden penny" poll-tax, amounting to one gulden annually. He openly declared that the possessions of the Jews were his personal property, and forbade them to sell or mortgage anything. And still Emperor Wenceslaus was not the worst of rulers in the eyes of the Jews. The rabbi, Avigedor Kara, of Prague, boasted his friendship; and the Jews of Germany whispered significantly to one another that his allegiance to the teaching of Christ was very weak.

This storm of spoliation and persecution had no far-reaching consequences in the history of the German Jews. It could not affect their abject condition, for they had been too long accustomed to turn their cheeks submissively to the smiter. Quite different were the effects of a contemporary persecution in Spain. Here the very heart of the Jewish race was attacked, and the results made themselves felt in the history of the whole Jewish people. The Spanish Jews had until then been more hated than despised; the horrors of this persecution, however, so thoroughly cowed their spirits, so paralyzed their energies, and humbled their pride, that they, too, became the scorn of their oppressors. As in Prague, the outbreak was the work of an ecclesiastic and a mob, but here it assumed the vastest proportions, and developed permanent results, the operations of which were disastrous in the extreme. It arose in Seville through the agitation of a fanatical priest, Ferdinand (Ferrand) Martinez, who seemed to consider implacable hatred of the Jews as the essence of his religion. His discourses were devoted to stirring up the populace against them, and he thundered against their hardened infidelity, their pride, their heaped-up riches, their greed, and their usury. In Seville he found the people only too ready to listen to him, for there the Jews were hated with special intensity. The citizens could not forgive them the important part they had played in the civil war between Don Pedro and Don Henry II, and particularly the suspicious circumstances of the death of Joseph Pichon, who had been so popular among them. As long as Don Juan I lived, Martinez took care to restrain the mob from open violence, for though the king regarded the Jews with but little affection, he was in the habit of punishing lawless outbreaks with the utmost severity. No sooner was he dead, however, than the bigoted cleric thought he might dare the utmost. The circumstances of the government were favorable to the development of his plans. The new monarch, Henry III, was a boy of only eleven years of age, and in the council of regency discord reigned, threatening to involve the country in another civil war.

One day (March 15, 1391)—a memorable day, not only for the Jews and for Spain, but for the history of the entire world, for on that day the first germ of the monstrous Inquisition was created—Martinez, preaching as usual against the Jews, deliberately incited the mob to riot in the expectation that many Jews would abjure their religion. The passions of the multitude became inflamed, and broke out in wild uproar. The authorities of the city, the Mayor (Alguacil mayor), Don Alvar Perez de Guzman, and two of the magistrates interposed to protect the Jews, arresting two of the ringleaders in the riot, and ordering them to be flogged. This proceeding excited the fanatical mob only the more. In their fury they put a large number of Jews to death, and threatened with a like fate the governor of the city, Don Juan Alfonso, and the officials who were attempting to shield the unfortunate Hebrews. A few of the leading Jews of Seville, perceiving that the local authorities were not strong enough to grapple with the rising, hurried to the court of the young king, and appealed to the council of regency to stop the slaughter of their brethren. Their representations were favorably received. Messengers were dispatched forthwith to Seville with instructions to tell the populace to abstain from further outrage. The local nobility seconded the action of the king, and, ranging themselves on the side of the Jews, succeeded in mastering the rioters. When the Christian inhabitants of the neighboring towns showed a disposition to imitate the scenes enacted in Seville, the council of regency also sent messengers thither armed with the same powers. Thus, for a brief moment, the threatened Jew-hunt was delayed, but by no means suppressed. It was soon renewed with greater violence, and on a far more extended scale. The young king and a few of the members of the council of regency were probably earnest in their desire not to permit the massacres, but, unfortunately, they were not sufficiently interested to take adequate precautions against them. One such precaution should have been to silence the outrage-monger, Ferdinand Martinez, or at least to prohibit his inflammatory harangues; but they did nothing of the kind. They left him perfectly free to level his poisonous eloquence at the Jews, and he was not slow to take advantage of their inaction. Encouraged by the dissensions in the government, and the disorder which consequently reigned throughout the entire land, he again set himself to stir up the rabble of Seville, and this time with greater success. Hardly three months after the last outbreak, the mob resumed (June 6th, 1391) its holy work of massacre by setting fire to the Jewish quarter (Juderia) and slaughtering its inhabitants. The result was that, of the important and wealthy community of Seville, which had numbered 7,000 families, or 30,000 souls, but few remained. Murder counted not more than 4,000 victims, but to escape death the majority permitted themselves to be baptized. Women and children were sold into Mahometan slavery by the bloody rioters. Of the three synagogues of Seville two were transformed into churches. Among the large number who sought refuge from fire and sword at the baptismal font was Samuel Abrabanel, the ancestor of the afterwards celebrated Abrabanel family, and an ornament of his community in the reign of Don Henry II, with whom he possessed great influence. He adopted the Christian name of Juan de Sevilla.

From Seville the persecution swept like a raging torrent over a large portion of Spain. Its progress was stimulated more by a craving for plunder than by fanatical eagerness to proselytize. Cordova, the parent community of the Peninsula, the mold in which the high character of Spanish Judaism had been cast, was the next scene of its activity. Here also many Jews were cruelly murdered, and a large number forced to embrace Christianity. On the fast day commemorating the fall of Jerusalem (Tammuz 17th—June 20th) the population of the capital, Toledo, rose against the largest Jewish community in Spain. The blood of the believers in the unity of God, who steadfastly refused to change their faith, deluged the streets. Among the many martyrs who fell at Toledo were the descendants of the Asheri family. They met death with the same unflinching courage as their German brethren. Jehuda ben Asher II, one of Asheri's great-grandsons, who lived in Burgos, but happened to be at Toledo, took with his own hands the lives of his mother-in-law and wife, and then his own. Here also a large number went over to Christianity. About seventy communities were visited by this terrible persecution, among them those of Ecija, Huete, Logroño, Burgos, Carrion, and Ocaña. At Ascalona not a single Jew remained alive. The thoroughly maddened Christian population meditated a similar fate for the Moors, or Mahometans, living in the kingdom of Seville. The more prudent among them, however, pointed out the danger of such a step, reminding them that the Christians living in the Mahometan kingdom of Granada, or held as prisoners by the Moors on the other side of the straits of Gibraltar, might be sacrificed in retaliation. The massacre of the Moors was consequently abandoned. The Jews alone were made to drain the cup of bitterness to the dregs, because they were too weak to protect themselves. Nothing demonstrates more impressively that the clergy had succeeded in transforming the people into a race of cut-throats.

In the kingdom of Aragon, where both ruler and people were opposed to Castile, and, as a rule, held that to be wrong which in the latter state was considered right, the hatred and persecution of the Jews were promoted with the same zeal. Here the government was in the hands of the weak but well-meaning king, Juan I, who, absorbed by his love of music and the chase, wielded but little authority, and was the laughing-stock of his generally uncultured subjects. About three weeks after the outbreak at Toledo, the inhabitants of the province of Valencia rose against the Jews (Ab 7th—July 9th). Of the 5,000 souls that constituted the Jewish community in the city of Valencia, not one was left. Some 250 were murdered, a few saved themselves by flight, and the rest embraced Christianity. Throughout the length and breadth of the kingdom the defenseless Jews were attacked with fire and sword, the community of Murviedro alone being spared.

The sanguinary madness then crossed the sea, and alighted on the island of Majorca. In the capital, Palma, a crowd of roughs and sailors paraded the Monte-Zion street, in which the Jews resided, and holding aloft a cross, rudely formed by tying together two cudgels, shouted "Death to the Jews" (August 2d—Ellul 1st). One sturdy Jew, assaulted by the rabble, ventured to defend himself, and severely punished his assailants. Hereupon the mob broke out in uncontrollable violence, and 300 martyrs fell to its fury. Among the victims was the rabbi, En-Vidal Ephraim Gerundi, whose controversy with Solomon Zarfati has already been referred to. A large number of Jews here also sought safety in baptism.

Three days later, as if by previous arrangement, the Jew-massacres began in Barcelona, one of the proudest homes of Jewish intelligence. The great wealth which the Jews of this city had acquired by their extensive maritime commerce appears to have excited the envy of the Christians, and tempted them to outrage. On the 5th August, a Sabbath, on which was held a minor festival in honor of Mary, the mob attacked the Jews as if to honor their queen of heaven with human sacrifices. In the first assault, close upon 250 victims fell. The larger portion of the community were harbored and cared for in the citadel by the governor of the town; but here again the rabble opposed the nobility. They attacked the citadel with crossbows, laid siege to it in due form, and ultimately set it on fire. When the imprisoned Jews saw that there was no longer a chance of being saved, a large number slew themselves with their own hands, or threw themselves from the walls. Others sallied forth from the fortress to meet their assailants in the open field, and fell in honorable combat. Among the martyrs was the noble Chasdaï Crescas' young and only son, then on the eve of his marriage. Eleven thousand Jews are said to have been baptized on this occasion. Only a very few escaped, and not one remained in Barcelona. The same fate befell the communities of Lerida, Gerona, and other towns, in each case a large number of Jews being murdered, some being baptized, and a very few escaping by flight. In Gerona, where the community was distinguished for rigid piety, the number of converts to Christianity was exceedingly small, the rabbis setting their flocks an example by their steadfastness and contempt for death. In Catalonia, as in Valencia, but few Jews were spared, and they owed their good fortune to the protection received —in exchange, of course, for large sums of money— in the castles of the nobility. In Aragon itself the outbreaks were not so serious, as the Jewish communities had made a timely and prudent offer of all their wealth for the protection of the court.

For three months fire and sword raged unresisted in the majority of the Spanish Jewries. When the storm abated, the Jews remaining were so broken in spirit that they did not venture forth from their places of refuge. The sad occurrences were described in a heart-breaking, tearful epistle to the community of Perpignan, which Chasdaï Crescas, who had been robbed of an only son and his entire fortune, penned in answer to their sympathetic inquiries. Thus, to Spanish Jews came the tragical fate which had befallen their German brethren, hardly half a century before, at the time of the Black Death. They also had acquired materials for bitter songs of lamentation, which they inserted in the Jewish liturgy. But the consequences of the persecution were even more terrible than the persecution itself. Their pride was completely crushed, and their spirit permanently darkened. They who had formerly held their heads so proudly aloft, now slunk timidly along, anxiously avoiding every Christian as a possible murderer or instigator of murderous assaults. If hundred Jews were assembled, and a single rough abused them, they fled like a flock of frightened birds. This persecution gave them their first experience of the bitterness of exile, for, notwithstanding many untoward circumstances, they had always imagined themselves secure and at home in Spain. Now, for the first time, their haughty demeanor was humbled. They were no longer the men who had so valiantly wielded the sword in the armies of Don Pedro. In Portugal alone the Jews were free from fanatical attacks. Its king, Don João I, enjoyed a popularity to which, in a crisis, he was able to appeal. As his instructions were cheerfully obeyed, he was able to preserve order and put down outbreaks with a firm hand. The chief rabbi, Don Moses Navarro, brought under his notice the two bulls of the popes Clement VI and Boniface IX, in which force was forbidden in converting Jews. The king immediately issued an order (July 17th, 1392) prohibiting persecutions. Wide publicity was given to the bulls in every town in Portugal, and they were inserted among the statutes of the realm. Portugal thus became an asylum for the persecuted Jews of Spain.

The Jews of the south of France were not entirely exempted from the horrors of this persecution. The tempest which had crossed the sea to the island of Majorca also whirled over the snow-capped Pyrenees, and caught up the Jews of Provence in its deadly eddies. No sooner was intelligence received of the bloody massacres of the Jews of Spain than the populace of Provence rose, and began to plunder and murder their Jewish neighbors.

The Jews in France had been permitted to settle in the country only for a specified time, and, although this term was frequently extended, their thoughts were necessarily always directed towards possible banishment. They were compelled to amass and keep in readiness sufficient money to enable them, at any moment, to start life afresh in another land. Like their ancestors in Egypt, they were ready for an exodus, their loins girded, their shoes on their feet, and their staffs in their hands. Although the acquisition of land was allowed them, they were obliged to concentrate themselves on the money business, and pursue the advantages offered by each moment. Necessity made them usurers. Some among them charged a higher rate of interest than permitted by the privileges granted them, and exacted even compound interest from dilatory debtors. But it was the king himself who forced them to immoderate, exasperating usury, by the extravagant demands he made upon their purses to meet the expenses of his wars, and the Jews could fulfill his demands only by transgressing the laws, but their exactions naturally rendered them hateful in the eyes of the general public. That Jewish creditors frequently had ill-intentioned or tardy Christian debtors imprisoned to force them to discharge their liabilities tended to increase the bitterness. The exercise of this right was regarded as a triumph of "the children of the devil over the children of heaven." The public became so angered at their possessing the privilege that the king, Charles VI, was obliged to abolish it. On the other hand, the necessity of maintaining the privilege was shown to be so imperative—the Jews being threatened with the entire loss of their outstanding debts—that the king and parliament had to grant it a month later in a modified form. They permitted the Jews to imprison only the debtors who, in their bonds, made themselves answerable with their bodies.

A trifling circumstance sufficed to kindle into a flame these embers of Jew-hatred in France. A wealthy Israelite, Denys Machault, of Villa-Parisis, became a convert to Christianity, and then suddenly disappeared. The affair became the subject of strange rumors. Some said that he had been murdered by Jews; others that he had been hurried abroad with a view to providing him with an easy means of returning to Judaism. The clergy interested themselves in the mystery, fanatical appeals were made to the people, and, eventually, the Paris tribunals prosecuted seven prominent Hebrews. A commission of priests and lawyers subjected the accused to the rack, and extorted the confession that they had advised Denys Machault to abandon his new faith. The commission condemned them to the stake as promoters of apostasy from Christianity. Parliament substituted an apparently milder punishment. It ordered the accused to be scourged in three of the public places of Paris, kept in goal until Denys Machault re-appeared, and then, stripped of all their possessions, expelled the country. From the publicity given to this affair, it created an extraordinary sensation, and still further inflamed the popular passions against the Jews.

For about three months the court extended a protecting wing over the unfortunate Jews, but soon withdrew it in face of the stormy, menacing clamor of the clergy and people. At last the enemies of the Jews prevailed upon the king to promulgate the order of banishment. Doubtless with malice aforethought the day chosen for the issue of the decree was the solemn Fast of Atonement (September 17th, 1394), when the Jews were afflicting their souls during the entire day in the synagogues. The prolonged term granted for their sojourn in the country not having expired, it became necessary to put forward an excuse for ignoring the convention. The royal decree was not able to impute to the Jews specific crimes or misdemeanors, and, consequently, confined itself to vague generalities. It had been reported to his majesty by trustworthy persons, including many of his lieutenants and other officials, that complaints had been made concerning offenses committed by the Jews against the Christian religion and the special laws drawn up for their control. That meant that they had encouraged baptized Jews to recant, and had practiced extortionate usury—the latter Charles had partly approved and partly condoned. The decree then stated that his majesty had made the irrevocable law that henceforth no Jews should be allowed to reside or tarry in any part of France, either in Languedoil or Languedoc (northern and southern France).

Thus, ninety years after their first expulsion by Philip le Bel, and after a second sojourn of thirty-four years, the French Jews were compelled once more to grasp the wanderer's staff. Charles, however, dealt more leniently with them than his heartless ancestor. They were not, as before, robbed of all their possessions, and turned adrift stripped to the skin. On the contrary, Charles VI issued orders to the prevôt of Paris and his provincial governors, instructing them to see that no harm come to the Jews, either in their persons or their chattels, and that they cross the frontier safely. Time was also allowed them up to the 3d November to collect their debts. They did not leave France until the end of 1394 or the beginning of the following year. To some of the nobility and towns the expulsion was not a welcome measure. Thus, the Count de Foix wished at all hazards to retain the community of Pamier, and had to be forced by royal officers to expel the Jews. In Toulouse twelve Jewish families, and in the vicinity seven more, remained behind, so that they must have received special indulgences. Jews also remained in the provinces not directly dependent on the French crown—in the

Dauphiné, in Provence proper, and in Arles, these being fiefs of the German empire. The flourishing seaport, Marseilles, possessed a Jewish community for a long time after the expulsion. Even the popes of Avignon tolerated Jews in Avignon and Carpentras, the chief towns of their small ecclesiastical province of Venaissin; and here they remained until very recent times, using a ritual of their own, which differed from that of their Spanish and their French brethren. The papacy had now little to fear from the helpless, enfeebled Jews; hence, doubtless, this parade of toleration.

The exiles who failed to find an asylum in the tolerant principalities of France emigrated to Germany and Italy; only a few directed their steps to Spain, formerly the most hospitable refuge for persecuted Jews. Since the massacres of 1391 that country had become a purgatory to the native Jews, and so long as foreign Jews could find a shelter elsewhere, they naturally avoided its frontiers. French communities migrated in a body to Piedmont, and settled in the towns of Asti, Fossano, and Moncalvo, where they could maintain unchanged their old synagogue ritual. The fate of the larger number of the French exiles may be described in the words of Amos: "As if a man did flee from a lion, and a bear met him; or went into the house, and leaned his hand on the wall, and a serpent bit him." Almost everywhere they were met with a storm of barbarity, not unfrequently stirred up against them by baptized Jews. In Germany an apostate named Pessach, who, with Christianity, had adopted the name of Peter, brought serious accusations against his brethren in race, with a view to bringing about another persecution. To the usual charges that the Jews called Jesus the crucified or the hanged, and that they cursed the Christian clergy in one of their prayers, Pessach-Peter added others. He stated that an abusive allusion to Jesus was contained in the sublime Alenu prayer, which pictures the future reign of God on earth, and he made other lying and ludicrous charges. The result was that a large number of the Jews of Prague were arrested and imprisoned (August 3d, 1399). Among them was the foremost and, perhaps, only really learned German Jew of the Middle Ages, Lipmann (Tab-Yomi) of Mühlhausen, a scholar accomplished alike in Biblical and Talmudical lore, who had read not only Karaite authors, but also the New Testament in a Latin version. The clergy called upon him to answer Pessach-Peter's charges. His defense was forcible, but seems to have had little effect, for on the day Emperor Wenceslaus was deposed, and Rupert of the Palatinate elected his successor (August 22d, 1400), seventy-seven Jews were executed, and three weeks later three more led to the stake.

CHAPTER VI.

JEWISH APOSTATES AND THE DISPUTATION AT TORTOSA.

The Marranos—The Satirists—Pero Ferrus of Alcala, Diego de Valencia, and Villasandino—Astruc Raimuch and Solomon Bonfed—Paul de Santa Maria and his Zealous Campaign against the Jews—Joshua Ibn-Vives—Profiat Duran (Efodi)—Meïr Alguades—The Philosophy of Crescas—Death of Henry III of Castile and Unfavorable Change in the Position of the Jews—Messianic Dreams of the Kabbalists—Jews seek an Asylum in Northern Africa—Simon Duran—Geronimo de Santa Fé, Vincent Ferrer and Benedict XIII—Anti-Jewish Edict of Juan II—Special Jewish Costume—Conversion of Jews owing to Ferrer's Violent Efforts—Disputation at Tortosa—The Jewish Spokesmen at the Conference—Incidents of the Meeting—Geronimo instigates the Publication of a Bull for the Burning of the Talmud—Pope Martin V befriends the Jews.

1391—1420 C.E.

THE baptized Jews who had abandoned their faith during the terrible persecution of 1391 became a source of considerable trouble to their Spanish brethren. They had embraced the cross only to save their lives, or the lives of those dear to them; for, surely, they had found no convincing demonstration of the truth of the Christian religion in the violence of its missionaries, or in the death agonies of their brethren in race who had perished rather than apostatize. Dazed and broken-hearted, these forced converts (Anusim) to Christianity felt more intense antipathy to their new religion than when they had been openly opposed to it. It was natural for them to resolve to take the first opportunity of casting away their disguise, and returning to Judaism with increased zeal. Many of these new Christians emigrated to the neighboring Moorish countries; to Granada or across the straits to Morocco, Tunis, or Fez, where the people, wiser and more tolerant than Christian Europe, gladly opened their doors to a wealthy and industrious race. The majority, unable to leave Spanish territory, yet averse to wholly discarding their ancient faith, joined in Jewish ceremonies and celebrations whilst outwardly appearing Christians. The kings of Castile, Aragon and Majorca, who had disapproved of conversions by mob violence, allowed the Jews to do as they pleased. The authorities either did not or would not see their relapse into Judaism, and the Inquisition had not yet been established in Spain. These forced converts gradually formed themselves into a peculiar class, outwardly Christians, at heart Jews. By the populace, who nicknamed them Marranos, or "The Damned," they were regarded with more distrust and hatred than the openly observant Jews, not because of their secret fidelity to Judaism, but on account of their descent and inborn intelligence, energy, and skill. Baptized Jews, who had been glad to disencumber themselves of their Judaism, shared in these feelings of aversion. They were the worldlings who valued wealth, rank, and luxury above religion, or the over-educated whose philosophy had led them to skepticism, and whose selfishness induced them to welcome a change which brought them out of the narrow confines of a small community, and opened up a wider world to them. Their hearts had never been with Judaism, and they had adhered to it only out of respect or a certain compunction. To them, forced baptism was a relief from chafing fetters, a welcome coercion to overcome scruples which had always sat lightly upon them. For their own advantage they simulated devotion to Christianity, but were on that account neither better nor more religious men. The unscrupulous among them found special pleasure in the persecution of their former religion and its followers. To gratify their malice, they brought charges against rabbis and other representative Jews, or any member of the community, thus endangering the existence of the whole body of Jews in the country. It was bad enough that the latter had been robbed of so many able and learned men —physicians, authors, poets—and that the church had been enriched by their wealth and intelligence; but these very forces were used to inflict further mischief on the Jews that had remained steadfast. Knowing the faults of their former brethren, the converts could easily attack them. Don Pero Ferrus, a baptized Jew, made the community and rabbis of Alcala the target for his ridicule. In a poem he represents himself exhausted from want of sleep finding repose at last in the synagogue of this town, when suddenly he is disturbed, and scared away without mercy by "Jews with long beards and slovenly garments come thither for early morning prayer." A sharp rejoinder to this effort of Ferrus' "buffoon tongue" was put forth by a Jewish poet in the name of the Alcala community. Spanish poetry reaped considerable advantage from these passages at arms. Verse, up to that period starched, solemn, and stately as the punctilious ceremonial of the Madrid court, in the hands of Judæo-Christian satirists acquired the flexibility, wit and merriment of neo-Hebraic poetry at its best. This tone and style were gradually adopted by Christian poets, who borrowed expressions from Jewish writers to give point to their epigrams. Not only the apostate, the monk, Diego de Valencia, used Hebrew words in lampoons on the Jews, but the same practice was adopted with surprising dexterity by the Christian satirist, Alfonso Alvarez de Villasandino, the "poet prince" of his day. A malicious critic might have been inclined to say that Spanish poetry was in process of being Judaized.

A few of the new-Christians showed as active a zeal in the propagation of Christianity as if they had been born Dominicans, or as if they felt isolated in their new faith among the old Christians, and yearned for the companionship of their former friends. A newly-baptized physician, Astruc Raimuch, of Fraga, who, as a Jew, had been a pillar of orthodoxy, exerted himself to make converts, taking to himself the name of Francisco God-flesh (Dios-Carne). He spread his snares particularly with a view to entrapping one of his young friends. A fluent writer of Hebrew, Astruc-Francisco drew up a letter in that language, dwelling on the decline of Judaism and enthusiastically propounding the dogmas of Christianity. His applications of Biblical texts to the doctrines of the Trinity, Original Sin, Redemption, and the Lord's Supper, appear almost droll in Hebrew. His friend's answer was meek and evasive, every word carefully weighed to avoid offending the delicate sensibilities of the church and its zealous servants. More spirited was the reply of the satirical poet, Solomon ben Reuben Bonfed, who in rhymed prose set himself to confute Astruc-Francisco's arguments with unsparing incisiveness. Apologizing in his introduction for interfering between two friends, he proceeded to point out that as a Jew the questions discussed concerned him nearly, whilst the misstatements made rendered it impossible for him to remain silent. Solomon Bonfed examined somewhat minutely the dogmas of the Incarnation, Original Sin, and Transubstantiation, showing them to be irrational and untenable. He justly said: "You twist and distort the Bible text to establish the Trinity. Had you a Quaternity, you would demonstrate it quite as strikingly and convincingly from the books of the Old Testament."

Of all the Jews baptized in 1391, however, none inflicted so much injury on his former brethren as Rabbi Solomon Levi of Burgos (born 1351—1352, died 1435), who as a Christian rose to very important ecclesiastical and political dignities under the name of Paul Burgensis, or de Santa Maria. Previous to his change of creed he had been a rabbi, and he was well versed in Biblical, Talmudical, and Rabbinical literature. As a Jew he was extremely orthodox and punctilious, passing in his own circle for a pillar of the faith. His nature was, however, shrewd and calculating. Ambitious and vain to the last degree, he soon began to regard as too narrow his sphere of action within the walls of the college, which during a long period counted him amongst its students and teachers. He longed for a life of bustling activity. To obtain a state appointment, he sought access to court, and began to live like a grandee, with equipage and horses and numerous retinue. It was his ambition to become a Jewish Almoxarif or even to obtain a higher appointment. His occupations bringing him into daily contact with Christians, and frequently involving him in religious controversies, he devoted some attention to church literature, in order to be able to make a display of learning. The massacres of 1391 dissipated his last hope of obtaining high preferment as a Jew, and he consequently resolved, in his fortieth year, to be baptized. To derive the best advantage from his conversion, the new Christian, Paul de Santa Maria, caused it to be understood that he had embraced Christianity willingly, as a result of the convincing arguments put forth in the theological writings of the schoolman Thomas Aquinas. The Jews received such protestations with distrust. Knowing him well, they did not scruple to ascribe his conversion to a craving for rank and power. After his change of creed, his family, wife and sons, renounced him.

For a commoner, the only road to high office lay through the church. Solomon-Paul knew this well, and at once proceeded to Paris and attended the University, where he pursued theology. His knowledge of Hebrew gave him a great advantage, and helped him to distinguish himself. It was not long before the quondam rabbi became a duly ordained Catholic priest. Then he betook himself to the papal court at Avignon, where the haughty, obstinate, and proselytizing cardinal, Pedro de Luna, reigned as anti-pope under the title of Benedict XIII. Here, during the stormy church schism, favorable opportunities for intrigue and personal advancement presented themselves. Paul won the pope's favor by his shrewdness, zeal, and eloquence. He was appointed archdeacon of Trevinjo and canon of Seville, his first steps on the ladder of the Catholic hierarchy. He abandoned himself to the most ambitious dreams: he might become a bishop, a cardinal, and why not the pope? The times were propitious. He boasted that he was descended from the most ancient and the noblest branch of the Hebrew race, the tribe of Levi, the same that had given birth to Mary, the mother of Jesus. He was not an ordinary priest sprung from the people, but had ancestors bound to be acknowledged and distinguished by the church. On the recommendation of the pope, he was later on overwhelmed with honors and favors by the king of Castile, Don Henry III, and his ambition was satisfied.

The apostasy of so respected a rabbi as Solomon Burgensis not only created the greatest astonishment among Jews, but filled them with anxiety. Would this example not find imitators in a time of so much trouble and temptation? Would it not bias waverers, or at least encourage pretending Christians to persevere in the course begun? The prevailing disquietude was increased when it was found that after his own conversion Paul considered it his duty to convert his former co-religionists. To this end he left no stone unturned. With voice and pen he assailed Judaism, seeking his weapons in Jewish literature itself. Not long after his conversion he addressed a letter to his former acquaintance, Joseph (José) Orabuena, physician in ordinary to King Charles III of Navarre, and chief rabbi of the Navarrese communities, in which he stated that he acknowledged and honored Jesus as the Messiah whose advent had been foretold by the prophets, and invited Orabuena to follow his example. To another chief rabbi, Don Meïr Alguades, physician in ordinary to the Castilian king, Don Henry III, Paul de Santa Maria addressed a Hebrew satire in prose and verse, in which he ridiculed the innocent celebration of the Jewish feast of Purim. As if grudging the Jews the moderate pleasures in which they indulged during this festival, he exaggerated their love of drink, and boasted of his own sobriety. Paul evinces in this satire considerable skill in handling the new-Hebrew language, but, notwithstanding his opportunities, he exhibits little wit.

As soon as he had acquired a position at the papal court at Avignon, he devoted himself to calumniating the Jews with a view to bringing about new persecutions. His purpose became so obvious that the cardinal of Pampeluna himself, and other ecclesiastics, ordered him to desist. It is true the Jews had to pay dearly for his silence. He also intrigued against Chasdaï Crescas. So far did this apostate carry his enmity to Judaism that he advised the king, Don Henry III, to abstain from employing both Jews and new-Christians in state offices. Did he wish to render impossible the rivalry of some fellow-Hebrew, his superior in adroitness? In his writings Paul de Santa Maria exhibited as much hatred of Judaism as of Jews. While the Franciscan monk, Nicholas de Lyra, a born Christian, held up the works of Jewish commentators like Rashi as models of simple exegesis, the former rabbi found every observation of a Rabbinical writer insipid, nonsensical, and scandalous. On the other hand, the most ridiculous commentary of a church writer was to him a lofty, unsurpassable work.

Thoughtful Jews were not slow to recognize their bitterest foe in this new-Christian, and they prepared for a severe struggle with him, notwithstanding that their choice of weapons was limited. Christians were not only free to say what they pleased in demonstration and defense of their doctrines, but could appeal to the summary authority of the sword and the dungeon. Jews were forced to all kinds of circumlocution and ambiguity to avoid provoking the violence of their adversaries. The gallant stand of a mere handful of Jews against power and arrogance should excite the admiration of all whose sympathies are not with victorious tyranny, but with struggling right.

The campaign against Paul de Santa Maria was opened by a young man, Joshua ben Joseph Ibn-Vives of Lorca (Allorqui), a physician and an Arabic scholar, who had formerly sat at the feet of the renegade rabbi. In an humble epistle, as though a docile pupil were addressing an illustrious master, Joshua Allorqui administered many a delicate reproof to his apostate teacher, and at the same time, by his naïve doubts, dealt destructive blows at the fundamental doctrines of Christianity. He observes in his introduction that the conversion of his beloved teacher had to him more than to others been a source of astonishment and reflection, as his example had been a main support of his own religious belief. He was at a loss to conceive the motives of the sudden change. He could not think that he had been led away by desire for worldly distinction, "for I well remember," he says, "how, surrounded by riches and attendants, thou didst yearn for thy former humble state with its life of retirement and study, and how it was thy wont to speak of thy high position as empty mockery of happiness." Nor could he suppose that Paul's Jewish convictions had been disturbed by philosophic doubt, as up to the moment of his baptism he had conscientiously observed all the ceremonial laws, and had known how to discriminate between the kernel of philosophic truth which harmonizes with religion and the pernicious shell which so often passes for the real teaching. Could it be that the sanguinary persecution of the Jews had led him to doubt the possibility of the enduring power of Judaism? But even this theory was untenable, for Paul could not be unaware of the fact that only a minority of Jews live under Christian rule, that the larger numbers sojourn in Asia, and enjoy a certain degree of independence; so that if it pleased God to allow the communities in Christian lands to be extirpated, the Jewish race would not by any means disappear from the face of the earth. There remained, continued Joshua Vives of Lorca, the assumption that Paul had carefully studied Christianity, and had come to the conclusion that its dogmas were well founded. He begged him, therefore, to impart to him the convictions at which he had arrived, and thus dissipate the doubts which he (Joshua) still entertained as to the truth of Christianity. Allorqui then detailed the nature of his doubts, covertly but forcibly attacking the Christian system. Every sentence in this epistle was calculated to cut the Jew-hating new-Christian to the quick. The evasive and embarrassed reply, which Paul indited later on, clearly indicated how he had winced under this attack.

The philosopher, Chasdaï Crescas, also came forward in gallant defense of the religion of his fathers. He composed (1396) a polemical treatise (Tratado), in which he tested philosophically the Christian articles of faith, and demonstrated their untenableness. This work was addressed to Christians more than to Jews, and was particularly intended for the perusal of Spaniards of high rank whose friendship Chasdaï Crescas enjoyed. Hence it was written not in Hebrew but in Spanish, which the author employed with ease, and its tone was calm and moderate. Chasdaï Crescas set forth the unintelligibility of the doctrines of the Fall, the Redemption, the Trinity, the Incarnation, the Immaculate Conception, and

Transubstantiation, and examined the value of baptism, the coming of Jesus, and the relation of the New Testament to the Old, with dispassionate deliberation, as if he did not know that he was dealing with questions which might at any moment light the fires of an auto-da-fé.

At about the same time an accomplished Marrano, who had relapsed into Judaism, published a pungent attack on Christianity and the new-Christians. In the entire history of Judæo-Christian controversy no such stinging satire had been produced on the Jewish side as that now issued by the physician, astronomer, historical student, and grammarian Profiat Duran. During the bloody persecution of 1391 in Catalonia, Profiat Duran, otherwise Isaac ben Moses, or, as he called himself in his works, Efodi (Ephodæus), had been forced to simulate conversion to Christianity. He was joined by his friend David Bonet Buen-Giorno. Both resolved at a convenient opportunity to abandon their hated mask and emigrate to Palestine, where they could freely acknowledge Judaism. Their affairs being arranged, Profiat Duran traveled to a seaport town in the south of France, and there awaited his friend. The latter, in the meantime, was sought out by or came across the Jew-hating apostate, Solomon Paul de Santa Maria, and was prevailed upon to remain a Christian. What was Profiat Duran's astonishment when he received a letter announcing, with much exultant vaporing, the definite acknowledgment of Christianity by En Bonet, who exhorted him also to remain in the pale of his adopted faith. The letter contained an enthusiastic panegyric of Paul de Santa Maria, who had been taken into the favor of the king of Castile. Profiat Duran could not remain silent. In reply, he inflicted punishment on his friend, and more particularly on the proselytizing Paul, in an epistle characterized by the keenest irony, which has not yet lost its sting. It pretends to assent to everything advanced by Bonet, and to confirm him in his resolve to remain a Christian. "Be not ye like your fathers" (Altehi ka-Abothecha) is the refrain throughout, and so artfully is this admonition employed that Christians used it (under the title Alteca Boteca) as an apology for Christianity. Whilst thus pretending to criticise the errors of the older faith, Profiat Duran dwells on the Christian dogmas, naïvely describing them in their most reprehensible form. He concentrates on the weaknesses of Christianity the full light of reason, Scriptural teaching and philosophic deduction, apparently with no desire to change his friend's intention. A portion of the satire is directed against the Jew-hater Paul de Santa Maria, upon whom Bonet had bestowed unstinted praise. "Thou art of opinion that he may succeed in becoming pope, but thou dost not inform me whether he will go to Rome, or remain at Avignon"—a cutting reference to the papal schism distracting the church. "Thou extollest him for having made efforts to free Jewish women and children from the obligation of wearing the Jew badge. Take the glad tidings to the women and children. For myself, I have been told that he preached mischief against the Jews, and that the cardinal of Pampeluna was compelled to order him to be silent. Thou art of opinion that he, thy teacher, will soon receive the miter or a cardinal's hat. Rejoice, for then thou also must acquire honors, and wilt become a priest or a Levite." Towards the end Profiat Duran changes irony into a tone of seriousness: he prays his former friend not to bear as a Christian the name of his respected father who, had he been alive, would sooner have had no son than one faithless to his religion. As it is, his soul in Paradise will bewail the faithlessness of his son. This satirical epistle was circulated as a pamphlet. Its author sent copies not only to his former friend, but also to the physician of the king of Castile, the chief rabbi, Don Meïr Alguades. So telling was the effect produced, that the clergy, as soon as they discovered its satirical character, made it the subject of judicial inquiry, and committed it to the flames. At the request of Chasdaï Crescas, Profiat Duran wrote another anti-Christian work, not, however, a satire, but in the grave language of historical investigation. In this essay he showed, from his intimate acquaintance with the New Testament and the literature of the church, how in course of time Christianity had degenerated.

Favored and promoted by the anti-pope, Benedict XIII, of Avignon, Paul of Burgos rose higher and higher; he became bishop of Carthagena, chancellor of Castile and privy counselor to the king, Don Henry III. His malice did not succeed in prejudicing the king against the Jews, or inducing him to bar them from state employment. Don Henry had two Jewish physicians, in whom he reposed especial confidence. One, Don Meïr Alguades, an astronomer and philosopher, he appointed, perhaps in imitation of Portugal, to the chief rabbinate of the various Castilian communities. He was always in the king's train, and it is probable that to some extent he influenced him favorably towards his co-religionists. The other was Don Moses Zarzel (Çarçal), who celebrated in rich Spanish verse the long wished for birth of an heir to the Castilian throne, borrowing the beauties of the neo-Hebraic poetry to do honor to the newly-born prince, in whose hands, he prophesied, the various states of the Pyrenean Peninsula would be united. The calm, as between two storms, which the Spanish Jews enjoyed during the reign of Don Henry was favorable to the production of a few literary fruits, almost the last of any importance brought forth in Spain. None of these works was epoch-making; they were useful, however, in keeping alive the spirit of better times, and in preventing the treasures of Jewish literature from being forgotten. Profiat Duran managed to make people forget his baptism and to settle down quietly in Spain or Perpignan, where he commentated Maimuni's philosophy, and some of Ibn-Ezra's works. He also composed a mathematical and calendarial essay (Chesheb-Efod) and an historical account of the persecutions to which his race had been subjected since the dispersion. His best work is a Hebrew grammar ("Maasé Efod," written about 1403), in which he summarizes the results of older writers, rectifies their errors, and even attempts to formulate the principles of Hebrew syntax.

A production of more than common merit was written by Chasdaï Crescas, now on the brink of the grave, his spirits shattered by persecution. He was a profound, comprehensive thinker, whose mind never lost itself in details, but was forever striving to comprehend the totality of things. His scheme for a work treating, in the manner of Maimuni, of all phases and aspects of Judaism, investigating the ideas and laws out of which Jewish teaching had gradually developed, and reharmonizing the details with the whole where the connection had ceased to be apparent, bears witness to the extraordinary range of his learning and the perspicacity of his mind. The work was to be at once a guide to Talmudical study and a practical handbook. Death appears to have prevented the accomplishment of this gigantic enterprise, only the philosophic portion, or introduction, being completed. In this introduction Chasdaï Crescas deals, on the one hand, with the principles of universal religion, the existence of God, His omniscience and providence, human free-will, the design of the universe, and, on the other, with the fundamental truths of Judaism, the doctrines of the creation, immortality, and the Messiah.

Crescas was less dominated by the Aristotelian

bias of mediæval philosophy than his predecessors. It had lost its halo for him; he perceived its weaknesses more clearly than others, and probed them more deeply. With bold hands he tore down the supports of the vast edifice of theory constructed by Maimuni on Aristotelian grounds to demonstrate the existence of God and His relation to the universe, and, conversant with the whole method of scholastic philosophy, he combated it with destructive force.

While the philosophy of his day appeared to him thus vague and illusory, he considered the foundations of Judaism unassailable, and set himself to show the futility of the criticisms of the former. The acknowledgment of Divine omniscience led him to the daring statement that man in his actions is not quite free, that everything is the necessary result of a preceding occurrence, and that every cause, back to the very first, is bound to determine the character of the final action. The human will does not follow blind choice, but is controlled by a chain of antecedent circumstances and causes. To what extent can the doctrine of reward and punishment be admitted, if the will is not free? Chasdaï Crescas' answer to this is that reward and punishment wait on intentions, not on actions. He who, in purity of heart, wishes to accomplish good—which must, of course, necessarily follow—deserves to be rewarded, as the man who willingly promotes evil, deserves punishment. The highest good to which man can aspire, and the end of all creation, is spiritual perfection, or bliss everlasting, not to be obtained, as the philosophers imagine, by filling the mind with metaphysical theories, but only through the active love of God. This is the substance of all religion and particularly of Judaism. From this point of view it may with justice be said that "the world was created for the sake of the Torah," for the aim of the Law is to lead to immortality by means of ideas and commandments and the guidance of thoughts and actions.

Chasdaï Crescas, the first to distinguish between universal religion and specific forms, such as Judaism and Christianity, propounded, deviating from Maimuni's system, only eight peculiarly Jewish tenets. His just objection to Maimuni's thirteen articles of faith was that they were either too many or too few, inasmuch as they blended indiscriminately fundamental truths common to all religions, and teachings peculiar to Judaism.

Together with Profiat Duran and Chasdaï Crescas, Don Meïr Alguades, the Castilian chief rabbi, appeared, in the brief interval between two bloody persecutions in Spain, as a writer of philosophic works. He was not an independent inquirer; he merely translated the ethics of Aristotle (1405, in collaboration with Benveniste Ibn-Labi) into Hebrew, making the work accessible to Jews, who, in practical life, lived up to its principles better than the Greeks, who produced them, or the Christians, who, in the pride of faith and church doctrine, considered themselves above the necessity of conforming to the requirements of morality.

Throughout the reign of Don Henry III of Castile the life of the Jews was tolerable. The young but vigorous monarch severely punished Fernan Martinez, the prime mover in the massacres of 1391, as a warning against further excesses. He permitted the Jews to acquire land, renewed the law of his ancestor, Alfonso XI, and relieved his Jewish tax-farmers and finance administrators from restrictions. As soon as he died (the end of 1406) the affairs of the Jews again took an unfavorable turn, foreshadowing unhappy times. The heir to the crown, Juan II, was a child, barely two years old. The regency devolved on the queen-mother, Catalina (Catherine) of Lancaster, a capricious, arrogant and bigoted young woman, who imagined that she ruled, while she was herself ruled by her various favorites. The co-regent, Don Ferdinand, later king of Aragon, who was intelligent and kind, allowed himself to be guided by the clergy. By his side in the council of state sat the apostate rabbi, Solomon *alias* Paul de Santa Maria, another and more mischievous Elisha-Acher, in whose eyes Judaism was an abomination, and every Jew a stumbling-block. The deceased king, Don Henry III, had appointed him executor of his will and tutor to his heir; he consequently had an influential voice in the council of the regency. What a prospect for the Jews of Castile! It was not long before they were made to feel the hostile spirit of the court. First it exhibited itself in attempts to humiliate the more notable Jews who had intercourse with the court circle and the grandees of the kingdom, and occupied positions of distinction. The intention was to dismiss them from these positions with the reminder that they belonged to a despised caste.

An edict was issued (October 25th, 1408), in the name of the infant king, reviving the anti-Jewish statutes of the code of Alfonso the Wise. "Whereas the exercise of authority by Jews may conduce to the prejudice of the Christian faith," their occupation of posts in which they might possess such authority was forbidden for all future time. Every Jew permitting himself to be invested with official functions, either by a nobleman or a municipality, was to be fined twice the amount of the revenue of such post, and, if his fortune did not suffice to make up the required amount, it would be confiscated, and the delinquent become liable to a punishment of fifty lashes. A Christian appointing a Jew to a post of influence would also be punished with a fine. To insure the working of the edict, it was enacted that the informer and the court of law concerned in a case should secure each one-third of the confiscated estates. Officials were charged to make the edict known everywhere, and carefully to watch that its injunctions were carried out. It is impossible not to suspect the hand of Paul de Santa Maria in this decree. No one knew better than he the strong and the weak points in the character of the Spanish Jews, and he doubtless calculated that Jewish notables, in danger of losing their official employment and high social position, would go over to Christianity, while the faithful, excluded from intercourse with Christian society and from participation in the public life of the country, would suffer a decline similar to that of the German Jews.

At the same time he vented his hate on Meïr Alguades, the physician of the dead king. The queen-regent had no cause to injure this Jewish notable; only Paul could desire his ruin, because he was the mainstay of his opponents and the leader of those who held him up to contempt. With the object of procuring his downfall, a vindictive accusation was trumped up against him. While the queen-mother, with the infant king, was staying at Segovia, some priests charged a Jew of the town with having bought a consecrated host from the sacristan, in order to blaspheme it. They further stated that the holy wafer had worked such terrible wonders while in the possession of the Jew, that in fear and trembling he had delivered it up to the prior of a monastery. Whether this story was fabricated, or whether there was a grain of truth in a bushel of fiction, it is impossible to say; it sufficed, however, to attract the serious attention of the bishop, Velasquez de Tordesillas, who caused a number of Jews to be arrested as accomplices in the crime, among them Don Meïr Alguades. Criminal proceedings were formally commenced by order of the queen-regent, and Alguades and his fellow-prisoners were subjected to torture, and confessed their guilt. It is stated that in his agony Meïr Alguades made a confession of another kind—that the king, Henry III, had come by his death at his hands. Although everybody knew that the king had been ailing from his youth, Don Meïr—who must have been specially interrogated while under torture as to whether he had poisoned the king—was put to death in the most inhuman manner. He was torn limb from limb. The same fate befell the other prisoners. Still not satisfied, the bishop of Segovia accused some Jews of having bribed his cook to poison his food, and they also were put to death. At about this time one of the synagogues in Segovia was transformed into a church.

The troubled times, projecting shadows of a still more unhappy future, produced the melancholy phenomenon of another Messianic frenzy. Again it arose in the minds of mystics. The Zohar having adroitly been raised to the dignity of an approved authority, the Kabbala daily acquired more influence, although it was not studied in proportion to the zeal with which its authority was advocated. Three Kabbalists were particularly active in exciting the emotions and turning the heads of the people—Abraham of Granada, Shem Tob ben Joseph, and Moses Botarel. The first composed (between 1391 and 1409) a Kabbalistic work, a farrago of strange names of the Deity and the angels, of transposed letters, and jugglery with vowels and accents. Abraham of Granada had the hardihood to teach that those who could not apprehend God by Kabbalistic methods belonged to the weak in faith, were ignorant sinners, and like the depraved and the apostate were overlooked by God, and not found worthy of His special providence. He thought that the relinquishment of their religion by cultured Jews was explained by their fatal application to scientific study, and their contempt for the Kabbala. On the other hand, he professed to see in the persecutions of 1391, and in the conversion of so many prominent

Jews to Christianity, the tokens of the Messianic age, the suffering that must precede it, and the approach of the redemption. Shem Tob ben Joseph Ibn-Shem Tob (died 1430) accused the Jewish philosophers, Maimuni, Gersonides, and others, of seducing the people to heresy and infidelity, and with being the real cause of apostasy in troubled times. In a work entitled "Emunoth" he made violent attacks on Jewish thinkers and philosophic studies generally, and taught that the salvation of Israel lies in the Kabbala, the oldest Jewish tradition, and the genuine, pure truth. The entire book is composed of grave charges against the more enlightened school of Jewish thinkers, and panegyrics of Kabbalistic nonsense.

These two men, Abraham of Granada and Shem Tob, though narrow-minded, were sincere, differing in this respect from Moses Botarel (or Botarelo), also a Spaniard, from Cisneros, in Castile, who pursued his course with fraudulent intent. He gave out that he was a thaumaturge and prophet; he announced himself even as the Messiah. He prophesied that in the spring month of 1393 the Messianic age would be ushered in by extraordinary marvels. Later on he wrote a work full of lies and delusions. In his pride and boastfulness, he addressed a circular letter to all the rabbis of Israel, declaring that he was in a position to solve all doubts, and throw light on all mysteries, that he was the chief of the great Synhedrin, and a great deal more in the same charlatanic strain.

As in the days of the oppression by the Visigothic kings, an asylum for persecuted Jews was formed on that portion of the African coast facing Spain. Many of the north African towns, such as Algiers, Miliana, Constantine, Buja, Oran, Tenes, and Tlemçen, were filled with Jews fleeing from the massacres of 1391, and with new-Christians anxious to get rid of the Christianity which they had been forced to embrace, but which they hated cordially. Almost daily there came fresh troops of refugees from all parts of Spain and Majorca. They transplanted to their new fatherland their intelligence, wealth, industry, and commercial enterprise. The Mahometan Berber princes, then more tolerant and humane than the Christians, received them without imposing a poll tax. At first the Mahometan population grumbled a little at so sudden and considerable an increase in the number of inhabitants, fearing that the price of provisions would be raised. When, however, the narrow-mindedness and selfishness of their complaints were pointed out to them by an intelligent kadi they were satisfied, and the Jews were allowed to settle in their midst in peace. The small Berber communities formed since the cessation of the Almohade persecution a century before, acquired greater importance through this immigration. The new-comers preponderated in numbers over the native Jews, so that the latter, to a certain extent, were forced to adopt the Spanish communal organization and the Sephardic ritual. The Spaniards, in fact, became the leading element in the old African communities.

The distinguished rabbi, Isaac ben Sheshet-Barfat, who had escaped from Spain and settled in Algiers, was recognized by the king of Tlemçen as chief rabbi and judge of all the communities. This he owed to the influence of one of his admirers, Saul Astruc Cohen, a popular physician and an accomplished man, who not only practiced his art gratuitously, but spent his fortune in relieving both Mahometan and Jewish poor. In the name of the king the local rabbis were forbidden to assume clerical or judicial functions without the authority of the chief rabbi, Isaac ben Sheshet. This in no way detracted from the esteem in which Ben Sheshet was held, and applications for the decision of difficult questions continued to pour in upon him. In

Algiers he continued to oppose wrong-doing with the conscientiousness and impartiality that had always characterized him. Among the members of his community was a mischievous personage (Isaac Bonastruc?), who had considerable influence with the Algerian authorities. Actuated by self-interest he was desirous of stopping the daily increasing immigration of Marranos, and to this end persuaded the kadi to impose a tax of one doubloon on every immigrant. Finding that troops of fugitives continued to arrive, he set himself to work upon the selfishness of the community, so that they might oppose any further influx of their brethren. Fifty-five new-Christians, who had recanted, from Valencia, Barcelona, and Majorca, were waiting to land in the harbor of Algiers, but were refused permission by Jews. This was tantamount to throwing them on the mercy of Christian executioners. Such selfishness and injustice the chief rabbi, Isaac ben Sheshet, could not tolerate, and he laid the ban on the heartless Jews, who tried to escape the punishment. So determined was his attitude that, with the assistance of Astruc Cohen and his brother, the Marranos were ultimately brought safe to land. In Africa Ben Sheshet-Barfat worked for nearly twenty years, promoting the welfare of his co-religionists and the interests of religion and morality. His declining years were embittered by the persistent attacks of a young rabbi, Simon ben Zemach Duran, an able Talmudist, who had emigrated from Majorca.

Ben Sheshet was succeeded on his death by Simon Duran (born 1361, died 1444). The community of Algiers elected him on condition that he did not seek a ratification of his appointment from the king, probably because the authority derived by his predecessor from the royal confirmation had been too uncontrolled. Simon Duran, an accomplished mathematician and physician, was the first Spanish-Jewish rabbi to take pay. He publicly excused himself for doing so, on the ground of his necessitous circumstances. During the persecutions in Majorca a portion of his large fortune had been lost, and the remainder had been sacrificed in bribing the informers who threatened to deliver him as a Judaizing Christian to the Dominican Moloch. He had arrived in Algiers almost a beggar, and the healing art, by which he had hoped to earn a subsistence, had brought him nothing, physicians enjoying but little consideration among the Berbers. Subsequently Simon Duran justified the payment of rabbis from the Talmud. Were the abbots, bishops, and princes of the church equally conscientious?

As if the Jews of Spain had not had enough enemies in the poor, indolent burghers and nobles, who regarded their opulence with so much jealousy, in the clergy, who cloaked their immorality with zeal for the propaganda of the faith, or in the upstart converts, who sought to disguise their Jewish origin by a show of hatred of their former brethren, there arose at about the beginning of the fifteenth century three new Jew-haters of the bitterest, most implacable type. One was a baptized Jew, another a Dominican friar, and the third an abandoned anti-pope. On these three men, Joshua Lorqui, Fra Vincent Ferrer, and Pedro de Luna, or Benedict XIII, the responsibility must rest for the events which directly conduced to the most terrible tragedy in the history of the Jews of Spain. Joshua Lorqui of Lorca assumed on his baptism the name Geronimo de Santa Fé, became physician in ordinary to the Avignon pope, Benedict, and, like his teacher, Solomon-Paul de Santa Maria, considered it his mission in life to draw his former brethren over to Christianity by every possible means. Vincent Ferrer, afterwards canonized, was one of those gloomy natures to whom the world appears a vale of tears, and who would wish to make it one. In saint-like virtue, indeed, he stood alone among the clergy and monks of his day.

The pleasures of life had no charm for him; for gold and worldly distinction he thirsted not; he was penetrated with true humility, and entered on his work with earnestness. Unfortunately, the degeneracy and foulness of society had impressed him with the fantastic idea that the end of the world was at hand, and that mankind could be saved only by adopting the Christian faith and a monastic mode of life. Vincent Ferrer consequently revived flagellation. He marched through the land with a troop of fanatics who scourged their naked bodies with knotted cords, and incited the masses to adopt the same form of penance, believing that it would bring about the salvation of the world. Gifted with a sympathetic voice, an agreeable manner, and considerable eloquence, this Dominican friar soon obtained ascendancy over the public mind. When amid sobs he recalled the sufferings of Jesus, and depicted the approaching end of the world, the emotions of his auditors became violently agitated, and he could lead them to good or to evil. He had given up a high position at the papal court to lead the life of a flagellant and barefooted friar. This helped to increase the number of his admirers and disciples, for renunciation of position and wealth on the part of an ecclesiatic was without parallel. Ferrer, however, abused his power by the promotion of sanguinary deeds. He directed his fanatical denunciations not only against Jews and heretics, but even against friends who had helped to raise him from the dust. The terrible demoralization of the church is illustrated in this monk. The wrangling of three contemporary popes, each declaring himself to be the vicegerent of God, one of whom, John XXIII (1410—1415), had exhausted the catalogue of vices and deadly sins, a pirate, a trafficker in indulgences, an assassin, and a debauchee—all this did not so strikingly indicate the prevailing degeneracy as the fanatical excesses of one really pure, moral nature like

Vincent Ferrer. The dove had become transformed into a venomous snake, the lamb into a rapacious beast. So much viciousness cannot be spontaneous in human character, in the adherents of Christianity; it must have been derived from the Christian teaching itself.

Unlike Wycliffe and other reformers, Ferrer did not raise his voice against the shortcomings of the church, but devoted himself to Jews and heretics, whom he hated as adversaries of Christianity and opponents of the infallibility of the pope. With pen and voice he opened a crusade against Jews, which he sustained for several years. His most vehement invective was aimed at the Spanish new-Christians, who during the massacres of 1391 had gone over to the church, but still largely conformed to Judaism. Partly from fear of incurring the severe punishment attaching to apostasy, partly won over by the fiery eloquence of the preacher, the Marranos made a contrite confession of faith, which Ferrer regarded as a great victory for the church, a triumph for the truths of Christianity, leading him to hope that the conversion of the entire body of Jews might be vouchsafed to him. By his influence with the people, who honored him as a saint, he was very useful to the kings of Spain in putting down popular risings during the civil wars without bloodshed. Encouraged by the consideration of the Castilian royal family, Ferrer craved permission not only to preach in the synagogues and mosques, but to force Jews and Mahometans to listen to his addresses. A crucifix in one arm, the Torah in the other, escorted by flagellants and spearmen, he called upon the Jews, "with a terrible voice," to enrol themselves under the cross.

Seraphic as he was, Vincent Ferrer was not averse to the employment of force. He represented to the Spanish rulers that the Jews should be strictly isolated, as their intercourse with the Christian population was calculated to injure the true faith. His suggestions met with too ready a response. Through him and the other two conversionists, unspeakable sorrows were brought upon the Spanish Jews; indeed, the years from 1412 to 1415 may be reckoned among the saddest in the sorrowful history of the Jewish people. Shortly after Ferrer's appearance at the most Christian court, the regent Donna Catalina, the Infante Don Ferdinand, and the apostate Paul Burgensis de Santa Maria, in the name of the child-king, Juan II, issued an edict of twenty-four articles (January 12th, 1412), the aim of which was to impoverish and humiliate the Jews, and reduce them to the lowest grade in the social scale. It ordered that they should live in special Jew-quarters (Juderias), provided with not more than one gate each, under pain of confiscation of fortune and personal chastisement. No handicraft was to be exercised by them; they were not to practice the healing art, nor transact business with Christians. It goes without saying that they were forbidden to hire Christian servants and fill public offices. Their judicial autonomy was abolished, not only in criminal cases, in which they had long ceased to exercise it, but also in civil disputes. The edict prescribed a special costume for the Jews. Both men and women were to wear long garments, in the case of males, of coarse stuffs. Whoever dressed in the national costume, or in fine materials, became liable to a heavy fine; on a repetition of the offense, to corporal punishment and confiscation of property. The wearing of the red Jew badge was, of course, insisted upon. Males were prohibited from shaving the beard or cutting the hair under pain of one hundred lashes. No Jew was to be addressed, either in conversation or in writing, by the title "Don," to the infringement of which a heavy fine was also attached. They were interdicted from carrying weapons, and might no longer move from town to town, but were to be fixed to one place of abode. The Jew detected in an evasion of the latter restriction was to lose his entire property, and be made a bondman of the king. Grandees and burghers were sternly enjoined to afford not the slightest protection to Jews.

It is not unwarrantable to assume the influence of the apostate Paul de Santa Maria in the details of these Jew-hating laws. They singled out the most sensitive features of the Jewish character, pride and sense of honor. Wealthy Jews, in the habit of appearing in magnificent attire and with smoothly-shaven chins, were now to don a disfiguring costume, and go about with stubbly, ragged beards. The cultivated, who as physicians and advisers of the grandees had enjoyed unrestricted intercourse with the highest ranks, were to confine themselves to their Jew quarter, or be baptized, baptism being the hoped-for result of all these cruel restrictions, enforced with merciless vigor. A contemporary writer (Solomon Alami)describes the misery caused by the edict: "Inmates of palaces were driven into wretched nooks, and dark, low huts. Instead of rustling apparel we were obliged to wear miserable clothes, which drew contempt upon us. Prohibited from shaving the beard, we had to appear like mourners. The rich tax-farmers sank into want, for they knew no trade by which they could gain a livelihood, and the handicraftsmen found no custom. Starvation stared everyone in the face. Children died on their mothers' knees from hunger and exposure."

Amid this tribulation the Dominican Ferrer invaded the synagogues, crucifix in hand, preached Christianity in a voice of thunder, offering his hearers enjoyment of life and opportunities of preferment, or threatening damnation here and hereafter. The Christian populace, inflamed by the passionate eloquence of the preacher, emphasized his teaching by violent assaults on the Jews. The trial was greater than the unhappy Castilian Jews could bear. Flight was out of the question, for the law forbade it under a terrible penalty. It is not surprising, then, that the weak and lukewarm among them, the comfort-loving and wordly-minded, succumbed to the temptation, and saved themselves by baptism. Many Jews in the communities of Valladolid, Zamora, Salamanca, Toro, Segovia, Avila, Benavente, Leon, Valencia, Burgos, Astorga, and other small towns, in fact, wherever Vincent Ferrer preached, went over to Christianity. Several synagogues were turned into churches by Ferrer. In the course of his four months' sojourn (December, 1412—March, 1413) in the kingdom of Castile, this proselyte-monger inflicted wounds upon the Jews from which they bled to death.

When, however, he repaired to the kingdom of Aragon—summoned thither to advise on the rival claims of several pretenders to the throne—and when through his exertion the Castilian Infante, Don Ferdinand, was awarded the Aragonese crown (June, 1414), a trifling improvement took place in the condition of the Castilian Jews. The regent, Donna Catalina, issued a new edict in the name of her son (17th July). In this document the Jews were still interdicted the exercise of handicrafts, but were allowed, under a multitude of conditions, to visit markets with their merchandise. The prohibition to hire Christian or Mahometan domestics was confirmed; but, on the other hand, the employment of day-laborers and gardeners for the fields and vineyards of Jews, and shepherds for their flocks, was permitted. The new law triflingly allowed Jews to trim their hair and to clip with shears, but not entirely remove, their beards; a fringe of hair was ordered to be left on the chin, and shaving with the razor was forbidden, as though the queen-regent and her sage counselors were anxious that Jewish orthodoxy should not be wronged. The new decree conceded the wearing of dress materials of a value of sixty maravedis (under the former edict the value had been fixed at half this sum), but imposed a funnel-shaped head-covering, to which it was forbidden to attach tassels. The vehemence with which the edict declaimed against the ostentation of Jewish women disclosed its female authorship. Under this decree, freedom of domicile was once more accorded to Jews. It is noteworthy that the new edict applied only to Jews, whereas its predecessor restricted Mahometans as well.

With the transfer of the fanatical Ferrer to Aragon, the communities of that kingdom began to experience trials and misfortunes. The newly-elected king, Don Ferdinand, owed his crown to Ferrer, for as arbitrator between the rival pretenders he had warmly espoused his cause, proclaimed him king, and united the populace in his favor. Ferdinand consequently paid exceptional veneration to his saintliness, appointed him his father-confessor and spiritual adviser, and granted him his every wish. Foremost among Ferrer's aspirations was the conversion of the Jews, and to advance it the king commanded the Jews of Aragon to give every attention to his discourses. The zealous proselytizer made a tour of the kingdom, vehemently denouncing the Jews in every town he visited. His intimidations succeeded in converting a large number, particularly in Saragossa, Daroca, Tortosa, Valencia, and Majorca. Altogether Ferrer's mission to the Jews of Castile and Aragon is said to have resulted in not less than 20,500 forced baptisms.

This, however, did not end the woes of Spanish Jews. Pope Benedict XIII had still worse troubles in store for them, employing as his instrument his newly-baptized Jewish physician, Joshua Lorqui, otherwise Geronimo de Santa Fé. This pope, deposed by the council of Pisa as schismatic, heretic and forsworn, deprived of his spiritual functions and put under the ban, projected the conversion of the entire body of Jews in Spain to the church, at that time the object of universal opprobrium. On the Pyrenean peninsula he was still regarded as the legitimate pope, and from this base of operations he used every effort to procure a general acknowledgment of his authority. He was not slow to perceive that the general conversion of the Jews would powerfully assist his design. If it were vouchsafed to him to overcome at last the obstinacy, blindness and infidelity of Israel, and to bring it under the sovereignty of the cross—would it not be the greatest triumph for the church and for himself? Would it not put all his enemies to shame? Would not the faithful range themselves under the pope who had so glorified the church? What better proof could he give that he was the only true pontiff?

To promote this scheme, Benedict, by the authority of the king, Don Ferdinand, summoned (towards the end of 1412) the most learned rabbis and students of Scripture in the kingdom of Aragon to a religious disputation at Tortosa. The apostate Joshua Lorqui, who was well read in Jewish literature, was to prove to the Jews, out of the Talmud itself, that the Messiah had come in the person of Jesus. The design was to operate on the most prominent Jews, the papal court being convinced that, their conversion effected, the rank and file would follow of their own accord. Geronimo carefully selected the names of those to be invited, and the pope or the king attached a punishment to their non-attendance. What were the Jews to do? To come or to remain away, to accept or to refuse, was equally dangerous. About twenty-two of the most illustrious Aragonese Jews answered the summons. At their head was Don Vidal ben Benveniste Ibn-Labi (Ferrer), of Saragossa, a scion of the old Jewish nobility, a man of consideration and culture, a physician and neo-Hebrew poet. Among his companions were Joseph Albo, of Monreal, a disciple of Chasdaï Crescas, distinguished for his philosophic learning and genuine piety; Serachya Halevi Saladin, of Saragossa, translator of an Arabic philosophic work; Matathias Yizhari (En Duran?), of the same town, also a polished writer; Astruc Levi, of Daroca, a man of position; Bonastruc Desmaëstre, whose presence was most desired by the pope, because he was learned and distinguished; the venerable Don Joseph, of the respected Ibn-Yachya family, and others of lesser note.

Although the Jewish notables summoned to the disputation were men of liberal education, and Don Vidal even spoke Latin fluently, none of them possessed that stout-heartedness and force of character which impress even the most vindictive enemy, and which Nachmani so conspicuously displayed when alone he encountered two of the bitterest adversaries of Judaism—the Dominican General De Penyaforte and the apostate Pablo Christiani. A succession of humiliations and persecutions had broken the manhood of even the proudest in Jewry, and had transformed all into weaklings. They were no match for perilous times. When Benedict's summons reached them, they trembled. They agreed to act with circumspection and calmness, not to interrupt their opponent, and, above all, to be united and harmonious, but they disregarded these resolutions, exposed their weakness, and eventually broke up into factions, each of which took its own course.

Duly commissioned by his schismatic master, the renegade Geronimo drew up a program. In the first place, proofs were to be adduced from the Talmud and cognate writings that the Messiah had already come in the person of Jesus of Nazareth. The papal court flattered itself that this would bring about widespread conversion of the Jews, but, in case of failure, there was to follow a war of extermination against the Talmud on account of the abominations it contained, and the support it afforded the Jews in their blindness. Geronimo de Sante Fé accordingly composed a treatise on the Messianic character and Divinity of Jesus as illustrated in Jewish sacred writings. He collected all the specious arguments, the sophistries and text twistings which his predecessors had developed from their obscure, senseless, Scriptural interpretations, added nonsense of his own, declared playful Agadic conceits to be essential articles of faith, and refuted Jewish views of the questions discussed. He enumerated twenty-four conditions of the coming of the Messiah, and exerted himself to show that they had all been fulfilled in Jesus. His fundamental contention was that the Christians constituted the true Israel, that they had succeeded the Jewish people in Divine favor, and that the Biblical terms, mountain, tent, temple, house of God, Zion and Jerusalem were allegorical references to the church. An instance of his ridiculous arguments may be mentioned. Like John of Valladolid, he saw in the irregular formation of a letter in a word in Isaiah a deep mystery, indicating the virginity of Mary, and the realization of the Messianic period by the advent of Jesus. From another prophetic verse he expounded the immaculate conception of Jesus in so indecent a manner that it is impossible to repeat his explanation. This treatise, which blended the Patristic and the Rabbinic spirit, having been examined by the pope and his cardinals, was ordered to serve as the theme of the disputation.

No more remarkable controversy was ever held. It occupied sixty-eight sittings, and extended, with few interruptions, over a year and nine months (from February, 1413, until the 12th November, 1414). In the foreground stands a pope, abandoned by almost the whole of Christendom, and hunted from his seat, anxious for a favorable issue, not for the glorification of the faith, but for his own temporal advancement; by his side, a baptized Jew, combating Rabbinical Judaism with Rabbinical weapons; and in the background, a frenzied Dominican preacher with his escort of flagellants, promoting a persecution of the Jews to give force to the conversionist zeal of Tortosa. The helpless, bewildered Jews could only turn their eyes to heaven, for on earth they found themselves surrounded by bitter enemies. When, at their first audience with Pope Benedict (6th February, 1413), they were asked to give their names for registtation, they were seized with terror; they imagined their lives in jeopardy. The pope quieted them with the explanation that it was only a customary formality. On the whole he treated them at first with kindness and affability, the usual attitude of princes of the church when they have an end to attain. He assured them that no harm would befall them; that he had summoned them merely to ascertain whether there was any truth in Geronimo's statement that the Talmud attested the Messianic character of Jesus, and he promised them the fullest freedom of speech. At the end of the first audience he dismissed them graciously, assigned quarters to each of the notables, and gave instructions that their comfort should be cared for. A few prophesied from this friendly reception a successful issue for themselves and their cause, but they knew little of Rome and the vicegerents of God.

A few days later the disputation began. When the Jewish notables entered the audience hall, they were awe-struck by the splendor of the scene: Pope Benedict, on an elevated throne, clad in his state robes; around him the cardinals and princes of the church, resplendent in jeweled vestments; beyond them nearly a thousand auditors of the highest ranks. The little knot of defenders of Judaism trembled before this imposing and confident array of the forces of Christianity. The pope himself presided, and opened the sitting with an address to the Jews. He informed them that the truth of neither Judaism nor Christianity was to be called into question, for the Christian faith was above discussion and indisputable, and Judaism had once been true, but had been abrogated by the later dispensation. The disputation would be confined to the single question, whether the Talmud recognized Jesus as the Messiah. The Jews were consequently limited to mere defense. At a sign from the pope, the convert Geronimo stood forth, and, after a salutation of the papal toe, delivered himself of a long-winded harangue, abounding in Christian, Jewish, and even scholastic subtleties, and full of praise of the magnanimity and graciousness of the pope in endeavoring to bring the Jews into the way of salvation. His text, applied to the Jews, was a verse from Isaiah: "If ye be willing and obedient, ye shall eat the good of the land; but if ye refuse and rebel, ye shall be devoured with the sword"—which disclosed the final argument of the church. In reply, Vidal Benveniste, who had been elected spokesman by the notables, delivered a speech in Latin, which evoked a compliment from the pope. Don Vidal exposed Geronimo's malignity in threatening the sword and other punishments before the arguments on either side were heard. The pope acknowledged the justice of the reproof, and said in extenuation that Geronimo had still the boorishness derived from his Jewish origin. The notables plucked up courage to petition the pope to release them from further controversy, giving as their reason that their opponent employed scholastic methods of reasoning, in which it was impossible for them to follow him, as their faith was founded not on syllogisms but on tradition. The pope naturally declined to accede to this request, but invited them to continue the discussion on the following day, and had them escorted to their quarters by officers of high rank.

Overwhelmed with anxiety, the Jewish notables and the entire community of Tortosa assembled in the synagogue to implore help of Him who had so often stood by their fathers in their hours of need, and to pray that acceptable words might be put into their mouths, so that by no chance expression they should provoke the wild beasts seeking to devour them. Serachya Halevi Saladin gave expression to the gloomy feelings of the congregation in his sermon.

For a time the controversy retained its friendly character. Geronimo quoted obscure Agadic passages from the Talmud and other Hebrew writings to establish his astounding contention that the Talmud attests that Jesus was the Messiah. Generally the pope presided at the disputations, but occasionally grave matters affecting his own position necessitated his absence. The maintenance of his dignity was threatened by the convening of the council of Constance by the Christian princes, which constituted itself the supreme court in the conflict between the three popes. Consequently, Benedict had to hold frequent consultations with his friends. On these occasions, his place was taken by the general of the Dominicans or the chamberlain of the papal palace. The proofs adduced by Geronimo in support of his statements were so absurd that it should have been easy for the Jewish delegates to refute them. But their words were wilfully misinterpreted, so that in several instances it was recorded in the protocol that they had conceded the point under discussion. A few of them consequently committed their refutations to writing; but they still met with arbitrary treatment. Some points raised by them were condemned as not pertinent to the discussion. The Jewish delegates, who had entered on the controversy with unwilling hearts, were exhausted by the talking and taunting, and were anxious to avoid retort. Suddenly the pope threw aside his mask of friendliness, and showed his true disposition by threatening them with death. Sixty-two days the war of tongues had lasted, and the representatives of Judaism showed no sign of their much-hoped-for conversion. Their power of resistance appeared to grow with the battle. So, in the sixty-third sitting, the pope changed his tactics. At his command Geronimo now came forward as the censor of the Talmud, accusing it of containing all kinds of abominations, blasphemy, immorality and heresy, and demanding its condemnation. A few new-Christians, among them Andreas Beltran (Bertrand) of Valencia, the pope's almoner, valiantly seconded this demand.

Geronimo had prepared, at the instance of the pope, a treatise with this purpose in view. He had collected all the extravagances accidentally uttered by one or two of the hundreds of Agadists figuring in the Talmud. Shameless malice or ignorance dictated manifestly false accusations against the Talmud. Thus, he stated that it permitted the beating of parents, blasphemy, and idolatry, also the breaking of oaths, provided that on the previous Day of Atonement the precaution had been taken to declare them invalid. Conscientiousness in respect to oaths and vows he thus construed as perfidy, and, like Nicholas-Donin, drew the conclusion that the Jews did not fulfill their obligations towards Christians. Of course, he revived the calumny of Alfonso of Valladolid, that the Jews cursed the Christians in their daily prayers. Every inimical reference in the Talmud to heathens or Jewish Christians, Geronimo interpreted as applying to Christians, a fabrication with disastrous consequences, inasmuch as the enemies of the Jews repeated these deadly charges without further inquiry. When the attacks on the Talmud unexpectedly became the subject of discussion, the Jewish representatives defended the arraigned points, but were so hard pressed that they split up into two parties. Don Astruc Levi handed in a written declaration, setting forth that he ascribed no authority to the Agadic sentences quoted incriminating the Talmud; that he held them as naught, and renounced them. The majority of the notables supported him. To save the life of the whole they sacrificed a limb. Joseph Albo and Ferrer (Don Vidal) alone maintained their ground, declaring that the Talmudic Agada was a competent authority, and that the equivocal passages had a different meaning from that ascribed to them, and were not to be interpreted literally. So the machinations of the pope and his creatures had at least succeeded in bringing about a division in the ranks of the defenders of Judaism.

The principal object of the disputation—the conversion of the Jews *en masse* through the example of their most prominent leaders—was not attained. All the means employed failed—the benignant reception, the threats of violence, the attack on Jewish convictions. An expedient, calculated entirely for effect, had also been tried, which, it was thought, would so mortify the notables that, dazed and overwhelmed, they would throw down their arms and surrender at discretion. The fanatical proselytizer Vincent Ferrer had returned from Majorca to Catalonia and Aragon, and, surrounded by his terror-inspiring band of flagellants, had renewed his mission to the Jews, amid dismal chants and fiery exhortations to embrace the cross. Again he succeeded in winning over many thousands to Christianity. In the great Jewish communities of Saragossa, Calatajud, Daroca, Fraga and Barbastro, the conversions were limited to individuals; but smaller congregations, such as those of Alcañiz, Caspe, Maella, Lerida, Alcolea and Tamarite, hemmed in by hostile Christians, who spared neither limb nor life, went over in a body to Christianity. All these proselytes were gradually brought, in small and large troops, to Tortosa, and conducted, at the order of the pope, into the audience hall, where, before the entire assembly, they made public profession of the Christian faith. Living trophies, they were intended to shadow forth the impending victory of the church, dishearten the defenders of Judaism, and press upon them the conviction that, as in their absence the Jewish communities were melting away, all resistance on their part was in vain. It is no small merit that Don Vidal, Joseph Albo, Astruc Levi, and their companions refused to yield to the pressure. The pope saw his hopes shattered. Not a single notable wavered, and conversions of large masses did not take place. The great communities of Aragon and Catalonia remained true to their faith, with the exception of a few weaklings, amongst them some relations of Vidal Benveniste. The council of Constance would soon meet, and Benedict would be unable to appear before it as the triumphant conqueror of Judaism—would have no special claim to preference over the other two competing popes.

In his disappointment he vented his spleen on the Talmud and the already restricted liberties of the Jews. At the last sitting of the disputation he dismissed the Jewish notables with black looks, from which they easily divined his evil intentions. Various obstacles prevented him from putting them into force for six months, when (May 11th, 1415) they were embodied in a bull of eleven clauses. The Jews were forbidden to study or teach the Talmud and Talmudic literature; all copies of the Talmud were to be sought out and confiscated. Anti-Christian works, written by Jews, especially one entitled "Mar Mar Jesu," were not to be read under pain of punishment for blasphemy. Every community, whether large or small, was prohibited from possessing more than one simple, poorly appointed synagogue. The Jews were to be strictly separated from Christians, were not to eat, bathe, or do business with them. They were to occupy no official posts, exercise no handicrafts, not even practice medicine. The wearing of the red or yellow Jew badge was also enjoined by this bull. Finally, all Jews were to be forced to hear Christian sermons three times a year—during Advent, at Easter, and in the summer. In the first sermon the Prophets and the Talmud were to be used to prove that the true Messiah had come; in the second, their attention was to be directed to the abominations and heresies contained, according to Geronimo's treatise, in the Talmud, alone responsible for their infidelity; and in the third it was to be impressed upon them that the destruction of the temple and the dispersion of the Hebrew people had been predicted by the founder of Christianity. At the close of each sermon the bull was to be read aloud. The strict execution of this malignant edict was confided by the pope to Gonzalo de Santa Maria, son of the apostate Paul, who had been taken over to Christianity by his father.

Fortunately, the vindictive schemes of Pope Benedict never came into active operation. While he was still engaged in tormenting the Jews, the council of Constance decreed his deposition. As he had obstinately opposed the advice of the king, Don Ferdinand, and the German emperor, Sigismund, to lay aside the tiara of his own initiative, he was abandoned by his Spanish protectors. The weapons he had employed recoiled upon himself. His last adherents were drawn from him by Vincent Ferrer's fanatical preaching. The flagellant priest not only exhorted the king of Aragon to renounce "this unfrocked and spurious pope," but he held forth everywhere—in the churches and the open streets—that "a man like this pope deserves to be pursued to death by every right-thinking Christian." Deserted by his protectors, his friends, and even his protégés, there now remained to Pedro de Luna, of all his possessions, only the small fortress of Peñiscola, and even here King Ferdinand, urged on by Santa Maria, the pope's creature, threatened him with a siege. In the end this ambitious and obstinate man covered himself with ridicule by attempting to continue to play the part of pope in his tiny palace. He appointed a college of four cardinals, and pledged them before his death not to recognize the pope elected at Constance, but to choose a successor from among their own body. When he died, his college elected two popes instead of one. Such was the infallibility of the church, into the pale of which it was sought to force the Jews. What became of the malicious apostate, Joshua Lorqui-Geronimo de Santa Fé, after the fall of his master, is not known. In Jewish circles he was remembered by the well-earned sobriquet of "The Calumniator" (Megadef). King Ferdinand of Aragon, who had always allowed himself to be influenced by enemies of the Jews, died in 1416. His death was followed, after a short interval, by that of the Jew-hating regent, Catalina of Castile, the instrument of Vincent's Jew-hunt (1418), and finally by that of Vincent himself (1419), who had the mortification to see the flagellant movement, to which he owed his saintly reputation, condemned by the council of Constance, he himself being compelled to disband his "white troop."

Although the chief persecutors of the Jews had disappeared, the unhappy conditions created by them remained. The exclusive laws of Castile and the bull of Pope Benedict were still in force. Ferrer's proselytizing campaigns had severely crippled the Spanish, and even foreign communities. In Portugal alone they met with no success. The Portuguese ruler, Don João I, had other interests to pursue than the conversion of Jews. He was then occupied in that first conquest on the coast of Africa, opposite to Portugal, which laid the foundation of the subsequent maritime supremacy of the Portuguese. When Vincent Ferrer petitioned King João for permission to come to Portugal in order to make the pulpits and streets resound with his dismal harangues on the sinfulness of the world and the blindness and obstinacy of the Jews, the Portuguese king informed him that he "might come, but with a crown of red-hot iron on his head." Portugal was the only refuge on the Pyrenean peninsula from the proselytizing rage of the flagellant preacher, and many Spanish Jews who had the means of escaping fled thither. Don Judah Ibn Yachya-Negro, held in high esteem by King João I, and, perhaps, appointed by him chief rabbi of Portugal, represented to him the horrors of enforced baptism, and the necessary insincerity of the professions of unwilling converts. The king consequently issued his commands that the immigrant new-Christians should not be interfered with or delivered up to Spain.

In other parts of Europe, where the fanatical Dominican had been, or whither reports of his deeds or misdeeds had penetrated, the Jews were forced to drain the cup of bitterness to the dregs. In Savoy, which Vincent Ferrer had visited, they were obliged to hide themselves with their holy books in mountain caves. In Germany, persecutions of Jews had always found a congenial soil, and they were promoted by the anarchy which prevailed during the reign of Sigismund and the sessions of the council of Constance. Even the Italian communities, though for the most part undisturbed, lived in continual anxiety, lest the movement strike a responsive chord in their politically distracted land. They convened a great synod, first at Bologna, then at Forli (1416—1418), to consider what measures might be adopted to avert the threatened danger.

Happily, at this moment, after a long schism, bitter strife and a plurality of anti-popes, the council of Constance elected a pope, who, though full of dissimulation, was not the most degraded in the college of cardinals. Martin V, who was said by his contemporaries to have appeared simple and good before his election, but to have shown himself afterwards very clever and not very kind, received the Jews with scant courtesy when, during his progress through Constance, they approached him carrying lighted tapers in festive procession, and offered him the Torah with a prayer for the confirmation of their sufferance. From his white palfrey with silk and gold trappings he answered them: "You have the law, but understand it not. The old has passed away, and the new been found." (The blind finding fault with the seeing.) Yet he treated them with leniency. At the request of Emperor Sigismund, he confirmed the privileges granted to the Jews of Germany and Savoy by the preceding emperor, Rupert, denouncing attacks on their persons and property, and the practice of converting them by force. The emperor, who may be accused of thoughtlessness but not of a spirit of persecution, thereupon issued his commands to all the German princes and magistrates, cities and subjects, to allow his "servi cameræ" the full enjoyment of the privileges and immunities which had been given them by the pope (February 26th, 1418). A deputation of Jews, commissioned by the Italian synod, also waited upon the now generally acknowledged pope, and craved his protection. Even the Spanish Jews appear to have dispatched an embassy to him, consisting of two of their most distinguished men, Don Samuel Abrabanel and Don Samuel Halevi. When the Jews complained of the insecurity of their lives, the attacks on their religious convictions, and the frequent desecration of their sanctuaries, the pope issued a bull (January 31st, 1419), with the following preamble:

"Whereas the Jews are made in the image of God, and a remnant of them will one day be saved, and whereas they have besought our protection, following in the footsteps of our predecessors we command that they be not molested in their synagogues; that their laws, rights, and customs be not assailed; that they be not baptized by force, constrained to observe Christian festivals, nor to wear new badges, and that they be not hindered in their business relations with Christians."

What could have induced Pope Martin to show such friendly countenance to the Jews? Probably he had some idea of checkmating by this means the Jew-hating Benedict, who still played at being pope in his obscure corner. The principal consideration probably was the rich gifts with which the Jewish representatives approached him. Although at the council of Constance no cardinal was poorer than Martin, and his election was in great measure owing to this fact, on the throne of St. Peter he showed no aversion to money. On the contrary, everything might be obtained from him if money were paid down; without it, nothing.

CHAPTER VII.

THE HUSSITES. PROGRESS OF JEWISH LITERATURE.

The Hussite Heresy—Consequences for the Jews involved in the Struggle—Jacob Mölin—Abraham Benveniste and Joseph Ibn-Shem Tob in the Service of the Castilian Court—Isaac Campanton, the Poet Solomon Dafiera—Moses Da Rieti—Anti-Christian Polemical Literature—Chayim Ibn-Musa—Simon Duran and his Son Solomon—Joseph Albo as a Religious Philosopher—Jewish Philosophical Systems—Edict of the Council of Basle against the Jews—Fanatical Outbreaks in Majorca—Astruc Sibili and his Conversion to Christianity.

1420—1442 C.E.

MEANWHILE history received a fresh impulse, which, although coming from weak hands, produced a forward movement. The spreading corruption in the church, the self-deifying arrogance of the popes and the licentiousness of priests and monks revolted the moral sense of the people, opened their eyes, and encouraged them to doubt the very foundations of the Roman Catholic system. No improvement could be expected from the princes of the church, the jurists and diplomatists who met in council at Constance to deliberate on a scheme of thorough reform. They had only a worldly object in view, seeking to gloss over the prevailing rottenness by transferring the papal power to the high ecclesiastics, substituting the rule of an aristocratic hierarchy for papal absolutism. A Czech priest, John Huss, of Prague, inspired by the teachings of Wycliffe, spoke the magic word that loosened the bonds in which the church had ensnared the minds of men. "Not this or that pope," he said in effect, "but the papacy and the entire organization of the Catholic church constitute the fundamental evil from which Christendom is suffering." The flames to which the council of Constance condemned this courageous priest only served to light up the truth he had uttered. They fired a multitude in Bohemia, who entered on a life and death struggle with Catholicism. Whenever a party in Christendom opposes itself to the ruling church, it assumes a tinge of the Old Testament, not to say Jewish, spirit. The Hussites regarded Catholicism, not unjustly, as heathenism, and themselves as Israelites, who must wage holy war against Philistines, Moabites, and Ammonites. Churches and monasteries were to them the sanctuaries of a dissolute idolatry, temples to Baal and Moloch and groves of Ashtaroth, to be consumed with fire and sword. The Hussite war, although largely due to the mutual race-hatred of Czechs and Germans, and to religious indignation, began in a small way the work of clearing the church doctrine of its mephitic elements.

For the Jews, this movement was decidedly calamitous, the responsibility for which must rest, not with the wild Hussites, but with the Catholic fanaticism stirred up against the new heresy. The former went little beyond denunciations of Jewish usury; at the most, sacked Jewish together with Catholic houses. Of special Hussite hostility to the Jews no evidence is forthcoming. On the other hand, Catholics accused Jews of secretly supplying the Hussites with money and arms; and in the Bavarian towns near the Böhmerwald, they persecuted them unmercifully as friends and allies of the heretics. The Dominicans—the "army of anti-Christ" as they were called—included the Jews in their fierce pulpit denunciations of the Hussites, and inflamed the people and princes against them. The crusades against the Hussites, like those against the Mahometans and Waldenses, commenced with massacres of Jews. Revived fanaticism first affected the Jews in Austria—a land which, like Spain, passed from liberal tolerance of Jews to persecution, and in bigotry approximated so close to the Iberian kingdom that it ultimately joined it. The mind of Archduke Albert, an earnest and well-intentioned prince, was systematically filled with hatred against the "enemies of God." Fable after fable was invented, which, devoid even of originality, sufficed to drive to extreme measures a man of pure character, ignorant of the lying devices of the Jew-haters. Three Christian children went skating in Vienna; the ice broke through, and they were drowned. When the anxious parents failed to find them, a malicious rumor was set on foot that they had been slaughtered by Jews, who required their blood for the ensuing Passover celebration. Then a Jew was charged with a crime calculated to incense the populace to a still greater degree. The wife of the sacristan of Enns was said to have purloined the consecrated host from the church, and sold it to a wealthy Jew named Israel, who had sent it to a large number of Jewish communities in and out of Austria. The charges of Jewish murders of Christian children and Jewish profanations of hosts had not lost their charm in the fifteenth century, and their inventors could calculate their effect with accuracy. By order of the archduke, the sacristan's wife and her two accomplices or seducers, Israel and his wife, were brought to Vienna, examined, and forced to confess. The records of the case are silent as to the means employed to obtain the avowal of guilt; but the procedure of mediæval Christendom in such trials is well known.

Archduke Albert issued the order that in the early morning of the 23d May, 1420 (10th Sivan), all the Jews in his realm should be thrown into prison, and this was promptly done. The moneyed Jews were stripped of their possessions, and the poor forthwith banished the country. In the gaols, wives were separated from their husbands, and children from their parents. When from helplessness they fell to hopelessness, Christian priests came to them with crosses in their hands and honeyed words on their lips to convert them. A few of the poorer-spirited saved their lives by accepting baptism. The more resolute slew themselves and their kinsfolk by opening their veins with straps, cords, or whatever they found to hand. The spirit of the survivors was broken by the length and cruelty of their imprisonment. Their children were taken from them, and immured in cloisters. Still they remained firm, and on the 13th March (9th Nisan), 1421, after nearly a year's confinement, they were committed to the flames. In Vienna alone more than a hundred perished in one field near the Danube. Another order was then issued by Archduke Albert, forbidding Jews to stay thenceforth in Austria.

The converts proved no gain to the church. The majority seized the first opportunity of emigrating and relapsing into Judaism. They bent their steps to Bohemia, rendered tolerant by the Hussite schism, or northwards to Poland and southwards to Italy. How attached the Austrian Jews were to their religion is shown by the conduct of one clever youth. Having received baptism, he had become the favorite of Duke Frederick, afterwards the German emperor, but, although living in luxury, he was seized with remorse for his apostasy, and boldly expressed his desire to return to Judaism. Frederick exerted himself to dissuade his favorite from this idea. He begged, entreated, and even threatened him; he sent a priest to advise him; all, however, in vain. Finally, the duke handed the "obstinate heretic and backslider" over to the ecclesiastical authorities, who condemned him to the stake. Unfettered and with a Hebrew song on his lips the Jewish youth mounted the scaffold.

In the meantime, the devastating war broke out between the fierce Hussites and the not less barbarous Roman Catholics, between the Czechs and the

Germans. A variety of nationalities participated in the sanguinary struggle as to the use of the cup by the laity in the eucharist. Emperor Sigismund, who found it impossible to subdue the insurrection with his own troops, summoned the imperial army to his standard. Wild free-lances, men of Brabant and Holland, were taken into his pay. From all quarters armed troops poured into the Bohemian valleys and against the capital, Prague, where the blind hero, Zisca, bade defiance to a world of foes. On the way, the German imperial army exhibited its courage by attacks on the defenseless Jews. "We are marching afar," exclaimed the mercenaries, "to avenge our insulted God, and shall those who slew him be spared?" Wherever they came across Jewish communities, on the Rhine, in Thuringia and Bavaria, they put them to the sword, or forced them to apostatize. The crusaders threatened, on their return from victory over the Hussites, to wipe the Jewish people from the face of the earth. Jewish fathers of families true to their faith gave orders that, at a certain signal, their children should be killed to avoid falling into the hands of the bloodthirsty soldiery. Letters of lamentation over the threatened disaster, calling upon him to implore the intervention of heaven, were addressed from far and near to the illustrious rabbi of Mayence, Jacob ben Moses Mölin Halevi (Maharil, born 1365, died 1427), the most pious rabbi of his time. His arrangement of the synagogue ritual and melodies is used to this day in many German communities, and their colonies in Poland and Hungary. Jacob Mölin ordered a general fast, accompanied by fervent prayer, and his instructions were circulated from one community to another throughout the land. The German congregations forthwith assembled for solemn mourning and humiliation, and fasted during four days between New Year and Atonement (8th—11th September, 1421), and for three successive days after Tabernacles, the observance being as strict as on the most sacred fast days of the Jewish calendar. It was a time of feverish tension for the German Jews. In their despair they prayed that victory might be vouchsafed to the Hussites, and it seemed as if their supplications were heard. For, shortly afterwards, the imperial army and its mercenary allies assembled near Saatz were stricken with such terror at the news of Zisca's approach, that they sought safety in disorderly flight, disbanding in all directions, and hurrying home by different routes. Famished and footsore, a few of the very men who had vowed death and extirpation to the Jews, appeared at the doors of their houses, begging for bread, which was gladly given them. Privation had so reduced the fugitives that they could not have harmed a child.

The Dominican clergy commissioned to preach against the Hussites did not cease to foster Catholic hatred of Jews. From their pulpits they thundered against heretics and Jews alike, cautioning the faithful against holding intercourse with them, and consciously and unconsciously inciting to attacks on their persons and property. The Jews flew for help to the pope, Martin V—doubtless not with empty hands—and again obtained a very favorable bull (23d February, 1422), in which Christians were enjoined to remember that their religion had been inherited from Jews, who were necessary for the corroboration of Christian truth. The pope forbade the monks to preach against intercourse between Jews and Christians, and declared null and void the ban with which transgressors had been threatened. He recommended to Catholics a friendly and benevolent attitude towards their Hebrew fellow-citizens, severely denounced violent attacks upon them, and confirmed all the privileges which had from time to time been granted by the papacy. This bull was, however, as ineffectual as the protection which

Emperor Sigismund had so solemnly promised the Jews. A persecuting spirit continued to animate the Christian church. The monks did not cease to declaim against the "accursed" Jewish nation; the populace did not refrain from tormenting, injuring and murdering Jews; even succeeding popes ignored the bull, and restored the odious canonical restrictions in all their stringency. Turning a deaf ear to both pope and emperor, the citizens of Cologne expelled the Jewish community, perhaps the oldest in Germany. The exiles took up their abode at Deutz (1426). In the South German towns, Ravensburg, Ueberlingen and Lindau, the Jews were burnt because of a lying blood accusation (1431).

The literary work of the German Jews was, as a consequence, poor and inconsiderable. Anxiety and persecution had deadened their intellect. Even in Talmudical study the German rabbis hardly rose above mediocrity, and gave nothing of consequence to the world. Some rabbis were installed by the reigning prince; at least Emperor Sigismund commissioned one of his Jewish agents, Chayim of Landshut, "to appoint three rabbis (Judenmeister) in Germany." Under such auspices, appointments were probably determined less by merit than by money. For a college, in which students were prepared for the rabbinate, a heavy tax had to be paid, notwithstanding that the instruction was given gratuitously. Besides Jacob Mölin, only one name of importance emerges from the darkness of this period, Menachem of Merseburg, or, as he was generally called, Meïl Zedek. He wrote a comprehensive work on the practice of the Talmudic marriage and civil law, which the Saxon communities adopted for their authoritative guidance. He, at least, departed from the beaten track of his older contemporaries or teachers, Jacob Mölin and Isaac Tyrnau, who attached value to every insignificant detail of the liturgy. By and by Menachem of

Merseburg was recognized as an authority, and an excellent regulation drawn up by him received universal assent. Among the Jews at that period, marriages took place at a very early age; girls in their teens were hurried into matrimony. According to Talmudical law a girl, under age, who had been given in marriage by her mother or brothers and not by her father, was permitted, on attaining her majority, in her twelfth year, and even much later under some circumstances, to dissolve her union without further ceremony than a declaration of her intention to do so, or the contracting of another marriage (Miun). Menachem of Merseburg felt the indecency of so sudden and often capricious a dissolution of marriage, and he decided that formal bills of divorce should be required.

The literary achievements of the Spanish Jews during this period were not of a higher character; they exhibited unmistakable signs of decay, notwithstanding that their situation had become more tolerable since the death of the bigoted and wanton queen regent, Catalina, and the fall of the anti-pope, Benedict XIII, and his Jewish accomplices. Don Juan II—or, rather, his favorite, Alvaro de Luna, to whom the management of the state was confided—stood too much in need of the assistance of Jewish financiers during the frequently recurring civil wars and insurrections to do anything to offend them. Hence, during his reign, restrictive laws against the Jews seem to have been enacted only to be broken. Jews were again admitted to public employment, regardless of the fact that such appointments had been sternly forbidden both by kings and popes. An influential Jew, Abraham Benveniste, surnamed Senior, distinguished for his intelligence and wealth, was invested with a high dignity at the court of Don Juan, and was thus in a position to frustrate threatened persecutions of his co-religionists. Also Joseph ben Shem Tob Ibn-Shem Tob, a cultivated and fruitful writer, proficient in philosophic studies, was in the service of the state under Juan II. On the one hand, the cortes did not fail to remind the king that by his father's laws and by papal decrees the Jews were excluded from public offices, and, on the other hand, Pope Eugenius IV, successor to Martin V, strained every effort to humiliate the Jews and harden their lot, even forbidding Don Juan to befriend them; but these representations were of no avail. To the cortes of Burgos the king replied evasively that he would cause an examination to be made of the laws promulgated in regard to the Jews by his father, and of the papal bulls, and he would take care to observe everything calculated to promote the service of God and the welfare of the state. Against the pope's interference with his crown-rights he entered a protest.

This king gave permission to the no less noble than wealthy rabbi, Abraham Benveniste, to hold a meeting of delegates from various communities in the royal palace of Avila (1432). These delegates were to bring harmony into the state of moral and religious disorder caused by the attacks of the masses in 1412—1415. The smaller communities were without teachers, the large ones without rabbis and preachers. Many of them had been reduced to poverty, and the richer members were unwilling to contribute to the support of religious institutions. Evil ways and denunciations by the unscrupulous had acquired the upper hand, because the representative men and the few rabbis did not venture to punish the evildoers. Abraham Benveniste, therefore, framed a statute (the law of Avila), which compelled people to establish schools and colleges, to introduce order into the communities, and to punish miscreants. Juan II confirmed this statute.

The literature of the Spanish Jews, however, was powerless to recover itself. Despite the calm succeeding the storm, it seemed to wither like autumn leaves. The decline was most marked in the department of Talmudic study. After the emigration of Isaac ben Sheshet and the death of Chasdaï Crescas, no Spanish rabbi obtained more than local authority and reputation. The only upholder of the traditions of the rabbinate was Isaac ben Jacob Campanton, who lived to be more than a hundred years old (born 1360, died at Peñafiel 1463); but he produced only one work (Darke ha-Talmud), which exhibited neither genius nor learning. Still, in his day, Campanton passed for the Gaon of Castile. Neo-Hebraic poetry, which had blossomed so profusely on Spanish soil, faded and drooped. Of those who cultivated it during this period only a few are remembered—Solomon Dafiera, Don Vidal Benveniste, the leading speaker on the Jewish side at the disputation of Tortosa, and Solomon Bonfed. The most gifted was the last. He was ambitious to emulate Ibn-Gebirol; but he possessed little more than the sensitiveness and moroseness of his great exemplar, like him imagining himself to be the sport of fortune, with a prescriptive right to lamentation.

The Jews of Italy failed to distinguish themselves in poetry even during the Medici period, in spite of the high culture which, with the Hussite movement, was eating away the foundations of mediæval Catholicism. Since Immanuel Romi, the Jews of Italy had produced but one poet; even he was not a poet in the noblest sense of the word. Moses ben Isaac (Gajo) da Rieti, of Perugia (born 1388, died after 1451), a physician by profession, a dabbler in philosophy, and a graceful writer in both Hebrew and Italian, might have passed for an artist if poetry were a thing of meter and rhyme, for in his sublimely conceived poem both were faultless. His desire was to glorify in poetry Judaism and Jewish antiquity, the sciences, and the illustrious men of all ages. He employed an ingenious form of verse, in which the stanzas were connected by threes by means of cross-rhymes. But Da Rieti's language is often rough, many of his allusions show want of taste, and where he should rise to lofty thought he sinks into puerilities. Only in one respect does his work mark an advance in neo-Hebrew poetry. He breaks entirely with the traditional Judæo-Arabic method of a single rhyme. There is variety in his versification; the ear is not wearied by monotonous repetition of the same or similar sounds, and the lines fall naturally into stanzas. He also avoids playing on Biblical verses, the objectionable habit of Judæo-Spanish poets. In a word, Da Rieti supplied the correct form for neo-Hebrew poetry, but he was unable to vivify it with an attractive spirit. Yet the Italian Jews adopted a part of his poem into their liturgy, and recited extracts daily.

From the Apennine Peninsula let us turn back to the Pyrenean, where the pulsation of historic life among the Jews, though gradually becoming weaker, still was stronger than in the other countries in which they were dispersed. The two branches of intellectual activity which formerly, in their palmy days, had exercised every mind—the severe study of the Talmud and the airy pursuit of the poetic muse—had lost their predominance in the Spanish Jewries. The systematic study of the Scriptures also was no longer properly cultivated. The literary activity of this period was almost exclusively directed towards combating the intrusiveness of the church, repelling its attacks on Judaism, and withstanding its proselytizing zeal. Faithful and strong-minded Jewish thinkers held it a duty to proclaim their convictions aloud, and to admonish waverers and strengthen them. The more the preaching monks, especially apostates of the stamp of Paul de Santa Maria, Geronimo de Santa Fé, and Pedro de la Caballeria, exerted themselves to prove that the Christian Trinity was the true God of Israel, taught and typified in the Bible and the Talmud, and the more the church stretched forth its tentacles towards the Jews, straining every nerve to fold them in its fatal embrace, the more necessary was it for the synagogue to watch over its sacred trust, and guard its holy of holies from idolatrous desecration. It was especially necessary that the weaker-minded should be spared confusion in religious and doctrinal matters. Hence Jewish preachers devoted themselves more than ever to expounding the doctrine of the unity of God in their pulpits. They pointed out the essential and irreconcilable difference between the Jewish and the Christian conception of the Deity, and characterized their identification as false and impious. The time resembled that other epoch in Jewish history when Hellenized Jews tried to induce their brethren to deny God, and were supported by the secular arm. Some preachers, in their zeal, went to extremes. Instead of relying exclusively on the convincing demonstrations in the Bible text, or on the attractive illustrations of the Agada, they resorted to the armory of scholasticism, employing the formulæ of philosophy and, in the presence of the Torah, and by the side of the Hebrew prophets and the Talmudical sages, quoted Plato, Aristotle, and Averroes.

This controversial literature, cultivated on a large scale, was designed to defend Judaism against calumny and abuse, rather than to convert a single Christian soul. Its aim was to open the eyes of Jews, so that ignorance or credulity might not lead them into the snares prepared for them. Doubtless it also desired to stir up the new-Christians, and to re-animate their Jewish spirit beneath the disguise they had assumed to save their lives. Hence the majority of the polemical writings of the day were merely vindications of Judaism from the old charges fulminated by Nicholas de Lyra a century before, or more recently by Geronimo de Santa Fé and others, and widely circulated by the Christian clergy. Solomon-Paul of Burgos, who had been appointed bishop of his native town, wrote, in his eighty-second year (1434, a year before his death), a venomous tract against Judaism—"Searching the Scriptures" (Scrutinium Scriptuarum)—in the form of a dialogue between a teacher and his pupil, the unbelieving Saul and the converted Paul. Solomon-Paul does not seem to have retained much of the wit which, according to Jewish and Christian panegyrists, had at one time distinguished him—it had probably become blunted amid the luxurious ease of the episcopal palace—for his tract, devoutly Christian and Catholic in tone, is pointless and dull. Another ex-rabbi who devoted himself to attacking Judaism was Juan de España, also called Juan the Old (at Toledo), a convert who in old age had embraced Christianity under the influence of Vincent Ferrer's proselytizing efforts. He wrote a treatise on his own conversion and a Christian commentary on the seventy-second Psalm, in both of which he asserted the genuineness of his change of creed, and urged the Jews to abjure their errors. How many weak-minded Jews must have been influenced by the zeal, earnest or hypocritical, of such men as these, belonging to their own race, and learned in their literature!

It is impossible to exaggerate the services of the men who, deeply impressed with the gravity of the crisis, threw themselves into the breach, with exhortations to their co-religionists to remain faithful to their creed. In defiance of the dangers which menaced them, they scattered their inspiriting discourses far and wide. Foremost among them were the men who had distinguished themselves at the Tortosa disputation by their unyielding attitude and their courage in withstanding the unjustifiable attacks upon the Talmud—Don Vidal (Ferrer) Ibn-Labi and Joseph Albo. The former drew up in Hebrew a refutation of Geronimo's impeachment of the Talmud (Kodesh ha-Kodashim), and the latter circulated, in Spanish, an account of a religious controversy he had sustained with an eminent church dignitary. Isaac ben Kalonymos, of a learned Provençal family named Nathan, who associated a great deal with learned Christians, and frequently had to defend his religious convictions, wrote two polemical works, one entitled "Correction of the False Teacher," directed against Geronimo's libelous essay, and the other, called "The Fortress," of unknown purpose. He also compiled a laborious work of reference intended to assist others in defending Judaism from attack. Isaac Nathan, in his intercourse with Christians, often had to listen to criticisms of Judaism, or evidences drawn from the Hebrew Bible, in favor of Christian dogmas, which he found were always based on false renderings of Hebrew words. To put an end to these illusory outgrowths of prevailing ignorance of the original text of the Scriptures, or, at least, to lighten the labors of his brethren in refuting them, he resolved to compile a comprehensive digest of the linguistic materials of the Bible, by which the actual meaning of each word should be made clear. According to the plan adopted, any one can ascertain, at a glance, both how often a certain word occurs in the Bible, and its varying meanings according to the contexts. The work thus undertaken by Isaac Nathan was of colossal scope, and occupied a long series of years (September, 1437—1445). It was a Bible concordance, that is, the verses were grouped alphabetically under the reference words according to roots and derivations. The existing Latin concordances served in a measure as models, although their purpose was the less ambitious one of assisting preachers to find texts. Isaac Nathan, who produced various other works, by this concordance rendered inestimable and lasting service to the study of the Bible, although his labor was of a purely mechanical kind. Originating from the temporary needs of the polemical situation, it has been, and will ever remain, a powerful weapon for ensuring the triumph of Judaism in its struggles with other religious systems.

The philosopher, Joseph Ibn-Shem Tob (born 1400, died a martyr 1460), who was a voluminous writer, a popular preacher, and a frequenter of the Castilian court, also entered the lists against Christianity to expose the fallacy and unreasonableness of its dogmas. In his frequent intercourse with Christians of distinction, both clerical and lay, he found it necessary to make himself thoroughly acquainted with Christian theology that he might adduce cogent arguments in reply to those who wished to convert him, or in his presence made the oft-reiterated statement of the falsity of Judaism. Occasionally a regular controversy in defense of his creed was forced upon him. The fruits of his studies and thought he committed to writing in the shape of a small treatise, entitled "Doubts of the Religion of Jesus," in which he criticised with unsparing logic the dogmas of Original Sin, Salvation, and Incarnation. Besides, he wrote, for the instruction of his brethren, a detailed commentary on Profiat Duran's satire on Christianity, and made available for them, by means of a Hebrew translation, Chasdaï Crescas' polemical work against the Christian religion, originally written in Spanish. Strange to say, the Spanish Jews preferred, as a rule, Hebrew books to those in the language of their adopted country.

Among the authors of polemical works against Christianity a contemporary of Joseph Ibn-Shem Tob deserves special mention. History has hitherto forgotten Chayim Ibn-Musa, from Bejar, in the neighborhood of Salamanca (born about 1390, died about 1460), a physican, versifier and writer, who had access to the Spanish court and the grandees through his medical skill, and so, frequent opportunities of discussing questions of doctrine with ecclesiastics and learned laymen. A colloquy preserved by Chayim Ibn-Musa illustrates the spirit which prevailed in Spain before the hateful Inquisition silenced all freedom of speech. A learned ecclesiastic once asked Ibn-Musa why, if Judaism, as he maintained, was the true faith, the Jews could not possess themselves of the Holy Land and Jerusalem? Ibn Musa replied that they had lost their country through the sins of their fathers, and could regain it only by perfect atonement and purgation. He, in turn, propounded a question: Why are the Christians no longer in possession of the Holy Sepulcher? and why does it, together with all the sites associated with the Passion, continue in the hands of Mahometan infidels, notwithstanding that Christians, by means of confession and absolution, and through the medium of the nearest available priest, can free themselves at any moment from sin? Before the ecclesiastic could bethink himself of a suitable reply, a knight, who had formerly been in Palestine, interposed: The Mahometans are the only people who deserve to possess the site of the Temple and the Holy Land, for neither Christians nor Jews hold houses of prayer in so much honor as they. The Christians, during the night before Easter (Vigils), perpetrate shameful abominations in the churches at Jerusalem, abandon themselves to debauchery, harbor thieves and murderers, and carry on bloody feuds within their precincts. They dishonor their character in the same way as the Jews profaned their Temple. Therefore, God, in His wisdom, has deprived the Jews and the Christians of the Holy City, and has intrusted it to the Mahometans, because, in their hands, it is safe from desecration. To his observation the Christian priest and the Jewish physician could oppose only abashed silence.

Chayim Ibn-Musa devoted himself to the task of discrediting the chief sources of the materials of Christian attacks on Judaism, the writings of the Franciscan Nicholas de Lyra. He not only refuted the assertions put forward in those works, but deprived them of the soil upon which they fed. The ever-recurring controversies between Jews and Christians led to no conclusions, and left each party in the belief that it had gained a victory, because they generally turned on secondary questions, the disputants never discussing fundamental premises, but wrangling, each from his undemonstrated basis. Chayim Ibn-Musa wished to introduce method into these controversies, and to lay down clear principles for the defense of Judaism. Accordingly, he drew up rules which, strictly observed, were bound to lead to a definite result. In the first place, he advised Jews invariably to hold fast in a disputation to the simple meaning of the Scriptures, always to take the context into account, and especially to avoid allegorical or symbolical methods of interpretation, which left Christian polemics free to introduce arbitrary theories. Further, Jewish disputants were to announce that they ascribed no authority in matters of belief either to the Chaldaic translation of the Bible (Targum) or to the Greek (Septuagint), these being the sources of the false proofs adduced by Christians. He counseled them to abandon even Agadic exegesis, and not to hesitate to declare that it had no weight in determining the doctrines of Judaism. These and similar rules Chayim Ibn-Musa applied to the writings of Nicholas de Lyra, successfully refuting them from beginning to end in a comprehensive work, justly entitled "Shield and Sword."

The anti-Christian polemical literature of this period was further enriched by two writers, father and son, living in Algiers, far removed from the scenes of the Christian propaganda. But Simon ben Zemach Duran and his son, Solomon Duran, were Spaniards by birth and education. In his philosophic exposition of Judaism, the former devoted a chapter to Christianity, maintaining, in answer to Christian and Mahometan objections, the inviolability of the Torah. This chapter, entitled "Bow and Buckler," and described as being "for defense and attack," proves the contention of older writers, and more recently of Profiat Duran, that Jesus' intention was not to abolish Judaism. The rabbi of Algiers exhibits extraordinarily wide acquaintance with the literature of the New Testament and thorough familiarity with church doctrine, combats each with weapons taken from its own arsenal, and criticises unsparingly.

Solomon Duran I (born about 1400, died 1467), who succeeded his father in the Algerian rabbinate, combined with profound Talmudic knowledge a decided leaning towards a rationalistic apprehension of Judaism. Unlike his father and his ancestor, Nachmani, he was a sworn enemy of the Kabbala. During his father's lifetime and at his request, he wrote a refutation of the shameless, lying accusations brought against the Talmud by Geronimo de Santa Fé. In an exhaustive treatise ("Letter on the Conflict of Duties") he deals sharply with Geronimo's sallies. He repels the accusation that the Talmud teaches lewdness, and proves that it really inculcates extreme continence. Jews who regulate their lives according to Talmudical prescriptions scrupulously abstain from carnal sins, holding them in great abhorrence, and pointing with scorn at persons guilty of them. How, asks Solomon Duran, can Christians reproach Jews with unchastity—they, whose holiest men daily commit sins which dare not be mentioned to modest ears, and which have become proverbial as "Monk's sin" (peccato dei frati).

Religious philosophy, which had been raised to

the perfection of a science only by Jewish-Spanish thinkers, had its last cultivators in Spain during this period. The same men who protected Judaism against the onslaughts of Christianity defended it against benighted Jews who wished to banish light, and, like the Dominicans, desired to establish blind faith in the place of reason and judgment. Zealots like Shem Tob Ibn-Shem Tob and others, biased by their narrow Talmudical education, and misled by the Kabbala, saw in scientific inquiry a byroad to heresy. Perceiving that for the most part cultivated Jews succumbed to the proselytizing efforts of Vincent Ferrer and Pope Benedict, men of the stamp of Shem Tob were confirmed in their belief that philosophic culture, nay, reflection on a religious topic, irretrievably lead to apostasy. The logical result of religious impeachment of science was the condemnation of Maimuni and all the Jewish thinkers who had allowed reason to have weight in religious questions. Against this form of bigotry Joseph Albo entered the lists with a complete religio-philosophical work (Ikkarim, "fundamental teachings"), in which he attempted to separate the essential doctrines of Judaism from the non-essential, and to fix the boundary line between belief and heresy.

Joseph Albo (born about 1380, died about 1444), of Monreal, one of the principal representatives of Judaism at the Tortosa disputation, who, probably through the intolerance of Pope Benedict, had emigrated to Soria, was a physician and a pupil of Chasdaï Crescas, hence well acquainted with the physical sciences and the philosophic thought of his time. Although a strict adherent of Talmudical Judaism, he was, like his teacher, not averse to philosophic ideas. Indeed, he tried to reconcile them, without, of course, permitting Judaism to yield a jot to philosophy. Albo had not, however, the profundity of his teacher; as a thinker he was superficial, commonplace, and incapable of writing with logical sequence. On the advice of his friends, he undertook to investigate in how far freedom of inquiry in religious matters was possible within the limits of Judaism. At the same time he wished to fix the number of articles of faith and to decide the question whether the number thirteen adopted by Maimuni was correct, or whether it could be increased or lessened without justly bringing a charge of heresy on him who made the change. Thus originated his religio-philosophical system, the last on Spanish soil. Albo's style differs widely from that of his predecessors. He was a preacher—one of the cleverest and most graceful—and this circumstance exercised marked influence on his method of exposition. It is easy, comprehensible, popular and captivating. Albo has the knack of explaining every philosophic idea by a striking illustration, and of developing it by skillful employment of Bible verses and Agadic aphorisms. What his style thus gained, on the one hand, in intelligibility and popularity, it lost, on the other, through a certain redundancy and shallowness.

It is a remakable fact that Albo, who thought that he was developing his religio-philosophical system exclusively in the native spirit of Judaism, placed at its head a principle of indubitably Christian origin; so powerfully do surroundings affect even those who exert themselves to throw off such influence. The religious philosopher of Soria propounded as his fundamental idea that salvation was the whole aim of man in this life, and that Judaism strongly emphasized this aspect of religion. His teacher, Chasdaï Crescas, and others, had considered man's aim the bliss of the future life, to be found in proximity to the Deity and in the union of the soul with the all-pervading spirit of God. According to Albo highest happiness consists not so much in the exaltation of the soul as in its salvation. That is the nucleus of Albo's religio-philosophical system.

Man attains only after death the perfection for which he is destined by God; for this higher life his mundane existence is but a preparation. How can he best utilize his term of preparation? There are three kinds of institutions for the reclamation of man from barbarism and his advancement to civilization. The first is Natural Law, a sort of social compact to abstain from theft, rapine and homicide; the second is State Legislation, which cares for order and morals; and the third is Philosophical Law, which aims at promoting the enduring happiness of man, or, at least, at removing obstacles in the way of its realization. All these institutions, even when highly developed, are powerless to assist the real welfare of man, the redemption of his soul, his beatitude; for they concern themselves only with actions, with proper conduct, but do nothing to inculcate the views or supply the principles which are to be the mainsprings of action. If the highest aim of man be eternal life or beatitude after death, then there must be a Divine Legislation, without which man in this world must always be groping in darkness and missing his highest destiny. This Divine Legislation must supply all the perfections lacking in its mundane counterpart. It must have for its postulate a perfect God, who both wishes and is able to promote the redemption of man; it must further bear witness to the certainty that this God has revealed an unalterable Law calculated to secure the happiness of man; and finally it must appoint a suitable requital for actions and intentions. Hence this Divine Legislation has three fundamental principles: the Existence of God, the Revelation of His Will, and just Retribution after Death. These are the three pillars on which it rests, and it requires none other.

Judaism, then, according to Albo, is a discipline for eternal salvation. It is "the Divine Legislation" (Dath Elohith), and, as such, comprises many religious laws—613 according to the customary calculation—to enable each individual to promote his own salvation. For even a single religious precept fulfilled with intelligence and devotion, and without mental reservation or ulterior motive, entitles man to salvation. Consequently, the Torah, with its numerous prescriptions, is not intended as a burden for its disciples, nor are the Jews threatened, as Christian teachers maintain, with a curse in the event of their not observing the entire number of commandments. On the contrary, the object is to render easy the path to higher perfection. Therefore, the Agada says that every Israelite has a share in Eternal Life (Olam ha-ba), for each one can obtain this end by the fulfillment of a single religious duty.

Arrived at this point, the religious philosopher of Soria propounds the question whether Judaism can ever be altered as previous dispensations were by the Sinaitic Revelation. This question required specially careful consideration, as Christians always maintained that Christianity was a new revelation, as Judaism had been in its time; that the "New Covenant" took the place of the "Old," and that by the Gospel, the Torah had been fulfilled, *i. e.*, abrogated. Albo had acknowledged the existence of rudimentary revelations previous to that of Sinai, and to avoid being entrapped by the consequences of his own system he put forward a peculiar distinction. That which God had once revealed by His own mouth direct to man was, by virtue of that fact, unalterable and binding for all time; but that which had been communicated only by a prophetic intermediary might suffer change or even annulment. The Ten Commandments which the Israelites had received direct from God, amid the flames of Sinai, were unalterable; in them the three cardinal principles of a divine legislation are laid down. On the other hand, the remaining prescriptions of Judaism, imposed on the people solely through the mediation of Moses, were open to change or even revocation.

But this instability of a portion, perhaps a large portion, of the Jewish religious law was only a theory, propounded simply as a possibility. In practice the obligations of the Torah were to be regarded as binding and unalterable, until it should please God to reveal other laws through the medium of a prophet as great as Moses, and in as open and convincing a manner as on Sinai. Hitherto no prophet had made good his claim so far as to render necessary the rescinding of any portion of Judaism.

Albo's religious system is far from satisfactory. Based upon the Christian doctrine of salvation, it was compelled to regard faith, in a Christian sense, as the chief condition of the soul's redemption, and the ordinances of Judaism as sacraments, similar to baptism or communion, upon which salvation was dependent. Nor is the development of his theory strictly logical. Too often the arts of the preacher take the place of severe reasoning, and for the illustration of his ideas he indulges in prolix sermons in exposition of Biblical and Agadic texts.

A bolder thinker than Albo, but, like him, a preacher, was his junior contemporary, Joseph Ibn-Shem Tob. At one time, when in disgrace with the king of Castile, and leading a wandering life, he held forth every Sabbath to large audiences. He had been well schooled in philosophy. His Kabbalistical, gloomy and fanatical father, who denounced philosophy as a primary source of evil, damned Aristotle to hell, and even accused Maimuni of heterodoxy, must have been scandalized when his son Joseph plunged deep, and with all his heart, into the study of Aristotle and Maimuni. But Joseph did not hesitate to stigmatize the error of his father and of those who thought the employment of philosophic methods opposed to the interests of religion. He, on the contrary, held that they were essential for the attainment of the higher destiny to which all men, especially Israelites, are called. The cultured, philosophical Jew who intelligently discharges all the religious duties of Judaism obviously realizes his high aim much sooner than the Israelite who practices his ceremonial blindly, without wisdom or understanding. Science is also of great value in enabling human intelligence to discriminate error. It is the nature of man's imperfect intellect to foster truth and error side by side; but knowledge teaches how to distinguish between the true and the false. On the other hand, gaps in philosophical teaching are bridged over by the Sinaitic Law. In so far as the latter conceives the happiness of man in the survival of the spirit after the destruction of the body, it is immeasurably the superior of philosophy. Judaism also names the means of attaining eternal happiness —the conscientious fulfillment of religious obligations. On this point, Joseph Shem Tob's view approximates that of Joseph Albo. In his eyes, also, the commandments of Judaism have a sacramental character, but he does not emphasize salvation so much as Albo. Joseph Ibn-Shem Tob went so far, however, as to deny that the objects of the religious laws were knowable, and, to a certain extent, ascribed to them a mystical influence.

None of these writings of the first half of the fifteenth century, philosophical or polemical, was the fruit of leisure and an unfettered spirit. All were stimulated into existence by the urgent necessities of the times, and were put forth to protect the religious and moral treasure-house from pressing danger. In order not to succumb, Judaism was forced simultaneously to strengthen itself from within and ward off attacks from without.

It was, indeed, more than ever necessary for Judaism to arm itself, doubly and trebly; its darkest days were approaching. Again the grim church fiend arose, and the gruesome shadow of its extended wings swept anxiously across Europe. As in the time of Innocent III, so again at this period the church decreed the degradation and proscription of the Jews. The old enactments were solemnly renewed by the official representatives of Christendom, assembled in Œcumenical Council at Basle, where they had declared their infallibility, and even sat in judgment on the papacy. Curious, indeed! The council could not arrange its own concerns, was powerless to bring the mocking Hussites back to the bosom of Mother Church, despaired of putting an end to the dissoluteness and vice of the clergy and monks, yet gave its attention to the Jews to lead them to salvation. Leprous sheep themselves, they sought to save unblemished lambs! The Basle church council, which sat for thirteen years (June, 1431—May, 1443), examining all the great European questions, gave no small share of its attention to the Jews. Their humiliation was necessary for the strengthening of Christian faith—such was the ground on which the council proceeded at its nineteenth sitting (September 7th, 1434), when it resolved to revise the old and devise new restrictions. The canonical decrees prohibiting Christians from holding intercourse with Jews, from rendering them services, and from employing them as physicians, excluding them from offices and dignities, imposing on them a distinctive garb, and ordering them to live in special Jew-quarters, were renewed. A few fresh measures were adopted, new in so far as they had not previously been put forward by the highest ecclesiastical authorities. These provided that Jews should not be admitted to university degrees, that they should be made, if necessary, by force, to attend the delivery of conversionist sermons, and that at the colleges means should be provided for combating Jewish heresy by instruction in Hebrew, Chaldee, and Arabic. Thus the Œcumenical Council, which gave itself out as inspired by the Holy Ghost, designed the conversion of all Jews. It adopted the program of Penyaforte, Pablo Christiani, and Vincent Ferrer, who had counseled systematic application of pressure to induce the Jews to abandon "their infidelity." On the baptized Jews, too, the Basle church council bestowed special attention. They were to be favored, but also carefully watched, lest they marry Jews, keep the Sabbath and Jewish feasts, bury their dead according to Jewish rites, or, in fact, follow any Jewish observances.

A fanatical paroxysm broke out afresh in various towns of Europe, commencing in the island of Majorca. The remnant of the congregation of Palma was hated alike by the priests and the mob, and both gave a willing ear to the rumor that the Jews, during Holy Week, had crucified the Moorish servant of a Jew, and put him to the torture. The reputed martyr was still living, but, nevertheless, Bishop Gil-Nunjoz caused two Jews to be imprisoned as ringleaders. Thereupon arose a contest between the bishop and the governor, Juan Desfar, the latter maintaining that as the Jews were the property of the king, he alone could condemn them. The bishop was obliged to hand over the Jews, who were locked up in the governor's jail. The priests, however, incited the mob against the governor and the Jews, and before Juan Desfar could arrange for a hearing, the people were prepossessed against him. A court composed chiefly of Dominicans and Franciscans was called together, and employed the rack as the most effectual means of obtaining the truth from the witnesses. One of the accused put to the torture acknowledged all that was desired, and pointed out any Jews who happened to be mentioned as his accomplices. An unprincipled Jew named Astruc Sibili, who lived in strife with many members of the community, and feared to be involved in the blood accusation, came forward as the denouncer of his co-religionists. Apparently of his own accord Astruc Sibili acknowledged that the servant had been crucified, and pointed out several Jews as the murderers. Although he kept himself clear from all complicity in the matter, Astruc Sibili was soon punished for his denunciations—he was thrown into prison as an accomplice. The fate of the informer and the flight of several Jewish families, justly fearing a repetition of massacres, from Palma to a mountain in the vicinity, excited the Christian inhabitants yet more. The fugitives were pursued, placed in fetters, and brought back to the city, their flight being considered a proof of the guilt of the entire community. Astruc Sibili and three others were condemned to be burnt at the stake, but their punishment was commuted to death by hanging, on condition that they be baptized. To this they agreed, considering baptism the last straw by which their lives might be saved. The whole community, men, women and children, two hundred in all, went over to Christianity to escape a horrible death. The priests had ample employment in baptizing the converts. How little they believed in the imputed crime of the condemned was shown when, the gallows being reached, the priests, encouraging the mob to do the same, demanded the pardon of the condemned. The governor yielded to the voice of the people, and by a procession and amid singing they were escorted to the church, where a *Te Deum* was chanted. Thus ended the community of Majorca, which had lasted over a thousand years, and had greatly contributed to the well-being of the island. With it disappeared the prosperity of this fruitful and favored island. Simon Duran, deeply grieved at the secession of the community of Palma, which he had lovingly cherished, silenced his conscience with the thought that he had not been remiss in exhortation.

CHAPTER VIII.

CAPISTRANO AND HIS PERSECUTION OF THE JEWS.

Pope Eugenius IV, under the Influence of Alfonso de Cartagena, changes his Attitude towards the Jews—His Bull against the Spanish and Italian Jews in 1442—Don Juan II defends the Jews—Pope Nicholas V's Hostility—Louis of Bavaria—The Philosopher Nicholas of Cusa and his Relation to Judaism—John of Capistrano—His Influence with the People is turned against the Jews—Capistrano in Bavaria and Würzburg—Expulsion of the Breslau Community—Expulsion of the Jews from Brünn and Olmütz—The Jews of Poland under Casimir IV—Capture of Constantinople by Mahomet II—The Jews find an Asylum in Turkey—The Karaites—Moses Kapsali—Isaac Zarfati—Position of the Jews of Spain—Persecutions directed by Alfonso de Spina—The Condition of the Marranos.

1442—1474 C.E.

About the middle of the fifteenth century, venomous hatred of Jews, become characteristic of Spain and Germany, began to increase, and at the end of that century reached its highest development. In Spain it was stimulated principally by envy of the influential positions still enjoyed by Jews in spite of misfortune and humiliation; in Germany, on the contrary, where the Jews moved like shadows, it arose from vague race-antipathy, of which religious differences formed only one aspect. An unfortunate event for the German communities was the death of Emperor Sigismund (towards the end of 1437) at the moment when the council of Basle was casting a threatening glance in their direction. This prince was not a reliable protector of the Jews. Often enough he bled them to relieve his ever-recurring pecuniary embarrassments, and he even charged them with the expenses of the council of Constance. But so far as lay in his power he set his face against the bloody persecutions of his Hebrew subjects. He was succeeded as German king and emperor by the Austrian Archduke Albert, who had already distinguished himself by inhumanity towards Jews. Albert II was a deadly enemy of Jews and heretics. He could not exterminate either, for the Hussites had courage and arms, and the Jews were an indispensable source of money; but whenever it was sought to injure them he gladly assisted. When the town council of Augsburg decided to expel the Jewish community (1439), the emperor joyfully gave his consent. Two years were granted them to dispose of their houses and immovables; at the end of that time they were one and all exiled, and the grave-stones in the Jewish cemetery used to repair the city walls. Fortunately for the Jews, Albert reigned only two years, and the rule of the Holy Roman Empire, or rather the anarchy by which it was convulsed, devolved on the good-natured, weak, indolent, and tractable Frederick III. As a set off, two fanatical Jew-haters now arose—Pope Eugenius IV and the Franciscan, John of Capistrano, a cut-throat in the guise of a lowly servant of God.

Eugenius, whom the council of Basle had degraded step by step, depriving him of his dignities and electing another pope in his place, ultimately triumphed through the treachery of some of the principal members of the council and the helplessness of the German princes, and was again enabled to befool the Christian nations. Eugenius, though of narrow, monkish views, was at first not unfavorably disposed towards the Jews. At the beginning of his pontificate, he confirmed the privileges granted Jews by his predecessor, Martin V, promised them his protection, and forbade their forcible baptism. But he was soon influenced in an opposite direction, and developed extraordinary zeal in degrading the Jews and withdrawing all protection from them. The prime mover in this conversion seems to have been Alfonso de Cartagena, a son of the apostate Paul de Santa

Maria. Appointed bishop of Burgos on the death of his father, Alfonso warmly espoused the cause of Pope Eugenius at the council of Basle, and hence rose high in the favor of the pontiff. He alone could have been the author of the complaints against the pride and arrogance of the Castilian Jews which induced the pope to issue the bull of 1442. This document was addressed to the bishops of Castile and Leon (10th August, 1442), and was to the effect that it had come to the knowledge of his Holiness that the Jews abuse the privileges granted them by former popes, blaspheming and transgressing to the vexation of the faithful and the dishonor of the true faith. He felt himself compelled, therefore, to withdraw the indulgences granted by his predecessors—Martin and other popes—and to declare them null and void. At the same time Eugenius repeated the canonical restrictions in a severer form. Thus, he decreed that Christians should not eat, drink, bathe, or live with Jews (or Mahometans), nor use medicines of any kind purveyed by them. Jews (and Mahometans) should not be eligible for any office or dignity, and should be incompetent to inherit property from Christians. They were to build no more synagogues, and, in repairing the old, were to avoid all ornamentation. They were to seclude themselves from the public eye during Passion Week, to the extent even of keeping their doors and windows closed. The testimony of Jews (and Mahometans) against Christians was declared invalid. Eugenius' bull emphatically enjoined that no Christian should stand in any relation of servitude to a Jew, and should not even kindle a fire for him on the Sabbath; that Jews should be distinguished from Christians by a peculiar costume, and reside in special quarters. Furthermore, every blasphemous utterance by a Jew about Jesus, the "Mother of God," or the saints, was to be severely punished by the civil tribunals. This bull was ordered to be made known throughout the land, and put in force thirty days later. Heavy penalties were to be exacted for offenses under it. If the culprit was a Christian, he was to be placed under the ban of the church, and neither king nor queen was to be exempt; if a Jew, then the whole of his fortune, personal and real, was to be confiscated by the bishop of the diocese, and applied to the purposes of the church. By means of circular letters, Eugenius exhorted the Castilian ecclesiastics to enforce the restrictions without mercy. He dared not be outdone in Jew-hatred by the council of Basle. At about the same time, or perhaps earlier, Eugenius issued a bull of forty-two articles against the Italian Jewish communities, in which, among other things, he ordered that, under pain of confiscation of property, Jews should not read Talmudic literature.

The papal bull for Castile was proclaimed in many of the towns, as it would appear, without the consent of the king, Juan II. The fanatics had won the day; all their wishes were fulfilled. The misguided people at once considered Jews and Mahometans outlawed, and proceeded to make violent attacks on their persons and property. Pious Christians interpreted the papal ordinances to mean that they were not to continue commercial relations of any kind with the Jews. Christian shepherds forthwith abandoned the flocks and herds committed to their charge by Jews and Mahometans, and plowmen turned their backs upon the fields. The union of towns (Hermandad) framed new statutes for the more complete oppression of the proscribed of the church. In consternation the Jews appealed to the king of Castile. Their complaints had all the more effect upon him as their damage meant damage to the royal exchequer. Accordingly, Juan II, or rather his favorite, Alvaro de Luna, issued a counter decree (April 6th, 1443). He expressed his indignation at the shamelessness which made the papal bull an excuse for assaults on the Jews and Mahometans. Canonical, royal and imperial law agreed in permitting them to live undisturbed and unmolested among Christians. The bull of Pope Eugenius placed Jews and Mahometans under certain specific restrictions; but it did not follow that they might be robbed, injured or maltreated, that they might not engage in trade or industry, nor work as weavers, goldsmiths, carpenters, barbers, shoemakers, tailors, millers, coppersmiths, saddlers, rope-makers, potters, cartwrights or basket-makers, or that Christians might not serve them in these pursuits. Such service involved neither relaxation of Christian authority nor dangerous intimacy with Jews. Nor did it appear that the avocations mentioned conferred any of that prestige which solely the bull was designed to deny to Jews.

Christians should certainly abstain from the medicines of Jewish or Moorish physicians, unless compounded by Christian hands; but this did not mean that skillful doctors of the Jewish or the Mahometan faith should not be consulted, or their medicines not used, when no Christian physician was available. Juan II imposed upon the magistracy the duty of safeguarding the Jews and Mahometans, as objects of his special protection, and instructed them to punish Christian offenders with imprisonment and confiscation of goods. He furthermore ordered that his pleasure be made known throughout the land by public criers, in the presence of a notary.

Whether this sophistical decree was of any real use to the Jews is doubtful. Don Juan II had not much authority in his kingdom, and was obliged to make frequent concessions to hostile parties, with whom his own son occasionally made common cause. The Castilian Jews were consequently abandoned to the arbitrary authority of the local magistrates during the remainder of the reign of this well-meaning but weak monarch, and were obliged to come to terms with them whenever protection was required against violence or false accusations. Did any misfortune threaten a Jew, then the tailor would fly to his princely patron, or the goldsmith to a grandee of high position, and seek to avert it by supplications or gold. It was truly no enviable situation in which the Jews found themselves.

Eugenius' successor, Pope Nicholas V (March, 1447—March, 1455), continued the system of degrading and oppressing the Jews. As soon as he ascended the throne of St. Peter he devoted himself to abolishing the privileges of the Italian Jews, which Martin V had confirmed and Eugenius had not formally revoked, and subjecting them to exceptional laws. In a bull, dated June 23d, 1447, he repeated for Italy the restrictions which his predecessor had formulated for Castile, re-enacting them in the fullest detail, not even omitting the prohibition against the lighting of fires for Jews on the Sabbath. But though Nicholas' bull was only a copy, it had much more real force than the original; for its execution was confided to the pitiless Jew-hater and heretic-hunter, John of Capistrano. On him devolved the duty of seeing, either in person or through his brother Franciscans, that the provisions of the bull were literally obeyed, and infractions strictly punished. If, for example, a Jewish physician provided a suffering Christian with the means of regaining health, Capistrano was authorized to confiscate the whole of the offender's fortune and property. And the saintly monk, with heart of stone, was just the man to visit such a transgression with unrelenting severity.

The Jew-hatred of the council of Basle and the popes spread like a contagion over a wide area. The fierce and bigoted Bavarian Duke of Landshut, Louis the Rich—"a hunter of game and Jews"—had all the Jews of his country arrested on one day (Monday, October 5th, 1450), shortly after his accession to power. The men were thrown into prison, the women shut up in the synagogues, and their property and jewelry confiscated. Christian debtors were directed not to pay their Jewish creditors more than the capital they had originally borrowed, and to deduct from that the interest already paid. After four weeks of incarceration the unhappy Jews were obliged to purchase their lives from the turbulent duke for 30,000 gulden, and then, penniless and almost naked, they were turned out of the country. Gladly would Louis have meted out the same treatment to the large and rich community of Ratisbon, which was within his jurisdiction. As, however, his authority was recognized only to a limited extent, and as the Jews of the city were under the protection of the council and its privileges, he was obliged to content himself with levying contributions. Many Jews are said to have been driven by anxiety and want into embracing Christianity.

As the rest of the European Jews regarded their Spanish brethren as an exalted and favored class, so the papacy directed special attention to them in order to put an end to their favorable position in the state. Either on the proposition of the king to modify the severe canonical restrictions against Jews, or on the petition of their enemies to confirm them, Pope Nicholas V issued a new bull (March 1st, 1451). He confirmed the old exclusions from Christian society and all honorable walks of life, and entirely abolished the privileges of the Spanish and the Italian Jews.

The unpitying harshness of canonical legislation against the children of Israel was unconsciously based on fear. All-powerful Christianity dreaded the influence which the Jewish mind might exert on the Christian population in too familiar intercourse. What the papacy concealed in the incense-clouds of its official decrees was disclosed by a philosophical writer and cardinal standing in close relation with the papal court. Nicholas de Cusa (from Cues on the Moselle), the last devotee of scholasticism, into which he tried to introduce mystic elements, enthusiastically advocated, in the face of the dissensions of Christendom, a union of all religions in one creed. The church ceremonies he was prepared to sacrifice, nay, he was ready to accept circumcision, if, by such means, non-Christians could be won over to the belief in the Trinity. He feared, as he distinctly said, the stiffneckedness of the Jews, who cling so stubbornly to their monotheism ; but he consoled himself with the reflection that an unarmed handful could not disturb the peace of the world. It is true, the Jews were unarmed ; but, mentally, they were still powerful, and Nicholas resolved to devote himself to the task of depriving them of intellectual strength. The pope had appointed him legate for Germany, where he was to reform church and cloister (1450—1451). But the cardinal also occupied himself with the Jewish question. At the provincial council of Bamberg he put into force the canonical statute concerning Jew badges, which provided that men should wear round pieces of red cloth on their breasts, and women blue stripes on their head-dresses—as if the branding of Jews could heal the dissolute clergy and their demoralized flocks of their uncleanness. The only result of the isolation of the Jews was their protection from the taint of prevailing immorality. The cardinal was not successful in purifying the clergy, or in putting an end to the fraud of bleeding hosts and miracle-working images, against which he had exclaimed so loudly. The church remained corrupt to the core. There would have been abundant cause to fear the Jews, if they had been permitted to probe the suppurating wounds.

Especially troublesome to the church were the thousands of baptized Jews in Spain, who had been driven into its fold by the massacres, pulpit denunciations, and legal restrictions to which their race was exposed. Not only the lay new-Christians, but also those who had taken orders or had assumed the monk's garb, continued to observe, more or less openly, the Jewish religious laws. The sophistry of the converts, Paul de Santa Maria and Geronimo de Santa Fé, regarding the testimony in the Old Testament and the Talmudic Agada to the Messiahship of Jesus, the Incarnation of God, the Trinity and other church dogmas, impressed the Marranos but little. In spite of baptism, they remained stiff-necked and blind, *i. e.*, true to the faith of their fathers. Don Juan of Castile, at the instigation of his favorite, Alvaro de Luna, who was anxious to strike at his arch-enemies, the new-Christians, complained to Pope Nicholas V of the relapses of the Marranos, and the pontiff knew of no remedy but force. He addressed rescripts to the bishop of Osma and the vicar of Salamanca (November 20th, 1451), empowering them to appoint inquisitors to inquire judicially into cases of new-Christians suspected of Judaizing. The inquisitors were authorized to punish the convicted, imprison them, confiscate their goods and disgrace them, to degrade even priests, and hand them over to the secular arm—a church euphemism for condemning them to the heretic's stake. This was the first spark of the hell-fire of the Inquisition, which perpetrated more inhumanity than all the tyrants and malefactors branded by history. At first this bull seems to have been ineffectual. The times were not ripe for the bloody institution. Besides, the Christians themselves helped to keep up the connection of the baptized Jews with their brethren in race. They denied equal rights to new-Christians of Jewish or Mahometan origin, and wished to exclude them from all posts of honor. Against this antipathy, inherent in the diversity of national elements, the pope was compelled to issue a bull (November 29th, 1451), but it was powerless to uproot the prejudice. It could be removed only by higher culture, not at the dictation of a church chief, even though he boasted of infallibility.

How absurd, then, to continue driving such proselytes into the church! Yet this was done by the Franciscan monk, John of Capistrano (of Neapolitan origin), who is responsible for immense injury to the Jews of many lands. This mendicant friar, of gaunt figure and ill-favored appearance, possessed a winning voice and an iron will, which enabled him to obtain unbounded influence, not only over the stupid populace, but also over the cultivated classes. With a word he could fascinate, inspire, or terrify, persuade to piety or incite to cruelty. Like the Spanish Dominican, Vincent Ferrer, the secret of Capistrano's power lay not so much in his captivating eloquence as in the sympathetic modulations of his voice and the unshakable enthusiasm with which he clung to his mistaken convictions. He himself firmly believed that, with the blood he had gathered from the nose of his master, Bernard of Sienna, and his *capuche*, he could cure the sick, awake the dead and perform all kinds of miracles, and the misguided people not only believed but exaggerated his professions. His strictly ascetic life, his hatred of good living, luxury and debauchery, made an impression the deeper from its striking contrast to the sensuality and dissoluteness of the great bulk of the clergy and monks. Wherever Capistrano appeared, the people thronged by thousands to hear him, to be edified and agitated, even though they did not understand a syllable of his Latin addresses. The astute popes, Eugenius IV and Nicholas V, recognized in him a serviceable instrument for the restoration of the tottering authority of St. Peter. They rejoiced in his homilies on the infallibility of the papacy and his fiery harangues on the extermination of heretics, and the necessity of withstanding the victoriously advancing Turks. They offered no objection if, at the same time, he thought proper to vent his monkish gall upon harmless amusements, pastimes and the elegancies of life, seeing that they themselves were not disturbed in their enjoyments and pleasures. Among the standing themes of Capistrano's exciting discourses—second only to his rancor against heretics and Turks, and his tirades against luxury and sports—were his denunciations of the impieties and the usury of Jews. This procured his appointment by Pope Nicholas to the post of inquisitor of the Jews, his duty being to superintend the enforcement of the canonical restrictions against them. He had in Naples occupied the position of inquisitorial judge for the Jews, on the nomination of Queen Joanna, who had empowered him to punish with the severest penalties any failure to observe the ecclesiastical law or wear the Jew badge.

When this infuriate Capuchin visited Germany, he spread terror and dismay among the Jews. They trembled at the mention of his name. In Bavaria, Silesia, Moravia, and Austria, the bigotry of the Catholics, already at a high pitch on account of the Hussite schism, was further stirred by Capistrano, and, the Bohemian heretics being beyond its reach, it vented itself upon Jews. The Bavarian dukes, Louis and Albert, who had on one occasion before driven the Jews out of their territories, were made still more fanatical by Capistrano. The former demanded of certain counts, and of the city of Ratisbon, that they expel the Jews. The burgomaster and town council, however, refused, and would not withdraw the protection and the rights of citizenship which the Jews had enjoyed from an early period. But they could not shield them from the hostility of the clergy. Eventually even the Ratisbon burghers, despite their good will for their Jewish fellow-citizens, fell under the influence of Capistrano's fanaticism, and allowed themselves to be incited to acts of unfriendliness. In the midwife regulations, promulgated during the same year, occurs a clause prohibiting Christian midwives from attending Jewish women, even in cases where the lives of the patients were at stake.

The change of public feeling in respect to the Jews, brought about by Capistrano, is strikingly illustrated by the conduct of one eminent ecclesiastic before and after the appearance of the Capuchin in Germany. Bishop Godfrey, of Würzburg, reigning duke of Franconia, shortly after his accession to the government of the duchy, had granted the fullest privileges to the Jews. More favorable treatment they could not have desired. For himself and his successors he promised special protection to all within his dominions, both to those settled and those who might settle there later. They were to be freed from the authority of the ordinary tribunals, lay and ecclesiastical, and to have their disputes inquired into and adjudicated by their own courts. Their rabbi (Hochmeister) was to be exempt from taxes, and to be allowed to receive pupils in his *Yeshiba* at his discretion. Their movements were to be unrestricted, and those who might desire to change their place of residence were to be assisted to collect their debts, and provided with safe-conduct on their journeys. It was further promised that these privileges should never be modified or revoked, and the dean and chapter unanimously recognized and guaranteed them "for themselves and their successors in the chapter." Every Jew who took up his abode within Bishop Godfrey's jurisdiction was provided with special letters of protection. But after Capistrano had begun his agitation, how different the attitude towards Jews! We soon find the same bishop and duke of Franconia issuing, "on account of the grievous complaints against the Jews in his diocese," a statute and ordinance (1453) decreeing their banishment. They were allowed until the 18th January of the following year to sell their immovables, and within fourteen days after that date, they were to leave, for "he (the bishop) would no longer tolerate Jews in his diocese." The towns, barons, lords, and justices were enjoined to expel the Jews from their several jurisdictions, and Jewish creditors were deprived of a portion of the debts owing to them. When Jews were concerned, inhuman fanaticism could beguile a noble-hearted prince of the church and an entire chapter of ecclesiastics into a flagrant breach of faith.

Capistrano's influence was most mischievous for the Jews of Silesia. Here he showed himself in truth to be the "Scourge of the Jews," as his admirers called him. The two chief communities in this province, which belonged half to Poland and half to Bohemia, were at Breslau and Schweidnitz, and the Jews composing them, not being permitted to possess real property, and being, besides, largely engaged in the money traffic, had considerable amounts of money at their command. The majority of the nobles were among their debtors, and several towns were either themselves debtors or had become security for their princes. Hence it is not unlikely that some debtors of rank secretly planned to evade their liabilities by ridding themselves of the Jews. At any rate the advent of the fanatical Franciscan afforded an opportunity for carrying out such a design.

Capistrano came to the Silesian capital on the invitation of the bishop of Breslau, Peter Novak, who found himself unable to control his subordinate ecclesiastics. Summoning the clergy to his presence, the Franciscan preacher upbraided them for their sinful, immoral, and sensual lives. The doors of the church in which the interview took place were securely bolted, so that no lay ear might learn the full extent of the depravity of the ministers of the

Gospel. But nearer to his heart than the reclamation of the clergy was the extermination of the Hussites, of whom there were many in Silesia, and the persecution of the Jews. The frenzied fanaticism with which Capistrano's harangues inspired the people of Breslau directed itself principally against the Jews. A report was spread that a Jew named Meyer, one of the wealthiest of the Breslau Israelites, in whose safe-keeping were many of the bonds of the burghers and nobles, had purchased a host from a peasant, had stabbed and blasphemed it, and then distributed its fragments among the communities of Schweidnitz, Liegnitz, and others for further desecration. It need hardly be said that the wounded host was alleged to have shed blood. This imbecile fiction soon reached the ears of the municipal authorities, with whom it found ready credence. Forthwith all the Jews of Breslau, men, women and childen, were thrown into prison, their entire property in the "Judengasse" seized, and, what was most important to the authors of the catastrophe, the bonds of their debtors, worth about 25,000 Hungarian gold florins, confiscated (2d May, 1453). The guilt of the Jews was rendered more credible by the flight of a few of them, who were, however, soon taken. Capistrano assumed the direction of the inquiry into this important affair. As inquisitor, the leading voice in the prosecution of blasphemers of the consecrated wafer by right belonged to him. He ordered a few Jews to be stretched on the rack, and personally instructed the torturers in their task—he had experience in such work. The tortured Israelites confessed. Meantime another infamous lie was circulated. A wicked baptized Jewess declared that the Breslau Jews had once before burnt a host, and that, on another occasion, they had kidnaped a Christian boy, fattened him, and put him into a cask studded with sharp nails, which they rolled about until their victim gave up the ghost. His blood had been distributed among the Silesian communities. Even the bones of the murdered child were alleged to have been found. The guilt of the Jews appeared established in these various cases, and a large number, in all 318 persons, were arrested in different localities, and brought to Breslau. Capistrano sat in judgment upon them, and hurried them to execution. At the Salzring—now Blücherplatz—where Capistrano resided, forty-one convicted Jews were burnt on one day (2d June, 1453). The rabbi (Phineas?) hanged himself; he had also counseled others to take their own lives. The remainder were banished from Breslau, all their children under seven years of age having previously been taken from them by force, baptized, and given to Christians to be brought up. This was Capistrano's wish, and in a learned treatise he explained to King Ladislaus that it was in consonance with the Christian religion and orthodoxy. The honest town clerk, Eschenloer, who did not venture to protest aloud against these barbarities, wrote in his diary, "Whether this is godly or not, I leave to the judgment of the ministers of religion." The ministers of religion had transformed themselves into savages. The goods of the burnt and banished Jews were, of course, seized, and with their proceeds the Bernardine church was built. It was not the only church erected with bloody money. In the remaining Silesian towns the Jews fared no better. Some were burnt, and the rest chased away, stripped almost to the skin.

When the young king, Ladislaus, was petitioned by the Breslau town council to decree that from that time forward no Jew would be allowed to settle in Breslau, not only did he assent "for the glory of God and the honor of the Christian faith," but he added, in approval of the outrages committed, "that they (the Silesian Jews) had suffered according to their deserts," a remark worthy of the son of Albert II, who had burnt the Austrian Jews. The same monarch also sanctioned—doubtless at the instigation of Capistrano, who passed several months at Olmütz—the expulsion of the Jews from the latter place and from Brünn.

The echoes of Capistrano's venomous eloquence reached even Poland, disturbing the Jewish communities there from the tranquillity they had enjoyed for centuries. Poland had long been a refuge for hunted and persecuted Jews. Exiles from Germany, Austria and Hungary found a ready welcome on the Vistula. The privileges generously granted them by Duke Boleslav, and renewed and confirmed by King Casimir the Great, were still in force. The Jews were, in fact, even more indispensable in that country than in other parts of Christian Europe; for in Poland there were only two classes, nobles and serfs, and the Jews supplied the place of the middle class, providing merchandise and money, and bringing the dead capital of the country into circulation. During a visit which Casimir IV paid to Posen shortly after his accession, a fire broke out in this already important city, and, with the exception of its few brick houses, it was totally destroyed. In this conflagration, the original document of the privileges granted the Jews a century before by Casimir the Great perished. Jewish deputations from a number of Polish communities waited upon the king, lamenting the loss of these records, so important to them, and praying that new ones might be prepared according to existing copies, and that all their old rights might be renewed and confirmed. Casimir did not require much persuasion. In order that they might live in security and contentment under his happy reign, he granted them privileges such as they had never before enjoyed in any European state (14th August, 1447). This king was in no respect a slave of the church. So strictly did he keep the clergy within bounds that they charged him with persecuting and robbing them. He forbade their meddling in affairs of state, saying that in such matters he preferred to rely on his own powers.

Either the king was misled by a false copy of the original charters, or he desired to avail himself of the opportunity of enlarging their scope without appearing to make fresh concessions ; at all events, the privileges accorded under the new statute were, in many respects, more considerable than those formerly enjoyed by the Jews. Not alone did it permit unrestricted trading and residence all over the then very extensive kingdom of Poland, but it annulled canonical laws often laid down by the popes, and only recently re-enacted by the general church council of Basle. Casimir's charter mentioned that Jews and Christians might bathe together, and in all respects enjoy free intercourse with each other. It emphatically decreed that no Christian could summon a Jew before an ecclesiastical tribunal, and that if a Jew was so summoned, he need not appear. The palatines in their several provinces were enjoined to see that the Jews were not molested by the clergy, and generally to extend to them powerful protection. Furthermore, no Jew might be accused of using Christian blood in the Passover ceremonies, or of desecrating hosts, "Jews being innocent of such offenses, which are repudiated by their religion." If a Christian charged an individual Jew with using Christian blood, his accusation had to be supported by native, trustworthy Jewish witnesses and four similarly qualified Christian witnesses, and then the accused was to suffer for his crime, and his co-religionists were not to be dragged into it. In the event, however, of the Christian accuser not being in a position to substantiate his charge by credible testimony, he was to be punished with death. This was a check on ever-recurring calumny with its train of massacres of Jews. Casimir also recognized the judicial autonomy of the Jewish community. In criminal cases between Jews, or between Jews and Christians, the ordinary tribunals were not to interfere, but the palatine, or his representative, assisted by Jews, was to adjudicate. In minor law-suits the decision was to rest with the Jewish elders (rabbis), who were permitted to inflict a fine of six marks in cases where their summonses were not obeyed. To keep the authority of the Jewish courts within reasonable bounds, Casimir's charter enacted that the ban should be pronounced on a Jew only with the concurrence of the entire community. Truly, in no part of Christian Europe were the Jews possessed of such important privileges. They were renewed and issued by the king with the assent of the Polish magnates. Also the Karaite communities of Troki, Luzk, etc., received from Casimir a renewal and confirmation of the privileges granted them by the Lithuanian Duke Witold in the thirteenth century.

The clergy looked with jealous eyes on this complaisance to the Jews, and zealously worked to induce the king to change his friendly attitude. At the head of the Polish priesthood thus hostile to the Jews stood the influential bishop and cardinal of Cracow, Zbigniev Olesnicki. The protection accorded the Jews and Hussites by the king was to him a source of deep chagrin, and, to give effective vent to his feelings, he sent in hot haste for the heretic-hunter Capistrano. Capistrano entered Cracow in triumph, and was received by the king and the clergy like a divine being. During the whole of his stay in Cracow (August 28th, 1453, to May, 1454), aided by Bishop Zbigniev, he stirred up King Casimir against the Hussite heretics and the Jews. He publicly remonstrated with him on the subject, threatening him with hell-fire and an unsuccessful issue to his war with the Prussian order of knights, if he did not abolish the privileges enjoyed by Jews, and abandon the Hussite heretics to the church. It was easy to predict a defeat at the hands of the Prussian knights, seeing that the pope and the whole of the Polish church were secretly assisting them against Casimir.

Therefore, when the Teutonic knights, in aid of their Prussian allies, took the field against Poland, and the Polish army, with King Casimir at its head, was ignominiously put to flight (September, 1454), the game of the clerical party was won. They spread the rumor that the disaster to Poland was a consequence of the king's favor to Jews and heretics. To retrieve his fallen fortunes, and to undertake a vigorous campaign against the Prussians, Casimir needed the assistance of Bishop Zbigniev, and the latter was in a position to make his own terms. The Jews were sacrificed—the king was compelled to give them up. In November, 1454, Casimir revoked all the privileges he had granted the Jews, on the ground that "infidels may not enjoy preference over the worshipers of Christ, and servants may not be better treated than sons." By public criers the king's resolve was made known throughout the land. Besides, Casimir ordered that the Jews of Poland wear a special costume to distinguish them from Christians. Capistrano was victorious all along the line. Through him the Jews were abased even in the land where they had been most exalted. The results of this misfortune were not long in showing themselves. The Jewish communities mournfully wrote to their brethren in Germany, "that 'the monk' had brought grievous trouble," even to those who lived under the scepter of the king of Poland, whose lot had formerly been so happy that they had been able to offer a refuge to the persecuted of other lands. They had not believed that an enemy could reach them across the Polish frontier; and now they had to groan under the oppression of the king and the magnates.

Meanwhile, heavy but deserved judgment descended on Christendom. After an existence of more than a thousand years the sin-laden Byzantine empire, which had stood its ground for centuries in spite of its rottenness, had at length collapsed with the fall of Constantinople (May 29th, 1453). The Turkish conqueror, Mahomet II, had given New Rome over to slavery, spoliation, massacre, and every horror and outrage, yet had, by no means, requited the wrongs she had inflicted on others and herself. From Constantine, the founder of the Byzantine empire, who placed a blood-stained sword in the hands of the church, to the last of the emperors, Constantine Dragosses, of the Palæologus family, everyone in the long series of rulers (with the exception of the apostate Julian) was more or less inspired by falsehood and treachery, and an arrogant, hypocritical, persecuting spirit. And the people, as well as the servants of state and church, were worthy of their rulers. From them the German, Latin and Slavonic peoples had derived the principle that the Jews ought to be degraded by exceptional laws, or even exterminated. Now, however, Byzantium itself lay shattered in the dust, and wild barbarians were raising the new Turkish empire on its site. Heavy vengeance had been exacted. Mahomet II, the conqueror of Constantinople, threw a threatening glance at the remainder of Europe, the countries of the Latin Church. The whole of Christendom was in danger ; yet the Christian rulers and nations were unable to organize an effective resistance against the Turkish conquerors. The perfidy and corruption of the papacy now bore bitter fruit. When the faithless pope, Nicholas V, called upon Christendom to undertake a crusade against the Turks, his legates at the diet of Ratisbon were compelled to listen to unsparing denunciation of his corruption. Neither the pope nor the emperor, they were told, had any real thought of undertaking a war against the Turks; their sole idea was to squander upon themselves the money they might collect. When the Turks made preparations to invade Hungary, and threatened to carry the victorious crescent from the right to the left side of the Danube, Capistrano preached himself hoarse to kindle enthusiasm for a new crusade. His tirades had ceased to draw. Their only effect was to assemble a ragged mob of students, peasants, mendicant friars, half-starved adventurers and romantic fanatics. The ghost of mediævalism vanished before the dawn of a new day.

It seems almost providential that, at a moment when the persecutions in Europe were increasing in number and virulence, the new Turkish empire should have arisen to offer an hospitable asylum to the hunted Jews. When, three days after the chastisement which he inflicted on Constantinople, the sultan, Mahomet II, proclaimed that all the fugitive inhabitants might return to their homes and estates without fear of molestation, he gave a benevolent thought to the Jews. He permitted them to settle freely in Constantinople and other towns, allotted them special dwelling-places, and allowed them to erect synagogues and schools. Soon after his capture of Constantinople, he ordered the election of a Greek patriarch, whom he invested with a certain political authority over all the Greeks in his new dominions, and also nominated a chief rabbi to preside over the Hebrew communities. This was a pious, learned, upright Israelite, named Moses Kapsali. Mahomet even summoned this rabbi to the divan, and singled him out for special distinction, giving him a seat next to the mufti, the Chief Ulema of the Mahometans, and precedence over the patriarch. Moses Kapsali (born about 1420, died about 1495), also received from the sultan a kind of political suzerainty over the Jewish communities in Turkey. The taxes imposed upon the Jews he had to apportion among communities and individuals; he had to superintend their collection and to pay them into the sultan's exchequer. He was furthermore empowered to inflict punishment on his co-religionists, and no rabbi could hold office without his sanction. In short, he was the chief and the official representative of a completely organized Jewish communal system.

This favorable situation of the Jews had a stimulating effect on the degenerate Karaites, who migrated in considerable numbers from Asia, the Crimea and southern Poland, to take up their abode with their more happily placed brethren in Constantinople and Adrianople. The Karaites, whose fundamental principle is the study and reasonable interpretation of the Bible, were in so lamentable a state of ignorance, that their entire religious structure had become a system of authorized dogmas and traditions more rigid even than that of the Rabbanites. The extent of their intellectual decline may be measured by the fact that in the course of a century they failed to produce a single moderately original theological writer. Those with a bent for study were compelled to sit at the feet of Rabbanite teachers and receive from them instruction in the Scriptures and the Talmud. The proud masters of Bible exegesis had become the humble disciples of the once despised Rabbanites. The petrifaction of Karaism is illustrated by an event in European Turkey. A Karaite college, consisting of Menachem Bashyasi, his son Moses Bashyasi, Menachem Maroli, Michael the Old, his son Joseph, and a few others, had permitted the lights necessary for the Sabbath eve to be prepared on Friday, so that the holy day need not be spent in darkness. The college gave adequate reasons for the innovation. According to a Karaite principle, not only an ecclesiastical authority, but any individual is justified in abolishing an ancient custom, or annulling former decisions, if he can cite sufficient exegetical authority. Nevertheless, stormy opposition arose (about 1460) against this decision, aimed at a custom derived, perhaps, from Anan, the founder of Karaism, and hence possessing the sacredness conferred by the rust of seven centuries. Schism and friction were the result. The section of the community which ventured to prepare the lights required for the Sabbath eve was abused, and charged with heresy. Moreover, the schism relating to the commencement of the festivals was still unhealed. The Palestinian Karaite communities and their neighbors continued to distinguish between an ordinary and a leap year by the state of the barley harvest, and to regulate their festivals by the appearance of the new moon. On the other hand, the communities in Turkey, the Crimea, and southern Poland, used the calendar of the Rabbanites. These hereditary differences were eating more and more into the solidarity of the sect, for there was no means of composing them, and agreeing upon uniform principles.

The conspicuous decrepitude of Karaism and the ignorance of its followers afforded the Rabbanites in the Turkish empire an opportunity for reconciling them to Talmudic Judaism, or, at least, overcoming their bitter hostility towards it. Rabbanite teachers, Enoch Saporta, an immigrant from Catalonia, Eliezer Kapsali, from Greece, and Elias Halevi, from Germany, stipulated that their Karaite pupils, whom they instructed in the Talmud, should thenceforward abstain, in writing and in speech, from reviling Talmudic authorities, and from desecrating the festivals of the Rabbanite calendar. In the difficult position in which studiously inclined Karaites found themselves, they could not do otherwise than give this promise. The Turkish chief rabbi, Moses Kapsali, was of opinion that, as the Karaites rejected the Talmud, they might not be taught in it. But he was a disciple of the strict German school, which, in its gloomy ultra-piety, would allow no concessions, even though the gradual conversion of a dissenting sect could be effected.

When contrasted with the miserable condition of the Jews in Germany, the lot of those who had taken up their abode in the newly-risen Turkish empire must have seemed unalloyed happiness. Jewish immigrants who had escaped the ceaseless persecutions to which they had been subjected in Germany expressed themselves in terms of rapture over the happy condition of the Turkish Jews. Unlike their co-religionists under Christian rule, they were not compelled to yield up the third part of their fortunes in royal taxes; nor were they in any way hindered in the conduct of business. They were permitted to dispose of their property as they pleased, and had absolute freedom of movement throughout the length and breadth of the empire. They were subject to no sumptuary laws, and were thus able to clothe themselves in silk and gold, if they chose.

The fruitful lands taken from the slothful Greek Christians were occupied by them, and offered rich reward to their industry. Turkey was, in short, correctly described by an enthusiastic Jew as a land "in which nothing, absolutely nothing, is wanting." Two young immigrants, Kalmann and David, thought that if German Jews realized but a tenth part of the happiness to be found in Turkey, they would brave any hardships to get there. These two young men persuaded Isaac Zarfati, who had journeyed in Turkey in earlier times, and whose name was by no means unknown in Germany, to write a circular letter to the Jews of the Rhineland, Styria, Moravia and Hungary, to acquaint them with the happy lot of Jews under the crescent as compared with their hard fate under the shadow of the cross, and to call upon them to escape from the German house of bondage and emigrate to Turkey. The lights and shadows of his subject could not have been more sharply defined than they are in Zarfati's letter (written in 1456), whose graphic, often somewhat too artificial language does not readily lend itself to translation:

"I have heard of the afflictions, more bitter than death, that have befallen our brethren in Germany—of the tyrannical laws, the compulsory baptisms and the banishments. And when they flee from one place, a yet harder fate befalls them in another. I hear an insolent people raising its voice in fury against the faithful; I see its hand uplifted to smite them. On all sides I learn of anguish of soul and torment of body; of daily exactions levied by merciless extortioners. The clergy and the monks, false priests, rise up against the unhappy people of God and say: 'Let us pursue them even unto destruction; let the name of Israel be no more known among men.' They imagine that their faith is in danger because the Jews in Jerusalem might, peradventure, buy the Church of the Sepulcher. For this reason they have made a law that every Jew found upon a Christian ship bound for the East shall be flung into the sea. Alas! how evilly are the people of God in Germany entreated; how sadly is their strength departed! They are driven hither and thither, and they are pursued even unto death. The sword of the oppressor ever hangs over their heads; they are flung into the devouring flames, into swift flowing rivers and into foul swamps. Brothers and teachers! friends and acquaintances! I, Isaac Zarfati, from a French stock, born in Germany, where I sat at the feet of my teachers, I proclaim to you that Turkey is a land wherein nothing is lacking. If ye will, all shall yet be well with you. The way to the Holy Land lies open to you through Turkey. Is it not better for you to live under Moslems than under Christians? Here every man may dwell at peace under his own vine and his own fig-tree. In Christendom, on the contrary, ye dare not clothe your children in red or in blue, according to your taste, without exposing them to insult and yourselves to extortion; and, therefore, are ye condemned to go about meanly clad in sad-colored raiment. All your days are full of sorrow, even your Sabbaths and the times appointed for feasting. Strangers enjoy your goods; and, therefore, of what profit is the wealth of your rich men? They hoard it but to their own sorrow, and in a day it is lost to them for ever. Ye call your riches your own—alas! they belong to your oppressors. They bring false accusations against you. They respect neither age nor wisdom; and, though they gave you a pledge sealed sixty-fold, yet would they break it. They continually lay double punishments upon you, a death of torment and confiscation of goods. They prohibit teaching in your schools; they break in upon you during your hours of prayer; and they forbid you to work or conduct your business on Christian feast-days. And now, seeing all these things, O Israel, wherefore sleepest thou? Arise, and leave this accursed land for ever!"

Isaac Zarfati's appeal induced many Jews to emigrate forthwith to Turkey and Palestine. Their grave demeanor, extreme piety, and peculiar apparel at once distinguished them from the Jews of Greece and the Orient, and ere long the newcomers exercised considerable influence upon the other inhabitants of the countries in which they settled.

There were peculiar circumstances connected with the prohibition of the emigration of Jews to Palestine. The Jewish inhabitants of Jerusalem had obtained permission from a pasha to build a synagogue on one of the slopes of Mount Zion.

The site of this synagogue adjoined a piece of land owned by Franciscan monks, or rather containing the ruins of one of their chapels, known as David's chapel. When this permission was given to the Jews, the monks raised as much clamor as though all Palestine, including the Holy City, had been their peculiar inheritance since the beginning of time. They forthwith carried their complaints to the pope, and represented that, if the Jews were permitted to take such liberties as this, it would not be long before they took possession of the Church of the Holy Sepulcher itself. The pope at once issued a bull directing that no Christian shipowner should convey Jewish emigrants to the Holy Land. As the Levantine trade was at that time almost entirely in the hands of the Venetians, the doge was prevailed upon to issue stringent orders to all the shipmasters of the mainland and the islands not to give passage to Palestine to any Jews.

It is, indeed, strange that, while the Christian powers were under the impression that they had hemmed in the children of Israel on all sides like hunted animals, the Turks of Eastern Europe opened a way of escape to them. Ere another half century had passed, their Spanish brethren, savagely hunted from the Peninsula, were destined to seek the same asylum.

It must, however, be admitted that under the sway of the Castilian king, Henry IV, and that of John II, of Aragon, the condition of the Spanish Jews was one of comparative peace and comfort. But it was the calm that went before the storm. The doubly impotent Castilian king was gentle to a degree ill-befitting a ruler of men. Although, as Infante, Don Henry had allowed himself to be persuaded by his partisans to replenish his exhausted coffers by plundering the houses, not only of the Jews, but also of the new-Christians or converts from Judaism, he had no personal antipathy to the people of Israel. A Jewish physician was his confidential minister. Not long after his accession to the throne he had even sent him to the Portuguese court on the most delicate mission of obtaining the hand of the young, beautiful princess of Portugal for his sovereign. The Jewish diplomatist brought his mission to a successful conclusion, but was assassinated in the hour of his success.

In spite of the papal bull and the repeated ordinances of the cities, Don Henry employed a Jewish farmer of taxes, one Don Chacon, a native of Vitoria; and he, too, fell a sacrifice to his office. A rabbi, Jacob Ibn-Nuñez, his private physician, was appointed by Henry to apportion and collect the tribute of the Jews of Castile; while Abraham Bibago, yet another Jew of eminence, stood high in the favor of John II of Aragon.

The example of the courts naturally affected the greater nobles, who, when their own interests were not concerned, troubled themselves very little about ecclesiastical edicts. The practice of medicine was still entirely in the hands of Jews, and opened to them the cabinets and the hearts of kings and nobles. It was in vain that papal bulls proclaimed that Christians should not employ Jewish physicians. There were few or no Christians who understood the healing art, and the sick had no recourse save to the skill of the Jews. Even the higher clergy had but little regard for the bulls of Eugenius, Nicholas, and Calixtus. They had too much care for the health of the flesh to refuse the medical aid of the Jews on account of a canonical decree. Most of the tyrannical restrictions belonging to the minority of John II and the times of the regent Catalina were completely forgotten. Only on one point did Henry insist with rigor. He would not permit the Jews to clothe themselves luxuriously. This was partly on account of his own preference for simplicity of dress, partly because he was desirous that the envy of Christians should not be excited against them. Under the mild rule of Don Henry, the Jews who had been more or less compulsorily baptized either returned to their faith, or at least observed the Jewish ritual unmolested. During the Feast of the Passover they lived upon rice entirely in order, on the one hand, to partake of nothing leavened, and, on the other, to avoid the suspicion of Judaism.

Hatred of the Jew, which burnt most fiercely in the great towns, naturally made it impossible for the orthodox to behold without indignation this favoritism towards the supposed enemies of their faith, and they made use of a weapon whose efficacy had been proved in other lands. The cry went forth: The Jews have put Christian children to death! Then came the report that "a Jew in the neighborhood of Salamanca had torn a child's heart out;" or, "Jews elsewhere have cut pieces of flesh out of a living Christian child," and so on. By means of such rumors, the fanaticism of the mob was speedily inflamed, the magistrates took up the matter, and the accused Jews were thrown into prison.

The king, well aware of the origin and object of these accusations, had them thoroughly sifted, with the result that the innocence of the accused was completely established. Nothwithstanding this fact, the enemies of the Jews maintained their guilt. Some insiuuated that the judges had been bribed; while others asserted that the new-Christians had exerted themselves in behalf of their kinsmen, and that the king himself was partial to them.

Among all their enemies the man who raged most bitterly and fiercely against the Spanish Jews was a preacher in Salamanca, Alfonso de Spina, a Franciscan monk, of the same order and opinions as Capistrano. Instead of the venomed tongue, he used the poisoned pen against them. This man enjoyed a certain amount of fame, because he happened to have accompanied Alvaro de Luna, the once all-powerful minister of John II, to the scaffold as his confessor. This bigoted priest thundered unceasingly from the altar steps against the Jews and their patrons, and especially against the new-Christians as secret adherents of their former faith. As his preaching did not appear to him to produce sufficient effect, De Spina issued, in 1460, a virulent work in Latin, directed against Jews, Moslems, and other heretics, under the title "Fortalitium Fidei." In this book he collected everything that the enemies of the Jews had ever written or said against them. He reproduced every absurd legend and idle tale that he could procure, and seasoned the whole collection with every device of rhetoric that his malice could suggest. In his opinion it was only right and natural that all Moslems and heretics should be exterminated root and branch. Against the Jews, however, he proposed to employ apparently lenient measures. He would simply take their younger children from them, and bring them up as Christians, an idea for which he was indebted to the scholastic philosopher, Duns Scotus, and his fellow Franciscan, Capistrano. De Spina most deeply deplored that the various laws for the persecution of the Jews, promulgated during the minority of John II, were no longer in force under his successor. In most trenchant words he rebuked the king, the nobles and the clergy for the favor that they showed to Jews; and, in order to inflame the mob, he untiringly retailed all the old fables of child-murder, theft of the host, and the like, in the most circumstantial narrative, and insinuated that the partiality of the king permitted these abominable crimes to go unpunished.

The fanaticism aroused by Alfonso de Spina was by no means without effect; indeed, the most lamentable consequences ere long resulted from it. A monk, crucifix in hand, proposed a general massacre of the Jews of Medina del Campo, near Valladolid, and his words were favorably received. The inhabitants of the town fell upon the Jews, and burnt several of them alive with the sacred books which they happened to find in their possession. Murder was naturally followed by plunder of the victims' goods. The king had the ringleaders of this outrage punished; but this was all that he could do. He was unable to prevent a recurrence of such scenes. He had been compelled to recognize the abject position of the Jews officially in the statute book which his advisers, his secret enemies, Don Pacheco, Marquis of Villena, and the Count of Valencia, prepared at his request. Don Pacheco, who by his intrigues brought both king and country to confusion, was himself of Jewish blood, his mother, who had married a Spanish noble, being the daughter of a Jew named Ruy Capron. Notwithstanding this fact, he included the most odious enactments in Don Henry's revised statute book. All the earlier disabilities were revived: the exclusion of Jews from all offices, even from practice as apothecaries, the wearing of distinctive badges, restriction to the Jewries of towns, and even confinement to their houses during Holy Week.

The civil war kindled by the intrigues of Don Pacheco and other courtiers through the burlesque deposition of Don Henry in Avila, and the coronation of his younger brother, Alfonso, bore more heavily on the Jews than even on the general population of Castile.

In 1467 Alfonso's party had by treason become master of Segovia, and immediately a riot against the Jews began here. The enemies of this unhappy people spread the report that, on the suggestion of their rabbi, Solomon Picho, the Jews of the little community of Sepulveda, not far from Segovia, had during Holy Week so cruelly tortured a Christian child that it died upon the cross (April, 1468). On the motion of Bishop Juan Arias, of Avila, of Jewish race, several Jews (eight or sixteen, according to different accounts), whom the popular voice had accused, were hauled from Sepulveda to Segovia, and there condemned to the stake, the gallows and the bowstring, whereupon the Christians of Sepulveda fell upon the few remaining Jews of the community, massacred some, and hunted the rest from the neighborhood. Is it not strange that in Castile and in Silesia, in Italy and in Poland, the selfsame accusations were raised, and followed by the same sentences?

Scarcely was Alfonso's party dissolved by the death of its puppet king before another sprang up, which professed to defend the rights of the Infanta Isabella, sister of Don Henry. The utter weakness which Henry betrayed encouraged the rebels to make the most outrageous assaults upon his prerogatives. The cortes convened at Ocaña in 1469, wishing to humiliate him, took up the Jewish question. They reminded him of the laws of his ancestors, and told him to his face that he had violated these laws by endowing Jews with the chief offices in the collection of the royal revenues. They further asserted that, owing to this distinguished example, even princes of the church had farmed out the revenues of their dioceses to Jews and Moslems, and that the tax-farmers actually levied their contributions in the churches. In conclusion, they insisted that the edicts be once more stringently enforced, and that heavy penalties be imposed for their transgression.

The finances of this monarch, who, in consequence of his liberality and the expense of putting down the ever-recurring revolts against his authority, was in constant need of money, would have been in a sorry condition had he intrusted them to Christian tax-farmers. The latter bid only a small amount for the privilege; moreover, they might have made use of the rebellious factions to rid themselves of their obligations. A king who said to his treasurer: "Give to these that they may serve me, and to those that they may not rob me; to this end I am king, and have treasures and revenues for all purposes" —such a king could not dispense with Jewish financiers.

Thus there existed, in Castile, an antagonism between the edicts against the Jews and the interests of the state; and this antagonism roused the mob, inspired alike by ecclesiastical fanaticism and envious greed against their Jewish fellow-townsmen, to the perpetration of bloody outrages. The fury of the orthodox was also excited against the new-Christians, or Marranos, because, happier than their former fellow-believers, they were promoted to the highest offices in the state by reason of their superior talents.

The marriage of the Infanta Isabella with Don Ferdinand, Infante of Aragon, on the 19th of October, 1469, marked a tragical crisis in the history of the Spanish Jews. Without the knowledge of her royal brother, and in open breach of faith—since she had solemnly promised to marry only with his consent—she had followed the advice of her intriguing friends, and had given her hand to the Prince of Aragon, who, both in Jewish and in Spanish history, under the title of "The Catholic," has left an accursed memory behind him. Don Abraham Senior had promoted this marriage, hoping by it to increase the welfare of his brethren. Many new complications arose in Castile out of this union. Isabella's partisans, anticipating that under her rule and that of her husband the persecution of the Jews would be made legal, took up arms in Valladolid, Isabella's capital, and fell upon the new-Christians (September, 1470). The victims assumed the defensive, but were soon compelled to surrender. Thereupon they sent a deputation to Henry, begging him to protect them. The king did, indeed, collect troops, and march against the rebellious city, but he had to be grateful that he himself was well received by the citizens, and could not think of punishing even the ringleaders.

Two years later the new-Christians underwent a persecution, which surely must have caused them to repent having taken shelter at the foot of the cross. The religious populace blamed the Marranos, not altogether without reason, for confessing Christianity with their lips while in their souls they despised it. It was said that they either did not bring their children to be baptized, or if they were baptized, took them back to their houses and washed the stain of baptism off their foreheads. They used no lard at their tables, only oil; they abstained from pork, celebrated the Jewish Passover, and contributed oil for the use of the synagogues. They were further said to have but small respect for cloisters, and were supposed to have profaned sacred relics and debauched nuns. The new-Christians, were, in fact, looked upon as a cunning and ambitious set of people, who sought eagerly for the most profitable offices, thought only of accumulating riches, and avoided hard work. They were believed to consider themselves as living in Spain as Israel did in Egypt, and to hold it to be quite permissible to plunder and outwit the orthodox. These accusations were not by any means merited by the new-Christians as a body, but they served to inflame the mob, and caused it to hate the converts even more bitterly than the Jews themselves.

The outbreak above referred to arose as follows: A certain princess was going through the streets of Cordova with the picture of the Virgin under a canopy, and a girl, a new-Christian, either by accident or design, poured some water out of a window on the canopy. The consequence was a frenzied rising against the converted Jews. An excited smith incited the Christian mob to avenge the insult offered to the holy picture—for it was said that the girl had poured something unclean upon it—and in an instant her father's house was in flames. The nobles sought to defend the Marranos, and in the skirmish, the smith was killed. This so enraged the already furious mob that the men-at-arms were forced to retire. The houses of the new-Christians were now broken into, plundered, and then reduced to ashes; while those who had not been able to save themselves by flight were massacred in the most barbarous manner (March 14th—15th, 1472). The fugitives were hunted like wild beasts in the chase. Wherever they were seen, the most horrible death inevitably awaited them. Even the peasant at work in the field struck them down without ado. The slaughter which thus began at Cordova spread rapidly from town to town. Those of the Cordovan fugitives who had found a temporary refuge in Palma lost no time in seeking a stronghold to afford them protection from the tempest of persecution. One of their company, Pedro de Herrera, held in the highest respect both by his fellow-sufferers and the governor, De Aguilar, went to Seville to seek an interview with the duke of Medina-Sidonia, lieutenant-governor of the province. He asked for the fortress of Gibraltar as a city of refuge for himself and his brethren, under their own command. In return, he promised to pay a considerable yearly tribute. The duke had signified his consent to this proposition, and the new-Christians had betaken themselves to Seville to sign the contract, when the friends of the duke took alarm. They believed that the Marranos were not to be trusted, and expressed the fear that they might enter into an alliance with the Moors, and deliver the key of the Spanish coast into their hands. The duke, however, insisted upon completing the contract, whereupon the opponents of the scheme gave the signal to the mob of Seville, which instantly rose against the new-Christians in an outburst of fanatical frenzy. It was with difficulty that the governor protected them. They were forced to return hastily to Palma, were waylaid by the country people, and ill-treated and plundered (1473).

Thus the plan of Pedro de Herrera and his friends served only to bring greater misery upon them, endangering the whole body of new-Christians as well as the Jews themselves. As early as this, the idea took shape among both the converted and the unbaptized Jews to leave the now inhospitable Peninsula and emigrate to Flanders or Italy.

Attacks upon the new-Christians were now so frequent that they suggested to the cunning and ambitious minister, Pacheco, the means of carrying out a *coup d'état*. This unscrupulous intriguer, who for two decades had kept Castile in constant confusion, saw with secret chagrin that the reconciliation of Don Henry with his sister and successor bade fair to completely annul his influence. To bring about new complications he determined to gain possession of the citadel (Alcazar) of Segovia, at that time occupied by the king. With this end in view, he instigated, through his dependents, another assault upon the baptized Jews, during the confusion of which his accomplices were to seize Cabrera, the governor of the castle, and, if possible, the king himself. The conspiracy was betrayed only a few hours before it was to be carried into action; but the attack upon the new-Christians was perpetrated. Armed bands perambulated the streets of Segovia, broke into the houses of the Marranos, and slew every man, woman and child that fell into their hands (May 16th, 1474).

The crowning misfortune of the Jewish race in Spain came in the death of Don Henry in the following December. The rulers of the united kingdoms of Aragon and Castile now were his sister, the bigoted Isabella, who was led by advisers hostile to the Jews, and Ferdinand, her unscrupulous husband, who pretended to be excessively pious. Sad and terrible was the fate that impended over the sons of Jacob throughout the length and breadth of the Pyrenean Peninsula.

CHAPTER IX.

THE JEWS IN ITALY AND GERMANY BEFORE THE EXPULSION FROM SPAIN.

Position of the Jews of Italy—The Jewish Bankers—Yechiel of Pisa—His Relations with Don Isaac Abrabanel—Jewish Physicians, Guglielmo di Portaleone—Revival of Learning among Italian Jews—Messer Leon and Elias del Medigo—Pico di Mirandola, the Disciple of Medigo—Predilection of Christians for the Kabbala—Jochanan Aleman—Religious Views of Del Medigo—German Rabbis immigrate into Italy—Joseph Kolon, his Character and his Feud with Messer Leon—Judah Menz an Antagonist of Del Medigo—Bernardinus of Feltre—Jews banished from Trent on a False Charge of Child-Murder—The Doge of Venice and Pope Sixtus IV befriend the Jews—Sufferings of the Jews of Ratisbon—Israel Bruna—Synod at Nuremberg—Emperor Frederick III.

1474—1492 C.E.

THE Spanish Jews would have belied their native penetration and the wisdom born of bitter experience had they not foreseen that their position would ere long become unbearable.

Because they did foresee it, they turned their gaze towards those countries whose inhabitants were most favorably disposed towards Jews. Italy and the Byzantine Empire, just wrested from the cross, were now the countries of greatest toleration. In Italy, where men saw most clearly the infamy of the papacy and the priesthood, and where they had most to suffer from their selfishness, the church and her servants were utterly without influence over the people. The world-wide commerce of the wealthy and flourishing republics of Venice, Florence, Genoa and Pisa, had in a measure broken through the narrow bounds of superstition, and enlarged men's range of vision. The interests of the market-place had driven the interests of the church into the background. Wealth and ability were valued even in those who did not repeat the Catholic confession of faith. Not only the merchants, but also the most exalted princes were in need of gold to support the mercenary legions of their Condottieri in their daily feuds. The Jews, as capitalists and skillful diplomatists, were, therefore, well received in Italy. This is proved by the fact that when the city of Ravenna was desirous of uniting itself to Venice, it included among the conditions of union the demand that wealthy Jews be sent to it to open credit-banks and thus relieve the poverty of the populace.

Jewish capitalists received, either from the reigning princes or the senates, in many Italian cities, extensive privileges, permitting them to open banks, establish themselves as brokers, and even charge a high rate of interest (20 per cent). The archbishop of Mantua in 1476 declared in the name of the pope that the Jews were permitted to lend money upon interest. The canonical prohibition of usury could not withstand the pressure of public convenience. The Jewish communal regulations also tended to guard the bankers from illegal competition, for the rabbis threatened with the ban all those members of the community who lent money on interest without proper authorization.

A Jew of Pisa, named Yechiel, controlled the money market of Tuscany. He was, by no means, a mere heartless money-maker, as the Christians were wont to call him, but rather a man of noble mind and tender heart, ever ready to assist the poor with his gold, and to comfort the unfortunate by word and deed. Yechiel of Pisa was also familiar with and deeply interested in Hebrew literature, and maintained friendly relations with Isaac Abrabanel, the last of the Jewish statesmen of the Peninsula. When Alfonso V of Portugal took the African seaboard towns of Arzilla and Tangier, and carried off Jews of both sexes and every age captive, the Portuguese community became inspired with the pious desire to ransom them. Abrabanel placed himself at the head of a committee to collect money for this purpose. As the Portuguese Jews were not able to support the ransomed prisoners until they found means of subsistence, Abrabanel, in a letter to Yechiel of Pisa, begged him to make a collection in Italy. His petition was heeded.

The Jews of Italy were found to be desirable citizens, not only for their financial ability, but also for their skill as physicians. In his letter to Yechiel, Abrabanel asked whether there were Jewish physicians in the Italian states, and whether the princes of the church employed them. "Physicians," he said, "possess the key to the hearts of the great, upon whom the fate of the Jews depends."

A celebrated Jewish doctor, Guglielmo (Benjamin?) di Portaleone, of Mantua, first was physician in ordinary to Ferdinand of Naples, who ennobled him; he next entered the service of Duke Galeazzo Sforza, of Milan, and in 1479 became body physician to Duke Ludovico Gonzaga. He was the founder of a noble house and of a long line of skillful Italian physicians. There even arose an intimate relation between Jews and Christians in Italy. When a wealthy Jew—Leo, of Crema—on the marriage of his son, arranged magnificent festivities which lasted eight days, a great number of Christians took part, dancing and enjoying themselves to the intense displeasure of the clergy. Totally forgotten seemed the bull in which Nicholas V had quite recently forbidden under heavy penalties all intercourse of Christians with Jews, as well as the employment of Jewish physicians. In place of the canonically prescribed livery of degradation, the Jewish doctors wore robes of honor like Christians of similar standing; while the Jews connected with the courts wore golden chains and other honorable insignia. The contrast between the condition of Jews in Italy and that of their brethren in other lands is well illustrated by two similar incidents, occurring simultaneously in Italy and Germany, but differing greatly in their issues.

The mother of a family in Pavia, in consequence of differences with her husband, had given notice of her desire to be received into the Catholic Church. She was put into a convent where she was to be prepared for baptism. The bishop's vicar, with other spiritual advisers, was earnestly occupied with the salvation of her soul, when she was suddenly seized with remorse. The bishop of Pavia, far from punishing her for this relapse, or seeking to oppose her desire, interceded for her with her husband. He advised him to take her out of the convent forthwith, and testified most favorably as to her behavior, so that her husband, a descendant of the family of Aaron, might not be obliged, under the Jewish law, to put her away.

In the same year a spiteful fellow in Ratisbon, Kalmann, a precentor (Chazan), took the fancy to turn Christian. He frequented the convent, attended church, and at length the bishop received him in his house, and instructed him in the Christian religion. To curry favor with the Christians he calumniated his fellow-believers by asserting that they possessed blasphemous writings against Christianity. Kalmann also came to rue the step he had taken. He secretly attended the synagogue, and at length, during the absence of the bishop, left his house, and returned to the Jews. The clergy of Ratisbon were infuriated against him, arraigned him before the Inquisition, and charged him with having sought to blaspheme the church, God, and the blessed Virgin. He was specially charged with having said that, if baptized, he would remain a Christian only till he found himself at liberty. On the strength of this, he was condemned, and put to death by drowning.

Wherever even a little indulgence was granted the Jews, their dormant energy revived; and the

Italian Jews were able to display it all the sooner from the fact that they had gained a certain degree of culture in the days of Immanuel and Leone Romano. They took an active part in the intellectual revival and scientific renascence which distinguished the times of the Medici. Jewish youths attended the Italian universities, and acquired a liberal education. The Italian Jews were the first to make use of the newly-discovered art of Gutenberg, and printing-houses soon rose in many parts of Italy—in Reggio, Ferrara, Pieva di Sacco, Bologna, Soncino, Iscion, and Naples. In the artistic creations of the time, however, in painting and sculpture, the Jews had no share. These lay outside their sphere. But several educated Jews did not a little for the advancement and spread of science in Italy. Two deserve especial mention: Messer Leon and Elias del Medigo, the latter of whom not only received the light of science, but also shed it abroad.

Messer Leon, or, by his Hebrew name, Judah ben Yechiel, of Naples, flourished between 1450 and 1490, and was both rabbi and physician in Mantua. In addition to being thoroughly versed in Hebrew literature, he was a finished Latin scholar, and had a keen appreciation of the subtleties of Cicero's and Quintilian's style. Belonging to the Aristotelian school, he expounded several of the writings of the philosopher so highly esteemed in synagogue and church, and wrote a grammar and a book on logic, in the Hebrew language, for Jewish students. More important than these writings is his Hebrew rhetoric (Nófeth Zufim), in which he lays down the laws upon which the grace, force and eloquence of the higher style depend, and proves that the same laws underlie sacred literature. He was the first Jew to compare the language of the Prophets and Psalmists with Cicero's—certainly a hardy undertaking in those days when the majority of Jews and Christians held the Scriptures in such infinite reverence that a comparison with profane pagan literature must have seemed a species of blasphemy. Of course, this was possible only in the times of the Medici, when love for Greek and Latin antiquities rose to positive enthusiasm. Messer Leon, the learned rabbi of Mantua, was liberal in all respects. He was never weary of rebuking the formal pietists for striving to withhold foreign influences from Judaism, as though it could be profaned by them. He was rather of opinion that Judaism could only gain by comparisons with the culture of the ancient classical literatures, since thereby its beauty and sublimity would be brought to light.

Elias del Medigo, or Elias Cretensis (1463–1498), the scion of a German family that had emigrated to Crete, is a striking figure in later Jewish history. He was the first great man produced by Italian Judaism. His was a mind that shone clearly and brilliantly out of the clouds which obscured his age; the mind of a man of varied and profound knowledge, and of both classical and philosophical culture. So completely had he assimilated the Latin literary style that he was able, not only to issue works in that language, but also to present Hebrew syntax under Latin analogies.

Medigo kept aloof from the vacuity of Italian sciolists, who were under the spell of the newly-discovered neo-Platonic philosophy introduced by Ficinus. He gave allegiance to those sound thinkers, Aristotle, Maimuni, and Averroes, whose systems he made known to Christian inquirers in Italy, by tongue and pen, through the medium of translations and in independent works. That youthful prodigy of his time, Count Giovanni Pico di Mirandola, made the acquaintance of Medigo, and became his disciple, friend and protector. Mirandola, who was a marvel by reason of his wonderful memory, wide erudition, and dialectic skill, and was, moreover, on friendly terms with the ruling house of the Medicis in Tuscany, learnt from his Jewish friend the Hebrew language, and the Arabic development of the Aristotelian philosophy, but he might also have learnt clearness of thought from him.

On one occasion a quarrel on a learned subject broke out in the University of Padua. The professors and students were divided into two parties, and, according to Christian custom, were on the point of settling the question with rapier and poniard. The University, acting with the Venetian senate, which was desirous of ending the dispute, called upon Elias del Medigo to act as umpire. Everyone confidently expected a final settlement from his erudition and impartiality. Del Medigo argued out the theme, and by the weight of his decision brought the matter to a satisfactory conclusion. The result was that he became a public lecturer on philosophy, and discoursed to large audiences in Padua and Florence. The spectacle was, indeed, notable. Under the very eyes of the papacy, ever striving for the humiliation and enslavement of the Jews, Christian youths were imbibing wisdom from the lips of a Jewish teacher. Against the protectors of Jews in Spain it hurled the thunders of excommunication, while in Italy it was forced passively to behold favors constantly showered upon the Jews by Christians.

Pico di Mirandola, a scholar rather than a thinker, took a fancy to plunge into the abysses of the Kabbala. He was initiated into the Kabbalistic labyrinth by a Jew, Jochanan Aleman, who had emigrated from Constantinople to Italy. Aleman, himself a confused thinker, made him believe that the secret doctrine was of ancient origin, and contained the wisdom of the ages. Mirandola, who had a marvelous faculty of assimilation, soon familiarized himself with the Kabbalistic formulæ, and discovered confirmations of Christian dogma in them; in fact, he found far more of Christianity than of Judaism. The extravagances of the Kabbala demonstrated in his eyes the doctrines of the Trinity, the Incarnation, Original Sin, the Fall of the Angels, Purgatory, and Eternal Punishment. He lost no time in translating several Kabbalistic writings from Hebrew into Latin in order to bring this occult lore to the knowledge of Christian readers. Among the nine hundred points which Pico, at the age of twenty-four, pledged himself to defend—to which end he invited all the learned of the world to Rome, and undertook to pay the cost of their journeys—was this: No science affords more certainty as to the Godhead of Christ than Kabbala and magic! Even Pope Sixtus IV (1471—1484) was by this means so strongly attracted to the Kabbala that he was eager to procure Latin translations of Kabbalistic writings for the benefit of the Catholic faith.

It is a striking proof of his sober mind and healthy judgment that Elias del Medigo kept himself aloof from all this mental effeminacy and childish enthusiasm for the pseudo-doctrine of the Kabbala. He had profound contempt for the Kabbalistic phantom, and did not hesitate to expose its worthlessness. He had the courage openly to express his opinion that the Kabbala is rooted in an intellectual swamp, that no trace of this doctrine is to be found in the Talmud, that the recognized authorities of ancient Judaism knew nothing of it, and that its supposed sacred and ancient groundwork, the Zohar, was by no means the work of the celebrated Simon bar Yochaï, but the production of a forger. In short, he considered the Kabbala to be made up of the rags and tatters of the neo-Platonic school.

Del Medigo had, in fact, very sound and healthy views on religion. Although a warm adherent of Judaism, entertaining respect also for its Talmudic element, he was yet far from indorsing and accepting as truth all that appears in the Talmud. When requested by one of his Jewish disciples, Saul Cohen Ashkenasi, of Candia, to give his confession of Jewish faith, especially his views on the signs which distinguish a true religion, Elias Cretensis issued a small but pregnant work, "The Investigation of Religion" (Bechinath ha-Dath), which gives a deep insight into his methods of thought.

It cannot be maintained that Del Medigo suggested novel trains of thought in his work. In general, the Italians were not destined to endow Judaism with new ideas. Moreover, he occupied the standpoint of belief rather than of inquiry, and his aim was to defend, not to cut new paths. Standing alone in the mental barrenness of his age, Del Medigo's sound views are like an oasis in the desert. He must be credited, too, with having recognized as deformities, and with desiring to remove, the additions to Judaism by Kabbalists and pseudo-philosophers.

Unfortunately, the rabbis who emigrated from Germany to Italy assumed an attitude distinctly hostile to philosophical investigation and its promoters, Elias del Medigo and Messer Leon. With their honest, but one-sided, exaggerated piety, they cast a gloomy shadow wherever their hard fate had scattered them. Fresh storms breaking over the German communities had driven many German Jews, the most unhappy of their race, into transalpine lands. Under Emperor Frederick III, who for half a century had with astounding equanimity beheld most shameless insults to his authority on the part of an ambitious nobility, a plundering squirearchy, a demoralized clergy, and the self-seeking patricians of the smaller towns, the Jewish communities but too often saw their cup of bitterness overflow. Frederick himself was by no means hostile to them. On the contrary, he frequently issued decrees in their favor. Unhappily, his commands remained for the most part a dead letter, and his laxity of rule encouraged the evil-minded to the commission of the most shameful misdeeds. It was dangerous for the German Jews to go beyond the walls of their cities. Every man was their foe, and waylaid them to satisfy either his fanaticism or his cupidity. Every feud that broke out in the decaying German empire brought misery to them.

Among exiles from Mayence were two profound Talmudic scholars. They were cousins, by name Judah and Moses Menz. The former emigrated to Padua, and there received the office of rabbi, while the latter at first remained in Germany, and then passed over to Posen. As the result of expulsion or oppression, many rabbis were emigrating from all parts of Germany, and on account of their superior Talmudic knowledge these German emigrants were elected to the most distinguished rabbinical positions in Italy. They re-indoctrinated with their prejudice and narrowness of vision the Italian Jews, who were making determined efforts to free themselves from the bonds of the Middle Ages.

The most distinguished rabbis of Italy were at that time Judah Menz and Joseph Kolon, and precisely these two were most inimical to any liberal manifestation within Judaism, and most strenuously opposed the advocates of freedom. Joseph ben Solomon Kolon (flourished 1460—1490) was of French extraction, his ancestors having been expelled from France; but he passed his youth in Germany, and belonged to the German school. He subsequently lived with his relatives in Chambéry until the Jews were hunted out of Savoy. With many companions in misfortune he went to Lombardy, where he gained his living by teaching; finally he became rabbi of Mantua. Endowed with extraordinary penetration, and fully the equal of the German rabbis in the depth of his Talmudic learning, Joseph Kolon was celebrated in his day as a Rabbinical authority of the first magnitude, and his academy rivaled the German school itself. He was consulted by both German and Italian communities. On scientific subjects and all matters outside the Talmud he was as ignorant as his German fellow-dignitaries. A resolute, decided nature, Joseph Kolon was a man of rigid views on all religious matters. His ruggedness involved him in unpleasant relations with Moses Kapsali in Constantinople, and in a heated controversy with the cultured Messer Leon in his own community. However well they might agree for a time, Joseph Kolon, the strict Talmudist, and Messer Leon, the cultured man of letters, could not long tolerate each other. When the conflict between them broke out, the whole community of Mantua took sides in their feud, and split into two parties as supporters of the one or the other. The strife at length became so keen that in 1476—1477 Duke Joseph of Mantua banished them both from the city; after which Kolon became rabbi of Pavia.

Still more strained were the relations between the rabbi Judah Menz and the philosopher Elias del Medigo. The former (born 1408, died 1509), a man of the old school, of comprehensive knowledge of Talmudic subjects, and of remarkable sagacity, was most resolutely opposed to scientific progress and freedom in religious matters, and after his expulsion from Mayence transplanted the narrow spirit of the German rabbis to Padua and Italy in general.

The relatively secure and honorable position of the Jews in Italy did not fail to rouse the displeasure of fanatical monks, who sought to cover with the cloak of religious zeal either their dissolute conduct or their ambitious share in worldly affairs. The colder the Christian world grew towards the end of the fifteenth century with regard to clerical institutions, the more bitterly did the monastic orders rage against the Jews. Preaching friars made the chancels ring with tirades against them, and openly advocated their utter extermination. Their most desperate enemy at this time was the Franciscan Bernardinus of Feltre, a worthy disciple of the bloodthirsty Capistrano. The standing text of his sermons was: Let Christian parents keep a watchful eye on their children lest the Jews steal, ill-treat, or crucify them.

He held up Capistrano, the Jew-slayer, as the type and model of a true Christian. In his eyes friendly and neighborly intercourse with Jews was an abomination, a most grievous sin against canonical law. Christian charity, he admitted, directs that Jews, being human, be treated with justice and humanity; but at the same time the canonical law forbids Christians to have any dealings with them, to sit at their tables, or to allow themselves to be treated by Jewish physicians. As the aristocracy everywhere, in obedience to their own interests, took the part of the Jews, Bernardinus inflamed the lower classes against the Jews and their patrons. Because certain Jewish capitalists had been successful, he depicted all Jews as vampires and extortioners, and roused the ill will of the populace against them. "I, who live on alms and eat the bread of the poor, shall I be a dumb dog and not howl when I see the Jews wringing their wealth from Christian poverty? Yea! shall I not cry aloud for Christ's sake?" Such is a fair specimen of his preaching.

Had the Italian people not been actuated by strong good sense, Bernardinus would have become for the Jews of Italy what, in the beginning of the same century, the Dominican, Vincent Ferrer, had been to the Jews of Spain, and Capistrano, to the communities of Germany and the Slav countries. The authorities sorely hindered Bernardinus in his business of Jew-baiting, and his bloodthirsty sermons mostly failed of effect. When he was conducting his crusade in Bergamo and Ticini, Duke Galeazzo, of Milan, forbade him to proceed. In Florence, in fact everywhere in Tuscany, the enlightened prince and the senate took the part of the Jews with vigor. The venomous monk spread the report that they had allowed themselves to be bribed with large sums by Yechiel of Pisa and other wealthy Jews. As Bernardinus was inciting the youth of the city against the Jews, and a popular rising was imminent, the authorities ordered him to quit Florence and the country forthwith, and he was compelled to submit (1487). Little by little, however, by dint of untiring repetition of the same charges, he managed so far to inflame public opinion against the Jews that even the Venetian senate was not always able to protect them. Finally, he succeeded in bringing about a bloody persecution of the Jews, not, indeed, in Italy, but in the Tyrol, whence it spread to Germany.

While Bernardinus was preaching in the city of Trent, he remarked with no little chagrin the friendly relation between Jews and Christians. Tobias, a skillful Jewish physician, and an intelligent Jewess, named Brunetta, were on most friendly terms with the upper classes, enjoying their complete confidence. This roused his ire not a little, and he made the chancels of Trent ring with savage tirades against the Jews. Some Christians called him to account for his hatred of Jews, remarking that though they were without the true faith, those of Trent were worthy folk. The monk replied: "Ye know not what misfortune these good people will bring upon you. Before Easter Sunday is past they will give you a proof of their extraordinary goodness." It was easy for him to prophesy, for he and a few other priests had arranged a cunning plan, which not only brought about the ruin of the community of Trent, but also caused the greatest injury to the Jews of various countries. Chance aided him by creating a favorable opportunity.

In Holy Week of 1475 a three-year-old child, named Simon, the son of poor Christian parents, was drowned in the Adige, and the corpse was caught in a grating close to the house of a Jew. In order to anticipate misrepresentation of the event, he hurried to Bishop Hinderbach to give him notice of the occurrence. The bishop took two men of high position with him, went to the place, and had the body carried into the church. As soon as the news spread, Bernardinus and other hostile priests raised a fierce outcry against the Jews, saying that they had tortured and slain the child, and then flung it into the water. The body of the supposititiously illtreated child was exhibited, in order to inflame the fury of the populace against them. The bishop had all the Jews of Trent, high and low, cast into prison, commenced proceedings against them, and called a physician, Matthias Tiberinus, to testify to the violent death of the child. A baptized Jew, one Wolfkan, from Ratisbon, an engrosser, came forward with the most fearful accusations against his former co-religionists. His charges the more readily found credence as the imprisoned Jews confessed under torture that they had slain Simon, and drunk his blood on the night of the Passover. Brunetta was said to have supplied the weapons for the purpose. A letter also was said to have been found in the possession of a rabbi, Moses, which had been sent from Saxony, asking for Christian blood for the next Passover. Only one of the tortured victims, a man named Moses, endured every torment without confirming the lying accusations of his enemies. The result was that all the Jews of Trent were burnt, and it was resolved that no Jew should thenceforth settle in the city. Four persons only became converts to Christianity, and were pardoned.

The bishop of Trent, Bernardinus, and the monks of all orders made every effort to utilize this occurrence for the general ruin of the Jews. The corpse of the child was embalmed, and commended to the populace as a holy relic. Thousands made pilgrimages to its remains, and ere long it was believed by the faith-drunken pilgrims that they had seen a halo about the remains of the child Simon. So much was said about it that even its inventors came to believe in the martyrdom. From every chancel the Dominicans proclaimed the new miracle, and thundered against the infamy of the Jews. Two lawyers from Padua who visited Trent in order to convince themselves of the truth of the occurrence were almost torn to pieces by the fanatical mob. It was imperative that the marvel be believed in, and so the Jews of all Christian countries were jeopardized anew. Even in Italy they dared not go outside the towns lest they be slain as child-murderers.

The doge, Pietro Mocenigo, and the Venetian senate, on the complaint of the Jews about the insecurity of their lives and property, issued orders to the podesta of Padua energetically to defend them against fanatical outbreaks, and to forbid the preaching friars to inflame the mob against them. The doge accompanied the orders with the remark that the rumor that Jews had slain a Christian child in Trent was a fabrication, a device invented by their enemies to serve some purpose. When Pope Sixtus IV was urged to canonize little Simon he steadfastly refused, and sent a letter to all the towns of Italy, on October 10th, 1475, forbidding Simon of Trent to be honored as a saint until he could investigate the matter, and thus he allayed the popular excitement against the Jews. The clergy, nevertheless, permitted the bones of Simon to be held sacred, and instituted pilgrimages to the church built for his remains.

Through this circumstance Jew hatred in Germany gained fresh vigor. The citizens of Frankfort-on-the-Main exhibited, on the bridge leading to Sachsenhausen, a picture representing in hideous detail a tortured child, and the Jews leagued with the devil in their bloody work. The news of the child-murder in Trent spread like wildfire through the Christian countries, and became the source of new sufferings to Jews. Nowhere were these sufferings so severe as in the free city of Ratisbon, containing one of the oldest Jewish communities in South Germany. It was held to be not only very pious but of distinguished morality, and it was considered a high honor to intermarry with the Jews of Ratisbon. Within the memory of man no native Jew had been brought before the tribunal for any moral lapse. The community was regarded as the most learned in the land, and the parent of all German communities. It possessed chartered liberties, which the emperors, in consideration of a crown-tax, were accustomed to renew on their accession. The Jews of Ratisbon were half recognized as burghers, and mounted guard with the Christians as militia. One might almost say that the Bavarian princes and corporations vied with each other in favoring them—of course, merely to share their purses. In the latter half of this century they had become a veritable bone of contention between the Duke of Bavaria-Landsberg and Frederick III, who, hard pressed on all sides, not only in the empire, but even in his own possessions, hoped to fill his empty coffers with the wealth of the Jews.

In addition to these the Kamerau family made claims upon the Jews of Ratisbon, as well as the town council, and, of course, the bishop. These contradictory and mutually hostile demands made the position of the Jews anything but a bed of roses. First from one side and then from another came orders to the council to imprison the Jews, their chiefs, or their rabbi, at that time the sorely-tried Israel Bruna, until, worn out by confinement, they decided to pay what was claimed. The council did indeed seek to shield them, but only so long as no danger threatened the citizens, or the Jews did not compete with the Christian guildmembers.

To escape these cruel and arbitrary extortions, prudence directed that they place themselves under the protection of one of the Hussite nobles or captains. They would thus enjoy more security than was possible under the so-called protection of the emperor, since the fiery Hussites were not a little feared by the more sluggish Germans. Although they had to some extent abandoned their heretical fanaticism, and had taken service under the Catholic sovereigns, their desperate valor was still a source of terror to the orthodox clergy. The event proved that the Jews had acted wisely in appealing to their protection.

A bishop named Henry was elected in Ratisbon, a man of gloomy nature, to whom the sentiment of mercy was unknown, and he naturally insisted on the enforcement of the canonical restrictions against the Jews. As examples to others, for instance, he mercilessly punished a Christian girl who had entered the service of a Jew, and a Christian barber who had let blood for a Jewish customer. His animosity was contagious. On one occasion, when the Jewish midwife was sick, and a Christian was about to attend some Jewish women, the council actually dared not give her the required permission without the episcopal sanction.

Bishop Henry and Duke Louis, one in their hatred of Jews, now pursued what seemed to be a preconcerted plan for the ruin or conversion of the Jews of Ratisbon. On the one hand, they obtained the acquiescence of the pope, and on the other, the assistance of influential persons on the city council. Their campaign began with attempts at conversions and false accusations, for which they availed themselves of the assistance of a couple of worthless converted Jews. One of these, Peter Schwarz by name, wrote slanderous and abusive pamphlets against his former co-religionists. The other, one Hans Vayol, heaped the vilest calumnies upon the aged rabbi, Israel Bruna, amongst other things charging him with purchasing from him a seven-year-old Christian child and slaughtering it, and the rabbi of Ratisbon, already bowed down by sorrow and suffering, was charged with the death of the child.

Israel Bruna (of Brünn, born 1400, died 1480) was one of those sons of sorrow who seem to fall from one misfortune into another. He appears to have been exiled from Brünn, where he was recognized as a Rabbinical authority, and after many wanderings, to have traveled by way of Prague to Ratisbon. He settled there, and wished to perform the functions of rabbi for those who might place confidence in him. But a Talmudic scholar who resided in the city, one Amshel, a layman, not an elected rabbi, raised objections to his competitor, and forbade Israel Bruna to hold discourses before disciples, to deal with matters of divorce, to exercise any Rabbinical functions, or to divide the honors of the office with himself. As each had his followers, a schism arose in the community of Ratisbon. His two teachers, Jacob Weil and Isserlein, upholders of the freedom of the Rabbinical office and pronounced opponents of spiritual officialism, took the part of the persecuted Israel Bruna, with whom David Sprinz, a rabbi of Nuremberg, also took sides. These men proved in the clearest manner that any Jew is competent to assume Rabbinical functions, provided he possesses the requisite knowledge, is authorized by a recognized teacher, and leads a pious and moral life. They further adduced in favor of Israel Bruna the fact that he contributed his quota to the communal treasury, and was therefore a worthy member of the community. The breach nevertheless remained open, and Israel Bruna was often exposed to insults from the opposite party. Once when he was about to hold a discourse, several of the ringleaders left the lecture-room, and were followed by many others. Disciples of his opponent secretly painted crosses on his seat in the synagogue, wrote the hateful word "heretic" (Epicuros) beside them, and offered other insults to him. As time went on, after the death of the great rabbis, Jacob Weil and Israel Isserlein, Bruna was recognized as a Rabbinical authority, and from far and near questions were sent to him. His misfortunes, however, did not cease. When Emperor Frederick demanded the crown-tax from the community of Ratisbon, Duke Louis opposed the payment, and the council was unable to decide which side to assist. The emperor thereupon threw Israel Bruna into prison to force him to threaten his people with the ban if they did not pay over the third part of their possessions. He was released only on bail of his entire property; and, in addition, the fearful charges of child-murder and other capital crimes were raised against the decrepit old man by the converted Jew, Hans Vayol. Bishop Henry and the clergy were only too ready to gratify their hatred of Jews by means of this accusation, and the besotted populace gave all the more credence to the falsehood, as rumors of the death of Christian children at the hands of Jews daily increased. No one in Ratisbon doubted that gray old Israel Bruna had foully murdered a Christian child, and he was on the point of being put to death on the demand of the clergy. To withdraw him from the fury of the mob, the council, which feared to be made answerable, imprisoned him.

In the meantime the anxious community appealed, not only to the emperor, but also to the Bohemian king, Ladislaus, more feared than the emperor; and ere long stringent directions came from both to release the rabbi instantly without ransom. The council, however, excused itself on the plea of fear of the bishop and the mob. Thereupon followed a mandate from the emperor to defer the execution of Israel Bruna until he came to the diet at Augsburg. The council was still less satisfied with this order, for it feared to lose its jurisdiction over the Jews. It accordingly prepared to take decisive action in the matter. The accuser, Hans Vayol, was led on the stone bridge, where the executioner stood in readiness. He was informed that he must die, and admonished not to go into eternity with a lie on his lips. The hardened sinner maintained his accusations against the Jews in general, but confessed that the rabbi, Israel Bruna, was innocent of the charge of child-murder, and on receipt of another rescript from the emperor, Vayol was banished, and the rabbi released from prison. He was, however, compelled to take an oath that he would not revenge himself for his long sufferings. This poor, feeble graybeard —how could he have avenged himself?

At this juncture the news of the martyrdom of Simon of Trent reached Ratisbon, and added fuel to the fire. Bishop Henry was delighted to have an opportunity of persecuting the Jews with impunity in the interest of the faith. He had heard something of this child-murder on his journey to Rome. On his return, he urged the council to institute a rigid inquiry respecting the Jews accused by Wolfkan. The result of the extorted confessions was the imprisonment of the whole community. Sentinels stood on guard day and night at the four gates of the Jewry of Ratisbon, and permitted no one to enter or go out. The possessions of the whole community were confiscated by the commissioners and judges who took an inventory of everything. A horrible fate threatened the unhappy children of Israel.

This trial, which caused considerable attention in its day, proved quite as prejudicial to the citizens as to the Jews themselves. Immediately after the inquiry began, several Jews of Ratisbon had betaken themselves to Bohemia and to the emperor, and tried by every means to save their unhappy brethren. They knew that to explain their righteous cause gold, and plenty of it, would be above all things necessary. For this reason several Bavarian rabbis assembled in a synod at Nuremberg, and decided that the Bavarian communities and every individual not absolutely impoverished should contribute a quota to make up the amount necessary to free the accused Jews of Ratisbon. When the safety of their brethren was in question, the Jews, however fond they might be of money, were by no means parsimonious. The intercession of the Bohemian nobles under whose protection several of the Ratisbon community had placed themselves led to no result. Far more efficacious were the golden arguments which the ambassadors of the community laid before Emperor Frederick and his advisers. It is only just to say that this usually feeble sovereign displayed considerable ability and firmness in this inquiry. He was so strongly convinced of the falsehood of the blood accusation against the Jews that he would not allow himself to be deceived by any trickery. He dispatched rescript after rescript to the council of Ratisbon, ordering the immediate release of the imprisoned Jews, the cessation of the durance of the community, and the restoration of their property. The council, through fear of the bishop and the duke, delayed the execution of the order, and the emperor became furious at the obstinacy of the citizens when news was brought to him that, in spite of the imperial command, they had already executed some of the Jews. He thereupon declared the city to have fallen under the ban of the empire on account of its obstinate disobedience, and summoned it to answer for its contumacy. At the same time he sent the imperial chancellor to deprive the city of penal jurisdiction and to threaten it with other severe penalties.

Frederick, as a rule weak, showed surprising firmness on this occasion. New and shameless charges were nevertheless brought by the clergy against the Jews. In Passau they were accused of having bought consecrated wafers from a Christian, and profaned them; whereupon certain marvels were said to have occurred. For this the bishop of Passau had a great number of Jews put to death, some "mercifully" by the sword, others at the stake, and others by means of red-hot pincers. In memory of this inhumanity and "to the glory of God," a new church was built near the scene of the atrocities. A Jew and a Jewess of Ratisbon were accused of complicity in this crime, and thrown into prison with the others. All the details were brought to the notice of the emperor in order to rouse his anger. He, however, maintained his conviction that the Jews of Ratisbon were innocent, and issued a new order to the effect that those in prison on the charge of profaning the host were neither to be tortured nor put to death, but to be treated like other prisoners. In vain the council sent deputy after deputy to the imperial court. Frederick roundly declared, "In justice and honor I neither can nor will permit these Jews to be slain, and the men of Ratisbon who have so long hardened themselves in their disobedience shall certainly not sit in judgment upon them."

Thus, after long resistance, the council was compelled to kiss the rod, and give a written promise to release the imprisoned Jews, and not to drive any out of the city on account of this trial. Further, the city was sentenced to pay a fine of 8,000 gulden into the imperial exchequer and to find bail in 10,000 gulden—which latter burden, strangely enough, the Jews had to bear. An appeal to the pope was out of the question, since experience had taught that "the papal court was even more greedy of gold than the imperial."

When the community of Ratisbon was informed of this conclusion of the affair, and of the conditions under which it could gain its freedom—by paying not only the sum imposed upon itself, but also the fine of the city and the costs of the proceedings—it refused. The delegates said that the total exceeded the possessions of the Jews, as they had been deprived, for three long years, of freedom and all opportunity of earning money. They preferred their present miserable state to becoming beggars. So they remained two years longer in durance, partly on account of lack of money, and partly by reason of the excessive bail demanded. They were finally set at liberty on taking an oath that they would not take revenge, nor convey their persons or their goods out of the city of Ratisbon.

All the Jews living in Suabia were expelled, doubtless in consequence of false accusations in connection with the child-murder of Trent. As late as in the eighteenth century, the shameless falsehood was repeated, and in many parts entailed upon the Jews the sacrifice of life and property.

CHAPTER X.

THE INQUISITION IN SPAIN.

Jewish Blood in the Veins of the Spanish Nobility—The Marranos cling to Judaism and manifest Unconquerable Antipathy to Christianity—Ferdinand and Isabella—The Dominicans, Alfonso de Ojeda, Diego de Merlo, and Pedro de Solis—The Catechism of the Marranos—A Polemical Work against the Catholic Church and Despotism gives a Powerful Impulse to the Inquisition—The Tribunal is established in 1480—Miguel Morillo and Juan de San Martin are the first Inquisitors—The Inquisition in Seville—The "Edict of Grace"—The Procession and the Auto-da-fé—The Numbers of the Accused and Condemned—Pope Sixtus IV and his Vacillating Policy with Regard to the Inquisition—The Inquisition under the first Inquisitor General, Thomas de Torquemada; its Constitutions—The Marranos of Aragon—They are charged with the Death of the Inquisitor Arbues—Persecutions and Victims—Proceedings against two Bishops Favorable to the Jews, De Avila and De Aranda.

1474—1483 C.E.

A JEWISH poet called Spain the "hell of the Jews;" and, in very deed, those foul fiends in monks' cowls, the inventors of the Holy Inquisition, made that lovely land an Inferno. Every misery, every mortal pang, conceived only by the most extravagant imagination of poet; every horror that can thrill the heart of man to its lowest depths, these monsters in the garb of humility brought upon the Jews of the Hesperian Peninsula.

These Calibans also said, "'Burn but their books;' for therein lies their power." The Dominicans wished to destroy not only the bodies, but the very soul and spirit of the Jews. Yet they were not able to quench the life of Judaism. They only succeeded in transforming the Spanish paradise into one vast dungeon, in which the king himself was not free. The Inquisition, created by the begging friars, wounded the Jew deeply, yet not mortally.

His wounds are now almost healed; but Spain suffers still, perhaps beyond hope of cure, from the wounds dealt by the Inquisition. Ferdinand the Catholic and Isabella the Bigot, who, through the union of Aragon and Castile, laid the foundation for the greatness of Spain, prepared the way, at the same time, by the establishment of the Inquisition, for her decay and final ruin.

The new-Christians, who dwelt by hundreds and thousands throughout the kingdoms of Aragon and Castile, were so many thorns in monkish flesh. Many of them held high offices of state, and by means of their wealth wielded great and far-reaching influence. They were also related to many of the old nobility; indeed, there were few families of consequence who had not Jewish blood in their veins. They formed a third part of the townspeople, and were intelligent, industrious, and peaceful citizens. These Marranos, for the most part, had preserved their love for Judaism and their race in the depths of their hearts. As far as they could, they observed Jewish rites and customs, either from piety or from habit. Even those who, upon philosophical grounds, were indifferent to Judaism, were not less irreconcilably hostile to Christianity, which they were compelled to confess with their lips. Although they did not have their children circumcised, they washed the heads of the infants immediately after baptism. They were, therefore, rightly looked upon by the orthodox clergy either as Judaizing Christians, or as apostate heretics. They took no count of the origin of their conversion, which had been accomplished with fire and sword. They had received the sacrament of baptism, and this condemned them and their descendants to remain in the Christian faith, however hateful it might be to them. Rational legislation would have given them liberty to return to Judaism, and, in any case, to emigrate, in order to avoid scandal. But the spiritual powers were full of perversity. That which demands the freest exercise of the powers of the soul was to be brought about by brute force, to the greater glory of God!

During the lifetime of Don Henry IV the clerical members of the cortes of Medina del Campo had persistently advanced the proposal that a court of Inquisition be instituted to bring recusant or suspected Christians to trial, and inflict severe punishment with confiscation of goods. Unfortunately for the clericals, the king was by no means zealous for the faith or fond of persecution; and so this decision of the cortes, like many others, remained a dead letter. The Dominicans, however, promised themselves greater results under the new sovereigns—Queen Isabella, whose confessors had reduced her to spiritual slavery, and Don Ferdinand, who, by no means so superstitiously inclined, was quite ready to use religion as the cloak of his avarice. It is said that the confessor, Thomas de Torquemada, the incarnation of the hell-begotten Holy Inquisition, had extorted from the Infanta Isabella a vow that, when she came to the throne, she would devote herself to the extirpation of heresy, to the glory of God and the exaltation of the Catholic faith. She was now queen; "her throne was established; and her soul was sufficiently beclouded to believe that God had raised her solely to cleanse Spanish Christianity from the taint of Judaism."

The prior of a Dominican monastery, Alfonso de Ojeda, who had the ear of the royal consorts, made fearful representations to them as to the offenses of the new-Christians against the faith. Aided by two others of like mind, he strained every nerve to set the Inquisition in motion against the Marranos; and the papal nuncio in Spain, Nicolo Franco, supported the proposition of the monk for a tribunal to call them to account for their transgressions.

Without further consideration Don Ferdinand, seeing that his coffers would be filled with the plunder of the accused, gave his assent to the scheme. The more scrupulous queen hesitated, and the royal pair decided to appeal to the pope for advice. The two Spanish ambassadors at the court of Rome, the brothers Francisco and Diego de Santillana, earnestly pressed the pope and the college of cardinals to grant the request of their sovereigns. Sixtus IV, from whom anything, good or bad, could be obtained for gold, immediately grasped the money-making aspect of the Holy Inquisition. In November, 1478, he issued a bull empowering the sovereigns to appoint inquisitors from among the clergy, with full authority to sit in judgment on all heretics, apostates, and their patrons, according to the laws and customs of the ancient Inquisition, sentence them, and—most important point of all—confiscate their goods.

Isabella, who had been somewhat favorably influenced in behalf of the new-Christians, was not inclined to adopt rigorous measures to begin with. At her direction, the archbishop of Seville, Cardinal Mendoza, prepared a catechism in 1478 for the use of new-Christians, and issued it to the clergy of his diocese, in order that they might instruct the Marranos in the articles, the sacraments, and the usages of the Christian religion. The authors of this measure displayed strange simplicity in believing that the baptized Jews would allow an antipathy, which every day found new incitement, to be appeased by the dry statements of a catechism. The Marranos naturally remained in what the church considered their blindness; that is to say, in the purity of their monotheism and their adherence to their ancestral religion.

It happened that a Jew or a new-Christian grievously offended the sovereigns by the publication of a small work in which he exposed at once the idolatrous cult of the church and the despotic character of the government. Hereupon the queen became more and more inclined to assent to the proposals for the establishment of the bloody tribunal. The work made so strong an impression that the queen's father-confessor, in 1480, published a refutation by royal command. The attitude of the court became more and more hostile to new-Christians, and when the commission appointed by the sovereigns to inquire into the improvement or obstinacy of the Marranos reported that they were irreclaimable, it was authorized to frame the statute for the new tribunal. The commission was composed of the fanatical Dominican, Alfonso de Ojeda, and the two monks—one in mind and order—Pedro de Solis and Diego de Merlo.

Had demons of nethermost hell conspired to torment innocent men to the last verge of endurance and to make their lives one ceaseless martyrdom, they could not have devised more perfect means than those which the three monks employed against their victims.

The statute was ratified by the sovereigns, and the tribunal of the Holy Inquisition was appointed on September 17th, 1480. It was composed of men well fitted to carry out the bloody decree: the Dominican Miguel Morillo, inquisitor in the province of Roussillon, and renowned as a converter of heretics by means of torture; Juan de San Martin; an assessor, the abbot Juan Ruez, and a procurator fiscal, Juan Lopez del Barco. These men were formally confirmed by Sixtus IV as judges in matters of faith, and of heretics and apostates. The tribunal was first organized for the city of Seville and its neighborhood, as this district stood immediately under royal jurisdiction, and, therefore, possessed no cortes, and because it contained a great many Marranos. Three weeks later the sovereigns issued a decree calling upon all officials to render the inquisitors every assistance in their power.

It is noteworthy that as soon as the creation of

the tribunal became known, the populace everywhere looked upon it with displeasure, as though suspicious that it might be caught in the net spread for the Marranos. While the cortes of Medina del Campo proposed the establishment of a court for new-Christians, the great popular assembly at Toledo in the same year—the first after the accession of Ferdinand and Isabella—maintained absolute silence on the question, as though it desired to have no share in the unholy work. The mayor and other officials of Seville proved so disinclined to assist the inquisitors that it was necessary to issue a second royal decree on December 27th, 1480, directing them to do so. The nobles, allied with the converted Jews either through blood or friendship, stood stoutly by them, and sought by every means to protect them against the new tribunal.

As soon as the new-Christians of Seville and the neighborhood received news of the establishment of the Inquisition, they held a meeting to consider means of turning aside the blow aimed at them. Several wealthy and respected men of Seville, Carmona and Utrera, among them Abulafia, the financial agent of the royal couple, prepared to do battle with their persecutors. They distributed money and weapons among the people, to enable them to defend themselves. An old man urged the conspirators to armed resistance; but the conspiracy was betrayed by the daughter of one of its members, and all fell into the hands of the tribunal. Others, who had collected their possessions, and fled to the province of Medina-Sidonia and Cadiz, under whose governors they hoped to receive protection against the threatened persecution, were deceived, for the Inquisition went to work with remorseless severity. As soon as it had taken up its quarters in the convent of St. Paul at Seville, on January 2d, 1481, it issued an edict to the governor of Cadiz and other officials to deliver up the Marranos and distrain their goods. Those who disobeyed were threatened not only with excommunication, but also with the punishment assigned, as sharers of their guilt, to all who showed sympathy to heretics—confiscation of goods and deprivation of office.

The Inquisition inspired so much terror that the nobility lost no time in imprisoning those to whom they had lately promised protection, and in sending them in custody to Seville. The number of these prisoners was so great that the tribunal was soon obliged to seek another building for its functions. It selected a castle in Triana, a suburb of Seville. On the gate of this house of blood were inscribed, in mockery of the Jews, certain verses selected from their Scriptures:—"Arise, God, judge Thy cause;" "Catch ye foxes for us," which plainly showed the utter heartlessness of their judges. Fugitives when caught were treated as convicted heretics. So early as the fourth day after the installation of the tribunal, it held its first sitting. Six Marranos who had either avowed their old religion before their judges, or made horrible confessions on the rack, were condemned and burnt alive. The tale of victims grew to such proportions that the city authorities set apart a special place as a permanent execution ground, which subsequently became infamous as the Quemadero, or place of burning. Four huge caricatures of prophets distinguished this spot, existing to the present day to the shame of Spain and Christianity. For three hundred years the smoke of the burnt-offering of innocence ascended to heaven from this infernal spot.

With that mildness of mien which skillfully covers the wisdom and the venom of the serpent, Miguel Morillo and his coadjutors gave to the new-Christians guilty of relapse into Judaism a certain time in which to declare their remorse. Upon doing this they would receive absolution, and be permitted to retain their property. This was the Edict of Grace; but it was not wanting in threats for those who should permit the time of respite to elapse, and be denounced by others as backsliders. The full vigor of the canonical laws against heresy and apostasy would then be exercised against them. The credulous in crowds obeyed the summons. Contritely they appeared before the tribunal, lamented the awful guilt of their lapse into Judaism, and awaited absolution and permission to live in peace. But now the inquisitors imposed the condition that they declare by name, position, residence and other particulars all persons of their acquaintance whom they knew to be apostates. This declaration they were to substantiate on oath. In the name of God they were asked to become accusers and betrayers—the friend of his friend, the brother of his brother, and the son of his father. Terror, and the assurance that the betrayed should never know the names of their betrayers, loosed the tongues of the weak-hearted, and the tribunal soon had a long list of heretics upon whom to carry out its bloody work.

Not only the hunted Marranos, every Spaniard was called upon by an edict of the inquisitors to become an informer. Under threat of excommunication every one was bound to give, within three days, a list of acquaintances guilty of Jewish heresy. It was a summons to the most hateful vices of mankind to become allies of the court: to malice, hatred and revenge, to sate themselves by treachery; to greed, to enrich itself; and to superstition, to gain salvation by betrayal.

And what were the signs of this heresy and apostasy? The Inquisition had published a very complete, practical guide on the subject, so that each informer might find good grounds for his denunciation. The following signs of heresy were set forth: if baptized Jews cherished hopes of a Messiah; if they held Moses to be as efficacious for salvation as

Jesus; if they kept the Sabbath or a Jewish feast; if they had their children circumcised; if they observed the Jewish dietary laws; if they wore clean linen or better garments on the Sabbath, laid tablecloths, or lit no fire on this day, or if they went barefoot on the Day of Atonement, or asked pardon of each other. If a father laid his hands in blessing on his children without making the sign of the cross; if one said his prayers with face turned to the wall, or with motions of the head; or if he uttered a benediction (Baraha, Beracha) over the wine-cup, and passed it to those seated at the table with him, he was to be deemed recalcitrant. As a matter of course, neglect of the usages of the church was the strongest ground for suspicion and accusation. Again, if a new-Christian repeated a psalm without adding the Gloria; or if he ate meat on fast-days; or if a Jewish woman did not go to church forty days after her lying-in; or if parents gave their children Jewish names, the charge of heresy was held proved.

Even the most innocent actions, if they happened to coincide with Jewish usages, were regarded as signs of aggravated heresy. If anyone, for instance, on the Jewish Feast of Tabernacles accepted gifts from the table of Jews, or sent them; or if a new-born child was bathed in water in which gold coins and grains of corn had been placed; or if a dying man in his last moments turned his face to the wall—all such actions were held to be signs of heresy.

By such means unscrupulous people were given ample opportunity for denunciation, and the tribunal was enabled to accuse of heresy the most orthodox proselytes when it desired to destroy their influence or confiscate their property. Naturally the dungeons of the Inquisition were soon filled with Jewish heretics. Fully 15,000 were thrown into prison at the outset. The Christian priests of Moloch inaugurated the first auto-da-fé, on January 6th, 1481, with a solemn procession, repeated innumerable times during the following three hundred years. The clergy in their gorgeous vestments and with crucifixes; the grandees in black robes with their banners and pennons; the unhappy victims in the hideous San Benito, short and clinging, painted with a red cross, and flames and figures of devils; the accompanying choir of a vast concourse—so the executioners with proud bearing and the victims in most miserable guise marched to the place of torment. Arrived there the inquisitors recited their sentence on the victims. To the horror of the scene was added the ghastly mockery that the tribunal did not execute the sentence of death, but left it to the secular judge; for the church, though steeped to the lips in blood, was supposed not to desire the death of the sinner. The Jewish heretics were given to the flames forthwith, or, if penitent, they were first strangled. In the first auto-da-fé, at which the bishop, Alfonso de Ojeda, preached the inauguration sermon, only six Judaizing Christians were burnt. A few days later the conspirators of Carmona, Seville, and other towns, and three of the most wealthy and respected of the Marranos, among whom was Diego de Suson, the possessor of ten millions, and Abulafia, formerly a Talmudic scholar and a rabbi, were burnt to death. On the 26th of March seventeen victims suffered death by fire on the Quemadero. In the following month a yet greater number were burnt; and up to November of the same year 298 burnt-offerings to Christ gasped out their lives in flame and smoke in the single district of Seville. In the archbishopric of Cadiz no less than 2,000 Jewish heretics were burnt alive in the course of that year, most of them being wealthy or well-to-do, their possessions, of course, going to the royal exchequer. Not even death afforded a safeguard against the fury of the Holy

Office. These ghouls of religion tore from their graves the corpses of proselytes who had died in heresy, burnt them, confiscated their possessions in the hands of their heirs, and condemned the latter to obscurity and poverty that they might never aspire to any honorable office. Here was a splendid field for the avarice of the king. When it was impossible to convict a wealthy heir, it was only necessary to establish proofs of a relapse to Judaism against his dead father, and then the property fell partly to the king, partly to the Holy Inquisition!

Many Marranos saved themselves by flight from the clutches of the merciless persecutors, and took refuge in the neighboring Moslem kingdom of Granada, in Portugal, Africa, Provence, or Italy. Those who reached Rome approached the papal court with bitter complaints about the savage and arbitrary proceedings of the Inquisition against themselves and their companions in misery. As the complainants did not come with empty hands, their cause usually obtained a ready hearing. On the 29th of January, 1482, the pope addressed a severe letter to Ferdinand and Isabella, censuring the conduct of the Inquisition in no measured terms. He stated that he had been assured that the proceedings of the tribunal were contrary to all forms of justice, that many were unjustly imprisoned, and subjected to fearful tortures. Innocent people had been denounced as heretics, and their property taken from their heirs. In this letter the pope admitted that he had issued the bull for the institution of the Inquisition without due consideration!

Sixtus further stated that, in strict justice, he ought to depose the inquisitors, De Morillo and San Martin; but out of consideration for their majesties he would allow them to remain in possession of their offices, only so long, however, as no further complaints were made against them. Should protests again be raised he would restore the inquisitorial office to the bishops, to whom it properly belonged. The pope refused the request of Don Ferdinand to institute in the other provinces of the united kingdom extraordinary tribunals for the trial of heretics.

But Don Ferdinand also knew how to apply the golden key to the papal cabinet, and obtained a bull sanctioning the establishment of the Inquisition in the provinces of Aragon. In this bull, dated February 11th, 1482, Sixtus appointed six monks and clerics as chief inquisitors, among them Thomas de Torquemada, general of the Dominicans of Avilo, a monk already infamous for his bloodthirsty fanaticism. In another letter, of the 17th of April, he invested these men with discretionary powers, in virtue of which they were able to dispense with certain forms of common law, the hearing of witnesses and the admission of pleaders for the defense. Thus were fresh victims brought to the stake.

In the kingdom of Aragon, however, where the nobility and the middle class had a weighty voice in public matters, the condemnation of Jewish heretics without formal trial raised such formidable opposition that Cardinal Borgia, afterwards the infamous Alexander VI, and the king himself, petitioned the pope for a modification of the conditions governing the practice of the tribunal. In a letter of the 10th of October, Sixtus excused himself from making any radical changes in consequence of the absence of the cardinals, who had fled from Rome in mortal fear of the plague. But he abrogated the conditions which too flagrantly violated the principles of common law; that is to say, he ordered that accuser and witnesses should be confronted with the accused, and that the process should be conducted in public.

The Inquisition also met with great opposition in Sicily, an appanage of the kingdom of Aragon. The people and even the authorities took the part of the new-Christians, and shielded them from the persecution of their bloodthirsty judges. Christians themselves openly charged that the victims were not executed out of zeal for the faith, but from insatiable greed which sought ceaseless confiscations. The bigoted Isabella was sorely troubled at having her pious desire to devote the proselytes to death thus evilly represented, and even the pope behaved as though it wounded him to the heart. (February, 1483.)

Sixtus IV had the greatest interest in maintaining friendly relations with the Spanish court, and, therefore, made every concession with regard to the Inquisition. As it often happened that Christian proselytes condemned by the tribunal, who had succeeded in escaping to Rome, purchased absolution from the papal throne, with the infliction of only a light, private penance, the sovereigns saw that their efforts to purge the Christian faith by the extermination of Jewish proselytes, especially by the confiscation of their goods, were most unpleasantly thwarted. The court, therefore, insisted that the pope appoint a judge of appeals in Spain itself, so that the rulings of the Inquisition might not be reversed in foreign countries, where all kinds of unfavorable influences might be brought to bear. The pope agreed to this proposition, and appointed Inigo Manrique chief judge of appeals in cases in which the condemned moved for a revision of their trial. This measure was, however, of very doubtful benefit to the unfortunate culprits, for upon what ground could they base their appeal when the trial had been conducted in secret, and neither accuser nor witnesses were known to them? It is altogether likely, too, that the tribunal did not leave them very much time to institute proceedings for the revision of the verdict. Between the passing of the sentence and the last act of the auto-da-fé only a very short interval elapsed.

Another measure of the Spanish court, calculated to deprive the accused of the last hope of acquittal, was approved by the pope. Baptized Jews, or new-Christians descended from them, frequently held bishoprics, and were naturally favorably inclined to their unfortunate and persecuted brethren in race. At the request of the Spanish court, the pope issued a bull decreeing that no bishop, vicar, or member of the upper clergy descended from a Jewish family, whether paternally or maternally, should sit as a judge in any court for the trial of heretics. From this prohibition there was only a step to the condemnation of clergy of Jewish blood to the stake. Both his own frame of mind and his political position now inclined the pope to encourage the sovereigns in the prosecution of their bloody work. He reminded them that Jesus had established his kingdom on earth solely by the extirpation of idolatry and the extermination of idolators, and he pointed to the recent victories which the Spaniards had gained over the Moslems in Granada as the reward of heaven for their efforts towards the purification of the faith—that is to say, for the burning of new-Christians and the confiscation of their goods.

Had his Holiness, Sixtus IV, not been infamous as a monster of depravity, sensuality and unscrupulousness, who appointed boys that he had himself abused to bishoprics and the cardinal dignity, and who bestowed no clerical office without payment—as his contemporary, Infessura, the chancellor of Rome, has recorded—his conduct with regard to the Holy Inquisition would have been sufficient to brand him with immortal infamy. Within a short period he published the most contradictory decisions, and did not take the trouble to veil his inconsistency with the most flimsy pretense. Scarcely had he proclaimed the utmost rigors against Judaizing heretics, and appointed a tribunal of appeals, than he partly abrogated these bulls, and issued another prescribing milder proceedings to the Inquisition, only to alter this policy in its turn.

The hated Marranos, among them the high-spirited Juan de Seville, had exerted themselves to procure from the papal court a decree to the effect that those who had undergone private penance in Rome should not be submitted to the oppression and persecution of the avaricious king and his bloodthirsty inquisitors, but should be regarded and treated as orthodox Christians. At first the pope consented, and issued a bull on August 2d, 1483, "to be held in eternal remembrance and as guide for the future," in which he especially directed that rigor be tempered with mercy in dealing with the new-Christians, seeing that the severity of the Inquisition had overstepped the bounds of justice. The bull enacted that all new-Christian who had confessed their remorse to the confessor-general in Rome, and had been assigned a penance, should not be pursued by the Inquisition, and should have their trials suppressed. It exhorted the king and queen, "by the bowels of Jesus Christ," to remember that in mercy and kindness alone may man resemble God, and that, therefore, they might in this follow in the steps of Jesus, whose peculiar attribute it was to show mercy and to pardon. The pope permitted this bull to be copied indefinitely, each copy to have the authority of the original, in order that the papal attitude with regard to new-Christians might be made universally known. Sixtus concluded with the statement that he issued this bull entirely of his own motion, not in obedience to external influence, although it was well known in high circles that it had been bought with new-Christian gold. The sovereigns, however, would have nothing to do with mercy or forbearance; they desired the death of the culprits and the possession of their property. Nor was the pope really inclined to mild measures. A few days later, on August 13th, he recalled this bull, excusing himself to the king for its tenor, and said that it had been issued in too great haste. Such was the consistency and infallibility of his Holiness, Pope Sixtus IV!

In vain Don Juan de Seville, who had procured the promulgation of the favorable bull, endeavored to circulate it. He failed to find any clerical official in Spain to copy and confirm it. He, therefore, applied to the Portuguese archbishop of Evora, who caused it to be copied by his notary and recognized as authentic. The Inquisition, however, was extremely suspicious of those who had sought and obtained indulgences at Rome, and Don Juan de Seville and his companions fell at length into its hands, and were severely punished.

Terrible though the tribunal had hitherto been; though many thousands of compulsory proselytes and their descendants, during its three short years of existence, had been cast into the flames, left to rot in its dungeons, driven from their country, or reduced to beggary, it was child's play compared with what it became when placed under the control of a priest whose heart was closed to every sentiment of mercy, whose lips breathed only death and destruction, and who united the savagery of the hyena with the venom of the snake. Until now the Inquisition had been confined to southern Spain, to the districts of Seville and Cadiz, and the Christian province of Andalusia. In the remaining provinces of Spain it had hitherto been unable to get a footing, in consequence of the resistance offered to its introduction by the cortes. Through the opposition of the people, the wicked will of the inquisitors Morillo and Juan de San Martin had remained inoperative; their uplifted arm was paralyzed by innumerable difficulties. If here and there a few courts were held in the remaining districts of Spain, they were isolated and without organization, and were thus unable to furnish each other with victims. King Ferdinand thus had not yet collected treasure enough, nor had the pious Isabella beheld a sufficient number of new-Christians writhing in the flames. For their joint satisfaction they now persuaded the pope to appoint an inquisitor-general who should constitute, direct, and supervise the several courts, that none of the suspected Marranos might avoid their fate, and that the opposition of the populace might be broken down by every species of terrorism. In cold blood, and with little interest even for the faith itself, the pope assented; and in May, 1483, appointed the Dominican, Thomas de Torquemada, hitherto prior of a monastery in Segovia, inquisitor-general of Spain. There are certain men who are the embodiment of good or evil sentiments, opinions and principles, and fully illustrate their extremest consequences. Torquemada was the incarnation of the Holy Inquisition with all its devilish malice, its heartless severity, its bloodthirsty ferocity.

"Out of Rome hath arisen a savage monster of such wondrous shape and hideous appearance that at the sound of its name all Europe trembles. Its carcass is of iron, tempered in deadly poison, and covered with scales of impenetrable steel. A thousand venom-dropping wings support it when it hovers over the terrified earth. Its nature is that of the ravening lion and the snake of the African desert. Its bite is more terrible than that of the hugest monster. The sound of its voice slays more speedily than the deadly glance of the basilisk. From its eyes and mouth stream fire and ceaseless lightnings. It feeds on human bodies, and its drink is human tears and blood. It excels the eagle in the speed of its flight, and where it broods its black shadow spreads the gloom of night. Though the sun shine never so clearly, the darkness of Egypt follows in its track. Wheresoever it flies, every green meadow that it touches, every fruitful tree on which it sets foot, withers and dies. With its destroying fangs it roots up every herb that grows, and with the poison of its breath it blasts the circle in which it moves to a desert like that of Syria, where no green thing grows, no grass-blade sprouts."

Thus did a Jewish poet, Samuel Usque, himself singed by its flames, depict the Inquisition.

The inscription which the poet Dante placed upon the portal of Hell—

> "All hope abandon, ye who enter here!"

would have been even more suitable to the dungeons of the Holy Inquisition, which the cruel energy of Torquemada now established in nearly all the great towns of Spain. He at once instituted three new tribunals in Cordova, Jaen and Villareal (Ciudad-Real), and, later on, one in Toledo, the capital of southern Spain. The offices of the Inquisition were entirely filled by him with hypocritical and fanatical Dominicans, whom he made the tools of his will, so that they worked like an organism with a single head, ready at his word to perpetrate the most hideous barbarities with a composure that cannibals might have envied. In those days Spain was filled with the putrefaction of the dungeon, the stench of corpses, and the crackling of the flames in which were burning innocent Jews, forced into a faith the falsity of which was demonstrated by every action of the servants of the church. A wail of misery piercing bone and marrow went through that lovely land; but their Catholic majesties paralyzed the arm of every man prompted by mercy to put a stop to the butchery. At the court itself there sat a commission on the affairs of Jewish Christians, of which the inquisitor-general held the presidency.

Don Ferdinand wished to perpetuate the jurisdiction of the Inquisition in his hereditary lands, in order to fill his purse with the spoils of the new-Christians settled there. During the assembly of the cortes at Tarazona, in April, 1484, he laid his plans before his privy council, and canceled the ancient privileges of the country, which had existed from the earliest times, and which provided that no native of Aragon, whatever his crime, should suffer confiscation of his property. The inquisitor-general accordingly appointed for the archbishopric of Saragossa two inquisitors who rivaled himself in bloodthirsty fanaticism, the canon, Pedro Arbues de Epila, and the Dominican, Gaspard Juglar. A royal ordinance was now issued to all officials and nobles, directing them to give every assistance to the inquisitors. The grand justiciary of Aragon, though of Jewish origin, and other dignitaries, were obliged to take an oath that they would spare no efforts to exterminate the culprits condemned by the tribunal.

Torquemada, the very soul of the Inquisition, now decided to publish a code for the guidance of the judges, so that the net might be drawn as closely as possible round his victims. The whole body of inquisitors was assembled to consider this design, and, under the title of "Constitutions," issued, on October 29th, 1484, a code of laws, calculated to inspire the utmost horror had no more been done than commit them to paper. It has been asserted that the monkish inquisitors merely copied the anti-Jewish enactments of the councils under the Visigothic kings. It is true that the decrees of Receswinth threatened with death, by fire or stoning, all new-Christians convicted of adherence to Jewish customs. The comparison is, nevertheless, incorrect. For not the enactments against heresy, but their enforcement, distinguishes the "Constitutions" of the Inquisition as the most hideous ever fashioned by human wickedness. It was as though the most malicious demons had taken counsel to discover how they might bring innocent human beings to destruction.

One decree ordained a respite of thirty days for those who of their own free will would tender confession of their relapse to Judaism. These were to be spared all punishment and confiscation of goods with the exception of a moderate fine. They were, however, compelled to put their confession into writing, to give exact answers to all questions put to them, and especially to betray their fellow-offenders, and even those whom they only suspected of Judaizing tendencies. Those who confessed after the expiration of the time of respite were to lose all their property, even that which they had possessed at the time of their falling away from Christianity, and though it had passed into other hands. Only new-Christians under twenty years old were exempted from loss of property in the event of later confessions; but they were compelled to bear a mark of infamy composed of flaming crosses, the San Benito, upon their clothing, and to take part in the processions and attend high mass in this guise. Those whose remorse awakened after the appointed day were indeed to receive indulgence, but they were to remain branded for life. Neither they nor their descendants were ever to hold any public office, nor to wear any garment embroidered with gold, silver or pearls, or made of silk or fine wool, and they were condemned to bear the "fiery cross" for ever. Should the inquisitors discover that the confession of a penitent was insincere, it was their duty to deny him absolution, to treat him as a recalcitrant, and to consign him to the flames. If a penitent made only a partial confession of his sins, he, too, was condemned to death. The evidence against a Judaizing Christian might, when not otherwise convenient, be taken through other persons. It was not necessary to place this testimony before the accused in full detail, but merely as an abstract. If, in spite of the evidence laid before him, he maintained that he had never relapsed into Judaism, he was condemned to the flames as impenitent. Inconclusive proofs of relapse brought against a Marrano stretched him upon the rack; in case he confessed under torture, he was submitted to a second trial. If he then adhered to what he had confessed under torture he was condemned; if he denied it, he underwent the torture again. In those cases in which an accused person failed to answer to the summons issued against him, he was condemned as a contumacious heretic, *i. e.*, his property was confiscated.

In the face of such proceedings—the parody of a trial—and the pre-determination on the part of the judge to consider the accused guilty, how was it possible for any Marrano to prove his innocence? The dungeon and the rack frequently made the accused so indifferent to their fate and so weary of life that they made confessions as to themselves, their friends and even their nearest relatives which appeared to vindicate the necessity for the Inquisition. The trial of every new-Christian involved others in apparent guilt, and brought new examinations and new accusations in its train, thus furnishing an ever-increasing number of victims to the Holy Office.

The towns of the kingdoms of Aragon and Valencia had from the first manifested the greatest displeasure at the introduction of the Inquisition. Up to this period they had been less despotically governed than Castile, and were exceedingly jealous of their freedom. Above everything the Aragonese valued, as the apple of their eye, the privilege which forbade the confiscation of goods even on account of the gravest offenses. Now the officers of the Inquisition were to be invested with unlimited power over life and property. The new-Christians, who held high offices and influential positions in Aragon, were naturally eager to foment and increase the discontent. In Teruel and Valencia, in 1485, disastrous popular risings broke out against the Inquisition, and were quelled only after great bloodshed.

The Marranos and those of Jewish descent did not, however, surrender their project of paralyzing the Inquisition in Aragon. Some of the highest dignitaries of state were numbered among them ; as, for example, Luis Gonzalez, royal secretary of state for Aragon; Alfonso de Caballeria, the vice-chancellor; his brother, the king's major-domo; Philip Clemente, chief notary; and such high hidalgos as the Counts of Aranda, together with many knights, among whom were the valiant Juan de Abadia, whose sister was burnt for heresy, and Juan Perez Sanchez, whose brothers were at court.

As soon as the first victims fell under the Inquisition in Saragossa, influential new-Christians brought pressure to bear upon the cortes to induce them to protest, both to the king and to the pope, against the introduction of the tribunal into Aragon. Commissioners were sent to the royal and papal courts to effect in person the repeal of the ordinances. They expected but little trouble in Rome, for there everything was to be had for money. With the king it seemed to be a matter of much greater difficulty. Ferdinand remained obstinately fixed in the resolution to exterminate the Jewish Christians by means of the Inquisition, and to acquire their property. When the commissioners sent news to their friends in Aragon of the failure of their efforts, Perez Sanchez conceived a plot to remove Pedro Arbues, chief inquisitor for Aragon, in order to cripple the activity of the Inquisition by terrorism, and to force the king to give way. He imparted his project to his friends, and many bound themselves to stand by him. In order to win over the entire body of new-Christians, and to induce them to stand firmly together, the leaders of the conspiracy laid them under contribution for the expenses of carrying out the project. A hidalgo, Blasco de Alagon, collected the money, and Juan de Abadia undertook to hire the assassins, and to see that the death of Arbues was achieved. This conspiracy was joined by many distinguished persons of Jewish descent in Saragossa, Tarazona, Calatayud, Huesca and Barbastro.

Juan de Abadia procured two trustworthy men, Juan de Esperaindo and Vidal de Uranso, with four assistants, to accomplish the death of the inquisitor Arbues. The intended victim appears to have suspected the plot, for he protected his body with a shirt of mail and his head with a species of steel cap. Before daybreak on the 15th of September, 1485, as he was entering the church with a lantern to hear early mass, the conspirators followed him. As soon as he had fallen on his knees, Esperaindo struck him on the arm with his sword, while Vidal wounded him in the neck. He was borne out of the church bathed in blood, and died two days later. The conspirators took instant flight. As soon as the news of the attack on the chief inquisitor spread in Saragossa it produced a violent reaction. The orthodox Christians assembled in crowds crying in tones of fury: "To the flames with the Jew-Christians! They have murdered the chief inquisitor!" The Marranos would have been massacred in a body there and then, had not the royal bastard, the youthful Archbishop Alfonso of Aragon, mounted his horse, and restrained the crowd by an armed force, promising them the fullest satisfaction by the severe punishment of the guilty persons and their accomplices.

King Ferdinand made good use of the unfortunate conspiracy in the establishment of the Inquisition in Aragon. The sovereigns carried public mourning for the murdered Arbues to the verge of idolatry. A statue was consecrated to his memory, in honor of his services to religion and the extermination of Jewish heretics. The Dominicans were by no means displeased at the death of the chief inquisitor. They were, in fact, in need of a martyr to enable them to surround their tribunal of blood with a halo of glory. They used every effort to raise Pedro Arbues to the rank of saint or Christian demi-god. It was not long before they fabricated a divine communication from the sainted heretic-slayer, in which he exhorted all the world to support and carry forward the Holy Inquisition, and soothed the scruples of the members of the tribunal, on account of the enormous number of men they had consigned to the flames, by assuring them that the most honorable places in heaven awaited them as the reward of their pious efforts.

The unsuccessful conspiracy of the Marranos in Saragossa afforded a vast number of fresh victims to the Christian Moloch. A few of the conspirators made full confession, and so the inquisitors soon had a complete list of the culprits. These were pursued with redoubled vigor as Judaizing heretics and enemies of the Holy Office. Those who had borne a leading part in the conspiracy, as soon as they fell into the hands of their judges, were dragged through the streets of Saragossa, their hands were hewn off, and they were then hanged. Juan de Abadia escaped this dishonorable fate by killing himself in prison. More than two hundred Jewish Christians were burnt as accomplices, a yet greater number were condemned to perpetual imprisonment, among them a high dignitary of the Metropolitan Church of Saragossa, and not a few women of gentle birth. Francisco de Sante-Fé also died at the stake. Even those who had given shelter to the conspirators for a brief period during their flight were compelled to attend an auto-da-fé as penitents, and lost their civil rights. How far the inhumanity of the persecutors went is especially shown by one of the punishments inflicted. A conspirator, Gaspard de Santa Cruz, had been successful in making his escape to Toulouse, and there died in peace. The Inquisition, not content with burning him in effigy, laid hands upon his son as an accomplice in his father's flight, and condemned him to travel to Toulouse to communicate his sentence to the Dominicans of that city, and to desire them to exhume the body of his father and burn it. The weak son performed his disgraceful mission, and brought back to Saragossa the certificate of the Dominicans to the effect that the corpse of the father had been dishonored on the prayer of the son.

Certain towns of northern Spain, such as Lerida and Barcelona, still obstinately resisted the introduction of the Inquisition. Their resistance proved vain. The iron will of Fernando and the bloodthirsty fanaticism of Torquemada overcame every obstacle, and the papal court was obliged to give its assent to every proposal. From that time forth the number of victims continued to increase. On the 12th of February, 1486, an auto-da-fé was celebrated in Toledo with 750 human burnt-offerings, while on the 2d of April in the same year, 900 victims were offered up, and on the 7th of May, 750. On the 16th of August twenty-five Jewish heretics were burnt alive in Toledo; on the following day two priests suffered; and on the 10th of December 950 persons were condemned to shameful public penance. In the following year, when the Inquisition was established in Barcelona and on the island of Majorca, two hundred Marranos suffered death by fire in these places alone. A Jew of that time, Isaac Arama, writes on this subject as follows: "In these days the smoke of the martyr's pyre rises unceasingly to heaven in all the Spanish kingdoms and the isles. One-third of the Marranos have perished in the flames, another third wander homeless over the earth seeking where they may hide themselves, and the remainder live in perpetual terror of a trial." So the tale of victims grew from year to year under the eleven tribunals which transformed the fair land of Spain into a blazing Tophet, whose flames soon reached and devoured the Christians themselves.

The pitiless persecution of the new-Christians had its origin perhaps even more in the racial hatred of the pure-blooded Spaniards towards the children of Judah than in religious fanaticism. Persons of Jewish descent, whom it was impossible justly to accuse of heresy, were included in the accusations simply because they held high offices. They were not permitted to enjoy any dignity or to exercise any influence in the country. The inquisitor-general, Torquemada, even laid hands upon two bishops of Jewish blood, De Avila and De Aranda, so that, if it were impossible to consign them to the flames, he might at least expel them from their sees.

CHAPTER XI.

EXPULSION OF THE JEWS FROM SPAIN.

Friendship of Marranos and Jews—Torquemada demands of the Rabbis of Toledo the Denunciation of Marranos—Judah Ibn-Verga—Jewish Courtiers under Ferdinand and Isabella—Isaac Abrabanel: his History and Writings—The Jews of Portugal under Alfonso V—The Ibn-Yachya Brothers—Abrabanel's Flight from Portugal to Spain—The Jews of Granada: Isaac Hamon—Edict of Banishment promulgated by Ferdinand and Isabella—Its Consequences—Departure from Spain—Number of the Exiles—Decline in the Prosperity of Spain after the Banishment of the Jews—Transformation of Synagogues and Schools into Churches and Monasteries—The Inquisition and the Marranos—Deza, the Successor of Torquemada.

1483—1492 C.E.

THE monster of the Inquisition, having poured out its wrath on the new-Christians, now stretched its arms over the Jews, and delivered them to a miserable fate. The connection between the Jews and the Marranos was too close for the former not to be made to participate in the misfortunes of the latter. They were in intimate relations with each other, were bound to each other by close, brotherly ties. The Jews experienced heartfelt pity for their unfortunate brethren, so unwillingly wearing the mask of Christianity, and strove to keep them in touch with the Jewish community. They instructed Christian-born Marranos in the rites of Judaism, held secret meetings with them for prayer, furnished them with religious books and writings, kept them informed of the occurrence of fasts and festivals, supplied them at Easter with unleavened bread, and throughout the year with meat prepared according to their own ritual, and circumcised their new-born sons. In Seville, in fact in the whole of Andalusia, there were countless new-Christians, baptized at the time of the furious attack upon the Jews by Ferdinand Martinez, and later during the persecution of 1391, so that it offered a good field for the activity of Jews who were endeavoring to bring back turncoat brethren into the ranks of Judaism. One of the most active in this work was Judah Ibn-Verga, of Seville, Kabbalist and astronomer, who was held in high estimation by the governor of Andalusia. The king and queen intended to call the Inquisition into existence here, and the first step was to separate the Jews from Christians, especially new-Christians, and to destroy every connecting link between them. The cortes of Toledo insisted on the enforcement of the stringent regulations—hitherto so frequently evaded—for special Jewish (and Moorish) quarters, but the strictly executed law of separation, made to take effect all over the kingdom, could not sever the loving relations existing between Jews and Marranos. In spite of all, the closest intercommunion was maintained, only more secretly, more circumspectly. The greater the danger of discovery, the the greater the charm of meeting, despite the Argus eyes of priestly spies and their myrmidons, for mutual solace and encouragement. These meetings of the Jews and Moors, from the secrecy with which they were conducted, and the danger attending them, wore a romantic aspect. A loving bond of union was thus created, which grew closer and stronger for every effort to loosen it.

The fiendish Torquemada strove by every possible means to destroy these ties. As soon as he had become grand inquisitor, he issued a command that Marranos should present themselves for confession, ordered the rabbis of Toledo to be convened, and exacted from them an oath that they would inform against new-Christians who observed Jewish rites and ceremonies, and would excommunicate Jews who refused to become witnesses against their own people. They were threatened with heavy punishment if they refused to take this oath (1485). What a tragical struggle for the rabbis of Toledo! They themselves were to lend a hand to wrench their faithful brethren from Judaism, and deliver them over to Christianity, or, rather, to the stake! Surely, they could not be brought to this, and preferred to suffer punishment! Judah Ibn-Verga, ordered by the inquisitors to deliver over pseudo-Christians who secretly clung to Judaism, chose to leave his native Seville, and fled to Lisbon, where he eventually died a martyr's death. Since the inquisitors could not attain their ends through Jews, who, despite all measures, continued their secret intercourse with new-Christians, they urged the king and queen to issue a mandate for the partial expulsion of the Jews from Andalusia, especially from Seville.

The Castilian and Aragonese Jews might have known, from these sad events, that their sojourn could not be of long duration; but they loved Spain too dearly to part from her except under compulsion. Besides, the king and queen often protected them from unfair treatment. When they removed to special Jewish quarters, Ferdinand and Isabella were at great pains to shield them from annoyance and chicanery. Moreover, under the rule of these Catholic sovereigns there were Jewish tithe and tax collectors, and, finally, the Jews relied upon the fact that they were indispensable to the Christians. The sick preferred to seek advice with Jewish physicians, the lower classes consulted Jews on legal questions, and even asked them to read the letters or documents which they received from the clergy. In addition to all this, it happened that, at the time when Torquemada was casting his snares over the Moors and Jews, the celebrated Abrabanel received an important post at the court of Castile, and enjoyed unlimited confidence. Under his protection the Spanish Jews hoped to be able to defy the fury of the venomous Dominicans. Abrabanel's favored position at court, the geniality of his character, his affection for the Hebrew race, his love of learning, and his tried wisdom, brought back the time of Samuel Nagrela, and lulled the Jews with false hopes.

Don Isaac ben Judah Abrabanel (born in Lisbon 1437, died in Venice 1509) worthily closes the list of Jewish statesmen in Spain who, beginning with Chasdaï Ibn-Shaprut, used their names and positions to protect the interests of their race. In his noble-mindedness, his contemporaries saw proofs of Abrabanel's descent from the royal house of David, a distinction on which the Abrabanels prided themselves, and which was generally conceded to them. His grandfather, Samuel Abrabanel, who, during the persecution of 1391, but probably only for a short time, lived as a Christian, was a large-hearted, generous man, who supported Jewish learning and its votaries. His father, Judah, treasurer to a Portuguese prince, was wealthy and benevolent. Isaac Abrabanel was precocious, of clear understanding, but sober-minded, without imagination and without depth. The realities of life, present conditions and events, he grasped with unerring tact; but what was distant, less obvious to ordinary perceptions, lay veiled in a mist which he was unable to penetrate or dispel. The origin of Judaism, its splendid antiquity, and its conception of God, were favorite themes with Abrabanel from his youth upward, and when still quite a young man he published a treatise setting forth the providence of God and its special relation to Israel. Philosophical conceptions were, however, acquired, not innate with him; he had no ability to solve metaphysical questions. On the other hand, he was a solid man of business, who thoroughly understood finance and affairs of state. The reigning king of Portugal, Don Alfonso V, an intelligent, genial, amiable ruler, was able to appreciate Abrabanel's talents; he summoned him to his court, confided to him the conduct of his financial affairs, and consulted him on all important state questions. His noble disposition, his sincerely devout spirit, his modesty, far removed from arrogance, and his unselfish prudence, secured for him at court, and far outside its circle, the esteem and affection of Christian grandees. Abrabanel stood in friendly intimacy with the powerful, but mild and beneficent Duke Ferdinand of Braganza, lord of fifty towns, boroughs, castles, and fortresses, and able to bring 10,000 foot-soldiers and 3,000 cavalry into the field, as also with his brothers, the Marquis of Montemar, Constable of Portugal, and the Count of Faro, who lived together in fraternal affection. With the learned John Sezira, who was held in high consideration at court, and was a warm patron of the Jews, he enjoyed close friendship. Abrabanel thus describes his happy life at the court of King Alfonso:

> "Tranquilly I lived in my inherited house in fair Lisbon. God had given me blessings, riches and honor. I had built myself stately buildings and chambers. My house was the meeting-place of the learned and the wise. I was a favorite in the palace of Alfonso, a mighty and upright king, under whom the Jews enjoyed freedom and prosperity. I was close to him, was his support, and while he lived I frequented his palace."

Alfonso's reign was the end of the golden time for the Jews of the Pyrenean Peninsula. Although in his time the Portuguese code of laws (Ordenaçoens de Alfonso V), containing Byzantine elements and canonical restrictions for the Jews, was completed, it must be remembered that, on the one hand, the king, who was a minor, had had no share in framing them, and, on the other, the hateful laws were not carried out. In his time the Jews in Portugal bore no badge, but rode on richly caparisoned horses and mules, wore the costume of the country, long coats, fine hoods and silken vests, and carried gilded swords, so that they could not be distinguished from Christians. The greater number of the tax-farmers (Rendeiros) in Portugal were Jews. Princes of the church even appointed Jewish receivers of church taxes, at which the cortes of Lisbon raised complaint. The independence of the Jewish population under the chief rabbi and the seven provincial rabbis was protected in Alfonso's reign, and included in the code. This code conceded to Jews the right to print their public documents in Hebrew, instead of in Portuguese as hitherto commanded.

Abrabanel was not the only Jewish favorite at Alfonso's court. Two brothers Ibn-Yachya Negro also frequented the court of Lisbon. They were sons of a certain Don David, who had recommended them not to invest their rich inheritance in real estate, for he saw that banishment was in store for the Portuguese Jews.

As long as Isaac Abrabanel enjoyed the king's favor, he was as a "shield and a wall for his race, and delivered the sufferers from their oppressors, healed differences, and kept fierce lions at bay," as described by his poetical son, Judah Leon. He who had a warm heart for all afflicted, and was father to the orphan and consoler to the sorrowing, felt yet deeper compassion for the unfortunate of his own people. When Alfonso conquered the port of Arzilla, in Africa, the victors brought with them, among many thousand captive Moors, 250 Jews, who were sold as slaves throughout the kingdom. That Jews and Jewesses should be doomed to the miseries of slavery was unendurable to Abrabanel's heart. At his summons a committee of twelve representatives of the Lisbon community was formed, and collected funds; then, with a colleague, he traveled over the whole country and redeemed the Jewish slaves, often at a high price. The ransomed Jews and Jewesses, adults and children, were clothed, lodged, and maintained until they had learned the language of the country, and were able to support themselves.

When King Alfonso sent an embassy to Pope Sixtus IV to congratulate him upon his accession to the throne, and to send him tidings of his victory over the Moors in Africa, Doctor John Sezira was one of the ambassadors. One in heart and soul with Abrabanel, and friendly to the Jews, he promised to speak to the pope in their favor and behalf. Abrabanel begged his Italian friend, Yechiel of Pisa, to receive John Sezira with a friendly welcome, to place himself entirely at his disposal, and convey to him, and to the chief ambassador, Lopes de Almeida, how gratified the Italian Jews were to hear of King Alfonso's favor to the Jews in his country, so that the king and his courtiers might feel flattered. Thus Abrabanel did everything in his power for the good of his brethren in faith and race.

In the midst of prosperity, enjoyed with his gracious and cultured wife and three fine sons, Judah Leon, Isaac and Samuel, he was disturbed by the turn of affairs in Portugal. His patron, Alfonso V, died, and was succeeded by Don João II (1481—1495), a man in every way unlike his father—stronger of will, less kindly, and full of dissimulation. He had been crowned in his father's lifetime, and was not rejoiced when Alfonso, believed to be dead, suddenly re-appeared in Portugal. João II followed the tactics of his unscrupulous contemporary, Louis XI of France, in the endeavor to rid himself of the Portuguese grandees in order to create an absolute monarchy. His first victim was to be Duke Ferdinand of Braganza, of royal blood, almost as powerful and as highly considered as himself, and better beloved. Don João II was anxious to clear from his path this duke and his brothers, against whom he had a personal grudge. While flattering the Duke of Braganza, he had a letter set up against him, accusing him of a secret, traitorous understanding with the Spanish sovereigns, the truth of which has not to this day been satisfactorily ascertained. He arrested him with a Judas kiss, caused him to be tried as a traitor to his country, sent him to the block, and took possession of his estates and wealth (June, 1483). His brothers were forced to fly to avoid a like fate. Inasmuch as Isaac Abrabanel had lived in friendly relations with the Duke of Braganza and his brothers, King João chose to suspect him of having been implicated in the recent conspiracies. Enemies of the Jewish statesman did their best to strengthen these suspicions. The king sent a command for him to appear before him. Not suspecting any evil, Abrabanel was about to obey, when an unknown friend appeared, told him his life was in danger, and counseled him to hasty flight. Warned by the fate of the Duke of Braganza, Abrabanel followed the advice, and fled to Spain. The king sent mounted soldiery after him, but they could not overtake him, and he reached the Spanish border in safety. In a humble but manly letter he declared his innocence of the crime, and also the innocence of the Duke of Braganza. The suspicious tyrant gave no credence to the letter of defense, but caused Abrabanel's property to be confiscated, as also that of his son, Judah Leon, who was already following the profession of a physician. His wife and children, however, he permitted to remove to Castile.

In the city of Toledo, where he found refuge, Isaac Abrabanel was honorably received by the Jews, especially by the cultured. A circle of learned men and disciples gathered round the famous, innocently persecuted Jewish statesman. With the rabbi, Isaac Aboab, and with the chief tithe-collector, Abraham Senior, he formed a close friendship. The latter, it seems, at once took him into partnership in the collection of taxes. Abrabanel's conscience pricked him for having neglected the study of the Law in following state affairs and mammon, and he attributed his misfortunes to the just punishment of heaven. He at once began to write, at the earnest entreaty of his new friends, an exposition of the books of the earlier prophets, hitherto, on account of their apparent simplicity, neglected by commentators. As he had given thought to them before, he soon completed the work. Certainly, no one was better qualified than Abrabanel to expound historical biblical literature. In addition to knowledge of languages, he had experience of the world, and the insight into political problems and complications necessary for unraveling the Israelitish records.

He had the advantage over other expositors in using the Christian exegetical writings of Jerome, Nicholas de Lyra, and the baptized Paul of Burgos, and taking from them what was most valuable. Abrabanel, therefore, in these commentaries, shed light upon many obscure passages. They are conceived in a scholarly style, arranged systematically, and before each book appear a comprehensible preface and a table of contents, an arrangement copied from Christian commentators, and adroitly turned to account by him. Had Abrabanel not been so diffuse in style, and not had the habit of introducing each Scriptural chapter with superflous questions, his dissertations would have been, or, at all events, would have deserved to be, more popular. Nor should he have gone beyond his province into philosophical inquiry. Abrabanel accepted the orthodox point of view of Nachmani and Chasdaï, merely supplementing them with commonplaces of his own. He was not tolerant enough to listen to a liberal view of Judaism and its doctrines, and accused the works of Albalag and Narboni of heresy, classing these inquirers with the unprincipled apostate, Abner-Alfonso, of Valladolid. He was no better pleased with Levi ben Gerson, because he had resorted to philosophical interpretations in many cases, and did not accept miracles unconditionally. Like the strictly orthodox Jews of his day, such as Joseph

Jaabez, he was persuaded that the humiliations and persecutions suffered by the Jews of Spain were due to their heresy. Yet, did German Jews, wholly untouched by heretical philosophy, suffer less than their brethren in Spain? Only a brief time was granted to Abrabanel to pursue his favorite study; the author was once more compelled to become a statesman. When about to delineate Judæan and Israelite monarchs, he was summoned to the court of Ferdinand and Isabella to be intrusted with the care of their finances. The revenues seem to have prospered under his management, and during his eight years of office (March, 1484—March, 1492) nothing went wrong with them. He was very useful to the royal pair by reason of his wisdom and prudent counsel. Abrabanel himself relates that he grew rich in the king's service, and bought himself land and estates, and that from the court and the highest grandees he received great consideration and honor. He must have been indispensable, seeing that the Catholic sovereigns, under the very eyes of the malignant Torquemada, and in spite of canonical decrees and all the resolutions repeatedly laid down by the cortes forbidding Jews to hold office in the government, were compelled to intrust this Jewish minister of finance with the mainspring of political life! How many services Abrabanel did for his own people during his time of office, grateful memory could not preserve by reason of the storm of misfortunes which broke upon the Jews later; but in Castile, as he had been in Portugal, he was as a wall of protection to them. Lying and fearful accusations from their bitter foes, the Dominicans, were not wanting. At one time it was said that the Jews had shown disrespect to some cross; at another, that in the town of La Guardia they had stolen and crucified a Christian child. From this tissue of lies, Torquemada fabricated a case against the Jews, and condemned the supposed criminals to the stake. In Valencia they were declared to have made a similar attempt, but to have been interrupted in the deed (1488—1490). That the Castilian Jews did not suffer extinction for the succor they afforded the unfortunate Marranos, was certainly owing to Abrabanel.

Meantime began the war with Granada, so disastrous for the Moors and Jews, which lasted with intervals for ten years (1481—1491). To this the Jews had to contribute. A heavy impost was laid upon the community (Alfarda—Strangers' Tax), on which the royal treasurer, Villaris, insisted with the utmost strictness. The Jews were, so to say, made to bring the fagots to their own funeral pyre, and the people, adding insult to injury, mocked them. In the province of Granada, which by pride had brought about its own fall, there were many Jews, their numbers having been increased by the Marranos who had fled thither to avoid death at the stake. Their position was not enviable, for Spanish hatred of Jews was strongly implanted there; but their creed was not attacked, and their lives were not in constant peril. Isaac Hamon was physician in ordinary to one of the last kings of Granada, and enjoyed high favor at court. One day a quarrel arose in the streets of Granada, and the bystanders implored the disputants to leave off in the name of their prophet, but in vain. But when they were bidden to give over in the name of the royal physician, they yielded. This occurrence, which testified that Isaac Hamon was held in more respect by the populace than the prophet Mahomet, roused certain bigoted Mahometans to fall upon the Jews of Granada and butcher them. Only those escaped who found refuge in the royal castle. The Jewish physicians of Granada came to the resolution henceforth not to clothe themselves in silken garments, nor ride on horseback, in order to avoid exciting the envy of the Mahometans.

After long and bloody strife the beautiful city of Granada fell into the hands of the proud Spaniards. Frivolous Muley Abu-Abdallah (Boabdil), the last king, signed a secret treaty with Ferdinand and Isabella (25th November, 1491) to give up the town and its territory by a certain time. The conditions, seeing that independence was lost, were tolerably favorable. The Moors were to keep their religious freedom, their civil laws, their right to leave the country, and above all their manners and customs, and were only required to pay the taxes which hitherto they had paid the Moorish king. The renegades—that is to say, Christians who had adopted Islam, or, more properly speaking, the Moorish pseudo-Christians—who had fled from the Inquisition to Granada, and returned to Islam, were to remain unmolested. The Inquisition was not to claim jurisdiction over them. The Jews of the capital of Granada, of the Albaicin quarter, the suburbs and the Alpujarras, were included in the provisions of the treaty. They were to enjoy the same indulgences and the same rights, except that relapsed Marranos were to leave the city, only the first month after its surrender being the term allowed for emigration; those who stayed longer were to be handed over to the Inquisition. One noteworthy point, stipulated by the last Moorish king of Granada, was that no Jew should be set over the vanquished Moors as officer of justice, tax-gatherer, or commissioner. On January 2d, 1492, Ferdinand and Isabella, with their court, amid ringing of bells, and great pomp and circumstance, made their entry into Granada. The Mahometan kingdom of the Peninsula had vanished like a dream in an Arabian Nights' legend. The last prince, Muley Abu-Abdallah, cast one long sad farewell look, "with a last sigh," over the glory forever lost, and retired to the lands assigned to him in the Alpujarras, but, unable to overcome his dejection, he turned his steps towards Africa. After nearly eight hundred years the whole Pyrenean Peninsula again became Christian, as it had been in the time of the Visigoths. But heaven could not rejoice over this conquest, which delivered fresh human sacrifices to the lords of hell. The Jews were the first to experience the tragical effect of this conquest of Granada.

The war against the Mahometans of Granada, originally undertaken to punish attempts at encroachment and breach of faith, assumed the character of a crusade against unbelief, of a holy war for the exaltation of the cross and the spread of the Christian faith. Not only the bigoted queen and the unctuous king, but also many Spaniards were dragged by this conquest into raging fanaticism. Are the unbelieving Mahometans to be vanquished, and the still more unbelieving Jews to go free in the land? This question was too pertinent not to meet with an answer unfavorable to the Jews. The insistence of Torquemada and friends of his own way of thinking, that the Jews, who had long been a thorn in their flesh, should be expelled, at first met with indifference, soon began to receive more attention from the victors. Then came the consideration that owing to increased opulence, consequent on the booty acquired from the wealthy towns of conquered Granada, the Jews were no longer indispensable. Before the banner of the cross waved over Granada, Ferdinand and Isabella had contemplated the expulsion of the Jews. With this end in view, they had sent an embassy to Pope Innocent VII, stating that they were willing to banish the Jews from the country, if he, Christ's representative, the avenger of his death, set them the example; but even this abandoned pope, who had seven illegitimate sons and as many daughters, and who, soon after his accession to the papal chair, had broken a solemn oath, was opposed to the expulsion of the Jews. Meshullam, of Rome, having heard of the pope's refusal, with great joy announced to the Italian and Neapolitan communities that Innocent would not consent to the expulsion. The Spanish sovereigns decided on the banishment of the Jews without the pope's consent.

From the enchanted palace of the Alhambra there was suddenly issued by the "Catholic Sovereigns" a proclamation that, within four months, the Spanish Jews were to leave every portion of Castile, Aragon, Sicily and Sardinia under pain of death (March 31, 1492). They were at liberty to take their goods and chattels with them, but neither gold, silver, money, nor forbidden articles of export—only such things as it was permitted to export. This heartless cruelty Ferdinand and Isabella sought to vindicate before their own subjects and before foreign countries. The proclamation did not accuse the Jews of extravagant usury, of unduly enriching themselves, of sucking the marrow from the bones of the people, of insulting the host, or of crucifying Christian children—not one syllable was said of these things. But it set forth that the falling away of the new-Christians into "Jewish unbelief" was caused by their intercourse with Jews. The proclamation continued that long since it would have been proper to banish the Jews on account of their wily ways; but at first the sovereigns had tried clemency and mild means, banishing only the Jews of Andalusia, and punishing only the most guilty, in the hope that these steps would suffice. As, however, these had not prevented the Jews from continuing to pervert the new-Christians from the Catholic faith, nothing remained but for their majesties to exile those who had lured back to heresy the people who had indeed fallen away, but had repented and returned to holy Mother Church. Therefore had their majesties, in council with the princes of the church, grandees, and learned men, resolved to banish the Jews from their kingdom. No Christian, on pain of confiscation of his possessions, should, after the expiration of a certain term, give succor or shelter to Jews. The edict of Ferdinand and Isabella is good testimony for the Jews of Spain in those days, since no accusations could be brought against them but that they had remained faithful to their religion, and had sought to maintain their Marrano brethren in it. A legend relates that their majesties were embittered against the Jews, because the Infante had found the picture of a crucified Holy Child in an orange which a Jewish courtier had given him.

The long-dreaded blow had fallen. The Spanish Jews were to leave the country, round which the fibers of their hearts had grown, where lay the graves of their forefathers of at least fifteen hundred years, and towards whose greatness, wealth, and culture they had so largely contributed. The blow fell upon them like a thunderbolt. Abrabanel thought that he might be able to avert it by his influence. He presented himself before the king and queen, and offered enormous sums in the name of the Jews if the edict were removed. His Christian friends, eminent grandees, supported his efforts. Ferdinand, who took more interest in enriching his coffers than in the Catholic faith, was inclined to yield. Then the fanatical grand inquisitor, Torquemada, lifted up his voice. It is related that he took upon himself to rush into the presence of the king and queen, carrying the crucifix aloft, and uttering these winged words: "Judas Iscariot sold Christ for thirty pieces of silver; your highnesses are about to sell Him for 300,000 ducats. Here He is, take Him, and sell Him!" Then he left the hall. These words, or the influence of other ecclesiastics, had a strong effect upon Isabella. She resolved to abide by the edict, and, of bolder spirit than the king, contrived to keep alive his enmity against the Jews. Juan de Lucena, a member of the royal council of Aragon, as well as minister, was equally active in maintaining the edict. At the end of April heralds and trumpeters went through the whole country, proclaiming that the Jews were permitted to remain only till the end of July to set their affairs in order; whoever of them was found after that time on Spanish ground would suffer death.

Great as was the consternation of the Spanish Jews at having to tear themselves from the beloved land of their birth and the ashes of their forefathers, and go forth to an uncertain future in strange lands, among people whose speech they did not understand, who, perhaps, might be more unfriendly towards them than the Spanish Christians, they had to bestir themselves and make preparation for their exodus. At every step they realized that a yet more cruel fate awaited them. Had they been able, like the English Jews at the end of the thirteenth century, and the French a century later, to take their riches with them, they might have been able to provide some sort of miserable existence for themselves; but the Jewish capitalists were not permitted to take their money with them, they were compelled to accept bills of exchange for it. But Spain, on account of its dominant knightly and ecclesiastical element, had no places of exchange like those in Italy, where commercial notes were of value. Business on a large scale was in the hands, for the most part, of Jews and new-Christians, and the latter, from fear, had to keep away from their brethren in race. The Jews who owned land were forced to part with it at absurd prices, because no buyers applied, and they were obliged to beg the Christians for even the meanest thing in exchange. A contemporary, Andreas Bernaldez, pastor of Los Palacios, relates that the most magnificent houses and the most beautiful estates of the Jews were sold for a trifle. A house was bartered for an ass, and a vineyard for a piece of cloth or linen. Thus the riches of the Spanish Jews melted away, and could not help them in their day of need. In Aragon, Catalonia and Valencia, it was even worse with them. Torquemada, who on this occasion exceeded his former inhumanity, forbade the Christians to have any intercourse with them. In these provinces Ferdinand sequestrated their possessions, so that not only their debts, but also the claims which monasteries pretended to have upon them were paid. This fiendish plan he devised for the benefit of the church. The Jews would thereby be driven to despair, and turn to the cross for succor. Torquemada, therefore, imposed on the Dominicans the task of preaching Christianity everywhere, and of calling upon the Jews to receive baptism, and thus remain in the land. On the other side, the rabbis bade the people remain steadfast, accept their trials as tests of their firmness, and trust in God, who had been with them in so many days of trouble. The fiery eloquence of the rabbis was not necessary. Each one encouraged his neighbor to remain true and steadfast to the Jewish faith. "Let us be strong," so they said to each other, "for our religion, and for the Law of our fathers before our enemies and blasphemers. If they will let us live, we shall live; if they kill us, then shall we die. We will not desecrate the covenant of our God; our heart shall not fail us. We will go forth in the name of the Lord." If they had submitted to baptism, would they not have fallen into the power of the blood-stained Inquisition? The cross had lost its power of attraction even for lukewarm Jews, since they had seen upon what trivial pretexts members of their race were delivered over to the stake. One year before the proclamation of banishment was made, thirty-two new-Christians in Seville were bound living to the stake, sixteen were burned in effigy, and 625 sentenced to do penance. The Jews, moreover, were not ignorant of the false and deceitful ways in which Torquemada entrapped his victims. Many pseudo-Christians had fled from Seville, Cordova and Jaen, to Granada, where they had returned to the Jewish faith. After the conquest of the town, Torquemada proclaimed that if they came back to Mother Church, "whose arms are always open to embrace those who return to her with repentance and contrition," they would be treated with mildness, and in private, without onlookers, would receive absolution. A few allowed themselves to be charmed by this sweet voice, betook themselves to Toledo, and were pardoned—to a death of fire. Thus it came about that, in spite of the preaching of the Dominicans, and notwithstanding their indescribably terrible position, few Jews passed over to Christianity in the year of the expulsion from Spain. Among persons of note, only the rich tax-collector and chief rabbi, Abraham Senior, his son, and his son-in-law, Meïr, a rabbi, went over, with the two sons of the latter. It is said that they received baptism in desperation, because the queen, who did not want to lose her clever minister of finance, threatened heavier persecution of the departing Jews, if these did not submit. Great was the rejoicing at court over the baptism of Senior and his family. Their majesties themselves and the cardinal stood as sponsors. The newly-baptized all took the family name of Coronel, and their descendants filled some of the highest offices in the state.

Their common misfortune and suffering developed among the Spanish Jews in those last days before their exile deep brotherly affection and exalted sentiments, which, could they have lasted, would surely have borne good fruit. The rich, although their wealth had dwindled, divided it fraternally with the poor, allowing them to want for nothing, so that they should not fall into the hands of the church, and also paid the charges of their exodus. The aged rabbi, Isaac Aboab, the friend of Abrabanel, went with thirty Jews of rank to Portugal, to negotiate with King João II, for the settlement of the Jews in that country, or for their safe passage through it. They succeeded in making tolerably favorable conditions. The pain of leaving their passionately loved country could not be overcome. The nearer the day of departure came, the more were the hearts of the unhappy people wrung. The graves of their forefathers were dearer to them than all besides, and from these they found parting hardest. The Jews of the town of Vitoria gave to the community the Jewish cemetery and its appertaining grounds in perpetuity, on condition that it should never be encroached upon, nor planted over, and a deed to this effect was drawn up. The Jews of Segovia assembled three days before their exodus around the graves of their forefathers, mingling their tears with the dust, and melting the hearts of the Catholics with their grief. They tore up many of the tombstones to bear them away as memorial relics, or gave them to the Moors.

At last the day arrived on which the Spanish Jews had to take staff in hand. They had been accorded two days respite, that is, were allowed two days later than July 31st for setting forth. This date fell exactly upon the anniversary of the ninth of Ab, which was fraught with memories of the splendor of the old days, and had so often found the children of Israel wrapped in grief and misery. About 300,000 left the land which they so deeply loved, but which now became a hateful memory to them. They wandered partly northwards, to the neighboring kingdom of Navarre, partly southwards, with the idea of settling in Africa, Italy or Turkey. The majority, however, made for Portugal. In order to stifle sad thoughts and avoid the melancholy impression which might have moved some to waver and embrace the cross in order to remain in the land, some rabbis caused pipers and drummers to go before, making lively music, so that for a while the wanderers should forget their gnawing grief. Spain lost in them the twentieth part of her most industrious, painstaking, intelligent inhabitants, its middle class, which created trade, and maintained it in brisk circulation, like the blood of a living organism. For there were among the Spanish Jews not merely capitalists, merchants, farmers, physicians and men of learning, but also artisans, armor and metal workers of all kinds, at all events no idlers who slept away their time. With the discovery of America, the Jews might have lifted Spain to the rank of the wealthiest, the most prosperous and enduring of states, which by reason of its unity of government might certainly have competed with Italy. But Torquemada would not have it so; he preferred to train Spaniards for a blood-stained idolatry, under which, in the sunlight of the Lutheran Reformation, pious men were condemned to chains, dungeons, or the galleys, if they dared read the Bible. The departure of the Jews from Spain soon made itself felt in a very marked manner by the Christians. Talent, activity, and prosperous civilization passed with them from the country. The smaller towns, which had derived some vitality from the presence of the Jews, were quickly depopulated, sank into insignificance, lost their spirit of freedom and independence, and became tools for the increasing despotism of the Spanish kings and the imbecile superstition of the priests. The Spanish nobility soon complained that their towns and villages had fallen into insignificance, had become deserted, and they declared that, could they have foreseen the consequences, they would have opposed the royal commands. Dearth of physicians was sternly felt, too. The town of Vitoria and its neighborhood was compelled, through the withdrawal of the Jews, to secure a physician from a distance, and give him a high salary. In many places the people fell victims to quacks, boastful bunglers, or to the superstition of deceiving or self-deceived dealers in magic. In one word, Spain fell into a condition of barbarism through the banishment of the Jews, and all the wealth which the settlement of American colonies brought to the mother country only helped to render its inhabitants more idle, stupid, and servile. The name of the Jews died out of the country in which they had played so important a part, and the literature of which was so filled with Jewish elements that men of intelligence were constantly reminded of them. Schools, hospitals, and everything which the Jews could not or dared not take away with them, the king confiscated. He changed synagogues into churches, monasteries or schools, where the people were systematically kept ignorant, and trained for meanest servility. The beautiful synagogue of Toledo, which Don Pedro's Jewish statesman, Samuel Abulafia, had erected about a century and a half before, was transformed into a church (de neustra Señora de San Benito), and, with its Moorish architecture, its exquisite columns, and splendid proportions, is to this day a magnificent ornament to the city. In the other cities and towns of Spain, which live in the chronicles of Jewish history, in Seville, Granada, Cordova, in densely-populated Lucena, Saragossa and Barcelona, every trace was lost of the sons of Jacob, or of the Jewish nobility, as the proud Jews of Spain styled themselves. Jews, it is true, remained behind, Jews under the mask of Christianity, Jewish Christians, or new-Christians, who had afforded their departing brethren active help. Many of them had taken charge of their gold and silver, and kept it till they were able to send it on by the hands of trusted persons, or had given them bills of exchange on foreign places. These negotiations were often of no avail, for when the fanatical king and queen heard of them, they sent for the treasure left behind, or sought to prevent the payment of the checks.

Great as were the obstacles, the Marranos did not cool in their zeal for their exiled brethren. They pursued those guilty of inhuman brutality to the wanderers with bitter hatred, and delivered them over to the Inquisition—turning the tool against its makers. At the instigation of the Marranos, the brother of Don Juan de Lucena, the powerful minister of Ferdinand, was thrown into the prison of the Inquisition, kept there under a strong guard, and none of his relatives allowed to see him, the minister, whose position exempted him from the power of the Inquisition, having counseled the banishment of the Jews, and practically assisted in it, and his brother having relentlessly confiscated the property they had left behind. Torquemada complained that Don Juan was persecuted by the new-Christians on account of his faith. The Marranos, now more than ever on their guard, lest they give the slightest offense, had to cross themselves assiduously, count their beads, and mumble paternosters, while inwardly they were attached more than ever to Judaism. Frequently their feelings outran their will, they broke the bonds of silence, and this was productive of heavy consequences. Thus a Marrano in Seville, on seeing an effigy of Christ set up in church for adoration, cried out, "Woe to him who sees, and must believe such a thing!" Such expressions in unguarded moments naturally afforded the best opportunity for inquiry, imprisonment, the rack and autos-da-fé, not merely for the individual caught in the act, but for his relatives, friends, and everybody connected with him who had any property. It had, moreover, grown to be a necessity to the people, hardened by the frequent sight of the death agonies of sacrificial victims, to witness a solemn tragedy of human sacrifice now and again. It is, therefore, not astonishing, that under the first inquisitor-general, Thomas de Torquemada, in the course of fourteen years (1485—1498) at least two thousand Jews were burned as impenitent sinners. He was so hated that he lived in constant fear of death. Upon his table he kept the horn of a unicorn, to which the superstition of the time ascribed the power of nullifying the effect of poison. When Torquemada went out, he was attended by a body-guard (Familares) of fifty, and two hundred foot-soldiers, to protect him from assault. His successor, the second inquisitor-general, Deza, erected still more scaffolds; but it soon came to pass that the men of blood butchered each other. Deza before his death was accused of being secretly a Jew. When the persecutions against the remaining Moors and Moriscos, and against the followers of the German reformer Luther, were added to those of the Marranos, Spain, under the wrath of the Holy Inquisition, became literally a scene of human slaughter. With justice nearly all the European princes, and even the parliament of Paris, bitterly blamed the perverseness of Ferdinand and Isabella in having driven out so useful a class of citizens. The sultan Bajasid (Bajazet) exclaimed: "You call Ferdinand a wise king, he who has made his country poor and enriched ours!"

CHAPTER XII.

EXPULSION OF THE JEWS FROM NAVARRE AND PORTUGAL.

The Exiles from Navarre—Migration to Naples—King Ferdinand I of Naples and Abrabanel—Leon Abrabanel—Misfortunes of the Jews in Fez, Genoa, Rome, and the Islands of Greece—The Sultan Bajazet—Moses Kapsali—Spanish Jews in Portugal—The Jewish Astronomers, Abraham Zacuto and José Vecinho—The Jewish Travelers, Abraham de Beya and Joseph Zapateiro—Outbreak of the Plague among the Spanish Jews in Portugal—Sufferings of the Portuguese Exiles—Judah Chayyat and his Fellow-Sufferers—Cruelty of João II—Kindly Treatment by Manoel changed into Cruelty on his Marriage—Forcible Baptism of Jewish Children—Levi ben Chabib and Isaac Caro—Pope Alexander VI—Manoel's Efforts on Behalf of the Portuguese Marranos—Death of Simon Maimi and Abraham Saba.

1492—1498 C.E.

THE Jews of northern Spain, in Catalonia and Aragon, who turned their steps to neighboring Navarre, with the idea of seeking shelter there, were comparatively fortunate. Here at least was a prospect of a livelihood, and a possibility of looking round for other places of refuge. The Inquisition had met with courageous resistance from the rulers and the people of Navarre. When some Marranos, concerned in the murder of Arbues, the inquisitor, fled to this kingdom, and the bloodthirsty heresy-mongers demanded that they be given up to the executioners, the town of Tudela declared that it would not suffer such unrighteous violence to people who had sought its protection, and closed the gates against their emissaries. In vain did king Ferdinand, who had an eye upon Navarre, threaten it with his anger. The citizens of Tudela remained firm. A Navarrese prince, Jacob of Navarre, suffered for the shelter he gave to a hunted Marrano. The inquisitors suddenly arrested, imprisoned and sentenced him, as an enemy of the Holy Office, to shameful exposure in a church, where his list of offenses was publicly read out, and absolution promised him only if he submitted to flagellation from priestly hands. Several other towns of Navarre gave protection to the fugitives, and about 12,000 Castilian wanderers took up their quarters in Navarre. Count of Lerin probably received the greater number of these. But the Jews enjoyed only a few years of peace in Navarre; for upon the vehement urging of King Ferdinand, who followed the fugitives with bitterest enmity and persecution, the king of Navarre gave them the choice between wandering forth again and baptism. The greater number adopted Christianity, because there was only a short time for preparation, and no time for thinking. In the community of Tudela, so famous for steadfast piety, 180 families submitted to baptism.

Also those Castilian Jews were fortunate who, instead of indulging themselves in the vain hope that the edict would be recalled, did not stay until the last day, but made their way, before the end of the respite, to Italy, Africa, or Turkey. They did not lack the means of getting away. The Spanish Jews had such widespread repute, and their expulsion had made so much stir in Europe, that crowds of ships were ready in Spanish seaports to take up the wanderers and convey them to all parts, not only the ships of the country, but also Italian vessels from Genoa and Venice. The ship-owners saw a prospect of lucrative business. Many Jews from Aragon, Catalonia and Valencia desired to settle in Naples, and sent ambassadors to the king, Ferdinand I, to ask him to receive them. This prince was not merely free from prejudice against the Jews, but was kindly inclined towards them, out of compassion for their misfortunes, and he may have promised himself industrial and intellectual advantage from this immigration of the Spanish Jews.

Whether it was calculation or generosity, it is enough that he bade them welcome, and made his realm free to them. Many thousands of them landed in the Bay of Naples (24th August, 1492), and were kindly received. The native Jewish community treated them with true brotherly generosity, defrayed the passage of the poor not able to pay, and provided for their immediate necessities.

Isaac Abrabanel, also, and his whole household, went to Naples. Here he lived at first as a private individual, and continued the work of writing a commentary upon the book of Kings, which had been interrupted by his state duties. When the king of Naples was informed of his presence in the city, he invited him to an interview, and intrusted him with a post, in all likelihood in the financial department. Probably he hoped to make use of Abrabanel's experience in the war with which he was threatened by the king of France. Whether from his own noble impulses, or from esteem for Abrabanel, the king of Naples showed the Jews a gentle humanity which startlingly contrasted with the cruelty of the Spanish king. The unhappy people had to struggle with many woes; when they thought themselves free of one, another yet more merciless fell upon them. A devastating pestilence, arising out of the sad condition to which they had been reduced, or from the overcrowding of the ships, followed in the track of the wanderers. They brought death with them. Scarcely six months had they been settled on Neapolitan soil when the pestilence carried numbers of them off, and King Ferdinand, who dreaded a rising of the populace against the Jews, hinted to them that they must bury their corpses by night, and in silence. When the pest could no longer be concealed, and every day increased in virulence, people and courtiers alike entreated him to drive them forth. But Ferdinand would not assent to this inhuman proceeding; he is said to have threatened to abdicate if the Jews were ill-treated. He had hospitals erected for them outside the town, sent physicians to their aid, and gave them means of support. For a whole year he strove, with unexampled nobility, to succor the unfortunate people, whom banishment and disease had transformed into living corpses. Those, also, who were fortunate enough to reach Pisa found a brotherly reception. The sons of Yechiel of Pisa fairly took up their abode on the quay, so as to be ready to receive the wanderers, provide for their wants, shelter them, or help them on their way to some other place. After Ferdinand's death, his son, Alfonso II, who little resembled him, retained the Jewish statesman, Abrabanel, in his service, and, after his resignation in favor of his son, took him with him to Sicily. Abrabanel to the last remained faithful to this prince in his misfortunes (January, 1494, to June, 1495).

After the conquest of Naples by the weak-headed knight-errant king of France, Charles VIII, the members of the Abrabanel family were torn apart and scattered. None of them, however, met with such signal misfortune as the eldest son, Judah Leon Medigo (born 1470, died 1530). He had been so well beloved at the Spanish court that they were loath to part with him, and would gladly have kept him there—of course, as a Christian. To attain this end, a command was issued that he be not permitted to leave Toledo, or that his one-year-old son be taken from him, baptized immediately, and that in this manner the father be chained to Spain. Judah Abrabanel, however, got wind of this plot against his liberty, sent his son, with his nurse, "like stolen goods," secretly to the Portuguese coast; but as he himself did not care to seek shelter in the country where his father had been threatened with death, he turned his face towards Naples. His suspicions of the king of Portugal were only too speedily justified. No sooner did João hear that a relative of Abrabanel was within his borders than he ordered the child to be kept as hostage, and not to be permitted to go forth with the other Jews. Little Isaac never saw his parents and grandparents again. He was baptized, and brought up as a Christian. The agony of the father at the living death of his lost child was boundless. It gave him no rest or peace to his latest hour, and it found vent in a lamentation sad in the extreme. Yet what was the grief for one child, compared with the woes which overtook the thousands of Jews hunted out of Spain?

Many of them found their way to the nearest African seaport towns, Oran, Algiers and Bugia. The inhabitants, who feared that their towns would be overcrowded from such a vast influx, shot at the Jews as they landed, and killed many of them. An eminent Jew at the court of Barbary, however, addressed the sultan in behalf of his unhappy brethren, and obtained leave for them to land. They were not allowed to enter the towns, probably because the pestilence had broken out among them, too. They could only build themselves wooden huts outside the walls. The children collected wood, and their elders nailed the boards together for temporary dwellings. But they did not long enjoy even this miserable shelter, as one day a fire broke out in one of the huts, and soon laid the whole camp in ashes.

Those who settled in Fez suffered a still more terrible lot. Here also the inhabitants would not admit them, fearing that such an influx of human beings would raise the price of the necessaries of life. They had to encamp in the fields, and live on roots and herbs like cattle. On the Sabbath they stripped the plants with their teeth, in order not to desecrate the holy day by gathering them. Starvation, pestilence, and the unfriendliness of the Mahometan people vied with each other in inflicting misery upon the Jews. In their awful despair, fathers were driven to sell their children as slaves to obtain bread. Mothers killed their little ones that they might not see them perish from the pangs of hunger. Avaricious captains took advantage of the distress of the parents to entice starving children on board their vessels with offers of bread, and, deaf to the cries and entreaties of the parents, carried them off to distant lands, where they sold them for a good price. Later, the ruler of Fez, probably at the representation of the original Jewish inhabitants, proclaimed that Jewish children who had been sold for bread, and other necessaries of life, should be set at liberty.

The descriptions by their contemporaries of the sufferings of the Jews make one's hair stand on end. They were dogged whithersoever they went. Those whom plague and starvation had spared, fell into the hands of brutalized men. The report got about that the Spanish Jews had swallowed the gold and silver which they had been forbidden to carry away, intending to use it later on. Cannibals, therefore, ripped open their bodies to seek for coin in their entrails. The Genoese ship-folk behaved most inhumanly to the wanderers who had trusted their lives to them. From avarice, or sheer delight in the death agonies of the Jews, they flung many of them into the sea. One captain offered insult to the beautiful daughter of a Jewish wanderer. Her name was Paloma (Dove), and to escape shame, the mother threw her and her other daughters and then herself into the waves. The wretched father composed a heartbreaking lamentation for his lost dear ones.

Those who reached the port of Genoa had to contend with new miseries. In this thriving town there was a law that Jews might not remain there for longer than three days. As the ships which were to convey the Jews thence required repairing, the authorities conceded the permission for them to remain, not in the town, but upon the Mole, until the vessels were ready for sea. Like ghosts, pale, shrunken, hollow-eyed, gaunt, they went on shore, and if they had not moved, impelled by instinct to get out of their floating prison, they might have been taken for so many corpses. The starving children went into the churches, and allowed themselves to be baptized for a morsel of bread; and Christians were merciless enough not merely to accept such sacrifices, but with the cross in one hand, and bread in the other, to go among the Jews and tempt them to become converted. Only a short time had been granted them on the Mole, but a great part of the winter passed before the repairs were completed. The longer they remained, the more their numbers diminished, through the passing over to Christianity of the younger members, and many fell victims to plagues of all kinds. Other Italian towns would not allow them to land even for a short time, partly because it was a year of famine, partly because the Jews brought the plague with them.

The survivors from Genoa who reached Rome underwent still more bitter experiences; their own people leagued against them, refusing to allow them to enter, from fear that the influx of new settlers would damage their trade. They got together 1,000 ducats, to present to the notorious monster, Pope Alexander VI, as a bribe to refuse to allow the Jews to enter. This prince, himself unfeeling enough, was so enraged at the heartlessness of these men against their own people, that he ordered every Roman Jew out of the city. It cost the Roman congregation 2,000 ducats to obtain the revocation of this edict, and they had to take in the refugees besides.

The Greek islands of Corfu, Candia, and others

became filled with Spanish Jews; some had dragged themselves thither, others had been sold as slaves there. The majority of the Jewish communities had great compassion for them, and strove to care for them, or at all events to ransom them. They made great efforts to collect funds, and sold the ornaments of the synagogues, so that their brethren might not starve, or be subjected to slavery. Persians, who happened to be on the island of Corfu, bought Spanish refugees, in order to obtain from Jews of their own country a high ransom for them. Elkanah Kapsali, a representative of the Candian community, was indefatigable in his endeavors to collect money for the Spanish Jews. The most fortunate were those who reached the shores of Turkey; for the Turkish Sultan, Bajazet II, showed himself to be not only a most humane monarch, but also the wisest and most far-seeing. He understood better than the Christian princes what hidden riches the impoverished Spanish Jews brought with them, not in their bowels, but in their brains, and he wanted to turn these to use for the good of his country. Bajazet caused a command to go forth through the European provinces of his dominions that the harassed and hunted Jews should not be rejected, but should be received in the kindest and most friendly manner. He threatened with death anyone who should illtreat or oppress them. The chief rabbi, Moses Kapsali, was untiringly active in protecting the unfortunate Jewish Spaniards who had come as beggars or slaves to Turkey. He traveled about, and levied a tax from the rich native Jews "for the liberation of the Spanish captives." He did not need to use much pressure; for the Turkish Jews willingly contributed to the assistance of the victims of Christian fanaticism. Thus thousands of Spanish Jews settled in Turkey, and before a generation had passed they had taken the lead among the Turkish Jews, and made Turkey a kind of Eastern Spain.

At first the Spanish Jews who went to Portugal seemed to have some chance of a happy lot. The venerable rabbi, Isaac Aboab, who had gone with a deputation of thirty to seek permission from King João either to settle in or pass through Portugal, succeeded in obtaining tolerably fair terms. Many of the wanderers chose to remain in the neighboring kingdom for a while, because they flattered themselves with the hope that their indispensableness would make itself evident after their departure, that the eyes of the now blinded king and queen of Spain would be opened, and they would then receive the banished people with open arms. At the worst, so thought the refugees, they would have time in Portugal to look round, decide which way to go, and readily find ships to convey them in safety to Africa or to Italy. When the Spanish deputies placed the proposition before King João II to receive the Jews permanently or temporarily in Portugal, the king consulted his grandees at Cintra. In presenting the matter, he permitted it to be seen that he himself was desirous of admitting the exiles for a pecuniary consideration. Some of the advisers, either from pity for the unhappy Jews, or from respect for the king, were in favor of granting permission; others, and these the majority, either out of hatred for the Jews, or a feeling of honor, were against it. The king, however, overruled all objections, because he hoped to carry on the contemplated war with Africa by means of the money acquired from the immigrants. It was at first said that the Spanish refugees were to be permitted to settle permanently in Portugal. This favor, however, the Portuguese Jews themselves looked upon with suspicion, because the little state would thus hold a disproportionate number of Jews, and the wanderers, most of them penniless, would fall a heavy burden upon them, so that the king, not of an amiable disposition, would end by becoming hostile to all the Jews in Portugal. The chief men, therefore, of the Jewish-Portuguese community met in debate, and many gave utterance to the cruel view that they themselves would have to take steps to prevent the reception of the Spanish exiles. A noble old man, Joseph, of the family of Ibn-Yachya, spoke warmly for his unfortunate brethren; but his voice was silenced. There was no more talk of their settling in Portugal, but only of the permission to make a short stay, in order to arrange for their journey. The conditions laid down for the Spanish Jews were: Each one, rich or poor, with the exception of babes, was to pay a stipulated sum (eight gold-cruzados, nearly one pound) in four instalments; artisans, however, such as metal-workers and smiths, who desired to settle in the country, only half of this amount. The rest were permitted to stay only eight months, but the king undertook to furnish ships at a reasonable rate for transporting them to other lands. Those found in Portugal after the expiration of this period, or not able to show a receipt for the stipulated payment, were condemned to servitude. On the promulgation of these conditions, a large number of Spanish Jews (estimated at 20,000 families, or 200,000 souls) passed over the Portuguese borders. The king assigned to the wanderers certain towns, where they had to pay a tax to the inhabitants. Oporto was assigned to the families of the thirty deputies, and a synagogue was built for them. Isaac Aboab, the renowned teacher of many disciples, who later took positions as rabbis in Africa, Egypt and Palestine, died peacefully in Oporto; his pupil, famous as a geographer and astronomer, Abraham Zacuto, pronounced his funeral oration (end of 1492). Only a few of his fellow-sufferers were destined to die a peaceful death.

The feverish eagerness for discovering unknown lands and entering into trading relations with them, which had seized on Portugal, gave practical value to two sciences which hitherto had been regarded as the hobby or amusement of idlers and dilettanti—namely, astronomy and mathematics, the favorite pursuits of cultured Jews of the Pyrenean Peninsula. If India, the land of gold and spices, upon which the minds of the Portuguese were set with burning desire, was to be discovered, then coasting journeys, so slow and so dangerous, would have to be given up, and voyages made thither upon the high seas. But the ships ran the risk of losing their way on the trackless wastes of the ocean. Venturesome mariners, therefore, sought astronomical tables to direct their way by the courses of the sun and the stars. In this science Spanish Jews had the mastery. A Chazan of Toledo, Isaac (Zag) Ibn-Said, had published astronomical tables in the thirteenth century, known under the name of Alfonsine Tables, which were used with only slight alterations by the scientific men of Germany, France, England and Italy. As João II of Portugal now wished to send ships to the Atlantic for the discovery of India by way of the African sea-coast, he summoned a sort of astronomical congress for the working out of practical astronomical tables. At this congress, together with the famous German astronomer, Martin Behaim, and the Christian physician of King Rodrigo, there sat a Jew, the royal physician, Joseph (José) Vecinho, or de Viseu. He used as a basis the perpetual astronomical calendar, or Tables of the Seven Planets, which Abraham Zacuto, known later as a chronicler, had drawn up for a bishop of Salamanca, to whom he had dedicated it. Joseph Vecinho, together with Christian scientists, also improved upon the instrument for the measurement of the altitude of the stars, the nautical astrolabe, indispensable to mariners. By its aid Vasco da Gama first found it possible to follow the seaway to the Cape of Good Hope and India, and thus, perhaps,

Columbus was enabled to discover a new continent. The geographical knowledge and skill of two Jews, Rabbi Abraham de Beya and Joseph Zapateiro de Lamego, were also turned to account by King João II, who sent them to Asia to obtain tidings of his emissaries to the mythical land of Prester John.

Although King João thus employed learned and skillful Jews for his own ends, he had no liking for the Jewish race: he was indifferent, or rather inimical, to them directly they came in the way of his bigotry. In the year in which he dispatched Joseph Zapateiro and Abraham de Beya to Asia, at the instigation of Pope Innocent VIII he appointed a commission of the Inquisition for the Marranos who had fled from Spain to Portugal, and, like Ferdinand and Isabella in Spain, delivered over those who had Jewish leanings, either to death by fire or to endless imprisonment. Some Marranos having taken ship to Africa, and there openly adopted Judaism, he prohibited, under penalty of death and confiscation, baptized Jews or new-Christians from leaving the country by sea. On the breath of this heartless monarch hung the life or death of hundreds of thousands of Jewish exiles.

Against those unfortunates in Portugal, not only evil-minded men, but nature itself, fought. Soon after their arrival in Portugal, a cruel pestilence began to rage among them, destroying thousands. The Portuguese, who also suffered from the plague, believed that the Jews had brought it into the country; and, indeed, all that they had suffered, the oppressive heat at the time of their going forth, want, misery, and all kinds of devastating diseases, may have developed it. A considerable number of the Spanish refugees died of the plague in Portugal. The population on this account murmured against the king, complaining that the pestilence had followed in the track of the accursed Jews, and established itself in the country. Don João, therefore, had to insist more strenuously than he otherwise would have done upon the condition that all who had settled in Portugal should leave at the expiration of the eight months. At first he put ships at their disposal, at moderate rates of transportation, according to his agreement, and bade the captains treat their passengers with humanity, and convey them whither they wished to go. But these men, inspired by Jew hatred and avarice, once upon the seas, troubled themselves but little about the king's orders, since they had no need to fear complaints about their inhumanity. They demanded more money than had originally been bargained for, and extorted it from the helpless creatures. Or, they carried them about upon the waste of waters till their stock of provisions was exhausted, and then demanded large sums for a fresh supply of food, so that at last the unfortunates were driven to give their clothes for bread, and were landed anywhere in a nearly naked state. Women and young girls were insulted and violated in the presence of their parents and relatives, and disgrace was brought upon the name of Christian. Frequently these inhuman mariners landed them in some desolate spot of the African coasts, and left them to perish from hunger and despair, or to fall a prey to the Moors, who took them prisoners.

The sufferings of the exiled Jews who left Portugal in ships are related by an eye-witness, the Kabbalist, Judah ben Jacob Chayyat, of a noble and wealthy family. The vessel on which he, his wife, and two hundred and fifty other Jews, of both sexes and all ages, had embarked, left the harbor of Lisbon in winter (beginning of 1493), and lingered four months upon the waves, because no seaport would take them in for fear of the plague. Provisions on board naturally ran short. The ship was captured by Biscayan pirates, plundered and taken to the Spanish port of Malaga. The Jews were not permitted to land, nor to set sail again, nor were provisions given them. The priests and magistrates of the town desired to incline them to the teaching of Christ by the pangs of hunger. They succeeded in converting one hundred persons with gaunt bodies and hollow eyes. The rest remained steadfast to their own faith, and fifty of them, old men, youths, maidens, children, among them Chayyat's wife, died of starvation. Then, at last, compassion awoke in the hearts of the Malagese, and they gave them bread and water. When, after two months, the remainder of them received permission to sail to the coasts of Africa, they encountered bitter sufferings in another form. On account of the plague they were not permitted to land at any town, and had to depend upon the herbs of the field. Chayyat himself was seized, and flung by a malicious Mahometan into a horrible dungeon full of snakes and salamanders, in order to force him to adopt Islamism; in case of refusal, he was threatened with death by stoning. These continuous, grinding cruelties did not make him waver one instant in his religious convictions. At last he was liberated by the Jews of a little town, and carried to Fez. There so severe a famine raged that Chayyat was compelled to turn a mill with his hands for a piece of bread, not fit for a dog. At night he and his companions in misery who had strayed to Fez slept upon the ash-heaps of the town.

Carefully as the Portuguese mariners strove to conceal their barbarities to the Jews, their deeds soon came to light, and frightened off those who remained behind from emigrating by sea. The poor creatures, moreover, were unable to raise the necessary money for their passage and provisions. They, therefore, put off going from day to day, comforting themselves with the hope that the king would be merciful, and allow them to remain in Portugal. Don João, however, was not a monarch whose heart was warmed by kindness and compassion. He maintained that more Jews had come into Portugal than had been stipulated for, and insisted, therefore, that the agreement be strictly carried out. Those who remained after the expiration of eight months were made slaves, and sold or given to those of the Portuguese nobility who cared to take their pick from them (1493).

King João went still further in his cruel dealings with the unhappy Spanish Jews. The children of from three to ten years of age whose parents had become slaves, he ordered to be transported by sea to the newly-discovered San Thomas or Lost Islands (Ilhas perdidas), there to be reared in the tenets of Christianity. The weeping of the mothers, the sobbing of the children, the rage of the fathers, who tore their hair in agony, did not move the heartless despot to recall his command. Mothers entreated to be allowed to go with their children, threw themselves at the king's feet as he came out of church, and implored him to leave them at least the youngest. Don João had them dragged from his path "like bitches who had their whelps torn from them." Is it to be wondered at that mothers, with their children in their arms, sprang into the sea to rest united in its depths? The Islands of San Thomas, whither the little ones were taken, were full of lizards and venomous snakes, and inhabited by criminals transported thither from Portugal. Most of the children perished on the journey, or became the prey of wild beasts. Among the survivors it happened that brothers and sisters, in ignorance of their relationship, married each other. Perhaps the king's barbarity to the Jews must be accounted for by the bitter gloom which mastered him at the death of his only legitimate son.

After the death of João II, who sank in wretchedness into his grave (end of October, 1495), he was succeeded by his cousin Manoel, a great contrast in disposition to himself—an intelligent, amiable, gentle-minded man, and a lover of learning. There seemed some prospect of a better star's rising upon the remnant of the banished Jews in Portugal. King Manoel, finding that the Jews had remained in his kingdom beyond the allotted time only from fear of many forms of death upon the ocean, gave all the slaves their freedom. The money which, beside themselves with joy, they offered him for this, he refused. It is true that his ulterior motive, as Bishop Osorius tells us, was to win them over to Christianity by clemency. The Jewish mathematician and astronomer, Abraham Zacuto, who had remained in Lisbon, having come thither from northern Spain, where he had taught his favorite science even to Christians, was made chief astrologer Zacuto served the king not merely in the latter capacity. Although a man of limited understanding, unable to rise above the superstition of his day, he had sound knowledge of astronomy, and published a work upon that science, besides preparing his astronomical tables. He also invented a correct metal instrument for measuring the altitude of the stars, to replace the clumsy and inaccurate wooden one used hitherto by mariners.

Under King Manoel, in whose reign Portugal's domains were enlarged by acquisitions in India and America, the Jews were able to breathe awhile. It appears that soon after ascending the throne he issued a command that the accusations against them for murdering children should not be recognized by courts of justice, since they were malicious, lying inventions. Nor would he allow the fanatical preaching friars to utter denunciations against them.

Very short, however, was the gleam of happiness for the Jews under Manoel: the somber bigotry of the Spanish court changed it into terrible gloom. No sooner had the young king of Portugal mounted the throne than their majesties of Spain began to entertain the idea of marriage relations with him in order to turn an inimical neighbor into a friend and ally. They proposed marriage with their younger daughter, Joanna, who afterwards became notorious on account of her jealous disposition and her madness. Manoel lent a willing ear to the proposal of an alliance with the Spanish court, but preferred the elder sister, Isabella II, who had been married to the Infante of Portugal, and had soon after become a widow. Isabella had strong repugnance to a second marriage; but her confessor knew how to overrule her objections, and made her believe that if she consented she would have opportunity to glorify the Christian faith. The Spanish court had marked with chagrin and vexation that the Portuguese king had received the Jewish and Mahometan refugees, and King Manoel's friendly treatment of them was a thorn in their flesh. Ferdinand and Isabella thought that by falling in with the Portuguese king's wishes, they would attain their end. They, therefore, promised him the hand of their eldest daughter upon condition that he join with Spain against Charles VII, and send the Jews out of Portugal, both the native and the refugee Jews. The conditions were very disagreeable to King Manoel, who was on good terms with France, and reaped great advantage from the wealth, energy, intelligence, and knowledge of the Jews.

He consulted with his lords and council upon this question, fraught with such importance for the Jews. Opinions upon it were divided. Manoel hesitated for some time, because his noble nature shrank from such cruelty and faithlessness. The Infanta Isabella spoke the deciding word. She entertained fanatical, almost personal hatred against the Jews. She believed or was persuaded by the priests that the misfortunes and unhappiness which had befallen King João in his last days were occasioned by his having allowed Jews to enter his kingdom; and, nourished as she had been at the breast of superstition, she was afraid of ill-luck in her union with Manoel if Jews were permitted to remain in Portugal. What dreary lovelessness in the heart of a young woman! Irreconcilable strife of feelings and thoughts was thus raised in the soul of King Manoel. Honor, the interest of the state, humanity, forebade his proscribing and expelling the Jews; but the hand of the Spanish Infanta, and the Spanish crown were to be secured only by the misery of the Jews. Love turned the balance in favor of hate. When the king was expecting his bride to cross the borders of his kingdom, he received a letter from her saying that she would not set foot in Portugal until the land was cleansed of the "curse-laden" Jews.

The marriage contract between Don Manoel and the Spanish Infanta, Isabella, then, was sealed with the misery of the Jews. It was signed on the 30th of November, 1496, and so early as the 24th of the following month, the king caused an order to go forth that all the Jews and Moors of his kingdom must receive baptism, or leave the country within a given time, on pain of death. In order to relieve his conscience, he showed clemency in carrying his edict into effect. He lengthened the term of their stay until the October of the following year, so that they had time for preparation. He further appointed three ports, Lisbon, Oporto, and Setubal, for their free egress. That he sought to allure the Jews to Christianity, by the prospect of honor and advancement, was so entirely due to the distorted views of the times, that he cannot be held responsible for it; as it was, only a few submitted to baptism.

Precisely Manoel's clement behavior tended to the greater misery of the Jews. Having ample time to prepare for their departure, and not being forbidden to take gold and silver with them, they thought that there was no need to hurrv. Perhaps the king would change his mind. They had friends at court who were agitating in their favor. Besides, the winter months were not a good time to be upon the ocean. The majority, therefore, waited until spring. In the meantime King Manoel certainly did change his mind, but only to increase their fearful misery. He was much vexed at finding that so few Jews had embraced Christianity. Very unwillingly he saw them depart with their wealth and their possessions, and sought ways and means to retain them, as Christians, of course, in his own kingdom. The first step had cost him a struggle, the second was easy.

He raised the question in council whether the Jews could be brought to baptism by force. To the honor of the Portuguese clergy it must be said that they expressed themselves as opposed to this. The bishop of Algarve, Ferdinand Coutinho, cited ecclesiastical authorities and papal bulls to the effect that Jews might not be compelled to adopt Christianity, because a free, not a forced, confession was required. Manoel, however, was so bent upon keeping the industrious Jews with him, that he openly declared that he did not trouble himself about laws and authorities, but would act upon his own judgment. From Evora he issued (beginning of April, 1497) a secret command that all Jewish children, boys and girls, up to the age of fourteen, should be taken from their parents by force on Easter Sunday, and carried to the church fonts to be baptized. He was advised by a reprobate convert, Levi ben Shem Tob, to take this step. In spite of the secrecy of the preparations, several Jews found it out, and were about to flee with their children from the "stain of baptism." When Manoel heard it, he ordered the forced baptism of children to be carried out at once. Heartrending scenes ensued in the towns where Jews lived when the sheriffs strove to carry away the children. Parents strained their dear ones to their breasts, the children clung convulsively to them, and they could be separated only by lashes and blows. In their despair over the possibility of being thus for ever sundered, many of them strangled the children in their embraces, or threw them into wells and rivers, and then laid hands upon themselves. "I have seen," relates Bishop Coutinho, "many dragged to the font by the hair, and the fathers clad in mourning, with veiled heads and cries of agony, accompanying their children to the altar, to protest against the inhuman baptism. I have seen still more horrible, indescribable violence done them." In the memory of his contemporaries lingered the frightful manner in which a noble and cultured Jew, Isaac Ibn-Zachin, destroyed himself and his children, to avoid their becoming a prey to Christianity. Christians were moved to pity by the cries and tears of Jewish fathers, mothers and children, and despite the king's commands not to assist the Jews, they concealed many of the unfortunates in their houses, so that at least for the moment they might be safe; but the stony hearts of King Manoel and his young wife, the Spanish Isabella II, remained unmoved by these sights of woe. The baptized children, who received Christian names, were placed in various towns, and reared as Christians. Either in obedience to a secret order, or from excessive zeal, the creatures of the king not only seized children, but also youths and maidens up to the age of twenty, for baptism.

Many Jews of Portugal probably embraced Christianity in order to remain with their children; but this did not satisfy the king, who, not from religious zeal, but from political motives, had hardened his heart. All the Jews of Portugal, it mattered not whether with or without conviction, were to become Christians and remain in the country. To attain this end, he violated a solemn promise more flagrantly than his predecessor. When the time of their departure came closer, he ordered the Jews to embark from one seaport only, that of Lisbon, although, at first, he had allowed them three places. Therefore, all who wished to go, had to meet in Lisbon—20,000 souls, it is said, with burning grief in their hearts, but prepared to suffer anything to remain true to their convictions. The inhuman monarch allowed them lodgings in the city, but he placed so many hindrances in the way of their embarkation, that time passed by, and the day arrived when they were to forfeit life, or at least liberty, if found upon Portuguese soil. He had all who remained behind locked in an enclosed space (os Estaõs) like oxen in stalls, and informed them that they were now his slaves, and that he could do with them as he thought fit. He urged them voluntarily to confess the Christian faith, in which case they should have honor and riches; otherwise they would be forced to baptism without mercy. When, notwithstanding this, many remained firm, he forbade bread or water to be given them for three days, in order to render them more pliable. This means did not succeed any better with the greater number of them: they chose to faint with starvation rather than belong to a religion which owned such followers as their persecutors. Upon this, Manoel proceeded to extreme measures. By cords, by their hair and beard, they were dragged from their pen to the churches. To escape this some sprang from the windows, and their limbs were crushed. Others broke loose and jumped into wells. Some killed themselves in the churches. One father spread his *tallith* over his sons, and killed them and himself. Manoel's terrible treatment comes into more glaring prominence when compared with his behavior to the Moors. They, too, had to leave Portugal, but no hindrances were placed in their way, because he feared that the Mahometan princes in Africa and Turkey might retaliate upon the Christians living in their domains. The Jews had no earthly protector, were weak and helpless, therefore, Manoel, whom historians call the Great, permitted himself to perpetrate such atrocities. In this fashion many native Portuguese and refugee Spanish Jews were led to embrace Christianity, which they—as their Christian contemporaries relate with shame—had openly scorned. Some, at a later period, became distinguished Rabbinical authorities, like Levi ben Chabib, afterwards rabbi in Jerusalem. Those who escaped with their lives and their faith attributed it to the gracious and wondrous interposition of God. Isaac ben Joseph Caro, who had come from Toledo to Portugal, there lost his adult and his minor sons ("who were beautiful as princes"), yet thanked his Creator for the mercy that in spite of peril on the sea he reached Turkey. Abraham Zacuto, with his son Samuel, also was in danger of death, although (or because) he was King Manoel's favorite, astrologer and chronicler. Both, however, were fortunate enough to pass through the bitter ordeal, and escape from Portugal, but they were twice imprisoned. They finally settled in Tunis.

The stir which the enforced conversion of the Jews caused in Portugal did not immediately subside. Those who had submitted to baptism through fear of death, or out of love for their children, did not give up the hope that by appealing to the papal court they might be able to return to their own faith, seeing that, as all Europe knew, Pope Alexander VI and his college of cardinals, as base as himself, would do anything for money. A witticism was then going the rounds of every Christian country:

> Vendit Alexander Claves, Altaria, Christum;
> Emerat ista prius, vendere jure potest.

Rome was a market of shame—a hill of Astarte—a mart of unwholesomeness—but there the innocent, also, could buy their rights. The Portuguese new-Christians now sent a deputation of seven of their companions in misery to Pope Alexander, and they did not forget to take a purse of gold with them. The pope and the so-called holy college showed themselves favorably inclined towards them, especially Cardinal de Sancta Anastasia took them under his patronage. The Spanish ambassador, Garcilaso, however, was instructed by their Spanish majesties to oppose them. Despite his influence the affairs of the Portuguese Jews must have taken a favorable turn, for King Manoel decided to make concessions. He issued a mild decree (May 30th, 1497), in which he granted amnesty to all forcibly baptized Jews, and a respite of twenty years, during which they were not to be brought before the tribunal of the Inquisition for their adherence to Judaism. It was said that it was necessary for them first to lay aside their Jewish habits, and accustom themselves to the ways of the Catholic faith, for which they needed time. Further, the decree ordered that, on the expiration of this term, a regular examination should be made of those accused of Judaizing practices, and if the case was decided against them, their goods should not be confiscated, as in Spain, but given over to their heirs. Finally, the decree ordained that those baptized physicians and surgeons who did not understand Latin might make use of Hebrew books of reference. Practically this allowed the enforced Christians to live in secret, without fear of punishment, as Jews, and to retain all their books. For, who, in Portugal, in those days, could distinguish a book of medicine from any other work in the Hebrew language? The students of the Talmud could thus follow their favorite researches and studies under the mask of Catholicism. This amnesty benefited the Portuguese Marranos, but not those who had immigrated into Portugal, by a clause which Manoel had inserted out of deference to the Spanish court, or, more particularly, to the Spanish Infanta Isabella. For she insisted that the Marranos who had fled out of Spain into Portugal should be delivered over to the Moloch of the Inquisition. In the marriage contract between the king of Portugal and the fanatical Isabella (August, 1497), it was expressly set down that all persons of the Hebrew race coming under condemnation of the Inquisition, who sought refuge in Portugal, must leave within a month's time.

Thus many thousand Portuguese Jews became pseudo-Christians, but with the firm resolve to seize the first opportunity to get away, so that in a free country they might openly practice a religion only the dearer to them for all they had suffered for it. Their souls, as the poet Samuel Usque writes, had not been stained by the baptism imposed on them. There were some Jews, however, who had refused baptism with all their might. Among them was Simon Maimi, apparently the last chief rabbi (Arrabi mor) in Portugal, a scrupulously pious man; also his wife, his sons-in-law, and some others. They were closely imprisoned, because they would not forswear Judaism, nor observe the rites of the church. To bring them to conversion, Simon Maimi and his fellow sufferers, official rabbis, were most inhumanly tortured. They were immured up to the neck in their prison, and left for three days in this fearful position. When they nevertheless remained firm, the walls were torn down; three had died, among them Simon Maimi, whose conversion was most important, because his example would have influenced the others. Two Marranos imperiled their lives to secure the corpse of the pious martyr, that they might inter it in the Jewish burial-ground, although it was strictly forbidden to bury the Jewish victims of Christian sacrifice otherwise than by the executioner's hands. A few Marranos secretly attended their deeply-lamented saint to his last rest, and celebrated a mourning service over his grave. Manoel permitted the few remaining Jews to depart not long after, probably on the death of Isabella, the instigator of all his barbarities to the Jews. She died at the birth of the heir to the thrones of Portugal and Spain, August 24th, 1498, and the Infante died two years later. One of the remnant dismissed was Abraham Saba, a preacher and Kabbalist author, whose two children were baptized by force and taken from him. The companions of Simon Maimi and his sons-in-law remained in prison a long time, were afterwards sent to Arzilla, in Africa, there condemned to work at the trenches on the Sabbath, and died at last a martyr's death.

Eighty years later, Manoel's great-grandson, the adventurous king, Sebastian, led the flower of the Portuguese people to fresh conquests in Africa. In a single battle the power of Portugal was broken, her nobility slain, or cast into prison. The captives were carried to Fez, and there, in the slave-market, offered for sale to the descendants of the barbarously treated Portuguese Jews. The unhappy Portuguese nobles and knights were, however, glad to be bought by Jews, as they well knew the mild and humane nature of the followers of the "God of vengeance."

CHAPTER XIII.

RESULTS OF THE EXPULSION OF THE JEWS FROM SPAIN AND PORTUGAL. GENERAL VIEW.

Widespread Consequences of the Expulsion—The Exiles—Fate of the Abrabanel Family—Leon Medigo—Isaac Akrish—The Pre-eminence of Jews of Spanish Origin—The North-African States: Samuel Alvalensi, Jacob Berab, Simon Duran II—The Jews of Algiers, Tripoli and Tunis—Abraham Zacuto, and Moses Alashkar—Egypt: Isaac Shalal, David Ibn-Abi Zimra—The Jews of Cairo—Selim I—Cessation of the Office of Nagid—Jerusalem—Obadyah di Bertinoro—Safet and Joseph Saragossi—The Jews of Turkey—Constantinople—Elias Mizrachi: the Karaites—The Communities of Salonica and Adrianople—The Jews of Greece—Elias Kapsali—The Jews of Italy and the Popes: Bonet de Lates—The Ghetto in Venice—Samuel Abrabanel and Benvenida Abrabanela—Abraham Farissol—The Jews of Germany and their Sorrows—Expulsion of the Jews from Various Towns—The Jews of Bohemia—Jacob Polak and his School—The Jews of Poland.

1496—1525 C.E.

THE expulsion of the Jews from the Pyrenean Peninsula, unwise as it was inhuman, forms in various ways a well-marked turning-point in the general history of the Jewish race. It involved not only the exiles, but the whole Jewish people, in far-reaching and mostly disastrous consequences. The glory of the Jews was extinguished, their pride humbled, their center displaced, the strong pillar against which they had hitherto leant broken. The grief caused by this sad event was shared by the Jews in every country which had news of it. They all felt as if the Temple had been destroyed a third time, as if the sons of Zion had a third time been condemned to exile and misery. Whether from fancy or pride, it was supposed that the Spanish (or, more correctly, the Sephardic) Jews were the posterity of the noblest tribe, and included among them descendants in a direct line from King

David; hence the Jews looked upon them as a kind of Jewish nobility. And now these exalted ones had been visited by the severest affliction! Exile, compulsory baptism, death in every hideous form, by despair, hunger, pestilence, fire, shipwreck, all torments united, had reduced their hundreds of thousands to barely the tenth part of that number. The remnant wandered about like specters, hunted from one country to another, and princes among Jews, they were compelled to knock as beggars at the doors of their brethren. The thirty millions of ducats which, at the lowest computation, the Spanish Jews possessed on their expulsion, had melted away in their hands, and they were thus left denuded of everything in a hostile world, which valued the Jews at their money's worth only. At the same period many German Jews were driven from cities in the East and in the West, but their misery did not equal that of the Spanish Jews. They had known neither the sweetness of a country that they could call their own, nor the comforts of life; they were more hardy, or, at least, accustomed to contempt and harsh treatment.

Half a century after the banishment of the Jews from Spain and Portugal, we everywhere meet with fugitives: here a group, there a family, or solitary stragglers. It was a kind of exodus on a small scale, moving eastwards, chiefly to Turkey, as if the Jews were to approach their original home. But their very wanderings, until they again reached secure dwelling-places, and in a measure were settled, were heartrending through the calamities of every description, the humiliations, the contumely, sufferings worse than death, that they encountered.

The ancient family of Abrabanel did not escape heavy disasters and constant migrations. The father, Isaac Abrabanel, who had occupied a high position at the court of the accomplished king, Ferdinand I, and of his son Alfonso, at Naples, was forced, on the approach of the French, to leave the city, and, with his royal patron, to seek refuge in Sicily. The French hordes plundered his house of all its valuables, and destroyed a choice library, his greatest treasure. On the death of King Alfonso, Isaac Abrabanel, for safety, went to the island of Corfu. He remained there only till the French had evacuated the Neapolitan territory; then he settled at Monopoli (Apulia), where he completed or revised many of his writings. The wealth acquired in the service of the Portuguese and Spanish courts had vanished, his wife and children were separated from him and scattered, and he passed his days in sad musings, out of which only his study of the Scriptures and the annals of the Jewish people could lift him. His eldest son, Judah Leon Medigo Abrabanel, resided at Genoa, where, in spite of his unsettled existence and consuming grief for the loss of his young son, who had been taken from him, and was being brought up in Portugal as a Christian, he still cherished ideals. For Leon Abrabanel was much more highly accomplished, richer in thought, in every way more gifted than his father, and deserves consideration not merely for his father's, but for his own sake. Leon Abrabanel practiced medicine to gain a livelihood (whence his cognomen *Medigo*); but his favorite pursuits were astronomy, mathematics, and metaphysics. Shortly before the death of the gifted and eccentric Pico de Mirandola, Leon Medigo became acquainted with him, won his friendship, and at his instigation undertook the writing of a philosophical work.

Leon Medigo, in a remarkable manner, entered into close connection with acquaintances of his youth, with Spanish grandees, and even with King Ferdinand, who had driven his family and so many hundred thousands into banishment and death. For he became the private physician of the general, Gonsalvo de Cordova, the conqueror and viceroy of

Naples. The heroic, amiable, and lavish De Cordova did not share his master's hatred against the Jews. In one of his descendants Jewish literature found a devotee. When King Ferdinand, after the conquest of the kingdom of Naples (1504), commanded that the Jews be banished thence, as from Spain, the general thwarted the execution of the order, observing that, on the whole, there were but few Jews on Neapolitan territory, since most of the immigrants had either again left it, or had become converts to Christianity. The banishment of these few could only be injurious to the country, since they would settle at Venice, which would benefit by their industry and riches. Consequently the Jews were allowed to remain a while longer on Neapolitan territory. But to exterminate the Spanish and Portuguese Marranos who had settled there, Ferdinand established the terrible Inquisition at Benevento. Leon Medigo for over two years was De Cordova's physician (1505—1507), and King Ferdinand saw him when he visited Naples. After the king's departure and the ungracious dismissal of the viceroy (June, 1507), Leon Abrabanel, having nowhere found suitable employment, returned to his father, then living at Venice, whither he had been invited by his second son, Isaac II, who practiced medicine first at Reggio (Calabria), then at Venice. The youngest son, Samuel, afterwards a generous protector of his co-religionists, was the most fortunate of the family. He dwelt amidst the cool shades of the academy of Salonica, to which his father had sent him to finish his education in Jewish learning. The elder Abrabanel once more entered the political arena. At Venice he had the opportunity of settling a dispute between the court of Lisbon and the Venetian Republic concerning the East-Indian colonies established by the Portuguese, especially concerning the trade in spices. Some influential senators discerned Isaac Abrabanel's correct political and financial judgment, and thenceforth consulted him in all important questions of state policy. But suffering and travel had broken his strength; before he reached seventy years, he felt the infirmities of old age creeping over him. In a letter of reply to Saul Cohen Ashkenasi, an inhabitant of Candia, a man thirsting for knowledge, the disciple and intellectual heir of Elias del Medigo, Abrabanel complains of increasing debility and senility. Had he been silent, his literary productions of that time would have betrayed his infirmity. The baited victims of Spanish fanaticism would have needed bodies of steel and the resisting strength of stone not to succumb to the sufferings with which they were overwhelmed.

We have a striking instance of the restless wanderings of the Jewish exiles in the life of one of the sufferers, who, though insignificant, became known to fame by his zeal to raise the courage of the unfortunate. To Isaac ben Abraham Akrish, a Spaniard, a great traveler and a bookworm (born about 1489, died after 1575), Jewish literature owes the preservation of many a valuable document. Akrish said, half in joke, half in earnest, that he must have been born in the hour when the planet Jupiter was passing through the zodiacal sign of the Fishes, a nativity which indicates a wandering life. For, though lame in both feet, he spent his whole life in traveling from city to city, on land and on sea. When a boy, Akrish was banished from Spain, and at Naples he underwent all the sufferings which seem to have conspired against the exiles. Thus he limped from nation to nation, "whose languages he did not understand, and who spared neither old men nor children," until in Egypt, in the house of an exile, he found a few years' rest. Who can follow all the wandering exiles, with sore feet, and still sorer hearts, until they somewhere found rest, or the peace of the grave?

But the very enormity of the misery they endured raised the dignity of the Sephardic Jews to a height bordering on pride. That they whom God's hand had smitten so heavily, so persistently, and who had undergone such unspeakable sorrow, must occupy a peculiar position, and belong to the specially elect, was the thought or the feeling existing more or less clearly in the breasts of the survivors. They looked upon their banishment from Spain as a third exile, and upon themselves as favorites of God, whom, because of His greater love for them, He had chastised the more severely. Contrary to expectation, a certain exaltation took possession of them, which did not, indeed, cause them to forget, but transfigured, their sufferings. As soon as they felt even slightly relieved from the burden of their boundless calamity, and were able to breathe, they rose with elastic force, and carried their heads high like princes. They had lost everything except their Spanish pride, their distinguished manner. However humbled they might be, their pride did not forsake them; they asserted it wherever their wandering feet found a resting-place. And to some extent they were justified. They had, indeed, since the growth of the tendency among Jews towards strict orthodoxy and hostility to science, and since their exclusion from social circles, receded from the high scientific position they had held, and forfeited the supremacy they had maintained during many centuries; yet they far surpassed the Jews of all other countries in culture, manners, and also in worth, as was shown by their external bearing and their language. Their love for their country was too great to allow them to hate the unnatural mother who had cast them out. Hence, wherever they went, they founded Spanish or Portuguese colonies. They carried the Spanish tongue, Spanish dignity and distinction to Africa, Syria, and Palestine, Italy and Flanders; wherever fate cast their lot they cherished and cultivated this Spanish manner so lovingly, that it has maintained itself to this day in full vigor among their descendants. Far from being absorbed by the rest of the Jewish population in countries which had hospitably received them, they considered themselves a privileged race, the flower and nobility of the Jewish nation, kept aloof from others, looked down upon them with contempt, and not unfrequently dictated laws to them. This arose from the fact that the Spanish and Portuguese Jews spoke the languages of their native countries (which by the discoveries and conquests of the sixteenth century had become the languages of the world) with purity, took part in literature, and associated with Christians on equal terms, with manliness, and without fear or servility. On this point they contrasted with the German Jews, who despised pure and beautiful speech, the very thing which constitutes a true man, and considered a corrupt jargon and isolation from the Christian world as proofs of religious zeal. The Sephardic Jews attached importance to forms of all kinds, to taste in dress, to elegance in their synagogues, as well as to the medium for the exchange of thought. The Spanish and Portuguese rabbis preached in their native tongues, and laid great stress on pure pronunciation and euphony. Hence their language did not degenerate, at least not in the first centuries after their expulsion. "In the cities of Salonica, Constantinople, Alexandria, Cairo, Venice, and other resorts of commerce, the Jews transact their business only in the Spanish language. I have known Jews of Salonica who, though still young, pronounced Castilian as well as myself, and even better." This is the judgment of a Christian writer about half a century after their expulsion.

The contempt which even Isaac Abrabanel, mild and broken though he was, entertained for the barbarous jargon spoken by German Jews is characteristic. He was surprised to discover in a letter, sent to him by Saul Cohen of Candia, a native of Germany, a finished Hebrew style and close reasoning, and freely expressed his astonishment: "I am surprised to find so excellent a style among the Germans (Jews), which is rare even among their leaders and rabbis, however gifted they may be in other respects. Their language is full of awkwardness and clumsiness, a stammering without judgment." This superiority of the Jews of Spanish descent in culture, bearing, social manners, and knowledge of the world, was appreciated and admired by other Jews, especially by German Jews, with whom they everywhere came into contact. Hence Spanish Jews could presume to play the rôle of masters, and frequently, in spite of their paucity of numbers, they dominated a majority speaking other tongues. In the century after their expulsion they are almost exclusively the leaders; the names of their spokesmen are heard everywhere; they furnished rabbis, authors, thinkers and visionaries, whilst German and Italian Jews occupied a humble place. In all countries, except Germany and Poland, into which they had not penetrated, or only as solitary individuals, the Sephardic Jews were the leaders.

The northern coast of Africa, and the inhabitable regions inland, were full of Jews of Spanish descent. They had congregated there in great numbers during the century from the persecution of 1391 to their total expulsion. From Safi (Assafi), the most southwestern town of Morocco, to Tripoli in the northeast, there were many communities, of varying numbers, speaking the Spanish language. Though mostly hated, arbitrarily treated, and often compelled by petty barbarian tyrants and the uncivilized, degenerate Moorish population to wear a disgraceful costume, yet prominent Jews found opportunities to distinguish themselves, to rise to high honors and acquire widespread influence. In Morocco a rich Jew, learned in history, who had rendered important services to the ruler of that country, was held in high esteem. At Fez, where there existed a community of five thousand Jewish families, who monopolized most trades, Samuel Alvalensi, a Jew of Spanish descent, was greatly beloved by the king, on account of his ability and his courage, and so trusted by the populace that it accepted him as its leader. In the struggle between the two reigning families, the Merinos and the Xerifs, he sided with the former, led one thousand four hundred Jews and Moors against the followers of the latter, and defeated them at Ceuta. A very numerous Jewish community of Spanish descent occupied the greater portion of Tlemçen, or Tremçen, an important town, where the court resided. Here Jacob Berab (born 1474, died 1541), fleeing from Spain, found a refuge. He was one of the most active men among the Spanish emigrants, and the most acute rabbi of his age. At the same time, he was a crusty, dogmatical and quarrelsome man, who had many enemies, but also many admirers. Born at Maqueda, near Toledo, Jacob Berab, after passing through many dangers, suffering want, hunger and thirst, reached Tlemçen, whence he went to Fez, the Jewish community of which chose him, a needy youth, for their rabbi, on account of his learning and sagacity. There he conducted a college until the fanatic Spaniards made conquests in northern Africa, and disturbed the quiet asylum that the Jews had found there.

The reduced community of Algiers was under the direction of Simon Duran II, a descendant of the Spanish fugitives of 1391 (born 1439, died after 1510), a son of Solomon Duran, the rabbi with philosophic culture. Like his brother, he was considered in his day a high rabbinical authority, and the advice of both was sought by many persons. Of as noble a disposition as his father, Simon Duran was the protector of his co-religionists and the sheet-anchor of the Spanish exiles who came within his reach, for he shunned neither cost nor danger when the religion, morals and safety of his compatriots were in question. Fifty fugitive Jews, who had suffered shipwreck, had been cast on the coast of Seville, where the fanatical Spaniards, in accordance with the edict, put them into prison, and kept them there for two years. They were in daily expectation of death, but finally they were pardoned—that is to say, sold for slaves. As such they reached Algiers in a deplorable condition; but by the exertions of Simon Duran they were redeemed for the sum of seven hundred ducats, which the small community managed to collect.

Two eminent Spanish Jews, the aged historian and astronomer, Abraham Zacuto, and a younger man, Moses Alashkar, found a refuge at Tunis. Zacuto, who had taught mathematics and astronomy to Christian and Mahometan pupils in Spain, and whose published writings were widely read and made use of, was nevertheless compelled to wander about like an outlaw, and had only with difficulty escaped death. He seems to have spent some quiet years at Tunis, where he completed his more celebrated than useful chronicle ("Sefer Yochasin," 1504), history it cannot be called. It is an epitome of Jewish history, with especial reference to the literature of the Jews. It has the merit of having promoted historical research among Jews, but lacks artistic arrangement and completeness. It is a mere compilation from works accessible to the writer, who has even failed to give a complete sketch of the history of his own times, the sufferings of the Spanish and Portuguese Jews. Zacuto's chronicle was a child of his old age and misery; he wrote it with a trembling hand, in fear of impending events, and without sufficient literary materials. On this account it must be judged leniently.

A contemporary of Zacuto at Tunis was Moses

ben Isaac Alashkar, as deeply learned a Talmudist as his teacher, Samuel Alvalensi. He was a correct thinker, and devoid of narrow one-sidedness. He plunged into the dark labyrinths of the Kabbala, yet, at the same time, raised his eyes to the bright heights of philosophy—a mental *mésalliance* possible in those days. Alashkar even defended Maimuni and his philosophical system against the charge of heresy brought by obscurantists.

Terrified by the perils which the Spanish arms foreboded to the Jews of northern Africa, Zacuto and Alashkar, with many others, appear to have quitted Tunis. They were but too well acquainted with the cruelties practiced against Jews by the ultra-Catholic Spaniards. The former went to Turkey, where he died shortly after his arrival (before 1515). Alashkar fled to Egypt, where his extensive learning and wealth secured for him an honorable position.

Egypt, especially its capital, Cairo, had become the home of many Jewish-Spanish fugitives, who had in a short time acquired an influence surpassing that of the original Jewish inhabitants. On their arrival, all the Jewish communities were, as of old, ruled by a Jewish chief justice or prince (Nagid, Reis). The office was then held by the noble and rich Isaac Cohen Shalal, a man of upright character, learned in the Talmud, who employed his wealth and the high esteem in which he was held by all, even including the Egyptian Mameluke sultan, for the benefit of his community and the fugitives who settled in their midst. He impartially promoted deserving men of the Spanish immigration to offices, whereby they gradually obtained paramount influence. The Spanish scholar, Samuel Sidillo (or Sid, Ibn-Sid), a disciple of the last Toledan rabbi, Isaac de Leon, highly venerated in his day on account of his piety and his profound rabbinical knowledge, found a refuge at Cairo. A Spanish fugitive who acquired still higher distinction was David Ibn-Abi Zimra (born 1470, died about 1573). A disciple of the mystic Joseph Saragossi, he was rich in knowledge and virtues, as well as in property and distinguished descendants, and he soon outshone the natives, acquiring the reputation of being the highest rabbinical authority in Egypt. Many other Spanish rabbinical scholars found rest in Egypt; to those already named, including Jacob Berab and Moses Alashkar, we may add Abraham Ibn-Shoshan, all eventually becoming official rabbis.

Political changes in Egypt placed the Spaniards at the head of the Jewish communities in that country. The land of the Nile, together with Syria and Palestine, whose conquest was so difficult a task for the sultans of Constantinople, finally became the well-secured prey of Selim I, who won a splendid victory over the Mameluke sultan in a decisive battle not far from Aleppo (1517). His march from Syria to Egypt was a triumphal progress. Selim spent the summer of that year in remodeling the order of things in Egypt, reducing it to a real dependency of Turkey, turning it, in fact, into a province, ruled by a viceroy, a pasha entirely devoted to him. Abraham de Castro, a Jew of Spanish descent, was appointed by Selim master of the mint for the new Turkish coinage, and, by his wealth and influence, he acquired great weight among Turkish officials and the Egyptian Jews. De Castro was very benevolent; he annually spent three thousand gold florins in alms, and in every way took lively interest in the affairs of his co-religionists.

Selim, or his viceroy, appears to have introduced an entirely new order into the management of the Egyptian Jews. For ages a chief rabbi and judge had ruled all the communities; the person holding the office had possessed a kind of princely power, similar to that formerly exercised by the princes of the exile in Babylon. The chief rabbi or prince

(Nagid) nominated the rabbis of the communities, had the supreme decision of disputes among Jews, confirmed or rejected every new regulation, was even authorized to decree corporal punishment for offenses and crimes committed by Jews under his jurisdiction. From these functions he derived a considerable revenue, but all this ceased with the Turkish conquest. Every community was thenceforth declared independent in the election of its head, and allowed to manage its own affairs. The last Jewish-Egyptian prince or chief rabbi was deposed from his dignity, and betook himself with his riches to Jerusalem, where he became a benefactor of its growing community. The office of rabbi of Cairo was bestowed on the Spanish immigrant David Ibn-Abi Zimra, on account of his upright character, learning, benevolent disposition, and chiefly, probably, on account of his wealth. His authority rose to such a degree that he could venture to abolish a very ancient custom, which excessive conservatism had dragged along from century to century, like a dead limb. The Babylonian Jews had more than eighteen hundred years before adopted the Syrian or Seleucidan chronology (*Minyan Yavanim, Minyan Shetaroth*), in memory of the victory of the Syrian king Seleucus over the other generals of Alexander the Great. The Syrian empire and the Seleucidæ had perished long ago, Syria had by turns become the prey of Romans, Byzantines, Mahometans, Mongols and Turks; nevertheless, the Babylonian and Egyptian Jews had retained that chronology, employing it not only in historical records and secular papers, but also in the dating of documents of divorce and similar deeds. Whilst the Jews of Palestine and of Europe had gradually adopted other chronologies, as "After the Destruction of the Temple," or "Since the Creation" (*æra mundi*), the Babylonian and Egyptian Jews so pertinaciously adhered to the Seleucidan era as to declare invalid every letter of divorce not so dated. Ibn-Abi Zimra abolished this antiquated chronology, as far as Egypt was concerned, introducing in its stead the already accepted mode of reckoning from the Creation, and his innovation met with no opposition. The ascendency of the immigrant Sephardic Jews over the majority of the original community (the Mostarabi) was so great and so well established, that the former, in spite of the objections of the latter, succeeded in the bold attempt to abolish an ancient and beautiful custom, introduced by Maimuni himself. The Mostarabian Jews for more than three centuries had been accustomed to have the chief prayer said aloud in the synagogue, by the reader (Chazan), without themselves participating in it. But to the pious immigrants from the Peninsula this custom, though promoting decorum and devotion, appeared illegal, anti-Talmudic, if not heretical, and they zealously set to work to abolish it. Terrible sufferings had hardened the hearts of the Sephardic Jews, and they were but too ready to exercise the utmost severity in religious matters, and slavishly to follow the letter. The rabbi, David Ibn-Abi Zimra, was their leader.

During his term of office a great danger hovered over the Cairo community. The fourth viceroy of Egypt, Achmed Shaitan (Satan), harbored the design of severing Egypt from Turkey, and making himself its independent master. Having succeeded in his first measures, he proposed to the Jewish superintendent of the mint, Abraham de Castro, to have his name placed on the coins. De Castro pretended compliance, but asked for a written order. Having obtained it he secretly left Egypt, and hastened to the court of Solyman I, at Constantinople, to inform the sultan of the treacherous design of the pasha, which was thus frustrated. Achmed vented his rage on the Jews, threw some of them, probably De Castro's friends and relatives, into prison, and permitted the Mamelukes to plunder the Jewish quarter of Cairo. He then sent for twelve of the most eminent Jews, and commanded them within a short time to find an exorbitant sum of money, threatening them, in case of non-compliance, with a cruel death for themselves and their families. For greater security he retained them as hostages. To the supplications of the Jewish community for mercy and delay, the tyrant replied by more terrible threats. In their hopelessness the Jews of Cairo tnrned in fervent prayer to God. Meanwhile the collectors had got together a considerable sum, which they offered as a payment on account. But as it scarcely amounted to the tenth part of Achmed's demand, his private secretary had the collectors put in irons, and threatened them, and all the members of the community, with certain death on that very day, as soon as his master left his bath. At the very moment when the secretary uttered these words, the pasha was attacked in his bath by Mahomet Bey, one of his vizirs, and some other conspirators, and severely wounded. Achmed Shaitan made good his escape from the palace, but was betrayed, overtaken, cast into fetters and then beheaded. The imprisoned Jews were set free, and their community escaped a great peril. The Egyptian Jews for a long period afterwards commemorated the day of their deliverance (Adar 27th or 28th, 1524—a Cairoan Purim, Furin al-Mizrayim).

By the immigration of Spaniards and Portuguese, Jerusalem and other Palestinian cities also obtained a great increase of members to their congregations, and considerable importance. Here, too, the immigrants in a short time became the social and religious leaders. In the very brief period of seven years the number of Jewish families in the Holy City grew from scarcely seventy to two hundred, and again within the space of two decades (1495–

1521), it rose from two hundred to fifteen hundred. The influx of new settlers had largely augmented the prosperity of the Jewish inhabitants of Jerusalem. Whilst formerly nearly all the members of the community were in a state of destitution, three decades afterwards there were only two hundred receiving alms. And what is of greater importance, morality was greatly benefited by the immigrants. Jerusalem was no longer the den of robbers found by Obadyah (Obadiah) di Bertinoro (1470—1520), who had immigrated from Italy. The members of the community were no longer harassed to death, and driven to despair or voluntary exile by a rapacious, tyrannical and treacherous faction; harmony, union, a sense of justice, and peace had found an abode with them. There was indeed a show of excessive piety, but it no longer flagrantly contrasted with a revoltingly immoral mode of life. Obadyah di Bertinoro, the gentle and amiable Italian preacher, had greatly contributed to this improvement of the moral tone of Jerusalem; for more than two decades he taught the growing community, by precept and example, genuine piety, nobility of sentiment and relinquishment of barbarian coarseness. After his arrival at Jerusalem, he wrote to his friends: "If there were in this country one sagacious Jew, who knew how to lead a community gently and justly, not Jews only, but also Mahometans would willingly submit to him, for the latter are not at all hostile to the Jews, but full of consideration for strangers. But there is not one Jew in this country possessing either sense or social virtues; all are coarse, misanthropical and avaricious." Bertinoro did not anticipate that he himself would soften that coarseness, improve the morals, mitigate that immorality, ennoble that baseness. But his genial, amiable manner disarmed evil, and healed the sores he had discovered, lamented, and pitilessly exposed. Obadyah was the guardian angel of the Holy City, he cleansed it from pollution, and clothed it with a pure festival garment. "Were I to attempt proclaiming his praise," writes an Italian pilgrim to Jerusalem, "I should never cease. He is the man who is held in the highest esteem in the country; everything is done according to his orders, and no one dares gainsay his words. From all parts he is sought after and consulted; his merits are acknowledged by Egyptians and Babylonians, and even Mahometans honor him. Withal, he is modest and humble; his speech is gentle; he is accessible to every one. All praise him and say: He is not like an earthly being. When he preaches every ear listens intently; not the least sound is heard, his hearers are so silently devout." Exiles from the Pyrenean Peninsula supported him in his humane work.

To the intervention of Obadyah di Bertinoro, and of those who shared his opinions, probably were due the excellent ordinances which the community voluntarily imposed on itself, and for remembrance graved on a tablet in the synagogue. They were directed against the abuses which had crept in by degrees. These ordinances included amongst others the following decrees: In disputes between Jews, the Mahometan authorities are to be applied to only in the utmost necessity. The Jewish judge or rabbi is not to be allowed to compel wealthy members of the community to make advances for communal wants. Students of the Talmud and widows shall not contribute to the communal funds. Jews are not to purchase bad coin, and, if they acquire any accidentally, are not to pass it. The pilgrims to the grave of the prophet Samuel are not to drink wine, for men and women traveled together, the latter unveiled, and if the men had been excited by wine, great mischief might have ensued.

The Holy City acquired still higher importance by the immigration of Isaac Shalal, with his riches, experience, and authority.

Safet in Galilee, the youngest town of Palestine, next to Jerusalem acquired the largest Jewish population and considerable importance, which increased to such a degree that Safet not only rivaled, but excelled the mother-city. At the end of the fifteenth and the beginning of the next century it sheltered only some three hundred Jewish families, original inhabitants (Moriscos), Berbers, and Sephardim. It did not at first possess any eminent native expounder of the Talmud, who might have become a leader. It owed its importance and far-reaching influence to the arrival of a Spanish fugitive, under whose direction the community was strengthened. Joseph Saragossi became for Safet what Obadyah di Bertinoro had been for Jerusalem. Driven from Saragossa, he passed through Sicily, Beyrout and Sidon, in which latter place he resided for some time, and finally reached Safet, where he settled. Joseph Saragossi possessed a mild, fascinating character, and considered it the task of his life to preach peace and restore harmony in private and communal life. Even among Mahometans he worked in a conciliating and appeasing spirit, and on this account he was loved and revered as an angel of peace. At one time he wished to leave Safet. The inhabitants fairly clung to him, and promised him an annual salary of fifty ducats, two-thirds of which the Mahometan governor of the town offered to furnish. Joseph Saragossi transplanted the study of the Talmud to Safet, and also that of the Kabbala, as he was an ultra-pious mystic. Through him the hitherto untainted community became a nest of Kabbalists.

In Damascus, the half-Palestinian capital of Syria, there also arose, by the side of the very ancient Mostarabian community, a Sephardic congregation, composed of fugitives, and numbering five hundred Jewish families. Within a short time after their arrival, the Spaniards built a splendid synagogue at

Damascus, called Khataib. They speedily increased to such a degree as to separate into several congregations, according to the states from which they had originally come.

The main stream of the Jewish-Spanish emigration flowed towards Turkey in Europe; the greater part of the remnant of the three hundred thousand exiles found an asylum in that country, where the inhabitants did not take love as their watchword. The sultans Bajazet, Selim I and Solyman I, not only tolerated the fugitive Jews, but gave them a hearty welcome, and granted them the liberties enjoyed by Armenians and Greeks. A Jewish poet enthusiastically described the freedom of his co-religionists in Turkey. "Great Turkey, a wide and spreading sea, which our Lord opened with the wand of His mercy (as at the exodus from Egypt), that the tide of thy present disaster, Jacob, as happened with the multitude of the Egyptians, should therein lose and exhaust itself. There the gates of freedom and equal position for the unhindered practice of Jewish worship are ever open, they are never closed against thee. There thou canst renew thy inner life, change thy condition, strip off, and cast away false and erroneous doctrines, recover thy ancient truths, and abandon the practices which, by the violence of the nations among whom thou wast a pilgrim, thou wert compelled to imitate. In this realm thou art highly favored by the Lord, since therein He granteth thee boundless liberty to commence thy late repentance."

The immigrant Jews at first enjoyed very happy days in Turkey, because they were a godsend to this comparatively new state. The Turks were good soldiers, but bad citizens. The sultans, frequently on bad terms with Christian states, could place but indifferent trust in the Greeks, Armenians, and Christians of other national creeds; they looked upon them as born spies and traitors. But they could depend on the fidelity and usefulness of the Jews. Hence they were, on the one hand, the business people, and on the other, the citizen class of Turkey. They not only carried on the wholesale and retail commerce by land and sea, but were the handicraftsmen and the artists. The Marranos especially who had fled from Spain and Portugal manufactured for the warlike Turks new armor and firearms, cannons and gunpowder, and taught the Turks how to use them. Thus persecuting Christianity itself furnished its chief enemies, the Turks, with weapons which enabled them to overwhelm the former with defeat after defeat, humiliation on humiliation. Jewish physicians especially were held in high esteem in Turkey; they were for the most part clever disciples of the school of Salamanca, and, on account of their skill, higher education, secrecy and discretion, were preferred to Christian, and even to Mahometan doctors. These Jewish physicians, mostly of Spanish descent, acquired great influence with grand sultans, vizirs and pashas.

Sultan Selim had for his physician in ordinary Joseph Hamon, an immigrant probably from Granada. Hamon's son and nephew successively held the same office. The son, Moses Hamon (born 1490, died about 1565), physician to the wise sultan Solyman, on account of his skill and manly, determined character, enjoyed even higher reputation and influence than his father. He accompanied the sultan in his warlike expeditions, and brought back from Persia, whither he had followed Solyman on a triumphal progress, a learned man, Jacob Tus or Tavs (about 1535), who translated the Pentateuch into Persian. This version, accompanied by Chaldean and Arabic translations, was afterwards printed at the expense of Hamon, who was justly considered a protector of his brethren and a promoter of Judaism.

The Jews were also in great request in Turkey

as linguists and interpreters, they having acquired knowledge of many languages through their wanderings among foreign nations.

The capital, Constantinople, held within its walls a very numerous Jewish community, which was daily increased by new fugitives from the Peninsula, so that it became the largest in Europe, numbering probably thirty thousand souls. It had forty-four synagogues, consequently as many separate congregations. For the Jewish community in the Turkish capital and other towns did not form a close corporation, but was divided into groups and sections, according to their native places, each of which was anxious to retain its own customs, rites and liturgy, and to possess its own synagogue and rabbinical college. Hence there were not only Castilian, Aragonese and Portuguese congregations, but still more restricted associations, Cordovan, Toledan, Barcelonian, Lisbon groups (Kahals), besides German Apulian, Messinian and Greek. Every petty congregation apportioned among its members the contributions, not only for its worship, officials, the maintenance of the poor, its hospitals and schools, but also for the taxes payable to the state. These latter at first were trifling: a poll-tax on every one subject to taxation (charaj), and a kind of rabbinical tax levied on the congregation, according to the three different classes of property, of 200, 100 and 20 aspers. The family of the physician Hamon alone was exempt from taxes.

At first the native Jews, who formed the majority, had complete preponderance over the immigrants. The office of chief rabbi, after the death of the meritorious but unappreciated Moses Kapsali, was held by Elias Mizrachi, probably descended from an immigrant Greek family, who under the sultans Bajazet, Selim I, and perhaps also under Solyman, had a seat in the divan like his predecessor, and was the official representative of the whole body of Turkish Jews. He deservedly held this post on account of his rabbinical and secular knowledge, and upright, impartially just character. Elias Mizrachi (born about 1455, died between 1525 and 1527), a disciple of the German school, and a profound Talmudist and strictly pious man, was no enemy to science. He not only understood, but taught mathematics and astronomy, gave public lectures thereon, as also on the Talmud, and compiled handbooks on these subjects, some of which became such favorites as to be translated into Latin. In his youth he was a Hotspur, and had a feud with the Karaites in Turkey. But in his old age he felt more kindly towards them, and employed his weighty influence to avert a wrong which the ultra-pious were about to inflict on them. A few obscurantists, chiefly members of the Apulian congregation at Constantinople, attempted to interrupt, in a violent manner, the neighborly intercourse which for half a century had existed between Rabbanites and Karaites. They assembled the members of the congregation, and, with the Sefer Torah in their hand, excommunicated all who should henceforth instruct Karaites, whether children or adults, in the Bible or the Talmud, or even in secular sciences, such as mathematics, natural history, logic, music, or even the alphabet. Nor were Rabbanite servants any longer to take service with Karaite families. These fanatics intended to raise an insuperable barrier between the followers of the Talmud and those of the Bible. But the majority of the Constantinople community were dissatisfied with this bigoted measure. The tolerant Rabbanites of the capital held a meeting to frustrate the plan of the zealots. But the latter behaved so outrageously and with such violence, bringing a fierce rabble provided with cudgels into the synagogue where the consultation was to be held, that the conveners of the meeting had no chance of being heard, and the act of excommunication was carried by an insolent minority, in defiance of the sound arguments and opposition of the majority. Then Rabbi Elias Mizrachi openly and vigorously opposed this unreasonable, illegal and violent proceeding, showing in a learned discourse how unjust and opposed to the Talmud was the rejection of the Karaites. He impressed on the zealots the fact that by their intolerant severity they would bring about the decay of the instruction of the young, since hitherto emulation to surpass their Karaite companions had been a great incentive to Rabbanite scholars.

The Turkish Jews in those days had a kind of political representative, an advocate (Kahiya), or chamberlain, who had access to the sultan and his great dignitaries, and was appointed by the court. Shaltiel, otherwise an unknown personage, but said to have been of noble character, held the office under Solyman. With a population looking contemptuously on unbelievers, with provincial pashas ruling arbitrarily, and with fanatical Greek and Bulgarian Christians, instances of injustice and violent proceedings against the Jews in the Turkish empire were not of rare occurrence; on all such occasions the Kahiya Shaltiel interposed on behalf of his co-religionists, and, by means of money liberally spent at court, obtained redress.

The community next in importance in Turkey was that of Salonica (the ancient Thessalonica), which, though an unhealthy town, possessed attractions for the immigrants of Spain and Provence; for this once Greek settlement offered more leisure for peaceful occupation than the noisy capital of Turkey. Ten congregations at least were soon formed here, the most of Sephardic origin. Eventually they increased to thirty-six. Salonica, in fact, became a Jewish town, with more Jews than Gentiles. A Jewish poet, Samuel Usque, calls the town "a mother of Judaism, built on the deep foundation of the Lord, full of excellent plants and fruitful trees, such as are found nowhere else on earth. Their fruit is glorious, because it is watered by an abundance of benevolence. The greatest portion of the persecuted and banished sons from Europe and other parts of the earth have met therein, and been received with loving welcomes, as if it were our venerable mother, Jerusalem." Within a short period the Sephardic immigrants acquired complete supremacy over their co-religionists, even over the original community, so that the leading language of Salonica became Spanish, which German and Italian Jews had to learn, if they wished to maintain intercourse with the Spanish immigrants. The son of one of the last Jewish-Spanish ministers of finance, Judah Benveniste, had settled here. From his paternal inheritance he had saved enough to possess a noble library; he was the standard around which his heavily-tried brethren could rally. Representatives of Talmudic learning were naturally found among the sons of the Pyrenean Peninsula only, such as the Taytasaks, a family of scholars, and Jacob Ibn-Chabib, though even they were not men of the first eminence. Spanish immigrants, such as the physicians Perachyah Cohen, his son Daniel, Aaron Afia (Affius), and Moses Almosnino, also cultivated philosophy and astronomy to some extent. But the chief study was that of the Kabbala, in which the Spaniards, Joseph Taytasak, Samuel Franco, and others, distinguished themselves. Salonica in Turkey and Safet in Palestine in time became the chief seats of Kabbalistic extravagance. Of less importance was Adrianople, the former residence of the Turkish sultans, though there also, as at Nicopolis, communities in which the Sephardic element predominated were formed.

To the towns of Amasia, Broussa, Tria and Tokat in Asia Minor, the Spanish fugitives furnished inhabitants. Smyrna, which later on had a large Jewish population, was then of little importance. Greece, however, could show some large communities. Calabrese, Apulian, Spanish and Portuguese fugitives settled at Arta or Larta, by the side of the original inhabitants, Rumelians and Corfuites. They seem to have done well here, for we read that the Jewish youth were much given to gayety and dancing, thereby greatly offending the ultra-pious. Not unimportant communities existed at Patras, Negropont and Thebes. The Thebans were considered very learned in Talmudic lore. The rites of the community of Corfu were followed by the other Jews of Greece. There was an important community at Canea, on the island of Candia, belonging to Venice. At their head were two famous families, the Delmedigos, sons and relatives of the philosopher Elias del Medigo, and the Kapsalis, connections of the former chief rabbi of Turkey. Judah Delmedigo (the son of the teacher of Pico di Mirandola), and Elias ben Elkanah Kapsali, finished their studies under the same rabbi, Judah Menz, of Padua; nevertheless, they were not at one in their views. As both held the office of rabbi at Canea, there was constant friction between them. If the one declared anything to be permissible, the other exerted all his learning and ingenuity to prove the contrary; yet both were worthy men of high principle, and both were well versed in general literature.

Elias Kapsali (born about 1490, died about 1555) was a good historian. When the plague devastated Candia, and plunged the inhabitants into mourning, he composed (in 1523) a history of the Turkish dynasty in a very agreeable Hebrew style, in lucid and elevated language, free from pompous and barbarous diction. Kapsali merely aimed at relating the truth. Interwoven with the Turkish narrative was the history of the Jews, showing in gloomy colors the tragic fate of the Spanish exiles, as he had heard it from their own lips. Though in this composition he had the subsidiary intention of cheering the people during the continuance of the plague, his work may serve as a sample of a fine Hebrew historical style. It has, indeed, found imitators. Kapsali forsook the dry diction of the chroniclers, and as an historian was far superior to his predecessor, Abraham Zacuto. Considering that Kapsali was a rabbi by profession, and that in consultations and the giving of opinions he was bound to make use of a corrupt jargon, his work displays much versatility and talent.

Italy at this period swarmed with fugitive Jews. Most of those driven from Spain, Portugal and Germany first touched Italian soil, either to settle there under the protection of some tolerant ruler, or to travel on to Greece, Turkey, or Palestine. Strangely enough, among the masters of Italy the popes were most friendly to the Jews: Alexander VI, Julius II, Leo X, and Clement VII, were pursuing interests, or devoting themselves to hobbies, which left them no time to think of torturing Jews. The popes and their cardinals considered the canonical laws only in so far as they needed them for the extension of their power or to fill their money-bags. Totally oblivious of the decree of the council of Basle, which enacted that Christians were not to consult Jewish physicians, the popes and cardinals themselves chose Jews as their physicians in ordinary. It appears that, owing to the secret warfare, the intrigues and the frequent use of poison, which, since Alexander VI, had been rife in the curia, where every one looked on his companion as an enemy, Jewish physicians were in favor, because there was no danger of their offering a pope or cardinal a poisoned cup instead of a salutary remedy. Alexander VI had a Jewish physician, Bonet de Lates, a native of Provence, who practiced astrology, prepared an astronomical circle, and sent the pope the Latin description thereof with a fulsome dedication. Bonet de Lates afterwards became the favorite physician in ordinary to Leo X, and influenced his conduct. Julius II had for his physician Simon Zarfati, who in other respects also enjoyed his master's confidence. Cardinals and other high princes of the church followed their examples, and generally intrusted their sacred bodies to Jewish doctors, who consequently were much sought after in Italy. Following the example of the popes, the northern Italian cities received fugitive Jews, even pseudo-Christians re-converted to Judaism, from Spain and Germany, and admitted them to all the privileges of free intercourse. Even the popes permitted Marranos to settle at Ancona, notwithstanding their having been baptized. The most important communities in Italy were formed, after the annihilation of the Jews of Naples, by an influx from other countries into Roman and Venetian territory; in the latter, Venice and the flourishing city of Padua, in the former, Rome and the port of Ancona, receiving most of them. Two opposite views with regard to Jews swayed the council of the egotistical Venetian republic. On the one hand, this commercial state did not wish to lose the advantages that Jewish connections might bring, though at the same time it was loath to foster them, for fear of offending the Levantine Jews, their co-religionists in Turkey; on the other hand, the Venetian merchants were full of trade envy against Jews. Hence the latter were caressed or oppressed as the one or the other party predominated in the Signoria. Venice was the first Italian city wherein Jews resided which set apart a special quarter as a Ghetto (March, 1516).

As a rule the immigrant Jews, Spaniards or Germans, obtained supremacy in Italy over native Jews, both in rabbinical learning and communal relations. The Abrabanels played an important part in Italy. The head of the family, Isaac Abrabanel, indeed, was too much bowed down by age and suffering to exercise much influence in any direction. He died before Jewish affairs had assumed a settled condition. His eldest son, Leon Medigo, likewise made no impression on his surroundings; he was too much of a philosophical dreamer and idealist, a poetic soul averse to dealing with the things of this world. Only the youngest of the three brothers, Samuel Abrabanel (born 1473, died about 1550) left his mark on his contemporaries. He was considered the most eminent Jew in Italy, and his community venerated him like a prince. He alone inherited his father's financial genius, and, after his return from the Talmudic college at Salonica, appears to have availed himself of it, and to have been employed in the department of finance by the viceroy of Naples, Don Pedro de Toledo. At Naples he acquired a considerable fortune, valued at more than 200,000 zechins. He employed his wealth to gratify the disposition hereditary in his family to practice noble beneficence. The Jewish poet, Samuel Usque, gives an enthusiastic description of his heart and mind: "Samuel Abrabanel deserves to be called Trismegistus (thrice great); he is great and wise in the Law, great in nobility, and great in riches. With his wealth he is always magnanimous, a help in the sorrows of his brethren. He joins innumerable orphans in wedlock, supports the needy, and redeems captives, so that he possesses all the great qualities which make the prophet."

To increase his happiness heaven had given him a companion in life, the complement of his high virtues, whose name, Benvenida Abrabanela, was uttered by her contemporaries with devout veneration. Tender-hearted, deeply religious, wise and courageous, she was a pattern of refinement and high breeding, qualities more highly esteemed in Italy than in any other European country. Don Pedro, the powerful Spanish viceroy of Naples, allowed his second daughter, Leonora, to be on intimate terms with Benvenida, that she might learn by her example. When this daughter afterwards became Duchess of Tuscany, she kept up her acquaintance with the Jewish lady, and called her by the honored name of mother. This noble pair, Samuel Abrabanel and Benvenida, in whom tenderness and worldly wisdom, warm attachment to Judaism and social intercourse with non-Jewish circles were combined, were at once the pride and the sheet-anchor of the Italian Jews, and of all who came under their beneficent influence. Samuel Abrabanel, though not so well versed in the Talmud as his poetic worshiper represents him to have been, was a friend and promoter of Jewish knowledge. To fill the office of rabbi at Naples, he sent for David Ibn-Yachya and his young, courageous wife, who had fled from Portugal (1518); and, as the congregation was too small to pay his salary, Abrabanel paid it himself. In his house the learned Yachya lectured on the Talmud, and probably also on Hebrew grammar. He thus formed a center for Jewish science in southern Italy. Christian men of science also resorted to Abrabanel's house.

The chief seat of Talmudic or rabbinical studies was at that time at Padua, where presided not Italians but immigrant Germans. Judah Menz, of Mayence, even at his great age of more than a hundred years, exercised attractive power over studious disciples from Italy, Germany, and Turkey, as though from his lips they would learn the wisdom of a time about to pass away. To be a pupil of Menz, was considered a great honor and distinction. After he died, his son, Abraham Menz, undertook the direction of the college (1504—1526); but his authority was not undisputed. The native Jews have in no direction left names of note. The chronicles mention some famous Jewish-Italian physicians, who also distinguished themselves in other branches, such as Abraham de Balmes (1521), of Lecce, physician and friend of Cardinal Grimani. De Balmes possessed philosophical knowledge, and wrote a work on the Hebrew language, which was published with a Latin translation by a Christian. Other Jewish physicians of the same age were Judah, or Laudadeus de Blanis, at Perugia, a worshiper of the Kabbala, and Obadyah, or Servadeus de Sforno (Sfurno, born about 1470, died 1550), a physician of Rome and Bologna, who, besides medicine, studied biblical and philosophical subjects, and dedicated some of his Hebrew writings with a Latin translation to King Henry II, of France. But, as far as we are now able to judge of these highly praised compositions, they are mediocre, and the authors, even in their own times, enjoyed but local reputation. It is certain that De Balmes and Sforno are far beneath Jacob Mantin, who, driven from Tortosa to Italy, there distinguished himself as a physician and philosopher, leaving a famous name behind him. Mantin (born about 1490, died about 1549) was a great linguist; beside his native language and Hebrew, he understood Latin, Italian and Arabic. He was a deeply learned physician and philosopher, and translated medical and metaphysical works from Hebrew or Arabic into Latin. He was held in high esteem as physician by a pope and the ambassador of Charles V at Venice. But his learning was marred by his iniquitous character; envy and ambition led him to commit wicked deeds, to accuse and persecute innocent persons, even his own co-religionists.

In those days there lived in Italy a man, who, though not distinguished by any brilliant achievement, was superior to nearly all his co-religionists by a qualification better and rarer than literary ability. He was gifted with common sense and a fine understanding, which led him not to judge of things by appearances, or from a limited point of view. Abraham Farissol (born 1451, died about 1525), a native of Avignon, for reasons unknown, perhaps from want, had emigrated to Ferrara. He supported himself by copying books, and also, it would appear, by officiating as chorister at the synagogue. Though he was in needy circumstances, and confined within narrow surroundings, his perception was acute, his horizon wide, and his judgment matured. Like most of his learned contemporaries in Italy, he commented on the Bible, and his independence of thought in the midst of the dense credulity of his time constitutes his claim upon pre-eminence. He said of himself, "As regards miracles, I belong to those of little faith." Farissol was the first Jewish author who, instead of studying the starry firmament, astronomy and astrology (to which Jewish authors of the Middle Ages were but too much inclined), turned his attention to investigate the configuration and phenomena of our globe. He was influenced to undertake these studies by the marvelous discoveries of the southern coasts of Africa and India by the Portuguese, and of America by the Spaniards. Penetrating mediæval mist and the deceptive illusions of fancy, Farissol saw things as they actually are, and deeming it necessary to point them out, he scoffed at ignorant men who, in their pseudo-learned conceit, considered geography of no account. He had to show conclusively that the Book of books, the holy record of the Torah, attached importance to geographical data, in doing which he indicated a new point of view for the comprehension of the Bible: it was not to be explained by allegories and metaphysical or Kabbalistic reveries, but by actual facts and the plain meaning of the words.

Farissol had access to the court of the duke of Ferrara, Hercules d'Este I, one of the best princes of Italy, who vied with the Medici in the promotion of science. The duke took delight in his conversation, and often invited him to discuss religious questions with learned monks. It seemed as if frequent religious disputations and intellectual encounters were to be renewed on Italian soil. Farissol displayed philosophical calm, besides caution, and forbearance for the sensibilities of his opponents, when touching upon their weak points. At the request of the duke of Ferrara, Farissol wrote down in Hebrew the substance of his discourses with the monks, and reproduced it in Italian, to give his opponents an opportunity for refutation. But his polemical and apologetic work is of much less value than his geographical writings, which he completed in his old age, with one foot in the grave. They display Farissol's clear mind, common sense and extensive learning.

The Italian Jews had at least the right of free discussion with Christians. But as soon as they crossed the Alps into Germany they breathed raw air, politically as well as atmospherically. Few Sephardic fugitives visited this inhospitable land. The German population was as hostile to Jews as the Spanish. True, the Germans had no occasion to envy Jews on account of the position and influence of Jewish magnates at royal courts, but they grudged them even their miserable existence in the Jews' lanes in which they were penned up. They had been banished from some German districts, from Cologne, Mayence and Augsburg, and not a Jew was to be found in all Suabia. From other parts they were expelled at about the same time as from Spain. Emperor Frederick III to his last hour protected those outlawed by all the world. He even had a Jewish physician, a rarity in Germany, the learned Jacob ben Yechiel Loans, whom he greatly favored, and made a knight. Frederick is said on his deathbed to have strongly recommended the Jews to his son, enjoining on him to protect them, and not to listen to calumnious accusations, whose falsity he had fathomed. It appears that Jacob Loans also enjoyed the favor of Emperor Maximilian, whose lot it was to rule over Germany in very troublous times. He transferred this favor to Loans' relatives, for he appointed a certain Joseph ben Gershon Loans, of Rosheim, in Alsace, as official representative of all German Jews at the diet. This Joseph (Josselman, Joselin) was distinguished neither by his rabbinical knowledge, nor his position, nor riches; yet, to a certain extent, he was the official representative of German Judaism. His most striking qualities were untiring activity, when it was necessary to defend his unfortunate co-religionists, his love of truth, and fervent clinging to his faith and people. Born 1480, died 1555, for half a century he vigorously protected his co-religionists in Germany, and became security for them when the ruling powers insisted on special bail. The Jews, therefore, praised and blessed him as their "Great Defender."

But the very fact that the German Jews needed a defender proves that their condition was not easy. For Emperor Maximilian was not a man of decided character, but was swayed by all kinds of influences and insinuations; nor did he always follow his father's advice. His conduct towards the Jews, therefore, was always wavering; now he granted, or at least promised, them his protection; now he offered his help, if not for their sanguinary persecution, at least for their expulsion or humiliation. At times he lent ear to the lying accusations that the Jews reviled the host, and murdered infants, falsehoods diligently promulgated by Dominican friars, and, since the alleged martyrdom of young Simon of Trent, readily believed. Hence, during Maximilian's reign, Jews were not only expelled from Germany and the adjoining states, but were hunted down and tortured; they were in daily expectation of the rack, and of the martyr's death, so that a special confession of sins was drawn up for such cases, and the innocently accused, summoned to apostatize, sealed their confession with death, and joyfully sacrificed themselves for the One God. When, either with the sanction or by the passive permission of the emperor, Jews were banished, he felt no compunction in confiscating their property and turning it into money.

The emperor did not, indeed, expel the Nuremberg community, but for a pecuniary consideration gave the citizens leave to do so. Yet Christians presumed to reproach Jews with making money unjustly, whereas only the rich did so, and then only on a small scale. Immediately after the emperor's accession, the townsmen of Nuremberg appealed to him to permit the expulsion of the Jews on account of "loose conduct." This "loose conduct" was explained in the indictment to be the reception of foreign co-religionists, whereby the normal number of Jews had been excessively increased in the town; the practice of inordinate usury; fraud in recovery of debts, whereby honest tradesmen had been impoverished, and finally the harboring of rogues and vagabonds. To stir up hatred against them, and to confirm the Latin reading (*i. e.*, the educated) classes, in the illusion that Jews were blasphemers, revilers of the host and infanticides, the rich citizen, Antonius Koberger, had the venomous anti-Jewish *Fortalitium fidei* of the Spanish Franciscan, Alfonso de Spina, reprinted at his own expense. After long petitioning, Emperor Maximilian at last granted the prayer of Nuremberg, "on account of the fidelity with which the town had ever served the imperial house," abrogated the privileges enjoyed by the Jews, and allowed the town council to fix a time for their expulsion, stipulating, however, that the houses, lands, synagogues, and even the Jewish cemetery should fall to the imperial treasury. He, moreover, granted to Nuremberg the privilege of being forever exempt from receiving Jews within its walls (July 5th, 1598). The town council at first allowed four months only for the exodus—and the cultured, virtuous and humanity-preaching patrician, Willibald Pirkheimer, afterwards so strong a pillar of the Humanists, was then a member of the council! Upon the supplications of the unfortunate people, the short reprieve was prolonged by three months. But the Jews, summoned to the synagogue by the sheriffs, had to swear to leave the town by that time. At last, on March 10th, 1599, the much reduced community left Nuremberg, to which it had returned after the Black Death.

At about the same time the Jews of other German towns, Ulm, Nordlingen, Colmar, and Magdeburg, were sent into banishment.

The community of Ratisbon, then the oldest in Germany, was to fare still worse; even then it heard the warning voice to prepare for expulsion. Since the inhabitants of that imperial city, through the disputes with the Jews growing out of the false blood-accusation, had suffered humiliation and pecuniary loss at the hands of Emperor Frederick, the former friendly feeling between Jews and Christians had given way to bitterness and hatred. Instead of attributing to the right cause the troubles and misfortunes which had come upon the town by its attempted secession from the empire, the citizens charged the Jews with being the authors of their misfortunes, and vented their anger on them. The priests, exasperated by the failure of their plot against the Jews, daily stirred up the fanaticism of the populace, openly preaching that the Jews must be expelled. The millers refused to sell them flour, the bakers, bread (1499), for the clergy had threatened the tradespeople with excommunication if they supplied them with food. On certain days Jews were not admitted into the market place, on others they were allowed to make their purchases only after stated hours, when the Christians had satisfied their wants. "Under severe penalties," imposed by the senate, Christians were prohibited from making purchases for Jews; the former were to "secure the glory of God and their own salvation" by being cruel to the latter. The town council seriously discussed applying to Emperor Maximilian to give his consent to the expulsion of the Jews, allowing about twenty-four families to remain. For a few years more they were permitted to drag on a miserable existence. Besides Ratisbon, only two large communities remained in Germany, viz., at Frankfort-on-the-Main and Worms, and even these were often threatened with expulsion.

There were many Jews in Prague, but this town was not in Germany proper; Bohemia was counted a private possession of the crown, under the rule of Ladislaus, king of Hungary. The Bohemian Jews were not too well off under him; the Jewish quarter in Prague was often plundered by the populace. The citizens were sincerely anxious to expel the Jews from Bohemia. But the latter had their patrons, especially among the nobility. When, at a diet, the question of the expulsion or retention of the Jews arose, the decree was passed (August 7th, 1501) that the crown of Bohemia was for all time to tolerate them. If any one of them offended against the law, he only was to be punished; his crime was not to be visited on the whole Jewish community. King Ladislaus confirmed this decision of the diet, only to break it very shortly after, for the citizens of Prague were opposed to it, and spared no pains to frustrate its fulfillment. They so strongly prejudiced the king against the Jews as to induce him to decree their expulsion, and to threaten with banishment such Christians as should venture to intercede for them. By what favorable dispensation they remained in the country is not known. Though in daily expectation of expatriation, they grew reconciled to having their habitation on the verge of a volcano. A descendant of the Italian family of printers, Soncinus, named Gershon Cohen, established a Hebrew printing office at Prague (about 1503), the first in Germany, nearly four decades after the foundation of Hebrew printing offices in Italy.

The Prague community does not seem to have excelled in learning; for some time not a single scientific work, not even one on a Talmudic or rabbinical subject, issued from the press of Gershon; it merely supplied the needs of the synagogue, whilst Italian and Turkish offices spread important ancient and contemporary works. We find but one rabbinical authority mentioned in those days: Jacob Polak (born about 1460, died about 1530), the originator of a new method of Talmud study, a foreigner, and, with the exception of his namesake Jacob Berab, in the East, the most profound and sagacious Talmudist of his time. Curiously enough, the astonishing facility of ingenious disquisition on the basis of the Talmud (Pilpul), attributed to Polak, which attained its highest perfection in Poland, proceeded from a native of Poland.

After Italy and Turkey, Poland was in those days a refuge for hunted and exiled wanderers, chiefly for those from Germany. Here, as well as in Lithuania, united with Poland under one sovereign, Jews enjoyed a better position than in the neighboring lands beyond the Vistula and the Carpathians, though the monk Capistrano had for a while interrupted the good understanding between the government and the Jews.

Kings and the nobility were, to a certain extent, dependent on them, and, when other interests did not conflict, generally granted them privileges, because with their capital and commerce they were able to turn the territorial wealth of the country into money, and to supply its inhabitants, poor in coin, with the necessary funds. The farming of the tolls and the distilleries were mostly in the hands of Jews. It goes without saying that they also possessed land, and carried on trades. Against 500 Christian there were 3,200 Jewish wholesale dealers in Poland, and three times as many artificers, including workers in gold and silver, smiths and weavers. The statute of Casimir IV, so favorable to Jews, was still in force. For though, constrained by the fanatical monk Capistrano, he had abrogated it, yet in view of the advantages that the crown of Poland derived from the Jews, he re-enacted the same laws a few years after. The Jews were generally treated as citizens of the state, and were not compelled to wear ignominious badges; they were also allowed to carry arms. After the death of this politic king, two opponents arose against them: on the one hand, the clergy, who saw in the favored position of the Polish Jews an offense to Christianity, and on the other, the German merchants, who, long settled in Polish towns, had brought with them their guilds and old-fashioned prejudices, and hated the Jewish traders and artificers from sheer envy. United they succeeded in prejudicing the successors of Casimir, his sons John Albert and Alexander, against the Jews, so that their privileges were abolished, and the Jews themselves confined to particular quarters, or even banished altogether from certain towns (1496—1505). But the next sovereign, Sigismund I (1506—1548), was favorably disposed towards them, and repeatedly protected them against persecution and expulsion. The strongest supporters, however, of the Polish Jews were the Polish nobility, who hated the Germans from national and political antipathy, and therefore, both from policy and inclination, favored the Jews, and used them as their tools against the arrogant Germans. And since the nobles held the high official posts, the laws against Jews, to the vexation of the clergy and the guilds, remained a dead letter. Poland, therefore, was an asylum much sought after by persecuted Jews. If a Jew who had turned Christian, or a Christian, wished to become a Jew, he could do so as freely in Poland as in Turkey.

The rabbis were important agents for the crown. They had the privilege of collecting the poll-tax from the communities and paying it over to the state. Therefore, the rabbis of large towns, appointed or confirmed by the king, became chiefs in the administration of communal affairs, represented the Jews before the crown, and bore the title of chief rabbi. The rabbis retained the civil jurisdiction, and were authorized to banish unworthy members, and even to inflict the punishment of death. But in Poland, the country which for several centuries was to become the chief home of the Talmud and the nursery of Talmudic students and rabbis, which was long enveloped, as it were, in a Talmudic atmosphere, there were no prominent Talmudists at the beginning of the sixteenth century; it became the home of the Talmud only after the immigration of numerous German scholars. Coming from the districts of the Rhine and Main, from Bavaria, Suabia, Bohemia, and Austria, swarms of Jewish families settled on the banks of the Vistula and the Dnieper, having lost their fortunes, but bringing with them their most precious possessions, which they defended with their lives, and which they could not be robbed of, namely, their religious convictions, the customs of their fathers, and their Talmudic learning. The German rabbinical school, which at home had no breathing-space, established itself in Poland and Lithuania, in Ruthenia and Volhynia, spread in all directions, and, impregnated with Slavonic elements, transformed itself into a peculiar, a Polish school.

But the Jewish-German fugitives transplanted to Poland not only the knowledge of the Talmud, but also that of the German language, as then spoken; this they imparted to the native Jews, and it gradually superseded the Polish or Ruthenian tongue. As the Spanish Jews turned portions of European and Asiatic Turkey into a new Spain, the German Jews transformed Poland, Lithuania, and the territories belonging thereto, into a new Germany. For several centuries, therefore, the Jews were divided into Spanish and German speaking Jews, the Italian speaking members being too small in number to count, especially as in Italy the Jews were compelled to understand either Spanish or German. The Jews settled in Poland gradually cast off their German awkwardness and simplicity, but not the language. They honored it as a palladium, as a holy remembrance; and though in their intercourse with Poles they made use of the language of the country, in the family circle, and in their schools and prayers, they adhered to German. They valued it, next to Hebrew, as a holy language. It was a fortunate thing for the Jews that at the time when new storms gathered over their heads in Germany, they found on her borders a country which offered them a hospitable welcome and protection. For a tempest burst in Germany, which had its first beginnings in the narrow Jewish circle, but eventually drew on the Jews the attention of all Christendom. An eventful, historical birth, which was to change the face of European affairs, lay, so to speak, in a Jewish manger.

CHAPTER XIV.

REUCHLIN AND THE TALMUD.

Antecedents of the Convert John Pfefferkorn—Pfefferkorn and the Dominicans of Cologne—Hoogstraten, Ortuinus Gratius and Arnold of Tongern—Victor von Karben—Attacks on the Talmud and Confiscation of Copies in Frankfort—Reuchlin's Hebrew and Kabbalistic Studies—The Controversy concerning the Talmud—Activity on both Sides—Public Excitement—Complete Victory of Reuchlin's Efforts in Defense of Jewish Literature—Ulrich von Hutten—Luther—Revival of Hebrew Studies.

1500—1520 C.E.

WHO could have anticipated that from the German nation, everywhere considered heavy and stupid, from the land of lawless knights, of daily feuds about trifles, of confused political conditions, where everyone was both despot and slave, mercilessly oppressing his inferiors, and pitifully cringing to his superiors—who could have anticipated that from this people and this country would proceed a movement destined to shake European affairs to their center, create new political conditions, give the Middle Ages their death-blow, and set its seal on the dawn of a new historical era? A reformation of church and politics, such as enlightened minds then dreamt of, was least expected from Germany. Yet there slumbered latent powers in that country, which only needed awaking to develop into regenerating forces. The Germans still adhered to ancient simplicity of life and severity of morals, pedantic, it is true, and ludicrous in manifestation; whilst the leading Romance countries, Italy, France and Spain, were suffering from over-refinement, surfeit and moral corruption. Because the Germans had retained their original Teutonic dullness, the clergy could not altogether succeed in infecting them with the poison of their vicious teaching. Their lower clergy, compared with that of other European countries, was more chaste and modest. The innate love of family life and genial association, which the Germans have in common with Jews, preserved them from that moral depravity to which the Romance nations had already succumbed. In the educated circles of Italy, especially at the papal court, Christianity and its doctrines were sneered at; the political power they conferred alone being valued. But in Germany, where there was little laughter, except in taverns, Christianity was treated as a more serious matter; it was looked upon as an ideal, which had once been alive, and would live again.

But these moral germs in the German race were so deeply buried that it needed favorable circumstances to bring them to light, and cause them to stand forth as historical potencies. However much the Germans themselves may ignore it, the Talmud had a great share in the awakening of these slumbering forces. We can boldly assert that the war for and against the Talmud aroused German consciousness, and created a public opinion, without which the Reformation, like many other efforts, would have died in the hour of birth, or, perhaps, would never have been born at all. A paltry grain of sand caused the fall of an avalanche, which shook the earth around. The instrument of this mighty change was an ignorant, thoroughly vile creature, the scum of the Jewish people, who does not deserve to be mentioned in history or literature, but whom Providence seems to have appointed like some noisome insect involuntarily to accomplish a useful work.

Joseph Pfefferkorn, a native of Moravia, was by trade a butcher, and, as may easily be surmised, illiterate. His moral turpitude was even greater than his ignorance. He committed a burglary, was caught, condemned to imprisonment by Count de Guttenstein, and released only at the urgent prayers of his relatives, and on payment of a fine. It appears that he hoped to wash away this disgrace with baptismal water; the church was not scrupulous, and received even this despicable wretch, when at the age of thirty-six he presented himself, with wife and children, to be received into Christianity (about 1505?). He seems to have been baptized at Cologne; at any rate, he was kept and made much of by the ignorant, proud and fanatical Dominicans of that city. Cologne was an owls' nest of light-shunning swaggerers, who endeavored to obscure the dawn of a bright day with the dark clouds of superstition, hostile to knowledge. At their head was Hochstraten (Hoogstraten), an inquisitor or heretic-hunter, a violent, reckless man, who literally longed for the smell of burning heretics, and in Spain would have been a useful Torquemada. His counterpart was Arnold of Tongern (Tungern), a Dominican professor of theology. The third in the coalition was Ortuin de Graes, of Deventer (who Latinized his name to Ortuinus Gratius), the son of a clergyman. Ortuin de Graes entertained so violent a hatred against Jews that it could not have been due solely to religious zeal. He made it his special business to stir up the wrath of the Christians by anti-Jewish writings. But as he was too ignorant to concoct a book or even a pamphlet, he surrounded himself with baptized Jews, who had to supply him with materials. A Jew, who, during a persecution or for some reason, had become a convert to Christianity in his fiftieth year, and assumed the name of Victor von Karben, though he had but little Hebrew and rabbinical learning, was dubbed rabbi, in order to give more weight to his attacks on Judaism and to his confession of Christianity. It is not precisely known whether Victor von Karben, who sorrowfully stated that on his conversion he left his wife, three children, brothers and dear friends, voluntarily or by compulsion reproached the Jews with hating Christians and reviling Christianity. He supplied Ortuinus Gratius with materials for accusations against them, their Talmud, their errors and abominations, which Ortuinus worked up into a book. But Victor von Karben appears, after all, not to have been of much service, or he was too old (born 1442, died 1515) to assist in the execution of a deep scheme, destined to bring profitable business to the Dominicans, the heresy-judges of men and writings. But they needed a Jew for this purpose; their own order had not long before got into rather bad odor. Pfefferkorn was the very man for them. He lent his name to a new anti-Jewish publication, written in Latin by Ortuinus Gratius. It was entitled "A Mirror for Admonition," inviting the Jews to be converted to Christianity. This first anti-Jewish book with Pfefferkorn's name dealt gently with the Jews, even sought to show the groundlessness of the frequent accusations with regard to stealing and murdering Christian children. It entreats Christians not to banish the Jews, nor to oppress them too heavily, since to a certain extent they are human beings. But this friendliness was only a mask, a feeler put forth to gain firm ground. For the Cologne Dominicans aimed at the confiscation of the Talmudic writings, as in the days of Saint Louis of France. This was distantly pointed to in Pfefferkorn's first pamphlet, which endeavored to throw suspicion on the Talmud, and adduced three reasons to explain the stiff-necked unbelief of Jews: their practice of usury, the fact that they were not compelled to go to church, and their attachment to the Talmud. These obstacles once removed, Jews would throng to church in crowds. The pamphlet, therefore, admonished princes and people to check the usury of the Jews, to compel them to attend church and listen to sermons, and to burn the Talmud. It admitted that it is not just to infringe upon the Jews' claim to their writings, but Christians did not hesitate, in certain cases, to do violence to Jews, and compared with that the confiscation of the Talmudic books was a venial offense. This was the sole object of the pamphlet under Pfefferkorn's name. It was generally believed in Germany that the Cologne owls expected to do a good stroke of business; if they could induce the ruling powers to sequestrate all copies of the Talmud, Dominicans, as inquisitors, would have the disposal of them, and the Jews, who could not do without the Talmud, would pour their wealth into Dominican coffers to have the confiscation annulled. Hence, in the succeeding two years, still putting Pfefferkorn forward as the author, they published several pamphlets, wherein it was asserted to be a Christian duty to expel all Jews, like so many mangy dogs. If the princes would not do so, the people were to take the matter into their own hands, solicit their rulers to deprive the Jews of all their books except the Bible, forcibly take from them all pledges, above all, see that their children be brought up as Christians, and expel the adults as incorrigible rogues. It was no sin to do the worst to Jews, as they were not freemen, but body and soul the property of the princes. If they refused to listen to the prayer of their subjects, the people were to assemble in masses, even create a riot, and impetuously demand the fulfillment of the Christian duty of degrading the Jews. The masses were to declare themselves champions of Christ, and carry out his will. Whoso did an injury to Jews was a follower of Christ; whoso favored them was worse than they, and would hereafter be punished with eternal suffering and hell fire.

But Pfefferkorn, Ortuinus Gratius and the Cologne Dominicans had come too late in the day. Riots for the killing of Jews, though they were no less hated and despised than in the times of the crusades and of the Black Death, were no longer the fashion. Princes were little disposed to expel the Jews, since with them a regular revenue would disappear. Zeal for the conversion of Jews had considerably cooled down; in fact, many Christians pointed scornfully at baptized Jews, saying that they resembled clean linen: as long as it is fresh the eye delights in it, after a few days' wear it is cast aside as soiled. Thus a converted Jew, immediately after his baptism, is cherished by the Christians; when some days have passed he is neglected, avoided, and finally made sport of.

The German Jews, dreading new dangers from Pfefferkorn's zeal, endeavored to thwart him. Jewish physicians, usually held in high favor at the courts of princes, appear to have exerted their influence with their patrons to show the falsity of Pfefferkorn's accusations, and to render them ineffectual. Even Christians manifested their dissatisfaction with the machinations of the baptized Jew, and loudly proclaimed Pfefferkorn to be a worthless fellow and a hypocrite, who was not to be believed, his object being simply to delude the foolish, and fill his own purse. He, therefore, published a new pamphlet (March, 1509), which he impudently entitled "The Enemy of the Jews." This venomous libel reiterated all his former accusations, and showed how the Jews, by charging interest on interest, impoverished the Christians. He blackened the character of Jewish physicians, saying that they were quacks, who endangered the lives of their Christian patients. It was, therefore, necessary to expel the Jews from Germany, as Emperor Maximilian had driven them from Austria, Styria and Carinthia; or if allowed to remain, they were to be employed in cleansing the streets, sweeping chimneys, removing filth and carrion, and in similar occupations. But, above all, every copy of the Talmud, and all books relating to their religion, the Bible excepted, were to be taken from them. In order effectually to carry out this step, house to house visitation was to be made, and the Jews were to be compelled, if necessary by torture, to surrender their books. Ortuinus Gratius had a hand in the drawing up of this pamphlet, too.

These venomous writings in German and Latin were but means and preliminaries to a plan which was to realize the hopes of the Dominicans of Cologne, the public burning of the theological books of the Jews, or their conversion into a source of profit. They urged Emperor Maximilian, who did not easily lend himself to the commission of a deed of violence, to deliver the Jews, together with their books and purses, to their tender mercies. For this purpose they called in the aid of the bigotry of an unfortunate princess.

Kunigunde, the beautiful sister of Maximilian and favorite daughter of Emperor Frederick, in her youth had been the cause of much affliction to her aged sire. Without her father's knowledge she had married his declared enemy, the Bavarian duke, Albert of Munich. For a long time her deeply offended father would not allow her name to be mentioned. When her husband died in the prime of manhood (1508), his widow, perhaps repenting her youthful error, entered a Franciscan convent at Munich. She became abbess of the nuns of Sancta Clara, and castigated her body. The Dominicans hoped to turn to good purpose the gloomy character of this princess. They furnished Pfefferkorn with letters of introduction to her. With poisoned words he was to detail to her the shameful doings of the Jews, their blasphemies against Jesus, Mary, the apostles and the church in general, and to demonstrate to her that the Jewish books which contained all these abominations deserved to be destroyed. A woman, moreover a superstitious one, whose mind has been dulled in convent walls, is easily persuaded. Kunigunde readily believed the calumnies against

the Jews and their religious literature, especially as they were uttered by a former Jew, who could not but be acquainted with their habits and wickedness, and who assured her that after the destruction of the Jewish books all Hebrews would gradually be converted to Christianity. Pfefferkorn easily obtained from the bigoted nun what he wanted. She gave him a pressing letter to her imperial brother, conjuring him to put a stop to Jewish blasphemies against Christianity, and to issue a decree that all their writings, except the Bible, be taken from the Jews and burnt, lest the sins of blasphemy daily committed by them fall on his crowned head. Furnished with this missive, Pfefferkorn straightway went to Italy, to the camp of the emperor.

The fanatical letter of Kunigunde and the calumnies of Pfefferkorn succeeded in extorting from Maximilian a mandate, dated August 19th, 1509, giving the baptized miscreant full power over Jews. He was authorized to examine Hebrew writings anywhere in the German empire, and to destroy all whose contents were hostile to the Bible and the Christian faith. The Jews were enjoined, under heavy penalties to person and property, to offer no resistance, but to submit their books to Pfefferkorn's examination. Pfefferkorn, with the emperor's authority, returned triumphantly to Germany, to open his campaign against Jewish books or Jewish purses. He began his business, which promised profit, with the community at Frankfort, then the most important of Germany, where many Talmud scholars, consequently many copies of that work, besides many rich Jews, were to be found. On Pfefferkorn's demand, the senate assembled all the Jews in the synagogue, and communicated to them the emperor's order to surrender their books.

In the presence of clergymen and members of the senate, all prayer-books found in the synagogue were confiscated. It happened to be the eve of the Feast of Tabernacles (Friday, September 28th). By his own authority, or pretending to hold it from the emperor, Pfefferkorn forbade the Jews to attend the synagogue on the day of the feast; he intended to hold a house to house visitation on that day, for he was very anxious to get hold of copies of the Talmud. The clergymen present, however, were not so inconsiderate as to turn the feast of the Jews into mourning, but deferred the search for books till the following Monday. How did the Jews act? That they dared protest against this arbitrary proceeding proves that a new order of things had arisen. No longer as formerly in Germany did they submit, with the dumb submission of lambs, to spoliation and death. They appealed to the charters of various popes and emperors, granting them religious liberty, which included possession of their prayer-books and text-books. They demanded a delay of the confiscation in order to appeal to the emperor and the supreme court of judicature. The directors of the community of Frankfort immediately sent a deputy to the elector and archbishop of Mayence, Uriel von Gemmingen, in whose diocese Frankfort was situate, to induce him to forbid the clergy to co-operate in this injustice. When Pfefferkorn began his house to house visitation, the Jews protested so energetically that it had to be deferred until the senate decided whether or not their objection was to be allowed. The decision of the sapient senate was unfavorable; but when the confiscation was about to be commenced, a letter from the archbishop arrived, prohibiting the clergy from lending Pfefferkorn any assistance. This frustrated the scheme; for the senators also withdrew from the transaction as soon as they knew that the highest ecclesiastical dignitary in Germany sided with the Jews. The latter were not idle. For, though they did not know that the powerful Dominicans stood behind Pfefferkorn, they suspected that persons, hostile to the Jews, used this spiteful wretch to stir up persecution against them. They at once dispatched a defender of their cause to the emperor, and another to the German communities, far and near, to appoint a general synod, to be summoned for the succeeding month, to consider what steps should be taken, and to raise funds.

Temporarily this unpleasant business seemed to take a turn favorable to the Jews. The senate of Frankfort remained passive, except in laying an embargo on the packets of books belonging to Jewish booksellers, and forbidding their sale. The conduct of the archbishop was what benefited them most. Either from a sense of justice—he was generally fair in his dealings—from a kindly feeling for the Jews, from a dislike of Dominican heretic-hunting, or, finally, from jealousy of the emperor's interference with his functions, in giving so miserable a wretch as Pfefferkorn spiritual jurisdiction in his diocese, Uriel von Gemmingen took the part of the Jews. He addressed a letter to the emperor (October 5th), wherein he gently insinuated that he was to blame for having given full powers to so ignorant a man as Pfefferkorn, and asserted that to his knowledge no blasphemous or anti-Christian writings were in the possession of the Jews of his diocese, and hinted that if the emperor absolutely insisted on the examination and confiscation of Hebrew literature, he must employ an expert. He was so zealous on behalf of the Jews as to write to Von Hutten, his agent at the imperial court, to assist the Jews in laying their case before the emperor. In the meantime, not to betray his partisanship, he invited Pfefferkorn to Aschaffenburg, and informed him that his mandate from the emperor was faulty in form, whereby it became ineffectual, for the Jews would dispute its validity.

At this interview the name of Reuchlin was mentioned for the first time, whether by the archbishop or by Pfefferkorn is uncertain. It was suggested to request the emperor to appoint Reuchlin and Victor von Karben Pfefferkorn's coadjutors in the examination of Jewish books. Pfefferkorn, or the Dominican friars themselves, thought it necessary to secure the co-operation of a man whose learning, character and high position would render their proceedings more effective. Reuchlin, the pride of Germany, was to be made their associate, so as to disarm possible opponents. It was part of their scheme, too, to throw discredit, in one way or another, on the man whom obscurantists looked upon with disfavor, and who, to their vexation, first stimulated German and then European Christians in general to study the Hebrew language. But by these very artifices Pfefferkorn and his patrons not only spoilt their game, but raised a storm, which in less than a decade shook the whole edifice of the Catholic Church. It was justly said afterwards that the semi-Jewish Christian had done more injury to Christianity than all the blasphemous writings of the Jews could have done. John Reuchlin assisted in making the transition from the Middle Ages to modern times, and, therefore, his name is famous in the annals of the sixteenth century; but in Jewish history also he deserves honorable mention.

John Reuchlin, of Pforzheim (born 1455, died 1522), or Capnion, as his admirers, the students of the *humaniora*, called him, with his younger contemporary, Erasmus of Rotterdam, delivered Germany from the reproach of barbarism. By their example and incitement they proved that, with regard to knowledge of ancient Greek and Latin, a pure style and humanistic culture in general, Germans could not only rival, but surpass Italians. Besides his astonishing learning in classical literature and his elegant diction, Reuchlin had a pure, upright character, nobility of mind, integrity which was proof against temptation, admirable love of truth, and a soft heart. More versatile than Erasmus, his younger colleague, in preparing for and spreading humanistic and esthetic culture in Germany, Reuchlin also devoted himself to the study of Hebrew to acquire mastery of the language blessed by God, and thus emulate his pattern, the Church Father Jerome. His love for Hebrew grew into enthusiasm, when on his second journey to Rome he became acquainted at Florence with the learned youth, Pico di Mirandola, Italy's prodigy, and learned from him what deep, marvelous secrets lay hidden in the Hebrew sources of the Kabbala. After that Reuchlin thirsted for Hebrew literature, but could not quench his thirst. He could not even obtain a printed copy of the Hebrew Bible. Only in his mature age he found opportunities of acquiring a more profound knowledge of Hebrew. During his stay at Linz, at the court of the aged emperor, Frederick III, he made the acquaintance of the imperial physician and Jewish knight, Jacob Loans; and this Jewish scholar became his teacher of Hebrew language and literature.

Reuchlin devoted every hour that he could snatch from his avocations at court to this study, and mastered it so thoroughly that he was soon able to do without a teacher. His genius for languages stood him in good stead, and enabled him to overcome difficulties. He endeavored to turn to speedy account the Hebrew learning acquired with such zeal. He wrote a small work, "The Wonderful Word," a spirited panegyric of the Hebrew language, its simplicity, depth and divine character. "The language of the Hebrews is simple, uncorrupted, holy, terse and vigorous; God confers in it direct with men, and men with angels, without interpreters, face to face, ... as one friend converses with another." A Jew devoted to the antiquities of his race could not have spoken more enthusiastically. The work consists of a series of discussions between an Epicurean philosopher, a Jewish sage (Baruchias), and a Christian (Capnion), and its object is to prove that the wisdom of all nations, the symbols of pagan religions and the forms of their worship are but misconceptions and travesties of Hebrew truth, mysteriously concealed in the words, in the very shapes of the letters of the Hebrew tongue.

Reuchlin may have felt that his knowledge of Hebrew still left much to be desired; he, therefore, as ambassador of the elector palatine, whom he represented at the court of Pope Alexander VI (1498—1500), continued his study of Hebrew literature. Obadiah Sforno, of Cesena, then residing at Rome, became Reuchlin's second teacher of Hebrew. Thus the German humanist, already a famous man, whose Latin discourses were the admiration of Italians, sat at the feet of a Jew to perfect himself in Hebrew, nor did he disdain to accept instruction from a Jew whenever the opportunity offered, so highly did he esteem the Hebrew language.

Being the only Christian in Germany, or we may say in all Europe, sufficiently familiar with the sacred language, Reuchlin's numerous friends urged him to compile a Hebrew grammar, to enable the studiously inclined to instruct themselves. The first Hebrew grammar by a Christian, which Reuchlin designated as "a memorial more lasting than brass" (finished in March, 1506), was a somewhat poor affair. It gave only the essentials of pronunciation and etymology, together with a vocabulary, the imperfections of which need not surprise us, as it is the work of a beginner. But the grammar produced important results: it aroused a taste for Hebrew studies in a large circle of scholars, who thenceforth zealously devoted themselves to it; and these studies supplied a new factor towards the Lutheran Reformation. A number of disciples of Reuchlin, such as Sebastian Münster and Widmannstadt, followed in his footsteps, and raised the Hebrew language to the level of Greek.

But though Reuchlin went down into the Jews' lane to carry off a hidden treasure, he was at first no less intensely prejudiced against the Jewish race than his contemporaries. Forgetful of its former glory, and blind to the solid kernel, because enveloped in a repulsive shell, Reuchlin looked on the Jewish people as utterly barbarous, devoid of all artistic taste, superstitious, mean and depraved. He solemnly declared that he was far from favoring the Jews. Like his pattern, Jerome, he testified to his thorough-going hatred of them. At the same time as his Hebrew grammar he wrote an epistle, in which he traced all the misery of the Jews to their blind unbelief, instead of looking for its source in Christians' want of charity towards them. Reuchlin, no less than Pfefferkorn, charged the Jews with blasphemy against Jesus, Mary, the apostles and Christians in general; but a time came when he regretted this indiscreet lucubration of his youth. For his heart did not share the prejudices of his head. Whenever he met individual Jews, he gave them his affection, or at least his esteem; he probably found that they were better than Christians represented them to be. His sense of justice did not allow him to let wrong be done to them, much less to help in doing it.

When Pfefferkorn and the Cologne Dominicans approached Reuchlin, he was at the zenith of his life and fame. High and low honored him for his rectitude; Emperor Frederick had ennobled him; Emperor Maximilian appointed him counselor and judge of the Suabian League; the circle of humanists, the order of free spirits within and without Germany, loved, worshiped, almost deified him. Though hitherto no shadow of heresy had fallen on Reuchlin, who was on the best of terms with the Dominicans, yet the friends of darkness instinctively saw in him their secret enemy. His cultivation of science and classical literature, his anxiety for an elegant Latin style, his enthusiasm for Greek, by which all Germany had been infected, and worse than all, his introduction of Hebrew, his preference for "Hebrew truth," for the Hebrew text over the corrupt Latin Vulgate, which the church held as canonical and unassailable, were considered by the obscurantists as crimes, for which the Inquisition could not, indeed, directly prosecute him, but which secured him a place in their black book.

The order given to Pfefferkorn, the secret agent of the Dominicans of Cologne, to implicate Reuchlin in the examination of blasphemous Jewish writings, as said above, was a cunningly devised trap. On his second journey to the imperial camp, Pfefferkorn waited on Reuchlin at his own house, endeavored to make him a confederate in his venomous schemes against the Jews, and showed him the imperial mandate. Reuchlin declined the proposal somewhat hesitatingly, though he approved of destroying Jewish libels on Christianity; but he pointed out that the emperor's mandate was faulty in form, and that, therefore, the authorities would not willingly enforce it. Reuchlin is said to have hinted that, if invited to do so, he would interest himself in the matter. Pfefferkorn, in consequence, applied to the emperor for a second mandate, correct in form and unassailable. But the Jews had not been idle in endeavors to induce the emperor to revoke the mandate and restore their books.

The community of Frankfort had appointed Jonathan Levi Zion, a zealous member, to advocate their case with the emperor. The community of Ratisbon also had sent an agent to the imperial court. Isaac Triest, a man greatly beloved by the persons surrounding the emperor, took great pains to frustrate Pfefferkorn's plans. The Jewish advocates were supported by influential Christians, including the representative of the archbishop and the Margrave of Baden. They first adduced the charters guaranteeing religious liberty, granted to the Jews by emperors and popes, in accordance with which even the emperor had no right to interfere with the management of their private affairs, or to attack their property in the shape of religious books. They did not fail to inform the emperor that their accuser was a worthless person, a thief and burglar. The Jewish advocates thought that they had attained their end. The emperor had listened to their petition in an audience, and promised them a speedy reply. Their friendly reception led them to look for an immediate settlement of this painful affair; moreover, it was a good omen that Uriel von Gemmingen, their protector, was appointed commissary.

But they did not understand Maximilian's vacillating character. As soon as Pfefferkorn appeared before him, armed with another autograph letter from his sister, wherein the ultra-pious nun conjured him not to injure Christianity by the revocation of his mandate, the scales were turned against the Jews. The emperor was in reality secretly piqued that the despised Jews of Frankfort, in contempt of his mandate, had refused to give up the books found in their houses.

He thereupon issued a second mandate (November 10th, 1509), wherein he reproached the Jews with having offered resistance, and ordered the confiscation to be continued. But he appointed Archbishop Uriel as commissioner, and advised him to obtain counsel from the universities of Cologne, Mayence, Erfurt and Heidelberg, and to associate with himself learned men, such as Reuchlin, Victor von Karben, and the inquisitor, Hoogstraten, who was wholly ignorant of Hebrew. With this mandate in his pocket, Pfefferkorn hastened back to the scene of his activity, the Rhenish provinces. Archbishop Uriel appoined Hermann Hess, chancellor of the University of Mayence, his delegate, to direct the confiscation of Jewish books. Accompanied by him,

Pfefferkorn again repaired to Frankfort, and the book-hunt began afresh. Fifteen hundred manuscripts, including those already seized, were taken from the Frankfort Jews, and deposited in the town hall.

Worse than the emperor's vacillating conduct was the apathy shown by the large communities of Germany in the appointment of delegates to a conference to discuss and frustrate the malicious plans of Pfefferkorn, or rather, of the Dominicans. Smaller communities had contributed their share towards the expenses occasioned by this serious matter, but the larger and richer communities of Rothenburg on the Tauber, Weissenburg and Fürth, on which the Jews of Frankfort had counted most, displayed deplorable indifference. But when, in consequence of the second mandate, Jewish books were confiscated not only at Frankfort but also in other communities, more active interest was manifested. First the Frankfort senate was influenced in their favor. The Jewish booksellers were accustomed to bring their bales of books for sale to the spring Fair at Frankfort. Pfefferkorn threatened to confiscate these also, but the senate of Frankfort refused to assist in the measure, being unwilling to break the laws regulating the Fair. The Jewish booksellers, moreover, had safe-conducts each from the prince of his own country, protecting not only their persons, but also their property. The archbishop maintained sullen silence, but was inclined to favor the Jews. He did not call together the learned men whom the emperor had mentioned to examine the Jewish books, and did no more than he could help. Many princes, also, whose eyes had been opened to the ultimate results of this strange confiscation, seem to have made representations to the emperor. Public opinion was particularly severe on Pfefferkorn. But he and the Dominicans were not idle; they endeavored to win over the emperor and public opinion, and it is remarkable that the enemies of publicity should have opened the mouth of that hitherto silent arbitress, and rendered her powerful.

For this purpose there appeared another anti-Jewish pamphlet, with Pfefferkorn's name on the title-page, entitled, "In Praise and Honor of Emperor Maximilian." It blew clouds of incense into the emperor's face, and regretted that the charges against the Jews, from indifference and ignorance, were so little noticed in Christian circles. It reasserted that the Talmud, the usury of the Jews, and their facilities for making money, were the causes of their obstinately refusing to become Christians. Thus the Cologne Dominicans—always standing behind Pfefferkorn—by means of public opinion again attempted to put moral pressure on Maximilian.

But this public opinion must have spoken so strongly in favor of the Jews, that Maximilian was induced to take a step unusual for an emperor, namely, in a measure revoke his former commands, by directing the senate of Frankfort to restore to the Jews their books (May 23d, 1510), "till the completion of our purpose and the inspection of the books." Great was the joy of the Jews. They had escaped a great danger: not their religious books only, so dear to their hearts, but their position in the Holy Roman Empire had been at stake, since the Dominicans, in case of success, would not have stopped at the confiscation of books, but would have inflicted new humiliations and persecutions.

But the Jews triumphed too soon; the Dominicans and their confederate and tool, Pfefferkorn, would not so readily surrender the advantages already secured. A regrettable occurrence in the Mark of Brandenburg supplied fresh energy to their machinations, and a pretext for formulating an accusation. A thief had stolen some sacred emblems from a church, and when questioned as to the holy wafer, he confessed having sold it to Jews in the Brandenburg district. Of course, the thief was believed, and the bishop of Brandenburg entered on the persecution of the Jews with fiery fanaticism. The elector of Brandenburg, Joachim I, an ardent heretic-hunter, had the accused brought to Berlin. The accusation of reviling the host was soon supplemented by the charge of infanticide. Joachim had the Jews tortured, and then ordered thirty to be burnt. With firmness, songs of praise on their lips, these martyrs of Brandenburg met their fiery deaths (July 19th, 1510), except two, who, with the fear of the stake upon them, submitted to baptism, and suffered the seemingly more honorable fate of being beheaded. This is the first mention of Jews in Berlin and Brandenburg. The occurrence made a great stir in Germany, and the Cologne Dominicans employed it to induce the emperor to issue a new mandate for the confiscation of Jewish books, seeing that to the Talmud alone could be attributed the alleged hostility of the Jews to Christianity. They sheltered themselves behind the same go-between; the bigoted nun, the ducal abbess Kunigunde, to whom the diabolical wickedness of the Jews, as revealed by the above occurrence, was presented in most glaring colors, was again to influence the emperor. The Dominicans suggested to her how detrimental to Christianity must be the fact that the host-reviling and child-murdering Jews could boast of having had their books restored to them by order of the emperor, who thus, to a certain extent, approved of the abuse of Christianity which they contained. The abbess thereupon fairly assailed her brother, and at their interview at Munich besought him on her knees to reconsider the matter of the Jewish books. Maximilian was perplexed. He was loath to refuse his dearly beloved sister what she had so much at heart; on the other hand, he was not highly edified by Pfefferkorn's tissue of lies about the Jews. He found an expedient to appear just to both parties.

He issued a new mandate, the fourth in this affair (July 6th, 1510), addressed to Archbishop Uriel, directing him to resume the inquiry, but in another form. The indictment was not to be considered as proved, but was to be thoroughly investigated. The archbishop of Mayence was to take the opinions of the German universities named, and also of Reuchlin, Victor von Karben and Hoogstraten, to whom the emperor sent a special summons in official form. The final decision as to the character of the Jewish writings was to be communicated to him by Pfefferkorn, the originator of the inquiry. The Jews had reason to look forward with anxiety to the issue; their weal and woe depended on it.

It was fortunate for the Jews that the honest, truthful Reuchlin, so enthusiastically prepossessed for Hebrew and Kabbalistic literature, was asked to give his opinion of Jewish literature. The Cologne Dominicans, who had proposed him, thereby frustrated their own design, and as a further effect made him the enemy of their hostile endeavors. As soon as Reuchlin received the emperor's command, he set to work to answer the question, "Whether it was godly, laudable, and advantageous to Christianity to burn the Jewish writings," whereby the Talmud especially was meant. His judgment was extremely favorable to the writings in question, nor did he miss the chance of bestowing sundry side blows on the vile instigator Pfefferkorn. Jewish literature, the mistress of his heart, was to be charged as a culprit, and should he fail to defend her with all the powers of his mind? Reuchlin's opinion is conceived in the pedantic, heavy, juridical style then prevailing, but does not lack ability. He started from the correct point of view, that, in answering the question, the Jewish writings were not to be treated in the aggregate as a homogeneous literature, but that, excluding the Bible, they were to be divided into six classes. The class of exegetic works, such as those by R. Solomon (Rashi), Ibn-Ezra, the Kimchis, Moses Gerundensis and Levi ben Gershon, far from being detrimental to Christianity, he declared to be indispensable to Christian theology, the most learned Christian commentators of the Old Testament having taken the best of their work from the Jews, as from fountains whence flow the real truth and understanding of the Holy Scriptures. If from the voluminous writings of Nicholas de Lyra, the best Christian exegetist, all borrowed from Rashi were to be excised, the part left, which he himself had composed, might be comprised in a few pages. He, indeed, considered it a disgrace that many doctors of divinity, from ignorance of Hebrew and Greek, interpreted the Scriptures wrongly. The class of Hebrew writings on philosophy, natural sciences and the liberal arts were in no way distinguished from what might be found in Greek, Latin, or German works. With regard to the Talmud, against which the chief accusation was laid, Reuchlin confessed his inability to understand it; but other learned Christians understood no more of it than they might learn from its accusers, including Pfefferkorn. He was acquainted with many who condemned the Talmud without understanding it. But could one write against mathematics without having knowledge thereof? He was, therefore, of opinion that the Talmud was not to be burnt, even if it were true that it contained libels on the founders of Christianity. "If the Talmud were deserving of such condemnation, our ancestors of many hundred years ago, whose zeal for Christianity was much greater than ours, would have burnt it. The baptized Jews, Peter Schwarz and Pfefferkorn, the only persons who insist on its being burnt, probably wish it for private reasons."

To defend Kabbalistic writings, and save them from being burnt, was easy enough. Reuchlin had but to point to occurrences at the papal court, scarcely two decades ago. The learned and eccentric Count Pico di Mirandola had aroused enthusiastic admiration for the Kabbala, maintaining that it contained the most solid foundation of the chief doctrines of Christianity. Sixtus IV had caused some of the Kabbalistic writings to be translated into Latin. Reuchlin concluded his opinion by advising that their books should not be taken from the Jews, nor burnt, but that at every German university two professors of Hebrew be appointed for ten years, who might also be asked to teach modern, or rabbinical Hebrew; and thus the Jews might be led by gentle means and by conviction to embrace Christianity.

Unquestionably, since Jews had been ill-used and persecuted by Christians, they had not found so friendly an advocate as Reuchlin, who declared himself in their favor in an official document, intended for the chancellor of the empire, and the emperor himself. Two points on which Reuchlin laid stress were especially important to Jews. The first was, that the Jews were citizens of the Holy Roman Empire, and were entitled to its full privileges and protection. This was the first stammering utterance of that liberating word of perfect equality, which required more than three centuries for its perfect enunciation and acknowledgment. The mediæval delusion, that the Jews, by Vespasian and Titus' conquest of Jerusalem, had become the bondmen of their successors, the Roman and German emperors, was hereby partly dispelled. The recognition that Jews also had rights, which the emperor and the state, the clergy and the laity must respect, was the first faint, trembling ray of light after a long, dark night. The second point, which Reuchlin emphasized more positively, was of equal importance: that the Jews must not be considered or treated as heretics. Since they stood without the church, and were not bound to hold the Christian faith, the ideas of heresy and unbelief—

those terrifying and lethal anathemas of the Middle Ages—did not apply to them.

Of what use this judgment of Reuchlin was to the Jews, we discover by the decision of the faculties consulted—faculties to whom the Talmud, of course, was a book with seven seals. The Cologne Dominicans in a body, the theological faculty, the inquisitor Hoogstraten, and the gray-haired convert Victor von Karben, all mouthpieces of one mind, did not trouble themselves to prove that the Talmud was hostile to Christianity; they assumed it, and, therefore, quickly arrived at their decision, that the Talmudic writings, and all others, probably of the same stamp, were to be seized and burnt. But they went further; Hoogstraten, in particular, had the assurance to say that the Jews should be indicted. Experts were to extract and arrange heretical passages from the Talmud and other Jewish books; then the Jews were to be questioned whether or not they admitted the perniciousness of books containing such doctrines. If they admitted it, they could raise no objection to have them committed to the flames. If they obstinately persevered in treating such passages as portions of their creed, the emperor was to surrender them as convicted heretics for punishment to the Inquisition.

The faculty of the university of Mayence delivered a similar sentence, but went much further. They pronounced not only all Talmudic and rabbinical writings to be full of errors and heresy, but that even the Scriptures must have been contaminated and corrupted by them, especially in articles of faith, wherefore these were to be taken from the Jews, examined, and if their expectation was realized, the Jewish Bibles were to be thrown into the flames. This was a cunning device, because the Hebrew text of the Bible does not agree with the Latin Vulgate, the work of bunglers, used by the church. It was like arraigning an immaculate mother before her degenerate daughter, and telling her that if she did not adopt the vices of the latter, she did not deserve to exist. And it was a clever trick on the part of the Dominicans to get rid of the inconvenient Hebrew text, the "Hebrew truth," majestically shaking its head at the childish trifling of clerical interpretations. Had the theologians of Mayence and Cologne succeeded in enforcing their views, the Book received on Sinai, the words of the Prophets, the Psalms, monuments of a time of grace, would have been cast upon a blazing pyre, and a bastard, the corrupt Latin Vulgate, substituted for it. The Dominicans appear to have suspected that the plain sense of the words of the Bible would bring ruin upon them. Fortunately, the Cologne Dominicans themselves defeated their cunningly laid plan by an act of villainy.

Reuchlin had sent his opinion on Jewish literature in a sealed packet, and by a sworn messenger, to Archbishop Uriel, assuming that, being an official secret, it would be opened and read only by the archbishop and the emperor. But Pfefferkorn, who believed himself to be on the eve of avenging himself on the Jews, had it open in his hand even before the emperor had read it. How this occurred has never been cleared up. Reuchlin in plain words denounced the Cologne priests as unscrupulous seal-breakers. We ought almost to be grateful to them for having dragged an affair, originally enveloped in official secrecy, into publicity, thereby calling in another tribunal, and turning the peril of the Jews into a peril to the church. They had grown desperate over Reuchlin's opinion, because his voice had great weight with the emperor and his advisers. Therefore, the Dominicans, armed at all points, set to work to publish a refutation of Reuchlin's defense of the Jews and their books. It was written in German to render the cause popular, and incense the multitude so as to render it impossible for the emperor to listen to Reuchlin.

This libel, entitled "Handspiegel," spread abroad in thousands of copies, on a man so highly placed and honored, a judge of the Suabian League, a scholar of eminence, naturally caused a great sensation. Since the invention of printing it was the first furious attack on a dignitary, and being written in German, every one could understand it. Reuchlin's numerous friends were indignant at the insolence of a baptized Jew, who pretended to be more sound in faith than a born Christian in good standing. The Cologne Dominicans had permitted themselves to be guided by their envenomed hatred rather than by prudence. Reuchlin was compelled to take steps against such attacks, by which his honor was too deeply wounded for silence. He hastened to the emperor, and complained of Pfefferkorn, the rancorous calumniator, the ostensible author of the "Handspiegel." The emperor, by words and gestures, betrayed his indignation, and quieted the excited Reuchlin by the promise that the matter should be inquired into by the bishop of Augsburg. But amidst the press of business, in the confusion of Italian quarrels, the emperor forgot Reuchlin, the mortification he had suffered, and the redress promised him. The Frankfort autumn Fair was approaching, at which Pfefferkorn intended to offer for sale the remainder of the copies, and nothing had been done for or by Reuchlin.

Thus Reuchlin was compelled to make the Talmud a personal question, to appeal to public opinion, and thereby render the matter one of almost universal interest. He prepared a defensive and offensive reply to the "Handspiegel" for the Frankfort Fair. At the end of August, or beginning of September, 1511, his controversial pamphlet, entitled "Augenspiegel" (or Spectacles, a pair of spectacles being represented on the title-page), which has acquired historical celebrity, made its appearance. He designed to reveal to the German public the villainy of Pfefferkorn and his coadjutors, but unconsciously he revealed the defects of the Christianity of his time. It was a pamphlet which, we may say without exaggeration, was equivalent to a great action. It was directed against Pfefferkorn, and by implication against the Cologne Dominicans, the patrons and instigators of his calumnies. It relates in plain, honest language the progress of the whole affair: how the baptized "Jew" had made every effort to prove the Talmud dangerous, desiring to have it burnt, and had meant to turn Reuchlin to account in the matter. He publishes the missives of the emperor and of the archbishop addressed to him, and also his "Opinion." He reports how Pfefferkorn by dishonest means obtained possession of the "Opinion," and misused it to concoct a libel, containing no less than thirty-four untruths about him (Reuchlin). The tone of the "Augenspiegel" expresses the just indignation of a man of honor against a villain who has set a trap for him.

What roused the indignation of Reuchlin most was the charge that he had been bribed to write his defense of the Talmud. With honest anger he protested that at no time during his whole existence had he received from Jews, or on their behalf, a single penny, or any other reward. No less hurt was Reuchlin at the contempt expressed for his Hebrew scholarship, especially at the accusation that he had not himself composed his Hebrew grammar. His defense of the Jews is dignified. The scoundrel Pfefferkorn had reproached him with having learnt Hebrew from Jews, with whom, then, he must have had intercourse in defiance of the canon law. Thereupon Reuchlin says: "The baptized Jew writes that Divine law forbids our holding communion with Jews; this is not true. Every Christian may go to law with them, buy of or make presents to them. Cases may occur where Christians inherit legacies together with Jews. It is allowed to converse with and learn from them, as Saint Jerome and Nicholas de Lyra did. And lastly, a Christian should love a Jew as his neighbor; all this is founded on the law."

It may be imagined what excitement was created by Reuchlin's "Augenspiegel," written in German, when it appeared at the Frankfort Fair, the meeting-place of hundreds of thousands, at a time when there was no public press, and everyone readily lent his ear to a scandalous tale. To find that so distinguished a man as Reuchlin would set an accuser of the Jews in the pillory as a calumniator and liar, was something so new and surprising as to make readers rub their eyes, and ask themselves whether they had not hitherto been dozing. The Jews greedily bought a book in which for the first time a man of honor entered the lists on their behalf, and with powerful voice stigmatized the charges against them as calumnies. They rejoiced at having found a champion, and thanked God that He had not forsaken them in their tribulation. Who would find fault with them for laboring in the promulgation of Reuchlin's pamphlet? But by preaching against it in their pulpits, and by prohibiting its sale as far as they could, bigoted priests of the stamp of the Cologne Dominicans did most to disseminate it. From all directions, in learned and unlearned circles, congratulations were sent to Reuchlin, with expressions of satisfaction that he had so boldly and firmly settled the impudent Pfefferkorn and his abettors.

With the publication and circulation of Reuchlin's treatise, and his defense of the Talmud, commenced a struggle which every day became more serious, and at last assumed far greater proportions than the subject justified. For the bigots, still in the full power of their terrorizing might, did not hesitate to take up the challenge. Pfefferkorn's cause was also theirs. Yet a man had dared step forward boldly, not only to disapprove of the condemnation of the Talmud, but also to declare that the persecution of the Jews was unchristianlike; and that they ought, on the contrary, to be treated with sympathy and love. What audacity! It aroused in them such virtuous indignation that they shot beyond the mark, and committed such blunders that they damaged their cause irreparably.

Pastor Peter Meyer, of Frankfort-on-the-Main, who had not been able to obtain the prohibition of the sale of the "Augenspiegel," made the second mistake. He announced from the pulpit during service that Pfefferkorn would preach on the eve of the next "Feast of our Lady" against Reuchlin's Jewish writings, and he exhorted the faithful to attend in great numbers. Nothing could be more fatal than this error. Pfefferkorn with his disagreeable, repulsive face, distinctly Jewish features and coarse, vulgar look, preach before a Christian congregation in his Jewish-German jargon! Each word and each movement would provoke his hearers to laughter, and drive away even sincere devotion. Moreover, was it in accordance with Catholic law that a layman, above all a married layman, should officiate in the church? Not long before this a simple shepherd had been sentenced to be burned on account of unsanctioned preaching. To keep the letter of the law Pfefferkorn preached on the appointed day (September 7th, 1511), not in the church, but before the entrance, to a great crowd of people. It must have been very droll to see how this ill-favored Jew made the sign of the cross over believers, and spoke of the Christian faith in the Jewish jargon. Pfefferkorn's chief desire was to make the Jews and their well-wishers detestable, and to excite the hatred of his hearers against them.

Until now the chief mover of the whole scandal, the venomous and malicious master heretic-hunter, Jacob Hoogstraten, had kept behind the scenes, but had sent his followers to the front one by one: first Pfefferkorn, then Ortuinus Gratius and Arnold von Tongern. Henceforth he stood in the foreground himself, his insolent demeanor seeming to assume that priests and laymen must all bow before him, and sink under his frown in the dust, and that he had the right to tread statutes and customs under his feet. To save, by violent measures, the weakened authority of the order, all Dominicans had to make common cause, and apply their energy to carry through the condemnation of Reuchlin and the Talmud. The conflict spread over a wider area, and became an affair of the whole order.

Authorized by the provincial of his order, Hoogstraten, in his capacity as inquisitor, suddenly issued (September 15th, 1513) a summons to Reuchlin to appear at Mayence within six days, at eight o'clock in the morning, to be examined on the charge of heresy and of favoring the Jews. On the appointed day Hoogstraten, with a host of Dominicans, appeared in Mayence; they were confederates, chosen to sit as judges in the commission. Hoogstraten opened the session, acting at once as judge and accuser. He had prepared an unassailable bill of indictment against Reuchlin and the Talmud, and taken the precaution to seek allies, so that he might not stand alone in this weighty contest. Shortly before, he had addressed letters to four universities, begging them to express their opinion on Reuchlin's book, "Augenspiegel," in accordance with his own views, and all had fulfilled his expectations.

The accusation which he brought forward was, of course, that which Pfefferkorn and Arnold von Tongern had already made. It had for its basis: Reuchlin favors the Jews too much, treats "the insolent people" almost as members of the church, and as men on an equality with others, while his writings savor too much of heresy. Hoogstraten, therefore, instructed the court to pronounce sentence upon Reuchlin's "Augenspiegel": that it was full of heresy and error, too favorable to the unbelieving Jews, and insulting to the church, and therefore ought to be condemned, suppressed, and destroyed by fire. One must not overlook the great difference between a German and a Spanish inquisition court. Torquemada or Ximenes would have made short work of it, and condemned the book together with the author to the stake. Hoogstraten was not too kind-hearted for such a sentence; but he dared not venture so far, because he would have had all Germany, the ecclesiastical as well as the temporal rulers against him.

General indignation was aroused at the injustice of a trial carried on in violation of all rules. The students of the Mayence University, not yet tainted by the corruption of theology, their judgment not warped by casuistry, and not influenced by foreign considerations, loudly proclaimed their displeasure at this shameless proceeding of the Inquisition. They carried the doctors of jurisprudence with them, and this induced other earnest men to interfere.

To the surprise of the Dominicans, the aged, venerable Reuchlin appeared in Mayence, accompanied by two respected counselors of the Duke of Wurtemberg. The chapter now took great trouble to effect a reconciliation. But Hoogstraten, who wished to see smoke rise from the fagots, would agree to nothing, and delayed the negotiations till the 12th of October, the time when the final sentence would be pronounced. The inquisitor commanded all the ecclesiastics in Mayence to announce from the pulpit that everyone, Christian or Jew, if he would escape punishment, must give up all copies of the "Augenspiegel" to the flames. The people were promised thirty days' indulgence, if they assembled on the appointed day at the church square to celebrate the auto-da-fé and increase its splendor. On the 12th of October the place before the church in Mayence was thronged with spectators—the curious, the sympathetic, and the seekers after indulgence! Decked out like peacocks, the Fathers and Brothers of the Dominican order, and the theologians of the universities of Cologne, Louvain, and Erfurt, strutted along to the tribunal erected for them, and "the earth trembled under their feet." Hoogstraten, till now the accuser, again took his place among the judges. They were about to pronounce the formula of the curse, and have the fire kindled, when a messenger hastily arrived, bringing a letter from Archbishop Uriel, which turned them speechless.

Uriel von Gemmingen, like most bishops of his time, was more worldly-minded than spiritual, and had no canonical fanaticism against Jews. The presumptuousness of the Dominicans of Cologne and their unjust proceedings against Reuchlin angered him, too. Therefore, he issued a proclamation to the commissioners selected from his chapter, ordering that judgment be delayed for one month until a new agreement might be arrived at. If they did not consent, this letter deprived them of their privileges as judges of the inquisitorial court, and every thing hitherto decreed was null and void. Utterly dumbfounded, the Dominicans listened to the notary's reading of the document, which entirely frustrated their schemes and machinations. Hoogstraten alone boldly dared express his anger at the denial of their rights. The other confederates slunk away ashamed, followed by the jeers of the street boys, and the cry of the men, "O that these Brothers, who wished to outrage a just man, might be burnt at the stake."

If it is true, as the Dominicans relate, that the rabbis of Germany met in a synod in Worms, and found in the defeat of the Dominicans who raged against Reuchlin a sign of the downfall of the Roman (papist) hierarchy, they were certainly endowed with prophetic vision. It was also said that Reuchlin had secret intercourse with rabbis.

Reuchlin was by no means so situated as to be able to triumph over his enemies and those of the Jews. Though subdued for the moment, they were certainly not vanquished. He knew their cunning and malignity too well to give himself up to inactive enjoyment of his victory. He knew that their persecutions would only be redoubled in the future. Therefore, he hastened to announce his appeal to the pope, so that silence might be imposed from that quarter on his embittered enemies. But Reuchlin justly feared that with the vacillation and venality of the Vatican his cause would go badly, if the investigation were conducted beyond the jurisdiction of the pope by the Dominicans of Cologne. Therefore, he sent a Hebrew letter to Bonet de Lates, the Jewish physician of Pope Leo X, begging him to plead for the pope's favor in his cause.

Leo, of the celebrated family of the Medici, about whom his father had said that he was the wisest of his sons, had succeeded to the papal chair only a few months before. He was an aristocrat, more interested in politics than in religion, a Roman pagan rather than a Catholic priest, looking down with contempt from his Olympian heights on theological controversy as child's play. He only considered how best to steer between the two warring states or houses of Hapsburg and Valois, without endangering the temporal interest of the Roman Catholic hierarchy. With candor that would surprise us today, the pope ventured to say, "It is well known how useful this fable of Christ has been to us and ours!" With him now rested the decision, whether Reuchlin's "Augenspiegel" savored of heresy, and whether he duly or unduly favored the Jews. Leo, whose pontificate fell in a time when theological questions threatened to embroil all Europe, perhaps knew less of them than his cook. Much, therefore, depended on the light in which the conflict between Reuchlin and the Dominicans was placed before him. For this reason Reuchlin begged the physician Bonet de Lates, who had access to the pope and care of "the person of his Holiness," to win over Leo X, so that the trial might not take place in Cologne or its vicinity, where his cause would be lost. Reuchlin laid all the circumstances before him: how Pfefferkorn and the Cologne Dominicans had conspired against the Jews and the Talmud, and how only his extraordinary efforts had saved the Talmud from destruction. Had the Dominicans been able to get hold of and read this letter, they could have brought forward incontestable proof of Reuchlin's friendliness towards the Jews, for in it he wrote much that he had publicly denied.

It is natural that Bonet de Lates brought all his influence to bear in favor of Reuchlin. And it was probably owing to his zeal that Leo so soon (November 21st, 1513) issued instructions to the bishops of Speyer and Worms on the controversy between Reuchlin and Hoogstraten. Leo ordered that they be examined separately or together, by the bishops or by judges appointed by them, who, without the intervention of any other tribunal, were to pronounce judgment, to be accepted without appeal. The bishop of Worms, a Dalburg, with whom Reuchlin was on friendly terms, did not care to accept the commission. So the young bishop of Speyer, George, elector palatine and duke of Bavaria, appointed two judges, who summoned both parties to appear within a month before the tribunal in Speyer. Reuchlin came punctually, accompanied by a procurator and friends. Hoogstraten, on the other hand, trusting to the power of the Dominicans, did not present himself, nor send a competent representative. The judges commenced the suit, not with becoming energy, but with a certain half-heartedness, perhaps from fear of the revenge of the Dominicans. The trial was spun out over three months (January to April, 1514).

Only after Reuchlin had written two German papers on the matter in dispute and the progress of the proceedings, did the bishop deign to notice the evidence and pass judgment, which was wholly in favor of Reuchlin. He stated that the "Augenspiegel" contained not an iota of heresy or error, that it did not unduly favor the Jews, that, therefore, Hoogstraten had slandered the author, and silence should be imposed on him in this matter; that the writings might be read and printed by everyone, and that Hoogstraten be charged with the costs (111 Rhenish gold florins).

The Dominicans of Cologne gnashed their teeth, stormed and raged at the issue of the suit, and used every effort to overthrow the judgment of the apostolic court. At that time, on account of the disunion in Germany, it was very difficult to put into execution a judicial decree, and the Dominicans were not inclined to lessen the difficulty when the sentence was given against themselves. They laughed at the bishop of Speyer, calling him a stupid fellow. The notice of the verdict in Cologne was torn down by the bold Pfefferkorn. Hoogstraten had unofficially—that is to say, without giving notice to the bishop of Speyer, then acting as apostolic judge—appealed to the pope, although he had scouted the idea of such an appeal before. His hope of winning the suit against Reuchlin and securing the condemnation of the "Augenspiegel" was founded on the venality of the Vatican. "Rome will do anything for money," he frankly said; "Reuchlin is poor, and the Dominicans are rich; justice can be suppressed by money." Hoogstraten could also count on the good will of the cardinals, who inveighed against free inquiry. At all events, they could be depended upon to drag out the suit so long that Reuchlin's means would not suffice to meet the costs. Besides this, the Dominicans relied on obtaining from the universities, in particular the leading one of Paris, the condemnation of the "Augenspiegel," and using it to exert pressure upon the pope. All Dominicans, Thomists and obscurantists, both in and outside Germany, made common cause to work the downfall of Reuchlin.

This union of the Dominican party had the effect of binding together the friends of learning, the enemies of scholasticism, bigotry and church doctrine—in one word, the Humanists—and inducing them to take concerted action. Virtually a society of Humanists, a Reuchlinist party, was formed in western Europe, the members of which silently worked for one another and for Reuchlin: "One supported the other, and said to his comrade, Be brave." "All we who belong to the ranks of learning are devoted to Reuchlin no less than soldiers to the emperor." It was a formal alliance, which the supporters of Reuchlin loyally adhered to. So, in consequence of Pfefferkorn's bitter hostility to the Jews and the Talmud, two parties were formed in Christendom, the Reuchlinists and the Arnoldists, who waged fierce conflict with each other. It was a struggle of the dark Middle Ages with the dawn of a better time.

Young Germany was working with all its might on behalf of Reuchlin and against the bigots: besides Hermann von Busche, and Crotus Rubianus (Johann Jäger), there was the fiery Ulrich von Hutten, the most energetic and virile character of the time. In fact, Hutten's energy first found a worthy aim in the passionate feud between Reuchlin and the Dominicans. Formerly his fencing had consisted of passes in the empty air; his knightly courage and fiery genius had met only phantom adversaries. Now, for the first time, the youth of six-and-twenty had a clear perception of the relation of things; he saw a real enemy, to meet whom with his knight's sword and the sharper weapon of his intellect, in a life and death struggle, would be a praiseworthy, glorious undertaking. To destroy the Dominicans, priests and bigots, and establish the kingdom of intellect and free thought, to deliver Germany from the nightmare of ecclesiastical superstition and barbarism, raise it from its abjectness, and make it the arbiter of Europe, seemed to him the aim to toil for. As soon as Hutten was clearly conscious of this, he worked ceaselessly for his object, the first step towards its realization being to help Reuchlin, the leader in the struggle for humanism, to gain the victory over his mortal foes. A cardinal, Egidio de Viterbo, who delighted in the Hebrew language and in the Kabbala, openly sided with Reuchlin. He wrote to him, "The Law (Torah) revealed to man in fire was first saved from fire when Abraham escaped the burning furnace, and now a second time, when Reuchlin saved, from the fire, the writings from which the Law received light, for had they been destroyed eternal darkness would again have set in. So, exerting ourselves for your cause, we are not defending you, but the Law, not the Talmud, but the church." It is remarkable that the whole Franciscan order, from hatred of the Dominicans, took up Reuchlin's cause.

In almost every town there were Reuchlinists and anti-Reuchlinists, whose mutual hatred brought them at times to blows. The motto of one was, "Rescue of the 'Augenspiegel' and preservation of the Talmud," and of the other, "Damnation and destruction to both." Involuntarily the Reuchlinists became friends of the Jews, and sought grounds on which to defend them. The adherents of the Dominicans became fiercer enemies to the Jews, and sought out obscure books to prove their wickedness.

The report of this contest spread through Europe. At first limited to Germany, the controversy soon reached both Rome and Paris. Hoogstraten and the Dominicans worked with energy to have the judgment of Speyer overthrown, in the latter place by the greatest university, in the former by the papal see, and to have Reuchlin's writings sentenced to the flames. In both places they had powerful and influential allies, who devotedly and zealously worked for their party.

Reuchlin, although his suit had been lawfully won in the apostolic court in Speyer, was forced to take steps to counteract the appeal instituted by the intrigues of his enemies. And his friends succeeded in influencing the pope. Leo X appointed the cardinal and patriarch Dominico Grimani as judge of the inquiry. It was well known that this ecclesiastical prince cultivated rabbinical literature, and, as patron of the Franciscan order, hated the Dominicans, and took Reuchlin's side. Without doubt prominent Jews were working in Rome for Reuchlin, but, like the German Jews, they had the good sense to keep in the background, so as not to imperil the cause by stamping it as Jewish. Cardinal Grimani issued (June, 1514) a summons to both parties, but in consideration of Reuchlin's advanced years permitted him to send a representative, while Hoogstraten had to appear in person. Furnished with recommendations and a well-filled purse, the inquisitor appeared in Rome with undiminished confidence of obtaining a victory. What could not be obtained in Rome for money?

Reuchlin had nothing of the kind to offer; he was poor. He had not the magic wand which commands the gold of bigoted women, nor the conjurer's formula over father-confessors, who are apt treasure-diggers. But there was no lack of recommendations from his friends and well-wishers. Emperor Maximilian, who, much to his own regret, had originated all this disturbance, by lending ear to Pfefferkorn's stupidities and his sister's hysterical piety, often interceded with the pope for Reuchlin. The emperor wrote that he believed that the Cologne people wished to prolong the controversy illegally and through intrigue, in order to crush the excellent, inoffensive, learned and orthodox Reuchlin; that what he had written (in favor of the Hebrew Scriptures) had been written at the emperor's command, with a good object, and for the benefit of Christendom.

But the Dominicans defied public opinion, the commission appointed by the pope, and the pope. They spoke of the pope as of a schoolboy under their authority. If he did not give a decision in their favor, they threatened to withdraw their allegiance, and desert him, even risking a rupture with the church. They went so far as to threaten that in case Reuchlin proved victorious, they would ally themselves with the Hussites in Bohemia against the pope. So blinded was this faction by revengeful feelings, that from sheer obstinacy they would undermine Catholicism. Nor did they spare the majesty of the emperor; when they learned that Maximilian had interceded for Reuchlin with the pope, they heaped abuse on him.

The Dominicans built their hopes on the verdict of Paris, the head of all European universities. If this important school of divinity condemned Reuchlin's writings and the Talmud, then even the pope would have to submit. Every influence was, therefore, brought to bear to obtain a favorable opinion from Paris. In particular, the king of France, Louis XII, was worked on by his confessor, Guillaume Haquinet Petit, to influence the school of divinity in favor of the Dominicans. The political events which had set the German emperor and the French king at variance were also brought into play. Because the emperor of Germany was for Reuchlin, the king of France decided for the Dominicans and against the Talmud. But this decision was not easily obtained, for Reuchlin numbered many warm friends in Paris. The consultation was prolonged from May to the beginning of August, 1514.

Many of the voters spoke in favor of Reuchlin, and at the same time expressed their indignation at the unlawful proceedings; but they were cried down by the fanatics. Many French divines were guided by the example of Saint Louis, who, at the instigation of the baptized Jew, Nicholas Donin, and by command of Pope Gregory IX, had ordered the Talmud to be burnt three centuries before. The Parisian doctors, therefore, gave sentence that Reuchlin's "Augenspiegel," containing heresy, and defending with great zeal the Talmudic writings, deserved to be condemned to the flames, and the author to be forced to recant.

Great was the joy of the Dominicans, particularly those of Cologne, over this judgment. They believed their game to be won, and that the pope himself would be forced to submit. They did not delay in making known to the public this concession, so hardly won, by means of another libelous pamphlet.

The lawsuit, allowed to lag in Rome, was wilfully delayed still more by the Dominicans. The commission appointed had a close translation of the "Augenspiegel" prepared by a German in Rome, Martin von Grönigen; but the opposition found fault with it. Numerous hindrances blocked the progress of the suit, and at this stage cost Reuchlin 400 gold florins. The Dominicans had hoped so to impoverish their adversary, the friend of the Jews, that he would be incapacitated from obtaining justice. The prospect of seeing Reuchlin's cause triumphant at Rome diminished. Reuchlin's friends were, therefore, anxious to create another tribunal, and appeal from the badly advised or intimidated pope to public opinion.

During this tension of minds in small and great circles, whilst high and low ecclesiastics, princes and citizens, anxiously awaited news as to how the Reuchlin lawsuit had ended, or would end in Rome, a young Humanist (most likely Crotus Rubianus, in Leipsic), wrote a series of letters, which, for wit, humor and biting satire, had not been equaled in all literature. The "Letters of Obscurantists" (*Epistolæ Obscurorum Virorum*), published in 1515, in a great measure directed against the rascally Ortuinus Gratius, laid bare, in the language of the unpolished monks, their own baseness and insolence, their astonishing ignorance, their lust, their animosity and vileness, their despicable Latin, and still more contemptible morality, the absurdity of their logic, their foolish chatter—in short, all their intolerable vices were made so evident, and described so clearly, that even the half-educated could comprehend. All Reuchlin's enemies, Hoogstraten, Arnold von Tongern, Ortuinus Gratius, Pfefferkorn, their accomplices, and the Paris University, were lashed with whips and scorpions, so that no spot on them remained sound. This clever satire, containing more than Aristophanian scorn, made the stronger an impression as the Dominicans, the Thomists, the Doctors of Divinity, revealed themselves in their own persons, in their miserable meanness, placing themselves, metaphorically speaking, in the pillory. But it was inevitable that, in deriding the bigots and the papacy, the whole tyranny of the hierarchy and the church should be laid bare. For, were not the Dominicans, with their insolent ignorance and shameless vices, the product and natural effect of the Catholic order and institution? So the satire worked like a corroding acid, entirely destroying the already rotting body of the Catholic Church.

The Jews and the Talmud were the first cause of the Reuchlinist quarrel; naturally, they could not be left out of account in the letters of the Obscurantists. So it happened that the much despised Jews became one of the topics of the day.

A roar of laughter resounded through western Europe at the reading of these satirical letters. Everyone in Germany, Italy, France and England who understood Latin, was struck with the form and tenor of these confessions of Dominicans and scholastics. Their awkward vulgarity, dense stupidity, egregious folly, impurity of word and deed, stood so glaringly in contrast with their presumed learning and propriety, that the most serious men were moved to mirth. It is related that Erasmus, who, at the time of reading the letters, suffered from an abscess in the throat, laughed so heartily that it broke, and he was cured. The merry Comedy of the Fools put Reuchlin entirely in the right, and the Dominicans were judged by public opinion, no matter how the pope might deal with them. All were curious to know who could be the author. Some thought it was Reuchlin himself, others Erasmus, Hutten, or one of the Humanist party. Hutten gave the right answer to the question as to the author: "God himself." It appeared more and more clearly that so slight a cause as the burning of the Talmud had taken a world-wide significance, the will of the individual serving only to further the interests of all. In Rome and Cologne, far-seeing Reuchlinists discerned in it the work of Providence.

Only the German Jews could not indulge in merriment. The Dominicans had meantime worked in another way to obtain their object, or at least to have revenge on the Jews. Of what avail was it to the Jews that some enlightened Christians, having had their attention drawn to Judaism, were seized with so great a predilection for it that they gave expression to their new convictions in writing? Christendom as a whole was irrevocably prejudiced against Jewish teachings and their adherents. Erasmus rightly said,

"If it is Christian to hate the Jews, then we are true Christians." Therefore, it was easy for their enemies to injure them. Pfefferkorn had often pointed out that there were in Germany only three great Jewish communities, at Ratisbon, Frankfort and Worms, and that with their extermination, Judaism in the German kingdom would come to an end.

To bring about the expulsion of the Jews from Frankfort and Worms, their enemies had discoverd effective means. The young Margrave, Albert von Brandenburg, hitherto bishop of Magdeburg, who later attained melancholy renown in the history of the Reformation, had been elected to the archbishopric of Mayence. The enemies of the Jews, acting probably on a suggestion from Cologne, induced Archbishop Albert to issue an invitation to religious and secular authorities and to towns, principally Frankfort and Worms, to attend a diet in Frankfort, to discuss how the Jews might be banished and never be permitted to return. Obeying the invitation (January 7th, 1516), many deputies appeared. The program was to this purport: All the estates were to unite and take an oath to relinquish the privileges and advantages derived from the Jews, to banish all Jewish subjects and never, under any pretext, or for any term, permit them to return. This resolution was to be laid before the emperor for his confirmation.

The Jews of these places saw certain danger hanging over their heads. If at other times the German princes and rulers were disunited and indolent, in the persecution of Jews they were always united and energetic. Nothing remained for the Jews but to send a deputation to Emperor Maximilian, and implore him to grant them his favor and support them against so malevolent a measure. The emperor happily remembered that the Jews, even when ruled by various great or petty rulers, were in reality the servants of himself and the empire, and that their banishment would be an encroachment on his suzerainty. Maximilian hastened, therefore, to send a very forcible dispatch to Elector Albert and the chapter of Mayence, to the religious and secular authorities, and to the towns (January, 1516), expressing his displeasure at their conference, and forbidding them to meet again at the appointed time. So the Jews were for the moment saved. But the archbishop of Mayence, or in his absence the chapter, did not give up the pursuit of the desired object. The enemies of the Jews, the friends of the Cologne Dominicans, still hoped to turn the emperor against them. But the hope was vain; the Jews were not banished for the present.

Reuchlin's lawsuit, although delayed by the struggles of the two parties, whose time was taken up in plotting against each other's intrigues, made slow but perceptible progress. Hoogstraten, seeing that the commission would decide in favor of Reuchlin, vehemently demanded a decision by council, inasmuch as it was a question, not of law, but of faith. Pope Leo, who did not care to be on bad terms with either party, in opposition to his own repeated command had to yield to a certain extent. On the one side Emperor Maximilian and many German princes insisted upon having Reuchlin declared blameless and silencing the Dominicans; on the other side the king of France and young Charles (at that time duke of Burgundy), the future emperor of Germany, king of Spain and America, used threatening language towards the pope, demanding that the matter be taken up seriously, and that Reuchlin's book be condemned. Leo, therefore, considered it advisable to escape from this critical position. He submitted the matter for final decision to a court of inquiry, formed of members of the Lateran Council, then in session. Thus the dispute about the Talmud became the concern of a general council, and was raised to the dignity of a European question.

The council committee finally declared in favor of Reuchlin. Before Leo X could confirm or reject its decision, Hoogstraten and his friends influenced him to issue a mandate suspending the suit. This temporizing exactly suited Leo's character and his position between the excited rival parties. He hated excitement, which he would have brought on himself, if he had decided in favor of either party. He did not wish to offend the Humanists, nor yet the bigots, nor the German emperor, nor the king of France, nor the ruler of Spain. So the suit was suspended, and at any favorable opportunity could be taken up again by the Dominicans. Hoogstraten had to leave Rome in disgrace and dishonor, but he did not give up the hope of winning his cause in the end. He was a strong-willed man, who could not be discouraged by humiliations, and so unprincipled that falsehood and misrepresentations came easy to him.

If Pope Leo believed that at his dictation the conflict would cease, he overestimated the authority of the papacy, and mistook the parties as well as the real issue involved. Feeling ran too high to be quieted by a word from those in power. Neither party wished for peace, but for war, war to the knife. When Hoogstraten returned from Rome, his life was in danger. Furious Reuchlinists often conspired against him, and sought by polemical leaflets to exasperate public opinion still more against the Dominicans. Hutten, since his mature judgment had taken in the situation at Rome, was most eager to bring about the downfall of ecclesiastical domination in Germany.

The secret could be no longer kept, it was given out from the house-tops that there was dissension in the church. Not their foes, but the provincial of the Dominican order, Eberhard von Cleve, and the whole chapter, represented in an official letter to the pope that the controversy had brought them, the

Dominicans, into hatred and contempt; that they were held up to the mockery of all, and that they—so very undeservedly!—were decried, both in speech and writing, as the enemies of brotherly love, peace and harmony; that their preaching was despised, their confessional avoided, and that everything they undertook was derided, and declared to be only the result of pride and meanness.

Meanwhile the contention between Reuchlin and the Dominicans, especially Hoogstraten, developed in another direction, and affected Judaism at another point. The Kabbala formed the background of this movement. Out of love for this secret doctrine, supposed to offer the key to the deepest knowledge of philosophy and Christianity, Reuchlin had wished to spare the Talmud, because in his opinion it contained mystical elements. The youthful Kabbala became the patroness of the old Talmud. Reuchlin understood but little of Kabbalistic doctrines, but his eagerness for knowledge and his zeal spurred him on to study. Moreover, the attack by his adversaries upon his orthodoxy, honesty and erudition, had made it an affair of honor for him to prove convincingly that the Kabbala agreed with Christianity. But he was unfortunate in the choice of his Hebrew models. For a long time he sought a guide, until chance brought him to the most confused source of information: the foolish writings of the Kabbalist, Joseph Jikatilla, of Castile, which the convert Paul Riccio had lately translated into Latin. As soon as Reuchlin heard of this literary treasure of Joseph Jikatilla, he did not rest till he had obtained it, and again set about proving that the Kabbala was in agreement with Christianity.

Believing that the Kabbala reveals and confirms the highest truths, the mysteries of Christianity, Reuchlin composed a work on Kabbalist science, and dedicated it to Pope Leo X, giving new emphasis to his contention that the Jewish writings, instead of being burnt, should be cherished.

Reuchlin must have counted on the approval of the pope, to whom he dedicated the work, for having found new support for the tottering faith. He hoped that Leo X would at length grant him peace and rest by pronouncing judgment in the suit between himself and the Dominicans, which, though suppressed, was persistently urged by the latter. The Christianlike Kabbala was to be his intercessor at the Vatican. He did not stand alone in his foolish fondness for the secret doctrine. Not only the cardinals but the pope himself expected to gain much for Christianity by proper research into the Kabbala.

As the interest in the Reuchlin controversy began to flag, another movement started in Germany, continuing, as the other had begun, to shake the firm pillars of the papacy and the Catholic Church, and prepare the regeneration of Europe. The discussion aroused by the Talmud created an intellectual medium favorable to the germination and growth of Luther's reform movement. Destined soon to become a force in the world's history, even the Reformation arose from small beginnings, and needed most powerful protection not to be nipped in the bud. Martin Luther was a strong, straightforward, obstinate and passionately excitable character, holding with tenacity to his convictions and errors. By the opposition which he met, Luther finally came to the conclusion that each individual pope, consequently the papacy, was not infallible, and that the basis of faith was not the pope's will, but the Scriptural word.

The death of the old emperor, Maximilian, who had been unequal to the task of grappling with the theological perplexities called forth by himself, and the election of a new emperor, spun out for half a year, drew politics into the arena, and gave rise to a confusion in which the friends and foes of free religious thought and of gloomy orthodox faith were not distinguishable. Hutten and the Humanists favored Charles V, in whose own country, Spain, the Dominicans still had the upper hand, and where the flames from the stake were still unextinguished; but he was opposed by the pope. The Reuchlinist and the Lutheran cause, as it were, the Talmud and the Reformation, were merged into each other. So great a change had taken place that the electors assembled to elect an emperor declared against the obscurantists of Cologne and in favor of Reuchlin.

Instead of condemning the Talmud, Pope Leo X encouraged the printing of the work. Thus, through a movement incomprehensible to all its contemporaries, the unexpected took place: Reuchlin was justified, and the Talmud was justified, and in a measure favored by the pope. Indeed, Daniel Bomberg, a rich Christian publisher in Antwerp, in the same year brought out a complete edition of the Babylonian Talmud in twelve folio volumes, the model of all later editions.

A clever pantomime, which first appeared in Latin or French, and was soon translated into German, portrays Reuchlin as the originator of the great and growing movement. It represents a doctor, on whose back may be read the name of Capnion (Reuchlin), throwing a bundle of straight and crooked sticks on the stage, and then going away. Another figure (Erasmus), having in vain endeavored to put the bundle in order, shakes his head over the chaos, and disappears. Hutten also comes in. Luther appears in monk's dress, and with a firebrand kindles the crooked twigs. Another figure, in imperial robes, strikes with its sword the spreading fire, only giving it wider play. At length comes the pope, who, wishing to extinguish the fire, seizes a vessel, and pours the oil in it upon the flames, then clasps his hands on his head, while the bright flames shoot up never again to be stifled. Pfefferkorn and the Talmud should not have been missing in this dumb show, for they were the fuse that started the conflagration.

The situation was such that the slightest breath made the flames leap up. Luther had gained firmness and courage at the imperial diet of Worms, and by his speech, revealing fearlessness, completed the rupture with the papacy. Although urged by his own bigotry, besieged by obscurantists and exhorted by princes, Emperor Charles was disposed to condemn the reformer to the stake as a heretic, yet partly from consideration for Frederick, elector of Saxony, partly from policy, hoping thereby to hold the pope in check, he only declared him an exile a month later. Meanwhile Luther was already on his Patmos, the Wartburg, hidden and protected. Whilst in solitude he worked at a German translation of the Bible, ultra-reformers overthrew church regulations, altered the church services, did away with masses and priestly decoration, abolished the vows of monks, and introduced the marriage of priests—that is to say, the priests publicly acknowledged their former secret mistresses as their wives. The time was ripe for the Reformation, and it took firm hold of North Germany, Denmark and Sweden, extending to Prussia, Poland, and, on the other hand, to France and even Spain, the country of darkest and most bigoted ecclesiasticism and the home of persecution. Zwingli, the reformer of Switzerland, after much wavering, declared himself against the papacy; so, in that country, too, where there was more freedom of action than in submissive Germany, the new church service was introduced, the marriage of priests permitted, pictures and crucifixes destroyed, and monasteries done away with. A new order of things had set in; all-powerful Rome stood impotent before the new spirit. The enthusiasm of the Anabaptists began to arouse public feeling and transform all relations of life.

At first, Luther's Reformation affected the Jews but slightly. Catholics and innovators in every town, especially in Germany, were so occupied with fighting each other, that they had no leisure for the persecution of Jews; so there came a pause. Luther, whose voice even then was more powerful than that of the princes, at first defended them from numerous accusations. In his plain-spoken and fervent way, he said:

"This rage (against the Jews) is still defended by some silly theologians, and advocated by them; they declare insolently that the Jews are the servants of the Christians, and subject to the emperor. I beg you to tell me who will join our religion, be he the most amiable and patient of men, when he sees that they are treated so cruelly and inimically, and not only in an unchristian way, but even brutally. Most of the Passion preachers (in Holy Week) do nothing but make the sin committed by Jews against Christ heavier and greater, and embitter the hearts of believers against them."

In one of his works, the title of which, calculated to startle their antagonists, ran, "Jesus was born a Jew," Luther expressed himself against the indelible hatred of the Jews still more sharply:

"Those fools, the papists, bishops, sophists and monks, have hitherto so dealt with Jews, that every good Christian would rather have been a Jew. And if I had been a Jew, and seen such stupidity and such blockheads reign in the Christian Church, I would rather have been a pig than a Christian. They have treated the Jews as if they were dogs, not men; they have done nothing but revile them. They are blood-relations of our Lord; therefore, if it were proper to boast of flesh and blood, the Jews belong to Christ more than we. I beg, therefore, my dear papists, if you become tired of abusing me as a heretic, that you begin to revile me as a Jew."

"Therefore, it is my advice," continued Luther, "that we treat them kindly. Now that we drive them by force, treating them deceitfully and ignominiously, saying that they must have Christian blood to wash away the Jewish stain, and I know not what more nonsense,—prohibiting them from working amongst us, from living and having social intercourse with us, forcing them to be usurers, how can we expect them to come to us? If we would help them, so must we exercise, not the law of the pope, but that of Christian love—show them a friendly spirit, permit them to live and to work, so that they may have cause and means to be with us and amongst us."

These were words which the Jews had not heard for a thousand years. They show unmistakable traces of Reuchlin's mild intercession in their favor. Many hot-headed Jews saw in Luther's opposition to the papacy the extinction of Christianity and the triumph of Judaism. Three learned Jews went to Luther, and tried to convert him. Enthusiastic feelings were aroused among the Jews at this unexpected revulsion, especially at the blow dealt the papacy and the idolatrous worship of images and relics; the boldest hopes were entertained of the speedy downfall of Rome, and the approaching redemption by the Messiah.

But the Jewish religion gained much more by the Reformation than the Jewish race. Despised before, it became fashionable, so to say, in the early days of the Reformation. Reuchlin had expressed the modest wish that at the few German universities a professor of the Hebrew language might be appointed. Through his zeal for Hebrew (he had published, shortly before his death, a work on Hebrew accents and prosody), and through the increasing conviction that without this knowledge the Bible must remain a sealed book, princes and universities sought teachers, and instituted Hebrew professorships not only in Germany and Italy, but also in France and Poland. The light, graceful, classic muse, which had withdrawn many hearts from the church, was more and more neglected, and the serious Hebrew mother was sought out instead. Young and old did not hesitate to seek Jews from whom to learn Hebrew. A friendly connection was formed between Jewish masters and Christian pupils, to the intense vexation of bigots on both sides; and many prejudices died out by these means. The principal teacher of the Christians was a grammarian of German descent, Elias Levita (born 1468, died 1549). This poor man, who had to struggle for his daily bread, laid the foundation of the knowledge of the Hebrew language. The plundering of Padua—where, perhaps, he was born—brought him, by way of Venice, to Rome, where Cardinal Egidio de Viterbo, wishing to advance in his grammatical and Kabbalistic studies, took him into his house, supporting him and his family for more than ten years. Not only this church dignitary, but many other Christians of high position sat at Levita's feet. One was George de Selve, bishop of Lavour, the French ambassador, as learned as he was statesmanlike. Against the reproach of some bigoted rabbis, Levita defended himself by the remark that his Christian pupils all were friends of the Jews, and tried to promote their welfare. On the inducement of his patron, Egidio, he worked at a Hebrew grammar in the Hebrew language, the greater part of which was translated into Latin by Reuchlin's pupil, Sebastian Münster. Elias Levita had not a mind of great depth, nor did he propound a new theory on the structure of the Hebrew language. He rigorously adhered to the grammatical system of the Kimchis, because he did not know their predecessors. His usefulness consisted in his command over the whole Scriptural vocabulary, his pedagogic skill, and his gift of vivid presentation. Beyond the elements he did not go, but they perfectly satisfied the wants of the time. Only one deviation did Levita make from the beaten track. Against the firm belief of the time that the accents and the vowel signs in the Hebrew Bible were of ancient origin, having been revealed on Mount Sinai, or, at all events, introduced by Ezra, he maintained that they had not been known even at the time of the Talmud, because they had been superfluous when Hebrew was a living language. It can easily be imagined what a storm this opinion raised. It at once upset all preconceived notions. The bigots raised a cry against him as though he had by his assertion disowned Judaism. Elias Levita was, therefore, little liked by his brother

Jews, and associated more with learned Christians, which brought much blame from the over-pious, and produced evil consequences for his descendants.

He was not the only teacher of the Hebrew language and literature to Christians. As before him, Obadiah Sforno had given Reuchlin instruction in Hebrew, so at the same time as Levita, Jacob Mantino and Abraham de Balmes were engaged in instructing Christians.

Throughout Christendom there was a desire to know the Hebrew language. The printers reckoned on such good sales that in several places in Italy and Germany, even where there were no Jews, new and old Hebrew grammatical writings were published. Everyone wished to know Hebrew and to understand the Hebrew language and literature. Some years before the representatives of the church had considered the knowledge of Hebrew superfluous, or even a pernicious evil touching on heresy; but through the Reformation it became a necessary branch of divinity. Luther himself learnt Hebrew to be able to penetrate the meaning of the Bible.

The change of mind was most evident in France. The Paris university, the leader of thought, had by a majority condemned Reuchlin's "Augenspiegel" in favor of the Talmud and Hebrew studies; scarcely six years later there was a professorship and a printing press for Hebrew, and the confessor of King Louis, William Haquinet Petit, though a Dominican, the one whose slander had brought about the condemnation of Reuchlin's work, appeared as a patron of Hebrew literature.

At his advice King Francis I invited the bishop of Corsica, Augustin Justiniani, a man well read in Hebrew literature, to come to France. This young king felt, or at least showed, interest in learning and also in the study of Hebrew. He invited Elias Levita to come to France, and fill the professorship of Hebrew there, probably at the instigation of his admirer, De Selve. One must take into consideration what this signified at that time. In France proper, for more than a century, no Jew had been permitted to dwell, nor even to make a passing stay, and now a Jew was invited, not merely to reside there, but to accept an honorable post and instruct Christians. What heresy! Elias Levita, however, declined this flattering proposal; he would not have felt at ease there as the only Jew, and to urge the admission of Jews into France was not in conformity with his character. Justiniani undertook the task of introducing the study of Hebrew into France.

At the University of Rheims the French students made attempts to speak Hebrew. As there were not sufficient grammars, Justiniani had the wretched Hebrew grammar of Moses Kimchi printed. Yet more remarkable is it that in Paris, where three hundred years previously the Jewish orthodox party, with the help of the Dominicans, had burnt Maimuni's religious philosophical work, "Guide of the Perplexed," the Dominican Justiniani now caused a Latin translation of the same to be published (1520). Naturally, the Christian teachers of the Hebrew language remained dependent on their Jewish masters; they could not take a single step without them. Paulus Fagius, a reforming priest and disciple of Reuchlin, wishing to establish a Hebrew press in Isny, called upon Elias Levita to go there. This offer was accepted, for Levita was in difficulties, and could find no publisher for his Chaldean and Rabbinical dictionaries. Paulus Fagius was particularly pleased with these works, because they appeared to him to offer the key to the Kabbala, so much sought for by Christian scholars.

Through the agitation by Reuchlin and Luther the neglected science of the Bible was to a certain extent cultivated. Judaism and Christianity are both founded on the Sacred Writings, yet they were quite strange to the followers of both religions.

The glorious memorial of a much favored time was so shrouded and surrounded with a network of senseless explanations, so disfigured by these accessories, that its full value was completely unknown. Because everything was looked for in, and imported into, the Holy Scriptures, the true meaning was not discovered. To the Christian laity the Bible had been inaccessible for a long time, because the papacy, with instinctive fear, had forbidden its translation into the vernacular. So the faithful knew only fragments or isolated texts, and, owing to distorted interpretations, these not always correctly. Even the clergy were not familiar therewith, for they were acquainted only with the Roman Catholic Latin version, and in this the fundamental truths of the Bible were confused by perversions and errors. It was, therefore, a work of great importance that occupied Luther in his solitude on the Wartburg—the translation of the Bible, the Old and New Testaments, into German. For this purpose Luther had to learn Hebrew, and seek information from Jews. To his contemporaries it seemed as if God's Word had for the first time been revealed; this clear voice they had never before heard. A breath of fresh air was wafted on men, when the ramparts were broken down that had so long held its spirit imprisoned. Classical antiquity had improved the taste of a small circle. Hebrew antiquity rejuvenated the whole generation, once more infusing love of simplicity and naturalness. The Bible was soon translated into all European languages; the Catholics themselves were obliged to disregard the papal command, and render it into intelligible language for the people's use. The Jews also felt the want of the Holy Scripture in the vernacular. A translation into Spanish was made in Ferrara, by a Marrano, Duarte de Pinel, who had escaped from Portugal, and called himself Abraham Usque as a Jew.

The demand for Hebrew Bibles was so great that

Daniel Bomberg undertook the great work of publishing the Old Testament, with the commentaries of Rashi, Ibn-Ezra, Kimchi, Gersonides, and others. The sale of this rabbinical Bible was so rapid that new editions were continually appearing.

CHAPTER XV.

THE KABBALA AND MESSIANIC FANATICISM. THE MARRANOS AND THE INQUISITION.

Internal Condition of Judaism—Division in the Communities—The Lack of Interest in Poetry—Historical Studies—Leon Medigo's "Dialogues of Love"—Supremacy of the Kabbala—Messianic Hopes—The Marranos and the Inquisition—Henrique Nunes—The Traveler David Reubeni in Rome—Solomon Molcho—His Relations with David Reubeni—Joseph Karo and his "Maggid"—Clement VII—Molcho in Ancona and Rome—His Favor with the Cardinals—Death of Molcho—The Enthusiastic Regard in which he was held—Duarte de Paz—Paul III—Charles V and the Jews—Emanuel da Costa.

1500—1538 C.E.

It is astonishing, yet not astonishing, that the surging movement, the convulsive heaving that shook the Christian world from pole to pole in the first quarter of the sixteenth century scarcely touched the inner life of the Jews. Whilst among Christians a radical change took place, in thought, customs, studies, and even in language; whilst their ancient customs and usages were rejected or put aside in some places, and in others freshened up; in a word, whilst a new era started, everything remained unchanged with the Jews. Having had no "Middle Ages," they needed no new epoch. They needed no regeneration, they had no immoral course of life to redress, no cankering corruption to cure, no dam to raise against the insolence and rapacity of their spiritual guides. They had not so much rubbish to clear away. It must not be imagined, however, that within the pale of Judaism all was bright. The refining and civilizing thoughts of Judaism had not yet gained the upper hand. The people were wanting in spirituality, their guides in clearness of mind. Reliance on justification by works and scholastic sophistry were prevalent also among Jews. In the synagogue service spirituality was missing, and honesty in the world of business. The ritual retained all received from olden times, and became filled with unintelligible elements, so that, on the whole, it acquired an unattractive character. Sermons were unknown in German congregations and their offshoots; at best, Talmudical discourses, utterly unintelligible to the people, especially to women, and, therefore, leaving them cold and uninterested, were delivered. The Spanish and Portuguese preachers spoke in the beautiful language of their country, but their sermons were so full of pedantry that they were no more easily understood by the laity.

The breaking up of Jewish congregations into national groups was also a misfortune. The persecution of the Jews had thrown into the large towns of Italy and Turkey fugitives from the Pyrenees and from Germany, who failed to unite themselves with the existing congregations, yet did not amalgamate with each other. There were, therefore, in many towns, not only Italian, Romanic (Greek), Spanish, Portuguese, German, and, now and again, Moorish (African) congregations, but of each almost as many as there were provinces and towns in each country. For example, in Constantinople, Adrianople, Salonica, Arta (Larta) in Greece, and many other towns, there was a large variety of congregations, each of which had its own directors, ritual, rabbi, academy, charities, its own prejudices and jealousies. In the face of such division, nothing for the public benefit or general good could be accomplished. The spiritual leaders, although generally moral, and, as a rule, sincerely and fervently religious, humbled themselves before the rich members of their congregation, witnessing insolence and misconduct without daring to reprove them.

Worse than this splitting up into tiny congregations was the faintness, the narrow-mindedness, the self-abasement, not merely of German Jews, but of the Sephardic exiles. Only when it was necessary to die for the faith of their fathers did they show themselves heroic and full of courage; at other times their activity was expended on petty concerns. No new course was taken, not even at sight of the daily changes of the Christian world. The few who maintained themselves on the heights of science kept to the beaten track, served but to level it still more. The ruling idea was to elucidate old thoughts and old thinkers, and to write commentaries, yea, even super-commentaries. The Talmudists explained the Talmud, and the philosophical inquirers Maimuni's "Guide." Higher flight of fancy and greater spiritual insight were not possible. No sound of real poetry came from the lips of those nourished on it, not even a thrilling song of lamentation, putting their grief into words. The only circumstance testifying to change of position and times was interest in historical research, and that was almost entirely confined to the Jews of Pyrenean descent. The endless suffering which they had endured, they wished to preserve for future generations. Present misery brought before them the sorrows of early ages, and showed them that the history of the Jewish race was one long course of painful martyrdom.

Otherwise there was nothing new at this period. Freedom of philosophical inquiry was not favored. Isaac Abrabanel, the transmitter of the old Spanish Hebrew spirit, found in Maimuni's philosophical writings many heresies opposed to Judaism, and he condemned the free-thinking commentators who went beyond tradition. A Portuguese fugitive, Joseph Jaabez, laid on philosophy the blame for the expulsion of the Jews from Spain and Portugal. Free-thinking was the sin which had led Israel astray; thereon must the greatest restriction be laid.

A fresh spirit breathes in the philosophical work of the talented Leon Abrabanel, or Medigo. Its title, "Dialogues of Love" (Dialoghi d'amore), tells the reader that it is not tainted with the insipidity of commonplace philosophy. No one can better show the elasticity of the Jewish mind than this scion of the ancient noble family of Abrabanel. Torn from a comfortable home, thrown into a strange land, leading an unsettled life in Italy, his heart tortured by gnawing pain for the living death of his first-born, who had been snatched from him, Leon Medigo had enough intellectual strength to immerse himself in the Italian language and literature, and reduce his scattered philosophical ideas to perfect order. Hardly ten years after his flight from Spain he might have passed for a learned Italian, rivaling in style the polished writers of the Medici era, and even excelling them in extent of learning. With the same pen with which he wrote Hebrew verses to his son, who was being educated in sham Christianity in Portugal, admonishing him, "Remain continually mindful of Judaism, cherish the Hebrew language and literature, and keep ever before thee the grief of thy father, the pain of thy mother," he wrote his "Dialogues of Love," the outpourings of Philo's deep love for Sophia. This ostensible romance is the keynote of Leon Medigo's philosophical system, which sounds more like a philosophical idyll than a logical system. There is more imagination than reality, and his reflections are suggestive rather than true. Possibly Leon Medigo put his deeper thoughts into a work, now lost, entitled the "Harmony of Heaven." His "Dialogues of Love" throughout was far removed from Judaism. Leon Medigo paid high honor to "Hebrew truth," and endeavored to uphold the scriptural doctrine of creation out of chaos, in opposition to the principles of Greek philosophy, but he did not penetrate to the true spirit of Judaism. Therefore his work was valued by Christians more than by Jews. The Italians were proud to see—it was the first time—philosophical thought laid down in their own enthusiastically beloved language. The work became the favorite reading of the educated class, and in the space of twenty years went through five editions.

The Kabbala with its futilities soon took possession of minds no longer accustomed to strict logical discipline, and in a measure it filled the void. In the sixteenth century it first began to have sway over men's minds. Its adversaries were dead, or indisposed to place themselves in opposition to the ideas of the age, only too strongly inclined to mysteries, paradoxes and irrational fancies. Sephardic fugitives, Judah Chayyat, Baruch of Benevento, Abraham Levi, Meïr ben Gabbai, Ibn-Abi Zimra, had brought the Kabbala to Italy and Turkey, and with extraordinary energy won zealous adherents for it. Also, the enthusiasm felt for the Kabbala by Christian scholars, such as Egidio de Viterbo, Reuchlin, Galatino, and others, reacted upon the Jews. The doctrine, they reasoned, must have some deep truth in it, if it is so sought for by noble Christians. Preacher-Kabbalists expounded the doctrine from the pulpit, which had not been done before. On questions of ritual the Kabbalist writings were consulted, often as final authorities. No wonder that typical elements of the Zohar crept into the liturgy, conferring upon it a mystical character. With bold presumption the Kabbalists asserted that they alone were in possession of the Mosaic tradition, and that the Talmud and the rabbis must give place to them. In this way the secret doctrine with its tricks and fancies, which had hitherto unsettled only some few adepts, became known amongst all the Jews, and affected the sober minds of the people. The opposition of the rabbis to this interference in the ritual and religious life was rather weak, as they themselves were convinced of the sanctity of the Kabbala, and objected to the innovations only in a faint-hearted way.

The empty Kabbala could not fail to arouse enthusiasm in empty heads. With the Zoharist mystics, as with the Essenes, the expectation of the Messiah was the center of their system. To further the kingdom of the Messiah, or the kingdom of Heaven, or the kingdom of morality, and to predict, by means of letters and numbers, the exact time of its advent, was the labor in which they delighted. Isaac Abrabanel, although he did not favor the Kabbala, gave this Messianic enthusiasm his countenance. The accumulated sufferings of the few remaining Spanish and Portuguese Jews had broken the spirit of many, and robbed them of their hope of better times. The hopelessness and despair of his people, which, if they spread, would further the plans of the church, pained the faithful Isaac Abrabanel, and in order to counteract this dangerous tendency, he prepared three works, based upon the Bible (principally the Book of Daniel) and Agadic sayings, which, he believed, proved incontrovertibly that Israel would have a glorious future, and that a Messiah would unfailingly come. According to his reckoning, the advent of the Messiah must of necessity be in the year 1503, 5263 years after the creation of the world, and the end would come with the fall of Rome, about twenty-eight years later.

The support given to Messianic calculations by so thoughtful and respected a man as Isaac Abrabanel, together with Kabbalistic fancies, seems to have encouraged an enthusiast to predict the immediate realization of Messianic ideals. A German, Asher Lämmlein (or Lämmlin), appeared in Istria, near Venice, proclaiming himself a forerunner of the Messiah (1502). He announced that if the Jews would show great repentance, mortification, contrition and charity, the Messiah would not fail to come in six months. The people's minds, prepared by suffering and the Kabbalist craze, were susceptible to such convulsive expectations. Asher Lämmlein gained a troop of adherents, who spread his prophecies. In Italy and Germany he met with sympathy and belief. There was much fasting, much praying, much distribution of alms. It was called the "year of penitence." Everyone prepared himself for the beginning of the miracle. They counted so surely on redemption and return to Jerusalem that existing institutions were wilfully destroyed. The sober and thoughtful did not dare check this wild fanaticism. Even Christians are said to have believed in Asher Lämmlein's Messianic prophecy. But the prophet died, or suddenly disappeared, and with him the extravagant hopes came to an end.

But with the termination of the Lämmlein "year of penitence," the Jews by no means lost their hope in the Messiah; it was necessary to support them in their misery. The Kabbalists did not cease arousing this hope, ever and anon promising them its wonderful realization. Thirty years later a more important Messianic movement commenced, which, by reason of its extent and the persons implicated in it, was most interesting. The Marranos in Spain and Portugal played the principal part in it.

These most unfortunate of all unfortunates, who renounced the faith of their people, who in a measure estranged themselves from their own hearts, who were compelled to observe church rites most punctiliously, though they hated them in the depth of their souls, yet despite all this were repelled by the Inquisition and the hatred of Christians—these converts suffered, without exaggeration, the tortures of hell. The greater portion of them, in spite of all their struggles, could not bring themselves to love Christianity. How could they feel love for a creed whose followers daily required the sacrifice of human life, and on the slightest pretext sought victims among new-Christians? Under Deza, the second

Spanish chief inquisitor, almost greater horrors were perpetrated than 'under Torquemada. He and his tools, in particular Diego Rodriguez Lucero, a pious hangman in Cordova, had committed so many infamies that a good monk, Peter Martyr, pictured the Inquisition thirty years after its origin in glaring colors: "The archbishop of Seville (Deza), Lucero, and Juan de la Fuente have dishonored this province. Their people acknowledge neither God nor justice. They kill, steal, and violate women and maidens, to the disgrace of religion. The injury and unhappiness which these servants of the Inquisition have caused in my land are so great and widespread that everyone must grieve." Lucero (the luminous), called by his confederates, on account of his horrible deeds, Tenebrero (the dark one), brought destruction on thousands: he was insatiable for the blood of Hebrew martyrs. "Give me Jews to burn," is said to have been his constant cry. His fanaticism degenerated into cannibalistic fury.

The officers of the Inquisition had their hands full in consequence of his cruelty, and an ominous disturbance was growing in Cordova. The principal people of the place complained of the proceedings of the inquisitor Lucero, and applied to the chief inquisitor to have him removed from office. But Deza was at one with him, and so the discontented knights, nobles, donnas, priests and nuns, were all accused of favoring Jewish heresy. The third chief .inquisitor, Ximenes de Cisneros, was forbearing towards old Christians suspected of Judaizing, but condemned not a few converts of Jewish and Moorish descent to be burned. It was he who used threatening language against Charles V, when he proposed granting the Spanish Marranos freedom of belief for a fee of 800,000 gold crowns. He forbade his royal pupil to tolerate the Jews, as Torquemada had forbidden it to Charles' ancestors. His successors were not less orthodox, that is to say, not less inhuman.

Under them the victims were not Jews alone; Christians suffered with them. The reform movement in Germany was felt also in Spain. Luther's and Calvin's onslaught on the papacy, on priestcraft and ceremonies was brought over the Pyrenees through the connection of Spain and Germany, and owing to the nationality of Emperor Charles V. The emperor, so troubled with the Reformation in Germany, empowered the Holy Office to proceed against Lutheran doctrines in Spain, a most welcome task to the bloodthirsty monster. Henceforth, Jews, Mahometans and Lutheran Christians enjoyed equality; at every auto-da-fé martyrs of the three different religions perished together.

The Marranos in Portugal were differently placed from those in Spain. King Manoel, who had by force dragged the Jews to the baptismal font, in order not to drive them to despair had pledged his word that for twenty (or twenty-nine) years, their faith should not suffer molestation at the hands of the Inquisition. Relying on this promise the Portuguese Marranos followed Jewish observances with less secrecy than those of Spain. In Lisbon, where they mostly resided, they had a synagogue, in which they assembled, the more regularly as they outwardly complied with the Roman Catholic rites, and, therefore, in their own place of worship, with much contrition, implored forgiveness of God for their idolatry. The old instructed the young in the Bible and the Talmud, and impressed upon them the truths of Judaism, so as to guard them against the temptation of unreserved acceptance of Christianity. The Portuguese Marranos also had more freedom to emigrate, and left singly or in numbers for Barbary or Italy, and thence went on to Turkey. To check the emigration of the Marranos Manoel had issued an order that a Christian could conclude an exchange or barter with a convert only under pain of forfeiting his possessions, and could buy real estate from him only by royal permission; moreover, that no Marrano, with wife, children and servants, should leave the land without a special license from the king. But orders of this description were made only to be evaded. Spanish Marranos had every reason to envy their fellows in Portugal, and spared no trouble to escape beyond the frontier of the land where the stake was ready, and the fagots lighted for them. Very naturally the vindictive Spanish government opposed them, and induced Manoel to pass a law that no Spaniard could step on Portuguese soil unless he brought a certificate that he was not guilty of heresy.

The Portuguese Marranos, then, would have had a tolerable existence if popular hatred of them had not been so fierce. This unfriendliness after their baptism shows that they were hated less as followers of Judaism than as a different race, and an active, industrious, superior class. The Christians' dislike of them increased when the converts obtained the right of pursuing a trade, of collecting church tithes, of taking office, or even accepting ecclesiastical dignities preparatory to entering one of the orders. At first they showed their hatred by calling them insulting names, "cursed convert of a Jew" (*Judæo Marrano, converso*), till Manoel stopped this by law. Bad harvests, which for many years had brought famine into Portugal, now resulted in a plague, and this added fuel to popular animosity. It was commonly said, "The baptized Jews are grain speculators; they make the necessaries of life dear, and export grain to foreign countries." The person most hated was a Marrano upstart, John Rodrigo Mascarenhas, the farmer of taxes, and through him all the Marranos incurred hatred.

This feeling was employed by the crafty Dominicans to gain the expulsion of the favorites of King Manoel. They not only preached about the godlessness of the converts, but invented a miracle outright to excite the fanaticism of the people. The moment was opportune. The plague raged in Portugal, and swept away thousands daily, while continued drought threatened another bad harvest. Of these troubles, the Marranos alone were the cause, at least so everybody said. The Dominicans loudly proclaimed that, in one of their churches, in a mirror attached to a cross, the Virgin Mary had appeared in a glow of fire, and other astonishing miracles had been seen in it. They were practiced in such deceit. Many people flocked to the church to behold the marvel. On a Sunday after Easter (April 19th, 1506), the church was filled with devotional gazers, among them Marranos, who were compelled to attend.

A Dominican, in a passionate sermon, charged the people collected in the church to murder the accursed converts, because the king favored them; and two others, John Mocho and Fratre Bernardo, walked through the street, bearing crosses, and, crying "Heresy, heresy!" The scum of the populace in the turbulent capital was aroused, and, together with German, Dutch and French sailors, took this opportunity to plunder. Thus nearly 10,000 people went through the town, and killed Marranos, men, women and children, wherever they found them, in the streets, in the houses, or in hiding.

This, however, by no means ended the massacre; it continued two days longer. A German, who was in Lisbon, reported: "On Monday I saw things dreadful to say or write if one has not seen them." Women with child were flung from the windows and caught on spears by those standing underneath, and their offspring hurled away. The peasantry followed the example of the townspeople. Many women and girls were violated in this fanatical chase. The number of new-Christians slain is estimated at between 2,000 and 4,000.

By this slaughter the fate of the Portuguese Marranos was decided. The people were the more embittered against them because they had gained the favor of the king, and they longed for their extermination. Their lives hung on the chance of the continuance of the king's favor. Manoel declared by proclamation (March, 1507) that converts were to be treated as Christians, and that they should be permitted to emigrate; and by another order, that for sixteen years more they should not be liable to be arraigned before a tribunal for their religious conduct. The Christian population remained hostile to the converts, from racial antipathy and from envy of their industrial success, and Manoel himself was compelled to modify his attitude towards them.

The condition of the Portuguese Marranos changed under Manoel's successor João III (1522—1557), the blockhead who brought about the ruin of his country. As Infante he had been the declared enemy of the new-Christians. At first he respected his father's edict to place converted Jews on a par with Christians, and to allow no trial to take place regarding their religious belief within the prescribed time (1522—1524). For this indulgence the Marranos had to thank the old counselors of Manoel, who remembered the violent mode of their conversion, and on the other hand appreciated how much they had increased the prosperity of the little state. For the Marranos were a most useful class on account of their energy, their wholesale business, their public banks, and their skill as armorers and cannon founders. They were the only ones, too, possessed of a knowledge of medicine and physical science and all pertaining to it. There were in Portugal hardly any but Jewish, that is to say, Marrano physicians. When, however, other influences were brought to bear on João, and he gradually freed himself from these wise counselors, his fanatical detestation of the converts gained the upper hand. Queen Catherine, a Spanish Infanta, filled with admiration of the religious tribunal of her country, and the bloodthirsty Dominicans, envious of the power of their order in Spain, besieged the king with complaints of the disgraceful and wicked conduct of the Marranos towards the Christian faith, and urged him to put a stop to the proceedings of the Marranos by instituting an Inquisition. João III thereupon commissioned George Themudo to inquire into the life of the Marranos in Lisbon, their headquarters, and to report to him upon it. Themudo was probably not far from the truth when he informed the king (July, 1524) that some Marranos observed the Sabbath and the Passover, that, on the other hand, they joined in Christian rites and ceremonies as little as possible, were not present at mass and divine service, did not go to confession, did not ask that extreme unction be administered to the dying, were buried in unconsecrated ground, not in a churchyard, that they had no masses said for their departed relatives, and committed other offenses of a similar character.

But João was not satisfied with Themudo's report; the Marranos were put under an espionage system. A convert, an emigrant from Spain, named Henrique Nunes, who afterwards received from the church the honorary title Firme-Fé, was chosen by the king to spy upon them. In the school of the bloodthirsty Lucero he had acquired a fierce hatred of the Marranos, and it was his ardent wish to see the fagots kindled in Portugal. To him the king gave secret instructions to insinuate himself into the families of the converts, to associate with them as a brother and companion in adversity, to observe them and report upon all the information he could gain. Blinded by fanaticism and hatred of his own race, Nunes did not consider how contemptible a rôle, that of a common spy, was allotted to him. He undertook the work only too willingly, learned all the secrets of the unhappy Marranos in Lisbon, Evora and other places, and communicated all that he saw and heard in letters to the king. He betrayed with a brother's kiss those who showed him the hidden corners of their hearts. He informed the king not only that he found no Catholic prayer-books in their houses, that they had no holy images among their ornaments or on their plate, that they did not care for rosaries and other things of that kind, but he gave the names of the Jewish Marranos, making hateful accusations against them. As soon as João received the desired intelligence, he resolved to introduce the Inquisition on the Spanish model into his country, and secretly sent the trusty Nunes to Charles V in Spain to learn something more about it. The Marranos had got wind of this, and were so furious with the treacherous spy, that two of them followed him to punish his perfidy with death. These were Diego Vaz, of Olivença, and André Dias, of Vianna, who were Franciscans, or disguised themselves in monks' dress. They reached him not far from the Spanish frontier, near Badajoz, and killed him with sword and spear. They found letters on him about the installation of the Inquisition. The avengers, or murderers, as the orthodox Christians called them, were discovered, brought to trial, stretched on the rack to betray their accomplices, and finally condemned to the gallows. But the traitor Nunes was regarded as a martyr, almost canonized, and given the honorary title of "Firme-Fé" (Firm Believer).

One would have expected the fanatical king after this occurrence to pursue with greater zeal his object of establishing an Inquisition, so as to proceed against the Jewish Marranos whose names he had obtained from Nunes. The king did, indeed, institute a strict inquiry to discover the accomplices of the two Marrano monks. Contrary to expectation

João issued no restrictions against the Marranos. Also the inquiry about the conspirators for Nunes' death seems to have been intentionally protracted as much as possible. Documents plainly say that the king gave up the plan of establishing the Inquisition. A chance, the boldness of an adventurer, appears in the first instance to have brought about this favorable alteration in the mind of the weak, vacillating king.

Coming from the far East, and emerging from obscurity, appeared a man of whom it is hard to say whether he was an impostor or a foolish fanatic, and whether he intended to play the rôle of a Messianic or of a political adventurer, but he caused a great stir among Jews, affecting the Marranos in the extreme West. David, an Oriental by descent, long resident in Arabia and Nubia, suddenly appeared in Europe in a peculiar character, and by means of both fiction and truth started the wildest hopes. He declared himself a descendant of the old Hebrew tribe of Reuben, which, he alleged, still flourished in Arabia in independence, and he claimed to be a prince, the brother of a reigning Jewish king. He, therefore, called himself David Reubeni.

Loving travel and adventure, he journeyed much in Arabia, Nubia and Egypt, and came finally to Italy. The report was that he had been sent by his brother, who commanded 300,000 chosen warriors, and by the seventy elders of the land of Chaibar, to the European princes, especially to the pope, to obtain firearms and cannon with which to fight the Mahometan people, who hindered the union of the Jewish race on both sides of the Red Sea, and to assist the brave Jewish army to drive the Turks out of the Holy Land.

David Reubeni's appearance and manner were such as to inspire confidence. In both, there was something strange, mysterious and eccentric. He was of dark complexion and dwarfish in stature, and so excessively thin that continuous fasts reduced him almost to a skeleton. Possessed of courage and intrepidity, he had at the same time a harsh manner that admitted of no familiarity. He only spoke Hebrew, and that in so corrupt a jargon that neither Asiatic Jews nor those of southern Europe understood him. He came to Rome (February, 1524), and accompanied by a servant and an interpreter, rode on a white horse to the Vatican, and requested an interview with Cardinal Giulio, in the presence of other cardinals. Pope Clement also gave him audience, and accepted his credentials.

Clement VII (1523—1534), one of the most excellent popes, an illegitimate scion of the Florentine Medicis, was sensible and kind, and earnestly desired to see Italy freed from the barbarians, that is, the Germans. But he reigned at a time when Europe had lost its balance. On the one side Luther and his Reformation, which gained ground daily, threatened to undermine the papacy; and on the other, Charles V's powerful realm, Spain and Germany with Burgundy and a part of America, almost crushed Italy into servile dependence. If Clement quarreled with the emperor, the latter favored the Reformation, and set about restraining the papal power. If the pope became reconciled to him, the liberty of Italy was menaced. Thus, notwithstanding his firm character, he was continually wavering, and like most of his contemporaries had recourse to astrology, in order to learn from the stars what was beyond the wisdom of men.

To Pope Clement VII, David Reubeni seems to have handed letters of introduction from Portuguese captains or business agents, whom he may have met in Arabia or Nubia. These credentials the pope sent to the Portuguese court, and when they were there declared trustworthy, David was treated with the greatest distinction, and received all the honors due an ambassador. He rode through Rome on a mule, accompanied by ten Jews and more than two hundred Christians. The plan of a crusade against Turkey, by which the most dangerous enemy of Christianity would be driven out of the Holy Land by an Israelitish army, attracted the pope, because it promised to restore to him the control of military affairs, but its execution was thwarted by the complexities of his position. Even the most incredulous of the Jews could not conceal from themselves the astonishing fact that a Jew was treated with respect and politeness by the Vatican, and were convinced that there must be at least a grain of truth in David's report. Roman and foreign Jews pressed round him who seemed to open a hopeful future to them. Señora Benvenida Abrabanela, wife of the rich Samuel Abrabanel, sent him great sums of money from Naples, a costly silk banner embroidered with the Ten Commandments, and many rich garments. He, however, played his part in a masterly manner, keeping the Jews at a respectful distance.

At length a formal invitation came from the king of Portugal, summoning David Reubeni to his court. The latter left Rome, traveling by sea with a Jewish flag on his ship. In Almeirin, the residence of king João III near Santarem, where David arrived, like a wealthy prince, with a numerous retinue bearing beautifully embroidered banners, he was also treated with the greatest honor, and a scheme was discussed with him as to how the weapons and cannons could be transported from Portugal for the Israelite army in Arabia and Nubia. David's appearance in Portugal seems to have changed the feeling towards the Marranos, and João was persuaded to give up the intended persecution of them. For so great an undertaking João would need their support, their money and their advice. If he wished for an alliance with the Hebrew king and people, he must not persecute the half-Jews in his own country. So his zeal for the establishment of the Inquisition in Portugal suddenly cooled. One can imagine the astonishment and joy of the Marranos in Portugal, when they understood that not only might a Jew be admitted into Portugal, but that he was received at court, and treated with respect. Thus, then, had come the hour of deliverance of which they had so long dreamed. Unexpected help had come to them, freedom and deliverance from their anguish; they breathed again. Whether or not David Reubeni had declared himself the forerunner of the Messiah, did not matter to the Marranos; they believed it, and counted the days to the time when he would make them behold the new Jerusalem in all its splendor. They pressed round him, kissed his hands, and treated him as if he were their king. From Portugal the supposed message of salvation passed to Spain to the still more unfortunate Marranos there, who received it with ecstasies of joy. These poor people had fallen into a morbid, eccentric, irresponsible state of mind. Daily and hourly they suffered torments of soul, through having to join in religious customs which they abhorred with their whole heart. It was no wonder that many of them lost their mental balance, and became quite mad. In the vicinity of Herrara, a Marrano maiden proclaimed herself a prophetess; fell into trances and had visions; declared that she had seen Moses and the angels, and promised to lead her suffering companions into the Holy Land. She found many believers among the Marranos, and when this was discovered, she was burned together with thirty-eight adherents. Messianic expectation, that is, redemption through a miracle, made the atmosphere in which the Marranos breathed and lived. At the news of the arrival of an ambassador from a Jewish kingdom at the Portuguese court, a crowd of Spanish converts fled to Portugal to be near their supposed redeemer. David, who enjoyed the privilege of traveling about in Portugal, appears to have behaved very circumspectly: he gave them no promises, and did not encourage them openly to acknowledge Judaism. He knew well that he was walking on the edge of a precipice, and that one expression, one act of his directed towards bringing back new-Christians to Judaism might cost him his life. Nevertheless, all eyes were fastened on him; all were aroused and excited by the wonderful events which would certainly come to pass.

David Reubeni's appearance and the hopes it awakened took strongest hold upon one noble, talented, handsome youth; indeed, the whole course of his existence was changed. Diogo Pires (born about 1501, died a martyr, 1532), whose glowing, poetic imagination under more favorable circumstances might have accomplished much in the domain of the beautiful, became a tool in the hands of the self-proclaimed envoy from Chaibar. Pires, who was born a new-Christian, had acquired a good education; he understood and could speak Latin, the universal language of the time. He had risen to be royal secretary at a high court of justice, and was a great favorite at court. With Hebrew and rabbinic literature he must have been familiar from his earliest youth, and he had been initiated into the Kabbala, probably by one of the Marrano teachers. At the time when David and his chimerical plans made so much stir in Portugal, Diogo Pires was completely possessed by wild dreams and visions, all of which had a Messianic background. He hastened, therefore, to David, to ascertain whether his mission was in accordance with these visionary revelations. David Reubeni appears to have treated him with coldness, and to have told him plainly that his military embassy had nothing to do with Messianic mysticism. But Diogo Pires fancied the coldness of the alleged envoy to be owing to the circumstance that he had not accepted the sign of the covenant, and he forthwith proceeded to undergo the dangerous operation of circumcision. The consequent loss of blood laid him on a sick bed. David was highly incensed when Pires told him of this, as both of them would be in danger, if it came to the king's ears that a Marrano had so emphatically and openly declared himself a Jew; for it would be asserted that David had persuaded him to take this course.

After circumcision Pires (who took the name of Solomon Molcho) had yet more terrible visions, owing presumably to his bodily weakness. Their import always had reference to the Marranos and their redemption by the Messiah. According to his own account a strange being (Maggid), who communed with him from Heaven in a dream, charged him to leave Portugal and set out for Turkey. David Reubeni also had advised that he should leave Portugal with all speed, as the act of circumcision might involve also David in danger, and frustrate his schemes. Leaving Portugal cannot, then, have been difficult for Marranos. Diogo Pires (or Solomon Molcho) reached Turkey, and hoped for a Messianic mission and a martyr's death.

A great sensation was made there by this enthusiastic, handsome young Kabbalist, the new Jewish recruit. At first he gave himself out as a delegate from David Reubeni, of whose good reception at the papal and Portuguese courts rumors were current even in the East, and had not failed to inflame people's imagination. In Salonica, Joseph Taytasak's Kabbalistic circle took possession of him, and greedily listened to his dreams and visions. At Adrianople Molcho converted to the Kabbala the sober-minded Joseph Karo, who had left Spain when a boy, and had hitherto busied himself entirely with Talmudic learning. Enthusiasm is infectious. Karo fell into the same Kabbalistic enthusiasm as Molcho.

He also had his dream-prompter (Maggid), who taught him inelegant, mystical interpretations of Scriptural passages, and revealed the future. He was so faithful an imitator that, like Molcho, he lived in the most certain expectation of being burnt at the stake as a "burnt-sacrifice of a sweet savour unto the Lord." Molcho inoculated his followers with a longing for martyrdom. His captivating person, pure enthusiasm, romantic disposition, past career, astonishing knowledge of the Kabbala (though born a Christian), everything connected with him, raised up a host of adherents, who greedily listened to his mystic utterances, and believingly accepted them. He often preached, and words flowed like a torrent from his lips. Gray-headed men went with questions to the youth, seeking explanations of obscure verses of Scripture, or revelations of the future. At the urgent request of his friends in Salonica he published a brief abstract of his Kabbalistic sermons, the substance of which was: The advent of the Messiah is at hand; his reign will begin at the end of the year 5300 dating from the creation (1540). The sack and havoc of Rome (May 5th, 1527), confirmed the Messianic hopes of Kabbalistic zealots. Rome, the iniquitous Catholic Babylon, filled with the spoils of the whole earth, was taken by storm by German soldiers, mostly Lutherans, and was treated almost as a hostile city by order of the Catholic emperor, Charles V. The fall of Rome, according to Messianic and apocalyptic principles, had been predicted as a sign of the Messiah's advent. Now Rome had fallen. In Asia, Turkey, Hungary, Poland, and Germany, hopes of the coming of the Messiah were stirring in Jewish hearts, and were associated with the name of Solomon Molcho, who was to bring about their realization.

In Spain and Portugal the Marranos held yet more firmly to their visions of Messianic redemption, and to David Reubeni, whom, with or without his consent, they took for a forerunner of the Messiah. Their illusion was so complete that they boldly inaugurated enterprises which could only end in death for themselves. Several Spanish Marranos, condemned to the stake, had curiously enough found a place of refuge in Portugal (in Campo-Mayor), where they were suffered to remain unmolested. A company of young people from among them ventured to attack Badajoz, whence they had fled, for the purpose of rescuing some Marrano women languishing in the Inquisition dungeons. Their irruption greatly alarmed the inhabitants, but they succeeded in rescuing the unfortunate victims. The incident made a great stir in both countries, and led to most prejudicial results for the pseudo-Christians. This occurrence, as well as the denunciation of several Marranos for disrespect to an image of the Virgin Mary, again induced the king to consider the scheme of establishing a court of Inquisition. David Reubeni's favor with the king of Portugal was of brief duration. He was at first received by João III with extraordinary friendliness, and often admitted to audience (when conversation was carried on by means of an Arab and Portuguese interpreter), and received the distinct promise that eight ships and 4,000 firearms should be placed at his disposal to enable his brother, the alleged king of Chaibar, to make war upon the Turks and Arabs; but the king gradually cooled down. Miguel de Silva, Portuguese ambassador at the papal court while David was at Rome, had held the alleged Jewish prince of Chaibar to be an adventurer. He was recalled to Portugal, and opposing the other councilors, who were deluded by David's daring character, made strenuous efforts to deprive him of the king's favor. Moreover, the homage so remarkably and openly offered to him by the Marranos had roused suspicion concerning him. Miguel de Silva, intrusted with the commission to establish the Inquisition in Portugal, pointed out that the king himself, by favoring the alleged Jewish prince, plainly fortified the Marranos in their unbelief, or adherence to the Jewish cause. Then came the circumcision and flight of the royal secretary, Diogo Pires (Solomon Molcho). This occurrence gave great offense at the Portuguese court, and it was insinuated to the king that David had been his abettor.

Thus it came to pass that David Reubeni suddenly received orders to quit Portugal after he had tarried there and been treated with distinction for nearly a twelvemonth. Only two months' grace before embarkation was granted him. The ship that carried him and his retinue was cast away on the Spanish coast, and David was taken prisoner in Spain, where he was forced to appear before the Inquisition. However, before that could take place, Emperor Charles set him free, and David Reubeni betook himself to Avignon, under papal jurisdiction. As soon as King João broke with David Reubeni, every reason for sparing the Marranos vanished. The vacillating king was hard-pressed by the queen, the Dominicans, and some of the nobles, to decide on introducing the Inquisition. The bishop of Ceuta, Henrique, formerly a Franciscan monk and a fanatical priest, brought about the decision. In his diocese of Olivença five new-Christians were suspected of Jewish practices. He made short work of them. Without greatly troubling as to whether the tribunal of the Inquisition was or was not sanctioned by the pope, and legally established by the king, he prepared stakes and fagots, and burnt the victims to death, having condemned them without regular trial (about 1530). The people jubilantly applauded him, and celebrated the murder of these Jewish-Christians with bull-fights. Far from wishing to hide his deed, Henrique boasted of it, and pressed the king to commence in earnest the chastisement of the heretical and sinful new-Christians. João decided to address himself to Pope Clement respecting the organization of commissions of inquiry in Portugal.

But there were still some priests left from the previous reign who loudly raised their voices against this violent treatment of the Marranos. Two especially deserve to have their names made known to posterity—Ferdinand Coutinho, bishop of Algarve, and Diogo Pinheiro, bishop of Funchal. They had been witnesses of the inhuman cruelties with which, under Manoel, the Jews were driven to baptism, and in no way could recognize them as Christians, neither when there was question of punishing them for relapsing into heresy, nor of intrusting them with judicial power or spiritual benefice. Coutinho, untiring in ridicule of the mistaken zeal of the younger priests, reminded the king that Pope Clement VII himself had not long before allowed several Marranos to acknowledge Judaism openly in the very city of Rome. This pope, convinced of the injustice shown to new-Christians, with the consent of the college of cardinals had given them an asylum at Ancona, permitting them freely to confess themselves Jews. In Florence and Venice also they could live without molestation. Nay, the papal consistory itself had given out that the Portuguese Marranos were to be regarded as Jews. He considered, so Coutinho expressed himself in his friendly consideration of the question, that instead of the new-Christians, accused of outraging what Christians hold sacred, the witnesses ought to be punished for bearing false testimony. The new-Christians should be won to the true faith only by gentle means. At length the king decided to submit the question to the pope, who, should he sanction the establishment of the Inquisition, would at the same time absolve him from the promises made to the Marranos. The Portuguese ambassador at Rome, Bras Neto, received orders to obtain a bull to that effect from the pope. But what so easily, by a stroke of the pen, had been conceded to Spain, cost the king of Portugal many efforts and a struggle, and he was never able fully to enjoy his Inquisition.

Now the weak hand of the amiable Kabbalist Solomon Molcho seized the spokes of this revolving wheel. From the East he had gone to Italy to fulfill the Messianic mission with which he was inspired, or with which he was credited. He wished to speak fearlessly before princes, in the capital of Christendom, of the approaching redemption. At Ancona, where he arrived with followers towards the end of 1529, certain malevolent persons, according to his own story, persecuted him. They were in fact prudent men, who were informed of his life in the East, and feared that, as a result of his impetuous striving for martyrdom, evil consequences would ensue for Jews all over the world, or at least for the Marranos in Italy, Portugal and Spain. Molcho, when cited, is understood to have confessed fearlessly that he preferred Judaism because it taught the truth. The bishop of Ancona discharged him as one of the Portuguese Marranos to whom freedom of religious confession had been allowed by the pope and the cardinals, but forbade him to preach against Christianity. Molcho remained some time at Ancona, where his preaching became very popular, even priests and Christians of the higher classes coming to the synagogue. However, he seems to have compromised himself, and in consequence repaired to Pesaro with the duke of Urbino, Francesco Maria della Rovere I, who thought a settlement of Marranos in his little state would be advantageous. But there was no rest for Molcho; he burnt with impatience to be at Rome to prepare the way for the coming of the Messiah, though without any clear conception of what to do. He waited for some prompting from on high, which, he believed, could not fail him. In obedience to a vision he abandoned his retinue at Pesaro, and set out alone on horseback for Rome. At the first sight of the Eternal City his feelings overcame him, for Molcho, like Luther, held Rome to be the seat of anti-Christ; he sank into fervent prayer, imploring redemption and forgiveness of sin for Israel. A voice broke in upon his prayer, predicting in verses of the Bible, "Edom (Rome) shall be the heritage of Israel, his foot shall be unsteady, but Israel will gain the victory." In this mood he entered Rome, and took up his abode at an inn kept by Christians. He put on a tattered suit, blackened his face, wrapped dirty rags around his feet, and leaving his horse and clothes at the inn, he took his stand among the tribe of beggars on the bridge over the Tiber, opposite the pope's palace. This equipment was in accordance with Messianic tradition, which had it that the Messiah would tarry amongst the lepers and ragged beggars of Rome, to be summoned thence to triumph. For thirty consecutive days the Portuguese enthusiast led this miserable existence, neither eating meat nor drinking wine, but contenting himself with the scantiest and poorest fare, and waiting for the prophetic ecstasy.

In this condition of bodily tension and mental exaltation, Molcho fell into a deep sleep, and had a confused dream, noteworthy because part of it was afterwards fulfilled to the very letter. It was predicted in this vision that a devastating flood would break over Rome and a northern country, and his native land be panic-stricken by an earthquake, that when he himself reached his thirtieth year he would be raised to a higher degree, and clad in Byssus, because of his own free will he had devoted himself to death. He would return to Rome, but leave it again before the flood took place. Then the Holy Spirit, the spirit of wisdom and understanding, would rest on the Messianic king, the dead would rise from the dust, and God give His people glory.

Next morning, enfeebled by his long mortification and his troubled sleep, Molcho dragged himself back to his inn, and rested. He laid aside his disguise, and went out to hold converse with Jews (February, 1530). Being still a complete stranger in Rome, and in order to avoid the denunciation of his opponents, he gave himself out as a messenger from Solomon Molcho. In spite of this he was recognized, and denounced to the Inquisition as a seditious Marrano. He had some time previously entered into intercourse with the pope and some of the cardinals, to whom he predicted the flood. Clement VII, who for several years had been drinking of the cup of sorrow, and experiencing humiliations such as had fallen to the lot of few popes before him, who had been forced to crown at Bologna his deadly enemy, Charles V, as king of Italy and emperor of Rome (February 22d—24th, 1530), was but too readily inclined to listen to dreams and visions. Other unknown relations may have existed between the pope and Molcho, in consequence of which the latter was regarded with surprising favor by the pope. Molcho had friends also among the cardinals. Lorenzo Pucci, for example, grand penitentiary of the papal see, who had taken Reuchlin's part against the Dominicans, was attached to him. Hence, while the papal police were lying in wait for Molcho, at the gates of Rome, he escaped over the walls, and hastened to the pope, from whom he obtained a pontifical passport that guaranteed him against harm.

Furnished with this, Molcho came back secretly to Rome, and one Saturday suddenly appeared in the chief synagogue, where, to the astonishment of all present, he preached on a text taken from the prophetical portion. His adherents in Rome increased so largely that he preached in the synagogue every Sabbath until autumn, without meeting with opposition. He inspired his hearers, yet seemed powerless to disarm his opponents. Molcho was the Jewish Savonarola. He spoke with unshakable certainty of his visions, and even announced to the king of Portugal (through the ambassador, Bras Neto) the earthquake which threatened Lisbon, so that precautionary measures might be taken. Molcho was himself so firmly convinced that the flood would come to pass that, when the predicted time approached, he went to Venice. Molcho and David Reubeni, who meanwhile had returned from Avignon to Italy, again met face to face. They looked at each other coldly and with amazement; each expected miracles from the other. Each desired the other to acknowledge his sublime mission. They were both embarrassed. Molcho's eyes were opened on this occasion to the true character of his once-admired master. He no longer believed in Reubeni's ignorance, but felt convinced that, Talmudic and Kabbalistic learning not being in keeping with his character as an Arabian prince, it was assumed by him in order to deceive people. Molcho even recanted his declaration that he was David's emissary. "Before the God of heaven and earth I proclaim the truth, that my circumcision and the abandonment of my country were not counseled by flesh and blood (David), but took place at the express command of God." Molcho was a deluded enthusiast, whereas David was an adventurer intentionally deceiving others. After his unsuccessful attempt to win over the king of Portugal and Charles V to his schemes, David went to Venice with the purpose of influencing the president of that republic, which had close relations with the East. Remarkably enough he found sympathy there; the Venetian senate sent a man well acquainted with the country to question him respecting his plan and means of conquest in the East (1530).

Both Molcho and David were harassed by the more temperate Jews, who apprehended danger for themselves and their religion. While at Venice Molcho was poisoned by Jewish hands, and fell into a dangerous illness.

Meanwhile the inundation of Rome predicted really took place, transforming the city into a stormy lake, and causing great havoc (October 8th, 1530). At the same time a brilliant comet appeared, shooting out rays of light till the heavens seemed about to open. In Portugal the earth shook thrice, and the earthquake destroyed a number of houses in Lisbon, many persons being buried beneath the ruins (January 26th, 1531).

After the inundation of Rome, Molcho again appeared in that city, where he was honored as a prophet. The pope, to whom he had predicted the calamity, seems to have lavished his affections upon him, and he bestowed public marks of honor upon him. The Portuguese ambassador, Bras Neto, told him that if the king of Portugal had known how favored a man in God's sight was Molcho, and how well able to read the future, he would have permitted him to dwell in his dominions. And this was the moment when the ambassador received the mandate from his sovereign to work secretly for a bull from the papal see introducing the Inquisition against the Marranos! A more unfavorable time could not have been chosen. The affair was laid for decision before the grand penitentiary, Cardinal Lorenzo Pucci. But the latter, as well as Pope Clement, influenced by Solomon Molcho, strongly opposed the proposal from the beginning. Pucci straightforwardly said to the Portuguese ambassador, "The king of Portugal, like the king of Spain, is more attracted by the Marranos' wealth than concerned about the orthodoxy of their creed; let him rather leave them free to live according to their own law, and punish only those who, after voluntarily embracing Catholicism, relapse to the Jewish faith." For the moment Bras Neto was powerless. He even feared Molcho's influence with the pope, and kept his doings secret, lest anything come to the ears of the Marranos in Portugal, and they supply Molcho with money wherewith to bribe the pope's retainers to work against the establishment of the Inquisition.

All this time Molcho was untiringly persecuted by his fellow-believers, more especially by his enemy, Jacob Mantin, the learned but unscrupulous physician and philologist. This revengeful man came from Venice to Rome for no other purpose than to cause the ruin of him whom he gratuitously hated. He took the Portuguese ambassador fairly to task for allowing a former Portuguese Christian, who preached against Christianity, to remain at liberty in Rome. As the ambassador would not listen to him, Mantin carried his complaint to the Inquisition. He procured witnesses from Portugal who testified that Solomon Molcho had lived as a Christian in Portugal, and managed to have him cited before the congregation. Hereupon Molcho exhibited his passport from the pope, trusting with such support to remain unmolested; but the Inquisitors tore it from his hands, and betook themselves to the pope, to whom they represented how indecent it was that he should protect a scoffer at Christianity. Clement replied that he needed Molcho for a secret purpose, and requested that he be left undisturbed. When the Inquisition showed itself inclined to disregard his denunciation, Mantin raised new points against Molcho He contrived to get possession of the letter which some years before Molcho had written from Monastir to Joseph Taytasak, respecting his past life and his return to Judaism, translated it into Latin, and laid it before the tribunal. As the letter undoubtedly contained abuse against Edom, *i.e.*, against Rome and Christianity, the Inquisition was forced to take notice of it, and Clement also no longer dared set his face against Mantin's denunciation. The congregation now proceeded with the case, and sentenced Molcho to be burnt to death. A funeral pile was built up, and the fagots kindled. People came in crowds to the place to witness the attractive sight. A wretched victim brought thither in penitential shroud was thrown without ceremony into the fire. One of the judges informed the pope that the act of faith had been completed by the offender's death. The judge and the witnesses of the execution are said to have felt no small astonishment when Solomon Molcho alive was encountered in the pope's apartments.

It seems that Clement, to save his favorite's life, foisted in some one else, who ascended the scaffold, whilst Solomon Molcho was kept hidden in the pope's chambers.

The pope himself communicated this fact to the perplexed judge, enjoining silence in order that Jews and Christians might not have fresh fuel to feed their excitement. Solomon Molcho was saved, but he dared no longer remain in Rome; that was plain even to him, and he begged the pope to let him go. Escorted by a few faithful servants of the pope, Solomon Molcho rode out of Rome at night (February or March, 1531).

After Molcho's departure from Rome, especially after the death of Cardinal Lorenzo Pucci (August, 1531), a different feeling towards the Marranos sprang up. A Portuguese agent obtained from the pope, who was urged thereto by Emperor Charles and the grand penitentiary, Antonio Pucci, the successor to his uncle, the bull establishing the Inquisition, so long prayed for (December 17th, 1531), although Cardinals Egidio de Viterbo, Elias Levita's disciple, and Geronimo de Ghinucci, had declared against it. As though this mild-tempered pope were ashamed of allowing his former *protégés* to be persecuted, he bracketed the Lutherans with them. He was careful, too, not to permit the fanatical

Dominicans to acquire power over the Marranos. The king's confessor, a Franciscan, the gentle-minded Diogo de Silva, was appointed inquisitor general of Portugal. Three tribunals were established, at Lisbon, Evora, and Coimbra, with the "Constitutions" of the Spanish courts introduced by Torquemada, and improved, that is, made severer, by his successors. After the king and the grandees had withdrawn their protection, the Portuguese Marranos were in a far worse plight than their Spanish brethren. The populace had long so hated them that even otherwise upright Christians turned informers, whereas in Spain spies had to be specially hired for the purpose.

When the Inquisition began its execrable work many of the Marranos naturally contemplated leaving the country. But flight was not easy; it was with them as with their forefathers when they came out of Egypt—the foe behind, the sea, with all its dangers and terrors, in front. A law was made (June 14th, 1532) strictly forbidding emigration to Africa, not even excepting the Portuguese colonies. Captains were warned, under penalty of death, not to carry Marranos, and all Christians were prohibited from buying real estate of new-Christians; these were not permitted to send their goods away to foreign countries, nor effect exchanges at home. Nevertheless, many of them prepared for emigration, in order "to flee from the land touched by the poisonous serpent (the Inquisition); but before they could even set foot on board ship, they and their wives and children were seized, and hurried away to gloomy dungeons, whence they were dragged to the stake. Others perished in the waves of the sea before they could reach the vessel which was to bring them to a place of safety. Many were drawn forth from the most hidden retreats, and burnt to death. Those who escaped from the claws of this bloodthirsty monster found no relief in strange lands—they were imprisoned in Flanders, arrested in France, unkindly received in England. In addition to such torments many lost their fortunes, and, in consequence, their lives. Those who reached Germany succumbed in extreme misery on the Alps, leaving wives about to become mothers, who, on cold and deserted roads, brought forth children, and endured a new form of misfortune."

Nevertheless, the Marranos did not intermit their attempts to escape, but prosecuted them with increased caution. No other way out of their troubles was left. Appeals to justice and humanity, and the urging of their chartered rights and privileges, found none but deaf ears in the cabinet.

Marranos who escaped to Rome made bitter complaints to Pope Clement of the inhumanity with which the Inquisition persecuted them and their brethren, and urged that the king had obtained the bull by fraud, inasmuch as the facts of the case had not been set before the papal consistory in a proper light. They especially complained that emigration was prohibited, in direct opposition to the legal equality which had been granted. Clement VII, who regretted that he had issued the bull, to which he had been forced, sympathized with their grievances. He may have felt, too, that the fires of the Inquisition, employed against those who were neither Catholics nor willing converts, branded the Catholic Church, and gave the Lutherans more material to continue their hostile assaults, to depict it as bloodthirsty and a just object of hatred. Moreover, he was well aware that the Inquisition had been introduced into Portugal only because Spain and his arch-foe, Emperor Charles, desired it, with the object of placing Portugal in an unequivocally dependent condition. Hence Clement revolved a plan to revoke the bull. At this time Solomon Molcho and David Reubeni resumed their mystical activity, and conceived the daring scheme of going to the emperor at Ratisbon, where the Reichstag was then assembled. With a floating banner, embroidered with the letters "Machbi" (initials of the Hebrew words of the verse, "Who is like unto thee among the gods, O Lord"), they traveled from Bologna, by way of Ferrara and Mantua, to Ratisbon. Emperor Charles gave them audience, and they probably pleaded the cause of the Jews earnestly. An unwarranted and improbable report affirms that they attempted to convert the emperor to the Jewish faith. But they were not so heedless as to make this attempt. They simply petitioned the emperor to permit the Marranos to arm themselves, and, joining the Jewish tribes, attack the Turks. Joslin of Rosheim, who was also in Ratisbon, vainly warned them not to make this request. The end was that Charles put them both in chains (June—September, 1532), and carried them fettered to Mantua. The banner was left at Ratisbon. An inquisition, at the emperor's wish, was set on foot at Mantua, and Molcho was condemned to be burnt to death for relapse and heresy. While the emperor was diverting himself by triumphal processions, festivals, hunting, plays, and all imaginable merrymakings, the funeral pile of the Lisbon Marrano was built up, and set on fire. They led him to the place of execution with a gag in his mouth, for his eloquence was so powerful and persuasive that emperor and tribunal feared its effect on the crowd. He was, therefore, forced to keep silence. But when the executioners were ready to throw him into the blazing fire, a courier from the emperor arrived, removed the gag, and asked him in the emperor's name, whether he repented of his transgressions and was willing to return to the bosom of the church; if so, he should be pardoned. As might have been expected, Molcho replied that he had longed to die a martyr, "a burnt-sacrifice, of a sweet savour unto the Lord," that he repented him of only one thing

—that he had been a Christian in his youth. Come life, come death, he commended his soul unto God. Then he was thrown into the midst of the flames, and died with unshaken constancy.

Molcho was the victim of a phantasmagoria, a delusion, into which, at feud with reality, he allowed himself to fall. The rich gifts bestowed on him by nature—a handsome person, glowing imagination, quick perception, ready enthusiasm—which would have been steps on the ladder of fortune for any character less fantastical, only served to ruin him, because, swept into the vortex of the Kabbala, he fondly hoped to accomplish the work of redemption. David Reubeni had not even the martyr's crown. Charles carried him to Spain, and cast him into a dungeon of the Inquisition, in which he was still living three years afterwards. It appears that he was at length put to death by poison. As a Jew, the Inquisition had no power over him. But many of the Spanish Marranos who had had intercourse with him, and whose names he probably betrayed on the rack, were burnt to death.

Enthusiasm for Molcho was so great that a mistaken faith was pinned to him, and various fictions respecting him were invented. In Italy and Turkey numbers believed that he had on this occasion, as once before, escaped death. Some said that they had seen him a week after his auto-da-fé; others gave out that he had visited his bride at Safet. Joseph Karo, whose name was soon to be widely known, longed for martyrdom like Molcho's. Even the circumspect Joseph Cohen of Genoa, a careful historian, averse to belief in miracles, was dazed, and knew not what to think of the affair. An Italian Kabbalist, Joseph of Arli, would not abandon the hope that the time of the Messiah, as announced and prepared by Molcho, would soon dawn on the Jewish world. Molcho's death, according to him, would soon find avengers. By a childish transposing of the letters of two verses in Isaiah (Notaricon), he predicted the downfall of the religion of Jesus from various causes: Luther's agitation, the many new sects springing up among Christians, the recent sack of Rome, and the mutually inimical attitude of the pope and the emperor.

The Kabbalist of Arli was ill-disposed towards the pope, though unreasonably so, for he was certainly not guilty of Molcho's death; on the contrary, the pope had to look on while the emperor, to gain his own ends, executed one, and imprisoned the other, of his favorites. However, Clement seems to have made a countermove. He strove to bring about the revocation of the fatal bull authorizing the institution of the Inquisition in Portugal, or at least to make it less drastic in its effects. The Marranos knew this, and made every effort to win the papal curia to their side. As soon as they understood that Solomon Molcho, their most successful advocate, was no longer to be reckoned upon, they sent another envoy to Rome, to bring their grievances before the pope and defend their cause. This new advocate of the Marranos, Duarte de Paz, was the very opposite in character to Molcho: cool-headed, far removed from any extravagance, cunning, calculating, bold, and eloquent, initiated into all the trickery of diplomacy, possessing profound knowledge of human nature, and able to make use of men's foibles for his own ends. Duarte de Paz for nearly eight years looked after the interests of Portuguese new-Christians. He was himself of Marrano descent, and as a reward for his services to the Portuguese court in Africa had obtained an important post and the confidence of King João III. Chosen by the king to perform a secret mission, and made a knight of the order of Christ (styled also Commendatore) on the day of his departure, he set out, not for the appointed place, but for Rome, to work for the Marranos. Duarte de Paz entwined the threads of his intrigues so intricately that to this day it is impossible to ascertain exactly whom he deceived, whether the king or the Marranos. His clients, the Marranos, kept him well supplied with money, which, for good or evil, was almighty at the pope's court. Duarte de Paz obtained substantial successes in return for his pains and his presents. Clement was convinced anew that most atrocious injustice was done the new-Christians in demanding Catholic orthodoxy from those who had been dragged with brutal force to be baptized, and in denying them liberty to journey beyond the confines of Portugal. The pope issued an apostolical brief (October 17th, 1532) stopping the proceedings of the Inquisition until further notice. Duarte de Paz continued his efforts in order to procure a general pardon for all Marranos denounced or imprisoned. It appears that intrigues were set on foot in favor of the Marranos even at the court of João III. The party in favor of the Inquisition worked for Spanish interests, and, in view of the probability of the king's remaining without issue, was eagerly bent on making the Portuguese crown one with the Spanish. On the other side, the national party, which sought to preserve the independence of Portugal, seems to have been against the Inquisition. Hence plotting and counter-plotting continued for several years to such an extent, that the inquisitor general, Diogo de Silva (appointed by the pope himself), declared that he would not undertake so great a responsibility, and resigned his office. Duarte de Paz obtained a second extraordinarily important brief from Pope Clement. The pope recognized as fair and legitimate the reasons urged by new-Christians to justify their lack of attachment to the church.

"Since they were dragged by force to be baptized, they cannot be considered members of the church, and to punish them for heresy and relapse were to violate the principles of justice and equity. With sons and daughters of the first Marranos the case is different, they belong to the church as voluntary members. But, as they have been brought up by their relatives in the midst of Judaism, and have had their example continually before their eyes, it would be cruel to punish them according to the canonical law for falling into Jewish ways and beliefs; they must be kept in the bosom of the church through gentle treatment."

By this brief Clement VII abrogated the power of the Portuguese Inquisition, ordered that denunciation of Marranos should be carried before his own tribunal, and granted to all a thorough absolution or amnesty for past defection from the church. Those languishing in the dungeons of the Inquisition were to be set free, the banished allowed to return, and those robbed of their goods to have them restored. Clement declared, with the peculiar untruthfulness of the papacy, from which even the best popes were unable to free themselves, that he had issued this brief of his own accord, without the suggestion of the Marranos, although the whole world knew the contrary, and counted up how many scudi the see had received for the letter. Clement also declared all who should resist this brief, clergy as well as laity, to be under the ban, and urgently pressed his envoy, Marco della Ruvere, to make it known throughout Portugal. To do Pope Clement VII justice, it must be said that he steadfastly defended the cause of humanity towards the unhappy Marranos against the bloodthirsty spirit of the Christianity of his time, though it must be admitted that other and not quite pure motives may have conduced to his action—viz., hatred of Charles V, who upheld the proposal for a Portuguese Inquisition, and greed for the sums of money paid him and his retainers. The thought of delivering the Marranos to the tender mercies of those bloody-minded wretches in Portugal was not to be lightly endured. Although the question had been thoroughly discussed, Clement appointed a commission, consisting of the two neutral cardinals, De Cesis and Campeggio, to consider the matter once more. The grand penitentiary, Antonio Pucci, Cardinal de Santiquatro, could not be excluded, although a partisan of the Portuguese court. Nevertheless, this commission officially attested the perpetration of devilish atrocities by the Inquisition against pseudo-Christians. In consequence of their report, Clement VII (July 26th, 1534), feeling that his end was near, issued a brief to the nuncio at the Portuguese court to press the release and absolution of imprisoned Marranos. There were about twelve hundred of them, and it may be doubted whether this brief effected their deliverance. Clement's death (September 25th, 1534) brought to naught his good intentions and the Marranos' hopes.

Intrigues concerning the Inquisition were woven anew under his successor, Paul III Farnese (1534—1549), at first to the prejudice of the Marranos, though this pope belonged to the old school of worldly-minded, diplomatic, by no means bigoted princes of the church. He was a subtle schemer, and paid more attention to earthly than to heavenly powers. Paul III was specially well-disposed to Jews. If a description by a narrow-minded bishop (Sadolet of Carpentras) is true only to a small extent, it still proves that this friendliness must have been remarkable. "No pope has ever bestowed on Christians so many honors, such privileges and concessions as Paul III has given to the Jews. They are not only assisted, but positively armed with benefits and prerogatives." Paul III had a Jewish physician in ordinary, Jacob Mantin, who dedicated some of his works to him.

As soon as Paul III had ascended the papal chair, the king of Portugal deemed it most important to procure a revocation of Clement's bulls and briefs in favor of the Marranos, and opposed to the Inquisition. But Duarte de Paz, the Marranos' advocate, who had been given an aid in Diogo Rodrigues Pinto, spared no effort to oppose the contemplated change of policy. Gold also was not wanting.

Duarte de Paz, although apparently engaged in a traitorous correspondence with the king, Don João, offered Cardinal Santiquatro, the partisan of Portugal, a yearly pension of 800 crusados, if he would give his support to the Marranos. The pope, diplomatically cautious as he was, and disinclined to bind himself, decided at first (November 3d, 1534), that Clement's brief should not be promulgated. But when he learned that it had already taken effect, he ordered the case to be again considered, and for that purpose named two cardinals, Ghinucci and Simoneta, of whom the first decidedly favored the Marranos, having published a work in their defense. The result of their investigation was that Paul III emphatically admonished the Portuguese court to obey Clement VII's bull of absolution. He was decidedly opposed to the imprisonment of Marranos in inaccessible dungeons and against the confiscation of their property. But the Catholic kings of that day showed obedience to the papal see only as long as it suited them and their interest; so João III paid but small heed to the pope's admonition. His envoy even advised him, in order to carry on the Inquisition, to cut himself adrift from the Romish Church as England had done. A complete web of intrigues was spun over this affair in Rome and Portugal. In Portugal the court was on the one side, and the Marrano leaders, Thomé Sarrão and Manuel Mendes, with the papal legate on the other—at Rome, Duarte de Paz and Pinto, against or with the Portuguese ambassador and against Cardinal Santiquatro.

Disgusted and wearied, Paul III, who did not readily give up an intention once formed, issued a new, decisive bull (October 2d, 1535), giving absolution to the Marranos, and protecting them against all clerical and civil penalties for relapse and heresy, provided that they would not be guilty of similar offenses in future. The Inquisition in Portugal, which for the sake of appearance could not proceed without the authorization of the pope, was once again arrested. The nuncio set to work energetically, made the bull known throughout Portugal, and carried matters so far, that even the inimically disposed Infante Don Alfonso opened the prison doors to free those whose release was so pressingly recommended by Rome. Altogether there were eighteen hundred Marranos liberated (December, 1535).

At first dazed as by a sudden blow, the Portuguese court later on set every lever in motion once more to obtain sovereign power over the Marranos and their property. It did not shrink from assassination to gain its ends. One day Duarte de Paz was attacked on the high road by assassins, and left lying there for dead, covered with fourteen wounds (January, 1536). All Rome believed the murderers to be hirelings of the Portuguese court. The pope was greatly provoked at this crime, and sent physicians to pay every attention to the procurator, who eventually recovered. Nevertheless, with respect to the Inquisition, the pope had to comply with the wishes of the Portuguese court, which had at last found out the right way to reach its goal. It had recourse to the victorious Charles V, urgently requesting him to manage the affair. Just at that time the emperor had fought a hard battle near Tunis with the Mahometan Barbarossa, who, supported by Turkey, had disquieted all Christendom. After many struggles, the numerous host of Christians, led by Charles himself, gained the day, and Barbarossa was defeated.

When Charles arrived in Rome after a triumphal progress through Italy, he asked the pope, as a reward of his victory for Christianity, to authorize the Inquisition in Portugal Paul III did not yield without a struggle. He always returned to the contention that the Portuguese Marranos were originally dragged by force to be baptized, and that, therefore, the sacrament had no hold upon them.

Unfortunately for the Marranos, their means for satisfying the greed of the papal court for gold were exhausted. Their advocate, Duarte de Paz, had promised exorbitant sums for the frustration of the Inquisition, and had misappropriated to his own use part of the money intrusted to him. The pseudo-Christians thus found themselves obliged, when pressed for payment by the papal nuncio, to declare that they were not in a position to redeem the exaggerated promises of Duarte de Paz. Moreover, this commerce between the nuncio and Marranos was betrayed, and the latter had to exercise yet greater caution. Hence interest in the Marranos gradually cooled down at the pope's court. As the emperor put increasing pressure on Paul III to authorize the Inquisition in Portugal, the pope at last sanctioned the tribunal for the Portuguese dominions (May 23d, 1536). The pope, friend of the Jews as he was, granted his sanction with a heavy heart, forced thereto by pressure from the emperor. He added all sorts of restrictions, that for the first three years the method of procedure in current civil courts must be adhered to, *i. e.*, open confrontment with witnesses—at least as regarded that class of Marranos which was not greatly esteemed—and that the confiscation of condemned Marranos' goods should take place only after the expiration of ten years. Personally, the pope recommended gentle measures in dealing with pseudo-Christians. Don João's joy at the ultimate fulfillment of his heart's desire was so great that he accepted the conditions. But the concession was only a pretense; in reality, the same rigor was employed against the Portuguese Marranos as against the Spanish. The admonition published by the Inquisition, that it was everyone's duty, under penalty of excommunication or a yet more severe punishment, to denounce any Jewish observances or expressions of the new-Christians, differed in no respect from that published by the first bloodthirsty Spanish inquisitor, Torquemada. In November of the same year, after the expiration of the thirty so-called days of grace, the bloody tribunal began its revolting and abominable activity, once again outraging and dishonoring human nature. The Portuguese Inquisition was conducted with almost more cruelty than the Spanish, because, on the one hand, its introduction had cost so much trouble, and the public mind was thereby embittered; on the other, because the Portuguese Marranos were more steadfast than their Spanish brethren, and finally, because the common people supported the Inquisition, and took part against the new-Christians. João III even made them wear a distinguishing mark to separate them visibly from other Christians.

They did not, however, accept their defeat inactively, but rather set to work with all imaginable energy to bring about a revocation of the bull. The most subtle intrigues were again commenced at the papal court. Duarte de Paz once more displayed his diplomatic skill. The Marranos raised complaints of the cruel dealings of the judges, who neglected to obey the pope's instructions. More especially they complained that liberty to emigrate and dispose of their real estate was still denied them.

In a memorial to the pope they ventured on almost threatening language:

"If your Holiness despises the prayers and tears of the Hebrew race, or despite our hopes, refuses to redress our grievances, as would beseem the vicar of Christ, then we protest before God, and with tears and cries that shall be heard afar off will we protest in the face of the universe, that our lives, our honor, our children, who are our blood, our very salvation made the butt of persecution, we will nevertheless try to hold ourselves aloof from the Jewish faith; but if tyranny ceases not, we will do what no one of us would else think of, *i. e.*, return to the religion of Moses, and abjure Christianity, which we are made to accept by main force. We solemnly cry aloud that we are victims, by the right which that fact gives us—a right which your Holiness recognizes. Leaving our native land, we will seek protection among less cruel peoples."

The nuncio who had returned from Portugal, knowing by long years of experience the position of men and affairs, managed to convince the pope that his sanction of the Inquisition was a mistake, and as Paul III had only given way to momentary pressure, a change of sentiment soon followed, and he repented the step he had taken. He went so far as again to submit his bull to a committee which was to examine its legality. To this commission the Marranos' friend, Cardinal Ghinucci, was elected along with another of like mind, Jacobacio. They contrived to prejudice the third member, the honest but narrow-minded Cardinal Simoneta, against the Inquisition, so that he begged the pope to right matters by the revocation of his former bull. Another nuncio was sent to Portugal, with authority within certain limits to nullify the proceedings of the Inquisition against the Marranos, to protect the latter, and particularly to render easier their emigration from Portugal. The pope sent a brief (dated August, 1537) after the nuncio, empowering and, to some extent, encouraging all to give protection and assistance to the accused Marranos—in fact, to do exactly what in Portugal was held to be conniving at and participating in heresy. The king must have been considerably puzzled. Here he was at length in possession of a bull, a tribunal, a grand inquisitor and his colleagues—the whole apparatus of a slaughter-house for the glory of God—and he might just as well have had nothing at all.

An incident again turned the chances of the game in favor of the king and the fanatics. One day (February, 1539) a placard was discovered fastened on the door of the Lisbon Cathedral: "The Messiah has not yet appeared—Jesus was not the Messiah, and Christianity is a lie." All Portugal was indignant at such blasphemy, and a strict investigation was set on foot to find out the offender. The king offered a reward of 10,000 crusados (ducats). The nuncio also offered 5,000 crusados, as he, with many others, was of opinion that this was a blow from some enemy of the Marranos, designed to excite the king's fanaticism to a higher degree, and to get the nuncio into trouble. To turn aside suspicion the new-Christians posted a notice on the same place—"I, the author, am neither a Spaniard nor a Portuguese, but an Englishman, and though you raise your reward to 20,000 crusados, you will not find me out." After all, the writer turned out to be a Marrano, one Emanuel da Costa. He confessed everything when cited before the Inquisition. The civil court then took him in hand, and put him on the rack to make him name his accomplices. Finally, after both hands had been cut off, he was burnt to death. The Marranos foresaw evil consequences for themselves, and took to flight. The king made the best of this opportunity to enforce the rules of the Inquisition with increased severity and bloodthirstiness, and to thwart the nuncio's efforts. The maddest fanatics were at once elected inquisitors, to the great anger of the pope and his nuncio. João Soares, whom the pope himself once described as "not a learned, but a most daring and ambitious, monk, with opinions and ideas of the very worst kind, who takes pride in his enmity to the apostolic see," was now given unbounded power over the lives of the new-Christians, and his colleague was Mallo, an arch-foe of the new-Christians. For the Marranos the state of affairs grew worse every day. On three points the pope showed immovable firmness: the Infante Don Henrique must not remain grand inquisitor; Marranos accused of heresy should have the witnesses' (that is, their accusers') names announced to them; finally, after sentence is passed they should be allowed recourse to the papal court of appeals. Indeed, Paul III caused a new bull to be drawn up (October 12th, 1539)—a supplement of that issued three years before—which throughout was of a favorable tenor to new-Christians, and would completely have crippled the Inquisition. But this likewise remained a dead letter. After this, fires for the obstinate heretics were kindled more frequently than ever, and more victims were sacrificed (from ten to forty a year) without permitting them to appeal to the pope. The denounced and suspected Marranos filled the prisons.

A contemporary poet, Samuel Usque, gives a dreadful picture of the tortures of the Portuguese Inquisition, which he himself had experienced in his youth:

"Its institution deprived the Jews of peace of mind, filled their souls with pain and grief, and drew them forth from the comforts of home into gloomy dungeons, where they dwelt amid torment and sighs of anguish. It (the Inquisition) flings the halter round their necks, and drags them to the flames; through its decrees they must see their sons murdered, husbands burnt to death, and brothers robbed of life; must see their children made orphans, the number of widows increased, the rich made poor, the mighty brought low, the nobly born transformed into highway robbers, chaste, modest women housed in lewd, ignominious dwellings, through the poverty and desertion in its wake. It has burnt numbers to death, not one by one, but by thirties, by fifties at a time. Not content with mere burning and destroying, it leads Christians to boast of such deeds, to rejoice when their eyes behold the members of my body (the sons of Jacob) burning to death in the flames, kindled with fagots dragged from afar on men's shoulders. Those baptized against their will, steal about overpowered with fear of this savage monster (the Inquisition); they turn their eyes on every side lest it seize them. With ill-assured hearts they pass to and fro, trembling like a leaf, terror strikes them suddenly, and they stay their steps lest it take them captive. When they sit down together to eat, every morsel is lifted to their mouths in anguish. The hour that brings repose to all other beings only increases their anxiety and exhaustion. At times of marriage and the birth of children, joy and feasting are turned into mourning and disquietude of soul. In fine, there is no moment not paid for by a thousand deadly fears. For it suffices not that they make themselves known as Christians by outward signs. Fire rages in their hearts, their tortures are innumerable."

Is this an exaggerated description? Did the poet's imagination transform petty sufferings into the pains of martyrdom? Every word of it is corroborated by an assembly of cardinals, officially gathered to investigate the proceedings of the Portuguese Inquisition against the Marranos.

"When a pseudo-Christian is denounced—often by false witnesses—the inquisitors drag him away to a dismal retreat where he is allowed no sight of heaven or earth, and least of all to speak with his friends, who might succor him. They accuse him on obscure testimony, and inform him neither of the time nor the place where he committed the offense for which he is denounced. Later on he is allowed an advocate, who often, instead of defending his cause, helps him on the road to the stake. Let an unfortunate creature acknowledge himself a true believing Christian, and firmly deny the transgressions laid to his charge, they condemn him to the flames, and confiscate his goods. Let him plead guilty to such and such a deed, though unintentionally committed, they treat him in a similar manner under the pretense that he obstinately denies his wicked intentions. Let him freely and fully admit what he is accused of, he is reduced to extremest necessity, and condemned to the dungeon's never-lifting gloom. And this they call treating the accused with mercy and compassion and Christian charity! Even he who succeeds in clearly proving his innocence is condemned to pay a fine, so that it may not be said that he was arrested without cause. The accused who are held prisoners are racked by every instrument of torture to admit the accusations against them. Many die in prison, and those who are set free, with all their relatives bear a brand of eternal infamy."

As the Inquisition grew more and more severe and bloodthirsty, the Portuguese new-Christians clung with increasing tenacity to the last anchor of hope left—to the pope and their other protectors. They had found a new advocate and mediator, who gave promise of being more honest and energetically active on their behalf. The battle between the Portuguese court and the papal see blazed up afresh. It was war to the death, not for those immediately concerned, but for the miserable beings who, in spite of self-repression, could not become reconciled to Christianity, yet were not courageous enough to suffer for Judaism—who would give up neither convictions, wealth, nor position. To influence the pope, or at least those about his person against the Marranos, the Infante and grand inquisitor Henrique had a list of the delinquencies of the new-Christians made out and sent to Rome (February, 1542). The Marranos, also, to wrest the weapons from their opponents' hands, in Rome and elsewhere, and for all times to refute the lying reports and statements of the Portuguese court, drew up a bulky memorial (1544), detailing their troubled lot, from the time of King João II and Manoel, who forced them to accept Christianity, until the most recent times, and verifying their statements by documentary evidence—a monument of everlasting disgrace to that age.

Yet these reciprocal indictments led to no settlement. At length, when they saw that nothing would stop the execrable activity of the Inquisition now it had once been called into existence, the pope and the Marranos felt how extremely important it was for them to secure at least two concessions. First, free right of emigration from Portugal for new-Christians; second, a general absolution (Perdaõ) for those already denounced or imprisoned, provided they would promise to give up their Jewish creed and remain good Christians in the future. But these were the very points on which the king and the Dominicans would not yield. As though in defiance of the pope, the king issued an ordinance (July 15th, 1547), that for three years longer no new-Christian might leave Portugal without express permission or payment of a large sum of money.

Paul III felt himself crippled. He might shudder at the cruelties of the Portuguese Inquisition—the vast sums which the Marranos spent on him and his sycophants might be ever so much needed to aid in carrying out his policy in Italy and in prosecuting war against the Protestants, yet he dared not show too stern a determination to thwart the court at Lisbon. He, too, was in the power of Catholic fanatics. To fight the Protestant heretics and reinstate the papal dignity, he had authorized the institution of the order of Jesuits (1540), who inscribed their banner with the watchword of the church militant.

He had agreed to the proposition of the fanatical Pietro Caraffa for an Inquisition at Rome (1542). Loyola and Caraffa now lorded it over Rome, and the pope was only their tool. Moreover, the council of Trent was to be convened to settle the standard of faith, whereby the Protestants were to be humbled, and their influence crushed. Paul III needed ardent fanatical helpers to keep the lukewarm up to the mark. Such men only Spain and Portugal could furnish. In Portugal the most friendly reception had been accorded the Jesuits. Thus the pope could offer only mild opposition to the Portuguese court, and proffer requests where he should have given orders.

At the council, Bishop Balthasar Limpo was a worthy representative of the fanatical king of Portugal, and dared use language against the pope which should have shown him clearly that he was no longer master in his own house. The bishop vehemently asked Paul III to sanction the Inquisition against relapsed new-Christians irrevocably, and censured his sympathy with them. He justly remarked:

"As Christians, and under Christian names, they leave Portugal by stealth, and take with them their children, whom they themselves have carried to be baptized. As soon as they reach Italy they give themselves out for Jews, live according to Jewish ordinances, and circumcise their children. This takes place under the eye of the pope and the papal see, within the walls of Rome and Bologna, and it happens because his Holiness has granted to heretics the privilege that in Ancona no one may molest them on account of their belief. Under these circumstances it is impossible for the king to grant them the right of free departure from the land. Perhaps his Holiness asks it in order that they may settle in his states as Jews, and the papal see derive advantage in that way. Instead of hindering the establishment of the Inquisition in Portugal, it should have been his Holiness' duty to have introduced it long since into his own dominions."

The pope could have given answer to such an harangue, had he possessed a clear conscience, and in very deed and truth preached Christianity as a religion of gentleness and humanity. But since he had need of blind fanaticism to keep up obstinate warfare with Protestantism, and on the outbreak of the war against the latter had issued the murderous bull ("Of the cross"), wherein Catholics, in the name of the vicar of Christ, were called upon to "smite the Protestants to death," he could make no reply when Limpo spoke. He was caught in his own trap. Yet, he tried to save one thing, the Marranos' free right of emigration from Portugal; on this condition he would give way to the Portuguese court. But new-Christians wishing to depart from the land would be required to give security that they would not emigrate to infidel countries, such as Turkey or Africa. To this also Bishop Limpo gave a convincing reply:

"Does it, then, make any difference whether these heretics take refuge under infidel governments, or come to Italy? At Ancona, Ferrara, or Venice, they are circumcised, and then go on to Turkey. They have papal privileges, forsooth, so that nobody dare ask them if peradventure they are Jews! They wear no distinguishing marks, and can go undisguised and free whithersoever they like, can observe their ceremonies, and attend their synagogues. Oh, how many attend these who were baptized in their youth in Portugal, or were condemned to death, or burnt in effigy! Give them free right of emigration, let them set foot in the land of the infidel, and they can openly confess themselves as Jews. The king will never allow, no theologian—do I say theologian?—no simple Christian could advise such a thing. Instead of his Holiness' exerting himself to insure the safety of the secret Jews, let him increase the number of Inquisitions in his own states, and punish not alone Lutheran heretics, but Jewish heretics also, who seek refuge and protection in Italy."

Yet another circumstance compelled Paul III to show a yielding disposition. Charles V, inspired thereto by his victory over the Protestants (April, 1547), sought to set himself above the papacy, and would have liked to see a new ritual established, agreeable to Protestants as well as to Catholics. This was tantamount to declaring war against the pope. The latter was, therefore, forced to break with the emperor, and that he might not stand unsupported against so powerful a foe, Portugal and the central Catholic states had to be won over to his side. To conciliate Portugal he sent thither a special commissary provided with bulls and briefs, wherein he partially sanctioned the Inquisition, though requesting that it be used with mildness. Above all, however, new-Christians accused of heresy and so-called relapse were not to be sentenced, for the present, but to be made answerable for their conduct in the future. Even then, for the first ten years, the property of relapsed heretics was not to be touched, but to descend to their heirs. He consented to the restriction of Marrano emigration, so strenuously insisted upon by the Portuguese court.

Prisons of the Inquisition at Lisbon, Evora, and other cities were thrown open in obedience to the pope's general absolution for new-Christians, and eighteen hundred set at liberty (July, 1548). Soon after this all the Marranos were called together, and forced to abjure their Judaizing tendencies. From that moment only were they recognized as complete Christians, and liable to be punished in case of heretical transgression. The pope, in a brief, desired the king to see that the tribunals deal mercifully even with the heretics, since they fulfilled Jewish observances only from habit. Thus, throughout his life, Pope Paul III took the part of the Marranos. Nevertheless, they fell victims to their tragic fate. It was cruel injustice to demand an open confession of Catholicism from them, when they protested against it with all their hearts, and then to punish them when detected in the performance of Jewish rites or ceremonies. On the other hand, the state could never allow a whole class of the population outwardly belonging to the church to be left in a certain sense free to hold the church in derision. Justice certainly demanded that the Marranos should have liberty of choice either to emigrate or confess themselves genuine members of the church. But, as the court acknowledged, their loss meant ruin to the state, for the Marranos of Jewish descent formed the most profitable class of the city population. Their capital and far-reaching business transactions increased the revenue, caused a general circulation of money, and made raw materials imported from the Indian and African colonies available. Without them the wealth of the whole country would be capital idly and unprofitably stored. Marranos were also the only artisans, and on them depended industrial prosperity. Plainly, the state could not afford to lose them, and, therefore, the king tried to turn them into good Christians by the terrors of the Inquisition, so as to keep a certain hold on the profit and utility of their presence. He labored in vain. Every year fresh victims perished at the stake; yet the survivors did not become more faithful believers. The Portuguese court, unlike the Spanish, never derived enjoyment from the Inquisition. Portuguese new-Christians, in spite of their confession, were not yet true Christians, on whom the penalty of heresy could legally, according to canonical laws, be inflicted by the Inquisition. After Paul's death, (November, 1549), Julius III was petitioned to give absolution to the Marranos. Even the succeeding popes, who favored reaction and persecution, allowed the Portuguese Inquisition to continue more as an accomplished fact than as a legal institution. Half a century later, a pope (Clement VIII) condemned the judicial murders of the Inquisition, and once more issued a general amnesty for condemned Marranos.

CHAPTER XVI.

STRIVINGS OF EASTERN JEWS FOR UNITY. SUFFERING IN THE WEST.

Efforts towards Unity—Jacob Berab proposes the Re-introduction of Rabbinical Ordination into Palestine—Successful Opposition of Levi ben Chabib—Joseph Karo—His Connection with Solomon Molcho and his Messianic Visions—Karo's Religious Code—Converts to Judaism at the Era of the Reformation—Expulsion of the Jews from Naples and Prague—Their Return to the latter Town—Dr. Eck—Martin Luther and the Jews—Moses Hamon—Jewish Histories by Joseph Cohen, the Ibn-Vergas, and Samuel Usque—Elegy of Samuel Usque—Reaction in the Catholic Church: Loyola establishes the Order of Jesuits—The Censorship of Books—Eliano Romano and Vittorio Eliano—Fresh Attacks on the Talmud—Paul IV and his anti-Jewish Bulls—Persecution of the Marranos by the Inquisition in Ancona—Joseph Nassi—The Levantine Jews—Expulsion of the Jews from Austria and Bohemia—Relations of Popes Pius IV and V to the Jews.

1538—1566 C.E.

EVERY fresh column of smoke rising from the fires of the Inquisition in Spain and Portugal drove Marranos, singly or in groups, far away to the East, to Turkey, beyond the shadow of the cross. They no longer felt safe even in Italy, since the popes, against their own higher convictions, allowed themselves to be overborne concerning the Inquisition. In Turkey a little Jewish world was thus by degrees formed, on which even the sultan's despotic rule did not encroach, however much individuals might be exposed to arbitrary treatment. Here, as in Palestine, where numbers and prosperity had raised them in their own estimation, they could indulge in dreams of obtaining some degree of independence, might strive for national and religious unity, and hope to realize their wild Messianic fancies. The career of the Mantuan martyr, Solomon Molcho, did not fail to leave an impression; his words echoed in the ears of his brethren. At Safet, the largest congregation in

Palestine, where he had made a long stay, forming intimate relations and awakening hopes, the fulfillment of his Messianic predictions was looked for even after his death. The completion of the round number 5300 from the creation of the world (1540) seemed to be a suitable year for the coming of the Messiah. But the Messianic period, according to then prevailing ideas, would not come suddenly; the Israelites had to do their part in preparing the way. Maimuni, the highest authority, had taught that the Messianic time would or must be preceded by the establishment of a universally recognized Jewish court of justice, or Synhedrion. Hence the necessity was felt of having authorized and duly appointed judges, such as existed at the time of the Temple and the Talmud in Palestine, of re-introducing, in fact, the long-disused ordination (Semichah). There was no hindrance to be feared from the Turkish state. As it was, the rabbis had their own civil and even criminal jurisdiction; but these rabbis (who were also judges), being appointed by the community, had not the warrant of authority required by Talmudic rules. Obedience was given them, but they also met with opposition. Authority was conventional, not built on the foundation of Talmudic Judaism. No unity of legislation and exposition of the Law was possible while every rabbi was absolute in his own congregation, not subject to some higher authority. It was, therefore, a need of the times to create a sort of religious supreme court, and where should that be done but in Palestine? The sacred memories connected with that country could alone lend the dignity of a Synhedrion to a college of rabbis. Teaching that was to meet with universal acceptance could proceed from Zion alone, and the word of God only from Jerusalem.

How excellent and necessary it was to re-introduce the ordination of rabbis by a higher authority had been discussed by many, but only one, the acute-minded but obstinate and daring Jacob Berab, had the energy to set about doing the thing. After much journeying from Egypt to Jerusalem, and thence to Damascus, Berab, in his old age, settled at Safet. He was in good circumstances, and, owing to his wealth and intellect, enjoyed marked respect and consideration. He determined to give a definite direction to the aimless ideas floating in men's minds with regard to the coming of the Messiah. This was certainly a praiseworthy aim, but some little ambition was undoubtedly mixed up in his plan : to be himself the highest authority, perhaps the chief of the Synhedrion in Palestine, and consequently revered throughout the East, and even by the whole Jewish race. The first step was difficult. Ordination could be lawfully given only by those who themselves had been ordained, and there had been no such for a very long time. An utterance of Maimuni happily offered ground for a new departure, viz., when wise men gathered together in Palestine shall agree to ordain one of their number, they have the right to do so, and the ordained rabbi can also ordain others. At that time no community in Palestine, in point of numbers, could compare with Safet, which had grown through frequent immigrations till it contained more than 1,000 Jewish families. Safet, or rather the Talmudists of that city, therefore, had it in their own hands, if they could only agree, to re-establish the dignity of the Synhedrion, even in the face of opposition from other congregations, because the Safet party was in the majority. The officiating and non-officiating rabbis of Safet, men without name or fame, had far too high a respect for Berab's intellectual power, Talmudic learning, and wealth, to gainsay his proposition, or put any obstacle in his path. A hint from him sufficed to bring together five and twenty men ready to confer on him the dignity of an ordained judge and rabbi. Thus ordination was re-established (1538), and the focus for a new Synhedrion determined. It rested with Jacob Berab to ordain as many colleagues as he pleased. From principles laid down in the Talmud he demonstrated in a lecture the legality of the step, and confuted every possible objection. One after another, Talmudists in other congregations in Palestine announced their assent to this innovation. By this step Berab and his followers thought that they had reached the first stage of preparation for the Messianic age. In fact, this renewal of ordination, if not able to bring about the Messianic times, might very well have been the nucleus of Jewish unity. A re-established Synhedrion in the Holy Land would have had a grand sound in Europe, might have exercised special attraction, and brought still more immigrants to Palestine. Persecutions of Jews in Italy and Germany, the war of extermination against Marranos in Spain and Portugal, a thirst for what was eccentric and out of the common in an age distinguished by strongly excited longing for the Messiah, all this would have been sufficient inducement to allure rich, educated Jews from western lands to the East. With the help of their capital, and founded on the authority of a Synhedrion, a Jewish community having the character of a state might have been organized, and Berab was the right person to carry out so great a scheme with perseverance —not to say stubbornness.

But difficulties immediately arose. It was to be expected that if the congregation at Jerusalem and its representatives were not consulted with regard to an act so pregnant with consequences, there would be danger that the whole arrangement would be declared null and void, for the Holy City should have the first vote in a matter of such weight for the Holy Land. Jacob Berab saw this perfectly well, and proposed, as the first exercise of his newly-acquired dignity, to ordain the head of the Jerusalem college of rabbis. Levi ben Jacob Chabib, who held that position, was born in Zamora, and was of about the same age as Berab. As a youth, in the times of forced baptism, under King Manoel, he had become a pseudo-Christian, received a baptismal name, made the sign of the cross, and performed other ceremonies of the Catholic Church with a heart full of despair. At the first favorable opportunity he fled from Portugal, cast off his assumed garb of Christianity, sought safety in Turkey, and finally betook himself to Jerusalem. There, by virtue of the wide range of his Talmudic learning, more extensive than profound, he became as rabbi the first person in the community. He deserved its gratitude by caring for the physical and spiritual welfare of his congregation, especially for piloting it through the disturbed state into which it was in danger of falling afresh through the new arrivals from various countries, who were disinclined to submit to law and order. Levi ben Chabib had also some knowledge of mathematics, astronomy, and the calculation of the calendar. Between himself and Jacob Berab, with whom he had lived for some time in Jerusalem, there was no friendly relationship. On several occasions they had come into collision, though Levi ben Chabib had always behaved in a friendly, unassuming manner, and avoided whatever might wound his opponent. Their relations of late years had been more intimate, but Levi ben Chabib could not forget how slightingly Jacob Berab had treated him.

And now, as chief rabbi of Jerusalem, he was invited to recognize the election of Jacob Berab as the first lawfully ordained rabbi-judge, member of the Synhedrion, and by his consent to approve of the same. Jerusalem was thereby subordinated to Safet, and he himself to Jacob Berab. This was a real offense, for Berab had not thought it worth while to ask the consent of the Jerusalem college beforehand, but had haughtily made his innovation known through a decree, in which, by virtue of the dignity conferred upon him, he designated Levi ben Chabib an ordained judge. At the same time he had made it evident that disapproval from Jerusalem would disturb him but little, since it could only be regarded as the opposition of a minority to the majority at Safet. The moment for taking an important step towards Jewish unity had come, and it found Levi ben Chabib, whose vote at all events was of importance, wanting in magnanimity. Resentment gained the upper hand; he forgot that in earlier days it had been also his desire to re-establish the ordination of rabbis. As soon as a notification of the act at Safet reached him, he immediately and emphatically declared himself against the election. His antagonism seems, however, to have found no response in Jerusalem, for only one of his rabbinical colleagues, Moses de Castro, adopted his view, the remainder acquiesced in Berab's action. In Talmudical and rabbinical law arguments could not fail to be discoverable against the revival of ordination and the Synhedrion. Such a confused host of opinions exists therein, that arguments may be found for or against almost anything. Berab and the electors obedient to his nod themselves furnished their opponents with an objection. Rabbinical Judaism is so thoroughly practical that it offers no foothold for romantic enthusiasm and sentimentality. The Jews of Safet dared not give utterance to their underlying hope that through ordination the Messianic time would be brought nearer. Though the rabbis might be filled with Messianic hopes, such a motive for the re-introduction of ordination would have sounded too fantastic and ridiculous in their own ears. Other plausible grounds were not just then to be found. The calendar of festivals, which had formerly been prepared by ordained members of the college, had been fixed for a thousand years, and could not now be meddled with. Other cases where the Talmud required an ordained judge were of too rare occurrence to permit that the necessity of ordination be proved on that head. The people of Safet, therefore, made the most of a reason meant to appear practical and suited to the times, which was nevertheless very far-fetched. Many Marranos were to be found in Palestine who had been forced during their outward assumption of Christianity to commit what according to the Talmud were deadly sins. With contrite hearts they repented of their transgressions, and longed for forgiveness and atonement—they had not given up the Catholic doctrine of outward penance when they cast off the mask of Christianity. Such forgiveness of sins, however (Berab made it appear), could be theirs only when the scourging prescribed by the Law (39 stripes) was inflicted; again, this punishment could be decreed only by a lawfully ordained college. Therein lay the necessity for ordination.

If Levi ben Chabib was disposed to extend his antipathy from the originator to the execution of his work, there would be no difficulty in proving this reason for the scheme invalid. Not content with this, he brought forward a host of sophistries. Jacob Berab had not expected such antagonism at Jerusalem from Levi ben Chabib and his colleague, Moses de Castro, because he credited them either with less courage or more self-denial, and it embittered him extremely. It was all the more painful to him since their opposition was calculated to wreck his whole undertaking. How could he hope to prove it acceptable to Asiatic, European, and African Jews, when Jerusalem, the Holy City, would have none of it? And without such acceptance, how could he make it the central point of a re-organization? Besides, his life was in danger at Safet, probably through denunciation to the Turkish authorities, who were willing to grasp at any opportunity to get hold of his property. Berab had to leave Palestine for a time. He consecrated four Talmudists, as

Judah ben Baba had done in Hadrian's time, so that the practice of ordination might not immediately fall to the ground. These four were chosen not from the elder, but from the younger rabbis, among them Joseph Karo, the enthusiastic adherent of Solomon Molcho and his Kabbalistic Messiahship, who entered heart and soul into the ordination scheme. Such preference, shown to younger and more pliable, if more gifted men, stirred up still more ill-will in Jerusalem. The two rabbis of Palestine in the epistles exchanged on the subject (written with a view to publication) grew more and more bitter against each other, so offensive indeed that the most passionate excitement cannot excuse their language. In reply to Levi ben Chabib's censorious remark: "One who is consecrated and ordained should have not only learning, but holiness also," Jacob Berab made a spiteful reference to Levi's compulsory adoption of Christianity: "I have never changed my name; in the midst of distress and despair I kept always in the way of the Lord." He upbraided Levi ben Chabib with still having somewhat of Christian dogma sticking to him. This thrust reached his opponent's heart. The latter confessed that in the day of forced baptisms in Portugal his name had been changed, that he had been made a Christian, and that he had not been able to die for the religion of his fathers. But he brought forward his youth as an excuse; he had not been twenty years old, had remained a pseudo-Christian scarcely a year, and he hoped that the flood of tears which he had shed since then, and which he still shed, would wipe out his sin before God. After this humiliation Levi ben Chabib's violence against Berab knew no bounds. He flung the grossest insults at him, and declared that he hoped never more to meet him face to face. Through this intemperate violence of the chief rabbi of Jerusalem and Berab's death, which followed immediately after (January, 1541), the system of ordination fell to the ground.

Joseph Karo alone, one of the ordained, refused to give in. This remarkable man, who later on had so deep an influence on Jewish history (born 1488, died 1575), when a child, was driven from Spain with his parents. He early learned the bitter lessons of suffering, and after long traveling about, came to Nicopolis in European Turkey. He studied the text of the Mishnah so assiduously that he knew it by heart. Later on Karo left Nicopolis to settle at Adrianople, where, on account of his extraordinary Talmudical learning, he was looked up to with respect, and found disciples. In his thirtieth year he undertook the gigantic work of furnishing Jacob Asheri's Code with a commentary, authorities, and corrections, to which he devoted twenty years of his life (1522—1542). Twelve years more were spent in a further revision (1542—1554). His imagination, kept in entire inactivity by such a dry task, was fired by the appearance of Solomon Molcho. That young enthusiast from Portugal made so overpowering an impression upon him, that Karo allowed himself to be initiated into the tortuous mazes of the Kabbala and to share Molcho's Messianic dreams. After this time his mind was divided between dry rabbinical scholarship and the fantastic ideas of the Kabbala. He kept up a correspondence with Molcho during the latter's stay in Palestine, and formed plans for going thither himself. Like Molcho, he prepared for a martyr's death, "as a burnt-sacrifice, an offering made by fire, of a sweet savour unto the Lord," and like Molcho, he had strange visions, which, according to his belief, were inspired by some superior being. This superior being (Maggid) was not an angel, or an imaginary voice, but—oddly enough—the Mishnah personified, who descended to him, and generally at night whispered revelations, because he had devoted himself to its service. Joseph Karo had these visions (which he for the most part committed to paper), not for a short period of time, but at intervals, to the end of his life, for nearly forty years. Part of them were afterwards published, and it is melancholy to see what havoc the Kabbala played with the intellect of that day. The superior being (or the Mishnah) laid the heaviest penances on Karo, forbade him to indulge in meat and wine, and went to the extent of prohibiting much drinking of water. If he was guilty of any fault, sleeping too long, being late at prayers, or slightly neglecting his study of the Mishnah, the mother Mishnah appeared, and made the most tender remonstrances. She certainly made astonishing revelations to him. These predictions were far from being mere deceptions, but were the promptings of a tumultuous epoch, or an excited imagination, such as is found in the warm, luxurious East oftener than in the cold, sober North.

Joseph Karo was so full of the thought that he was called to play a part in Palestine, and die as a martyr, during the time of preparation for the Messiah as begun by Solomon Molcho, that he left Adrianople. He stayed for some time at Salonica, a place swarming with Kabbalists. At length, he arrived in Safet, that nest of Kabbalists, with a companion of like mind, Solomon Alkabez, a dull, spiritless writer, whose song of welcome for the Sabbath bride (Lecha Dodi) has become more famous than its author. At Safet, Joseph Karo experienced the joy of seeing part of his fantastic dreams fulfilled; he was ordained by Berab as a member of the Synhedrion. After Berab's death Karo dreamed of nothing but his future greatness; he was to bring about ordination, and to be recognized by the sages of Palestine and foreign countries as a patriarch and leader of the Jews in Palestine. He would educate the best Talmudists, so that disciples of his school only would be accepted. Everyone would do him reverence as the holy likeness (Diokna Kadisha), and he would work miracles. Like Molcho, he was to die a martyr's death, that the name of

God might be hallowed; but his resurrection would soon afterwards follow, and he would enter into the Messianic kingdom.

All these advantages and prerogatives were to be won by a single achievement, which of itself would make the Jews into one great people, and gain him universal admiration. When his thorough commentary on Jacob Asheri's Code was completed, printed, published, and in circulation, when he had elaborated a comprehensive code of religious law grounded on that work, he would surely be acknowledged as patriarch and lawgiver in all Israel. His guardian angel had whispered to him that he would be made worthy to train many disciples and to see his writings printed and circulated throughout Israel. Even the supernatural worlds would ask, "Who is the man with whom the King of kings is well pleased, the patriarch of Palestine, the great writer of the Holy Land?" He would be enabled to publish his commentary, elucidations, and decisions without fault or error.

Devoted piety, fantastical imagination, and some degree of ambition inspired the author, who elaborated, for the whole Jewish race, the final code of religious law, destined to end all wavering, uncertainty, and antagonism of opinion. Kabbalistic enthusiasm combined with the Messianic hopes excited by Solomon Molcho, and the ceremony of ordination administered by Berab, gave Karo no rest, until by means of a comprehensive written work he had accomplished these hopes, at least so far as religious unity was concerned. Yet several decades were to elapse before the Jewish world received this gift, a colossal work which required years for its completion. Joseph Karo's astounding, incessant industry had to eke out lack of genius. Such a work could be accomplished only by religious devotion and inspiration united with a fantastic imagination. Of all his lofty dreams one only was actually realized, that he would be chief rabbi of Safet after Jacob Berab's death, and would be acknowledged as a rabbinical authority, the latter coming about only gradually. But his authority was not absolute; he had a rival in Berab's best disciple, Moses de Trani.

While the Jews of the East were rejoicing in a measure of peace and independence, and were able to indulge in Messianic speculations, and endeavoring, although by mistaken means, to bring about an ideal state of things, the Jews of the West were subjected to fresh persecutions instituted against them. The old accusations of their harmful influence upon mankind, their child-murder, their hostile attitude towards Christianity, which had ceased for a time during the excitement of the Reformation, were again heard. The bigoted ecclesiastical policy, espoused by those who sought to maintain their position against the ever-increasing strength of Lutheranism, reacted upon the Jews, and brought fresh sufferings upon them, principally in Catholic countries. To the old accusations was added a new one, which prejudiced also Lutherans against them. The Lutheran and Calvinistic Reformation, which had extended into England and Poland, had opened the eyes of many concerning religion and Christianity, and led them to find much that even the Reformers considered essentials of Christianity to be false, mistaken, and blasphemous. The Bible translated into most European languages gave thoughtful readers an opportunity of forming a religious system for themselves differing wholly from the dogmas of Rome, Wittenberg, or Geneva. In reading the Bible the Old Testament came before the New, and in the transition from one to the other many perceived that much in the two was irreconcilable; that the doctrine of the unity of God in the prophets was in direct contradiction to the doctrine of the Trinity propounded by the Church Fathers.

Besides this, the Reformation had had in view not only religious freedom, but also political deliverance from the iron yoke of the princes, in whose eyes the people were nothing, of importance only for the payment of taxes and the forced service of bondmen. Now it struck not a few that the Hebrew Scriptures make the people the source of all power, and condemn the despotism of kings, whilst evangelical Christianity does not recognize a people, but only humble believers, whom it exhorts to bow the neck to the yoke of tyrants. The contrast between the Old and the New Testament, the one teaching active virtue together with a God-fearing life, the other glorifying passive virtue together with blind faith, could not be overlooked by eyes sharpened through deep research into the Bible.

Among the host of religious sects which the Reformation called forth in the first decades, there arose some which nearly approached Judaism, and whose adherents were stigmatized by the ruling party as half-Jews or Judaizers (Judaïzantes, Semijudæi). These found the doctrine of the Trinity a stumbling-block, and maintained that God must be conceived as an absolute Unity. Michael Servetus, an Aragonese, perhaps instructed by Marranos in Spain, wrote a pamphlet on the "Errors of the Doctrine of the Trinity," which created a great sensation, and brought him some faithful adherents; but he was burnt at the stake by Calvin at Geneva. The Reformers had retained the fanatical intolerance of the Catholic Church! Notwithstanding this, a sect of believers in the Unity (Unitarians, Anti-trinitarians) arose which rejected the identification of Jesus with God. In England, where Catholicism had been overthrown only by the whim of a tyrant, Henry VIII, to gratify his sensual desires, a religious-political party began to be formed, which proposed to take the Old Testament system of government and adapt it to English circumstances. It appeared to recognize only Old

Testament types, and not to take any account of the praying brethren and sisters of the New Testament. Many kept the Sabbath as the day of rest appointed by God, but with their windows closed. Some eccentric Christians conceived a predilection for the Jews as the successors of the patriarchs, as the remnant of that people whom God had once favored with the fullness of His grace, as the direct descendants of the great prophets, on this account deserving the highest respect.

Among the innumerable pamphlets appeared one, a dialogue between a Jew and a Christian, in which the grounds of the Christian dogmas were overthrown by texts out of the Old Testament. Publications of this sort helped to make the Jews obnoxious to the Reformers, too. The adherents of the new faith in a measure simulated hatred of Jews in order to avert from themselves the suspicion that they wished to undermine Christianity, and set up Judaism in its place. The Jews, therefore, had enemies on both sides, and were soon compelled to relinquish the illusion that Catholicism was overthrown, and that the new religion was in sympathy with them.

When the peasants of South Germany, Alsatia, Franconia, and elsewhere, trusting too readily in the evangelical freedom proclaimed by Luther, attempted to throw off the yoke of their oppressors, the few Jews in Germany found themselves between two fires. On the one hand they were accused by the nobility and the upper classes of supporting the rebellious peasants and citizens with their money, and egging them on; and, on the other, the peasants attacked them as the confederates and abettors of the rich and the nobility. The fanatical priest, Balthasar Hubmaier, who had agitated the expulsion of the Jews from Ratisbon, was the adviser of the peasants of the Black Forest, and probably the author of the twelve written demands (articles) which the peasants had proposed. Instead of becoming milder and more humane by his apostasy from the Roman Catholic, he became still more fanatical as an adherent of the Anabaptist faith. He had no doubt excited the rage of the townspeople, who wished to free themselves from their debts to their Jewish creditors, and that of the peasants who desired to enrich themselves with the property of the Jews. The province of the Rheingau among other things demanded that no Jew should be allowed to remain in the district. The annals of the age of the Reformation thus continue to present year after year accounts of banishments, tortures, and restrictions. But, after all, times had improved. There were no longer sudden attacks, massacres, wholesale murders—simply expulsions, mere exile into poverty. Only events of deep and far-reaching effect can find a place here.

In Naples, where the Spaniards ruled, the ultra-Catholic party had long tried to introduce the Inquisition against the Marranos who resided there. When Charles V returned from his victorious expedition in Africa, this party tried to induce him to banish the Jews from Naples, because the Marranos were but strengthened in their unbelief by intercourse with them. But Donna Benvenida, the noble wife of Samuel Abrabanel, who was held in high respect by the Spaniards, so ardently entreated the emperor to revoke the decree of banishment, and her young friend, the daughter of the viceroy, so warmly supported her request, that he could not refuse them. It is also possible that Abrabanel's money may have had something to do with it. But a few years afterwards, Charles ordered the Neapolitan Jews to wear the badge of shame on their dress, and in case of transgression to suffer punishment in their person and property, or leave the country. They chose the latter alternative, probably by the advice of Samuel Abrabanel. They probably realized that persecution would not end there, but that it would form the prelude to harsher treatment. But this voluntary exile was turned into banishment, and every Jew who should venture to show himself again in Naples, was threatened with severe punishment (1540—1541). Many turned their steps towards Turkey, a few went to Ancona, under papal protection, or to Ferrara, under the rule of Duke Hercules II, who passed for a friend of the Jews. Those who emigrated by sea suffered much hardship, and many of them were taken by pirates, and carried to Marseilles. The Marranos who were living there did much for them, and King Henry II also treated them humanely. As he could not keep them in his country, he sent them in his ships to Turkey. Samuel Abrabanel also left Naples, although he was offered the exceptional license to remain there; but he refused to separate himself from the lot of his unhappy co-religionists. He settled in Ferrara, and lived there for about ten years. His noble wife, highly respected by Leonora, the daughter of the viceroy of Naples, now the Duchess of Tuscany, survived him.

A year later, the Jews of Bohemia experienced a milder, so to speak, more decent form of hatred. There had been many fires in the towns, especially in Prague. The Jews and shepherds were accused of having hired incendiaries. The Jews were also charged with having betrayed to the sultan the secret preparations for war against the Turks. The Bohemian diet therefore resolved to banish all Jews from Bohemia, and King Ferdinand, brother of Charles V, gave his assent. They were compelled to start on their exile with all their belongings (Adar, 1542), for of the numerous Jews of Prague only ten persons or families received permission to remain there. Many of them found their way into Poland and Turkey, then the two most tolerant countries. The innocence of those who had suffered death, and of the banished Jews, was established in the course of the same year. A few of the notables interceded for their recall, for they were more indispensable than trade jealousy, fanaticism, and the hatred of race would confess. Thus those who had settled near the Bohemian frontier were able to return to their home. But for this favor they were obliged to pay a tax of 300 schock groschen, and were ordered to wear a badge of yellow cloth as a mark by which they might be distinguished.

At the same time two persons of exalted rank and great influence, the one on the Catholic, the other on the Protestant side, attacked the Jews so mercilessly, that it is a marvel that they were not exterminated to a man. The cause of provocation in one instance was as follows:—About Easter, a peasant boy, four years old, from the duchy of Neuburg in Bavaria, was missed, and suspicions arose that he was with the Jews. After Easter the boy was discovered by means of a dog, and enemies of the Jews pretended to see signs of Jewish torture on his body. Upon this the bishop of Eichstädt caused certain Jews to be seized and dragged to his residence that they might be tried, and sent a request to the neighboring princes to seize the Jews in their domains. But the inquiry did not prove the guilt of the Jews. On this occasion Duke Otto Henry of Neuburg warmly espoused the cause of the Jews, and exerted his influence to oppose the bishop of Eichstädt. The latter moved heaven and earth to have them banished at least. A courageous writer, probably at the suggestion of the duke, boldly defended the Jews against the prejudice of Christians in a pamphlet. This publication, "Little Book about the Jews," the author of which was a Lutheran pastor (perhaps Hosiander), for the first time placed the whole falsehood and malice of the accusation of the murder of Christian children in a clear light. The author, who professed to have had much intercourse with Jews, and to have become thoroughly acquainted with their language, laws, and customs, declared emphatically that a shameful injustice was done to Jews by these perpetual accusations of child-murder. The wealth and the pure faith of the Jews were the reasons. On the one hand, avaricious and cruel princes, or impoverished nobles or citizens, who owed money to Jews, invented such tales in order to be able to use violence against them; and on the other, such fables were invented by monks and the secular clergy in order to make new saints and fresh shrines for the encouragement of pilgrimages. In the long period since the dispersion of the Jews among Christians, no one had asserted, till within the last 300 years, that they had murdered Christian children. These idle tales had become current only since monks and priests practiced so much deception with pilgrimages and miraculous healings. For the priests feared no one more than Jews, because the latter disregarded human invention, and understood the Scripture better than the priests, who, therefore, persecuted the Jews to the utmost, slandered them, and caused them to be hated. They even wished to burn their sacred books. Therefore, it was fair to assume that priests had invented the story of the murder of the child in the province of Neuburg. The author further points out that till the third century the Christians were accounted child-murderers and shedders of blood in the heathen world. The confessions of Jews themselves, which were quoted in confirmation of the accusations, had been made under torture, and could not be received as evidence.

Fanatical Catholic priests, especially the bishop of Eichstädt, saw with indignation that Jews, instead of being abhorred and persecuted, were glorified in this book, and hastened to efface the impression. Dr. John Eck, so notorious in the history of the Reformation, a favorite of the bishop of Eichstädt, was commissioned to write an answer, to prove the crime of bloodguiltiness, and to defame the Jews. This lawyer-theologian, with the broad shoulders of a butcher, the voice of a seditionist, and the disputativeness of a sophist, who had brought the Catholic Church, which he intended to defend against the Lutherans, into discredit by his vanity and his intemperate habits, this unprincipled disputant gladly undertook to belabor the Jews. In 1541 he wrote a hostile reply to the above-mentioned pamphlet, in which he set himself to prove "the evil and wickedness brought about by Jews in all the German territories and other kingdoms." He revived the old accusations against baptized Jews, patched together old wives' tales about the cruel nature of the Jews, raked up the false stories about Trent and Ratisbon uttered by Jews when undergoing torture, and added his own experiences to them. Eck was so shameless as to bring proofs of the cruelty of the Jewish character from the Old Testament. To cast infamy upon them he even slandered the Old Testament heroes held sacred by the church. In verbose language and with a false show of learning he maintained that Jews mutilated the children of Christians, and used their blood in the consecration of their priests, to assist their wives in child-birth, and to heal sickness; and that they desecrated the host. He exclaimed indignantly: "It is a great mistake that we Christians leave the Jews so much freedom, and grant them protection and security." Probably on the petition of Jews against these accusations, the emperor, Charles V, renewed their privileges, and declared them innocent of shedding the blood of Christians.

It is not edifying to find that Luther, the champion against obsolete prejudices, the founder of a new faith, agreed completely on the subject of Jews with his mortal enemy, Dr. Eck, who, with the same effrontery, had employed similar falsehood against himself. These two passionate opponents were of one heart and soul in their hatred of Jews. Luther had become greatly embittered with advancing age. He had lost much among his own followers by his obstinacy and persistent caviling, had disturbed the unanimity of those of the same way of thinking, and in his own camp created a breach which caused infinite harm to the Reformation for several centuries. His hard disposition had steadily gained the mastery over his gentle religion and humility, and his monkish narrowness could not at all comprehend Judaism with its laws, which brought forth and developed not the faith, but the morality and elevation, of man. He became enraged when his colleagues, Karlstadt, Münzer, etc., referred for example to the year of Jubilee, and the enfranchisement of the slaves and serfs. A pamphlet, in the form of a dialogue, in which Judaism was involved in a contest with Christianity, probably written by a Christian, was now sent to him; this was too much for him. Could Judaism be so bold as to think of measuring itself against Christianity! Luther at once set about writing a passionate, stinging pamphlet, "Concerning the Jews and their Lies" (1542), which, in spitefulness, exceeded the writings of Pfefferkorn and Eck.

Luther began by saying that he had made up his mind not to write anything further about Jews, nor against them, but because he had learnt that "this miserable, wicked people" dared entice Christians to join them, he wished to warn weak-minded men not to allow themselves to be befooled. Luther's principal argument, in proof of the truth of Christianity against the denial of the Messiahship of Jesus by the Jews, is written in very monkish style. Because the Christians, for more than a thousand years, had robbed them of all the rights of man, had treated them as evil beasts, had trodden them under foot, lacerated, and slain them: in a word, because they had fallen into distress through the harshness of Christians, therefore, they must be rejected, and the Saviour of the world must have appeared!

This is mediæval logic. But it exceeds the limits of indulgence towards the peculiarities of a strong character, when Luther, in his uncharitableness towards Jews, employs language such as was usual with those who burnt Jews at the stake. "Why should the Jews complain of hard captivity among us?" he says. "We Christians suffered persecution and martyrdom at their hands for nearly 300 years, so that we might well complain that they took us captive and killed us. And to this very day we know not what devil brought them into our land" (as if Jews had not dwelt in some districts of what is now Germany long before Germans were there). "We did not bring them from Jerusalem; besides that, no one keeps them: the country and the roads are open to them, let them return to their own land. We will gladly give them presents, if we can but be rid of them, for they are a heavy burden upon us, a plague, a pestilence, a sore trial." Luther, like Pfefferkorn and Eck, stated with malicious delight how the Jews were often driven out by violence "from France and recently from Spain by our beloved Emperor Charles (an historical blunder); this year also from the entire dominion of Bohemia, although one of their securest nests was in Prague; also from Ratisbon, Magdeburg, and many other places in my time."

Without appreciation of the heroic patience displayed by Jews in the midst of hostility, and untaught by history, Luther did nothing but repeat the lying accusations of the vindictive Pfefferkorn, whose falsehood and villainy had been palpably proved by the Humanists. In imitation of this arch-enemy of the Jews he wrote that the Talmud and the rabbis taught that it was no sin to kill the Goyim, that is, heathens and Christians, break an oath to them, or rob and plunder them, and that the one and only aim of Jews was to weaken the Christian religion. It is incomprehensible that Luther, who had taken the part of the Jews so strongly in the heat of the Reformation, could repeat all the false tales about the poisoning of the springs, the murder of Christian children, and the use of human blood. He also maintained, in agreement with Eck, from whom in other respects he was so widely divided, that the Jews were too prosperous in Germany, and in consequence had become insolent.

What is to be done with this wicked, accursed race, which can no longer be tolerated? asked Luther, and he gave an answer to the question which shows equal want of charity and wisdom. First of all the reformer of Wittenberg recommended that the synagogues be reduced to ashes, "to the honor of God and of Christianity." Next, Christians were to destroy the houses of the Jews, and drive them all under one roof, or into a stable like gypsies. All prayer-books and copies of the Talmud and the Old Testament were to be taken from them by force (as Luther's opponents, the Dominicans, had advised), and even praying and the use of God's name were to be forbidden under penalty of death. Their rabbis were to be forbidden to teach. The authorities were to prohibit the Jews from traveling, and to bar the roads against them, so that they must stay at home. Luther advised that their money be taken from them, and that this confiscated wealth be employed to establish a fund to maintain those Jews who should embrace Christianity. The authorities were to compel able-bodied Jews and Jewesses to forced labor, and to keep them strictly employed with the flail, the axe, the spade, the distaff and spindle, so that they might earn their bread in the sweat of their brow, and not live in idleness, feasting, and splendor. Christians were not to show any tender mercy to Jews. Luther urged the emperor and the princes to expel them from the country without delay, and drive them back into their own land. But anticipating that the princes would not consent to such folly, he exhorted the clergy and teachers of the people to fill the minds of their hearers with hatred of Jews. He observed that if he had power over Jews, he would assemble the best and most learned among them, and, under penalty of having their tongues cut out, force them to accept the Christian teaching, that there is not *one* God, but that there are *three* Gods. Luther even stirred up the robber-nobles against them. He had heard that a rich Jew was traveling through Germany with twelve horses. This Jew was known as the wealthy Michael, of Frankfort, the protégé of the Margrave of Brandenburg; if the princes did not close the road against him and his fellow-believers, Luther urged the robber-knights to do so, for Christians might learn from his pamphlet how depraved was the Jewish nation. These absurd charges Luther ascribed to a worthless convert, Anton Margaritha, the son of a rabbi of Ratisbon. He had become a Catholic, and being punished on account of calumnies, had turned Lutheran, and written a foolish book against the Jews, and from this book Luther had taken his unjust attacks upon them.

Shortly before his death he exhorted his hearers in a sermon to drive out the Jews:

"Besides all this you still have the Jews, who do great evil in the land. If they could kill us all, they would gladly do so, aye, and often do it, especially those who profess to be physicians—they know all that is known about medicine in Germany; they can give poison to a man of which he will die in an hour, or in ten or twenty years; they thoroughly understand this art. I say to you lastly, as a countryman, if the Jews refuse to be converted, we ought not to suffer them, or bear with them any longer."

In the reformer and regenerator of Germany, then, the Jews had almost a worse enemy than in the Pfefferkorns, Hoogstratens, and Ecks, certainly worse than in the popes till the middle of the century. But few heeded the words of those wretches, known to be sophists and liars, while Luther's uncharitable utterances were respected as oracles by the Christians of the new faith, and but too well followed out. As Jerome had infected the Catholic world with his openly avowed hatred of Jews, so Luther poisoned the Protestant world for a long time to come with his Jew-hating testament. Protestants became even more bitter against Jews than Catholics had been. The leaders of Catholicism demanded absolute submission to canonical law, but on this condition granted them permission to remain in Catholic countries ; Luther, on the other hand, required their absolute expulsion. The popes often issued exhortations to spare the synagogues; but the founder of the Reformation insisted upon their desecration and destruction. It was reserved for him to place Jews on a level with gypsies. This difference arose from the fact that the popes occupied the highest rank in life, and dwelt in Rome, the metropolis of the world, the center of affairs in the four quarters of the globe; thus they had no eye for petty events, and usually left the Jews unnoticed because of their small importance. Luther, on the other hand, who lived in a petty country town and amidst narrow surroundings, listened to all the gossip against Jews, judged them by the measure of a country bumpkin, and reckoned up every farthing that they earned against them. He, therefore, was the cause of their being expelled by Protestant princes. In Roman Catholic states the Dominicans alone were their deadly enemies.

This hatred followed the Jews even into Turkey. If there were neither Roman Catholics nor Protestants, there were Greek Catholic Christians. Turks and Greeks lived together in the towns of both Greece and Asia Minor. The latter, who would not give up their arrogance, but dared not display it towards the ruling Turks, persecuted the Jews with silent hatred, and took advantage of every opportunity to draw upon them the persecution of the government. On one occasion some of them gave rise to a persecution in the town of Amazia in Asia Minor. They caused a poor Greek, who was in the habit of associating with Jews, and had been supported by them, to disappear, and then accused some Jews of having murdered him. Hereupon the Turkish cadis seized the accused, put them to the torture, and forced them to acknowledge the murder. They were hanged, and a respected Jewish physician, Jacob Abi-Ayub, was burnt (about 1545). A few days afterwards a Jew recognized the Greek supposed to have been murdered, induced him to tell how he had been made to disappear, and brought him before the cadi. The latter, justly incensed against the malicious Greek accusers, had them executed. A similar accusation, the falseness of which was brought to light, was lodged against a Jew of the town of Tokat at about the same time.

These cruel occurrences suggested to Moses Hamon, Sultan Solyman's Jewish physician, to obtain a decree from the sultan that an accusation against Jews in Turkey of having murdered a Christian, and other malicious calumnies, should not be brought before the ordinary judges, but before the sultan himself.

Hatred against Jews, restrained in Turkey, raged the more openly in Christian countries. The republic of Genoa for a long time had not suffered a Jew to remain more than three days within its boundaries. Notwithstanding this, fugitives from Spain or Provence from time to time were received in the town of Novi, near Genoa; they went in and out of the capital itself, and were suffered to remain there. In the party differences between the patrician families, the little community, repulsed by the one side, was taken up by the other. Most of them were intelligent artisans, capitalists, or physicians. But again the Dominicans stirred up the people against them, and roused the professional jealousy of Christian physicians. Contrary to the wishes of Doge Doria, the Jews were driven out of Genoa (April, 1550), and, heralded by the sound of trumpets, a proclamation was made that henceforth no Jews should be suffered. This expulsion from Genoa is of importance, because a clever Jewish historian was included in it, whose fate represents in miniature the painful lot experienced by the Jewish race on a large scale.

The vicissitudes in the life of the nations, as well as the changes in the life of the Jewish people, especially since their cruel expulsion from Spain and Portugal, and the heartless persecution of the Marranos, at length brought some clear-seeing Jews to the conviction that history is not ruled by chance, but that a higher hand guides it, bringing to pass destined events by bloodshed and tears. Since the time of the crusades, no century had been richer in changeful, almost dramatic, events than the sixteenth, when not only fresh continents were discovered, but when a new spirit began to prevail among mankind, striving after new creations, but always kept down by the leaden weight of existing systems. This wealth of occurrences taught a few thoughtful Jews, mostly of Sephardic origin, to trace the work of Providence in the apparently whimsical and irregular course of universal and Jewish history. They considered history a comfort to that portion of mankind which had been overthrown, overridden, and downtrodden by the tumultuous course of events. And what race stood in more need of consolation than the Jewish, a martyr people apparently born only for sorrow, always eating its bread in tears? Almost at one and the same time, three enlightened Jews undertook the task of studying history, and placing before the Jewish reading world its brazen tables. These were the physician, Joseph Cohen, the learned Talmudist, Joseph Ibn-Verga, and the poet, Solomon Usque. All three began with the same fundamental idea. The spirit of the prophets, which recognized in the course of historical events the fittest means for instruction and improvement, had come upon them, incontestably showing that Jews even in their degradation are not like the gypsy rabble, neither having nor knowing a history; that, in fact, they stood higher than those who wielded the scepter and the sword, the rack and the club, for the subjugation of mankind.

The greatest of these historians was Joseph ben Joshua Cohen (born at Avignon, 1496, died 1575). His ancestors had come from Spain at the great expulsion, his father Joshua emigrating to Avignon, and thence moving to Novi, in Genoese territory. For a while he lived in Genoa, and was expelled thence. Joseph Cohen had studied medicine, devoting himself both to the theory and the practice. He appears to have been family physician to the doge, Andrea Doria. His heart beat warmly for his Jewish brethren, and he was zealous in his endeavors to lighten their unhappy lot. He once exerted himself to obtain the release of a father and son, cast into prison by the heartless Giannettino Doria, nephew and presumptive heir to the doge. But he succeeded in delivering only the father, the son did not escape till the stormy night of Fiesco's conspiracy. At the last expulsion from Genoa (1550), the inhabitants of the little town of Voltaggio begged him to settle amongst them as a physician, and he lived there for eighteen years. But history attracted him more than the practice of medicine, and he began to search for chronicles in order to write a sort of universal history in the form of annals. He began with the period of the decline of the Roman empire and the formation of the modern states, and represented the course of the world's history as a struggle between Asia and Europe, between the Crescent and the Cross; the former represented by the then powerful dominion of Turkey; the latter, by France, which had set up Charlemagne, the first emperor of a Christian realm. He connected the whole of European history with these two groups of nations. He included all the events and wars of Christendom, and of the Mahometan countries in "The Annals of the Kings of France and of the House of Othman," the title of his historical work. In the history of his own times, which he either witnessed himself, or obtained from the experience of contemporaries, he is an impartial narrator, and, therefore, his work is a trustworthy source of information. The Hebrew historical style, borrowed from the best books of the Bible, renders his account most forcible. The Biblical language and dramatic style give a charm to the work, and raise it above the level of a dry chronicle.

Joseph Cohen introduced the history of the various persecutions of the Jews at the different periods when they occurred. His chief aim was to point out the justice of God in the course of history, showing how violence and cunning met with their desert, and were cast down from the height attained. He sympathized with the sorrows which he described; therefore, he often wrote with intense bitterness.

Very different is another historical work of the same period, upon which three generations, father, son, and grandson, were employed. Judah Ibn-Verga, Kabbalist and astronomer, a member of the distinguished Ibn-Verga family, related to the Abrabanels, had noted down in a book some of the persecutions which Jews had undergone in different countries and at various times. Solomon Ibn-Verga, who had witnessed the expulsion of the Jews from Spain and Portugal, and who for a time had pretended to be a Christian, and then emigrated to Turkey as a Marrano, added several narratives to his father's notes.

He understood the Latin language, and so borrowed and added fresh material from various Latin documents. His son, Joseph Ibn-Verga, who belonged to the college of rabbis at Adrianople, completed the work by adding some of the events of his own times and the age immediately preceding, and then published the whole under the title of "Judah's Rod of Correction" (Shebet Jehuda). Joseph Ibn-Verga was also learned in Latin, and incorporated many narratives from Latin documents. This martyrology of the Ibn-Vergas, then, is not a unit, but a medley without plan or order, destitute even of chronological sequence. Imaginary conversations between Jews and Spanish or Portuguese kings are given as having actually taken place. But the Hebrew style is brilliant and graceful, without possessing biblical coloring like that of the historical works of Elias Kapsali and Joseph Cohen. Ibn-Verga sought (towards the end of the first part) to show the reason why the Jewish race, above all the Spanish Jews, were visited with so many intolerable trials, and found it in the preference once shown for the Jewish nation: "Whom God loves most He chasteneth most." But the chief sources of persecution were to be found in the division between Jews and Christians in the matter of food and drink, in the revenge taken by Christians for the crucifixion of Jesus Christ, in the offenses of Spanish Jews against Christian women, in the envy of their riches, and in the false oaths of which they were guilty. Ibn-Verga did not conceal the faults of his race; perhaps he exaggerated them. Joseph Ibn-Verga added a heartfelt prayer about the numerous sufferings which Israel had undergone, and was still enduring, the last causing the first to be forgotten. All the nations of the world were united in hatred to this race; all creatures in heaven and on earth allied in enmity against it; before a Jewish child began to prattle it was pursued by hatred and scorn. "We are despised like the lowest worms; may God soon fulfill His promises to His people."

The most original of the three historians, as well as of the three Usques, probably belonging to the same family, was Samuel, who had no doubt fled from the fire of the Inquisition in Portugal. He settled with his relations in Ferrara. Like Solomon Usque, known under his Spanish name of Duarte Gomez, he was a poet, but his muse did not occupy herself with foreign material, with imitations and adaptations, but created something original and peculiar. The brilliant and tragical history of the Israelite people had great attraction for him; it did not exist merely as a lifeless mass of learning in his memory, but lived in his heart as a fresh bubbling spring from which he drew comfort and inspiration. Biblical history with its heroes, kings, and men of God, the history subsequent to the Captivity, with its alternations of splendid victory and unhappy overthrow, the history since the destruction of the Jewish rule by the Romans, all the events and changes of these three periods were present to Samuel Usque's mind. The material gathered from many sources he transformed by the breath of poetry into a long, most touching lament and consolation in the Portuguese language, not in verse, but in elevated prose, more charming than a poetic garb. It is a conversation of three shepherds, Icabo, Numeo, and Zicareo, the first of whom laments with bitter tears the tragical fate of Israel since its appearance on the scene of history; the other two pour the balm of comfort into the broken heart of the unhappy shepherd, and show him that these sufferings are the necessary steps to the attainment of a glorious goal. Samuel Usque named this historical dialogue, "Consolation for the Sorrows of Israel." By his vivid picture of the Jewish past, he intended to give to the Portuguese fugitives in Ferrara and elsewhere, who had again attached themselves to Judaism, comfort in their great sorrow and suffering, and lead them to look forward to a happy future.

He represented the Israelite nation now as a mourning widow, wringing her hands in lamentation, and weeping day and night over the sufferings of her sons during thousands of years; now as a prophetess inspired by God, clothed in a radiant robe, whose eye pierces the darkness, and sees a glorious future, and whose lips utter wisdom, and pour balm on burning wounds. Though he was not a regular historian, yet no one has represented the principal features of Jewish history from the earliest times down to his own with so much light and life as Samuel Usque.

The external form of this historico-poetical dialogue is as follows: the shepherd, Icabo (or Jacob, the representative of the Jewish nation), laments in a lonely spot the misery of his flock, dispersed throughout all parts of the world, humiliated, and torn in pieces. "To what quarter of the globe shall I turn and find healing for my wounds, oblivion of my sorrows, and comfort in this grievous, heavy torment? The whole earth is full of my misery and my distress. I am like a poor, heavy-laden pilgrim in the midst of all the riches and delight of favored Asia. Amid the wealth of the gold of sun-burnt Africa, I am an unhappy, starving, fainting exile. And Europe, Europe! my hell upon earth! what shall I say of thee, thou who hast adorned thy greatest triumphs with the limbs of my flock? How can I praise thee, Italy, thou blasphemous and warlike land! Thou who hast fed upon the flesh of my lambs like a ravenous lion! Ye accursed pastures of France, which did furnish poisoned grass for my flocks to feed on! Thou proud, rough mountain-land of Germany, which hast taken my young, and dashed them in pieces from the tops of thy wild Alps! And you sweet, fresh streams of England, from you my flocks have drunk only bitter, brackish waters! Hypocritical, cruel, bloodthirsty Spain, in you voracious and ravening wolves have devoured, and still devour, my fleecy flocks!" The two shepherds, Numeo and Zicareo, attracted by the heart-rending lamentations of Icabo, induce him by much persuasion to tell them his sorrow, and thus obtain relief for his burdened heart. But not without a struggle does he bring himself to do this. He then describes to his two friends the former splendor of his flock, and thus brings before their eyes the prosperous days of Israel. Then he passes to the trials which God's flock has had to endure. Icabo is at length induced by gentle persuasion to relate the history of his unhappy race in detail, first its adverse fortunes, and its exile during the existence of the first Temple; then, in a second dialogue, the bitterness endured, and the exile till the second destruction of the Temple by the Romans; and in a third dialogue, the sufferings of his people during the long exile; the first forced baptism which Sisebut, king of the Visigoths, imposed upon the Jews of Spain; the expulsion of the Jews from England and France, Spain and Portugal; the horrors of the Inquisition, which Usque had himself beheld; and lastly, the desecration of a synagogue at Pesaro (1552). In this manner does Icabo (or Samuel Usque) go through the long range of Jewish history. He concludes this summary of sorrows thus:

"Scarcely hadst thou ceased to drink of the poisoned cup of the Babylonians, which had well-nigh proved fatal to thee, O Israel, when thou wast revived to endure the torments inflicted by the Romans; and when this double misfortune, which so cruelly tore thee in pieces, was at an end, thou wert indeed still living, but fast bound to suffering and misery, tortured by fresh pangs. It is the fate of all created beings to experience change; only not thine, for thy unhappy lot is not changed, and has no ending."

The friends offer comfort and consolation to Icabo. They say:

"Sorrows, be they never so great and intense, have an object. They have been partly incurred by a sinful life and by backsliding from God, and are intended to serve for the correction and purification of Israel. It is also a blessing that thy people is scattered abroad among all the nations of earth, that the wicked may not succeed in utterly destroying them. When the Spaniards drove thee out, and burnt thy people, God ordained that thou shouldst find a country ready to receive thee, where thou couldst dwell in freedom, namely, Italy."

The enemies who treated Israel so unmercifully were said to have received their punishment. The poet said of the Spaniards that Italy had become their grave; of France, that Spain had been its rod of correction; of Germany, that the Turks were its executioners, who made of it a wall against which to direct their cannon; and of England, that wild and savage Scotland was a perpetual thorn in its side. One great comfort was that all these sufferings, sorrows, and trials which came upon the Jewish race were literally announced and precisely foretold by the prophets. They had only served to elevate Israel, and as the prophecies of evil were verified, so they might trust that the prophecies of good would not remain unfulfilled.

The dialogues end with comforting prophecies in the feeling words of Isaiah. This edifying description served doubtless to sustain the Marranos in their newly-recovered creed, and to endure sufferings of every kind for it, even death itself.

Samuel Usque was of opinion that the sufferings of the Jewish people were soon to decrease, and that the long looked-for morning would soon follow the darkness of night. But the church showed him that this anticipation was ill-founded. He lived to see fresh tribulations arise in his immediate neighborhood, and a whole system of fresh persecutions put into practice, which the Jewish historian, Joseph Cohen, was able to record in his annals of Jewish martyrdom. These fresh troubles had their origin in the reaction which the Roman Catholic Church was ardently desirous to institute against the ever-growing Reformation. Two men strove at almost the same time, quite independently of each other, to re-establish declining Catholicism, and thereby laid snares in the way of the progress of the human race. A Neapolitan, Pietro Caraffa, and a Spaniard, Ignatius Loyola, both men of zeal, and ready to take the initiative, began with self-castigation, and ended by reducing the minds and bodies of others to bondage. The worm-eaten papacy, supposed to be crumbling away beneath the laughter and derision of its opponents, for which its very friends had nothing but a shrug of the shoulders, was raised by these two men to a height greater almost than in the time of Innocent III and his immediate successors, because it rested, not on the tottering foundations of dreamy belief, but on the firm ground of powerful conviction and reckless determination. Caraffa, afterwards Pope Paul IV, and Loyola, the founder of the order of Jesuits, so powerful to this day, were very much in earnest in impressing the minds of the faithful with the belief in the supremacy of the papacy and the pope's power to bind and to loose, both in heaven and on earth, they themselves being firmly convinced thereof. Caraffa re-established the discipline of the church which had grown lax, increased its severity, and placed a rod of iron in her hand. He introduced into the Catholic world at large the means which Torquemada, Deza, and Ximenes de Cisneros had employed in Spain to force Jews and Moors to become members of the church, namely, the stake. All who held a belief differing by so much as a hair's breadth from the papacy were to abjure it, or be burnt. Merciless force, which does not think, and destroys all independent thought, was to restore credit to the defamed church.

To regain possession of the minds which had striven to emancipate themselves, and to keep them in bondage, the Inquisition thought it in the highest degree necessary to watch the press. The press had brought mischief and schism into the church (so thought Caraffa and his associates); the press, then, must be gagged. Only what was approved by the pope and his followers was to be printed. Censorship of the press had been introduced by previous popes, but as anything had hitherto been obtainable by bribery, publishers had been able to print and disseminate seditious works against the existing church system, either with or without the knowledge of the clergy appointed to control such publications. The seditious controversial pamphlets in the Reuchlin quarrel, the famous "Letters," Von Hutten's shafts at the papacy, Luther's first pamphlets against the Romish Babylonian harlot, inflammable materials which, appearing in rapid succession, on all sides kindled the tow of which the church tent was woven, were the result of negligent censorship. This was now to be changed. The censorship was henceforth intrusted only to priests faithful to the papacy, and, either from conviction or from instincts of self-preservation, they exercised their office without leniency.

The Jews soon felt the effect of this fierce Catholic reaction, for they had no sort of protection, and owed their miserable existence only to neglect in the enforcement of the canonical laws against them. As soon as the church began seriously to put these hostile decrees into execution, the existence, or at least the peace, of the Jews was endangered. First of all the question of the Talmud was again raised, but not with the lukewarmness of forty years before. At that time Pfefferkorn and the Dominicans of Cologne could not hope to obtain a hearing before the papal chair for their proposal to burn the Talmud, but were obliged to have recourse to all sorts of ruses in order to gain over the emperor to their policy. Now a totally different spirit prevailed. The universal harm caused by the Talmud needed only to be hinted at by malicious converts for a decree to be at once issued against it. By such the fresh outcry against it was raised.

Elias Levita, the Hebrew grammarian, who had lived for a long time in the house of Cardinal Egidio de Viterbo, and had instructed many Christians in the Hebrew language, both personally and by his writings, and had also imparted to some a superficial knowledge of the Kabbala, left two grandsons, the children of his daughter, who were received in Christian circles. One of them, Eliano, had learnt Hebrew thoroughly, and was a proof-reader and copyist in several towns of Italy; his brother, Solomon Romano, had traveled much in Germany, Turkey, Palestine, and Egypt, and understood many languages: Hebrew, Latin, Spanish, Arabic, and Turkish. Eliano, the elder, had become a Christian under the name of Victor Eliano, and was a priest, later even a canon. Solomon Romano was so indignant at this that he hastened to Venice to persuade his brother to return to the bosom of Judaism. But instead of converting, he himself became converted. A Venetian patrician, much attached to the church, set about bringing him over to Christianity, and what he began, a Jesuit finished. Solomon Romano was baptized (1551), and assumed the name of John Baptista, to the great grief of his mother, who was still living. He became a Jesuit and afterwards an ecclesiastical writer, wrote upon the mysteries of the Christian faith, a Hebrew and Arabic catechism, and other similar works. This grandson of the grammarian Elias Levita, with two other converts, Joseph Moro and Ananel di Foligno, not content with having forsworn their religion, appeared before the pope, like Nicholas Donin, to denounce the Talmud, and repeated the same slanders, namely, that the books of the Talmud contained abuse of Jesus, the church, the whole of Christendom, and that they hindered the conversion of the Jews in a body. Julius III was by no means bigoted, least of all was he inimical to Jews. But it no longer lay with the pope to decide upon the Talmud; this task devolved on the court of the Inquisition, that is to say, on the fanatical Caraffa, and Julius III was obliged to approve and sign the decree laid before him by the inquisitor general (August 12th, 1553)—another proof of the emptiness of the boasted infallibility of the papacy. Leo X had encouraged the printing of the Talmud, and the third pope after him decreed its destruction. The officers of the Inquisition invaded the houses of the Roman Jews, confiscated the copies of the Talmud and compilations made from it, and burnt them with special malice on the Jewish New Year's Day (September 9th), so that the Jews might feel the grief at the destruction of their sacred books the more keenly. The inquisitors did not wage war against the Talmud in Rome only. Copies were burnt by hundreds of thousands throughout the whole Romagna, in Ferrara, Mantua, Venice, Padua, and in the island of Candia, which belonged to Venice. The officers of the Inquisition in their fury no longer distinguished between the Talmud and other Hebrew writings. Everything that fell into their hands became a prey to the flames; they even seized copies of the Holy Scriptures. The Jews of all Catholic countries were in despair; they were robbed by this confiscation of the rabbinical books which contain the precepts of a religious life, and in which there is no word referring to Christianity. They, therefore, appealed to the pope to revoke the decree, or at least to permit them the use of these harmless rabbinical writings. Julius III agreed to this latter request, and issued a bull (May 29th, 1554) that the Jews be compelled, under pain of corporal punishment, to give up all copies of the Talmud, but that the bailiffs be not allowed to seize other Hebrew works, or vex the Jews. Transgressors of this decree were to be visited with severe ecclesiastical punishment. Henceforward all Hebrew books were subjected to inspection before they were published, lest they contain a shadow of reproach against Christianity or Rome. The censors were mostly baptized Jews, who thus had the opportunity of tormenting their former brethren in faith.

Matters became worse for the Jews after the death of Julius III, as the college of cardinals insisted that all henceforth elected to the papacy should belong to the strictest church party, if possible, be monks. Cultivated dignitaries, interested in humanistic studies, who loved the arts and sciences, if such there still were, had fallen into disfavor.

Marcellus II, the first of the reactionary popes, was succeeded in the papal chair by the bigoted and fanatical Caraffa, under the name of Paul IV (May, 1555—August, 1559). He retained in old age all the violence and passion of his youth, and framed his policy accordingly. He hated not only Protestants and Jews, but also the Spaniards, the most useful tools of ecclesiastical fanaticism; he termed them and the bigoted king, Philip II, "worthless seed of the Jews and Moors." Soon after his accession to the papal chair he issued a bull, by which every synagogue throughout the Papal States was ordered to contribute ten ducats for the maintenance of the house of catechumens in which Jews were educated in the Christian faith. Still more severe was his second bull against the Jews (July 12th, 1555), which enforced the canonical laws against them with great harshness. They were to remain shut up in Ghettos, and were to possess only one synagogue; the rest were to be destroyed. They were not allowed to employ Christian servants, not even wet-nurses, and were forbidden to have intercourse with Christians in general. Every Jew was commanded to wear a green cap, and every Jewess a green veil, even outside the precincts of the city. They were not to be addressed as "Sir" by the Christian population. They were forbidden to own real estate, and those who had any were ordered to sell it within six months; thus they were compelled to part with their lands, worth more than 500,000 gold crowns, for a fifth of their value. But the severest blow was that Jewish physicians were prohibited from attendance on Christians, though so many popes owed their health to them. Heavy penalties were attached to the infringement of this edict. These cruel measures were carried out with extreme severity, and confiscation of copies of the Talmud was not interrupted. Thereupon, many Jews forsook Rome, which had become so malicious towards them, and betook themselves to more tolerant states, but they were maltreated on the way by fanatical mobs. Those who remained in Rome were treated in a most undignified manner by the pope First it was said that they had only made a feint of selling their lands, and had executed sham deeds of sale, and for this they were imprisoned; next the pope announced that those Jews who were not working for the common good should leave Rome within a given time. When the terrified Jews asked for an explanation of what was meant by "working for the general good," they received the Pharoah-like reply, "You shall know at the proper time."

Paul IV compelled them to do forced labor in repairing the walls of Rome, which he desired to fortify against the Spaniards, of whom he had wilfully made enemies. Once he, whom the Jews not unjustly called Haman, impelled by his fierce enmity against them, commanded his nephew to set fire to all their dwellings under the veil of the darkness of night. The latter was about to carry out the order, though unwillingly, when he met the sensible cardinal, Alexander Farnese, who advised him to delay the execution of the inhuman deed that the pope might have time to consider. The order was revoked on the following day.

The fanatical Pope Paul IV thus ill-treated the

Jews, but he raged with even greater fury against the Marranos in his dominions. Many, compelled to become Christians in Portugal, had found an asylum in Ancona, and received an indemnity from Pope Clement VII guaranteeing that they should not be molested by the Inquisition, but might confess Judaism. The next two moderate popes, Paul III and Julius III, had confirmed this privilege to the Marranos, convinced as they were that baptism, enforced by violence, could have no sacramental significance. The more violently the Inquisition now introduced into Portugal proceeded against the Marranos, like that in Spain, the more fugitives took refuge in Italy. They settled, with the property rescued, in Ferrara and Ancona, trusting in the privileges assured to them by the head of Catholic Christendom. But what did the vindictive Pope Paul IV care for an assurance of safety granted by his predecessors, and for a time tacitly recognized by himself, if it was in opposition to his notion of orthodoxy? His perverse spirit could not suffer those to live as Jews who had been sprinkled with baptismal water. Paul, therefore, issued a secret order that all the Marranos in Ancona, already numbering several hundreds, should be thrown into the dungeons of the Inquisition, a trial of their orthodoxy instituted, and their property sequestered (Elul—August, 1555). This was a severe blow to the Marranos, some of whom had been there for half a century, and had lulled themselves into a dream of security. Even those Marranos who were Turkish subjects, and were dwelling only for a short time in the flourishing seaport because of their trade with the Levant, were included in the accusation of Judaizing, and imprisoned, and their goods confiscated, as a matter of course. The furious pope thus cut off a considerable source of his revenue at the moment when he was about to plunge into a costly war with Spain.

But very few Marranos succeeded in escaping from the bailiffs of the Inquisition. They were all received by Duke Guido Ubaldo, of Urbino, and quartered in Pesaro, because he was then at enmity with the pope, and thought to transfer the trade of the Levant from Ancona to Pesaro by means of the connection of the Marranos with Turkey. Duke Hercules II, of Ferrara, also offered the Portuguese and Spanish Jews, from whatever country they might have fled, an asylum in his dominions, and formally invited them thither (December, 1555). Among those who escaped to Pesaro was a man then held in high repute, the celebrated physician Amatus (Chabib) Lusitanus (born 1511, died 1568), a sensible and intelligent man, a skillful physician, a noted scholar, and a man of equal conscientiousness and amiability. As a pretended Christian he had borne the name of João Rodrigo de Castel-Branco. He appears to have been driven from his home by the introduction of the Inquisition into Portugal. He had been for some time in Antwerp, then the most important city of Flanders, afterwards visited both Ferrara and Rome, but had permanently established himself at Ancona (about 1549), where he had openly assumed his family name of Chabib, and Latinized it under the form of Amatus Lusitanus. Although he openly professed himself a Jew, he was frequently summoned to the court of Pope Julius III to attend him in sickness. Sufferers came to him from far and near. The art of healing was to him a sacred office, which he fulfilled with his whole soul in the endeavor to prolong human life. Amatus was able to take a solemn oath—by God and His holy commandments—that he had always labored purely for the welfare of mankind, had never concerned himself about compensation, had never accepted valuable presents, had treated the poor without fee, and made no difference between Jews, and Christians, and Turks. Nothing ever hindered him in his devoted calling, neither family considerations, nor long distances. Amatus had many disciples of his art who were attached to him, and whom he regarded as his children. In his young days he had written medical works so highly esteemed that they were often printed during his lifetime. The greatest interest was excited by his seven "Centuries" (each dealing with a hundred cases of illness), in which he minutely described his remedies and their effect, and gave the characteristics of his patients. These "Cures" procured for him very extensive fame during his lifetime; they were frequently printed in Italy, France, Germany, and even in Spain, and were used by other physicians as text-books. Amatus received an invitation from the king of Poland to come to his court in the capacity of his private physician, an invitation which he did not accept.

This benefactor of mankind, the ornament of his time, was obliged to flee like a criminal from Ancona to Pesaro, and afterwards to journey even further, because he refused to make a ridiculous confession of faith before the bloodthirsty Inquisition of Paul IV, and did not wish to expose himself to the risk of death at the stake. More than a hundred Portuguese Marranos, unable to flee, had to pine in the dungeons of the Inquisition until their sentence was announced to them. This was to the effect that those who penitently made confession of the Catholic faith should be set at liberty, but be carried to the island of Malta, and forfeit all honors and dignities. Sixty Marranos agreed to this hypocrisy, but twenty-four of them, among them an aged woman, Donna Maiora, remained firm in the faith of their fathers, "The Lord our God is one God," and were burnt at the stake (May, 1556). Most of those to be transported to Malta escaped, and took refuge in Turkey. A cry of horror was heard from all Jews when the news of this shocking catastrophe was spread abroad. The sentence was as illegal as cruel, because, as has already been said, the religious freedom of the Marranos in Ancona had been solemnly confirmed by three popes in succession. The Portuguese Marranos in Turkey were completely stunned by this blow administered to their fellow-sufferers. They bethought themselves of means by which to be revenged on the insanely cruel pope. The peculiar position of the Jews in this century made it possible for them to entertain the idea of a struggle with their malicious enemy in the chair of St. Peter. A union of all the Jews of the East might furnish the means.

There lived at this time a noble Jewish lady, an ornament to her sex and her people by her grace, her intelligence, her character, and greatness of mind, one of those beings whom Providence seems to place in the world from time to time that the likeness of man to the Divine Image may not be quite forgotten. Donna Gracia Mendesia was a name which her Jewish contemporaries pronounced only with admiration and love. Blessed with ample means, which she expended wisely, and only for the benefit of others and for the elevation of mankind, she commanded an influence equal to that of a princess, and reigned over the willing hearts of hundreds of thousands. She was called the Esther of her time. But what anguish of mind she was obliged to endure before she dared openly to call herself Gracia (Hannah)! The waves of meanness and wickedness surged around her, but could not sully the purity of her soul. Born in Portugal (about 1510, died about 1568), of a Marrano family named Benveniste, she was married under the Christian name of Beatrice to a rich participator in the same unhappy fate, one of the house of Nassi, who had taken the baptismal name of Francisco Mendes. He had founded an extensive banking business, branches of which extended through Flanders and

France. The German emperor and ruler of two continents, Charles V, the king of France, and many princes besides, were debtors to the house of Mendes. A younger brother, Diogo Mendes, was head of the branch bank at Antwerp. When the husband of Beatrice died (before 1535), leaving her with one daughter named Reyna, and the terrible Inquisition, introduced into Portugal, threatened danger to her property and the lives of herself and her child, she betook herself to her brother-in-law at Antwerp, accompanied by a younger sister and several young nephews. She furnished poor Marranos with the means to flee from the fires of the Inquisition. The sums which pseudo-Christians paid to the emissaries and creatures of the pope to frustrate the Inquisition, went through her hands and her brother-in-law's. The Mendes family acquired a high position in Antwerp, where there were many Marranos. Mendesia's young, handsome and clever nephew, João Miques, associated with the first people in the city, and was much beloved by Maria, ruler of the Netherlands, formerly queen of Hungary, sister to Charles V.

Beatrice was by no means at ease in Antwerp. Affection for the religion in which she had been born, and which she was compelled to deny, and horror of the Catholic faith forced upon her, made Flanders just as hateful to her as Portugal. She longed for a country where she could freely follow the impulses of her heart, glowing with love to Judaism. She, therefore, importuned her brother-in-law, the head of the banking business, who had married her sister, either to go to Germany, or elsewhere, with her, or pay over her share of the property. Diogo Mendes fixed a time for this removal, but died before it arrived (1540—1546); he also left a widow and a daughter, Gracia the younger. This was the beginning of sorrowful days for Mendesia. She was recognized by her brother-in-law's will as the head of the widely-extended business, but could not settle the affairs of the house quickly enough to enable her to follow the wish of her heart, and betake herself to some tolerant land, where she could openly confess herself a Jewess. Besides, Charles V, in his covetousness, cast an eye upon the large property of the house of Mendes. An accusation was made by the imperial attorney-general that the deceased Diogo Mendes had secretly practiced Judaism. It may also have become known that he had supported the antagonists of the Inquisition by word and deed. It was, therefore, decreed that the whole of his property, being that of a heretic, should be forfeited to the exchequer. The order was issued that the goods and account-books of the house of Mendesia be seized and sealed. But the widow Mendesia succeeded in satisfying the avarice of the officials for the moment by bribes and the advance of a large loan. But it was impossible for her to leave Antwerp without exciting suspicion against herself and endangering her property still more. Thus she was obliged to remain there in great distress of mind for more than two years, until the loan was repaid by the emperor.

At length the hour of deliverance seemed to be at hand, when she might leave Antwerp, and proceed to Venice. A story circulated that her nephew, João Miques, had fled to Venice with her daughter Reyna, for whose hand several Christian noblemen had sued. Perhaps this was a story sedulously spread by the Mendes family so as to afford a pretext for their journey to Venice, and that no hindrance might be interposed. But this precaution was not successful. After her departure, Charles V again gave orders that her property, so far as it lay within his dominions, should be seized, because the sisters were secret Jewesses, and Mendesia the elder (as she was called) was compelled to pay large sums to avert this fresh calamity.

But misfortune, greater than any that she had yet experienced, was in store for her at Venice, from a quarter whence she least expected it, namely, from her younger sister. The latter, as reckless and scatter-brained as the elder was prudent and sedate, demanded her share of the property and her daughter's, to do with as she pleased.

But Donna Mendesia neither could nor would agree to this, she having been made sole manager of the property, and also guardian of her niece, still under age. Chafing at this guardianship, and probably guided by evil counselors, the younger sister took a step which turned out to her own disadvantage. She informed the Venetian government that her sister was about to emigrate to Turkey, and take with her all her wealth, there to resume her adherence to Judaism, while she herself and her daughter desired to remain Christians; and she asked the Venetian authorities to assist her in obtaining possession of her property, in order that she might use it as a good Christian in Venice. The rulers of Venice, seeing the prospect of a rich prize, did not hesitate to take up the accusation, cited the accused to appear before the legal authorities, and arrested her to prevent her flight. Her ill-advised or worthless sister also sent an avaricious, Jew-hating messenger to France, to take possession of the property there belonging to the Mendes family. This envoy, thinking himself insufficiently paid for his errand, denounced the younger sister also as a secret Jewess, and the French court confiscated the Mendes property in France. King Henry II also held himself exempt from repaying his debt to the family. The unfortunate Mendesia was meantime endeavoring to divert these blows aimed at herself and her property. Her nephew, João Miques, gave liberal assistance to prevent losses and to set his noble relative free. Either he or his aunt found a way to induce Sultan Solyman to embrace their cause. Such immense riches were about to be brought into his dominions, and the Venetian Republic, which existed only by his forbearance, dared deprive him of them? That roused his fury. His private physician, Moses Hamon, a Jew who hoped to win the hand of the rich heiress Reyna for his son, had disposed the sultan in favor of the Mendes family. A special messenger of state (Tshaus) was sent by the Porte to Venice, with instructions that the imprisoned Marrano was at once to be set free and allowed to depart unhindered for Turkey with all her property. In consequence of this a difference arose between the court of Turkey and the Republic of Venice, which afterwards led to animosities. An important part was thus thrust upon this poor lady against her will.

In the meantime she succeeded—no one knows how—in finding a place of refuge in Ferrara under the protection of the liberal-minded Duke Hercules of Este, where she resided for several years (about 1549 to 1553) under her Jewish name, a blessing and a comfort to her fellow-sufferers for their faith. Here she was able for the first time to exercise openly and freely her sublime virtue, her lively sympathies, her generosity, her genuine piety—in a word, all the nobility of her heart. Her wisdom and prudence were of great service to the Marranos in Italy. The poet Samuel Usque, who dedicated his beautiful work to her, spoke of her with enthusiasm and deep respect. He makes his Numeo, who plays the part of consoler in the dialogues, utter among other grounds of consolation for the sufferings of the Israelites, that they had met with unexpected help from this good woman:

"Who has not seen Divine Mercy reveal itself in human form, as it has shown, and still shows itself to thee a shield and defense against thy wretchedness? Who has not seen the heartfelt compassion of Miriam over again in the sacrifice of her own life to save that of her brethren? Or the great wisdom of Deborah in ruling her fellow-men? Or the infinite virtue and holiness of Esther in protecting the defenseless? Or the memorable exertions of the chaste widow Judith in order to deliver the besieged from terror? The Lord hath sent her down in our days from the midst of His holy angels, and united every virtue in one person, and for thy happiness it is that He hath placed this soul in the lovely form of the blessed Jewess Nassi. She it was who, at the beginning of the dispersion (of the Marranos), gave strength and hope to thy perishing sons, made hopeless by their want of means to escape the fire, and encouraged them to go forth on their pilgrimage. With bountiful hand did she succor those who had already set out on their wanderings in Flanders and other parts, and who, weakened by poverty and overcome by the perils of the sea passage, were in danger of getting no further, and strengthened them in their need. She did not withhold her favor even from her enemies. With her pure hand and her heavenly will has she freed most of this nation (of Marranos) from the depths of endless misery, poverty, and sin, led them into safe places, and gathered them together into obedience to the precepts of the true God. Thus did she become thy strength in thy weakness."

The two editors of the Ferrara Spanish Bible, Ahraham Usque and Athias, who dedicated it to "Her Highness the Señora Donna Gracia," described her invaluable services in a few words:

"We desire to dedicate the translation to your Grace, as the person whose deserts among our people will always occupy the foremost place. May you be pleased to accept it, to favor and protect it with the spirit which has always favored those who have asked help of you."

As she protected all three of the Usques, this eulogy may sound partial from their lips; but all, even the most conscientious rabbis of the time, were full of her praise, and wrote with equal enthusiasm, if not elegance, of her virtues:

"The noble princess, the glory of Israel, the wise woman who builds her house in holiness and purity, with her hand sustains the poor and needy, in order to make them happy in this world, and blessed in the world to come. Many are they whom she has rescued from death, and lifted up from the abasement of a worthless life, when they were languishing in a dungeon, and were given over to death. She hath founded houses wherein all may learn the law of God. She has given to many the means whereby they may not only live, but live in plenty."

After Donna Gracia Nassi had become reconciled to her sister, who probably saw that she endangered herself by assuming an antagonistic attitude towards Gracia, after she had seen her sister's child, the beautiful young Gracia, betrothed to her nephew Samuel Nassi in Ferrara, and after she had provided like a mother for all the members of her family, she carried out her long-cherished intention, and betook herself to the Turkish capital to escape the many annoyances to which she was subject in Christian territory. Her gifted nephew, João Miques, who was betrothed to her daughter Reyna, and who had undertaken long journeys to Lyons, Marseilles, Rome, and Sicily on business affairs, had by his adroitness prepared a good reception for her in Constantinople. With skillful diplomacy, acquired by intercourse with Christian statesmen, he obtained a hearty recommendation to Constantinople from M. de Lansac, the ambassador at the French court, with whom the Mendes-Nassi family had been at enmity, and so met with a favorable reception there. In Constantinople, João Miques made open avowal of Judaism, assuming the name of Joseph Nassi, and marrying his wealthy cousin Reyna. He did not go thither alone, but took with him a great following of 500 persons, Spanish, Portuguese, and Italian Jews. He made his appearance there as a prince; his tact, his knowledge of European affairs, and his wealth, procured him an entrance into the court circle, and secured the favor of Solyman. But his noble mother-in-law remained the principal manager of the large property of the family.

The Jewish inhabitants of Constantinople soon felt the beneficent hand of Donna Gracia and her son-in-law. They assisted the poor, established houses of prayer and schools, and made endowments for teachers of the Talmud. But their benevolence was not limited to Spaniards and Portuguese, it extended to Germans and beyond the city of Constantinople.

When the news came that Pope Paul IV had imprisoned the Marranos of Ancona with the intention of burning them sooner or later, the heart of Donna Gracia felt a terrible pang, as a mother when her children are in misfortune, for she had taken them all into her heart as her sons and brothers. She did not give herself up to useless lamentation, but at once joined with her son-in-law in taking active steps for their relief. She first addressed herself to Sultan Solyman, entreating him to demand that at least Marrano Jews from Turkey, in Ancona on business, be surrendered to him, and had the happiness of seeing this request fulfilled. Sultan Solyman addressed a letter to the pope (March 9th, 1556) in the haughty tone which Turkish rulers, in the consciousness of their power, assumed towards the Christian princes, weakened by disunion. He complained that his Jewish subjects had been unjustly imprisoned, whereby his treasury had suffered the loss of fully 4,000 ducats, besides a still greater diminution of revenues on account of injuries to Turkish Jews. The sultan insisted that the pope should at once set at liberty all Turkish Marranos in Ancona, and hinted that, in case his representation meet with an unfavorable reception, reprisals would be made upon Christians dwelling in his dominions. Paul IV was most unwillingly compelled to submit, set free the Turkish Jews, and allow them to depart uninjured. The remainder, who had no powerful partisan, were, as has been said, burnt. The Jews resolved to be revenged on the pope, and hoped for the active aid of Donna Gracia and her son-in-law in accomplishing this purpose.

Duke Guido Ubaldo, of Urbino, had received the Marranos from Ancona in Pesaro, only because he thought by this means to bring the Levantine trade of the Jews to his own port. The community of Pesaro, therefore, sent a dispatch to all the Turkish communities which had commercial relations with Italy, requesting that they no longer send their goods to Ancona, but to Pesaro. The commerce of the Turkish Jews was very considerable; everything passed through their hands, they competed with the Venetians, and sent out their own ships and galleys. The Jewish Levantine merchants had hitherto made Ancona the staple port for the wares shipped from Turkey to Europe, in order to lessen the pre-eminence of Venice. In the first ebullition of indignation at the shameful deed of Pope Paul IV, many of the Levantine Jews agreed to the proposal of the Jews of Pesaro (Elul—August, 1556), and resolved to punish him severely by entirely cutting off the important source of revenue arising from the commerce of the Levant. But as this measure was practicable only if all Jews trading with Italy were privy to it, the participators in the arrangement at first only agreed not to carry on trade with Ancona for eight months (till March, 1557).

The Jews of Pesaro and the Marranos formerly in the Turkish dominions, of course, made every effort to effect a general movement to place the pope and his seaport under ban. But the resident Jews of Ancona, not Marranos, were afraid that their interests would suffer injury by the removal of the trade of the Levant to Pesaro, and they lost no time in sending letters to the Jewish communities in Turkey, entreating them not to make any binding agreement, because they would incur great danger, owing to the passionate disposition of the pope, who would certainly drive them into misery if he learnt that the Jews intended to be revenged on him.

All eyes were, therefore, directed towards Constantinople, for thither the representatives of the commercial towns of Salonica, Adrianople, Broussa, Ancona, and the Morea had sent letters requesting that the matter be well weighed, and their interests regarded. Donna Gracia and Joseph Nassi, of course, had the principal voice, and they were resolved from the beginning to punish the inhuman pope severely. They had instructed their agents to send the goods belonging to their house to Pesaro. The Portuguese and some of the Spanish communities in Turkey agreed to make a decided stand and prohibit trade with Ancona under threat of exclusion from Jewish commercial circles. But some opposition was made in Constantinople itself, many of the merchants fearing that their interests would be endangered by the preference given to Pesaro. The matter was, therefore, in the hands of the rabbis of Constantinople. If they unanimously considered that the port of Ancona was to be avoided out of regard for the danger which threatened the Marranos of Pesaro, their authority would fall into the balance, and settle the question. Gracia and Joseph, therefore, influenced the rabbis, so that they decided to pronounce against the pope.

Two rabbis, however, were opposed to this decision. As no unanimous decision was made in the chief community of Constantinople, the Jewish merchants of the other Turkish communities were spared the imposition of restrictions upon their trade with Ancona. In vain Donna Gracia, who regarded the question as of the deepest interest, demanded an opinion from the rabbis of the community of Safet, which enjoyed the highest authority among the Jews of the East, in the persons of its two representatives, Joseph Karo and Moses di Trani. The ban of the rabbis against Pope Paul IV was not put into action. Whilst the rabbis were still consulting, that which Donna Gracia and her adherents had been fearing to their great grief came to pass. Duke Guido Ubaldo, disappointed in his expectation of seeing his port of Pesaro become the center of the Jewish Levantine commerce, and attacked by the pope for his favor towards Jews, ordered the Marranos to depart from Pesaro (March, 1558). It must be accounted a great merit in him that he did not surrender them to the officers of the Inquisition. Most of the exiles sailed eastward in hired ships ; but the pope's naval police lay in wait for them, and they escaped with difficulty. Some were taken prisoners, and treated as slaves. The skillful and humane physician, Amatus Lusitanus, a Marrano, who had resided for a short time in Pesaro, and then in Ragusa, restoring many Christians to life and health, was also obliged to quit Christian territory and take refuge in the town of Salonica, almost entirely peopled by Jews (1558–1559). This same year seems to have brought misfortune also to the Marranos of Ferrara, and the duke withdrew his protection from them, for the printing press of Abraham Usque was closed, and Joseph Nassi's brother, Don Samuel Nassi, was so badly treated by the duke, that he was obliged to call in the intercession of the Turkish court to enable him to remove to Constantinople in peace. One threatening glance from the infidel sultan had more effect upon Christian princes than the voice of justice and humanity.

The nearer Paul IV approached the grave, the more did he become incensed against the Jews. Two baptized Jews, named Sixtus Senensis, and Philip or Joseph Moro, at his command traveled through the Jewish communities situated in the Papal States and annoyed the Jews with their seditious sermons. The latter once forced his way into the synagogue at Recanate on the Day of Atonement (1558) with a crucifix, which the Jews regarded as an idolatrous image, and with violence placed it in the ark where the sacred Torah was kept. When the Jews turned him out for this insult to their sanctuary, he collected the furious mob round the house of God, and two Jews who had laid hands on him were seized and scourged by order of the chief magistrate. Pope Paul IV was most enraged against the Marranos and the Talmud. He tried to drive the former out of their most secret hiding-places.

Many pseudo-Christians of Spain and Portugal, unable to save themselves by flight, entered the orders, and, so to speak, howled with the wolves to escape being attacked by them. Paul IV, to whom complaints were made that Jewish Christians had joined the orders of monks, forbade them to receive Jews as members.

He went yet more thoroughly to work with the Talmud, of which not a copy was left in the Papal States or throughout the greater part of Italy, owners thereof being exposed to the heaviest penalty. The schools, for the most part, were closed. Had this condition of things become universal, great ignorance and stagnation would have spread among Italian Jews, and facilitated the great object of the pope—their conversion. But at this time a large school and an asylum for the persecuted Talmud arose in Cremona, a town of northern Italy, belonging to Milan. A Talmudist, Joseph Ottolenghi, from Germany, opened a school under the protection of the governor of Milan, teaching the Talmud and having rabbinical works printed. Every owner of a copy of the Talmud sent it secretly to Cremona, and thus very many were collected there, and thence exported to Germany, Poland, and the East. This scanty religious freedom the Jews retained also under the Spaniards, who were compelled to carry on war with Paul IV. After the pope had been obliged to submit to a disgraceful peace, he planned to have the Jewish writings in Cremona burnt. The Dominicans, who acted as the papal police, influenced the people, so as to be able to exert pressure upon the governor. Inflammatory papers were distributed in Cremona calling upon the people to kill the Jews (April 8th, 1559). A few days afterwards the governor was urged by two Dominicans, one of whom was Sixtus Senensis, a baptized Jew, to erect a pyre on which to burn copies of the Talmud, because it was said to contain nothing but blasphemies of Jesus.

The governor did not choose to give credence to the accusations against the Jews without further confirmation, so two witnesses stood up against the Talmud (April 17th), a baptized Jew, Vittorio Eliano, grandson, by a daughter, of the Jewish grammarian Elias Levita, and a worthless German Jew, Joshua dei Cantori. By them the Spanish governor of Milan was convinced of the injuriousness of the Talmud, and gave orders to his soldiery to make a house to house search among the Jews of Cremona and in the printing offices, to collect all the copies they could find, and make a great fire of them. Ten or twelve thousand books were burnt on this occasion.

Vittorio Eliano, the malicious proselyte, very nearly came to grief by this burning of the Talmud, for the Spanish soldiery, having received orders to wage war upon the writings of Jews, troubled themselves but little whether the contents were Talmudical, or otherwise, and they very nearly burnt the Zohar, the Kabbalistic text-book, the especial favorite of the papacy. Since the enthusiasm of Pico di Mirandola, still more of Reuchlin, Cardinal Egidio de Viterbo, and the Franciscan Galatino, for mysticism, the most orthodox of the Fathers and Princes of the church believed firmly that the Kabbala contained the mysteries of Christianity. The order of extinction issued against the Talmud, then, did not touch the Zohar. In fact, it was precisely under Pope Paul IV that it was first printed, with the consent of the Inquisition, in Mantua. The Kabbala was to rise out of the ruins of the Talmud. Thus the printing of the book which caused more permanent injury to Judaism than any blow hitherto aimed at it was aided. From envy of the Mantuan publishers, a Christian publisher, named Vincent Conti, of Cremona, printed the Zohar at the same time, because the sale promised very large profits in Italy and the East, and he even offered to furnish a larger book in order to cast suspicion upon the Mantuan edition. The baptized grandson of Elias Levita, the venomous canon Vittorio Eliano, had charge of this Cremona Zohar, and he did not hesitate to write a boastful Hebrew preface to attract buyers, and to have his own name mentioned in connection with it. Whilst it was being printed, the Spanish soldiers were searching for Jewish writings in Cremona, and found two thousand copies of the Zohar, which they were about to cast into the burning pile. Vittorio Eliano and his partners very nearly lost their outlay and their profits, but another convert, the above-named Sixtus of Siena, commissioned by the papal Inquisition to help in destroying the Talmud in Cremona, restrained the fury of the Spanish soldiery, and rescued the Zohar. Thus the Talmud was burnt, and the Zohar spared for the time being. It was a wise instinct of the enemies of the Jews which led them to spare this poisonous spring in the hope that adherents of the Zohar would the sooner renounce Judaism.

Spread abroad by the press, the Zohar came to be considered a canonical book, and for some time was as much quoted as verses from the Bible, and treated on an equality with the Holy Scriptures in all Hebrew works not strictly Talmudical. But the love of the papacy for the Kabbala did not last long. A few years later the Kabbalistic writings were included in the catalogue of books to be burnt (Index expurgatorius).

Paul IV's hatred of Jews and their writings was not confined to Italy, but, nourished by the fanatical spirit aroused by him, extended far and wide. Baptized Jews were always the tools employed in these persecutions. One named Asher, from Udine, brought accusations against Jewish works in Prague, and the authorities confiscated them one and all, even prayer-books, and sent them to Vienna (1559). The Jewish ministers were obliged to repeat the prayers in the synagogue by heart. A fire which broke out at about this time in the Jews' quarter of Prague, and by which a great number of their houses were reduced to ashes, displayed the fanatical hatred of Christians towards them still more clearly. Instead of hastening to the assistance of the unfortunate people, and joining in their rescue, they threw helpless women and children into the flames, and plundered the goods of the Jews. And as if the measure of misfortune were not full enough, Ferdinand I, chosen emperor about a year before, commenced the expulsion of the Jews from Bohemia and Prague in real earnest.

Emperor Ferdinand was, in reality, a mild prince, who sincerely desired to maintain peace between Catholics and Protestants, but he had an invincible dislike to Jews. It was he who first introduced the tickets of notification, or permits, for the Jews of Austria. He made a regulation by which every Jew resident in Austria who went on business to Vienna, should at once on his arrival announce himself to the marshal of the district, and state what was his business, and how long he intended to remain in the place. To this restriction Ferdinand added others, and at length commanded the expulsion of the Jews with their wives and children, their servants and all their goods and chattels, from Lower Austria. This decree of banishment was delayed for two years, but they were finally compelled to withdraw from the country.

Emperor Ferdinand destined the ancient community of Prague to the same fate. What may have been the reason is either easy or difficult for us to conceive, according to our way of thinking. The congregation of Prague was in very evil repute among other Jewish communities, being considered low, unprincipled, violent, and quarrelsome. Such fierce disputes arose regularly about the appointment of rabbis and the choice of the president, that the chief rabbis of Germany and Italy, at the instigation of the emperor, were obliged to arrange a system of election for the community of Prague. The reason of this sad state of things was no doubt that, on the recall of the Jews after the expulsion of twenty years previously, only the worst, none of the well-disposed, members had returned. Christians were, no doubt, very much overreached by this rabble, but Christians of the lower class were probably not better nor more conscientious. Christians treated their own brethren with the greatest leniency, but required the practice of the strictest virtue and uprightness from Jews. Discussions about the second expulsion of Jews from Prague were long carried on, for even the archdukes then in the land were opposed to it; yet the banishment took place (1561). The exiles were attacked, and plundered by robber knights. But it was clear then, as after the first expulsion, that the Christians of Prague, or at all events the nobility, longed for the Jews. Scarcely were they driven out when steps were taken to recall them, and this policy was favored by the princes.

But Emperor Ferdinand refused the request to allow the Jews to return, on the ground, genuine or assumed, that he had sworn to expel the Jews from Prague, and could not break his oath. Thereupon a noble Jew of Prague undertook a journey to Rome to procure from the new pope, Pius IV (the Jew-hating Paul IV was dead), the absolution of the emperor from his oath.

This noble man was Mordecai Zemach ben Gershon, one of the noted Soncin family of printers, whose ancestor, Gershon, or Girolamo, Soncino, founded not only beautiful Hebrew, but also Latin, type, and published both rabbinical works and Petrarch's poems. Members of this family with great success carried on Jewish printing establishments in several towns of Lombardy, in Constantinople, and in Prague. Although Mordecai Zemach had borne gross insults to his honor from the people of Prague, and his married daughter, a second Susannah, had been accused of adultery by false witnesses, and sentenced by cowardly rabbis, he yet showed himself ready to make the greatest sacrifices for the good of the people of Prague. He undertook the journey to Rome amidst many dangers and difficulties for the purpose above stated, and his exertions were crowned with success. The pope, at that time invested with the power to bind and to loose, relieved the emperor of his oath, and the latter felt his conscience lightened. His son Maximilian (afterwards emperor) took the Jews of Prague under his special protection, and thus the decree of banishment was recalled. Jews were again allowed to reside in Prague and a few other Bohemian towns, and were also re-admitted to Austria. But they had a troubled existence even under the best of the emperors, such as Maximilian II and Rudolph, for the official hand of the Catholic Church was heavy upon them.

The first consistent representative of the fanatical and persecuting Catholic Church, Pope Paul IV, was dead (1559), and the people of Rome cursed his memory and his system. The people flocked to the Capitol as in the old times of the Roman Republic, traversed the eternal city, set fire to the buildings of the Inquisition, maltreated the Dominicans and the bailiffs of that tribunal, tore down the arms of the pope, destroyed his statue, and rolled its head through the streets. With derisive laughter the Romans looked on while a Jew placed the cap that he and his brethren were compelled to wear on the statue of the very pope who had issued the order concerning it. But of what avail was this childish rage against the dead? The system survived its supporter for centuries. The Jesuits and the strict church party had got the upper hand in the Catholic

Church, and each pope, willingly or unwillingly, was obliged to submit to them. It was under Pope Pius IV, one of the best high priests of Rome, that the principles of the council of Trent were turned into decrees which enslave the minds of Catholics to this very day.

A deputation of the Jews of Rome waited upon the newly-chosen pope to do homage to him, and described in touching words the sorrows which his predecessors had brought upon them. Pius IV promised them relief, and issued a bull for the Jews of the Papal States (February 27th, 1562), which was certainly to their advantage, but the milder regulations only made the restrictions still remaining appear the harsher. The introduction to the bull is interesting, because it brings to light the hypocrisy of the papal curia:

"The precepts for your conduct issued by my highly venerated predecessor, out of his zeal for religion, have (as we are told) served some who coveted your goods as a pretext for false accusations against you, and have been interpreted contrary to the intention of my predecessor, thus causing you to be vexed and disquieted. Therefore, we decree, in consideration that Holy Mother Church grants and concedes much to Jews in order that the remnant of them may be saved, and in accordance with the example of our predecessors," etc.

All that the new pope conceded, however, was that Jews of the Roman dominions beyond the city be allowed to doff their distinguishing mark, the yellow cap, acquire land to the value of 1,500 ducats, trade in other things besides old clothes, and hold intercourse with Christians, but not to keep Christian servants. This was about all that one of the best popes granted, or dared grant. More important to the Jews of Rome was the point that the accusations of transgressing the harsh laws of Paul IV were not heard, as well as the charge of misdemeanor against those who had not given up their copies of the Talmud. The Italian Jews also made an effort to obtain from the pope the remission of the interdict against the Talmud. But this question was in the hands of the cardinals and bishops sitting in the council of Trent, and to carry out their object the Italian communities chose two deputies (October, 1563). As the council only approved the list of forbidden books previously made out in the papal office, the opinion of the pope and those who surrounded him served as a guide in the treatment of Jewish writings. The decision of this point was left to the pope, who afterwards issued a bull to the effect that the Talmud was indeed accursed—like all humanistic literature, including Reuchlin's "Augenspiegel and Kabbalistic writings"—but that it would be allowed to appear if the name Talmud were omitted, and if before its publication the passages inimical to Christianity were excised, that is to say, if it were submitted to censorship (March 24th, 1564). Strange, indeed, that the pope should have allowed the thing, and forbidden its name! He was afraid of public opinion, which would have considered the contradiction too great between one pope, who had sought out and burnt the Talmud, and the next, who was allowing it to go untouched. At all events, there was now a prospect that this written memorial, so indispensable to all Jews, would once more be permitted to see the light, although in a maimed condition. The printing of the Talmud was in fact undertaken a few years later at Basle.

But even this slight concession was withdrawn from the Jews of the Papal States when Pius IV was succeeded by a pope who held gloomy, monkish, intolerant institutions in higher esteem than human happiness and human life, and who carried the ecclesiastical aims of Caraffa and his colleagues to their extreme consequence. Pius V (1566—1572) outdid his pattern, Paul IV, in love of persecution and cruelty. This pope hated Jews no less than he hated Swiss Calvinists and French Huguenots. They soon felt the severity of the new ecclesiasticism.

Three months after his enthronement (April 19th, 1566), Pius V confirmed in every respect the restrictions which Paul IV had imposed on Jews; he even increased their severity, and disregarded the ameliorations of his predecessor as if they had never been granted. The former regulations, then, were enforced: exclusion from intercourse with Christians, prohibition to own lands, or to carry on any business except the trade in old clothes, compulsion to wear the distinctive Jew badge, and the refusal to permit more than one synagogue. But these edicts were not issued against the Jews in the Papal States only; they extended throughout the whole Catholic world. For at that day, in a period of spiteful reaction against Protestantism, the decrees of the pope made a far different impression from what they had produced previously, and found willing executors. Thus days of sorrow were again beginning for the Jews of Catholic countries.

Once more Joseph Cohen had to enter trials in his "Annals of Persecution," once more to collect the tears of his people in his "Vale of Weeping" (Emek ha-Bacha). The ecclesiastical tyrant, Pius V, often gave the opportunity. Under the pretext that the Jews of the Papal States had infringed his canonical laws, he caused a number of them to be thrown into prison, and their books to be collected and burnt. The prosperous community of Bologna was visited with especial severity, the blow being aimed at their property. In order to have a legal reason for robbery, confusing questions upon Christianity were put at a formal hearing before the tribunal of the Inquisition; for example, whether the Jews regarded Catholics as idolators; whether the forms of imprecation against the Minæans, and the "Kingdom of Sin" in the prayers referred to Christians and the papacy, and especially whether the story, in a work but little read, about a "Bastard, the Son of an Outcast," was intended to refer to Jesus.

A baptized Jew, named Alexander, had drawn up the points of accusation, and the prisoners were questioned upon them, under application of torture. Some of them succumbed to the pain, and confessed everything that the bloody tribunal asked them. Only the rabbi of Bologna, Ishmael Chanina, had the courage to declare even under torture, that if he should confess anything during the unconsciousness which might ensue from his sufferings, such confession would be null and void. As others, however, had confessed to slanders uttered by Jews against Christians, the papal curia had an excuse for its robberies. The rich and the upper classes were forbidden under the severest penalties to leave the town. But this foolish prohibition awakened in the minds of the Jews of Bologna the idea of leaving the place entirely and forever. By bribing the gatekeeper, they succeeded in escaping, with their wives and children, from the net spread for them, and fled to Ferrara. Pope Pius V was so incensed against the Jews for this act, that he informed the college of cardinals that all Jews were to be expelled from the Papal States. In vain some of the church dignitaries protested, showing how the Jews had been protected by the chair of St. Peter from time immemorial, that it had indeed pledged itself to shield the remainder of the Jews, in the hope that they might be saved. In vain did the commercial world of Ancona entreat the pope not to ruin by his own deed the commercial prosperity of the Papal States; his hatred of Jews stifled the voice of common sense, of justice, and of interest. The bull was issued (February 26th, 1569), that all Jews in the Papal States, except those of Rome and Ancona, should depart within three months; those who remained were to be reduced to slavery, and undergo even severer punishment.

There were at that time about 1,000 Jewish families

and 72 synagogues in the Papal States, excluding Rome, Ancona, and Bologna. In spite of the misery which threatened them, almost all included in this decree decided upon emigration, and only very few became Christians. The exiles also suffered loss of property, because they had not time to sell their estates, and collect the debts owing to them. The historian Gedalya Ibn-Yachya alone lost over 10,000 ducats by his debtors in Ravenna. The exiles dispersed, and sought protection in the neighboring little states of Pesaro, Urbino, Ferrara, Mantua, and Milan. The Jews of Avignon and Venaissin, the only communities remaining on French territory since the expulsion of the Jews from France two hundred years previously, were also ordered to leave. The reactionary princes of the church had long cast malicious glances upon them, for they had been particularly favored by the officials of the Papal States under the humanistic popes, Leo X, Clement VII, and especially Paul III. The curia received its only income from this district through their commerce. The Jews of Avignon, Carpentras, and other towns, owned great wealth and property of all kinds, and held lands.

Most of the Jews of the Italian and French ecclesiastical territories, like all expelled from Christian countries, went to Turkey, and there met with the kindest reception, if they were able to get so far without being attacked and maltreated by the robber-knights of the Order of Malta. It seemed almost as if there were to be an end of Jews in Christian Europe. Hatred, persecution, and banishment reigned everywhere. In Catholic dominions the fanaticism of the papacy prevailed, and in Protestant countries the narrowness of Lutheranism, sunk from its former height to the level of a child's quarrel.

Both seemed to desire the enforcement of the oft expressed thought of the arch-enemies of the Jews, that Jews have no right to dwell in the West.

CHAPTER XVII.

THE JEWS IN TURKEY. DON JOSEPH NASSI.

Joseph Nassi's Favor with Sultan Solyman—His Friendship for Prince Selim—Hostility of Venice and France to Nassi—Joseph Nassi restores Tiberias, and is created Duke of Naxos—The Vizir Mahomet Sokolli—The Turks, at the Instigation of Nassi, conquer Cyprus—Rebellion against Philip II in the Netherlands—Solomon Ashkenazi—Election of Henry of Anjou as King of Poland—Ashkenazi negotiates a Peace between Venice and Turkey—Gedalya Ibn-Yachya and Jewish Literature in Turkey—Joseph Karo compiles the "Shulchan Aruch"—Azarya deï Rossi—Isaac Lurya—The Jewish "Dark Age"—Spread of the Kabbala—Lurya's Disciple, Chayim Vital Calabrese—Death of Joseph Nassi—Esther Kiera and the Influence of Jewish Women in Turkey.

1566—1600 C.E.

AGAIN, as often before, the threads in the web of universal history were so involved that it was impossible to annihilate the Jews of Christendom even by systematic persecution. The sun, obscured on the Jewish horizon by gloomy clouds in the West, again rose bright in the East. Through a favorable turn of affairs a time was beginning in Turkey which, to the superficial observer, may seem a brilliant epoch. A Jew, who would have been burnt at the stake without ceremony in the countries of the cross, occupied a very influential position in the land of the crescent, rose to the rank of duke, and ruled over many Christians. All the Jews in Turkey, amounting to millions in number, rose with and by him to a free and honorable station, the envy of their despised and less numerous brethren in Christian Europe. With rage the Jew-hating Christian potentates saw their plans here and there frustrated by Jewish hands, and their internal complications rendered more and more involved and entangled. The down-trodden worm might yet become an annoyance to its tormentors. Joseph Nassi, or João Miques, the outlawed Marrano of Portugal, caused anxious hours to many a Christian ruler and diplomatist, who were obliged to flatter him in an abject manner, though they would have struck him dead like a dog if he had been in their power. The illustrious republic of Venice, the mighty kingdom of Spain, the conceited government of France, and even the haughty papacy, all saw themselves endangered by him.

João Miques, or Don Joseph Nassi, who had been well recommended to the Turkish court by French statesmen when first he entered Turkey, had become yet more popular by his agreeable presence, his inventive genius, his experience, and his knowledge of the Christian countries of Europe and their political situation. Sultan Solyman, who understood men well, soon took him into favor. He formed extensive plans for beginning a war with Spain and aiding the Mahometans on the coast of Africa against those who fed the stake. Joseph Nassi, through his riches, and through the attachment of his fellow-believers in Christian countries, was kept well informed as to what was going on in Christian courts, and could tell the sultan the state of political and military affairs, relieving the latter of the necessity of employing spies, or of permitting himself to be deceived by the Christian ambassadors at his court. Don Joseph could assist him with wise counsel, and thus as a Frankish bey soon became a very important person in Constantinople and was able to render material service to those of his own religion. His importance increased still more by a fortunate chance. Hatred and jealousy prevailed among the sons of Solyman, and the father preferred the younger on account of his military inclinations. The courtiers kept themselves aloof from the disregarded prince, Selim, and did not intercede with his father on his behalf. Only Joseph

Nassi pressed Selim's claims warmly on his father, and when the latter wished to show his favor to his son by making him a handsome present of 50,000 ducats in cash, and 30,000 in valuables, he chose his Jewish favorite as the bearer of the gift to Selim's residence in Asia Minor. The prince, overjoyed both at the gift and at this proof of favor, from that moment became very friendly towards the messenger, and assured him of his life-long gratitude. He made a favorite and confidant of the Jewish bey, and appointed him a member of the life-guard (Mutafarrica), an honor to which even the sons of Christian princes eagerly aspired, and to which a large salary was attached.

The ambassadors from Christian courts saw with vexation the growing influence of a Jewish favorite, acquainted with all their plots, upon the future sultan, and promulgated the falsest rumors about him. They reported to their courts that Joseph Nassi was leading the prince into all kinds of orgies and excesses, and was ruining him. The ambassadors of Venice and of France were most hostile, because he saw through their artful designs against the Turkish court, and was able to frustrate them, and especially because he had private quarrels with them. The government of Venice had imprisoned his mother-in-law, deprived her of some of her property, and also had treated him scornfully; the French court owed an immense sum (150,000 ducats) to the house of Mendes-Nassi, and did not think of repaying it. The French ambassador was, therefore, very eager for Joseph's ruin; he wrote to Henry II, that he should inform Sultan Solyman that Joseph Nassi made it his business to acquaint the enemies of France with all the negotiations carried on at the Turkish court, and that being a Spaniard he did this in the interest of Spain. But so far from punishing him, Prince Selim and the reigning sultan took up Joseph's cause, and urgently insisted that the court of France pay the debt owing their Jewish favorite. Henry II and his successor raised an objection to Joseph's well-founded demand, characteristic of the —shall we say, Christian?—morality of the time. They averred that both law and religion forbade the king to repay the debt to his Jewish creditor, because it was altogether prohibited for Jews to have business dealings in France, and that all their goods could be confiscated by the king. The sultan and his son did not, of course, recognize this code of morals, and insisted with a half-threat that Joseph Nassi should be satisfied. Joseph Nassi rose so high in favor with Sultan Solyman, that the latter gave him a tract of land in Palestine, on the Sea of Tiberias, to restore the city of Tiberias under his own rule, with the express privilege that only Jews should dwell therein. The deed of gift was signed by the reigning sultan, by Selim, the heir to the throne, and by his son Murad, so as to render it valid in the future, and not liable to dispute. Selim proposed to his father to reward Joseph's services still further, and to make him sovereign lord over Naxos and some other islands. But the vizir, Mahomet Sokolli, a Christian renegade, who watched the growing power of the Jewish favorite with jealous eyes, seems to have worked against this and to have upset the plan.

After Solyman's death, when Selim II entered his capital to receive the homage of his subjects (1566), and Joseph also presented himself to swear allegiance to the new sovereign, he created him on the spot Duke of Naxos, and of the Cyclades, Andro, Paro, Antiparo, Milo, twelve islands in all, which he gave him one after the other, and for which he had to pay but a small tribute. He also granted him the collection of the duties paid in the Black Sea on imported wines.

Thus a Jew was able to issue his commands in the following grandiose style: "We, Duke of the Ægean Sea, Lord of Andro." Joseph did not reside in the capital of his duchy, where he would have been too far away from the center of affairs, but remained in his handsome palace Belvedere near Constantinople, and deputed the government of the islands to a Spanish nobleman, a Christian named Coronello, whose father had been governor of Segovia. Jealously as the Christian princes regarded this Jewish duke, placed upon an equality with them, European affairs were in such a condition that they were forced not only to recognize, but even to flatter him. If they wished to gain anything at the Turkish court, they dared not ignore him, knowing how high he stood in Selim's favor, and of how much weight his opinion was in the divan. When an Austrian embassy from Emperor Ferdinand I arrived in Constantinople (after fresh victories gained by the Turks in Hungary) to sue for peace, and win the great dignitaries by gifts and annual subsidies, it was charged to make terms also with Joseph of Naxos. His bitterest enemies were obliged to dissemble their hatred. The two states which set themselves most to oppose him, namely, France and Venice, felt the power of the Jewish duke severely.

The king of France declined to pay the debt contracted with the Marrano house of Mendes and transferred to Joseph. The latter easily procured a firman from the sultan, by virtue of which he was allowed to seize all ships carrying the French flag which entered any Turkish harbor. Joseph of Naxos sent privateers as far as Algiers to make a raid upon French merchant vessels. At last he succeeded in getting possession of several vessels in the port of Alexandria, captured all the merchandise on board, and sold it to pay the debt owing to him (1569). The court of France raised a clamor, protested, stormed, but all in vain; Selim protected his favorite. A coolness arose in consequence in the diplomatic relations of the two countries, which was more injurious to France than to Turkey.

The French ambassador at the Porte was, therefore, very desirous to bring about the overthrow of Joseph of Naxos. Not only was his own honor concerned, but that of the French crown also. The French had often boasted in the European cabinets that their word had the greatest weight and influence at the Turkish court, and that they were in a position to lead the divan to determine upon war or peace at will. And now it was proved that a gross insult had been shown to the French flag by this very court, and that France was not even in a position to demand satisfaction from a Jew, the originator of the insult. The French ambassador, therefore, directed his efforts to turning this overthrow into triumph by compassing the fall of the influential Jew. An opportunity soon presented itself in the discontent of one of Joseph's agents. A Jewish physician, named David or Daud, one of the physicians in ordinary at the Turkish court, and also in the service of the duke, considered himself slighted and wronged by his superior, and a quarrel arose between them. As soon as the French ambassador got wind of this, he tried to fan the flame of dissension, promised Daud a sum of money and a place as interpreter at the French embassy with a yearly salary, and then entered into relations with him in order to obtain secret information about Joseph of Naxos. In his irritation Daud allowed himself to be led into hasty expressions. He promised to furnish the French ambassador with full proofs that Joseph of Naxos had carried on a correspondence traitorous to the Porte. He undertook to produce documents to prove that Joseph sent daily information to the pope, the king of Spain, the duke of Florence, the Genoese republic, in short, to all the enemies of the sultan, and kept them acquainted with every thing that went on at the Porte. Delighted at the opportunity of overthrowing the Jewish duke, he informed the king of France and the crafty queen-mother, Catherine de Medici, in cipher, that he would soon be in a position to bring the powerful enemy of French influence at the Turkish court to the scaffold (October, 1569).

The Jewish duke was placed in a position of the greatest danger, and with him probably all the Jews in the Turkish empire. If Daud had been able to push his hatred to the point of an open accusation, if French money could have supported the intrigue, and if the grand vizir, Mahomet Sokolli, the deadly enemy of Joseph, could have taken the matter in hand, the latter would have been lost. But the French ambassador thought it wise to treat the matter as a secret for a time.

In spite of this secrecy, the intrigues of Daud and the French ambassador were betrayed to Joseph of Naxos, and he was able to be beforehand with them. It was not difficult for him to convince Sultan Selim that he had always served him faithfully, and that of all his courtiers, he had been most sincerely attached to him. He obtained a decree from the sultan by which the traitor Daud was banished for life to Rhodes, the criminal colony of the Turkish empire. Either at the instigation of Don Joseph, or by their own impulse, all the rabbis and communities of Constantinople pronounced the severest form of excommunication upon Daud and two of his accomplices. The rabbinical colleges of the largest Turkish communities, Joseph Karo at their head, in servile flattery joined them, without first having convinced themselves of Daud's innocence or guilt. The extraordinary efforts of the French ambassador and court to procure the overthrow of Joseph were thus a complete failure, and left in the mind of the latter a feeling of only too justifiable bitterness, which induced him to strive the more to hinder and frustrate the diplomatic schemes of France.

Joseph of Naxos dealt even more severely with the state of Venice. Secret enmity prevailed between the

Jewish duke and the republic, which both tried in vain to conceal by compliments. Independently of the ill-treatment which his mother-in-law had undergone at the hands of the Venetian government, it had refused Joseph's request for a safe conduct through its dominions for himself and his brother. Selim, not very well disposed towards the Venetians, was often urged by his Jewish favorite to put an end to the long-existing peace between them, and to set about the conquest of the Venetian island of Cyprus. In spite of the disinclination of Mahomet Sokolli, the first vizir, who was favorable to the Venetians, the war was undertaken.

The sultan is said to have promised Joseph that he should become king of Cyprus, if the enterprise proved successful, and the duke of Naxos is said to have kept a banner ready in his house, with the inscription, "Joseph, King of Cyprus." His European alliances made this undertaking easy. Whilst Mahomet Sokolli was still raising difficulties about consenting to a naval war of this character, Joseph received the news that the arsenal in Venice had been destroyed by an explosion. Joseph and the party in the divan which he had gained over for war took advantage of the embarrassment thus caused to the Republic of Venice, and persuaded the sultan to allow the attacking fleet to sail at once. Nicosia, one of the chief towns of Cyprus, fell at the first assault, and the other, Famagusta, was closely besieged.

In this instance, as often before, all Jews were made answerable for the action of one. That the Venetian government, at the outbreak of the war, imprisoned all the Levantine merchants in Venice, for the most part Jews, and seized their goods, was only natural in the barbarous state of intercourse between one state and another. But that the senate, at the instigation of the hostile doge, Luis Mocenigo, came to the resolve (December, 1571) to expel all Jews from Venice, as fellow-conspirators of Joseph Nassi and of the Turkish empire, was a result of the race-hatred encouraged by Christianity. Happily, things did not go so far. Notwithstanding the endeavors of the fanatical pope, Pius V, to bring about a league of the Christian states against Turkey, to organize a crusade against the so-called unbelievers, and to drive the Turkish fleet from the waters of Cyprus, the town of Famagusta was obliged to yield to the Turkish commander, and so the whole island fell into the hands of Turkey. The Venetians were compelled to sue for peace, and they placed their whole hope of obtaining it upon an influential Jew, who was to negotiate it. In spite of the solemn determination of the Venetian senate that no one should venture to say a word in favor of Jews, they had to be tolerated, because it dared not quite break with the Jews in Turkey.

The power of the latter was, indeed, so great that they, generally the suppliants, were entreated for aid by Christians. A serious rebellion had arisen in the Netherlands against Spain and the morose king, Philip II, who wished to introduce the bloody tribunal of the Inquisition. The barbarous Alva was trying to suppress apostasy and to lead back the erring into the bosom of the Catholic church by hecatombs of human beings. The block was to support the cross. In this extremity, the rebels turned to Joseph of Naxos, who had dealings with some of the nobility of Flanders from the time of his residence there. Prince William of Orange, the moving spirit of the rebellion, sent a private messenger to Joseph of Naxos, entreating him to persuade the sultan to declare war against Spain, which would necessitate the withdrawal of the Spanish troops from the Netherlands. The Austrian emperor, Ferdinand, also condescended to address an autograph letter to the Jewish duke in order to obtain the favor of the Porte, increasing the grand vizir's envy. Sigismund Augustus, king of Poland, who was hoping for an important service from the Porte, also addressed him, gave him the title of "Serene Highness," and, what was of greater importance, promised favorable conditions to the Jews in his country, to ensure Joseph's approval of his plans.

We may almost say that the divan, or Turkish council of state, under Sultan Selim consisted of two parties trying to checkmate each other: the Christian party, represented by the first vizir, and the Jewish, headed by Joseph of Naxos. Through and besides him there were other Jews who, though only in subordinate positions, exercised influence—the men on the holders of office, the women on the ladies of the harem. Sultan Selim's goodwill towards Jews was so evident that a story became current that by birth he was a Jew, foisted into the harem as a prince, when he was a child. Even the grand vizir, Mahomet Sokolli, although an enemy of Joseph of Naxos and of Jewish influence, was forced to employ a Jewish negotiator and to intrust him with important commissions. The Venetian envoy, ordered to work secretly against the Jews at the Turkish court, himself assisted such a man in obtaining influence.

Solomon ben Nathan Ashkenazi, who, supplanting Joseph Nassi, conducted the diplomatic affairs of Turkey with Christian courts for nearly thirty years, was an unknown personage in Constantinople at the period when the duke of Naxos had a powerful voice in the divan. Descended from a German family of Udine, he began to travel early in life, and went to Poland, where he rose to be first physician to the king. On his removal to the Turkish capital, he placed himself as a subject of the Venetian republic under the protection of the diplomatic agents of Venice. Solomon Ashkenazi understood the Talmud, and was called rabbi, but displayed greatest intelligence and skill in the niceties of diplomatic technicalities, the disentanglement of knotty questions, in negotiations, settlements, and compromises. For these qualities he had been esteemed by successive Venetian agents in Constantinople. The first minister of the Turkish court recognized his diplomatic skill, attached him to his service, and trusted him to the end of his life with such commissions as required tact, wisdom, and discernment in their fulfillment. Whilst the Turkish arms were raised against the Venetians, Solomon Ashkenazi was beginning to weave the web for the future treaty of peace.

Christian cabinets did not suspect that the course of events which compelled them to side with one party or the other was set in motion by a Jewish hand. This was especially the case at the election of the Polish king. The death (July, 1572) of the last Polish king of the Jagellon family, Sigismund Augustus, who left no heir, necessitated a genuine election from an indefinite number of candidates, and this put the whole of Europe, at all events the cabinets and diplomatic circles, into the utmost excitement. The German emperor, Maximilian II, and the Russian ruler, Ivan the Cruel, were most intimately concerned in the election, as neighbors of Poland. The former did everything that he could to insure the choice of his own son, and the latter boasted that he or his son would be chosen king. The pope plotted for a Catholic prince to be placed on the throne of Poland; otherwise it was to be feared that the choice of a king in favor of the Reformation, already on the increase among the nobles and the townspeople of Poland, would strengthen the movement, and that the country would free itself from the papacy. On the other hand, the Protestant countries of Germany and England, and, above all, the adherents of the various sects of the new church in Poland itself, felt the greatest interest in securing the election of a sovereign of their own faith, or at least of one not an aggressive Catholic. To this was added the personal ambition of a powerful French queen, who interfered with a deft hand. The widowed queen, Catherine de Medici, as clever as false, who believed in astrology, and to whom it had been announced that each of her sons should wear a crown, wished to procure a foreign throne for her son, Henry of Anjou, so that the astrological prophecy might not be fulfilled by the death of her reigning son, Charles IX. She and her son, the king of France, therefore, set every lever in motion to place Anjou on the throne of Poland. Turkey also had important interests and a powerful voice in the election of the king of Poland. A tangle of cabals and intrigues was developed by the election. Each candidate sought to gain a strong party among the higher and lesser nobility of Poland, and also to gain the favor of the Porte. Henry of Anjou seemed at first to have some prospect of success, but this was imperiled by the bloody massacre of St. Bartholomew, in France, in which, at a hint from the king and the queen-mother, a hundred thousand Huguenots, great and small—men, women and children—were attacked, and murdered (August 26th, 1572). Such barbarity, planned and carried out in cold blood, had been unheard of in European history since the murderous attack made on the Albigenses in the thirteenth century by papal command. The Lutherans and other adherents of the Reformation in every country were completely stunned by this blow. The candidates for the throne of Poland sought to make capital out of it against Anjou. So much the more the French candidate, his mother, and his brother, were compelled to endeavor to gain over the Porte to their side. An ambassador extraordinary was dispatched to Constantinople with this object. So the choice of a king of Poland rested with a Jew who was in the background, for Solomon Ashkenazi governed the grand vizir completely, and ruled his will, and he managed foreign affairs in the sultan's name. Solomon decided in favor of Henry of Anjou, and won over the grand vizir to his side. When Henry of Anjou, by a combination of favorable circumstances, was at last chosen almost unanimously (May, 1573), the French ambassador boasted that he had not been one of the last in bringing about this election. But Solomon Ashkenazi ventured to write as follows to the king of Poland, afterwards king of France under the name of Henry III: "I have rendered your majesty most important service in securing your election; I have effected all that was done here" (at the Porte).

Great sensation was aroused throughout Christian Europe when this Jewish physician and diplomatist was appointed by the Porte to conclude the peace which he had for several years been trying to bring about with Venice, and thus to stand forth as a person of the highest official importance. The Jewish ambassador was not received without opposition by the illustrious republic. The subject was eagerly discussed in the senate, and the members of the government were against him. But, on the one hand, the grand vizir, Mahomet Sokolli, was resolved upon it, because Solomon enjoyed his unreserved confidence, and he wished through him to establish diplomatic relations for other purposes. On the other hand, the words of the Venetian consul, Mark Antonio Barbaro, who repeatedly assured his state that the Jewish diplomatist cherished the warmest sympathy with Venice, made a great impression. Under these circumstances, "Rabbi Solomon Ashkenazi," as he was termed, went to Venice in the capacity of envoy extraordinary from Turkey. When once he was acknowledged, the dignitaries of the republic, the doge, and the senators, paid him the greatest honor and attention, because the Turkish court was very sensitive on this point, and would have regarded want of due respect to its representative as an insult. Solomon was, therefore, received in state audience at the doge's palace, and there the act of peace between Turkey and Venice was signed by him on behalf of the former. The signoria showed him the most polite attentions during his stay in Venice (May to July, 1574), and all the European ambassadors in Venice paid him court.

Solomon was an angel of deliverance to his fellow-believers in Venice. Their joy at the honor shown by the authorities to one of their race was mingled with anxiety and sorrow on account of threatened expulsion. The doge Mocenigo had insisted upon the fulfillment of the decree of banishment previously issued against the Jews. Many Jewish families had already departed without waiting for the term to expire. Solomon had arranged with Jacopo Soranzo, the Venetian agent in Constantinople, to receive these unfortunates. On his return to Venice, Soranzo at once brought the question of the Jews to the consideration of the council of the doge and the Ten. He made them understand the injury to the republic which would arise by the expulsion of the Jews. Those driven out of Spain and Portugal had manufactured guns and other arms for the Turks, and it would be a serious matter to make enemies of a people who constituted a power in Turkey. To maintain friendship with this country would be the surest guarantee of peace, as neither the pope nor Spain could be trusted. This earnest appeal of Soranzo in favor of the Jews effected a change in the disposition of the doge and the Dieci (ten) towards them. The decree of banishment was revoked (July 19th, 1573), and Solomon's presence in Venice served to increase the joy of his fellow-believers, as he obtained for them the promise that they should never again be threatened with expulsion. Loaded with honors and enriched by a gift of ten pounds (weight) of gold, Solomon returned to Constantinople, where his position became more assured and his importance greater than ever. His son, who was residing in Venice for his education, was treated by the doge with the greatest consideration.

In consequence of the influence of Joseph of Naxos over Sultan Selim and of Solomon Ashkenazi over the prime minister, Mahomet Sokolli, the foreign Christian courts strove yet more earnestly to obtain the favor of the Turkish Jews in Stambul. If one of them wished to effect any object with the Porte, it first of all sought a Jewish negotiator, because without this aid there was no prospect of success. Even the morose Philip II of Spain, that incarnate hater of Jews and heretics, was obliged to turn to Jewish mediators in order to obtain peace with the Turks. The position of the Jews in Turkey, and above all in the capital, under the very eyes of their powerful protectors, was, therefore, extraordinarily favorable. They were able to put forth all their powers freely, and thus earned the wealth which then meant power, as it does now. The wholesale trade and customs dues were mostly in their hands; they also carried on wholesale shipping, and emulated the Venetians. They owned the largest and best houses, with gardens and kiosks, in Constantinople, equal to those of the grand vizir.

This prosperity, freedom, and security of the Turkish Jews could not fail to produce an exalted frame of mind, to open a prospect beyond the actual present, and to stir up their minds to activity. The mental fertility of the Spanish Jews, which brought so much that is beautiful and true to the light of day, was not exhausted or extinct in Turkey. The taste for history and events outside the Jewish world was not yet lost to them. Moses Almosnino, a favorite preacher at Salonica, while on a visit to

Constantinople to procure privileges for the community of Salonica, described life in the Turkish capital, with its contrasts of glowing heat and benumbing cold, its astonishing wealth and terrible poverty, its enervating luxury and severe privations, its extravagant generosity and heartless greed, exaggerated piety and callous indifference, which followed one another abruptly, without any gradual transition. In his Spanish work on the "Contrasts and Greatness of Constantinople," Almosnino described the power and development of the Turkish empire with the pen of a master. He had a taste for the sciences and philosophy, and worked out his sermons as well as his expositions of the Scriptures in a scientific shape.

The physician, Samuel Shulam, likewise a Spaniard by birth, also had a great taste for history. He led a life of adventure until he was taken up by a Jewish woman in Constantinople, named Esther Kiera, in high favor with the sultana. He published Zacuto's poor but useful chronicle at her expense (1566—1567). This favorite of the court-Jewess also translated from the Latin the interesting work of the old Jewish historian Josephus against the attacks of Apion, the Alexandrine enemy of the Jews, being the first Jewish writer to make use of it. The dark side of Jewish history, the thousand years' martyrdom of the Jewish race, was at the same time described by a more competent historian, the now venerable Joseph Cohen, of Spanish descent. His "Vale of Weeping" presents a long series of mournful scenes, tortures, death, and distress in every form, but he was enabled to conclude his history with the joyful tidings that the Venetians were eager, if only from policy, to pay honor to and distinguish a Jew, the Turkish ambassador Solomon Ashkenazi.

Even Hebrew poetry bore some blossoms at this period in Turkey, and although but autumn flowers, showing traces of damp mists and a pale sun, they form an agreeable contrast to the joyless wintry waste of other regions and times. But we are more interested in the originator of these efforts than in the productions themselves. He was a certain Ibn-Yachya of the Turkish branch of this widespread family. This family preserved nobility of heart and mind throughout a long line of generations. The great-grandfather Jacob Tam, the grandfather Gedalya Ibn-Yachya, the grandson Moses, and the great-grandson Gedalya Ibn-Yachya II, with all collateral branches, were without exception friends of learning, and shared their property with the poor. Moses Ibn-Yachya not only spent thousands of ducats on sufferers at the time of the plague, but even exposed himself to the risk of death in his attendance upon the sick. His son Gedalya, a wise man and an agreeable orator, imitated his father in all his virtues, and by his love for poetry excelled him in gifts of the mind. He formed a sort of school or circle of poetry, that is to say, he assembled from time to time, at his own expense, all those interested in neo-Hebrew poetry, to recite their poems, and urged those at a distance to send him the fruit of their muse in order to encourage their zeal for this beautiful but neglected art. Two poets distinguished themselves in this numerous circle, Jehuda Zarko and Saadio Longo. To them we may add Israel Najara, the prolific versifier, living in Damascus. It is true that the verses of these writers do not contain much real poetry, and that the authors deserve the name of poet only on account of the smoothness and euphony of their style. As a matter of course this group of poets extolled Gedalya Ibn-Yachya, their patron and protector, in their verses.

The Jews of Turkey also wrote Latin verses in the security and comfort of their present life. The writers were, of course, immigrant Marranos, who had learnt the language of their oppressors in the dungeons of Spain and Portugal. When the conscientious physician, Amatus Lusitanus, whose aid had been sought alike by kings and beggars, and who, on account of the intolerance of the reactionary policy, emigrated from Italy to Salonica, and there acquired new friends and admirers, fell a sacrifice to his devoted energy, and died of the plague, one of his friends, the Marrano Flavio Jacopo de Evora, composed a memorial to him in beautiful Latin verses to the following effect:

> He who so often recalled the breath well-nigh gone from the dying, and was, therefore, beloved by kings and peoples, lies far from the land of his birth, beneath the dust of Macedonia.

The exaltation of the Turkish Jews and their contentment with their present condition imbued them with thoughts of independence. Whilst the Jews of Christendom had no such thought, and from time immemorial considered themselves in a condition of subjugation to their masters, the Turkish Jews became familiar with the idea of regarding themselves as independent men.

Joseph of Naxos long cherished the thought of founding a Jewish state. The Jew and the statesman in him yearned for this, and the enormous wealth of his mother-in-law, over which he had control, was to serve him as the means for its execution. Even when a fugitive Marrano he had seriously put before the Republic of Venice the request that it give him one of its numerous islands, so that he might people it with Jewish inhabitants. But this was refused either on account of the narrow-mindedness of the Christians or the fear of mercantile competition. When later on Joseph stood high in favor with Prince Selim, and also with Sultan Solyman, he obtained from them, besides seven villages, the ruins of the city of Tiberias, for a small Jewish state to be peopled only with Jews. He sent one of his agents to superintend the re-building of

Tiberias. The Turkish prince gave the pasha of Egypt strict orders to assist the building in every way. The Arab occupants of the neighboring villages were compelled to render forced labor, and the new and beautiful houses and streets of the city of Tiberias were completed in a year. Joseph of Naxos wished to make it a manufacturing town to compete with Venice. He planted mulberry-trees for the cultivation of silk-worms, and introduced looms for the manufacture of silks ; he also imported wool from Spain for the making of fine cloth.

Joseph does not seem to have directed his full energy to the little Jewish state ; his plans were far more extensive, and thus New Tiberias never became an important place. He next endeavored to obtain the island of Naxos as a dukedom, together with the adjacent islands of the Ægean Sea, and when he was fortunate enough to be appointed duke by Sultan Selim, he thought no more about peopling his little island state with Jews ; perhaps it was not practicable. His mind was next set on becoming king of Cyprus. It is possible that he might have transformed this island of the goddess of beauty into a Jewish state had he obtained possession of it, but his enemy, the grand vizir, Mahomet Sokolli, prevented this. Thus his dreams of founding an independent Jewish state were dispelled. In reality, Joseph of Naxos did nothing of lasting importance for Judaism. He made various attempts, and then relaxed in his endeavors, or misspent his means.

The fact that Jews occupied an exceedingly favored position in Turkey for so long a period did not result in correspondingly enduring progress. They did not produce a single great genius who originated ideas to stimulate future ages, nor mark out a new line of thought for men of average intelligence. Not one of the leaders of the different congregations was above the level of mediocrity. The rabbis and preachers were deeply learned in their particular subjects, but kept to the beaten track, without making a new discovery or bequeathing an original contribution, even in their own department. Only one rabbi left to posterity an epoch-making work, which even yet possesses significance, disputed though it be; but even this work contained nothing new or original. Joseph Karo, chief rabbi of the city of Safet, in Palestine, completed, after many years of toil, a new book of religious ordinances, the "Shulchan Aruch." Religious impulses, mystical fanaticism, and ambition, had equal shares in the making of this book. For Joseph Karo was still subject to strange visions: he still believed that he would be recognized everywhere as the highest authority by the compilation of his religious code, a norm for Jewish religious life; and that, by this means, he would accomplish the revival of rabbinical ordination, in which Jacob Berab had failed; restore, in fact, the unity of Judaism, and thereby hasten the coming of the Messiah. He spent the whole of his life in collecting the vast material, in weighing the pros and cons of arguments, drawing conclusions and arranging them in their proper places. By doing this he supplied a serious want. There was no manual that embraced the whole field of religious observance. As the Talmud and the later religious codes to an even greater extent favored differences of opinion upon nearly every single point in matters of religion, ritual, law and the marriage state, disputes constantly occurred which led to altercation and divisions in the communities, for it rarely happened that two rabbis agreed upon any question that came up for discussion. Each was able to adduce reasons for or against any argument from the vast mass of rabbinical literature.

It was this confusion and divergence of opinion that Joseph Karo wished to check by means of his new religious Code. He embraced the whole of the vast field of Talmudic and rabbinical literature, although his intellect could not master it. By birth a Spaniard, he involuntarily preferred the views of Spanish authorities to those of French and German writers. Hence he allowed partiality to creep into his compilation. As a matter of course, too, Karo admitted various elements of mysticism, though only sparingly, as if unwilling to place the Zohar upon a level with the Talmud in matters of practical religious observance. He has embodied in his Code excellent precepts in regard to sanctity, chastity, brotherly love, morality, and honesty in business, drawn from the Talmud and the rabbinical writings; but they disappear in a sea of casuistical details and mere externals, in a patchwork of divisions and subdivisions, of "ifs" and "buts." In this work there appears an altogether different kind of Judaism from that revealed on Sinai, announced by the prophets, or even taught by Maimuni. But this Judaism thoroughly suited the ideas of the Jews of that period, and therefore Karo's Code was immediately hailed with delight, disseminated, and received as the infallible standard authority in Turkey, throughout the East, in Italy, and even in Poland.

Thus religious life received a certain finality and unity, but at the expense of spirituality and freedom of thought. From Karo Judaism received the form maintained up to the present time. His dream was partially fulfilled. His rabbinical writings became the common property of Judaism, and gave it religious unity. But he himself did not become the leader and head, as the "Spirit of the Mishna" had repeatedly promised him: he was only honored as one authority among many others. Still less did he restore the ordination of rabbi-judges as members of a Synhedrion, or hasten in any way the coming of the Messiah.

At that time there was a man in Italy, who not

only surpassed all his Jewish contemporaries in his spirit of inquiry and desire for truth, but who would have been able to purify Judaism from the dross of centuries of hardship, if the tendency of the age had not run counter to this endeavor, or if he had had greater courage in opposing it. Azarya ben Moses deï Rossi (born at Mantua about 1514, died in 1578), descended from an old Italian family, had buried himself so deeply in books, that his body bore traces of severe suffering from over-study. Feeble, yellow, withered, and afflicted with fever, he crept about like a dying man. Yet in this living corpse a powerful and healthy mind worked with great activity. He had thoroughly mastered the whole of Jewish literature, besides being well read in Latin historical works, and he had also practiced medicine. At the same time he led a wandering life. He dwelt for some time at Ferrara, then in Bologna, had to leave that city in consequence of the persecution and expulsion of the Jews under Pius V, and finally settled again permanently in Ferrara. He held intercourse with the greatest Jews, Christians, and Marranos of his age, and was regarded by all with astonishment as a marvel of learning. He did not allow the treasures of his knowledge to lie dead within him, but let them grow and spread luxuriantly. Ancient history possessed special attraction for him. But even more admirable than his vast reading was the use he made of it. He was the first to bring into contact and connection with one another two provinces of literature which were far apart—the Talmud and its offshoots, with Philo, Josephus, and the works of the Church Fathers, proving the truth of historical narratives from the mouths of many witnesses. Deï Rossi, too, was the only one not satisfied with the data of tradition; he accepted nothing as truth till he had subjected it to a searching examination.

Chance brought to light the mental treasures of Deï Rossi. Ferrara, where, after leaving Bologna, he had settled shortly before, had been visited by a terrible earthquake (November 18th, 1570), and the inhabitants were compelled to leave their ruined and crumbling houses and seek places of refuge outside the city. In one of the villages Deï Rossi happened to meet a learned Christian, who was trying to overcome the gloomy thoughts caused by the earthquake by reading a Greek book of Jewish antiquity. In conversation Deï Rossi became aware that his co-religionists, even those possessed of some culture, owing to their one-sided absorption in the Talmud or obsolete philosophical writings, knew nothing of their own brilliant literature of the period of the Second Temple, whilst Christians resorted to it to dispel melancholy thoughts. Encouraged by his Christian friend, he determined to translate into Hebrew the "Letter of Aristas," supposed to be the discourse of a Greek king about the wisdom of the Jews, in order to make it accessible to his fellow-believers. He completed this task in twenty days. This was the first-fruit of his learning, and it led him on to further undertakings. His principal work, "Light of the Eyes," consists chiefly of parallel passages from Talmudic and profane sources upon the same subjects. Deï Rossi's distinction rests upon the fact that he did not adhere to tradition, but applied the methods of scientific inquiry to what the multitude regarded as unassailable truths, and that he used profane sources in elucidating them. The actual results of this historical investigation, for the most part, have proved unsound. Strong as Deï Rossi was in removing obstructive rubbish, his power of reconstruction was small.

The value of his efforts appears in its proper light only if we compare them with the circumstances of his time, or with the works of contemporary writers on the same subject, as, for example, those of Gedalya Ibn-Yachya; to these they form a complete contrast.

A descendant of the Italian branch of the noble Ibn-Yachya family, Gedalya inherited taste for knowledge. He was born in 1515, and died in 1587. His wealth enabled him to satisfy his taste by collecting a magnificent library. In his voluntary and compulsory journeys in northern Italy—for he was a preacher, and owing to the intolerance of the popes had to lead an unsettled life—he had seen and read much, both in sacred and profane literature, but without independent judgment, without discrimination, and without appreciation of the essence of truth. Ibn-Yachya's abbreviated "History of the Jews," together with a chronicle of the world, called "The Chain of Tradition," at which he worked for nearly forty years, is a confused medley of authentic historical narratives and mere fables. But in spite, or perhaps because, of its legendary contents, his book has found more acceptance among Jews than the researches of Deï Rossi. When the first edition of the latter's "Light of the Eyes" found its way to Safet, the orthodox of that town declared its contents to be heretical. Joseph Karo commissioned Elisha Gallaico, one of the members of his rabbinical college, to draw up an indictment, to be distributed amongst all Jews, ordering Deï Rossi's work to be burned. The people of Safet likewise had an inquisition. But Joseph Karo died (in Nisan, *i.e.*, April, 1575) before he had signed the indictment. The Italian Jews were not so fanatical as to condemn Deï Rossi, for they knew him to be a pious and pure Jew. But the rabbis of Mantua employed the procedure of Ben Adret concerning the study of profane literature, that is, they forbade the reading of Deï Rossi's works by young people under twenty-five years of age. In consequence of this semi-official sentence of heresy, the book exercised but little influence upon the Jewish world of that day, or the generation immediately succeeding it, and has been appreciated only in quite recent times, when it created a new, enlightened view of history in Jewish circles. But in the Christian world Deï Rossi's work was noticed much sooner, and was annotated, and translated into Latin.

How, indeed, could a sober, critical method of inquiry have found favor in an age when the mystic, dazing Kabbala was the first authority, bidding men esteem blind credulity as the highest virtue, and exciting visionary enthusiasm to the highest pitch of fanatical intoxication? The visions of Solomon Molcho and Joseph Karo and their fond enthusiasm about the Messiah were sober compared with the excitement which reigned after their death, and celebrated a veritable witches' Sabbath. During the last three decades of the sixteenth century the Kabbala gained sole mastery in Palestine, conjured up apparitions, and encouraged orgies of mysticism. It spread thence over the whole of Turkey, Poland, Germany, and Italy, darkening and confusing men's minds, having an evil influence even upon their hearts, allowing no healthy thought to appear, or branding such thought as heretical and sinful. Once again, as in the early days of Christianity, Galilee, especially the district of Safet, became the scene of a host of evil spirits, of people possessed with devils, which challenged mystic exorcism, and revealed profound mysteries; and it is impossible to say whether the possessed appeared in consequence of the exorcisers, or the latter of the former. It was a period of Kabbalistic mania, coincident with profligacy and moral degradation, and its victims despised not only the sciences, but even the Talmud with its exhortations to sobriety. Then for the first time the Jewish world entered on a "dark age" of its own, with all the appropriate credulity, while only the last traces of such darkness were visible in Europe generally.

This tendency was exaggerated by two men, who by their fanaticism and visionary extravagance infected a continually widening circle. These were Isaac Lurya and his disciple Chayim Vital Calabrese.

Isaac Lurya Levi (born in Jerusalem in 1534, and died 1572) was descended from a German family. Left an orphan at an early age by the death of his father, young Isaac came to Egypt, to the house of a rich uncle, Mardochaï Francis, a tax-farmer, and began to study the Talmud. The dry study of the Talmud, which filled the mind with voluminous learning, unfruitful hairsplitting, and mere formulas, yet failed to satisfy the wants of the heart, seems to have become repugnant to Lurya, and to have driven him to fantastic mysticism. He preferred the awful loneliness of the Nile country to the noise of the school; abstraction in worlds of mysticism and devout praying to working out intellectual problems. He was greatly attracted by the Zohar, which had then been printed for the first time, and, widely spread abroad, had become accessible to everybody. The more familiar he became with the Kabbala through his absorption in the sounding emptiness of the Zohar, the more did he seek solitude, and the less intercourse had he with men. He even neglected his young wife, only visited his house from Sabbath to Sabbath, and spoke little, that little being only in Hebrew. Lurya is said to have spent several years in solitude in this manner, and the result was that like all whose reason is weaker than their imagination, he became a confirmed visionary. The mystic book, the Zohar, his constant companion in this seclusion, aided in exciting his imagination. Firmly convinced of its authenticity as the work of Simon bar Yochaï, and also of the divine character of all the fantasies and follies therein revealed, Lurya persisted in seeing in it high allusions and profound wisdom. In his heated imagination he even saw Elijah, the teacher of mysteries, face to face.

But what did the prophet Elijah, or the Zohar, or rather his own heated imagination, reveal to him? First he took the trouble to put system, unity, and logical order into the confusion and intricacies of the Zohar, as if connected thought could be expected in the idle chatter of a half imbecile. The hermit of Cairo sought to deduce from it how God had created and ordered the world by means of the mystic numbers (Sefiroth), or how the Godhead revealed itself in the forms of substances, or how it concentrated itself within itself in order to project the finite nature of created things from its own infinitude. Thus he evolved an extraordinarily complicated system of powers and opposing powers, forces and counter-forces, forms and degrees (Parsophin), in the four spheres of Separation, Creation, Formation, and Transformation; and he clothed these empty abstractions with such wondrous names, that he afterwards complained, with reason, that no one could understand his mystic system. Yet Lurya looked upon this intricate and complex theory of the creation as only a kind of introduction to what seemed to him a much more important and practical part of the Kabbala, whereby the divine order of the world (Olam ha-Tikkun) could be brought about. This practical Kabbala of Lurya rests upon a not less marvelous doctrine of souls, also based upon the visions of the Zohar.

Our souls, he says, reflect the close connection between the finite and the infinite, and, therefore, have a manifold character. The whole of the soul material to appear in temporal life was created with Adam, but each soul, according to its higher or lower degree, was fashioned in, from, or with the first man, out of high or low organs and forms. Accordingly, there are souls of the brain, the eyes, the hands, and the feet. Each of these must be regarded as an effluence, or spark (Nizuz), from Adam. By the first sin of the first man—for the Kabbala finds original sin necessary for its fanciful creations—the higher and the lower, the superior and the inferior souls, good and evil, became confused and mingled together. Even the purest beings thereby received an admixture of evil and the devilish element of the "husk" (Kelifa). But the moral order of the world, or the purification of the first man, cannot be brought about till the consequences of original sin, the confusion of good and evil, are obliterated and removed. From the most evil part of the soul material emanates the heathen world; the people of Israel, on the other hand, come from the good part. But the former are not quite without an admixture of the original good, while the latter are not free from an admixture of the corrupt and demoniac. This imperfection gives the continual impulse towards sin, and hinders the chosen fragment of the human race from following the law of God, the Torah. The Messianic period will put an end to the disturbance of divine order arising from the first sin, or abolish the disorder which has since crept in, and will introduce, or see introduced, the divinity of the world. Therefore, a complete separation of good from evil must take place, and this can only happen through Israel, if it or each of its members will lose or cast away the admixture of evil. For this purpose, men's souls (especially those of the Israelites) have to wander through the bodies of men and animals, even through rivers, wood, and stones. The doctrine of the transmigration of souls forms the center and basis of Lurya's Kabbala, but he has a peculiar development of the idea. According to this theory even the souls of the pious must suffer transmigration, since not even they are free from the taint of evil; there is none righteous upon earth, who does only good, and sins not. In this way, Lurya solved the difficulty, which former Kabbalist writers could not overcome.

But this separation of the good and evil elements in the world's soul material, the expiation and obliteration of original sin, or the restoration of the divine order in Adam, would require a long series of ages, owing to the impulse towards sin continually present. There are, however, means of hastening this process, and this was the really original doctrine that Lurya enunciated. Besides the transmigration of our souls, sinful and subject to demoniac forces as they are, there is another mode of expiation, the elevation or impregnation of the soul (Ibbur, *superfœtatio*). If a purified soul has neglected various religious duties here on earth, or has had no opportunity of fulfilling them, it must return to the earthly life, attach itself to the soul of a living human being, and unite and coalesce with it in order to retrieve this neglect. Or again, the departed spirits of men freed from sin appear again on earth to support the weak and wavering souls which cannot attain to good by their own efforts, strengthen them and lead them to the final goal. These pure spirits combine with weaker souls still struggling, and form a union with them, provided that they have some affinity with one another, *i. e.*, if they originate from the same spark or organ of Adam, since as a rule only similar (homogeneous) souls attract each other, while on the other hand dissimilar (heterogeneous) souls repel each other. According to this theory the banishment and dispersion of Israel have for their purpose the salvation of the world or of men's souls. The purified spirits of pious Israelites unite with the souls of men of other nationalities in order to free them from the demoniacal impurities that possess them.

Isaac Lurya imagined a complete system of the transmigration and combination of souls. It also seemed to him important to know the sex of a soul, for feminine souls are found in masculine bodies, and *vice versâ*, according to the transmigration and attraction in each case. It is especially important in contracting a marriage to know whether the souls of man and wife harmonize with each other in respect of origin and degree. By means of this secret the visionary of Cairo expected to solve the other mystery, namely, how good spirits may be conjured down from heaven, and in a measure compelled to enter the bodies of living men, and thus made to divulge revelations of the world beyond. Hereby he believed that he held the key to the kingdom of the Messiah and the regeneration of the world. Lurya also believed that he possessed the soul of the Messiah of the branch of Joseph, and that he had a Messianic mission. He saw spirits everywhere, and heard their whispers in the rushing of the waters, the movements of the trees and grass, in the song or twittering of birds, even in the flickering of flames. He saw how at death the souls were set free from the body, how they hovered in the air, or rose out of their graves. He held intimate intercourse with the saints of the Bible, the Talmud, and with the rabbis, in particular with Simon bar Yochaï. In short, Lurya was a ghost-seer and raiser of the dead, a second Abraham Abulafia, or Solomon Molcho, arousing hopes of the coming of the Messiah by Kabbalistic jugglery, but with all this fanaticism he was sober and sophistical. He introduced the casuistry of the Talmud into the Kabbala.

In Egypt, Isaac Lurya found little or no favor with his labyrinth of higher worlds and his theories of creation and redemption. To realize his scheme of redemption he migrated with his wife and child to Safet, the Jerusalem of mysticism, where the mystic doctrine flourished, and the Zohar, the spurious work of Moses de Leon, was exalted to the same level as the Law of Moses ben Amram. Almost the whole college of rabbis and the chief leaders of Safet were Kabbalists. This place was at the time a flourishing city inhabited only by Jews. The members of the community knew little of oppression or the cares of life, and so the Kabbalists could spin mystical theories to their hearts' content. They felt as safe under the favor that the Jewish Duke of Naxos found with the sultan, as if in a state of their own, politically independent. The Kabbalists had gone so far in their imitation of Catholicism that they had adopted auricular confession and the adoration of martyrs. And this was the stage on which Lurya, the creator of the new Kabbala, was to originate new aberrations.

At first (about 1569), he appears to have received little attention in the city of Kabbalists. Only through his acquaintance and connection with a still greater visionary, perhaps not quite so honest as himself, did he become a person of consequence, and infect everyone with his waking dreams. This man was the Italian Chayim Vital Calabrese (born 1543, died 1620), whose father, a copyist of the scrolls of the Law, had traveled to Palestine from Italy. Vital had learned nothing thoroughly in his younger days; he had only gained a smattering of the Talmud and mystic lore. He possessed a wild, extravagant imagination, and a decided inclination for adventure and sensation. For two years and a half Vital had occupied his time with alchemy and the art of making gold. From this mystic art he turned to Lurya's Kabbala. It is not known which of these two men first sought the other, but it is certain that each, without wishing it, deceived the other. Together they visited desolate places and graves, particularly the grave of Simon bar Yochaï, the feigned author of the Zohar, in Meïron. This was Lurya's favorite spot, because there he fancied he could draw down upon himself the spirit of this supposed chief of the mystics. Now and again Lurya sent forth his disciple to conjure up spirits, and for this purpose delivered to him certain formulas made up of the transposed letters of the name of the Deity. Of course, evil spirits fled before Vital's gaze, whilst good spirits attached themselves to him, and communicated their secrets.

It was Vital who spread sensational reports concerning the extraordinary, almost divine gifts of his master, and of his power over departed and living souls; doing so, it appears, with an artful calculation of effect and publicity. Lurya, once so isolated, now found himself surrounded by crowds of visitors; Kabbalists, young and old, came to listen to the new revelation. Several disciples attached themselves to him, and he communicated to them his confused thoughts, assigned to each the original Adamite soul that dwelt in him, the transmigrations which it had undergone before its present corporeal existence, and its functions on earth. It never occurred to these people, already enmeshed in the Kabbalistic net, to doubt the truth of these communications. The disciples that gathered round him Lurya formed into two classes: the "initiated" and the "novices."

Mystical conversations and notes, the interviewing and summoning of spirits, formed the occupation of Lurya and his followers. In short, Lurya was on the eve of founding a new Jewish sect. On the Sabbath he dressed in white, and wore a fourfold garment to symbolize the four letters of the name of God. The underlying fact of all his revelations and exertions was that he was the Messiah of the race of Joseph, the forerunner of the Messiah of David's line. This, however, he only furtively hinted to his disciples. His delusion was that the Messianic period would commence at the beginning of the second half of the second period of a thousand years since the destruction of the Temple, *i. e.*, in 1568.

The sudden death of the mystic, at the age of thirty-eight, conduced still more to his glorification. Death is wont to transfigure natures like his, and veneration for them increases as years roll on. With Eastern exaggeration, his disciples regarded him as even more than a worker of wonders; they called him the "Holy and Divine," and sought, for their own glory, to win adherents for him and his visionary extravagances. They declared that, if Lurya could only have lived five years longer, he would have improved the world so effectually, that the Messianic period would certainly have begun. Abraham Abulafia, who had evolved a Kabbalistic medley from his own consciousness, was declared a heretic, and persecuted. Isaac Lurya, who had done the same thing with the Zohar as a foundation, was almost deified.

After Lurya's death, Vital Calabrese came to the fore. He immediately usurped a kind of authority over his fellow-disciples, pretended that Lurya on his deathbed had appointed him his successor, and, in feigned obedience to a dying request of his master, took away from them the written notes given them by Lurya. Vital let it be understood that he was the Messiah of the race of Joseph. However, some disciples did not pay any attention to this, and forthwith taught in various countries what they had received from Lurya himself. This was especially done by Israel Saruk in Italy, whither he had traveled.

The harm that the Kabbalistic doctrines of Lurya caused in Jewish circles is inexpressible. Judaism became surrounded with so thick a husk of mysticism, that it has not even yet succeeded in entirely freeing itself, and showing its true kernel. Through Lurya's influence there was formed, side by side with the Judaism of the Talmud and the rabbis, a Judaism of the Zohar and the Kabbala. For it was due to him that the spurious Zohar was placed upon a level with, indeed higher than, the Holy Scriptures and the Talmud.

The mysticism of Lurya laid stress upon an idea which has been strangely neglected in Jewish circles, viz., devotion in prayer, but even this devotion degenerated into Kabbalistic trifling. Every word and every syllable of the ordained prayers was to be meditated on devoutly, so that one might reflect upon the worlds of the Sefiroth, the number of the names of God hidden therein, and many other things. Lurya's Kabbala certainly inculcated the preservation of an unruffled disposition, and interdicted dejection, or outbreaks of anger and ill-humor. But this serenity, from its mystical setting, received a touch of constraint and unpleasantness, like the laughter of a madman. The Sabbath, with its prayers and meals, forms the central point of Lurya's mystic teaching. He looked upon it as the visible representation of the world of the Sefiroth, as the embodiment of the Divinity (Shechinah) in temporal life, and all actions done or left undone on that day had an influence upon the higher world. Lurya's followers welcomed the Sabbath, "the mystic bride," with chanting, and for this purpose Lurya composed Chaldaic songs full of obscure and meaningless formulas. His Kabbala also introduced a second Day of Atonement. The "Day of Hosannas," the seventh day of the Feast of Tabernacles, was formerly observed as a day of festivity. Even Joseph Karo did not venture in his code to attribute a higher, mystical, religious function to this day. Lurya's school first raised it, on the authority of the Zohar, to the rank of a minor day of expiation, introduced the practice of holding a mystic vigil the previous night, and perceived in every leaf of the willow branches, and in the seven-fold processions round the scrolls of the Law, a higher, mystical meaning. In relation to morality, too, the mysticism of Lurya had a corrupting influence. It demanded a "harmony of souls" as a condition of marriage, and, therefore, whenever disagreement showed itself in married life, it was said that the marriage was not a union foreordained by the harmony of the Sefiroth.

Kabbalists, therefore, separated from their wives in consequence of the smallest dissension in married life, to seek out the harmonious soul predestined for them. Thus divorce became frequent in Kabbalistic circles. Kabbalists often left their wives and children in the West, and, migrating to the East, contracted a new marriage, or several new marriages, and the children of the different marriages knew nothing of one another.

These corrupting mystic doctrines did not remain a dead letter, but were forthwith put into practice by their adherents. Thus, the brilliance shed by the Jewish Duke of Naxos and other influential Jews at the Turkish court over their fellow-believers in the East, came to resemble the light of the will-o'-the-wisps that make the waters of a stagnant marsh gleam with a flickering light. The religious stagnation at the time was glaring indeed; there was a complete relapse into heathenism; and what was worse, there sounded no warning voice which recognized the mischief, or stigmatized, though ever so feebly, the corruption as it really was. Perhaps the feeling of complete security in which the Jews in Turkey reposed under mighty protectors of their own race had encouraged this religious disorder. In any case, it did not decrease as this protection gradually disappeared, when the influence of Joseph of Naxos ceased on the death of Sultan Selim in 1574. His successor, Sultan Murad III (1574—1595), left the Jewish duke in possession of his rank and offices according to his father's dying request. But he no longer had direct influence over the divan; he was supplanted by his adversary, the grand vizir, Mahomet Sokolli, and his rival, Solomon Ashkenazi, and could accomplish nothing without intrigues through the agency of the harem. Joseph Nassi did not long survive his partial disgrace; he died of calculus, on August 2d, 1579, sincerely lamented by the Jews. His accumulated treasures melted away even as his ambitious designs. The avaricious sultan, Murad, who slept upon heaps of gold in order that they might not be stolen from him, by the advice of Mahomet Sokolli confiscated all his property, ostensibly to cover his debts. The widowed duchess, Reyna Nassi, with difficulty retained her dowry of 90,000 ducats out of her husband's estate. This noble woman, although she certainly did not possess the spirit either of her mother, Donna Gracia, or of her husband, determined like these to spend her wealth in the interests of Jewish knowledge. She set up a Hebrew printing press in her palace of Belvedere, and afterwards in a village called Kuru-Gismu, on the European side near Constantinople. But she was misled by Joseph Askaloni, a business manager devoid of all taste, to whom she had intrusted the direction of her press, so that only writings of no importance, which had far better have remained in obscurity, were published in her establishment (1579—1598). And so this noble family of two men and two women, renowned in their own time, left no worthy or lasting memorial; and their deeds, prompted by the noblest intentions, have perished in the stream of the ages.

Duke Joseph having disappeared from the scene, the prestige of the Hebrew statesman, Solomon Ashkenazi, the peacemaker between Turkey and Venice, increased. But, much as he was able to accomplish by means of his diplomatic arts, he did not, like Joseph of Naxos, stand in the forefront of events as a Turkish dignitary, but rather remained in the background as a wise and silent mediator. Solomon Ashkenazi had no access to the sultan himself, but only held secret intercourse with the successive grand vizirs, whose right hand man he was. The negotiations between Turkey and Spain to procure a peace, or at least a *modus vivendi*, desired as it was by both sides, owing to pride on both sides, were delayed, broken off, and renewed.

These diplomatic discussions were conducted by Solomon, who possessed greater qualifications for that purpose than anyone else, and the matters in dispute were partially brought to a conclusion by him. He was particularly careful to maintain a good understanding between the Porte and Venice, and was on this account rewarded by the doge, his sons being allowed to live in Venice at the expense of the state.

Also Jewish women of wisdom and good sense, having skill in medicine, gained great influence by means of the harem under the sultans Murad III, Mahomet IV, and Achmed I. Among these women, Esther Kiera, widow of one Elias Chendali, specially distinguished herself. She was a great favorite with the sultana Baffa, herself the favorite wife of Murad, who influenced politics under her husband and afterwards during the reign of her son. If a Christian state wished to gain any object at the Porte, it had first to win over the Jewish go-between, Kiera. The Venetians particularly knew how to turn this fact to account. All ambitious persons who aimed at attaining high office paid respect to Kiera, and addressed her with flattery. Naturally, she enriched herself by her secret power, as did everyone in Turkey who, however strong or weak he might be, formed one of the spokes in the wheel of the state. She showed great interest in her race, supported the poor and suffering, fed the hungry, and comforted the sorrowful. Jewish science was helped by her generous hand. Zacuto's history, as mentioned before, was published at her expense. Naturally her position excited envy. Esther Kiera imprudently allowed herself to be implicated in the appointment of cavalry officers, first promising one man a high post and then bestowing it on another. The Turkish Spahis, the proudest class of soldiers, took this treatment very ill, plotted together, and demanded her head. The deputy grand vizir Chalil wished to save her and her sons, and allowed them to take refuge in his palace. But on the very steps Esther Kiera and her three sons were seized by the Spahis, torn to pieces, and their limbs hung upon the doors of the favored magnates who had received their posts through her influence.

Under Sultan Achmed I, another Hebrew woman, the widow of the statesman Solomon Ashkenazi, gained great consideration. She was so fortunate as to cure the young sultan of the smallpox, which shortly after his accession threatened his life, and for which the Turkish physicians knew no remedy. She was richly rewarded for nursing him back to health. But such signs of favor towards Jews became continually rarer in Turkey, and at last ceased altogether, as the empire sank into enervation, and each sultan became a Sardanapalus; while the harem, on the one hand, and the Spahis and Janissaries, on the other, held the reins of power. The glory of the Turkish Jews was extinguished like a meteor, and plunged into utter darkness, from time to time illuminated by fanciful visions. Extortion, robbery, and open deeds of violence, on the part of the pashas towards Jews, began to occur daily, since they were now deprived of a powerful protector at the Sultan's side. The center of Judaism was shifted to another stage.

CHAPTER XVIII.

THE JEWS IN POLAND.

Condition of Poland—Favorable Situation of the Jews in that Country—Anti-Jewish Party in Poland—The Jewish Communities—Judaizing Poles—Studies of the Jews—The Talmud in Poland—Solomon Lurya—Moses Isserles—The Historian, David Gans—"Zemach David"—Supremacy of the Polish Authorities in Rabbinical Matters—The Jewish Seminaries in Poland—The Disputations at the Fairs—Chiddushim and Chillukim—Stephen Bathori—His Kindness towards his Jewish Subjects—Sigismund III—Restriction on the Erection of Synagogues—Jewish Synods—Vaad Arba Arazoth—Mordecai Jafa—Christian Sects in Poland—The Socinians or Unitarians—Simon Budny—The Reformers and the Jews—Isaac Troki—"The Strengthening of Faith."

1566—1600 C.E.

POLAND, which in this century had become a great power by reason of its union with Lithuania under the sons of Casimir IV, like Turkey, was the refuge of the outlawed or persecuted. Canonical Christianity, with its love of persecution, had not yet struck firm roots there; and monarchical despotism, encouraged by priests in its obstinate determination to realize all its ends regardless of consequences, could not prevail against the independent spirit of the Polish nobility. The Starosts ruled unchecked in their provinces, like the English and Scottish lords and clans, and could ward off the encroachments of royalty. The reformed faith, that is to say Calvin's teaching, was readily received by the nobility and the middle classes. Poland, therefore, in this century, too, was a second Babylonia for the Jews, in which on the whole they were protected from bloody persecutions, where some of them could attain to respectable positions, and where they were allowed to develop their individuality without restraint. When the Jews were expelled from Bohemia, and turned their steps to Poland, they were kindly received. Indeed, so highly appreciated were they, that it was thought that the people could not do without them. When, attracted by the favored position of their brethren in Turkey, many prepared to migrate thither, the king made every exertion to retain them in his land either by persuasion or compulsion. It mattered very little what were the king's relations to them; for whether he was kindly or evilly disposed, the nobles protected those who dwelt on their estates from all attacks, in as far as their own interests were not injured thereby. Under some kings, the Jews received favors, under others, suffered restrictions, according as hostile or friendly influences preponderated.

But there was a party in Poland hostile to the Jews. It regarded with dissatisfied eyes their more favored position in that country as compared with the rest of Christendom, and endeavored to abrogate the statute of Casimir IV, still in force, giving protection against unduly severe persecution. It consisted, on the one hand, of the Catholic clergy which regretted the absence in the Polish legislation of canonical restrictions regarding Jews; on the other, of the German merchant and artisan class which feared Jewish competition.

There exists no estimate of the number of Jews in Poland at this time. It is said that there were 200,000 adults. The community at Posen numbered 3,000 members, and there were about as many in Cracow, or rather in the suburb Kazimierz, to which they had on a former occasion been banished. The third community in point of size was at Lublin. The Jews had many taxes to pay under different heads. For this purpose, indeed, they were received, and on this account tolerated in the country, and protected by the kings and the nobility, being almost the only ones in that impecunious land who possessed money. For this reason, also, the kings encouraged their commercial enterprises. When Sigismund Augustus, soon after his accession, negotiated for a prolongation of the peace with the Russian Czar, Ivan IV, called "the Terrible," he inserted the condition that the Jews of Lithuania be allowed, as formerly, to freely carry on trade with Russia. But Ivan absolutely refused this condition; he did not wish to see any Jews in his realm. "We do not want these men," he said, "who have brought us poison for our bodies and souls; they have sold deadly herbs among us, and blasphemed our Lord and Saviour." A Judaizing sect had been founded some seventy years before by a Jew called Zacharias, to which sect even some of the priests, and a metropolitan named Zosina belonged. This proselytizing sect continued to exist till the beginning of the sixteenth century, but its adherents were severely persecuted when discovered. On this account Jews were not allowed in Russia.

In consequence of the Reformation, which had made its way into Poland, a purer taste and a love of science and literature had developed there. Polish nobles fond of traveling brought back from Germany an interest in these matters, and sent their sons to study at the reformed universities of Wittenberg and Geneva. Schools arose in Poland where Jewish boys and youths were instructed together with Christians. The Polish Jews, it is true, did not devote themselves to science to a marked degree, but they were by no means so devoid of it as their German brethren.

Aristotle, that philosophical authority so familiar to the Hebrew world and so closely akin to the Hebrew spirit, found admirers also among Polish Jews. Even Maimuni's philosophic and religious writings found a few readers. Astronomy and medicine, two favorite sciences of the Jews from time immemorial, were studied also by Polish Jews.

Generally speaking, they did not share the intellectual degradation of the Jewish inhabitants of Germany. Among them the study of the Talmud received an impetus greater almost than in France in the times of the Tossafist schools. Of all the Jews in Europe and Asia those in Poland were the last to become familiar with the Talmud; as though desirous of making up for lost time, they cherished it with extravagant affection. It appeared as if the deep secrets of the Talmud were to be rightly understood and completely unraveled and appreciated only in Poland. Comprehensive erudition and marvelous insight were united in a surprising manner in the Polish students of this book, and everyone whom nature had not deprived of all talent devoted himself to its study. The dead letter received new life from the eager inspiration of the Jewish sons of Poland; in this land it exerted an influence of great force, striking sparks of intellectual fire, and creating a ceaseless flow of thought. The Talmudical schools in Poland henceforward became the most celebrated throughout the whole of European Judaism. All who sought sound learning betook themselves thither. To have been educated in a college of the Polish Jews was of itself a sufficient recommendation; and all who did not possess this advantage were considered inferiors.

The fame of the rabbinical schools of Poland was due to three men : Shalom Shachna, Solomon Lurya, and Moses Isserles. Solomon Lurya (born in Posen about 1510, died about 1573) came from a family of German immigrants. Had he been born in a better, a more intellectual epoch, he would have been one of the makers of Judaism, perhaps another Maimuni. But being the son of an age of decadence, he became only a profound and thorough Talmud scholar, in the higher sense of the word, not remaining satisfied with traditional data, but examining every single point and weighing it in the golden balance of critical exactitude. To the thorough and critical investigation of the great field of the Talmud his whole mental activity was devoted, and he possessed the greatest natural qualifications for such critical work. With his bold spirit of inquiry, ruthlessly subjecting everything to the severest examination, Lurya in any other age would have gone beyond the Talmud, if its contradictions had made themselves glaringly apparent to him. But by this son of an age of faith the whole book was regarded as an actual continuation of the revelation made at Sinai, an unassailable authority, which only needed to be properly understood, or which wanted perhaps a little rectification here and there, but as a whole contained the truth. Lurya was a strongly marked character, having all the acerbity and angularity commonly associated therewith. Injustice, venality, and hypocrisy, were so hateful to him, that he broke out into what was sometimes imprudent excess of zealous indignation. By reason of his distinct individuality and firmness, which he wished to assert everywhere, Solomon Lurya offended and hurt the vanity of not a few. He lashed in bitter terms those Talmudical scholars whose actions did not correspond to their teaching, and devoted themselves to the study of rabbinical literature only for the sake of discussion, or to gain a reputation. Hence he made many enemies, and in his own time was more feared than loved. In polemical discussion he was reckless and unsparing, and very naturally brought upon himself retaliation which only embittered him the more. Then he complained of persecution, and even of the ingratitude of his disciples, who, he said, had turned against him, and looked at everything in a gloomy light. He attacked the students of the Talmud, because, he said, the ignorant were so many and the possessors of knowledge so few, while their arrogance continually increased, and no one was content to take the position that properly belonged to him. No sooner was one of them ordained than he assumed the airs of a master, collected a troop of disciples around him for money, as people of rank hire a body-guard. "There are," he complained, "gray-headed rabbis with very little knowledge of the Talmud, who behave imperiously to congregations and to people of real knowledge, excommunicate and re-admit members, ordain disciples—all for their own selfish purposes." Solomon Lurya extended the sarcastic bitterness of his scorn to German experts in the Talmud, "who, in the case of people of wealth and authority, show indulgence towards the transgression of rabbinical precepts, while they spread evil reports about men of moderate means and strangers who are guilty of slight irregularities, such as going about with uncovered head."

However, things were not so bad in Jewish society as depicted by Lurya's bitter humor; and this is proved in the most conclusive manner by the recognition that this morose faultfinder himself received. Talmudical students, both young and old, even in his lifetime, were full of admiration for his achievements. While still betwixt youth and middle age, he undertook his principal work of elucidating and sifting Talmudic discussions with a view to establishing religious practice, and he continued this work up to the end of his life without completing it. Solomon Lurya performed this task with more thoroughness, clearness, and depth than his contemporaries and predecessors. But if he hoped, as it appears he did, to put an end to all variety and confusion of opinion, he made the same mistake as Maimuni and others. He only contributed to further entanglement of the knot. His numerous other writings bear the same impress of thoroughness and critical insight, but he could not reach the seat of the trouble any more than others who had made the attempt; it lay too deep.

By reason of his critical faculty, Lurya laid stress upon what his Polish and German fellow-students neglected as too trifling—namely, on grammatical correctness and precision in the distinction of the forms of speech. On the other hand, he was a declared enemy of scholastic philosophy. It appeared to him to be dangerous and fatal to faith.

Another leading rabbi in Poland was Moses ben Israel Isserles, of Cracow (born in 1520, died Iyar, 1572). The son of a greatly respected father, who had held the office of president of the community, he distinguished himself more by his precocity and comprehensive learning than by striking mental individuality. Inheriting so much property from his family that he dedicated one of his houses as a synagogue, Isserles was able to follow the bent of his genius with ease and comfort, devote himself to the Talmud, and make himself familiar with its mazes. He soon gained such a reputation that, while still almost a youth, he was nominated rabbi-judge in Cracow. At thirty years of age he had embraced the whole field of Talmudic and rabbinical literature as thoroughly as Joseph Karo, a man double his age.

Isserles also felt the need of collecting and giving finality to the widely scattered materials of rabbinical Judaism. But since Joseph Karo had forestalled him by the compilation of his Code, it only remained for him to rectify it, and comment upon it. For he regretted the omission of several elements in that work, especially the neglect of German rabbinical authorities and customs. This continuation of Karo's Code, or "Table," he called the "Mappa" or "Table-cloth." As the Jews in Germany had always been more scrupulous in their observances than those elsewhere, the additions and supplementations made by Isserles turned out to be burdensome. His decisions immediately received recognition, and to the present day form the religious standard, the official Judaism, of the German and Polish communities and those allied to them. It cannot quite be said that he contributed to its ossification, for he did not invent and introduce these burdens, but only noted and codified them; he followed the universal tendency. If Isserles had not arranged them into a religious code, some one else would have done so.

Isserles had taste also for other subjects besides the Talmud, especially for astronomy. He produced a commentary to Frohbach's astronomical work, "Theorica." He likewise had an inclination for philosophy, and pursued the subject rather deeply, though only through the medium of Hebrew works. Maimuni's "Guide" was his guide, too. On this account he had to submit to a sharp reproof from the proud Solomon Lurya. Isserles also had some taste for history, which led him to induce one of his disciples to occupy himself seriously with it. David Gans (born in Westphalia in 1541, died in Prague in 1613) had come to Cracow when a youth in order to study in the rabbinical academy there; but his natural taste for scientific subjects, history, geography, mathematics, and astronomy, was involuntarily aroused by Isserles, who brought him up, and guided his studies. Gans devoted himself to these subjects, and made the acquaintance of two great leaders in mathematics and astronomy, Kepler and Tycho de Brahe. He wrote several works on these subjects, of course in Hebrew. His chronicle (Zemach David), consisting of annals of Jewish and general history, has become celebrated. It was a very great thing for a German Jew to have devoted himself to studies outside of the ordinary track. But one cannot call David's historical work great. He introduced among Jews the dry, bare form of historical narrative formerly employed by monks, which at that time had already given place to a more artistic method. However, unimportant as David's chronicle is, it possesses some merit, because it reminded those wrapped up in the study of the Talmud that they were the last links of a long historical chain. The want of appreciation of history displayed by German Jews is indicated by the brief inscription placed on Gans' tomb, while there were no limits to the eulogies glorifying the memory of some obscure rabbinical dignitary. The study of the Talmud, prosecuted merely as an effort of memory, won greater fame for its votaries than devotion to any branch of science, however profoundly grasped.

The three great rabbinical lights, first both in rank and in priority of time, Shachna, Solomon Lurya, and Isserles, laid the foundation of the extraordinary erudition of the Polish Jews. Any complicated or generally interesting question, arising in Germany, Moravia, Bohemia, even in Italy and Turkey, was submitted to them, especially to Isserles, for final decision. The revoltingly vulgar actions of the community at Prague, against which the local college of rabbis was powerless, were brought before the rabbis of Poland, and attacked vigorously by them. Passionate disputes in Frankfort-on-the-Main, which threatened to produce persecution or expulsion, were settled, and a reconciliation effected from Poland. Thus this rabbinical triumvirate founded a kind of supremacy of Poland over the Jews of Europe, acknowledged on all sides, and the Polish rabbis maintained their position as leaders up to the end of the eighteenth century.

The triumvirate, whose numerous disciples rivaled each other in the study of the Talmud, gradually caused nearly all Polish Jews to become familiar with that book, and eligible for the rabbinical office. Even in small communities of only fifty members there were at least twenty Talmudical scholars, who in turn instructed at least thirty pupils. Everywhere there arose schools with rabbis at their head as teachers, whose chief duty was to deliver lectures, everything else being of secondary importance. Young men crowded to these establishments, where they could live free from care, their maintenance being defrayed out of the treasury of the community, or by wealthy private individuals. Children were put to the study of the Talmud at a tender age, certainly to the detriment of the natural development of their minds. It was the highest honor to conduct a rabbinical school, and their ambition was encouraged to strive for this object. Supervisors were nominated to watch over the industry of the students (Bachurim) and the children. Gradually a kind of syllabus with alternating themes, in use up to recent times, was introduced for the lectures on the Talmud in the summer and the winter term.

At the end of the term, the teachers and their numerous pupils went to the great Polish fairs, in summer to Zaslaw and Jaroslaw, in winter to Lemberg and Lublin. Thus several thousand students of the Talmud met, and there ensued a lively interchange of remarks and subtle disputations upon the subject-matter of rabbinical and Talmudic study. Public disputations were held, in which anyone might take part. The keener intellects received wealthy brides as a reward for their mental exertions. Rich parents took pride in having sons-in-law educated in Talmudic schools, and sought for them at the fairs. The Polish Jews, by reason of this fervent zeal, acquired a Talmudic deportment, so to speak, which showed itself in every movement and every utterance, by ungraceful shrugging of the shoulders and a peculiar movement of the thumbs. Every conversation, whether of a perfectly indifferent nature or even upon matters of business, resembled a disputation upon the Talmud. Talmudical words, designations, phrases, and allusions, passed into popular speech, and were understood even by women and children.

But this excessive study of the Talmud in Poland was of no real advantage to Judaism. It was not carried on in order to gain a proper understanding of the book, but merely to find something unique, rare, witty, striking, something to tickle the intellectual palate. In these meetings of thousands of students of the Talmud, masters and disciples, teachers and pupils, at the great fairs, every individual exerted himself to discover something new, startling, and casuistical, bringing it forward only to surpass all others, without caring whether it stood the test of proof, or was only relatively true, but merely to gain a reputation for sharp-wittedness. The chief endeavor of the Talmudical students of Poland was directed to bringing to light something new in Talmudic criticism, or in inventing something (Chiddush). The lectures of the heads of schools, and of all rabbis, had only this object in view—to set up something hitherto unsurpassed, to weave a net of sophistical Talmudical propositions, and to go still further in the process of incomprehensible hair-splitting (Chillukim). Hence the whole trend of Jewish thought in Poland was in a wrong direction. The language of the Jews in particular suffered from this cause, degenerating into a ridiculous jargon, a mixture of German, Polish, and Talmudical elements, an unpleasant stammering, rendered still more repulsive by forced attempts at wit. This corrupt speech, despising all forms, could be understood only by Jews, natives of the country. Together with their language the Polish Jews lost that which really constitutes a man, and were thus exposed to the scorn and contempt of non-Jewish society. The Bible had fallen gradually into the background in the course of development since the time of Maimuni; now in Poland knowledge of it was utterly lost. If anyone occupied himself with it, it was merely to derive the materials for wit, or false wit, from its pages.

The circumstances of the time were such that the Jews of Poland were able, to a certain extent, to form an independent state within the Polish state. Several kings in succession were favorable to them, according them extensive protective privileges, and seeing, as far as their power went, that these rights were respected. After the death of the last king of the Jagellon dynasty, Sigismund Augustus (1572), the Jews of Poland profited by the elective monarchy. Each newly-elected king above all needed money, which could be supplied only by Jews; or, he needed a party among the nobles, and this order, in general devoted to the Jews, obtained a preponderating influence as compared with the narrow-minded German middle class, hostile to Jews.

After a thirteen months' interregnum, occupied by election negotiations and intrigues, the sagacious prince of Transylvania, Stephen Bathori, gained the Polish throne, not without the co-operation of the Jewish agent, Solomon Ashkenazi, for Turkey had supported his election. Not long after his accession, he sent kind messages to the Jews, protected those in Lithuania against false and calumnious accusation of the murder of Christian children, and uttered his conviction that the Jews conscientiously obeyed the Hebrew law of not shedding human blood. His reign of nearly twelve years (1575—1586) forms a happy episode in the history of the Jews in Poland. Stephen Bathori, moreover, did not allow the privileges to remain a dead letter, but preserved them in full force. He allowed Jews (in 1576) to carry on all kinds of trade without restriction, even to buy and sell on Christian holidays, desired that the murder of a Jew, like the murder of a Christian, be punished by death, and made the city magistracies responsible for riots and injuries caused by Christian mobs in synagogues, cemeteries, and at Jewish funerals. The promoters of tumultuous attacks upon Jews, which occurred chiefly in the half-German city of Posen, were to be fined ten thousand Polish marks, and the magistrate who had not done his duty in protecting Jews was to be fined a similar sum. Bathori's reign was not, however, free from libelous attacks on the Jews. Where was there at that time in Christian Europe a single country in which the enemies of the Jews did not assail them? A Polish poet, Klonowicz, poured forth his scorn of their trade, usury, and arrogance, in Latin verses; the rulers, he said, robbed the Jews, only to be robbed by them in turn.

In the long reign of Sigismund III (1587—1632), the Swedish prince whose election gave a pretext for internal dissensions and civil wars, the Polish Jews fared better than might have been expected from a pupil of the Jesuits and a zealous Catholic. Although he caused dissenting Poles to be severely persecuted, the Jews under his government were by no means unhappy. At the diet in Warsaw (1592) he confirmed the ancient privileges of Casimir, considered to be in their favor. However, Sigismund III introduced one law, very disadvantageous to Jews, and disclosing the ecclesiastical bent of his mind. He ordained that the permission of the clergy had to be gained to build new synagogues, a regulation which, of course, rendered the practice of the Jewish religion dependent on a church eager for persecution.

Under this king the Jews in Poland introduced (1586—1592) an institution which had not existed in that particular form in Jewish history. It gave the Polish communities extraordinary unity, firmness, and strength, and hence secured respect both from their members and outsiders. Hitherto it had naturally come about that, at the meeting of rabbis and heads of schools with their followers at the great fairs, important questions were discussed, law cases were settled, and general consultations took place. The utility of such meetings may have become clearly apparent, and given rise to the idea of arranging regular conferences of the heads of communities, to draw up final, binding decisions. Both leaders and communities must have been actuated by a healthy spirit in agreeing to common action. The communities of the chief provinces, Little Poland, Greater Poland, and Russia, were the first to unite in instituting conferences (Vaad) at regular intervals, to take place at the great fairs of Lublin and Jaroslaw. The communities sent delegates, learned men of proved excellence, who had a seat and a vote in the synod. They chose a president, who directed the discussion of questions, and drew up a report of the session. Disputes in the communities, questions of taxation, religious and social regulations, the averting of threatened dangers, and help to brethren in distress, were the main points treated by the synods, and settled finally. The synods also exercised a literary censorship by granting permission for certain books to be printed and sold, and refusing it in the case of others which seemed to them harmful. Probably the Lithuanian Jews were represented at a later period, and the synods were called the Synods of the Four Countries (Vaad Arba Arazoth). These conferences had a very beneficial effect: they prevented long-standing dissensions, averted or punished acts of injustice, kept alive a feeling of union amongst the communities, directing them towards common action, thereby counteracting the narrowness and selfishness of merely local interests, which so greatly encouraged the dismemberment and isolation of communities, as, for example, in Germany. On this account the synod of Polish Jews was respected even abroad; and distant German communities or private individuals who had any complaint to make, applied to these supreme assemblies, certain to obtain relief. It is to the glory of the men who, for nearly two hundred years, presided over the synods, that their names, worthy of the remembrance of posterity, remained in obscurity, as though they had consciously suppressed their individuality in favor of the community at large. Still less is known of the originators of this institution, who succeeded in the difficult task of overcoming the anarchic tendency of the people, as Jews and as Poles, and of inducing them to subordinate themselves to one great end. It is conjectured that Mordecai Jafa, a rabbi from Bohemia (born about 1532, died 1612), who made many journeys, and suffered much sorrow, was the organizer of these regular conferences. He had been compelled, in his youth, to assume the wanderer's staff. In this way he came to Venice; here he occupied himself in drawing up a religious code more convenient than that of Joseph Karo. Apparently the search made by the Inquisition for copies of the Talmud rendered his stay in Venice unpleasant, and he again betook himself to Poland. There finally he officiated as a rabbi, first in Grodno, afterwards in Lublin, from about 1575 till the spring of 1592. In Lublin, one of the great fair towns, many thousands of Jews used to meet, and there were always undecided law-suits and disputes to be settled. Mordecai Jafa may very possibly have gained from this the idea of transforming these chance synods into regular conferences and of drawing up rules for them. His authority was sufficient to gain acceptance for his proposals, which satisfied an urgent need. When he left Lublin in his old age to take up the office of rabbi at Prague, the presidency of the synod seems to have been occupied by Joshua Falk Cohen, the head of a school at Lemberg (1592—1616), whose great academy was maintained by his rich and respected father-in-law. The frequent meetings of the Reformers in Poland, the Lutherans and Unitarians, with their respective sects, seem to have served as a model for the Jewish assemblies. Only the latter did not discuss hair-splitting dogmas, like the others, but decided practical questions of daily life.

Poland and Lithuania, superficially considered, presented the spectacle of a land honeycombed with religious divisions, from which a new form of Christianity was to arise. While in Germany the reforming movement and the opposition to it was subsiding, while the Titans who stormed the gates of heaven were settling down into ordinary parsons; while the new church in its turn was entering upon a process of ossification, and, after a short season of youthful ardor, was falling into the feebleness of old age; the waves of religious and sectarian separation were only now rising in Polish countries, and threatening a general inundation. The German colonies in Poland had transplanted the Reformation with them, and the Polish nobility thought it an imperative fashion to pay homage to this anti-papal innovation. Christianity in Poland and Lithuania, be it the new or the old church, was too young to be firmly rooted; and so the Reformation, finding little opposition, gained rapid admittance among the nobles and the bourgeoisie almost to its own discomfiture. Sigismund Augustus had allowed the movement free play; indeed, under the influence of the Radziwills of Lithuania, who stood close to his throne, he almost renounced the papacy altogether. Thus Poland became a free state in the widest sense, and an arena for the new teaching of the Augustine monk of Wittenberg. Even those thinkers or enthusiasts in Italy, Switzerland, or Germany, who wished to push the religious movement, but were persecuted either by the Catholics or the Reformers, found kindly welcome and protection under the Polish nobility, who were quite independent in their own districts.

Thus arose a sect in Poland which, logically developed, might have given a fatal blow to Christianity in general. The ashes of Servetus of Aragon, burned at the stake in Geneva, the author of a treatise, "On the Errors of the Trinity," seem to have been the seed for fresh dissensions in the church. A number of his disciples, Socinus, Blandrata, and Paruta, Italians of bold intellect, who undermined the foundations of Christianity, and were outlawed by Catholics and Reformers alike, passed over the Polish frontier, and were allowed not only to live there free, but also to speak freely. The attacks of the Socinians or Pinczovinians (as this sect, which flourished in Poland, was called) were directed mainly against the Trinity as a form of polytheism. Hence they received the name of Unitarians or anti-Trinitarians. There arose a swarm of sects who met at synodic conventions to find grounds of union, but separated with still further divisions and dissensions.

Among the Unitarians, or disbelievers in the Trinity, were some who partially approached Judaism, rejecting the veneration of Jesus as a divine person. They were scoffed at by their various opponents as "Half-Jews" (semi-judaizantes). To the strictest sect of Unitarians in Poland belonged Simon Budny, of Masovia, a Calvinist priest, who founded a sect of his own, the Budnians. He died after 1584. He possessed more learning than the other founders of sects, and also had a slight knowledge of Hebrew, which he had probably learned from Jews. Simon Budny made himself famous by his simple translation of the Old and the New Testament into Polish (published at Zaslaw, 1572). His intercourse with Jews is shown by his respect for the universally despised Talmud.

Although the movement of religious reform in Poland, in spite of the frequent synods, disputations, and protests, did not penetrate very deep, it was not without effect upon the Jews. They were fond of entering into discussions with the leaders or adherents of the various sects, if not to convert them to Judaism, yet to show their own superiority in biblical knowledge. Conversations upon religion between Jews and "Dissenters" (as all Poles who had seceded from Roman Catholicism were called) were of frequent occurrence. A Unitarian, Martin Czechowic (born about 1530, died 1613), from Greater Poland, a man of confused intellect, who had passed through all the phases of the religious movements of the day, and who finally became a schismatic, rejected the baptism of infants, and maintained that a Christian could not undertake any office of state. This Martin Czechowic had written a work to refute the objections of the Jews to the Messianic claims of Jesus, and had fought against the continued obligatoriness of Judaism with old and rusty weapons. A Rabbanite Jew, Jacob of Belzyce, in Lublin (1581), wrote a refutation, so effective that Czechowic found himself compelled to justify his thesis in a rejoinder.

Isaac ben Abraham Troki, of Troki, near Wilna (born 1533, died 1594), a Karaite, engaged still more actively than Jacob of Belzyce in disputations with the adherents of Polish and Lithuanian sects. He had access to nobles, princes of the church, and other Christian circles, was deeply acquainted with the Bible, well read in the New Testament, and in the different polemical, religious writings of his day, and thus able to produce thoroughly accurate statements. Shortly before his death (1593) Isaac Troki collected the results of his religious conversations in a work that was subsequently to serve as the arsenal for destructive weapons against Christianity. He entitled his work "The Strengthening of Faith." He not merely answered the numerous attacks made upon Judaism by Christians, but carried the war into the camp of Christianity. With great skill and thorough knowledge of his subject, he brought into prominence the contradictions and untenable assertions in the Gospels and other original Christian documents. It is the only book by a Karaite author worth reading. It certainly does not contain anything specially new; all brought forward in defense of Judaism and against Christianity had been far better said by Spanish authors of a previous period, especially by the talented Profiat Duran. Yet Troki's work had more success, for books have a fate of their own. This book was translated into Spanish, Latin, German, and French, and gained still greater fame from the attacks upon it by Christians. One of the dukes of Orleans undertook to refute the onslaught of this Polish Jew upon Christianity. And when Reason, awakened and strengthened, applied the lever to shake the foundations of Christianity and demolish the whole superstructure, it was to this store-chamber that she turned for her implements.

CHAPTER XIX.

SETTLEMENT OF JEWS IN HOLLAND.—FEEBLE ATTEMPTS AT ENFRANCHISEMENT.

Revival of Catholicism—Decay in European Culture—Ill-treatment of Jews in Berlin—Emperor Rudolph II of Austria—Diminution in the Numbers of Italian Jews—Pope Gregory XIII—Confiscation of Copies of the Talmud—Vigorous Attempts at the Conversion of Jews—Pope Sixtus V—The Jewish Physician, David de Pomis—Renewal of Persecution by Clement VIII—Expulsion from Various Italian States—The Censors and the Talmud—The Jews of Ferrara—Settlement of Jews in Holland—Samuel Pallache—Jacob Tirado and the Marranos in Amsterdam—Tolerant Treatment—The Poet, David Jesurun—Moses Uri—Hebrew Printing in Amsterdam.

1593—1618 C.E.

THE free spirit of the nations of Europe, which at the beginning of the century had taken so bold a flight, had broken the ancient bonds in which the church had long held minds captive, and cast the blight of doubt on the hitherto sacred authority of the wearer of the Roman purple—this spirit, which promised to bring the regeneration of civilized humanity and political freedom, seemed in the second half of the century to be utterly cast down. The papacy, or Catholicism, had recovered from its first feeling of terror, and collected itself. Extraordinarily strengthened by the council of Trent, it forged new chains to which the nations that had remained faithful, willingly submitted. The order of the Jesuits, restless and indefatigable champions, who not only disarmed their opponents, but even drew them over to their own ranks, had already reconquered much lost ground by their widespread plots, and had conceived new measures in order to win back with double interest what they had lost. Italy, a great part of southern Germany and the Austrian provinces,

France—after long civil wars and convulsions, after the blood-stained eve of St. Bartholomew, and the murder of two kings—as also to a great extent Poland and Lithuania, had once more become Catholic, as fanatically Catholic, too, as Spain and Portugal, the blazing hells of the Inquisition. In Lutheran and reformed Germany another papacy had gained the mastery, a papacy of dry formulas of belief, and slavery to the letter of the law. The Byzantine quarrel about shadowy dogmas and meaningless words divided the evangelical communities into as many sects and subsidiary sects as there were points of discussion, and had a harmful influence upon political development. Classical philology, at first liberalizing and suggestive, was neglected, owing to excessive belief in the Bible by the one party and the sway of authority over the other, and had degenerated into fanciful dilettanteism or learned lumber. The study of the Hebrew language, which for a time had kindled great enthusiasm, was similarly debased, or only carried on superficially for the purposes of ecclesiastical wrangling. The knowledge of Hebrew had always been considered, at any rate was now thought, in orthodox Catholic society, to be actual heresy. And the same was still truer of rabbinical literature. The learned Spanish theologian, Arias Montano, published the first complete polyglot Bible in Antwerp, at the expense of Philip II. He also compiled grammars and dictionaries of the Hebrew and cognate languages, in which regard was had to the older Jewish expositors. He, the favorite of Philip II, who had himself drawn up a list of heretical books, was accused by the Jesuits and the Inquisition of favoring heresy, suspected of secret conversion to Judaism, and stigmatized as a rabbi. Thus, Europe seemed to be actually making a retrograde movement, only with this distinction—what had formerly been cheery, naïve credulity now became sinister, aggressive fanaticism.

Refined ecclesiasticism, resulting in the tension which subsequently relieved itself in the general destructiveness of the Thirty Years' War, made the sojourn of Jews, both in Catholic and Protestant countries, a continual torture. Luther's followers in Germany forgot what Luther had so earnestly uttered in their favor, only remembering the hateful things of which, in his bitterness, he had accused them. The Jews of Berlin and the province of Brandenburg, for instance, had the sad alternative put before them of being baptized or expelled. A Jewish financier, the physician Lippold, favorite of Elector Joachim II, and his right hand in his corrupt, financial schemes, examined and tortured on the rack by Joachim's successor, John George, admitted, though afterwards recanting, that he had poisoned his benefactor. The Jews were driven also out of Brunswick by Duke Henry Julius. Catholic nations and princes had no cause to reproach their Protestant opponents with toleration or humanity in regard to Jews.

It was, in some respects, fortunate for the Jews of Germany and Austria, that the reigning emperor, Rudolph II, although a pupil of the Jesuits, educated in a country where the fires of the stake were always smoking, and a deadly enemy of the Protestants, was not greatly prejudiced against Jews. Weak and vacillating, he was not able to check the persecutions directed against them, but at least he did not encourage them. He issued an edict to one bishop (of Würzburg) that the Jews should not be deprived of their privileges, and to another (of Passau) that they should not be tortured on the rack. But, in order not to be decried by his contemporaries or by posterity as a benefactor of Jews, he not only maintained the heavy taxation of Jews in his crown land, Bohemia, but from time to time increased it. He also ordered the Jews to be expelled from the archduchy of Austria within six months.

In this position, robbed by Catholics and Lutherans alike, trampled down or driven into misery, barely protected by the emperor, but taxed under the pretense of enjoying this protection, the ruin and degradation of German Jews reached ever lower depths. They were so sorely troubled by the cares of the moment, that they neglected the study of the Talmud, once their spiritual food.

The Jews of Italy fared even worse at this time, and they, too, sank into misery and decay. Italy was the principal seat of the malicious and inexorable, ecclesiastical reaction, animated with the thought to annihilate the opponents of Catholicism from the face of the earth. The torch of civil war was hurled from the Vatican into Germany, France, and the Netherlands. And as the Jews, from the time of Paul IV and Pius V, had been upon the list of heretics, or foes of the church, their lot was not to be envied. With the loss of their independence, their numbers also decreased. There were no Jews living in southern Italy. In northern Italy, the largest communities, those of Venice and Rome, numbered only between 1,000 and 2,000 souls; the community in Mantua had only 1,844; and in the whole of the district of Cremona, Lodi, Pavia, Alessandria, and Casalmaggiore, there dwelt only 889 Jews. Pius V, by nature a sinister ecclesiastic delighting in persecution, who treated Jews as the cursed children of Ham, was succeeded by Gregory XIII (1572—1585), who had been skillfully trained to fanaticism by the Jesuits and the Theatine monks. As regards Jews, Gregory was a most consistent follower of the cruelty of his predecessor. In spite of repeated warnings, there were still many Christians in Italy, who, in their blindness, preferred Jewish physicians of proved excellence, such as David de Pomis, or Elias Montalto, to Christian charlatans. Gregory was desirous of prohibiting their employment. He renewed the old canonical law that Christian patients were not to be treated by Jewish physicians; not only visiting Christians who transgressed this command with severe penalties, but also punishing the Jewish physicians if they ventured to prolong the life of a Christian patient, or even alleviate his sufferings. His severity succeeded. Another of Gregory's edicts referred not to one profession, but to the Jewish race in general. He placed them under the Argus eye of the Inquisition. If any of them maintained or taught what was heretical, *i.e.*, obnoxious to the church; if he held intercourse with a heretic or an apostate, helped him or showed him sympathy, he was to be summoned by the Inquisition, and according to its verdict was to be condemned to confiscation of his property, the punishment of the galleys, or even sentenced to death. If, then, a refugee Marrano from Spain or Portugal was caught in Italy, and it was proved that a brother Jew had given him food or shelter, both might expect to be seized by the inexorable arm of the Inquisition of Italy. The anger of Pope Gregory XIII was poured forth also against the Talmud. The Jews were once more admonished to deliver up the Talmud and other works suspected of being hostile to the church. The Inquisitors and other spiritual authorities were appointed to institute search for these books everywhere. Anyone subsequently found in possession of them, even after declaring that the offending passages had been expunged, was rendered liable to severe punishment. Pope Gregory XIII's most zealous effort was directed to the conversion of Jews. This pope, who most heartily encouraged the Jesuits and their proselytizing school of thought, endowed a propagandist seminary of all nations—the curriculum included twenty-five languages—called the "Collegium Germanicum," issued a decree that on Sabbaths and holy days Christian preachers should deliver discourses upon Christian doctrine in the synagogues, if possible in Hebrew, and that Jews of both sexes, over twelve years of age, at least a third of the community, must attend these sermons. The Catholic princes were exhorted to support this vigorous attempt at conversion. Thus an ordinance of a half-mad, schismatic pope, Benedict XIII, issued in a moment of passionate excitement, was sanctioned, and even exaggerated in cold blood by the head of the united Catholic church, thereby exercising religious compulsion not very different from the act of Antiochus Epiphanes in dedicating the Temple of the one true God to Jupiter. It is characteristic of the views then prevailing, that the Jews were to provide salaries for the preachers, in return for the violence done their consciences! Like his predecessor, Pius V, Gregory spared no means to win over the Jews. Many allowed themselves to be converted either from fear or for their advantage; for Gregory's edicts did not remain a dead letter, but were carried out with all strictness and severity. The consequence was that many Jews left Rome.

The condition of the Jews in Rome was apparently altered under Gregory's successor, Sixtus V (1585—1590), who rose from the position of a swineherd to the office of the shepherd of Catholic Christendom, and whose dauntless energy in the government of the Papal States stamped him as an original type of character. He allowed Jews to be around him, and harbored Lopez, a Jewish refugee from Portugal, who made various suggestions as to the improvement of the finances. He went still further; he issued a bull (October 22d, 1586), which did away with almost all the restrictions made by his predecessors. Sixtus not merely granted Jews permission to dwell in all the cities of the Papal States, but also allowed them to have intercourse with Christians and employ them as assistants in business. He protected their religious freedom by special provisions, and extended to them an amnesty for past offenses, *i.e.*, for condemnations on account of the possession of religious books. Moreover, he forbade the Knights of Malta to make slaves of Jews traveling by sea from Europe to the Levant, or *vice versâ*, a practice to which these consecrated champions of God had hitherto been addicted. Pope Sixtus knew how to secure obedience to his command when it became law, and the Jews previously expelled now returned to the papal dominions. Under him the Jewish community at Rome numbered two hundred members. Finally he removed the prohibition which prevented Jewish physicians from attending Christian patients. The compulsory services instituted by his predecessor were the only ordinances that Sixtus V allowed to remain.

The permission, so important at that time, for Jewish physicians to have access to Christian patients, was probably gained for himself and his colleagues, by the then celebrated physician, David de Pomis (born 1525, died 1588). With medical knowledge he combined linguistic acquirements, and familiarity with Hebrew and classical literature, writing both Hebrew and Latin with elegance. In the course of his life he felt keenly the changes in the papal policy. He lost all his property through the hostile decrees of Paul IV, was kindly treated by Pius IV, and allowed by way of exception to practice among Christians in consequence of a splendid Latin discourse delivered before the pope and the college of cardinals. But he was again subjected to irritating restrictions by Pius V, and had to employ his skill in the service of petty, capricious nobles. To dispel the unconquerable prejudices against Jews, particularly against Jewish physicians, De Pomis wrote a Latin work, entitled "The Hebrew Physician," which affords favorable testimony to his noble mind and extensive culture. With considerable eloquence De Pomis maintained that the Jew was bound by his religion to love the Christian as his brother, and that a Jewish physician, far from wishing to do harm to his Christian patient, was wont to treat him with the utmost care and solicitude. He enumerated various Hebrew physicians who had attended princes of the church, cardinals and popes, had restored them to health, and had received distinctions from them and from cities. In conclusion, De Pomis adduced some proverbs from the Talmud in a Latin translation, to show that this much-calumniated book was not so harmful and corrupt as enemies of the Jews asserted. This apology for Judaism and Jewish physicians, dedicated to Prince Francisco Maria of Urbino, the elegant Latin style of which was highly praised by an experienced critic of the time, appears to have made an impression upon Pope Sixtus. De Pomis must certainly have been intimate with him, as he was allowed to dedicate to him his second important literary work, a dictionary of the Talmud in three languages.

The pope severely punished a Christian Shylock, because he claimed a pound of flesh from a Roman Jew as the result of a wager. This Christian, named Seche, had wagered with a Jew, named Ceneda, that St. Domingo would be conquered, and on winning his bet he claimed the penalty. On hearing of this, Sixtus condemned him to death, but afterwards mitigated the punishment to banishment, and allotted the same fate to Ceneda for wagering his body, the property of his sovereign.

The favorable attitude of Sixtus towards Jews encouraged them in the hope—to them a matter of conscience, of life itself—that the prohibition directed against the Talmud and the Hebrew Scriptures would be removed forever. Under the last two popes no copies of the Talmud had been allowed to appear without causing the possessor to incur the dangers of the watchful Inquisition. Nor was the possession of other perfectly harmless Hebrew works without risk, for as the Inquisitors and clerical authorities did not in the least understand them, they condemned all without exception as inimical to the church, a category which afforded ample room for denunciation. Whether the possessor of a Hebrew book should be condemned to lose his property, or be sent to the galleys, depended, in the last instance, upon the decision of baptized Jews acquainted with rabbinical literature. To escape these annoyances the communities of Mantua, Ferrara, and Milan addressed a request to Sixtus V to allow the Jews to possess copies of the Talmud and other books, provided these works were previously expurgated of the passages objectionable to Christianity. They referred to the decision of Pope Pius IV that the Talmud could not be entirely condemned, but that it contained passages worthy of censure, which were to be struck out by the censor's marks. A Jewish delegate, Bezalel Masserano, had gone to Rome, provided with 2,000 scudi, in order to lay the request of the Jews at the feet of his Holiness. It was granted in the bull of October 22d, 1586. Sixtus allowed the reprinting of the Talmud and other writings, though only after censorship. For this purpose two commissions were appointed, in which baptized Jews were naturally included as experts. The Italian Jews began to rejoice at being allowed to possess even a mutilated Talmud. But scarcely had the commission arranged the conditions of the censorship (August 7th, 1590), when the wise pope died, and the undertaking, just begun, of reprinting the mutilated Talmud was at once discontinued.

The regard paid Jews by Sixtus V arose not from any sentiment of justice, but from his passionate desire to amass treasure. "This pope bled Christians from the throat," says his biographer, "but he drew the blood of Jews from all their limbs." They often found themselves compelled to pay immense sums into the papal treasury.

With Clement VIII, however (1592—1605), the system of intolerance, practiced by Paul IV, Pius V, and Gregory XIII, once more came into vogue. He repeated the edict of expulsion against the Jews in the Papal States (February 25th, 1593), and allowed them to dwell only in Rome, Ancona, and Avignon. If a Jew were caught in any other papal city, he was to expiate his offense by the loss of his property and the penalty of the galleys. Clement re-imposed the old restrictions upon the Jews in the three cities mentioned, forbidding them either to read or possess the Talmud and other rabbinical writings. The Jews, expelled from the Papal States, seem to have been received by Ferdinand, Duke of Tuscany, who assigned Pisa to them as a dwelling-place (July, 1593). He allowed them to possess books of every kind and of all languages, including the Talmud, but the copies first had to be expurgated according to the regulations of the commission instituted by Sixtus V. So great was the fanaticism of the apostolic throne that even noble princes, like Ferdinand de Medici, of Tuscany, and Vicenzo Gonzago, of Mantua, did not venture to relax it. Even in places where, as a favor, the Jews were allowed to possess expurgated books, they were exposed to all kinds of annoyances and extortions. They had to pay the censors, mostly baptized Jews, for the mutilation of these writings, nor were they assured that even then their books would not again be confiscated, and the owners punished, merely because some obnoxious word or other had remained unobliterated. Woe to those who rubbed out one of the censors' marks! To avoid being exposed to vexation, Jews themselves laid hands upon their sacred literature, and expunged not only everything that referred to idolatry, but also everything that glorified the Jewish race, or made mention of the

Messiah and his future advent. As Italy, at that time, was the chief market for printed Hebrew works, the Jews in other countries received only mutilated copies, from which open or covert protests against Rome were completely obliterated.

Expulsion of the Jews from all Italian cities was the order of the day in the reign of this pope. Thus the Jews were expelled (in the spring of 1597) from the Milan district, *i.e.*, from the cities of Cremona, Pavia, Lodi, and others, to the number of about a thousand. They were forced to beg for shelter in Mantua, Modena, Reggio, Verona, and Padua. During their migrations, they were robbed by heartless Christians. The sword of the church hovered for a time also over the Jews in Ferrara, a town that had always been a safe refuge for them, and even for the new-Christians from Spain. The ducal race of De Este, whose representatives vied with the Medici in magnanimity and culture, had died out. The Jews of Ferrara felt themselves so identified with the fortunes of this princely house, that they offered public prayers in the synagogue on the occasion of the severe illness of the thoughtful Princess Leonore, whom two great poets have immortalized by placing her in the glorified heaven of poetry. She herself was a benefactress of Jews, and frequently protected them. But now the last representative of the race, Alfonso II, had died without heirs (1597), and, in opposition to his last wishes, Ferrara was incorporated into the Papal States by Clement VIII. The Jewish community, consisting chiefly of Marrano refugees, was prepared to endure banishment, as it could expect no mercy from this pope. They only asked Aldobrandini, the pope's relative, who had taken possession of Ferrara, to grant them a respite that they might make preparations for departure. As Aldobrandini saw that a great portion of the trade of the town was in the hands of Jews, he had sufficient consideration not to injure it, granted them permission to remain for five years, and had this decree carried out in spite of the fanatical wishes of Clement VIII, who had hoped to banish them. No fugitive new-Christian, however, could now stop in Ferrara without falling into the clutches of the bloody Inquisition. Thus the last refuge in Italy for this class of Jews was destroyed, and there was no longer any place of safety for them in all Christendom.

It seems providential that the Jewish race, which, at the end of the sixteenth century, had no longer a footing, properly speaking, in Europe or Asia, under Christianity or Islam, should have taken firm root in the empire of their obstinate foe, Philip II, of Spain, and should have been able from that vantage ground to gain a position of equality. Indeed, in the chain of causation it was the bloody Inquisition itself which helped gain them freedom. Holland, a land wrung from the sea, became for the hunted victims of a horrible, refined fanaticism, a resting-place where they could settle down, and develop their national characteristics. But what changes and vicissitudes they had to undergo before this almost undreamed of possibility could become reality! The northwest corner of Europe had hitherto been inhabited by only a few Jews. They suffered, as did their brethren, under the extravagances of excited fanaticism, were hunted down, and massacred at the time of the crusades and the Black Death, bearing all in silent obscurity and patience. When the country, under the name of the Netherlands, beneath the far-reaching scepter of Charles V, was united to Spain, the Spanish principle of hostility to Jews was transferred to it. The emperor issued command after command that the Jews in the cities of the Netherlands, small though their numbers were, should be expelled. Every citizen was required to make known to the royal officers the presence of Jews contrary to law. In consequence of the introduction of the Inquisition into Portugal, several Jewish families had betaken themselves, with all their wealth, industry, and skill, to the flourishing cities of the Netherlands, Brussels, Antwerp, and Ghent, in order to lead a religious life secure from danger. The severe edict of Charles V, and his repeated command not to allow their presence, extended to them. The magistrates duly fulfilled the commands of their ruler in this matter, because they feared that the presence of new-Christians would cause the Inquisition to be introduced—an evil which seemed to their anxious hearts to forebode great danger for themselves.

The people of the Netherlands could not escape the Inquisition. Although an appendage of Spain, were they not surrounded by Lutheran heretics, and did not these dwell in their very midst? So this institution was to be introduced among them also. This was one of the main causes of the revolt of the Netherlands, and of that long-continued war, so small in its beginnings, and so great in its results, that rendered powerless the might of Spain, and raised the tiny land of Holland to a power of almost the first rank. It seemed as if from every head that Alva struck off in the Netherlands, hundreds of others sprang, as from the Hydra of old. It was a matter of course that in this sanguinary struggle which transformed the whole land into an arena of battle, there was no place for Jews. Upon the advice of Arnheim and Zütphen, Alva had issued an edict that if Jews were found there, they were to be kept in custody until such time as he should pass judgment upon them. It was well known what this meant from his mouth.

The Portuguese Marranos, or new-Christians, who, even in the third generation, could not forget, and would not repudiate, their Jewish descent, turned their eyes towards the Netherlands, now wrestling for freedom, the more as the Inquisition was raging more furiously than ever, and dragging them to the dungeon or the stake. Since the first symptom of the decline of Spain's fortunes, since the collapse of the invincible Armada, by means of which Philip II had thought to carry the chains of actual and spiritual bondage not only to England, but, if possible, to the ends of the earth, there had arisen in the hearts of the pseudo-Christians, under the iron rule of this tyrant, an eager desire for freedom. As Italy was closed to them by the persecuting policy of the reactionary popes, their only hope of refuge was in the Netherlands.

An eminent Jew, Samuel Pallache, sent by the king of Morocco as consul to the Netherlands (about 1591), proposed to the magistrate of Middelburg, in the province of Zealand, to receive the Portuguese Marranos, and allow them religious freedom. In return, they would develop the city into a flourishing, commercial center by means of their wealth. The wise city fathers would willingly have agreed to this plan, but the war for religion and freedom, so passionately waged against the twofold despotism of Spain, had made even the reformed preachers fanatical and intolerant. They were opposed to the admission of Jews into Zealand.

But the Portuguese new-Christians did not abandon the idea of seeking security in the provinces of the Netherlands already freed from the Spanish yoke. They felt themselves drawn towards this republic by mighty bonds; they shared its fierce hatred against Spain with its thirst for human sacrifices, and against its fanatical king, Philip II. The great Protector, William of Orange, the soul of the struggle for independence, had uttered the idea of mutual toleration and friendly intercourse between different religious parties, creeds, and sects. Although this first germ of genuine humanity at first fell to the ground, the Marranos clung to it as affording hope of release from their daily torments. A courageous Marrano woman, Mayor Rodrigues, appears to have formed the plan of seeking a refuge for her family in Holland. She, her husband, Gaspar Lopes Homem, her two sons and two daughters, and several other members of this rich and respected family, were devotedly attached to Judaism, and weary of the pretense of following Christian customs, a pretense, after all, powerless to protect them from the horrors of the Inquisition. When a ship sailed from Portugal with a load of fugitive Marranos, under the leadership of one Jacob Tirado, Mayor Rodrigues intrusted to this vessel her charming and beautiful daughter, Maria Nuñes, and also her son. The mother appears to have relied upon the magic of her daughter's charms; the extraordinary beauty of Maria Nuñes was to serve as an ægis to these wanderers, surrounded by dangers on all sides, and secure to them a place of refuge. As a matter of fact, her beauty was successful in averting the first danger that threatened the party of refugees, consisting of ten persons, men, women and children. They were captured by an English ship making raids upon vessels sailing under the Spanish-Portuguese flag, and were taken to England. Maria Nuñes so bewitched the captain, an English duke, that he offered her his hand, thinking that she belonged to the rank of the Portuguese grandees; but she refused this honorable offer, because she wished to live as a Jewess. The beauty of the fair Portuguese prisoner made so great a sensation in London, that the virgin queen, Elizabeth, was curious to make the acquaintance of this celebrated beauty, inaccessible even to the love of a duke. She invited her to an audience, and drove with her in an open carriage through the streets of the capital. Probably owing to the mediation of Maria Nuñes, the fugitive Jews were allowed to leave England unharmed, and set sail for Holland. After enduring a most stormy voyage, they were able to make for the harbor of Emden, where, as in the rest of East Friesland, some few German Jews lived.

As soon as the Marranos became aware, by Hebrew letters and other signs, of the presence of brethren in this city, Jacob Tirado, the most eminent among them repaired to Moses Uri Halevi, who had the reputation of being a learned man, and on whose house Hebrew characters had been noticed. He discovered to him his own and his companions' intention to give up pseudo-Christianity, and to be received fully and, if possible, immediately into Judaism. But Moses Uri had scruples about taking such a decisive course, the apparent conversion of Christians to Judaism, in a small town, where nothing could long remain hidden. He, therefore, advised the fugitives to betake themselves to Amsterdam, where greater toleration was enjoyed, and promised to come to them with his whole family, to remain with them, and instruct them in Jewish doctrines. Accordingly, the Marranos, led by Tirado, arrived at Amsterdam (April 22d, 1593), sought an abode which would allow of their remaining together, and were received back into Judaism as soon as Moses Uri and his family came to them.

Moses Uri and his son arranged a house of prayer for the Marranos, and officiated as conductors of the services. Great zeal was shown, not only by Jacob Tirado, but also by Samuel Pallache, the consul, and a Marrano poet, Jacob Israel Belmonte, come thither from Madeira,who depicted the tortures of the Inquisition in verse, giving his poem the appropriate title of "Job." The youthful community was strengthened in numbers and in standing by fresh arrivals. An English fleet, which, under the Earl of Essex, surprised the fortress of Cadiz, and inflicted serious injuries upon the Spaniards (in the summer of 1596), conveyed several Marranos to Holland, amongst them a man of great originality, not without importance for posterity. Alonso de Herrera was descended from Jewish and ancient Spanish families. His ancestor was the great Gonsalvo de Cordova, the conqueror of Naples for Spain. He himself was the Spanish resident in Cadiz, and on the capture of this city was taken prisoner by the English. On being liberated he went to Amsterdam, became a Jew, and adopted the name of Abraham de Herrera (wrongly called Irira).

The Marranos in Amsterdam did not find the practice of their religion altogether easy. When this first Portuguese community was secretly celebrating its fourth Fast of Atonement (October, 1596), their Christian neighbors were surprised at the secret meeting of disguised figures in one house; they suspected treacherous assemblies of Catholic conspirators, and denounced them to the magistrates. Whilst the Jews were engaged in prayer, armed men suddenly rushed into the house, and spread terror amongst the assembled worshipers. As most of them, mindful of the cruelties of the Inquisition, and fearing a similar fate in Amsterdam, tried to save themselves by flight, the suspicions of the Amsterdam officials were increased. The latter searched for crucifixes and wafers, and led Moses Uri and his son, the leaders of the service, to prison. However, Jacob Tirado, who was able to make himself understood in the Latin language, succeeded in convincing the authorities that the assembly was not one of papists, but of Jews who had fled from the Moloch of the Inquisition. Moreover, that they had brought much wealth with them, and finally that they would induce many co-religionists to come from Spain and Portugal with their riches, and thus give an impulse to the trade of Amsterdam. Tirado's speech made a great impression. The prisoners were released, and the terrified Portuguese Jews were able to conclude the service of the Fast of Atonement.

Now that their religion was made known, they ventured upon the step of petitioning the magistrate to allow them to build a synagogue in which to hold their religious services. After much consideration the request was granted. Jacob Tirado bought a site, and in 1598 built the first Jewish temple in the north of Europe, called the "House of Jacob" (Beth Jacob). It was consecrated amid the enthusiasm of the little community.

The favorable news about the Marrano colonists, carried secretly to Spain and Portugal, afforded additional inducement to emigration. Mayor Rodrigues Homem, the first promoter of this course, also found an opportunity of escaping from Portugal and joining her beautiful daughter, Maria Nuñes (about 1598). She brought her younger son and daughter with her; her husband had probably died before this time. Simultaneously, barely escaping the Inquisition, another eminent family arrived from Portugal, that of Franco Mendes, including the parents and two sons, Francisco Mendes Medeïros, a cultured literary man, who took the Hebrew name of Isaac, and Christoval Mendes Franco, rich and benevolent, who called himself Mordecai. Both played important parts in the Amsterdam community, but subsequently caused a division.

Philip II lived to see the two races whom he had most savagely hated and persecuted, the Netherlanders and the Jews, in a measure join hands to destroy what he had created, for Holland derived advantage from the Jewish settlers from Portugal. Previously it had been one of the poorest states, and the bitter, destructive wars had made the land still poorer. The capital brought by the Marranos to Amsterdam was very acceptable, and benefited the whole country. The Dutch were now enabled to lay the foundations of their prosperity by taking the Indian trade out of the hands of the Portuguese, who had been connected with Spain in an unprofitable alliance. The capital of the fugitive Jews made it possible to found great transmarine companies and fit out trading expeditions, in which they participated. The connections, too, of the Portuguese Jews with their secret co-religionists in the Portuguese possessions in the Indies assisted the undertakings of Dutch merchants.

Philip II died in September, 1598, a terrible warning to obstinate, unscrupulous despots. His body was covered with abscesses and vermin, which made him such an object of horror that his trembling servants approached him only with disgust. The great empire which he bequeathed to his feeble son, Philip III, was likewise diseased. It was succumbing to its infirmities, and no longer possessed influence in the councils of Europe. The reins of government were loosened, and thus the new-Christians found it still easier to escape the clutches of the Inquisition. They now had a goal to which to direct their steps. An extraordinary occurrence in Lisbon had excited the most lukewarm apostate Jews to return to Judaism. A Franciscan monk, Diogo de la Asumção, of an ancient Christian family, had become convinced of the truth of Judaism and the falsity of Christianity by reading the Bible—Bible reading has its dangers—and had openly expressed his convictions to the other monks of his order. For what purpose had the Inquisition been instituted, if it were to let such crimes go unpunished? Diogo was thrown into a dungeon; but it was not necessary to extort confession, for he openly and without reservation admitted his offense, love for Judaism. The tribunal needed to put him to the rack only to induce him to denounce his accomplices, he having asserted that several of his fellow-monks shared his convictions. Certain learned theologians were charged to dissuade the apostate Franciscan from his belief, and remove so dark a stain from the order and Christendom in general; but in vain.

Diogo remained true to his belief in the truth of Judaism. After he had spent about two years in the dungeons of the Inquisition, he was finally burnt alive at a solemn auto-da-fé in Lisbon, in the presence of the regent (August, 1603).

The fact that a Christian by birth, a monk to boot, had suffered for the sake of Judaism, and had died steadfast in faith, made a powerful impression upon apostate Portuguese Jews, and impelled them to return publicly to the faith of their fathers. The Inquisition lost its terrors for them. They reverted to Judaism, without heeding whether or not they were rushing upon death. David Jesurun, a young poet, a favorite of the Muses since his childhood, on this account called "the little poet" by his acquaintances, celebrated the burning of the martyr, Diogo de la Asumção, in a fiery Portuguese sonnet:

> "Thou wast the gold, buried in the dark vaults of the tribunal of blood;
> And even as gold is purified from dross by flames,
> So, too, by flames would'st thou be purified.
> Thou wast as the phœnix, renewing his life,
> Disdaining to remain the slave of death.
> Thou wast consumed in the fire,
> Only to rise again from thine ashes,
> A burnt-offering
> Brought to God in the flames.
> In heaven dost thou laugh at those who tortured thee;
> And no more art called Brother Diogo,
> But Golden Phœnix, Angel, Sacrifice."

This eager young poet was fortunate enough to escape the Inquisition, and hastened to Amsterdam. He composed a powerful poem in Spanish on seeing this city, which seemed to him a new Jerusalem. Another young Marrano poet also reverted to Judaism through the tragic death of Diogo, the Franciscan. Paul de Pina, a man of some poetic talent, was inclined to religious enthusiasm, and was on the point of becoming a monk. This step caused great sorrow to his relative, Diego Gomez Lobato, at heart faithful to Judaism, and he wished to hinder him from apostasy. When he was about to make a journey to Italy, Diego, therefore, gave him a letter, addressed to the celebrated Jewish physician, Elias Montalto, known as Felix Montalto when professing Christianity. The letter was as follows: "Our cousin, Paul de Pina, is going to Rome to become a monk. Your Grace will do me the favor to dissuade him."

If this letter had fallen into the hands of the Roman or Portuguese Inquisition, it would have cost both the writer and his correspondent their lives. Elias Montalto endeavored to dissuade young De Pina from his purpose and win him back to the religion of his fathers. He seems to have succeeded only in so far that De Pina abandoned his journey to Rome, went off to Brazil, and then returned to Lisbon. The martyrdom of Diogo de la Asumção appears to have finally decided him against Christianity. He hastened to Amsterdam with the sad news (1604), became an eager convert to Judaism, and adopted the Hebrew name of Rohel Jesurun. He became a most enthusiastic Jew, an ornament to the Amsterdam community.

The loyalty to Judaism manifested by the Portuguese Marranos regardless of consequences naturally swelled the numbers of the victims of the Inquisition. Not long afterwards, one hundred and fifty of them were thrown into gloomy dungeons, tortured, and forced to confess. Even the regent of Portugal hesitated to burn so large a number. Moreover, the new-Christian capitalists had a certain amount of power over the Spanish court, to which, since the union of the two kingdoms, Portugal now belonged. The court owed them large sums which it could not pay in consequence of the increasing poverty of both countries. The Marranos offered to release Philip III from this debt, and give in addition a present of 1,200,000 crusados (£120,000), if the imprisoned Jews were pardoned. They also spent 150,000 crusados to persuade the councilors to make the king grant this favor. Hence the court manifested an inclination to mercy, and applied to Pope Clement VIII to empower the Inquisition to deal mildly with the sinners on this occasion. The pope remembered, or was reminded, that his predecessors, Clement VII and Paul III, had granted absolution to Portuguese Marranos. He did the same, and issued a bull pardoning the imprisoned Jews (August 23d, 1604). The Inquisition contented itself with the hypocritical repentance of its prisoners. Several hundred of them, clad in the garb of penitents, were led to the auto-da-fé at Lisbon (January 10th, 1605), not, however, to mount the stake, but to make public confession of their guilt, and be condemned to deprivation of all civic rights. All, or a large proportion, of those set free, repaired to their new place of refuge. Among them was Joseph ben Israel, who had thrice suffered torture, and escaped with shattered health and the loss of his property. He took with him his son Manasseh—or whatever his name may have been as a pseudo-Christian—then a child, subsequently destined to fill a distinguished rôle in Jewish history.

Moses Uri (born 1544, died 1620) at different times received into the Hebrew faith two hundred and forty-eight men, so greatly did the numbers of the community at Amsterdam increase. They sent to Salonica for a rabbi of Sephardic descent, by name Joseph Pardo, who well understood the character of the semi-Catholic members of the community. He put into their hands a book written in Spanish, Christian rather than Jewish in tone. The synagogue Beth Jacob, built by Tirado, no longer sufficed for the accommodation of its worshipers, and a new one had to be built in 1608, called "Neve Shalom." It was founded by Isaac Francisco Mendes Medeïros and his relatives. As the discoverers of a new country regard every step they take in it, every new path into which they strike out, and every person prominent in the enterprise, as important and worthy of remembrance, so the young Amsterdam community joyfully recorded everything that occurred in their midst at the commencement of their career.

The arrival of Isaac Uziel (died in 1620) was a piece of good fortune for this unique community. Apparently of a family of refugees, this rabbi could thoroughly sympathize with his companions in misfortune at Amsterdam. He was a poet, grammarian, and mathematician, but, above all, a preacher of rare power and influence, the first who dared arouse, with his mighty voice, the consciences of his hearers, lulled to sleep by the practice of Catholic customs, and warn them not to believe that they had purchased indulgence or remission for their sins, follies, and vices, by religious observances thoughtlessly practiced. Isaac Uziel did not spare even the most respected and powerful in the community, although he thereby drew upon himself their hatred, which went so far as to cause a split; on the other hand, he gained devoted followers, who celebrated him in spirited verse.

In this manner religious union was encouraged and faith strengthened among the Portuguese fugitives, who had so degenerated in religious matters. But as yet no arrangements had been made for the proper burial of their dead. They were compelled to bury them far away from the city, at Groede, in northern Holland. By the endeavors of the leading members of the community, they succeeded in obtaining a burial-ground, not too far from Amsterdam, in Ouderkerk, near Muiderberg (in April, 1614), at which they rejoiced greatly. The first person buried there was Manuel Pimentel, or, by his Jewish name, Isaac Abenacar, called "king of players" by the French king, Henry IV, who was in the habit of playing with him. Two years later, the body of an eminent and noble man, Elias Felice Montalto, was brought from far off to be buried in this peaceful spot. He had formerly professed Christianity, but afterwards became a faithful Jew, was a clever physician and elegant author, and lived in Livorno, Venice, and finally in Paris as private physician to Queen Maria de Medici. He died in Tours while on a journey with the French court, on February 16th, 1616. The queen caused his body to be embalmed, and taken to the cemetery at Ouderkerk, accompanied by his son, his uncle, and his disciple, Saul Morteira.

The Jews of Amsterdam were long compelled to pay a tax, for every corpse, to the churches past which the body was carried. On the whole, they were at first not tolerated officially, their presence was only connived at. They were distrusted as Catholic spies in the service of Spain, plotting treason disguised as Jews. Even when the authorities and the population in general had become convinced of their genuine hatred of Spain and Portugal, they were still far from being recognized and tolerated as an independent, religious body. For a short time the synagogues were closed, and public worship prohibited. Jewish refugees from the Spanish peninsula, on arriving in Havre, were thrown into prison. This intolerance in the country destined to be the first where religious freedom was to raise its temple, was chiefly caused by the passionate conflict between two parties of Reformers—the Remonstrants and Contra-Remonstrants. The former were more gentle in their exposition and practical application of Christianity than their opponents, the gloomy Calvinists, Dutch Independents. In Amsterdam the latter party predominated and persecuted their opponents, considered secret, treacherous adherents of Spain. Although the Remonstrants had cause to try to effect toleration for all sects, it was they who came forward as the accusers of the Jews. They complained to the chief magistrate of Amsterdam that all kinds of sects, even Jews, were tolerated in the capital of Holland, they being the sole exception.

The governor, Prince Maurice of Orange, was certainly favorable to Jews, but he could do nothing against the spirit of intolerance, and the independence of the cities and states. Consequently, even in Holland the Jewish question came up for discussion, and a commission was appointed for its settlement. Finally it was decided (March 17th, 1615) that every city, as in the case of Amsterdam, could issue a special regulation about Jews, either to tolerate them, or to expel them ; but in those cities where they were admitted, they were not to be forced to wear a badge. Upon the repeated complaints of the Remonstrants, the burgomaster, Reinier Pauw, laid before the council (October 15th, 1619) the question as to what was to be done in the case of the numerous fugitive Portuguese Jews who had intermarried with the daughters of the land, thereby causing great scandal and annoyance. Hereupon it was decided (November 8th), that intercourse between Jews and Christian women, even prostitutes, was to be strictly forbidden. On the other hand, permission was granted to Jews freely to acknowledge their religion.

As Amsterdam was not so wealthy as it afterwards became, it could not do without Jews, who had transferred to it their riches and their knowledge of affairs. The old-established prejudices against them disappeared more and more upon closer acquaintance. The Jews from Portugal betrayed neither by their cultured language, their demeanor, nor their manners, that they belonged to a despised caste ; on the contrary, their carriage was that of people of rank, with whom it was an honor for many a Christian burgher to be acquainted. They were, therefore, treated with a certain amount of consideration. Their number soon increased to four hundred families, with three hundred houses in the city, and before long, a

Hebrew printing press was set up in Amsterdam, without fear of the Argus eye of the censor.

The prosperity of Amsterdam, caused by the influx of Portuguese Jews, excited the envy of many Christian princes, and they invited the Jews into their dominions. Christian IV, king of Denmark, addressed a letter to the Jewish Council of Amsterdam (November 25th, 1622), asking them to encourage some of their members to settle in his state. He promised them freedom of worship, and other favorable privileges. The Duke of Savoy invited Portuguese Jews to come to Nice, and the Duke of Modena offered them the right of residence in Reggio, both granting them extensive privileges. Thus, in the midst of the gloomy persecution of Christendom, whose two religious factions were drawing the sword against each other in the Thirty Years' War, the Jews found pleasant little oases, as it were, from which they could recover their lost liberty, and gradually raise themselves from their heavy bondage.

CHAPTER XX.

THE DUTCH JERUSALEM AND THE THIRTY YEARS' WAR.

The Amsterdam Jewish Community — Its Wealth, Culture, and Honored Position—Zacuto Lusitano—Internal Dissensions—The Talmud Torah School—Saul Morteira, Isaac Aboab, and Manasseh ben Israel—The Portuguese Congregation in Hamburg —The First Synagogue — Lutheran Intolerance—John Miller—Jewish Colony in Brazil—The Chief Communities in Germany—Persecution in Frankfort — Dr. Chemnitz — The Vienna Congregation—Lipmann Heller—Ferdinand II's Zeal for the Conversion of Jews—Influence of the Thirty Years' War on the Fortunes of the Jews.

1618—1648 C.E.

THE Jewish race during its dispersion of nearly two thousand years may fitly be compared to a polyp. Though it was often wounded and cut to pieces, the parts severed from the whole did not die, but began an independent existence, developed organically, and formed a new rootstock. Driven from their original Palestinian home, the scattered members of this peculiar national organism assembled on the banks of the Euphrates and Tigris and in the palm district of Arabia. Doomed to ruin there, they emigrated to Spain with the Arabs, the most cultured people of the Middle Ages, and became the teachers of Europe, then plunged in barbarism. Expelled thence, weakened in heart and numbers, they proceeded eastwards, and, as again they found no resting-place, they settled in the north, always following advancing civilization. The admission of Jews to Holland was the first quivering dawn of a bright day after dense gloom. Amsterdam, the northern Venice, in the beginning of the seventeenth century, had become a new center for Jews; they rightly named it their new, great Jerusalem. In time this city became an ark of refuge for the

Jewish race in the new deluge. With every trial conducted by the Inquisition in Spain and Portugal on account of the Judaizing practices of the Marranos, with every burning pile set ablaze for convicted or suspected persons, the numbers of the Amsterdam community increased, as if the fanatics aimed at depopulating and impoverishing the Catholic countries to render the heretical states of the Netherlands populous and wealthy. The Amsterdam Portuguese community, consisting of more than four hundred members, already possessed three hundred stately houses and palaces in this city, raised by them to a flourishing seat of commerce. Their capital enabled them to carry on trade, for the most part on a large scale, and they were interested in the East and West India Companies, or conducted banking houses. But to usury, which made the Jews of other countries so hated, they were sworn foes. The synagogue dues imposed upon themselves give an approximate idea of the extent of their capital and trade. For every pound of goods exported or imported by them they were accustomed to pay a doit, and these taxes, exclusive of those on the receipts of merchants interested in trading companies, amounted to 12,000 francs annually.

Not on account of their wealth alone did they occupy a distinguished position in the new Batavian seat of commerce. The immigrant Marranos belonged for the most part to the educated class; in Spain or Portugal, their unnatural mother country, they had occupied positions as physicians, lawyers, government officials, officers, or clergymen, and were familiar with the Latin language and literature no less than with *belles-lettres*, and were accustomed to the usages of society. In the Netherlands, then the most civilized part of Europe, humanistic culture was in itself a recommendation. Hence, in Holland, cultivated Jews had intercourse with educated Christians on terms of equality, and obliterated the prejudices against the Jewish race. Some of them obtained a European reputation, and were connected with personages of high rank. Abraham Zacuto Lusitano (born 1576, died 1642), great-grandson of Zacuto, the historian and astronomer, was one of the most celebrated physicians of his time. He corresponded with Frederick, prince of the Palatinate, and his learned wife, the unfortunate couple that occupied the throne of Bohemia for a brief space, and was the cause of the Thirty Years' War. Zacuto's praise was sounded in poetry and prose by Christian as well as Jewish professional brethren. The Stadtholders of the Netherlands, princes of the house of Orange-Nassau, Maurice, Henry, and William II, like the founder of their race, William I, were well disposed towards Jews, and treated them as citizens with full rights. Even the Spanish and Portuguese kings, the persecutors of the Marranos in their own countries, condescended to show respect to the descendants of their hunted victims, to confer appointments upon them, and to intrust them with consular functions for their states.

The attachment of the Amsterdam Jews to their re-adopted religion, purchased with so many dangers, was deep, and was renewed at every accession of fresh fugitives, and every report of the martyrdom of their brethren on the burning pile of the Inquisition. This devotedness was reflected in their conduct, and embodied in verses composed in the language of their persecutors.

Paul de Pina, or Rëuel Jesurun, the poet, who had once been on the point of becoming a monk, composed for a sacred festival part songs in Portuguese, performed by seven youths to do honor to the first synagogue (Beth-Jacob) in 1624. The mountains of the Holy Land, Sinai, Hor, Nebo, Gerisim, Carmel, and Zethim (Mount of Olives), in melodious verses celebrated the excellence of the

Jewish religion, the Jewish Law, and the Jewish people. They praised the thousand merciful ways in which God had led His people from the earliest times to the present. The unity of God, the holiness of the Law, and the expectations of the Messianic age of grace, the more deeply felt by the Sephardic Marranos because they were newly acquired and dearly gained convictions—these were the inexhaustible themes of their poetry. But in the background of the splendid picture there always lowered the dreadful dungeon, the priests of Moloch, and the blazing flames of the Inquisition.

In this mood, exalted by the recollection of sufferings and torture endured, the members of the Amsterdam community, with full heart and bountiful hand, founded benevolent institutions of every description, orphan asylums, benevolent societies (brotherhoods), and hospitals, such as were not in existence in any of the older communities. They had the means and the disposition. Their piety was shown in charity and generosity. But, exalted though their mood was, they were men with passions, and dissensions arose in the young community. Many members, born and brought up in Catholicism, brought with them and retained their Catholic views and customs; they thought that they could combine them with Judaism. "Can one carry coals in his bosom without singeing his clothes?" From childhood the Marranos had heard and seen that one is allowed to sin, if from time to time he is reconciled with the church. Catholic priests of all ranks were at hand to effect the reconciliation, and by ecclesiastical means ward off future punishment from the sinner. In the eyes of most Marranos, the rites and ceremonies of Judaism took the place of the Catholic sacraments, and the rabbis of father-confessors. They believed that he who conscientiously observes Jewish rites, and in addition does a few other things, may yield to his desires without forfeiting his soul's welfare. At any rate, the rabbis could give him absolution. Hence the Marranos led a life far from perfect, especially in point of chastity. The first two rabbis of the Amsterdam community, Joseph Pardo and Judah Vega, in consideration of the circumstances were indulgent to these weaknesses and shortcomings. But the third, Isaac Uziel, did not restrain himself; with inexorable rigor he scourged the evil habits of semi-Jews and semi-Catholics from the pulpit. This severity wounded the attacked, but, instead of mending their ways, they were angry with the preacher, and several left the community and the synagogue, and combined to found a new one (the third) in 1618. At the head of the seceders was David Osorio; possibly he felt most deeply wounded by Uziel's severe sermons. For the new synagogue (Beth Israel) which the seceders erected, they chose David Pardo, the son of Joseph Pardo, as rabbi and preacher. He defended the acceptance of this office in the new body, founded to some extent in defiance of Isaac Uziel, by alleging that he wished to lessen dissension. However, the tension lasted for twenty years (1618—1639).

Meanwhile German Jews, whom the ravages of the Thirty Years' War had driven out of their Ghettos, sought the asylum of Amsterdam, and were admitted to its shelter. If the Amsterdam Council had at first merely connived at the immigration and settlement of Jews, at a later period it decidedly furthered their admission, because it perceived the important advantage which they brought the state. The immigrant German Jews naturally could not unite closely with the Portuguese community, because they differed, not only in language, but also in demeanor and manners. A wide chasm divided the Portuguese and the Germans of the same race and religion from each other. The former haughtily looked down upon the latter as semi-barbarians, and the latter did not regard the former as genuine Jews. As soon as a sufficient number had assembled, the German Jews formed a synagogue, with a rabbi of their own. Their first chief was Moses Weil. The breach within the Portuguese community was painfully felt. Jacob Curiel, a distinguished man, afterwards resident of the Portuguese court in Hamburg, by the greatest exertions brought about a reconciliation, and not till the union of the three synagogues in one single corporate body, in April, 1639, did the Portuguese community, by the harmonious co-operation of its powers, stand forth in all its splendor, and surpass all its elder sisters in the three divisions of the globe. The Amsterdam community in some points resembled the ancient Alexandrian Jewish congregation. Like the latter, it possessed great wealth, cultivation, and a certain distinction of character; but, like it, suffered from insufficient knowledge of Jewish religious and scientific literature. Nearly all Marrano members had to commence to learn Hebrew in advanced age!

On uniting the three communities, for which statutes were passed, the representatives took pains to obviate this ignorance of Hebrew. They founded an institute (Talmud Torah) in which children and youths might have instruction in the useful branches of Jewish theology. It was, perhaps, the first graded institution of the kind among Jews. It consisted, at first, of seven classes. Students could be conducted from the lowest step, the Hebrew alphabet, to the highest rung of the Talmud. It was at once an elementary school and a college for higher studies. Thorough Hebrew philology, elocution, and modern Hebrew poetry were also taught there, which was not usual in other Jewish schools. In the highest departments, the first rabbis, or Chachamim, at that time Saul Morteira and Isaac Aboab, gave instruction. These two men, with Manasseh ben Israel and David Pardo, formed the first rabbinical college. This richly endowed institute became a nursery for the training of rabbis for the Amsterdam community and its daughters in Europe and America. From it pupils went forth who labored in wider spheres; among whom may be mentioned, for the sake of contrast, the confused Kabbalist Moses Zacuto and the clear-headed Baruch Spinoza.

It was a misfortune for the Amsterdam community that its first spiritual guides, who exercised remarkable influence, were possessed of only mediocre talents, in some degree lacked mental poise. With the vast resources which this first Dutch community had at command, with the fund of culture characterizing its members, and their devotion to Judaism, its leaders might have brought about remarkable results, if they had possessed more independence, profounder intellect, and greater genius. The first Amsterdam rabbinical college had nothing of all this. David Pardo appears to have been of very little importance. Saul Levi Morteira (born about 1596, died 1660) was not even a distinguished preacher; his colleagues, Aboab and Manasseh ben Israel, far outshone him. His sermons, the only printed productions of his literary activity, have a philosophical complexion, but no depth of thought. Morteira followed the broad, beaten paths, repeating what had been thought and pointed out before him. Even in rabbinical learning he had no mastery, and was not considered an authority by contemporary Talmudists. His colleague, Isaac Aboab de Fonseca (born 1606, died 1693), was even less distinguished. He, also, was a Portuguese by descent, and, it seems, came to Amsterdam as a child with his mother, who was fifty years old at his birth. He was trained under Isaac Uziel, and acquired from him pulpit eloquence, if that can be learnt. Aboab became an excellent and beloved preacher. His style of speaking has been very well described by Antonio Vieira of Lisbon, a wise Jesuit, possessed of goodwill towards Jews. When once in Amsterdam, he heard Aboab and Manasseh ben Israel preach, and when asked how he liked them, he replied: "The one (Manasseh) says what he knows, and the other knows what he says." But a well-arranged, impressive, attractive sermon is not always the fruit of solid knowledge and clear conviction. At any rate, it was not with Aboab. In character he was vacillating, submissive to the influence of others, open to flattery, hence not independent. To this man was given the control of the Amsterdam community for nearly seventy years. Aboab was superstitious like the multitude, and, instead of leading, was led.

Far more distinguished was Manasseh ben Israel (born 1604, died 1657), a child of the Amsterdam community, to which his father had come broken down by the torture of the Inquisition, and robbed of all his property. Young Manasseh, eager for learning, was trained under Isaac Uziel, and while his knowledge of the Bible and the Talmud did not attain to perfect mastery, it was extensive and ready. Directed by his personal circumstances to the study of ten languages—including Portuguese as his mother tongue, and Latin as the literary language—Manasseh learnt to express himself in speech and writing with more or less perfection in all these languages and in an elevated style. A ready speaker by nature, he educated himself as a preacher, displaying all the lights and shadows of his profession. He became a prolific writer, and, though he died young, performed incomparably more than his colleagues. In the case of this amiable man, who rendered essential service to Judaism, we should not take the part of severe critics, nor inquire how large a share enthusiasm and a certain vanity had in his work. But history is a stern judge. What his contemporaries admired in Manasseh was not his profound intellect, nor his overpowering, far-reaching greatness, but his quiet, yielding, modest behavior, and his simple nature. He correctly and briefly described himself without under- or over-estimation: "I rejoice in the modest though happy talent of being able to describe, with a certain degree of order, the objects that the will presents to the mind." He brought no great and fruitful thoughts into the world, but fostered the intellectual offspring of others, treating them as his own. He knew rather than thought much. Although familiar with profane literature and Christian theology, he clung firmly not only to traditional Judaism, as represented by the rabbinical system, but also to the Kabbala, and, like his less educated colleagues, regarded every word in the Talmud and the Zohar as a profound truth. Like others, Manasseh ben Israel was subject to superstitions, which had a strong influence over him, and spurred on his will.

Such was the character of the men called to guide and instruct the young, ignorant, catholicizing, and tractable Amsterdam community. Great power was in their hand. Important affairs were discussed and decided at the public sittings of the rabbis (Maamad) with the trustees elected by the members. In religious matters the Chachamim alone decided, because the laity did not trust their own judgment. The decisions of the rabbis were binding on the members. Nobody might oppose them, because the government had a despotic character. The authorities allowed the board of trustees and the college of rabbis full liberty to inflict spiritual penalties on disobedient members. Of this liberty and this power the leaders made only too extensive a use. They had brought from Spain mischievous zeal in maintaining the faith pure and uprooting heresy. The Amsterdam rabbis introduced the innovation of bringing religious opinions and convictions before their judgment-seat, of constituting themselves a sort of inquisitional tribunal, and instituting autos-da-fé, which, even if bloodless, were not less painful to the sufferers. The character and organization of the largest Portuguese community in Europe had a powerful influence on the course of Jewish history. Branch communities were formed, which took for their model not only the organization, dignity, devoted piety, and benevolence, but also the follies and perversities, of their mother. The second community on Dutch soil was gradually formed at Rotterdam. Two brothers, as pious as wealthy, Abraham and David Pinto, laid the foundation of this community, and elected as Chacham and principal of the institute which they founded (Jesiba de los Pintos), a young man, Josiah Pardo, son of David Pardo, and son-in-law of Morteira, who, however, did not distinguish himself.

In Haarlem, also, the Jews were on the point of obtaining permission to settle. The Humanists and favorers of toleration, like Joseph Scaliger, the prince of philologists, were already rejoicing; but, in the end, intolerance prevailed, and nothing came of the movement. Instead, Portuguese communities arose in North Germany beyond the sea, and gradually in other cities of the Netherlands.

In Hamburg an important colony of the Amsterdam community was next formed. But there were difficulties in overcoming German prejudices and German pedantry. Against the advantages arising from the settlement of wealthy and intelligent Jews, which the Amsterdam people had quickly comprehended, the Hamburg citizens struggled hand and foot. For the fierce Lutherans it was an abomination to have Jews in their midst. A Jewish jeweler named Isaac, from Salzuflen, in Lippe, with twelve of his co-religionists, who were compelled to go in search of a new home, made an attempt to settle in Hamburg.

He presented a petition to the senate to receive them for twelve years, offering the sum of 9,000 marks and a yearly tax of 400 marks. The negotiator, Isaac, exhaustively set forth all possible reasons for the reception of Jews, and declared that they were willing to submit to any conditions. He adduced that Jews were tolerated not only in Catholic, but also in evangelical countries, both in the West, at Frankfort and Worms, and in northern Germany, in Hanover, Minden, Hildesheim, Göttingen, Norden, Dortmund, Hamm, Lippe, and Emden. All was in vain. Hamburg, then delighting in popish quarreling about orthodoxy and heresy, refused a home to Jews.

It is curious that Hamburg, at the very time when it so strongly opposed the temporary admission of Jews, harbored some in its midst without being aware of it. With these, under the mask of Portuguese papists, orthodox Christians had daily intercourse. Marrano fugitives had escaped from the Inquisition, settled in the North German free Hanse town, and passed as Portuguese "traders." Hearing that their brethren in Amsterdam, with whom they were in communication, openly professed Judaism, and were tolerated, they also lifted their mask, and wished to be recognized as Jews, but continued to have their children baptized. The strict Lutheran citizens raised a loud outcry, and demanded of the senate that the wealthy Jews who had been driven from Portugal and other places should be got rid of, and not be tolerated. But to this the senate did not like to accede; they felt shame at treating these Portuguese of noble demeanor and intelligent character as vagrants or Jews. To the secret Jews of Hamburg there belonged at that time the beloved and much-sought physician, Rodrigo de Castro (born about 1560 at Lisbon, died 1627 or 1628), who, in the violence of the pestilence, hastened with self-sacrifice to the bedsides of those stricken by the plague, and saved the lives of many. De Castro was also a skillful physician for women, and won the favor of the weaker sex, strong in sympathy and antipathy. Able physicians were not numerous, especially not in North Germany. Other "Portuguese," as the disguised Marranos in Hamburg called themselves, and were called, possessed capital, or, as agents, conducted important business for Spanish or Portuguese houses. In short, it did not seem practicable to send these Portuguese away. The senate, therefore, at first put off the citizens with an official denial that there were Jews among them; and afterwards admitted the presence of a smaller number than was correct—about seven Portuguese Jews "who have fire and smoke here," *i.e.*, households. But the Lutheran clergy in Hamburg behaved most intolerantly, excited people against the Portuguese Jews, and charged the senate with neglect of duty. That body, which guarded only the commercial interests, did not care to dispense with the Jews, but being unwilling to burden its conscience, or rather to incur the reproach of unchristian feeling, turned from the Hamburg clergy—the ministry—to a higher court, the theological faculties of Frankfort-on-the-Oder and Jena. The theological grounds of which the senate availed itself for the toleration of Jews are very ridiculous, and prove the ossification of Lutheranism at that time. The judgment of the Frankfort faculty proceeds upon these grounds, and indulges the hope that the Portuguese Jews—who for the sake of their convictions had given up honors, fortune, and a beloved home—would be converted to Christianity in Hamburg. The decision of the Jena faculty looks as if a professor of Dominican theology of a century before, in the time of Hoogstraten, had written it, and as if the index on the dial of history had stood still. Like the intolerant papists, the Lutheran theological faculty wished to compel Jews to listen to Christian preaching.

The senate, sufficiently protected on the ecclesiastical side by these two judgments, in February, 1612, with restrictions growing out of the German spirit or the German narrow-mindedness of that time, granted the Portuguese Jews free residence in Hamburg, avoiding a consideration of the consequences on both sides with pedantic scrupulousness. They really became protected Jews (*Schutzjuden*), who had to pay an annual charge or protection fee of 1,000 marks. They were not allowed to have synagogues, or private religious service according to Jewish customs, or to practice circumcision, but they might bury their dead in a cemetery of their own at Altona. There were then in Hamburg 125 adults of Marrano descent, among whom were ten capitalists, two physicians, and three artisans. It was an important article in the agreement that new-comers might obtain admission, "if the high and wise council found their qualifications of such a nature that it had no objection to take them under its protection." Thus the young, semi-tolerated Hamburg community grew from year to year, and within a decade several capitalists were added. The increase of the community through the accession of such settlers, admitted openly as Jews, no longer disguised as Portuguese, in 1617 rendered necessary a fresh agreement with the senate, enlarging their privileges in commercial respects, but diminishing them in point of citizenship. They could not possess houses or land, and had to dispose of any they might own. Exception was made in favor of the physician, Rodrigo de Castro, in consideration of his faithful services of many years, but even he could not bequeath his house to an heir.

The more the Portuguese Jews, by their capital and business connections, gained weight with commercial men in the senate, the more they broke through the boundaries drawn by narrow-minded legislation. When the bank at Hamburg, to which this city owed its commercial prosperity, was founded (1619—1623), no less than twelve Jewish capitalists supported it with their funds and efforts, as the Amsterdam Portuguese had done at the formation of the Dutch companies trading beyond the sea. The Portuguese Jewish settlers alone founded the important trade of Hamburg with Spain and Portugal. Hence they might assume that the senate, which held the reins of government, would connive at violations of the articles. They were especially anxious to be permitted to assemble for public worship, and this was directly forbidden. Relying on their indispensability, they quietly erected a synagogue in about 1626. It was Elihu Aboab Cardozo who risked this venture. They named it Talmud Torah, and appointed as Chacham, Isaac Athias, of Amsterdam, a disciple of Isaac Uziel.

This probably simple synagogue, consisting of two large rooms, caused wide dissension, and produced much bitterness. Emperor Ferdinand II, the terror of the Protestants, indignant that the arch-Lutheran city on the Elbe would not allow Catholics to build a church, sent a threatening letter to the senate, July 28th, 1627, because for the sake of trade a synagogue was openly permitted to Jews, while Roman Catholics were forbidden the exercise of their religion. Nothing more was needed to excite the Lutheran fanatics. If free exercise of their religion was granted to Jews, it must also be granted to Catholics, and even to Calvinists, they said. A frightful consequence indeed! When the ministry, or spiritual assembly, which had great power in Hamburg, reproached the senate on account of the violation of articles in the agreement with the Jews, and that body in turn arraigned the Jews, the latter declared that they had no synagogue, merely a place of meeting to read the Law of Moses, the Psalms, the Prophets, and other books of the Old Testament; if they prayed there, it was only for the welfare of the city and the government. The senate proceeded no further, because the Jews threatened that, in case they were denied the worship of God, they would leave Hamburg in a body, and transfer their capital and business connections to a neighboring place. That argument prevailed. But the clergy demanded nothing less than that a Christian rabbi be appointed to preach Christianity to Jews in the synagogue, or elsewhere. The physicians also viewed with indignation the popularity of their Jewish colleagues, and sought to bring not only them, but Jews generally, under suspicion, and stirred up the people against them.

But the community grew in prosperity from year to year, and the senate gladly received those who came with capital and business connections. Even if the descriptions by John Miller, the arch-foe of the Jews, appear exaggerated, yet an idea may be gathered from them of the wealth of the Portuguese Jews of Hamburg. "They strut along adorned with gold and silver, costly pearls, and precious stones. At their weddings they eat and drink from silver ware, and drive in such carriages as become only persons of exalted rank, and, moreover, have outriders and a large following." The extremely rich Texeira family, settled in Hamburg, lived in princely luxury. The founder of this banking house, Diego Texeira de Mattos, was called in Hamburg, like Joseph of Naxos in Constantinople, "the rich Jew." He was of Portuguese descent, bore a title of high nobility, and had previously been Spanish resident in Flanders. Over seventy years of age, he underwent the operation of circumcision in order to become a Jew in reality. By means of his wealth, and his connections with both the nobility and capitalists, Diego Texeira could play the aristocrat. He drove in a carriage lined with satin, and had liveried servants.

The Portuguese Jews already had three synagogues, the second built by Abraham Aboab Falero, the third by David de Lima. A German community, also, had gradually assembled at Hamburg, and built a house of prayer. And were the faithful followers of Luther to behold it calmly, although almost on his death-bed he had ordered the Jews to be treated as gypsies, and the tongues of the rabbis to be cut out? The Hamburg pastors could not endure it, they pressed the senate, and stirred up the citizens to withdraw even this small amount of religious toleration. Among them stood forth an arch-bigot, John Miller, senior at St. Peter's church, a Protestant inquisitor and chief persecutor, an abusive man given to scandal, who cast aspersions upon his reverend brethren from the pulpit and in libelous writings. With this virulent pastor, who considered himself a pillar of Lutheran orthodoxy, it was a matter of conscience thoroughly to hate and humiliate the Jews. In writing and in talking, in the pulpit and in the circle of his disciples, in private conversation and in official addresses, his favorite theme was the Jews and their humiliation. Everything in the Jews vexed him: their joy and feasting on Purim, their mourning on the anniversary of the destruction of the Temple, their dress, their friendship with Christians, and their funerals. The bigot was not wrong on some points, as, for instance, his censure of the hereditary failing of the Portuguese Marranos, as illustrated in their misconduct with Christian women, and of the way in which some of them challenged Christianity. A Jewish author (Jacob Jehuda Leon?) had composed a work entitled "Colloquium Middelburgense," a Latin dialogue between a rabbi and a Christian on the value or worthlessness of Christian doctrines, the gospels, and the ecclesiastical writings, in which the weak points of Christianity were laid bare. Miller composed a defense, or rather a libel, entitled, *Judaism, or the Jewish Doctrine*, a full account of the Jewish people's unbelief, blindness, and obduracy (1644). This was dictated neither by the Holy Ghost nor by Christian love. Luther's virulent language against Jews seemed an undeniable revelation to the pastor. Out of it spoke Lutheranism, pure and unadulterated, which had as little heart as the popery attacked by it, and the essence of which consisted of dry formulas of belief. Miller's absurdity and uncharitableness are not his own; they are part and parcel of the corrupt Lutheran church of the time. Three theological faculties, the arch-Lutheran faculty of Wittenberg, and those of Strasburg and Rostock, in reply to Miller's inquiry, decided that Jewish physicians should never be admitted to Christian patients. Thus, in the face of the seventeenth century, when the Thirty Years' War was teaching toleration with an iron rod, the leaders of Lutheranism were issuing a new edition of the decrees of the Visigothic councils against Jews. But, after all, times had changed. Christian IV, king of Denmark, Schleswig and Holstein, next to Gustavus Adolphus the champion of the Protestants, to whom Miller dedicated his book, had appointed Benjamin Musaphia, a Jewish physician, his medical attendant.

Even in Hamburg Miller's fanatical zeal did not meet with great success. The citizens gradually got accustomed to Jews, and learnt to respect them. Some of them were appointed business agents or residents even by high Catholic potentates. The king of Portugal first appointed Duarte Nuñes da Costa, and then Jacob Curiel, as his agents, and his Catholic majesty, Philip IV, elevated Immanuel Rosales, a Jewish author of Portuguese descent, to the dignity of count palatine. The Portuguese Jews, in general more favorably situated than their German brethren, felt so happy at Hamburg, that they called it their "little Jerusalem."

A colony of the Amsterdam mother-community was formed in Brazil, South America, discovered and peopled by Portuguese, and a number settled in the town of Pernambuco. Thither the Portuguese government had often transported Jewish offenders, *i.e.*, Marranos, whom it did not wish to deliver to the burning-pile, together with prostitutes, and other rabble. These disgraced Marranos assisted the Dutch in conquering Brazil, which became a Dutch colony, with a Stadtholder of its own, the intelligent John Maurice, of Nassau (1624—1636). Connections were immediately established between the Amsterdam and the Brazilian community, which threw off the mask of Christianity, and was almost spoilt by the favor of the Dutch. The Jews at Recife, near Pernambuco, called themselves "the holy community" (Kahal Kados), and had a governing body consisting of David Senior Coronel, Abraham de Moncado, Jacob Mucate, and Isaac Cathunho. Several hundred Amsterdam Portuguese, either by invitation, or of their own accord, sailed to Brazil to form business connections with the colony, and took with them the Chacham Isaac Aboab. He was the first Brazilian rabbi, settling probably at Recife. At Tamarica a community was formed, which had its own Chacham, Jacob Lagarto, the first Talmudical author in South America. Of course, the Brazilian Jews enjoyed perfect equality of rights with other citizens, for they rendered the Dutch essential services as advisers and warriors. When the native Portuguese, who bore the yoke of the Dutch impatiently, formed a conspiracy to get rid of the Dutch authorities at a banquet in the capital, and attack the colony bereft of government, a Jew gave warning, and saved the colony from certain destruction. Later, in 1646, when open war broke out between the Portuguese and the Dutch, and the garrison of Recife, exhausted by famine, was on the point of surrendering unconditionally, the Jews encouraged the governor to brave resistance.

A fanatical war of race and religion between the Portuguese and the Dutch devastated fair Brazil, and a famine ensued. The Jews vied with the Dutch in suffering and bravery. Isaac Aboab, the Chacham of the Brazil community, paints the sufferings of the war, which he himself endured, in lurid colors:

> Volumes would not suffice to relate our miseries. The enemy spread over field and wood, seeking here for booty and there for life. Many of us died, sword in hand, others from want; they now rest in cold earth. We survivors were exposed to death in every form; those accustomed to luxuries were glad to seize mouldy bread to stay their hunger.

At last, the States-General were compelled by European wars to surrender the colony to the Portuguese. The devoted zeal of the Jews for the political welfare of the Dutch was a firm bond, never afterwards dissolved, between them and the republic. The toleration and equal position of Jews in the Netherlands were ensured for ever.

Whilst the first ray of a better time glimmered in Holland, the rest of Europe was still full of darkness for Jews. In Germany especially, the Jew even in the seventeenth century continued to be an outcast for whom there was no sympathy. He was pelted with mud, his beard was singed, and he was treated almost worse than a dog. There were only three or four important communities in Germany: Frankfort-on-the-Main, with over 4,000 souls; Worms, with 1,400; Prague, with 10,000 at most; and Vienna, with 3,000: the rest did not number many. Hamburg was still a young community. In the West German free cities of Frankfort and Worms, almost stronger antipathy to Jews prevailed than in

Hamburg, having its root in the narrow-mindedness of the Philistine citizens and the guilds rather than in religious antipathy. Both cities treated the Jews within their walls as their "servi cameræ," and appealed in all seriousness to a deed of Emperor Charles IV, declaring that they had been sold to them in person and property. When Portuguese Marranos, wishing to remove from the Netherlands to Frankfort, and raise it to a commercial center of the first rank, like Amsterdam and Hamburg, asked permission to build a house of prayer there, the council roundly refused. The Jewish capitalists then addressed themselves to the lord of Hanau, and obtained very favorable terms.

The bitterness of the people of Frankfort against their Jewish neighbors was crystallized in a most revolting and absurd legislative enactment, entitled "the permissive residence of Jews" (Judenstättigkeit), and defining under what conditions or restrictions Jews might breathe the Frankfort air, or rather the pestilential atmosphere of the Jewish quarter. The city, chiefly Protestant, retained all the canonical restrictions introduced by the papacy for the purpose of branding Jews, such as, prohibiting them from having Christian servants or nurses, and requiring them to wear an opprobrious badge. They were treated exactly like criminals. Jews might not go outside their quarter except for necessary business, and two might not walk together, certainly not in the neighborhood of the town-hall, and especially not during Christian festivals or weddings, or if princes were staying in the city. They were also required to observe silence in their Ghetto, avoid offending Christian ears with any shrill sound, and see that strange Jews visiting them went to bed in good time. In fact, they might not harbor any strangers without the knowledge of the magistracy, nor even admit a patient into their hospital. They might not purchase food in the market at the same time as Christians. Though their business was jealously restricted, they were forced to pay more taxes than the Christian inhabitants. As they were obliged to wear special badges on their clothes, so they were required to have on their houses shields, with strange figures and names, such as "the garlic," "the ass," "the green or white shield," "red shield," "black shield." After these shield figures the inhabitants were named, "The Jew N of the ass," "the Jew N of the dragon." On the admission of a Jew, he was obliged to promise on oath to obey these stupid and heartless directions. Even this wretched existence depended on the favor of the magistrate, for in one paragraph the council reserved the power of depriving a Jew at any time of the right of residence. In such case the individual or family had to leave the city within a fixed space of time.

As the magistrate was empowered to deprive a single Jew of the right of residence, he could banish all from the city. This was inferred and demanded by the citizens or the guilds at variance with the council. They aimed at enlarging their liberties by limiting the aristocratic power of patricians in the magistracy, and they began with the Jews. The reason was that the councilors, in return for the substantial gratitude of the Jews, were indulgent in the administration of the laws issued against them; else they would not have been able to exist under the pressure of opprobrium and the "permissive residence." But this indulgence of the magistracy towards Jews was doubly hateful to the guilds. Hence they strove by all possible means to bring about the expulsion of the Jews from Frankfort. The Jews had obtained assurance of their safety as a community by charter from the emperor, but the decrees and threats of the emperor were little heeded at that time. At the head of the discontented guild-members stood the pastry-cook, Vincent Fettmilch, who, with his workpeople, belonged to the Reformers, a sect excluded from civic honors, and who sought to sate his fury against the Lutheran authorities by taking vengeance on the Jews. He was a daring man, who kept the councilors in awe, and openly called himself "the new Haman of the Jews." He was chosen by the citizens as their spokesman and ringleader, and deserved this leadership, for he executed his plans with much circumspection.

On an appointed day (27 Ellul = September, 1614, new style), while the community was assembled in the house of prayer, blow followed upon blow and thrust upon thrust, mingled with furious shouting, on the door of the Jewish quarter. Thereupon followed cries of anguish on the part of the Jews, who rushed hither and thither in despair and distracted flight. Bold youths and men seized weapons to ward off assaults or die manfully. On both sides fell the wounded and dead, until the superiority of numbers and the daring of the Fettmilch party decided the victory. Then all through the night until the next day followed plundering, desecration, and destruction of sacred places with brutal fury. The imperial commissioners could do nothing to check the riot; they were even compelled to put up a notice that the murderous band was not liable to punishment. Most of the Jews not sheltered by philanthropic citizens awaited death in trembling at the burial-ground, crouching together, many of them in shrouds. The rabble purposely left them in uncertainty as to the fate to which they were destined—life, death, or banishment—so that the Jews regarded it as a mercy from God when the fisherman's gate was opened in the afternoon of August 24th (new style), and they were allowed to depart, 1,380 in number, but without property of any kind. The advance of humanity, compared with earlier ages, is seen in the circumstance that compassionate Christians gave bread and other provisions to those who departed utterly destitute, and the smaller towns and villages sheltered them, though Fettmilch and the foes of the Jews had warned them against receiving the exiles.

It was long before the Frankfort Jews obtained satisfaction for these atrocious injuries. The magistracy and Emperor Matthias were equally impotent. Fettmilch's rabble for a whole year so tyrannized over the council that it could do nothing for the Jews. Some of the law faculties defended the robbers, by issuing an opinion that their attacks on the property of the Jews could not be regarded as theft, since they had occurred in the daytime or by torchlight. It was only by similar events at Worms that the end of the Frankfort troubles was hastened.

There the bitterness against one of the oldest German-Jewish communities, arising out of hatred of Jews and trade jealousy, took a different course. Not the guilds, but some members of the magistracy urged the banishment of the Jews, and the chief enemy of the Jews, instead of being a brutal but straightforward workman, was a crafty advocate and perverter of the law. Here, as in Frankfort, the chief motive was opposition to the magistracy, but the guild-members acted with more resolution and unanimity. The leader, adviser, and director of the committee of citizens was a learned lawyer, Dr. Chemnitz (Chemnitius), who thought that by lawyers' tricks he would be able to effect the banishment of the Jews with less danger than the Frankfort people had incurred by brutal violence. At first chicanery and insults of every sort were employed. The committee did not care to use violence, but strove to wear them out. It closed the outlets of the city against them, hindered them from purchasing food, drove their cattle from the meadows, and would not permit milk for Jewish children to be brought to the Jewish quarter.

After various movements, the Worms guilds, by Chemnitz's advice, assembled unarmed in the market place to take counsel, and sent a deputation to the Jews, ordering them "to retire from the city with bag and baggage" within an hour. The deputation reproached them with having caused the citizens to be suspected by the emperor, with having excited his hatred against them, and deprived them of every means of obtaining justice. The magistrates protested, but without effect, and so nothing remained for the Jews but to depart on the last day but one of the Passover (April 20th, 1615, new style). Fanaticism could not refrain from venting its fury on the holy places of the Jews, from devastating the synagogue which had stood for a thousand years, desecrating the burial-ground, and breaking to pieces several hundred tombstones, some of which gave evidence of the high antiquity of the community. The archbishop of Mayence and Count Louis of Darmstadt granted residence to the exiles in small towns and villages, and thus some of the exiles met their suffering brethren of Frankfort.

But the rejoicing of the foes of the Jews in Worms did not last long. The council, humiliated by the committee of citizens, secretly negotiated with Frederick, elector palatine, and, about ten days after the expulsion of the Jews, he moved infantry, cavalry, and cannon into the town, under the unavailing protest of the committee, and this soon brought the disorder to an end. Still it was nearly nine months before the Worms Jews were re-admitted by order of the elector palatine and the bishop of Speyer (January 19th, 1616, new style). Two months afterwards, the Jews of Frankfort were led back, as in triumph, with the sound of trumpets, and blowing of horns, by the commissioners of the electorate of Mayence and Darmstadt (Adar 20th = March 10th). Here the rioters were more severely punished than at Worms, because they had caused destruction, plundering, and bloodshed. Vincent Fettmilch, the pastry-cook, the Frankfort Haman, was hanged, and quartered, his house razed to the ground, and his family banished. The city was fined 175,919 florins by the emperor as compensation for the depredations committed on Jewish property. In memory of this extraordinary deliverance and honorable restoration, not an every-day occurrence in the German Empire, the Frankfort community appointed the day of their return (Adar 20th) to be observed as a feast-day, named Purim-Vincent, the day before being kept as a fast in memory of their sufferings.

The old "permissive residence" of the Jews in Worms and Frankfort was abolished by Matthias, who introduced a new regulation, recommended by the commissioners in 1617. This new arrangement still bore the impress of the Middle Ages. The old restrictions of the Jews, as to dress, occupation and movement, were retained, and, if possible, made more severe in some respects. The Jews were still considered outcasts, even by the emperor of the Holy Roman Empire and his councilors. "As they are privileged by the emperor, the council is to protect them, and no longer has the power to banish those who have obtained 'permissive residence.'" The Frankfort Jews, re-admitted at that time, did not need to renew their right of residence every three years as before, and transmitted it to their descendants. On the other hand, the number of Jews was fixed at 500. Not more than six new families a year could be granted "permissive residence," and only twelve couples a year could get married. A further restriction was that the Jews should not be called citizens of Frankfort; they were only hereditary protected dependents of the council. In addition to the old protection fee, there was a marriage and an inheritance tax. The restrictions in the new Jewish ordinance for Worms proved, if possible, still more oppressive.

The banishment of the Jews from two cities of western Germany, and their restoration had a favorable result for the German Jews. It was an advantage to all German communities that the emperor had emphatically insisted on, and by force of arms confirmed, the safety of the Jews. Emperor Ferdinand II, though a pupil of the Jesuits and a destroyer of Protestants, confirmed the inviolability of the Jews throughout the whole empire, especially in Frankfort and Worms, when the citizens of these places again thought of persecuting them. Hence it came about, that the destructive, cruel Thirty Years' War did not affect the Jews in Germany so severely as might have been expected. Of course, they did not fail to share the sufferings of the German nation, which, divided into two camps, drew the sword against its own breast, and made havoc of its own land. The Jews, like the rest of the population, had to submit to the plunderings and ravagings which leaders of armies, such as Mansfeld, Tilly, and Wallenstein, one after the other, brought upon flourishing cities.

Many a Jewish community was destroyed by the fury of war. But at least the Jews had nothing to fear from the internal foe, and, in the seclusion of their Ghettos, were perfectly secure from all attacks. The Catholic generals had orders from the emperor to spare the life and property of Jews, so that many a Protestant could lodge, and save his property, in the Jewish quarter. Before Wallenstein made the discovery that war is supported by war, and that a large army can obtain means for itself, the war carried on by Ferdinand II against the Protestant half of Germany required much money, and the imperial treasury had always been poor. But ready money was chiefly in the iron chests of Jewish capitalists. Hence, the financial springs, the Jews, had to be protected, if the war was to be carried on successfully. Consequently, the emperor, acting with careful consideration, impressed upon his generals to spare the Jews from all the hardships of war, including the quartering of troops. How dearly this tender treatment cost the communities is not known. The Bohemian Jews paid a considerable sum, and bound themselves to contribute 40,000 florins a year towards defraying the expenses of the war.

The court of Vienna invented another means of making Jews contribute to the war. It appointed Jewish capitalists as court Jews, granted them most extensive freedom of trade, freed them from the restrictions to which other Jews were subjected, even from wearing the yellow badge, in a word, afforded them and their families an exceptionally favored position.

The Jewish community of Vienna enjoyed great consideration during, or perhaps on account of, this war. Through the indifference of Spain, the center of Catholicism was transferred at that time from the Manzanares to the Danube, from Madrid to Vienna. The Jews, who by degrees re-assembled in Vienna, in spite of repeated banishment by the emperors, came into close relations with important European affairs. Court Jews and Jewish physicians repaired to Vienna with their retinue, *i.e.*, persons depending, or pretending to be dependent, upon them. The Viennese Jews at that time were considered to be exceedingly rich. As they lived scattered in various quarters of the city, they felt the necessity of assembling and having a common place for prayer. They applied to the emperor, and he granted them a site in what is now Leopoldstadt, released them from the jurisdiction of the municipal authorities, and even excused them from wearing the badge. At the very time when Protestant Hamburg citizens were jealously on the watch that no synagogue be granted to the Portuguese Jews, the arch-Catholic emperor allowed them to build in his capital a new synagogue with all its appurtenances (December, 1624). His "liberated," *i.e.*, privileged Jews were not required to quarter troops, or to contribute to the expenses of the war. The magistrates, of course, raised objections to the favor shown to Jews, and wished to turn the whole "swarm of Jews" out of the city. The court councilors, who desired to extort money, gave the citizens to understand that, for 20,000 florins, they might enjoy the satisfaction of seeing the Jews banished; but at the same time, they whispered to the Jews, that if they anticipated the payment of this sum, they might remain in Vienna. Probably the Jews prevailed.

The united and prosperous community looked about for a rabbinical leader, and, in February, 1625, made happy choice of Lipmann Heller, an amiable and learned man, at that time rabbi of Nikolsburg. He was no brilliant personage, but his talents stand out conspicuously from the dark background of the time. He forms an exception to the rabbis of that age, at least to those in Germany and Poland. He not only occupied himself with Talmudic learning, but was acquainted with branches of knowledge outside the rabbinical field. For instance, Heller had studied other than Jewish literature, and understood mathematics well. In the Talmudical department he could not compare with contemporary Poles of distinction, with Samuel Edles at Ostrog, Joshua Falk at Lemberg, Joel Serkes at Cracow, and many others. But if he was inferior to them in acuteness, more properly, subtlety, he surpassed them in profundity and lucidity.

Heller (born 1579, died 1654) possessed a mild nature, an attractive presence, and skill in speech, and could, therefore, frequent Christian circles. Far from the conceit which brooks no contradiction—a failing of most representatives of rabbinical learning in Poland—he prepossessed every one in his favor, and won all hearts by his modesty. He is one of those whom we involuntarily pity for having lived in such barbarous times. In a better age they might have labored with more success for Judaism. In his thirtieth year, at the same age as Maimuni, he completed a gigantic work, a comprehensive commentary on the Mishna (Tossafoth Yom-Tob, 1614—1617). This involved a much greater amount of work than his great predecessor, or Obadiah di Bertinoro, had been forced to devote to it, if we take into account how much the materials to be considered, examined, and tested, had increased in the interval.

Having been summoned to Vienna to the post of rabbi, he labored usefully for this young community. He drew up its constitution, and for the short time of his official career there was esteemed and beloved. With his peaceful disposition he should have remained at Vienna instead of allowing himself to be attracted by the seemingly superior qualities of the Prague community, where vulgarity and baseness, envy and malice, still prevailed. For this circle Heller was most unfit, but he was attracted to the Bohemian capital, where there was incomparably more study of the Talmud, and where he could hope to enjoy interchange of thought. Only too soon he had occasion to regret his acceptance of this office. As acting rabbi, Heller was president of the commission which had the thankless task of distributing the large yearly war tax of 40,000 thalers among the members of the Prague community and those of the country communities. With Heller's upright and pure character it may be assumed that he acted with the utmost conscientiousness, and that he did not knowingly overburden anyone. Nevertheless, some members complained of improper allotment, raised a quarrel in the community, and collected a large following, who threatened the commission with accusations. In vain did Heller raise his warning voice against the prevailing dissension, speaking from the pulpit, now in mild, now in severe terms. Contumacy combined with envy, and the discontented party accused him and the elders of the commission before the civil authorities of having with partiality spared the rich, and laid the burden of the tax on the shoulders of those with less means, compelling payment of the share imposed by threats of excommunication, imprisonment, and other punishments. The accusations against Heller must have been of a still more hateful nature. The drift was that in one of his works he had used offensive expressions against Christianity. To give emphasis to their calumny, they reported to a person close to the emperor, who prided himself much on his theological knowledge, that Heller had boasted in the hearing of the Stadtholder of Prague that he had beaten him in a disputation. At the same time the slanderers hinted that the accused rabbi was in possession of much property, which would fall to the imperial treasury in case he was found guilty. To gratify their revenge or their malicious spirit, the informers quite overlooked the fact that by this means they might bring on a persecution, not only of Prague Jews, but of all German Jews.

Their slander met with only too ready a hearing. A formal command from the emperor reached the Stadtholder of Prague to have Rabbi Lipmann Heller sent in chains to Vienna. In view of the military severity customary during the Thirty Years' War even the innocent had the worst to fear. However, Heller was so highly esteemed even by Christian officials, that the head of police, who was charged with his custody, behaved with extraordinary indulgence towards him, and he was allowed to travel to Vienna merely on bail. On arriving he waited on the chancellor, in order to learn particulars with regard to the accusation brought against him. The chancellor sternly alleged what led Heller to fear the worst—that he had written against the Christian religion. Thereupon Heller was put into prison, confined with criminal offenders, and a commission of clergy appointed to establish his guilt as a blasphemer. The sentence was that Heller properly deserved death, but that the emperor was willing to exercise mercy and allow the punishment of death to be commuted to a fine of 12,000 thalers, to be paid immediately, and that the incriminated writings were to be destroyed, The Prague slanderers who were not pleased with the sentence, did not rest till the emperor deprived Heller of the office of rabbi at Prague, and declared him unworthy to fill the rabbinical office wherever the emperor's scepter held sway. At last, after a confinement of forty days, he was liberated, with the loss of his office and his property, and without any prospect of an appointment elsewhere. The maligning of Lipmann Heller was not altogether without consequences to the Jews. The bigoted emperor and many of the clergy who had been led to notice the bearing of Jews towards Christianity conceived the idea of introducing in Vienna Pope Gregory XIII's plan of preaching sermons for the conversion of Jews. The emperor issued a decree in February, 1630, that Jews be compelled to listen to conversion sermons every Saturday morning between eight and nine, at least 200 members of both sexes in equal numbers to be present, among them forty young Jews, of from fifteen to twenty years of age. Every one summoned to hear the preachers was to be fined a thaler in case of absence, and a higher sum if the offense was repeated. Sleeping and talking during the sermon were punished. The fines were to be used in support of converted Jews. The conversion of Jews was a matter that the emperor had at heart, and he hoped much from these compulsory measures. However, this plan was not easily carried out. The court councilors, to whom the emperor committed the matter, were not proof against bribery, and followed the Jesuits, who laid less stress on catching Jewish souls than on the oppression of Protestants and the increasing of their own power.

The annals of the Thirty Years' War contain no record of special sufferings of the Jewish race. It seems almost as if Jews were better treated than Christians. At least, in Mayence, the Swedes, who resided there more than four years, from the end of 1631 to 1636, behaved more kindly to them than to others. They were not greatly impoverished, for they were able, three years after the departure of the Swedes, to build a synagogue at Mayence, and thus extend their community, a favor which it had not been in their power to enjoy for more than 150 years. The Thirty Years' War ended, as is well known, at Prague, on the very stage where it had begun. The Swedish general besieged the city on the Moldau, and had already captured one quarter. But the inhabitants resisted bravely, and the Jews were not behind the others, if not with arms, yet with labor, in the trenches, and with extinguishing apparatus. It was a Jew who brought intelligence to the emperor from the besieged city in order to obtain relieving forces. On account of their attachment to the imperial family, the Bohemian Jews obtained from Ferdinand III an extension of their rights, which consisted in the privilege of residing in all royal cities and domains, and in not being expelled without the knowledge of the emperor. It may be assumed that the Jews did not lose very much by the devastating war. While the Christian population was thoroughly impoverished, and had to contend with want—the chief circumstance which induced the rulers to conclude the Peace of Westphalia—the Jews had saved something. The booty of many cities went through their hands, and, even if they were exorbitantly taxed, and forced to pay heavy sums, they still derived some gain. Hence it came about that directly after the close of the Thirty Years' War, when great numbers of their fugitive brethren came from Poland through Germany, they could be supported in a brotherly way by the German communities; for the Jews of Poland, for the first time, were visited with a long-continued, bloody persecution. The cup of suffering was not to pass them by.

END OF VOL. IV.

INDEX.